Wissenschaftliche Untersuchungen
zum Neuen Testament · 2. Reihe

Herausgeber/Editor
Jörg Frey

Mitherausgeber / Associate Editors
Friedrich Avemarie · Judith Gundry-Volf
Martin Hengel · Otfried Hofius · Hans-Josef Klauck

173

John Lierman

The New Testament Moses

Christian Perceptions of Moses and Israel in the Setting of Jewish Religion

Mohr Siebeck

JOHN LIERMAN, born 1965; 1994 M.Div. Trinity Evangelical Divinity School, Deerfield, Illinois; 1997 M.A. Trinity Evangelical Divinity School, Deerfield, Illinois; 2003 Ph.D., Cambridge University; currently Adjunct Professor of New Testament, Fuller Theological Seminary Southwest and Adjunct Professor of Bible Studies, Grand Canyon University, Phoenix, Ariziona.

ISBN 3-16-148202-6
ISSN 0340-9570 (Wissenschaftliche Untersuchungen zum Neuen Testament 2. Reihe)

Die Deutsche Bibliothek lists this publication in the Deutsche Nationalbibliographie; detailed bibliographic data is available in the Internet at *http://dnb.ddb.de*.

© 2004 by Mohr Siebeck, Tübingen, Germany

The book was printed by Druckpartner Rübelmann GmbH in Hemsbach on non-aging paper and bound by Buchbinderei Schaumann in Darmstadt.

Printed in Germany.

For Mom and Dad

Preface

This book is a significantly revised and rewritten version of a dissertation accepted by the Faculty of Divinity and the Board of Graduate Studies of Cambridge University in 2002 for the degree of Doctor of Philosophy.

Thanks are in order first of all to my *Doktorvater*, Professor William Horbury, to whom I express the most profound and heartfelt gratitude for the skillful supervision, inexhaustible patience, and unflagging encouragement he gave me while the thesis that underlies this book was in preparation. His thorough acquaintance with source material and his scholarly acumen in fields of study so far flung that among persons of merely great erudition they lie in entirely separate areas of expertise were an inspiration to me throughout my enjoyable time under his supervision.

For numerous thoughtful comments and suggestions over the whole of the thesis I am also deeply grateful to Professor Christopher Rowland, Dr. Andrew Chester, and Professor Martin Hengel. Dr. Peter Head provided helpful criticism of selected portions as well. Their kind assistance greatly aided the revision of the study to its present form.

For helping to meet not only my own financial needs, but also those of Corpus Christi College and Cambridge University, I owe a debt of thanks to many.

I am grateful to the Committee of Vice-Chancellors and Principals of the Universities of the United Kingdom for a three-year Overseas Research Students Award, to the Cambridge Overseas Trust for the award of a three-year Bursary, and to the Master and the Tutor for Advanced Students of Corpus Christi College for the award of a Purvis Scholarship. The Tutor for Advanced Students at my matriculation was Dr. Paul Hewett, to whom I am grateful not only for the financial support he was instrumental in providing, but also for inviting me to matriculate at a college which provides such a supportive environment in which to do postgraduate research. Special thanks in this respect go also to the Master Professor Haroon Ahmed, the Warden of Leckhampton Dr. Chris Howe, and the Graduate Secretary Mrs. Margaret Cathie. Also, when my studies were interrupted by a lengthy period of illness Dr. C. J. B. Brookes, then the Tutor for Advanced Students at Corpus, saw that I was provided College Hardship funding. I remain grateful to Dr. Allan C. Carlson and Dr. Harold O. J. Brown of The Howard Center for Family, Religion and Society for taking me on as an Associate of the Center on Religion and Society, and to Dr. Steven Dilsaver for providing a one-year stipend for that position. I am grateful to the Trustees of the Crosse Fund and to the Managers of the Theological Studies Fund of the University of Cambridge for awarding me further support in the latter part of my research. Mr. Paul Riddington generously paid for private medical care for tendonitis, brought on in the line of (research) duty. My parents have provided for many needs as they have arisen and, as usual for parents, have received only a fraction of the thanks they deserve. Two other patrons who wish to remain anonymous also have my sincere thanks.

I have benefited from the support and assistance of many friends and colleagues in ways that are sometimes hard to quantify. Professor Horbury and his wife Katharine provided me with months of gracious hospitality in their home during the preparation of this book, chiefly asking in return only that I chop down a number of trees in their back garden, something I would have relished doing anyway. Dr. David Chapman was an encouraging friend and fellow researcher at the thesis stage, and he and his wife Tasha lavished delicious meals on me regularly, as if feeding me was some sort of privilege. Marko Jauhiainen gave me the computer on which nearly all my writing has been done since my own met its demise, and the rest of the Tyndale House community also provided camaraderie and support in all kinds of ways, especially the Warden, Dr. Bruce Winter, who undertook selfless and thoughtful pastoral care, the librarian Dr. Elizabeth Magba, research fellows Dr. David Instone-Brewer and Dr. Peter Williams, and the administrator, Mrs. Fiona Craig. For the work done in Phoenix, Jason and Jennifer Schumann gave me the use of their office and the freedom of their house, including the pantry and the refrigerator. A great many people seem to have fed me while I wrote this book. Not all can be named here, but I think warmly of each one.

I am grateful to Dr. Kris Burroughs for her (painfully) insightful comments on style, and for volunteering, as the last deadline neared, to share in the unrelenting tedium of indexing. Miss Helen Dalgleish ferreted out many "strange sentences!" and malapropisms throughout the whole of this study. No doubt a residue of errors persists, and responsibility for it, as well as for any persisting errors of fact or interpretation, can be laid at my door.

Phoenix, Arizona   John Lierman
28 September 2003

ad maiorem Dei gloriam

Table of Contents

Chapter 3
Moses as Priest and Apostle

Chapter 4
Moses as King

Chapter 5
Moses as Lawgiver

Chapter 6
Baptism into Moses

Chapter 8
Points of Contact with Christology

Chapter 9
Conclusion

Chapter 1

Introduction

1.1 Scope and Method

This is a study of the NT witness to how Jews and Jewish Christians perceived the relationship of Moses with Israel and with the Jewish people. This is a narrowly tailored study, focusing specifically on that relationship without treating Moses in the New Testament comprehensively. The study consults ancient writings and historical material to situate the NT Moses in a larger milieu of Jewish thought. It contributes both to the knowledge of ancient Judaism and to the illumination of NT religion and theology, especially Christology.

1.1.1 Focus

The basic plan of the study derives from the New Testament. The words "in the New Testament" could appropriately be appended in parentheses to each chapter title and each chapter aims to preserve and highlight the NT witness to Jewish perceptions of Moses.

The chapters divide along lines that throw the various NT presentations of Moses into sharpest relief. Sometimes those divisions may not accord with what might be expected from a study of Jewish literature generally. For example, the decision to separate treatment of Moses as Prophet from discussion of Moses as Priest could seem artificial given the intertwining of such roles in ancient Jewish (and non-Jewish) thought. The NT texts that prompt consideration of these motifs here, however, seem to treat them separately from one another; the key text on Moses' priesthood actually links it with a third role, that of an apostle. So in this case it seemed better to highlight the somewhat unusual NT treatment of Moses as a priest and keep it separate from ascriptions to Moses of the prophetic office, which by contrast is so typically associated with him.

At the same time, while commonly noticed, the prophetic office of Moses does not seem always to have been adequately appreciated, and separate treatment here facilitated a closer inspection in light of what the New Testament says on the subject. Since the New Testament seems to treat the themes separately with no obvious overlap it seemed both valuable and warranted to treat them separately here as well. The other chapters are

similarly focused to achieve the clearest possible impression of the way
Moses is presented in the New Testament.

Guided principally by that NT presentation, the chapters of this study
focus on the roles and relations of Moses to Israel. This happens not
because of any special interest in doing mosesology by titles or in "func-
tional mosesology" but because of this study's special focus on the relation
of Moses to Israel, as opposed to Moses as a static entity or Moses as the
subject of Jewish lore (though both come in for some consideration). It
seemed most effective to deal with some NT evidence by recourse to prosaic headings like "Moses as King" or "Moses as Lawgiver," but in those
cases it was not taken for granted what those titles mean. Part of the function of the chapters so named is to work out how NT (and other Jewish
writers) saw Moses in those roles, without relying too heavily simply on
the use of a given title or the naming of a given function. On the other
hand, in a chapter like "The Baptism into Moses" the best procedure
seemed to be to work outward from the basic datum to what it might imply
about Moses, whether or not that involved the affixing to him of a specific
title.

1.1.2 Arrangement

With the intent to arrange all the evidence in such a way as to throw the
strongest light possible on the New Testament, the most basic decision has
been to focus the chapters on aspects of the NT Moses, rather than devote
each chapter to one corpus of literature, to one Jewish community or author, or to one period of history. Thus, for example, there is not a chapter
on the Samaritan view of Moses and another on the rabbinic view of Moses, but rather there are chapters on Moses as King and on Moses as
Lawgiver in the New Testament, with rabbinic and Samaritan discussion
relevant to each theme distributed in each chapter accordingly.

The obvious weakness of the approach taken is that the study does not
present in one place the complete portrait of Moses from any one era.
Even the overall impression of Moses gained from the New Testament
does not finally emerge until the Conclusion.

Nonetheless, despite its weaknesses the chosen strategy seemed the best
way to proceed. It became apparent as work progressed that the NT evidence for Jewish estimation of Moses has not always been adequately
appreciated. This seemed to be the case not with just one aspect of Moses,
but with every theme considered. In some cases this malappreciation was
also true of extra-NT evidence that did not match academically accepted
paradigms of ancient Judaism.

Therefore, the chapter divisions here consciously underscore the ways
the New Testament presents Moses. Each chapter brings in the Jewish
literary context for its theme, drawing on all segments of Jewish tradition

from before, during, and after the period when the New Testament was authored.

This does not mean that all the Jewish evidence is forced into a single plane, as if no movement occurred in Jewish thought between the inter-testamental period and the Talmudic era, or between Palestine and Alexandria. To the contrary, the study highlights differences in the appreciation of Moses, particularly when a New Testament author looks to be the odd man out. Still, the position here is that the literature inherited by the Jews of the first century and the literature authored by them, along with later texts containing traditions that they passed on, can all, properly handled, be of assistance in understanding and interpreting the evidence of the New Testament.

A secondary concern reflected in the layout of this study is that some Mosaic motifs detected in the sources would threaten almost to disappear if the evidence for them were scattered across several chapters dealing with several different Jewish authors or epochs of Jewish history. This might be the case for example, for the priesthood and the apostleship of Moses; the former has tenuous support reaching right back into the Old Testament, while the latter seems first to arise in the New Testament itself. Proper appreciation of either seems in part to require gathering all the evidence for Jewish treatment of these ideas together in one place for consideration. Given the fragmentary and incomplete nature of the evidence for Judaism in the first century A.D., any evidence is worthy of close consideration. Here, with that in mind, the NT evidence for the Jewish conceptions of Moses was prioritized, with other evidence set in relation to it.

Of course, inspection of even plainly established motifs, such as the role of Moses as Lawgiver, may be facilitated by a diachronic approach that attempts to bring all the available evidence on the subject into focus at once. Again, this need not imply insensitivity to genre or to provenance. The intent rather is simply to highlight the conceptions of Moses evident in the New Testament, in part by locating them, when possible, in the stream of Jewish tradition.

A third consideration is that the usefulness of presenting Jewish attitudes toward Moses community by community or period by period, instead of theme by theme, is at least potentially illusory. In the case of tightly unified (or unifiable) corpora such as the works of Philo (perhaps combined with other Alexandrians), or the Palestinian Targums, Samaritan literature, or possibly even rabbinic literature, such an approach may yield meaningful results. More fragmentary evidence from late Second Temple Judaism, however, as well as evidence from Greco-Roman authors and other literature not easily bracketed within postulated Jewish communities, is harder to work up into chapter-length presentations. (Witness scholarly attempts to characterize "intertestamental Judaism" on the basis of scattered apocrypha and pseudepigrapha.) Where a single author is under consideration, such as Philo or Josephus, it is certainly reasonable to look for a single coherent impression of Moses or of any other figure. Rabbinic literature, by contrast, is the work of scores or perhaps hundreds of individuals, some named and some not. Rabbinic literature is also conservative by design and may be expected to harbor multifarious views carried forward by different traditions across hundreds of years. (Witness the extraordinary mélange of material accumulated by L. Ginzberg.) Literature of this kind may not yield the best results when treated like unified presentations of single authors.

Whatever approach is taken presents a risk of methodological forcing of the evidence. The appearance of homogeneity in a given presentation may arise as much from the selective and interpretive grid imposed by the scholar as from the data itself. The arrangement of the present study is not immune from this risk, but neither are the alternatives.

In sum, while the weaknesses of the plan chosen for this study are freely recognized, the strengths the plan offers are substantial and important enough to justify the approach taken here. Doubtless, at some point fresh appraisals of The Rabbinic Moses, or The Philonic Moses might complement this study. Here the focus is on The New Testament Moses.

1.1.3 Sources

The most important sources for this study are the *New Testament* texts themselves. Most NT passages that speak of Moses come in for at least some consideration, but those texts which say something directly concerned with the relation Moses was deemed to have to the Jewish people receive the closest attention. Other texts, for example those adding hagiographical color to the portrait of Moses, provide important background and context for the conclusions drawn from the more central passages.

The value of extra-NT and extrabiblical sources for illuminating NT concepts of Moses can hardly be doubted. If we lacked all other sources for Moses legends and the varied haggadic embellishments of his biblical biography we would both know of their existence and be able to make a fair reconstruction of their contents from the New Testament, so richly does it incorporate Jewish Moses lore. Above all other NT instances of Moses, the richly adorned account of Moses in the speech of Stephen shows how familiar early Christians were with Jewish embroideries of the Moses tale, embroideries more fully known from apocryphal, pseudepigraphal, and rabbinic literature. The casual reference to Jannes and Jambres in 2 Tim. 3:8 similarly indicates that early Christian writers were familiar with hagiographical expansions of the biography of Moses.[1]

Outside the New Testament, a number of ancient, often rather full, Jewish treatments of Moses survive, which, while widely separated chronologically, provide reliable guides to at least a selection of Jewish opinion about Moses at about the time of the origin of the New Testament. These include, above all, Philo's lengthy *De Vita Mosis* (along with numerous references to Moses in his other works) and the recasting of the Exodus-Deuteronomy narrative in the *Antiquities* of Josephus; also important are the account of Artapanus (preserved in fragments), the more highly-dramatized but still informative *Exagoge* of Ezekiel the Tragedian (also preserved in fragments), *The Assumption of Moses* (incomplete in places) and Pseudo-Philo's *Biblical Antiquities*. Ecclesiasticus and some instances of biblical interpretation from Qumran also include interesting material. Additionally, non-Jewish treatments of Moses sometimes at least partly reflect contemporary, Jewish ideas and therefore ought to be included in discussion.

Of all of these, perhaps the writings of *Josephus, Pseudo-Philo*, and the *Assumption of Moses* are most obviously relevant to NT study. These three are generally held to stem from Palestine, and from about the period when the New Testament was forming. The traditions they report are more likely than those of any other Jewish writers to have been known in the milieu of the first Christians. Their perspectives on Moses quite likely share something with the conceptions of Moses circulating among those who first converted to Christianity. Their value for illuminating the New Testament on that subject is therefore undoubted.[2]

Undoubtedly, *Philo* stands in a different part of the stream of Jewish tradition than, say, the Palestinian rabbis. This, however, only adds to his

---

[1] On introduction to these two figures and the book named for them see Emil Schürer, *The History of the Jewish People in the Age of Jesus Christ (175 B.C.-A.D. 135)*, rev. Geza Vermes, Fergus Millar, and Martin Goodman, vol. 3.2 (Edinburgh: T. & T. Clark, 1987), 781. Hebrews 11:23-28 appears not to be much influenced by extra-biblical legend, though the length of that pericope shows the importance of Moses in the early Church.

[2] Johannes Tromp, ed. and trans., *The Assumption of Moses: A Critical Edition with Commentary*, Studia in Veteris Testamenti Pseudepigrapha, ed. A.-M. Denis and M. de Jonge, vol. 10 (Leiden: E. J. Brill, 1993), 116-17 dates the *Assumption of Moses* to the first quarter of the first century A.D. Tromp, 93-111, 114-116, 120-23 presents a thorough review of the relevant scholarship, but see also especially the exchange between John J. Collins, "The Date and Provenance of the Testament of Moses," in *Studies on the Testament of Moses*, ed. George W. E. Nickelsburg, Jr., Septuagint and Cognate Studies, no. 4 (Cambridge, Mass.: Society of Biblical Literature, 1973), 15-32, and George W. E. Nickelsburg, Jr., "An Antiochan Date for the Testament of Moses," in the same volume, 33-37.

importance as a witness to a non-Palestinian, though not necessarily aberrant, Jewish tradition.[3] In fact, Philo claims to draw for material on Moses
not only on the Bible but also on the oral tradition of the Jewish elders
(*Mos.* 1.4), and there are signs of contact between his treatment of Moses
and the rabbinic midrash. His expressed dependence on Jewish tradition,
combined with his representation of an educated and philosophically sophi-
sticated sort of Jewish belief, mean that elements of the portrait of Moses
which appear both in Philo and in the more obviously Palestinian sources
should be regarded as very well-attested indeed. The *Exagoge* of *Ezekiel
the Tragedian*, as well as the writings of other Alexandrian Jews, such as
Artapanus and *Aristobulus*, are similarly valuable.

This study makes use of the *Targums*, as well as Samaritan and rabbinic
literature. Although their final, edited form is relatively late, these corpora
undoubtedly preserve material that is much earlier. The Targums in particular, though suspected of reflecting Talmudic Judaism, can point the way
toward how the Hebrew Bible was understood in an earlier day.[4] The
value of the Targums as witnesses to Jewish thought from long before their
final redaction stems from their role in transmitting vernacular traditions
conserved by regular liturgical use. (To the extent that a text comes in for
regular use in public services it is protected from the "drift" to which texts
that only see light in scribal halls and private studies may be subject, a
phenomenon seen at its most pronounced in congregational reactions to

---

[3] See Wayne A. Meeks, *The Prophet-King: Moses Traditions and the Johannine
Christology*, Supplements to *Novum Testamentum*, ed. W. C. van Unnik, et al., vol. 14
(Leiden: E. J. Brill, 1967), 100-102 on Philo as "Greek and Jew," and Erwin R.
Goodenough, *By Light, Light: The Mystic Gospel of Hellenistic Judaism* (New Haven,
Connecticut: Yale University Press, 1935; reprint, Amsterdam: Philo Press, 1969), 180-
81.

[4] Now we have manuscript evidence for written Targums from well before the turn
of the era, which further indicates the value of the Targums for NT study. "Targums
have long been recognised as part of the ancient literature of Judaism, but over the last
century scholars have been reluctant to draw on these for NT background, reckoning
that they reflect Talmudic Judaism. More recently there has been a renewed willingness to regard much targumic material as earlier, in some parts predating the destruction of the Temple. The discovery of targumic material at Qumran [4QtgJob,
11QtgJob, 4QtgLev] and an increased appreciation of the operation of synagogues at
the end of the Second Temple era have contributed to this new assessment," p. 424
from David Powys, "Appendix A: The Relevance of the Palestinian Targums," in
*"Hell": A Hard Look at a Hard Question: The Fate of the Unrighteous in New Testa-
ment Thought* (Carlisle: Paternoster, 1998), 424-432, which contains a thorough and
detailed discussion of the utility of the Targums for the study of the NT world. Powys,
424-25 also points out the lack of evidence for rabbinic redaction of the Palestinian
Targums (*Neofiti, Pseudo-Jonathan*, the Cairo Genizah Targum fragments, and the
Fragment Targum) apart from clearly interpolated passages, and urges the relevance of
these Targums especially for the study of late Second Temple Judaism.

even slight alterations in much-loved hymns.) Much the same can be said for the *rabbinic writings* as well since, although they are academic productions and did not have the same popular exposure enjoyed by the Targums, they self-consciously serve as preservers and repeaters of older tradition.

The profile of the *Samaritans* in the period of the New Testament may have been much higher, and more meaningful among Jews, than might now be guessed. In the first century they constituted a significant, expanding population in Palestine.[5] Josephus describes their territory as one of its three major divisions.[6] They had their own council (βουλή), which was of sufficient standing both to send an embassy to the governor of Syria, and thus to bring about the recall of Pilate to Rome.[7]

Samaritans had extensive intercourse with Jews, much of it, evidently, along theological lines, and the ties between Jewish and Samaritan communities were closer than usually supposed.[8] Of course, these links also became the sources of great tension, as is well known. Ben Sira already describes the Samaritans as a "perfidious people" (50:26), and other intertestamental writings are similarly vituperative, demonstrating the bad blood between the communities, but also their continued contact and interaction. Josephus reports a Samaritan desecration of the Temple under the governorship of Coponius (A.D. 6-9), again demonstrating ongoing contact and controversy between the two groups.[9] Even outside their homelands Samaritans and Jews were simultaneously both distinct and linked together: the Samaritan and Jewish communities of Alexandria maintained a running theological dispute that at one point led to a public debate under the patronage of Ptolemy Philometor.[10]

Undoubtedly the Jewish attitude toward Samaritans varied. In some earlier rabbinic traditions they could be seen as "almost Jewish," or at least more like Jews than Gentiles.[11] For example, *m. Dem.* 3.4 brackets Samaritans (כותים) with common Jews (עם הארץ), and not with non-Jews

---

[5] Nathan Schur, *History of the Samaritans*, Beiträge zur Erforschung des Alten Testamentes und des antiken Judentums, ed. Matthias Augustin and Michael Mach, no. 18 (Frankfurt am Main: Verlag Peter Lang, 1989), 44, 51.

[6] *B.J.* 3.48-50, the other two are Galilee and Judaea. In *Ant.* 13.50 he lists Samaria (with Peraea and Galilee) as one of three toparchies adjoining Judaea.

[7] Josephus, *Ant.* 18.88-89.

[8] Schur, *History of the Samaritans*, 43.

[9] *Ant.* 18.29-30. The Samaritans preserved memories of the incident. The destruction of the Samaritan sanctuary on Mt. Gerizim by John Hyrcanus in 128 B.C. was possibly the greatest source of bitterness between the two groups, see Schur, *History of the Samaritans*, 43.

[10] Josephus, *Ant.* 12.10; 13.74-81 (including some possibly fabulous embroidery).

[11] See Schnur, *History of the Samaritans*, 47-49.

(נכרים) for purposes of purity.[12] This once again demonstrates the (perhaps unwilling and distasteful) close community that existed between the
two groups. Samaritans are certainly prominent in the New Testament,
leading some scholars to think that the influence of Samaritan religion and
thought is especially pronounced among the early Christians.[13] All this
counts as more evidence for the relevance of Samaritan traditions for understanding Second Temple Judaism and the New Testament.

Problems of dating and provenance that attend study of Samaritan literature can be severe. Nonetheless, the paramount importance given to
Moses in Samaritan thought combined with the close links between Jews
and Samaritans in the Second Temple period suggests that Samaritan
literature stands to make an important contribution to this study. This is
particularly the case when the evidence gleaned from Samaritan sources
can be seen to ratify the apparent thrust of Jewish evidence more clearly
linked with the NT setting.

The targumic, rabbinic, and Samaritan corpora all attest, from roughly
the second century A.D. onwards, the continuing propagation among Jews
who used Aramaic and Hebrew (and among Samaritans) of traditions about
Moses apparently originating in earlier periods. Owing to the relatively
late dates at which such material was finally edited, its employment often
becomes entangled with difficulties regarding the date and provenance of
the specific tradition being considered at any one time. In nearly every
case, however, material from collections edited subsequent to the NT era is
of interest here not primarily because an early date can be confidently
assigned to a given line of thinking, but rather because even positions formulated at relatively late dates can attest the persistence of an idea or
theme arising at a much earlier time down to a later period. Naturally, writings generally considered to be relatively early, such as the Mishnah and
the halakhic midrashim, are given a measure of priority over those which
are widely acknowledged to be late, such as the later homiletic midrashim.
Likewise, both rabbinic and targumic traditions, generally speaking, are of
less moment than texts and traditions more certainly stemming from near
or within the first century itself.

---

[12] See also *m. Nid.* 4.1-2; 7.3, with Christine E. Hayes, *Gentile Impurities and
Jewish Identities: Intermarriage and Conversion from the Bible to the Talmud* (Oxford:
Oxford University Press, 2002), 111, 122-23. Josephus, *Ant.* 11.340-41 relates, with
irritation, that the Samaritans themselves claimed connection with the Jews.

[13] Further on the high profile of the Samaritans among the Jews in John Bowman,
"Samaritan Studies," *Bulletin of the John Rylands Library* 40 (1957-58): 298-99, who
argues, 298-308, that the Fourth Gospel was written with Samaritan theology clearly in
mind.

1.2 Need and Prospects for This Study

The figure of Moses has always been important in NT and Jewish studies alike, but some important opportunities for further investigation remain.

First, examination of the NT depiction of Moses often takes place solely as an adjunct to the study of NT Christology. The NT material on Moses, however, urgently needs to be considered for its contribution to the *understanding of contemporary Judaism* as well. While a variety of Jewish literature from the first century A.D. has been preserved, in many respects the New Testament contains the best of those sources. As M. Hengel puts it:

Denn daß das Neue Testament ohne die Kenntnis der zeitgenössischen jüdischen Geschichte und Religion historisch weithin unverständlich bleibt, wird heute kaum mehr bestritten. Daß es jedoch umgekehrt selbst eine wichtige Quelle für die Erforschung des Judentums seiner Zeit darstellt, wird erst allmählich erkannt.[14]

This study will seek to broaden and refine modern understanding of ancient Judaism by elucidating the (first of all Jewish) portrait of Moses found in the New Testament.

Second, the special theme of this study, *the relation of Moses to Israel and to the Jewish people*, seems particularly underexplored. The ancient conception of Moses' relationship to Israel, however, including his functions within that relationship and Israel's resultant disposition vis-à-vis Moses, is one of critical importance for understanding Jewish "ecclesiology." The same conception, especially as it stood in the Herodian age and the early Christian period, has significant bearing on the study of early Christian ecclesiology, and of the functions Christ was held to have in the Christian Church. On this score this study holds out the prospect of illuminating both ancient Judaism and early Christianity.

Third, when studies of Moses in the New Testament are undertaken, they usually look only at a single book or corpus of material (particularly the Fourth Gospel, where Moses has attracted special attention). At some stage, however, the NT material really requires treatment as a whole. This study examines the figure of Moses *across the whole New Testament*, while still respecting the distinctiveness of the various NT sources.[15]

---

[14] Martin Hengel, "Das Johannesevangelium als Quelle für die Geschichte des antiken Judentums," in *Judaica, Hellenistica, et Christiana: Kleine Schriften II*, ed. Martin Hengel with Jörg Frey and Dorothea Betz, WUNT, ed. Martin Hengel and Otfried Hofius, no. 109 (Tübingen: J. C. B. Mohr [Paul Siebeck], 1999), 294-95. See also A. F. Segal, "Conversion and Messianism: Outline for a New Approach," in *The Messiah: Developments in Earliest Judaism and Christianity*, ed. James H. Charlesworth, et al. (Minneapolis: Fortress Press, 1992), 299.

[15] Josef M. Kastner, "Moses im Neuen Testament" (Th.D. diss., Ludwig-Maximilians-Universität Munich, 1967) must be given his due here, as another effort to view Moses across the whole of the New Testament; others have made briefer attempts, such

Fourth, NT scholars have not been mistaken in supposing Moses to be important for early Christology — no doubt it is here that the figure of Moses has its chief importance for early Christianity. The *significance of Moses for early christology*, therefore, is clearly an important fourth arena of inquiry to which this study contributes. This is particularly so because the christological relevance of Moses can only be adequately assessed in light of the witness of the whole New Testament to the figure of Moses himself, properly contextualized within contemporary Judaism. The expectation of better understanding of first-century A.D. Christianity through this study has already been expressed. In particular, a fuller appreciation of the NT portrait of Moses will allow a better-informed assessment of the role of Moses in NT, and pre-NT, Christology.

1.3 Recent Study of Moses in the New Testament

Recent study of the figure of Moses in the New Testament and in ancient Judaism will now be surveyed. Research on the place Moses had in NT Christology is reviewed separately at the beginning of Chapter Eight.

J. Jeremias

A particularly influential effort to describe the figure of Moses in the New Testament is the *Theologisches Wörterbuch zum Neuen Testament* article by J. Jeremias (1942).[16] Jeremias summarizes Jewish thought about Moses in rabbinic writings and in the New Testament, though his treatment of individual NT books or corpora is limited to the assessment of Moses/Christ typology. That is, in the New Testament his interest lies in Christology.

For Jeremias, Moses is everywhere in the New Testament essentially the lawgiver. Jeremias alludes to the special, personal authority of Moses, implying a distinction between Moses merely mediating law and Moses creating law himself, a distinction that this study will take up in Chapter Five.[17] In addition to his role as lawgiver, Jeremias also views Moses in the New Testament as a prophet (principally of Christ).[18]

Jeremias calls attention both to what he identifies as the essentially Palestinian character of the NT portrait of Moses, as well as to what he considers

---

as J. Jeremias and his *TWNT* article (see next note). These studies, however, all have their shortcomings from the point of view of the present study, and clearly stand in a complementary position. See the review of past scholarship, below.

[16] J. Jeremias, "Μωυσῆς," in *Theological Dictionary of the New Testament*, ed. Gerhard Kittel, trans. and ed. Geoffrey W. Bromiley, vol. 4, *Λ-Ν* (Grand Rapids: Wm. B. Eerdmans, 1967), 848-73.

[17] Ibid., 864-65.

[18] Ibid., 865.

the characteristically Palestinian omission of exaggerated embellishment in that portrait:

There is no trace of the wild flights of imagination found in the Egyptian-Jewish legend. To summarise, it is plain that the Moses of the NT has nothing whatever to do with either the hero of the Moses romance or the ideal sage of Philo. This depiction is closer to that of the surrounding Palestinian world, though with the decisive distinction that it avoids glorifying of Moses and can repeatedly offer relentless criticism. The true basis is the OT.[19]

Jeremias has generally been vindicated in his evaluation of the NT depiction of Moses as an essentially Jewish portrayal, but the impression he gives both of a Palestinian Judaism cut off from Hellenism and Hellenistic Judaism, and of a consistent Palestinian avoidance of the glorification of Moses, has been shown less viable.

A. Descamps

A more ambitious effort in the study of Moses in the New Testament came in 1954 when the quarterly *Cahiers Sioniens* combined volume 8, numbers 2, 3, and 4 into a special edition entitled *Moïse: L'homme de l'alliance*. The edition was an attempt at a scholarly treatment of the figure of Moses across a broad diachronic front, from pre-historic times into the Muslim period, and includes treatments of Moses in the New Testament and in early Christian thought; these studies were complemented by articles on the figure of Moses in rabbinic tradition, and on Moses between the two Testaments.[20]

In that edition of *Cahiers Sioniens*, A. Descamps surveys the view of Moses in the non-Pauline portions of the New Testament, with emphasis on the view of Moses attributable to Jesus.[21] Descamps recognizes in Jesus' outlook chiefly an appreciation of the prophetic and the lawmaking activity of Moses, the latter extending as far as "l'autorité souveraine," an ascription of lawmaking authority that the present study will underline.[22] This authority is such that Descamps dubs the Judaism of the time "Mosaism," thus fore-shadowing the similarly strong formulations of Wayne Meeks (see below).

Descamps's treatment of non-Pauline Christian thought is devoted to the interpretation given by first-century Christianity to Jesus' doctrine concerning Moses and this "Mosaism."[23] Descamps sums up Moses in that strand of early Christian thought as a prophet, and, through parallels of the narratives of Moses and Jesus, as a type of Christ.[24] Descamps, however, treats views of the Law as equivalent to views about Moses himself (and vice versa), taking

---

[19] Ibid., 866.

[20] On these articles, see below, pp. 25, 26, 27..

[21] Albert Descamps, "Moïse dans les évangiles et dans la tradition apostolique," *Cahiers Sioniens* 8, nos. 2, 3, and 4 (*Moïse: L'homme de l'alliance*, 1954): 171-87.

[22] Ibid., 171.

[23] Ibid., 180.

[24] Ibid., 184-8.

his line away from the focus upon the portrayal of Moses himself which this study will seek to preserve, but which he regards as of minimal importance. Accordingly, in assessing Jesus' outlook on Moses as witnessed in the New Testament, he writes, "c'est de la Loi qu'il s'agira, la personne de Moïse ne se profilant ici qu'à l'arrière-plan."[25]

P. Démann

Filling out the treatment of the New Testament in *Moïse: L'homme de l'alliance*, P. Démann finds in the Pauline Moses chiefly a mediator of the Law.[26] Démann's treatment of the figure of Moses is quite brief, and it is also mainly concerned with typologies (in 1 Cor. 10:1-11 and 2 Cor. 3:7-18) built on the narrative of Moses' career, as opposed to the functions of Moses toward Israel.[27] He regards the rarity with which Paul mentions Moses as significant; even in Paul's great interpretation of the history of Israel in Gal. 3:6-4:7, he notes, Moses is mentioned only in 3:19, and there not by name.[28]

Like Jeremias, Démann holds that in Paul's writing we find none of the panegyric excitement about Moses that characterizes so much Hellenistic Jewish literature.[29] Like Descamps, Démann deliberately amalgamates references to the Law and references to Moses in a way which obscures Moses himself: a citation from the Pentateuch is evidence of Paul's attitude toward "Moses," which itself is a term tantamount to "Law." He writes, "Pour Paul apôtre comme pour Paul pharisien, Moïse, c'est la Loi."[30] As Descamps in the rest of the New Testament, so Démann also in Paul finds that "la figure historique de Moïse reste à l'arrière-plan."[31]

H. M. Teeple

Where other treatments involve studies of the figure of Moses itself (if sewn up within vaguely defined stereotypes [e.g., "the Lawgiver"], or converted into shapeless abstractions [e.g., "the Law"]), the focus of H. M. Teeple's revised doctoral dissertation (1957) is on the first-century notion of a prophet, secondarily of a prophet like Moses, and not on conceptions of Moses himself. Teeple attempts "to collect, organize, and evaluate the evidence for the hypothesis that some Jews and early Christians held a belief in the coming of a

---

[25] Ibid., 172; see 171.

[26] Paul Démann, "Moïse et la Loi dans la pensée de Saint Paul," *Cahiers Sioniens* 8, nos. 2, 3, and 4 (*Moïse: L'homme de l'alliance*, 1954): 189-242, a view which, as will be seen in Chapter Five, has much to commend it.

[27] Ibid., 190-98.

[28] Though an anonymous reference may be an especially reverent one. See below, p. 50.

[29] Ibid., 189.

[30] Ibid., 241.

[31] Ibid., 197.

Mosaic eschatological Prophet, i.e., the return of Moses or the coming of a Prophet like him in the new, eschatological age."[32] As he elsewhere put it, "The problem of this study is to discover the nature and influence in Judaism and early Christianity of the belief in the Mosaic eschatological Prophet."[33]

Teeple devotes the main body of his work simply to examining the many and various ways that Jews and Christians maintained and further developed the exaltation of the figure of Moses. The summary of the first century A.D. portrait of Moses which this involves is one of the stronger of such attempts, particularly since Teeple recognizes the ruling, lawgiving, and (in Philo), priestly functions of Moses, along with the prophetic role which is Teeple's main concern.[34] In particular, Teeple's sections on the functions of the Prophet-King and the Prophet-Lawgiver in Judaism[35] usefully anticipate much later work, notably that of Wayne Meeks (see below). To the discussion of the eschatological prophet in Judaism, as well as that of the prophet like Moses, he makes an important contribution; the main criticism offered here is that he does very little to adduce NT evidence for the Jewish (and Christian) conception of Moses himself.

C. K. Barrett

C. K. Barrett's *From First Adam to Last* (1962) contains an important, and sometimes overlooked, review of the portrayal of Moses in the Pauline epistles. Barrett specifically seeks "to reconstruct the working of Paul's mind, and in the light of this to see what he makes of the figure of Moses."[36] In this two-step process, and in the attempt to work "backward" into the thought-world which gave rise to Paul's statements concerning Moses (rather than "forward" into the significance of those statements for Christian theology), Barrett, after a fashion, parallels this study, which also will seek to enter the (broader, Jewish) thought-world which gave rise to the conceptions about Moses found throughout the New Testament, and so to shed light on what its writers make of Moses. Yet Barrett, reading Paul, assumes not that Moses influenced Christology, but that Christology influenced the depiction of Moses: "Paul works back from Christ to Moses, understanding Moses in the light of Christ, not Christ in the light of Moses."[37] In this regard, Barrett takes an approach much different from the thrust of this study.

---

[32] Howard M. Teeple, *The Mosaic Eschatological Prophet*, Journal of Biblical Literature Monograph Series, vol. 10 (Philadelphia: Society of Biblical Literature, 1957), v.

[33] Ibid., 1.

[34] Ibid., 32-37, 93, 108.

[35] Ibid., 102-110 and 110-15.

[36] C. K. Barrett, *From First Adam to Last: A Study in Pauline Theology* (London: Adam & Charles Black, 1962), 46-67, p. 51.

[37] Barrett, *From First Adam*, 60, also 49-50.

On one hand, Barrett finds that for Paul, Moses "certainly ... is a great man. He is one of the primary authorities, perhaps the primary authority, of the OT. A quotation may be introduced by the simple formula, Moses writes (Rom. 10:5)."[38] Moses is for Paul "a figure of glory,"[39] even (in the Exodus) a figure comparable, in rather an unexpected way, to Christ: "It was he [Paul] who decided that it was reasonable to parallel 'into Christ' with 'into Moses' [from 1 Corinthians 10:2]. ... Israelites were in a sense incorporated into him."[40]

Yet overall, Barrett finds, "Paul's treatment of Moses seems strikingly temperate."[41] Yes, "Moses remains a figure of glory, but instead of exalting his glory, as Philo and the Rabbis do, Paul minimizes it."[42] For example, "Moses was to the Rabbis ... the mediator, in the sense of intercessor and advocate. In contrast with this, Moses takes for Paul the character of a postman or telephone operator — an astounding reversal."[43]

For Barrett, then, Paul takes Moses to be both a "postman," and a "figure of glory." As if aware of the tension, commenting on 2 Corinthians 3 Barrett refers to what he calls Paul's "paradoxical glorification" of Moses.[44] Barrett never explicitly resolves the "glorious yet insignificant" Mosaic paradox he finds in Paul, yet he seems, almost despite himself, to come down on the side of glory. Absorb his summation of Paul's Moses as presented in the two most important Pauline texts, 1 Corinthians 10 and 2 Corinthians 3:

With a little alteration, both could be made to speak of Moses ... as sent by God to be a prince and redeemer . .... In I Cor. x he is at the same time the deliverer who leads his people through the desert and across the Red Sea, and the dispenser of baptism, and of spiritual food and drink. His people are baptized into him, so as to become one with him, his property, and his obedient subjects and devotees. In II Cor. iii he is an almost supernatural being, a θεῖος ἀνήρ, whose face is resplendent with divine glory. There seems to have been in Paul's time a tendency to make of Moses just such a divine, cult figure.[45]

Barrett goes on to compare this with what he accepts is the presentation of Moses in the murals of Dura-Europos "in the character of one of the great founders of new religions of the ancient world, as a canonized and almost deified hero, founder of the Jewish religion; a counterpart in some degree of Buddha and Christ."[46] This is not only a picture of Moses as "the central

---

[38] Ibid., 47 (sic).

[39] Ibid., 52.

[40] Ibid., 49-50.

[41] Ibid., 60.

[42] Ibid., 52.

[43] Ibid., 61-62.

[44] Ibid., 53.

[45] Ibid., 54.

[46] Ibid., 54, quoting M. Rostovtzeff, *Dura-Europos and Its Art* (Oxford: Clarendon Press, 1938), 108.

figure in Jewish religion," "the central figure in the drama of redemption, upon which the national, religious, and liturgical life of the people rested."[47] This is a picture of Israel as well, of what might be called the "inner constitution" of the Jewish people, and the function of Moses within that constitution.

Barrett stresses that this picture cannot be generalized to all Jews, and that particularly Jews with a more solid faithfulness to the revealed religion of Scripture would have used the sort of language in these quotations "as at most an illustration."[48] Of Paul in particular he writes:

In view of the material we have now briefly surveyed [texts from Philo, Artapanus, magical papyri which invoke Moses, and rabbinic literature] Paul's treatment of Moses seems strikingly temperate. For him Moses is no quasi-divine figure. Nor does he think of Christ as a new Moses, a 'latter redeemer' conceived on the model of the former. ... Paul works back from Christ to Moses, understanding Moses in the light of Christ, not Christ in the light of Moses.[49]

Despite this caveat (which is defended only by a further exegesis of Gal. 3:19), Barrett's assessment shows what a robust impression of Moses can be gained from the writings of Paul, an impression that may have been more influential both in (Pharisaic?) Judaism and in Christianity than is commonly conceded.

T. F. Glasson

T. F. Glasson (1963) mainly pursues allusions to Moses, or to the events of the wilderness wanderings, in the Fourth Gospel.[50] Glasson does not much attempt to develop a contemporary impression of the Moses figure, with the important exception of the prophethood of Moses, and the expected Prophet like him, regarding which he concludes that "the entire conception of a prophet like unto Moses, Deut. 18.15ff., is basic to the understanding of St John."[51] He even briefly tackles the idea of Moses as a prophet-king,[52] a theme dealt with more comprehensively by Teeple (above) and by Meeks (see below), and a Mosaic motif of interest to this study. Chiefly, however, Glasson's interest in his short book is to illuminate narrative parallels between the Gospel of John and elements of the OT account of Moses and the journey to the Promised Land. His interest in the use of the Moses narrative takes the focus away from

---

[47] Ibid., 58. N.B., with these words Barrett sums up his description of Moses in first-century Judaism, not in Paul, but the description seems to fit his summation of Paul and most of the Jewish literature he cites is applicable to the NT environment.

[48] Ibid., 58-59.

[49] Ibid., 60.

[50] T. F. Glasson, *Moses in the Fourth Gospel*, Studies in Biblical Theology, ed. C. F. D. Moule, et al., no. 40 (London: SCM Press, 1963).

[51] Ibid., 80.

[52] Ibid., 31-32.

Moses himself, and what the Evangelist and his community, etc., thought of him.

F. Bovon

In an essay published in 1978, F. Bovon explores the depiction of Moses in Luke-Acts.[53] He finds that Luke sees Moses with authority so great that he seems to incarnate the Law: "La Loi, c'est Moïse," he writes, in a refrain evidently especially popular among French scholars (e.g. Descamps and Démann, as cited above).[54] Nonetheless, for Bovon the principal quality of Moses in Luke is prophetic (Luke 24:27, 44-45).[55] While Moses, in Luke-Acts, may be summed up as both a prophet and a legislator, for Bovon the former decidedly overshadows the latter.[56] Such a compression of Moses into the scheme of "prophet" is, as should be becoming apparent, a common feature of NT scholarship.

M. R. D'Angelo

M. R. D'Angelo (1979) approaches the portrayal of Moses in Hebrews, and in the New Testament generally, as a product of Christology.[57] An individual NT author's view of Moses is "illustrative of the workings of his Christology upon the portrait of Moses as well as of the expectation of the prophet like Moses upon the Christology."[58] "Thus," she writes:

in dealing with the texts of the New Testament, it becomes possible and perhaps more useful … to look at the correspondence between Christ and Moses in order to see how an understanding of Christ, of Christianity, and of the relation of Christianity to Judaism has shaped an author's understanding of Moses.[59]

D'Angelo focuses in particular on the creativity of the author of Hebrews in conforming Moses to Christ (in a way that resembles Barrett's line on Paul, see above).[60] In a sense, then, the present study is, at least in its eighth chapter, a counter-proposal to D'Angelo, since it will suggest the opposite tack to

---

[53] François Bovon, "La figure de Moïse dans l'oeuvre de Luc," in *La figure de Moïse: Ecriture et relectures*, by Robert Martin-Achard, et al., Publications de la Faculté de Théologie de l'Université de Genève, no. 1 (Geneva: Labor et Fides, 1978), 47-65.

[54] Ibid., 48.

[55] Ibid., 50.

[56] Ibid., 50-53, 59.

[57] Mary Rose D'Angelo, *Moses in the Letter to the Hebrews*, Society of Biblical Literature Dissertation Series, ed. Howard Clark Kee, no. 42 (Missoula, Montana: Scholars Press, 1979).

[58] Ibid., 3; see pages 2-11, esp. 2-3.

[59] Ibid., 2.

[60] Ibid., 11-12.

hers: how an existing Moses tradition may have influenced the presentation of NT Christology.

D. Allison

D. Allison's *The New Moses* (1993) is distinguished from the present study both by its concentration on the Gospel of Matthew and by its emphasis on demonstrating Moses typology in Matthew rather than on elucidating Matthew's view of Moses himself.[61] To build his case, Allison shows how through many centuries both Jews and Christians used Moses as a type for an impressively large and disparate group of figures.[62] While exploring these typologies, Allison incidentally illuminates aspects of Moses' portrait that go beyond prophethood, such as kingship and redeemership. He also formulates an impressive description of the Jewish view of Moses as "the personification of authority," in which respect his speech was tantamount to God's speech.[63]

Allison's strong focus on typology, however, usually limits him to exploring ways in which the narrative of Moses in the Old Testament (and in legends) has been paralleled and alluded to by authors writing about other figures. Allison writes, "The First Gospel displays no independent interest in Moses,"[64] and the same might be said of Allison (and of many other NT scholars). Allison's study and this study are therefore complementary to each other, both in scope and in subject matter.

S. Harstine

Another recent study of the role Moses plays in a single NT book is S. Harstine's *Moses as a Character in the Fourth Gospel*. Harstine sets out "to investigate the function of Moses as a character in the Fourth Gospel" and "to examine the probable responses of ancient readers to that characterization."[65] Harstine's study of the Gospel of John is a strictly literary analysis, an attempt to discern "the role that Moses plays within the literary setting of the narrative" of the Gospel,[66] focusing on the relationship between Moses and the unfolding plot of the Gospel and the other characters of the Gospel, and the characterization of Moses that appears along the way.[67] For purposes of com-

---

[61] Dale C. Allison, Jr., *The New Moses: A Matthean Typology* (Edinburgh: T. & T. Clark, 1993).

[62] Ibid., 11-134.

[63] Ibid., 276.

[64] Ibid., 275.

[65] Stan Harstine, *Moses as a Character in the Fourth Gospel: A Study of Ancient Reading Techniques*, Journal for the Study of the New Testament Supplement Series, no. 229, ed. Stanley E. Porter, et al. (London and New York: Sheffield Academic Press, 2002), 37.

[66] Ibid., 14.

[67] Ibid., 37. Harstine, 72-75, sums up John's characterization of Moses mainly as "a witness," specifically in favor of Jesus.

parison, Harstine also pursues a similar analysis of the function of Moses as a character in the Synoptic Gospels and in the narratives of Second Temple Judaism.

All three of these investigations are useful, and in the breadth of material explored Harstine's work rivals this one. Since, however, Harstine's interest is in the function of Moses specifically as a background character in the Gospels (especially John), the Second Temple Jewish texts he reviews are limited to prose narrative texts from the period 200 B.C. to A.D. 200 that present Moses as a background character.[68] Because of his close focus exclusively on narrative employment of the figure of Moses in the Gospels and other Jewish literature, Harstine's study rather closely resembles the one by Allison (above), and like Allison's study, Harstine's study is less a rival to the present one than its complement.

J. Kastner

The unpublished dissertation by J. Kastner, "Moses im Neuen Testament," has received less attention that it deserves.[69]

Part One, "Die Grundlagen des ntl. Mosesbildes," takes in a review of pre- and post-NT Jewish literature on Moses. Kastner opens with a detailed examination of Moses as he is presented in the Old Testament. Through application of source-critical and other literary tools Kastner works out a history of the views of Moses in the various eras held to be represented by the several discernible strata of the Old Testament. This portion of his dissertation is therefore an intriguing, if necessarily somewhat speculative, diachronic study.

Kastner detects growing interest in Moses in Second Temple Judaism, expressed by increasing numbers of references to Moses in the sources and the accumulation of legendary embellishments of the biblical accounts.[70] Particularly in the Palestinian apocrypha one finds the tendency "Moses mit den höchsten Attributen zu verherrlichen und unter Zuhilfenahme der Legende sein Lebensbild zu ergänzen."[71]

While Qumran has not been a key source for Jewish views of Moses, Kastner also presents a very helpful summation of the view, in the Qumran texts he knew, of the *Endzeit* as a *Moseszeit*, and of the eschatological interpretation of Deut. 18:15-19 in the literature of Quman.[72]

Kastner then undertakes a further helpful review of the portrayal of Moses in rabbinic traditions, focusing particularly on haggadic developments.[73]

---

[68] Ibid., 96.

[69] Josef M. Kastner, "Moses im Neuen Testament" (Th.D. diss., Ludwig-Maximilians-Universität Munich, 1967).

[70] Ibid., 44.

[71] Ibid., 48.

[72] Ibid., 61-66 and 66-68.

[73] Ibid., 74-104.

In Part Two, "Moses im Neuen Testament," Kastner seeks to employ the appreciation of Moses gleaned from Part One in order better to understand the ways in which Moses motifs are used in the NT presentation of Christ and the *Heilszeit* inaugurated by Christ. Kastner's concern throughout this part is with Moses typology, and the way the NT writers exploit Moses typology, and not with the portrayal of Moses *per se* in the NT books.

His approach in the four Gospels (and Hebrews), is to pursue "Parallelisierung der Jesusgeschichte mit der Mosesüberlieferung."[74] That is, he is interested in the story of Moses, not the function(s) of Moses, and that for its typological value. Similarly in the letters of Paul, Kastner investigates the use of Moses as a source of typology for Christ and the Christian community.[75] In Acts as well, the burden of Kastner's work is in the elucidation of (christological) typology, so while a strong portrait of Moses as prophet emerges, it does so through exploration of the portrayal of Jesus as a prophet (like Moses).

Kastner finds the portrait of Moses implied by Acts to be especially positive, even by NT standards.[76] Perhaps this is because Kastner, like other NT scholars, basically views Moses as a prophet. In Hebrews, for example, Kastner finds Moses portrayed with great glory (the better to set off the glory of Jesus) but it is strictly the glory of a mediator, even though the glory of Jesus in that book reaches into other roles.[77] In his discussion of John, Kastner provides a lengthy review of (now older) scholarly discussion of the liveliness of the expectation of an eschatological Prophet like Moses,[78] and his study of Moses in John picks up that motif along with assorted allusions to the life of Moses.

Overall, then, Kastner's focus is significantly different from that of the present study. His focus is precisely on "Die Vorstellung von Jesus als der Erfüllung des weissagenden Mosestypos,"[79] and not on the NT presentation of Moses himself. Kastner's principal interest in Christology leads to appreciable differences between his study and this in the treatment of NT texts.

Also, for Kastner the New Testament authors handle and depict Moses almost exclusively as a mediator.[80] Though the Mosaic themes involved in NT typology that Kastner unearths are very varied, other roles Moses might be thought to play do not enter into Kastner's focus. For exmaple, in line with

---

[74] Ibid., 112. Cf. 140-43, and *passim*.

[75] E.g., ibid., 200-201.

[76] "Der atl. Mittler ist nicht Gegenbild, sondern Vorbild Jesu," ibid., 232.

[77] Ibid., 240-41, 243 ("Der Autor 'braucht' die relativ hohe Würde des Moses"), 247-56, 266-67.

[78] Ibid., 290-300.

[79] Ibid., 308.

[80] E.g., as in Hebrews, noted above. In John, Moses is Mittler des Gesetzes (271, 287).

this emphasis Kastner frequently treats "Moses" as standing for "Law of Moses," without discussion.[81] "Mediation" captures nearly everything that Kastner wishes to say about Moses in the New Testament, and his commitment to seeing Moses as a mediator has an appreciable flattening effect on his assessment of the NT presentation of Moses.

The difference between the present study and Kastner's is well-captured in their respective titles: where "Moses im Neuen Testament" examines the way the Moses figure found elsewhere in Jewish tradition is used in the New Testament, the present study focuses on the Moses figure portrayed in the New Testament itself.[82]

W. Meeks

Possibly the most influential NT study of Moses along the lines advocated here is by W. Meeks (1967).[83] In his introduction, Meeks cites John 6:14-15: "So when the men saw the sign which he had done, they said, 'This is truly the prophet who is coming into the world.' So Jesus, recognizing that they were about to come and seize him to make him king, fled to the mountain alone."[84]

"Who," Meeks asks, "is 'the prophet who is coming into the world'? Why does the 'sign' of the multiplication of loaves indicate his identity? Why is it so self-evident that 'the prophet' is to be made 'king'?"[85] Meeks sets out "to clarify the way in which the motifs represented by the two terms 'prophet' and 'king' in the Fourth Gospel not only are interrelated, but interpret each other" through "a study of similar combinations of the prophetic and royal motifs in representative sources from the Mediterranean religious world."[86]

Moses features in his study as a consequence of the recognition that "certain traditions about Moses provided for the Fourth Gospel not only the figure of the eschatological prophet, but the figure who combines in one person both royal and prophetic honor and functions."[87] Exegesis laid out in Meeks's second chapter shows the connection of Mosaic prophethood with kingship in the Fourth Gospel. The main body of Meeks's book surveys Moses traditions in Jewish sources (rabbinic and non-rabbinic), Samaritan sources, and Mandaean sources, showing that Moses was indeed widely understood in terms suitable for the role Meeks hypothesizes for him in John. Meeks's relatively

---

[81] E.g., ibid., 220, 222, 305.

[82] Kastner's work is reviewed with special reference to Mosaic Christology below, pp. 269-70.

[83] Wayne A. Meeks, *The Prophet-King: Moses Traditions and the Johannine Christology*, Supplements to *Novum Testamentum*, ed. W. C. van Unnik, et al., vol. 14 (Leiden: E. J. Brill, 1967).

[84] Meeks, 1 n. 1 prefers the *lectionem difficiliorem*, φευγει.

[85] Ibid., 1.

[86] Ibid., 1.

[87] Ibid., 29.

brief final chapter surveys the way Moses is actually portrayed in John; it is chiefly here that *The Prophet-King* and this study work some of the same ground.

Meeks's investigation is explicitly an "investigation of a narrow aspect of the Johannine christology."[88] He concludes that "the Johannine traditions were shaped, at least in part, by interaction between a Christian community and a hostile Jewish community whose piety accorded very great importance to Moses and the Sinai theophany." Further, "the depiction of Jesus as prophet and king in the Fourth Gospel owes much to traditions which the church inherited from the Moses piety."[89] Meeks's coverage of the extra-biblical material on Moses available to him is very thorough, and despite his primary interests he assesses Moses in that material in a range of roles, not simply as king or as prophet (though it is to these that he returns most of the time).[90]

The very success of Meeks's study draws attention to three *desiderata* that seem to have remained outstanding until now.

First, while he alludes to traditions, which "the church inherited from the Moses piety," his work only examines the figure of Moses in one Gospel.[91] Clearly it would be desirable to examine the view of Moses attested in the rest of the New Testament, since the other books as well should witness what "the church inherited from the Moses piety."

Second, Meeks is concerned with "a narrow aspect of the Johannine christology." This leads him, among other things, to focus his attention on two great themes of that Christology, prophethood and kingship, and it is chiefly these that he relates to Moses, though he is attentive to other themes as well, including most of those treated in this study. Surely, however, it would be desirable and useful to build a fuller picture of the appraisal — or appraisals — of Moses attested across the whole of the New Testament, taking into account all the ways in which Moses seems to be portrayed in the entire corpus.

Third, Meeks undertook his study realizing the importance of discovering how concepts like "king" and "prophet" could be joined in the portrayal of a single figure (namely, Jesus in the Fourth Gospel). The most important contribution of his book lies in showing how Jewish conceptions of Moses provided the template for the fusion of those roles in John's christology. The fact that the two most pronounced motifs in John's christology seem to be modeled on the fusion of the same motifs in Moses calls for investigation of whether other motifs in the broader christology of the whole New Testament might also be conjoined on the model given by Moses.

---

[88] Ibid., 16.

[89] Ibid., 318-19; his expression recalls the "Mosaism" of Descamps, see above, pp. 11-12.

[90] See his index, p. 352.

[91] See his index, pp. 338-41.

This study is intended in part to address these considerations stemming from Meeks's work.

1.4 Recent Study of Moses in Ancient Jewish and Graeco-Roman Writings

The study of Moses in the New Testament, valuable in its own right and the principal focus of this study, is also necessarily part of a larger project of studying the figure of Moses in ancient Judaism generally. In this field non-Jewish, as well as Jewish, authors can be useful witnesses.

Moses in the context of strictly (i.e. not Christian) Jewish material has received a good deal more scholarly attention than Moses in the New Testament, both because of the obvious importance of Moses to Judaism, and because studies focusing on Jewish literature naturally face little temptation to make a priority of Christology.

1.4.1 The Alexandrians: Artapanus, Aristobulus, and Ezekiel Tragicus

In a sense the father of the modern study of the figure of Moses in Judaism is J. Freudenthal (1875), who emphasized the importance of Moses in the great saga of the Jews as retold by Artapanus, and helped to show the importance of Moses for late Second Temple Judaism generally.[92] A large part of Freudenthal's work involved demonstrating that the legendary Moses of Artapanus had been taken up as the basis for most, if not all, subsequent Jewish retellings of the Exodus account,[93] from not only Alexandrian but also Palestinian sources, down into the midrash of the rabbinic period.[94] This indicates not simply the wide readership enjoyed by Artapanus, but more significantly the wide endorsement of the Artapanian view of the centrality and exaltation of Moses in Judaism (and in the Jewish history of the world).

Other scholars who have studied the Alexandrian writers on Moses have broadly ratified the conclusions of Freudenthal about the importance of Artapanus's embellished life of Moses, while carrying the discussion forward in various ways. J. G. M. Barclay (1996), makes more than some modern writers of the possible ascription of divine status to Moses by Artapanus,[95] though

---

[92] J. Freudenthal, "Die Trugschrift des Artapanos," in *Alexander Polyhistor und die von ihm erhaltenen Reste judäischer und samaritanischer Geschichtswerke*, vol. 2 in *Hellenistische Studien von Dr. J. Freudenthal* (Breslau: H. Skutsch, 1875), 143-74.

[93] Ibid., 162-165, 172. He, 169-71, concludes that Josephus used not Artapanus, but a source on which Artapanus relied.

[94] Ibid., 171-73.

[95] John G. M. Barclay, *Jews in the Mediterranean Diaspora from Alexander to Trajan (323 BCE-117 CE)* (Edinburgh: T. & T. Clark, 1996), 129.

G. Vermes (1954) minimizes the same possibility.[96] *P. M. Fraser* (1972) contributes a classicist's appreciation of the place of the accounts of Moses given by the historians Aristobulus and Artapanus, and by the playwright Ezekiel, in Hellenistic literature.[97] *C. R. Holladay* (1983, 1989, 1995) and *E. S. Gruen* (1998) also provide general commentary on the presentation of Moses in all three Alexandrians, though, like Fraser, their main interest is in the texts themselves, and not in Moses.[98]

For much the same reason that Artapanus has attracted scholarly attention, the audacity of the portrait of Moses in the *Exagoge* of Ezekiel the Tragedian attracts the attention of scholars of Judaism. Like Barclay and Vermes on Artapanus, *P. van der Horst* (1983, 1984) and *R. Bauckham* (1999) focus attention in somewhat contrasting ways on the implications of the *Exagoge* for the divinity of Moses, with van der Horst urging that Ezekiel endows Moses with full-fledged deity, and Bauckham taking the line that the divinity of Moses in the *Exagoge* is only a stylized representation of his leadership of Israel.[99]

1.4.2 The Alexandrians: Philo

The Alexandrian Jewish writer *par excellence* is Philo, and many of the scholars mentioned in the preceding subsection demonstrate how clearly he is the heir and propagator of Moses traditions set out by his predecessors in that

---

[96] (One of the *Moïse: L'homme de l'alliance* articles alluded to above:) Geza Vermes, "La figure de Moïse au tournant des deux Testaments," *Cahiers Sioniens* 8, nos. 2, 3, and 4 (*Moïse: L'homme de l'alliance*, 1954): 72-73.

[97] P. M. Fraser, *Ptolemaic Alexandria*, 3 vols., vol. 1, *Text* (Oxford: Clarendon Press, 1972; reprint, 1984), 694-96, Aristobulus; 704-708, Artapanus and Ezekiel the Tragedian, with the Letter of Aristeas treated pp. 696-704.

[98] Holladay, *Fragments from Hellenistic Jewish Authors*, vol. 1, *Historians*, Society of Biblical Literature Texts and Translations Pseudepigrapha Series, ed. Harold W. Attridge, Texts and Translations no. 20, Pseudepigrapha no. 10 (Chico, California: Scholars Press, 1983), vol. 2, *Poets*, SBLTTPS, ed. James C. Vanderkam, Texts and Translations no. 30, Pseudepigrapha no. 12 (Atlanta: Scholars Press, 1989), vol. 3, *Aristobulus*, SBLTTPS, ed. Martha Himmelfarb, Texts and Translations no. 39, Pseudepigrapha no. 13 (Atlanta: Scholars Press, 1995); Erich S. Gruen, *Heritage and Hellenism: The Reinvention of Jewish Tradition*, Hellenistic Culture and Society, ed. Anthony W. Bulloch, et al., no. 30 (Berkeley: University of California Press, 1998).

[99] Pieter W. van der Horst, "Moses' Throne Vision in Ezekiel the Dramatist," *Journal of Jewish Studies* 34 (1983): esp. 25-26 and "Some Notes on the *Exagoge* of Ezekiel," *Mnemosyne* 37, nos. 3-4 (1984): esp. 366-68; Richard Bauckham, "The Throne of God and the Worship of Jesus," in *The Jewish Roots of Christological Monotheism: Papers from the St. Andrews Conference on the Historical Origin of the Worship of Jesus*, ed. Carey C. Newman, James R. Davila, and Gladys S. Lewis, Supplements to the *Journal for the Study of Judaism*, ed. John J. Collins with Florentino García Martínez, vol. 63 (Leiden: Brill, 1999) esp. 55-57.

city. *M. Braun* (1938) in particular assesses Philo's life of Moses as a sanitized (i.e. less embarrassing to Jews) version of the one by Artapanus.[100]

Perhaps the most important modern writer on Philo is *E. R. Goodenough*. Philo was a special interest of Goodenough throughout his career. In *By Light, Light: The Mystic Gospel of Hellenistic Judaism* (1935) Goodenough sets out, almost entirely on the basis of Philo's writings, to deduce the contours of the mystery religion or "Mystic Judaism" into which, he believes, one section of Diaspora Judaism had evolved.[101] The Jewish Mystery, according to Goodenough, regarded Moses as its founder and leader: the supreme hierophant and mystagogue of Israel.[102] Perhaps for this reason, although Goodenough does not set out to study Moses *per se*, he devotes two chapters to him: "Moses as Presented to the Gentile Inquirer," and "The Mystic Moses."[103] The separate chapter on Moses for Gentiles reflects, in part, the fact that for non-Jews Moses was practically the emblem of Jews and Judaism.[104] (This would be one reason Jewish authors took such pains to get his portrait right.)

Philo's Moses, according to Goodenough, was competent to head Mystic Judaism because he was a divine incarnation;[105] he became the god — a substitute for God — of the whole nation.[106] "In Moses," Goodenough writes, "the gulf between the mortal and immortal ... has been bridged."[107] Goodenough claims that "Philo sees in Moses an active and present power," and even cites what he thinks is Philo's prayer to Moses.[108]

Goodenough develops his construct of Mystic Judaism almost exclusively from the writings of Philo and he freely concedes:

They were ... few who went quite beyond ordinary Judaism to what seemed to Philo the essential and only true Judaism ... [that is,] the Mystery of Judaism, which is by no means the religion of the Jews in general.[109]

---

[100] Martin Braun, *History and Romance in Graeco-Oriental Literature* (Oxford: Basil Blackwell, 1938), 26-31, 99-102, esp. 30-31; Braun is more interested in the Joseph Romance than in Moses. Freudenthal, "Die Trugschrift des Artapanos," 173 regards the accounts of Moses in Philo and Artapanus as parallel.

[101] See Erwin R. Goodenough, *By Light, Light: The Mystic Gospel of Hellenistic Judaism* (New Haven, Connecticut: Yale University Press, 1935; reprint, Amsterdam: Philo Press, 1969), 8-9; his thesis is set out succinctly on 7-8.

[102] Goodenough, *By Light, Light*, 215, 220-21.

[103] Ibid., 180-98, 199-234.

[104] See John G. Gager, *Moses in Greco-Roman Paganism*, Society of Biblical Literature Monograph Series, ed. Robert A. Kraft, no. 16 (Nashville and New York: Abingdon Press, 1972), 18, and discussion below, pp. 27-29.

[105] Ibid., 199-200

[106] Ibid., 223-29.

[107] Ibid., 197.

[108] Ibid., 233. See p, 193-94 below.

[109] Goodenough, *By Light, Light*, 230.

Thus Goodenough frankly confesses that his broader, and rather speculative, thesis about a Jewish Mystery is at best applicable to only one esoteric wing of Judaism.[110]

His appraisal of the Philonic Moses, by contrast, is hardly speculative at all, arising as it does simply from a close reading of Philo's works. It remains a useful synthesis whether or not his scheme for a Jewish Mystery is judged a success, and will be helpful at points in the course of this study.[111]

The divine aspect of the Jewish view of Moses was carried beyond Philo and Alexandria, but in evident debt to Goodenough, in *W. Meeks*'s article, "Moses as God and King" (1968, in the Goodenough memorial volume), which is "an analysis of some variations on the theme of Moses' heavenly enthronement in Philo, the midrash aggada, and Samaritan sources."[112]

1.4.3 The Palestinians: Josephus and Pseudo-Philo

Among the most obvious transmitters of Palestinian traditions are Josephus and Pseudo-Philo. The eclectic *Vermes* treats both together in the same article already referred to above, though his discussion is taken up with the haggadic embellishments recorded by the two ancient authors in what he characterizes as a Jewish catechism.[113] *P. Spilsbury* (1998) reviews the depiction of Moses in Josephus as part of his discussion of the role Moses plays in Josephus's theory of Jewish identity, a concern also relevant to the present study.[114] *M. Maher* (1996) demonstrates that the haggadic embellishments specifically of Artapanus seem to have been known both to Josephus and to Pseudo-Jonathan (the targumist), and that they go on to appear in the tenth-century *Chronicle of Moses*.[115]

---

[110] See also the rebuttal in Wilfred L. Knox, *St Paul and the Church of the Gentiles* (Cambridge: Cambridge University Press, 1939), ix-x.

[111] Louis H. Feldman, (tentatively) *Philo's Portrait of Moses in the Context of Ancient Judaism* (still in progress), is likely to shed further light on the subject.

[112] Wayne A. Meeks, "Moses as God and King," in *Religions in Antiquity: Essays in Memory of Erwin Ramsdell Goodenough*, ed. Jacob Neusner, 354-371, Studies in the History of Religions (Supplements to *Numen*), no. 14 (Leiden: E. J. Brill, 1968), p. 354.

[113] Vermes, "La figure de Moïse au tournant des deux Testaments," 86-92, (87).

[114] Paul Spilsbury, *The Image of the Jew in Flavius Josephus' Paraphrase of the Bible*, Texte und Studien zum Antiken Judentum, ed. Martin Hengel and Peter Schäfer, no. 69 (Tübingen: J. C. B. Mohr [Paul Siebeck], 1998), 94-146.

[115] Maher, "Targum Pseudo-Jonathan of Exodus 2.21," in *Targumic and Cognate Studies: Essays in Honour of Martin MacNamara*, ed. Kevin J. Cathcart and Michael Maher, Journal for the Study of the Old Testament Supplement Series, ed. David J. A. Clines and Philip R. Davies, no. 230 (Sheffield: Sheffield Academic Press, 1996), 82, 86-87, and 99, which extends the reach of such Artapanian traditions to several other Palestinian and Alexandrian writers.

1.4.4 Qumran

The Qumran and Judaean Desert texts have not been notable for their contribution to our understanding of the Jewish view of Moses, but they do contain some relevant material. In addition to the remarks provided by Vermes, just noted, who builds on the similar work by *N. Wieder* (1953) on the Mosaic implications of the titles given to the Interpreter of the Law in the Damascus Document,[116] *C. H. T. Fletcher-Louis* (1996), draws attention to the implications for a divine Moses in the Moses Apocryphon A of Qumran Cave Four.[117] The work of these scholars is consulted in the discussions below of Moses as a lawgiver and as a focus of Jewish loyalty.

1.4.5 The Apocrypha and Pseudepigrapha

Vermes, as noted above, looked at the wildly embellished narrative of Artapanus, but he also takes an interest in "the Palestinian apocrypha."[118] Under "Palestinian apocrypha" he includes diverse sources such as the writings from Qumran, 4 Ezra, Jubilees, the *Assumption of Moses*, and the Targums. In reviewing these writings, he focuses on the Law and other revelations said to have been received by Moses, and so on Moses principally as a lawgiver and a prophet (i.e. the usual categories for discussion of Moses).

In this literature especially, Vermes is well supplemented by *S. J. Hafemann*'s 1990 article which "surveys all of the major references to Moses in the Apocrypha and Pseudepigrapha," outlining the basic ways in which the figure and ministry of Moses functioned within that literature.[119] Hafemann's "Apocrypha and Pseudepigrapha," which come from the standard sets of so-named materials, include especially 2 Maccabees, 2 Baruch, Jubilees, the *Assumption of Moses*, and Pseudo-Philo's *Biblical Antiquities*. Hafemann's attention to the function of Moses as described in this literature resembles the focus of this study, though the only function that he really attends to is the manner in which Moses bears authority.

---

[116] Naphtali Wieder, "The 'Law-Interpreter' of the Sect of the Dead Sea Scrolls: The Second Moses," *Journal of Jewish Studies* 4, no. 4 (1953): 165-67.

[117] Crispin H. T. Fletcher-Louis, "4Q374: A Discourse on the Sinai Tradition: The Deification of Moses and Early Christology," *Dead Sea Discoveries* 3 (1996): 236-252.

[118] Vermes, "La figure de Moïse au tournant des deux Testaments," 63-92; he examines apocrypha, 74-86.

[119] Scott J. Hafemann, "Moses in the Apocrypha and Pseudepigrapha: A Survey," *Journal for the Study of the Pseudepigrapha* 7 (1990): (79-)104; reprised with less detailed argument in his *Paul, Moses, and the History of Israel: The Letter/Spirit Contrast and the Argument from Scripture in 2 Corinthians 3*, WUNT, ed. Martin Hengel and Otfried Hofius, no. 81 (Tübingen: J. C. B. Mohr [Paul Siebeck], 1995), 63-71.

1.4.6 Rabbinic and Other Jewish Literature

As already indicated above, *J. Jeremias*'s *TWNT* article includes a few dense pages on the view of "Moses in Later Judaism," which embrace in scope, if not in detail, the epoch spanning all the centuries from the early Hellenistic to the late rabbinic periods, distinguishing (somewhat artificially) between Hellenistic and Palestinian views, and assessing Moses overall as "für das Spätjudt die wichtigste Gestalt der ganzen bisherigen Heilsgeschichte."[120] As also already noted, *J. Kastner*'s "Moses im Neuen Testament" provides extensive and helpful reviews of intertestamental, Qumran, and rabbinic conceptions of Moses.

R. Bloch's study on Moses in rabbinic tradition is massive,[121] incorporating literature from the Septuagint down to late rabbinic works, but she intentionally focuses solely on one chapter of the history of Moses, that of his birth, a haggadic element of little intrinsic interest to the present study.[122]

Perhaps the wide extent to which the early, embellishing traditions survived in later tradition, interwoven with rabbinic midrash and haggadah, is revealed nowhere better than in *L. Ginzberg*'s compiled *Legends of the Jews* (1909-1928).[123] Ginzberg amalgamates an extraordinarily broad mass of material from a whole spectrum of sources. His detailed bibliographical notes make him a valuable resource on source material even if his own synthesis of Jewish legends produces a somewhat undifferentiated harmony of very distinct voices.

1.4.7 Study of Moses in Greek and Roman Writings

Besides the many treatments of what are really a relatively few key Jewish writings, a few efforts have been made to develop the picture of Moses found in the writings of Greek and Roman authors.

The premier such treatment is still that of *J. G. Gager* (1972), who examines the conception of Moses as recorded by a large number of pagan authors in the Greco-Roman world.[124] The questions Gager asks:

---

[120] J. Jeremias, "Μωυσῆς," in *Theologisches Wörterbuch zum Neuen Testament*, ed. Gerhard Kittel, vol. 4, *Λ-Ν* (Stuttgart: W. Kohlhammer, 1942), 854, "Μωυσῆς," *TDNT* 4.849(-56).

[121] Renée Bloch, "Quelques aspects de la figure de Moïse dans la tradition rabbinique," *Cahiers Sioniens* 8, nos. 2, 3, and 4 (*Moïse: L'homme de l'alliance*, 1954): 93-167 in this fascicle (211-285 in the volume).

[122] Ibid., 94-95.

[123] Louis Ginzberg, *The Legends of the Jews*, 7 vols., vols. 1 and 2 trans. Henrietta Szold, vol. 3 trans. Paul Radin, vol. 7, *Index*, by Boaz Cohen (Philadelphia: The Jewish Publication Society of America, 1913, 1920[sic], 1911[sic], 1913, 1925, 1928, 1938).

[124] John G. Gager, *Moses in Greco-Roman Paganism*, Society of Biblical Literature Monograph Series, ed. Robert A. Kraft, no. 16 (Nashville and New York: Abingdon Press, 1972).

What did they know, or claim to know, of him [Moses]? What did they think of him, and what factors (social, political, literary, etc.) influenced their evaluation of him? Where did they get their information? Was there anything like a fixed image, or images of Moses?[125]

are very similar to the questions this study asks about NT authors. Gager's study is extensive — he draws on about twenty ancient authors — and important — he himself was aware in 1972 of only two similar, but less ambitious, attempts in modern scholarship.[126]

All the Greco-Roman texts on Moses that Gager examines can also be found, with commentary, scattered in *M. Stern*'s massive *Greek and Latin Authors on Jews and Judaism* (1974, 1980),[127] along with Lactantius Placidus (sixth century A.D.), and Pseudacro (scholiast, date not known), whom Gager does not mention.[128]

Probably the earliest,[129] and most influential, pagan Greek writer about Moses is the great fourth-century B.C. ethnographer Hecataeus of Abdera, discussed by both Gager and Stern and more thoroughly by *B. Bar-Kochva* (1996).[130] Hecataeus's excursus on the Jews (in his *Aegyptiaca*) is actually a highly laudatory abstract of the career of Moses, much conformed to contemporary Greek ideals of the founding and political establishment of cities.[131] Hecataeus's account, "the first comprehensive account of Jews and Judaism in

---

[125] Ibid., 15.

[126] Ibid., 15-16.

[127] Menachem Stern, ed. and trans., *Greek and Latin Authors on Jews and Judaism Edited with Introductions, Translations, and Commentary*, 3 vols. Vol. 1, *From Herodotus to Plutarch*, vol. 2, *From Tacitus to Simplicitus*, vol. 3, *Appendixes and Indexes*, Fontes and Res Judaicas Spectantes (Jerusalem: The Israel Academy of Sciences and Humanities, 1974, 1980, 1984).

[128] Ibid., 2.685 and 2.656, respectively. Their references to Moses are incidental, though interesting. Both Stern and more especially Gager can now be supplemented with additional evidence from papypri. See Timothy B. Savage, *Power through Weakness: Paul's Understanding of the Christian Ministry in 2 Corinthians*, Society for New Testament Studies Monograph Series, ed. Margaret E. Thrall, no. 86 (Cambridge: Cambridge University Press, 1996), 107.

[129] Gager, *Moses in Greco-Roman Paganism*, 26; cf. Stern, *Greek and Latin Authors on Jews and Judaism*, 1.8-9.

[130] Bezalel Bar-Kochva, *Pseudo-Hecataeus' On the Jews: Legitimizing the Jewish Diaspora*, Hellenistic Culture and Society, ed. Anthony W. Bulloch, et al., no. 21 (Berkeley: University of California Press, 1996), 7-43, by way of introduction to his study of "Pseudo-Hecataeus"; see also Gager, *Moses in Greco-Roman Paganism*, 26-37; Stern, *Greek and Latin Authors on Jews and Judaism*, 1.20.

[131] Bar-Kochva, *Pseudo-Hecataeus' On the Jews*, 30-39; Stern, *Greek and Latin Authors on Jews and Judaism*, 1.21. The excursus is preserved in Diodorus Siculus, *Bibliotheca Historica* 40.3. The attribution to Hecataeus by Josephus of a different treatise, *On the Jews*, which he quotes in *Ap.* 1.183-204; 2.43, is widely contested (see, in favor, Stern, 1.22-24, and against, Bar-Kochva, 228-39, 249-52). Neither Moses nor the Exodus is mentioned in the Josephan text.

Greek literature,"[132] "deeply influenced, directly and indirectly, the contents of almost all ethnographical accounts of and references to the Jews and Judaism written by Hellenistic and Roman authors,"[133] making him a sort of Gentile Artapanus. Indeed, "especially the attribution to Moses of the settlement in Judea and the establishment of basic Jewish institutions and practices, became a vulgate in Greco-Roman literature."[134]

Non-Jewish writers can be important witnesses to Jewish thought on Moses. For example, for the highly influential Hecataeus Stern identifies a Jewish source, "probably an oral one,"[135] while Bar-Kochva concludes that Hecataeus's information was "certainly provided by Egyptian Jews, probably of priestly descent."[136] The evidently Jewish background to Hecataeus's summary of the work and legacy of Moses puts essentially Jewish traditions at the source of the first, and through it nearly all subsequent, Gentile treatments of Moses. Moreover, while Gentile authors will have respected the work of a significant ethnographer like Hecataeus, they also had recourse to more contemporary Jewish publications and colleagues, which to some extent will have freshened and clarified their impression of Jewish perspectives.[137]

1.5 Plan

This study focuses in six chapters on seven themes relevant to the relationship of Moses to Israel, which appear in the New Testament.

Chapter Two treats "Moses as Prophet." The prophetic ministry of Moses is acknowledged in the New Testament, and at the same time his prophetic role can be seen to be important underpinning for the other aspects of his ministry discussed in this study. The subject, however, has been dealt with extensively in the past (as seen in the above survey). Here accordingly the focus will be on some less-noticed aspects of the NT attributions to Moses of the role of prophet, and their links both with his role as ruler and with his general prestige as leader of his people.

---

[132] Bar-Kochva, *Pseudo-Hecataeus' On the Jews*, 18.

[133] Ibid., 211; this is explored, 211-17.

[134] Ibid., 18.

[135] Stern, *Greek and Latin Authors on Jews and Judaism*, 1.21.

[136] Bar-Kochva, *Pseudo-Hecataeus' On the Jews*, (25-)28, further developed, 28-39; "By and large, Hecataeus recorded the information provided by his Jewish informants," 36; "the excursus is, by and large, an *interpretatio Graeca* of Jewish history and life," 43.

[137] See, on Strabo for example, Gager, *Moses in Greco-Roman Paganism*, 40, 47, and in reply, Stern, *Greek and Latin Authors on Jews and Judaism*, 1.266; on Pseudo-Longinus (*De Sublimitate*), see Stern, 1.363.

Chapter Three, "Moses as Priest and Apostle," deals with two themes found linked together in Heb. 3:1-6. Neither office is ascribed to Moses so much as implied of him, through comparison with Jesus. The priesthood of Moses, however, is fairly prominent in contemporary literature, and it is unlikely that the implication of the Hebrews passage would be missed. The apostolate of Moses, on the other hand, may first come to light in Hebrews, at least under that specific rubric.

Chapter Four, "Moses as King," focuses on a role of Moses that by contrast seems never explicitly to be named in the New Testament. Thus scholars often neglect it even though it appears to lie behind several NT texts, which seem to make the most sense in a milieu in which Moses was seen as a king. Owing to the highly inferential nature of the NT evidence, this chapter gives a good deal of coverage to extrabiblical material which demonstrates the viability of the concept "Moses the King of Israel" in Judaism of the late Second Temple period. The important NT passages are considered in light of this evidence with a view to establishing that NT writers shared the wider view of Moses as king.

Chapter Five, "Moses as Lawgiver," turns to probably the most familiar element of Moses' ministry to Israel as depicted in the New Testament. Of all aspects of the NT portrait of Moses this is by far the easiest to detect. It is, however, frequently misconstrued or undervalued through amalgamation with his prophetic activity. Actually, Moses' lawgiving in the New Testament often seems less a matter of mediation and more a matter of his personal authority to make laws. Careful review of extra-biblical material current in the first century confirms this assessment as typical of at least some of first-century Judaism.

Chapter Six, "The Baptism into Moses," steps further into the background of the New Testament. The chapter is unusual in this study in that here it is more a question of how to explain the "baptism into Moses" of 1 Cor. 10:2 than of attempting in the first place to say something about Moses. On any reading, the very idea of baptism into Moses appears to invoke a conception of Moses as someone with whom a group could take on solidarity, or in whom it could enjoy corporate union. The chapter takes up proposals made in the past for a Pauline reference in 1 Cor. 10:2 to a rite which predates Christian baptism and explores conceptions of Moses which may have made it possible for him to be thought of as someone into whom his followers could be baptized.

Chapter Seven, "Moses the Focus of Jewish Loyalty," argues that beyond the more or less familiar qualities and functions attributed to Moses by NT writers and their fellow Jews, the New Testament and other texts show that Moses was considered a personal focus of Jewish loyalty. Although Moses was held to be subordinated to God, his function as a focus of loyalty means that pre-Christian, first-century Judaism possessed in some sense a binary focus of loyalty: God and his servant Moses. Some of the arguments of this chapter challenge in certain respects the scheme of Jewish monotheism put forward by R. Bauckham,[138] and are of special interest in this respect.

Chapter Eight turns to "Points of Contact with Christology." Each of the NT conceptions of Moses examined in the preceding chapters is paralleled by a very similar NT conception of Jesus. By no means was Moses the only paradigm employed in early Christology, but one outcome of this study, it is hoped, will be to show that the paradigm of Moses in NT Christology, though not forgotten, may hitherto have been under-appreciated in modern scholarship.

---

[138] E.g., in *God Crucified: Monotheism and Christology in the New Testament*, Didsbury Lectures, 1996 (Carlisle, Cumbria: Paternoster Press, 1998), 3-22, examined below, pp. 97-99.

Chapter 2

Moses As Prophet

What of Moses?
Is he not everywhere celebrated as a prophet?
—Philo
Quis Rerum Divinarum Haeres Sit 262

2.1 Introduction

Prophethood was one of the best-developed features of Moses in the first century A.D., enjoying extensive literary coverage in the period.[1] This chapter will review enough of that literature to give a feel for the background before looking at the way some key NT texts imply or characterize Moses' prophethood (perhaps not always in a way immediately apparent to the modern reader). The Lawgiving will receive special attention in Chapter Five.

2.2 Moses as Prophet in the Old Testament

"Dans la tradition biblique, Moïse fut avant tout considéré comme un prophète."[2] Numbers 12:6-8 and Deut. 34:10 may be better known, but the biblical text which labels Moses a prophet most clearly is Hos. 12:14(13), "By a prophet (וּבְנָבִיא) the Lord brought Israel from Egypt/and by a prophet (וּבְנָבִיא) he was kept."[3]

Elsewhere Moses is linked with the prophets by implication. This happens in a variety of ways, some quite subtle. For example, the biblical

---

[1] W. D. Davies, *The Setting of the Sermon on the Mount* (Cambridge: The University Press, 1964), 116-17.

[2] Albert Gelin, "Moïse dans l'Ancient Testament," *Cahiers Sioniens* 8, nos. 2, 3, and 4 (*Moïse: L'homme de l'alliance*, 1954): 43.

[3] The MT of Hos. 12:14 focuses the credit for the Exodus on the Lord, but *Targum Jonathan* renders that verse, "the Lord sent a prophet and [he] brought Israel up from Egypt" (נביא שלח יוי ואסיק ית ישראל ממצרים), a rendering which leaves ambiguous whether it was God or the prophet (Moses) who was the actual deliverer. Cf. Leivy Smolar and Moses Aberbach, *Studies in Targum Jonathan to the Prophets* (New York and Baltimore, 1983), 138 n. 61.

accounts of the call of Moses and the calls of several other prophets are found to follow the same basic structure of 1) theophany, 2) divine commission, 3) identification of an obstacle to the performance of the commission, and 4) divine provision for overcoming the obstacle (frequently involving the provision of a sign).[4]

While ordinarily the Old Testament does not give Moses a title, when it does those it gives him are particularly suited to a prophet; that is, they conform generally to the nomenclature of prophets elsewhere.[5] According to Psalm 105:26-27 the Lord sent Moses to perform "signs" and "wonders" (אתותיו ומפתים; LXX [104:26-27]: τὰ σημεῖα αὐτοῦ καὶ τὰ τέρατα) in Egypt, and of course the Pentateuch depicts him doing so there and performing miracles in the wilderness. As will be seen below, the performance of miraculous signs may have been construed as the veritable badge of a prophet in NT times, adding to the impression that in that period the scriptures would have been thought to depict Moses as a prophet.[6]

He was not just a prophet, of course; Moses was the greatest prophet, a prophet *sui generis*. According to Num. 12:6-8 Moses exceeded the

---

[4] Scott J. Hafemann, *Paul, Moses, and the History of Israel: The Letter/Spirit Contrast and the Argument from Scripture in 2 Corinthians 3*, WUNT, ed. Martin Hengel and Otfried Hofius, no. 81 (Tübingen: J. C. B. Mohr [Paul Siebeck], 1995), 49, nn. 47-62. Hafemann's list is a compressed synthesis of the structure laid out by Wolfgang Richter, *Die sogenannten vorprophetischen Berufungberichte: Eine literaturwissenschaftliche Studie zu 1 Sam 9,1-10, Ex 3f. und Ri 6,11b-17*, Forschungen zur Religion und Literatur des Alten und Neuen Testaments, ed. Ernst Käsemann und Ernst Wurthwein, no. 101 (Göttingen: Vandenhoeck & Ruprecht, 1970), 139 (Andeutung der Not, Auftrag, Einwand, Zusicherung des Beistandes, Zeichen); and N. Habel, "The Form and Significance of the Call Narratives," *Zeitschrift für die alttestamentliche Wissenschaft* 77, no. 3 (1965): 305-23, summed up, 316-20 (Divine Confrontation, Introductory Word, Commission, Objection, Reassurance, Sign; corresponding in Moses' case to Exod. 3:1-4a, 4b-9, 10, 11, 12a, 12 respectively); see below p. 52 nn. 98 and 99.

[5] "God's servant" in Exod. 14:31; Num. 12:7-8; Deut. 34:5; Josh. 1:1, 2, 7, 15; 8:31, 33; 9:24; 11:12, 15; 12:6; 13:8; 14:7; 18:7; 22:2, 4, 5; 1 Kings 8:56; 2 Kings 18:12; 21:8; 1 Chron. 6:49; 2 Chron. 1:3; 24:6, 9; Neh. 1:7, 8; 9:14; 10:29; Ps. 105:26; Dan. 9:11; Mal. 3:22(4:4); Wis. 10:16; Bar. 2:28; and in later writers, e.g. Josephus, *Ant.* 5.39; cf. 4.16, 317; "the man of God" in Deut. 33:1; 15; 1 Chron. 23:14; 2 Chron. 30:16; Ezra 3:2; Ps. 90:1, on which as a prophetic title see Rolf Rendtorff, "προφήτης κτλ," in *Theological Dictionary of the New Testament*, ed. Gerhard Friedrich, trans. and ed. Geoffrey W. Bromiley, vol. 6, Πε-Ρ (Grand Rapids: William B. Eerdmans, 1968, reprint, 1988), 809, and Henri Cazelles, with H.-J. Fabry, "מֹשֶׁה mōšeh," *Theological Dictionary of the Old Testament*, ed. G. Johannes Botterweck, Helmer Ringgren, and Heinz-Josef Fabry, trans. David E. Green, vol. 9, נָשָׂה־מָרַד *mārad-naqâ* [sic] (Grand Rapids: William B. Eerdmans, 1998), 39. Deut. 18:15; 34:10 also imply that he was a prophet.

[6] See below, pp. 52-63.

(other) prophets, because with him the Lord "spoke face to face, even openly" (פֶּה אֶל־פֶּה אֲדַבֶּר־בּוֹ וּמַרְאֶה; στόμα κατὰ στόμα λαλήσω αὐτῷ, ἐν εἴδει). According to Exod. 33:11 the Lord spoke to Moses "face to face (פָּנִים אֶל־פָּנִים; ἐνώπιος ἐνωπίῳ), just as a man speaks to his friend." Deuteronomy 34:10 states that since then there has been no prophet like Moses, whom the Lord knew face to face (פָּנִים אֶל־פָּנִים; πρόσωπον κατὰ πρόσωπον).[7]

A. Jepsen concludes that for pre-exilic Jews Moses' position was so unique, and his separation from the prophets so complete, that "er nicht in einem Atem mit diesen genannt werden darf."[8] There is no evidence that Moses' standing did anything but rise from that starting point throughout the post-exilic and Hellenistic periods, but at all times he continued to be seen as a prophet. In Second Temple Judaism and especially in the Herodian period, the biblical statements just reviewed were the starting point for portraying Moses as the greatest prophet of all.

2.3 Moses as Prophet in Writings of the Second Temple Period

2.3.1 Jubilees

The prologue to *Jubilees* does not explicitly call Moses a prophet, but it does report that he received revelations of "what (was) in the beginning and what (will be) at the end" (1:26; likewise 1:4).

2.3.2 Ben Sira

Ben Sira characterizes Joshua as "the successor of Moses in the prophetic office" (46:1; מְשָׁרֵת מֹשֶׁה בִּנְבוּאָה; καὶ διάδοχος Μωυσῆ ἐν προφητείαις), a statement which probably interprets Deut. 34:9 (with 34:10-12).[9] In the section on Moses himself (44:23b-45:5, which includes interesting features relevant to Chapter Seven of this study[10]), Ben Sira combines the Lawgiving with prophetic motifs, including the working of mira-

---

[7] The extant Targums to all these verses use the expression "speech opposite speech" (מְמַלֵּל לָקֳבֵל מְמַלֵּל et var.), and generally interpose the Memra of the Lord as that which Moses met, e.g., Cairo Genizah Fragment MS F2, Deut. 34:10, "whom the Memra of the lord knew speech opposite speech (מְמַלֵּל לָקֳבֵל מְמַלֵּל)," in Michael L. Klein, *Genizah Manuscripts of Palestinian Targum to the Pentateuch* (Cincinnati: Hebrew Union College Press, 1986), text and trans., 1.360-61.

[8] Alfred Jepsen, *Nabi: Soziologische Studien zur alttestamentlichen Literatur und Religionsgeschichte* (München: C. B. Beck'sche Verlagsbuchhandlung, 1934), 208. Jepsen, 208-209, theorizes about an ongoing tradition maintaining this distinction, perhaps energized at some stages by popular mistrust of the prophetic movement.

[9] Cf. the similar Josephus, *Ant.* 4.311.

[10] Notably on pp. 242 and 244 below.

cles (signs, in the LXX), to create the impression of the Lawgiving as the work of a prophet:

45:3   ויחזקהו לפני מלך   בד [. . . . .] מהר
        [. . . . .] ויר[.]   ויצוהו [.]ל[. . .]

("By his words he performed swift miracles;[11]/ he glorified him in the presence of a king.[12]// He gave him commandments for his people,/ and revealed to him his glory"[13]), and:

45:5   ויגישהו לערפל :   וישמיעהו את קולו
        תורת חיים ותבונה   וישם בידו מצוה

("[God] caused him to hear his voice,/ and led him into a cloud,// and put the commandment in his hand,/ the instruction of life and understanding.") Here, Moses the prophet mediates God's message to the people.

In the LXX tradition, Ecclus. 45:3 moves even closer to a "standardized" description of a prophet with the inclusion (admittedly in a fashion of uncertain significance) of signs: "By his words he caused signs to cease" (ἐν λόγοις αὐτοῦ σημεῖα κατέπαυσεν).[14] Ecclesiasticus 45:5, which reads in part, "and brought him into the dark cloud, and gave him commandments before his face" (ἔδωκεν αὐτῷ κατὰ πρόσωπον ἐντολάς), now recalls the description, in Exod. 33:11, Num. 12:7-8, and Deut. 34:10

---

[11] The margin supplies בדברו for the lacuna where characters have been erased; Rudolf Smend, *Die Weisheit des Jesus Sirach: Hebräisch und deutsch mit einem hebräischen Glossar* (Berlin: Georg Reimer, 1906), 1.49 supplies בד]בר פין [א]ת[ות] מהר. LXX: ἐν λόγοις αὐτοῦ σημεῖα κατέπαυσεν, "by his words he caused signs to cease"). Cf. (the prophet) Joshua (Sir. 46:4-5), Elijah (48:2-6), and Elisha (48:12-14), all wonder-workers, and see below on the signs of a prophet, pp. 52-63.

[12] LXX: κατὰ πρόσωπον βασιλέων; Wis. 10:16b also refers to "kings" withstood by Moses. See Peter Enns, "Egypt Had 'Kings'," in *Exodus Retold: Ancient Exegesis of the Departure from Egypt in Wis 15-21 and 19:1-9*, Harvard Semitic Museum Publications, ed. Lawrence E. Stager, Harvard Semitic Monographs, ed. Peter Machinist, no. 57 (Atlanta: Scholars Press, 1997), 45-52.

[13] Relying on Smend, *Weisheit des Jesus Sirach*, 1.49 (see his note, 2.427), who fills out the last line as ויצוהו [א]ל [העם]/ ויר[א]הו את כבודו:.

[14] W. O. E. Oesterley, *The Wisdom of Jesus the Son of Sirach or Ecclesiasticus in the Revised Version with Introduction and Notes*, The Cambridge Bible for Schools and Colleges, ed. (Old Testament) A. F. Kirkpatrick (Cambridge: Cambridge University Press, 1912), 304 n. 3 reasons that the meaning is that Moses brought about the removal of the plagues from Egypt, but also conjectures that "κατέπαυσεν may be a corruption for κατέσπευσεν," and notes the reverse corruption in 43:5. Other commentators assume such a corruption, e.g. Helge Stadelmann, *Ben Sira als Schriftgelehrter: Eine Untersuchung zum Berufsbild des vor-makkabäischen Sofer unter Berücksichtigung seines Verhältnisses zu Priester-, Propheten- und Weisheitslehrertum*, WUNT/2, ed. Martin Hengel, Otfried Hofius, and Otto Michel, no. 6 (Tübingen: J. C. B. Mohr [Paul Siebeck], 1980), 254, who interprets, "Bei ihm kommen die Wunderzeichen des Mose 'durch das Wort' zustande."

of Moses as the greatest prophet, with whom the Lord spoke "mouth to mouth" or "face to face."

2.3.3 Wisdom of Solomon

When Wisdom of Solomon treats an individual person it regularly applies an appropriate rubric as a way of summing up who the person was. Its special designation for Moses is, "a holy prophet" (προφήτης ἅγιος; 11:1).[15] Wisdom 10:15-16 also recalls the "wonders and signs" (τέρατα καὶ σημεῖα) which Wisdom worked through Moses at the time of the Exodus, a feature of his portrayal which, as will be shown later in this Chapter, is probably emblematic of a prophet.[16]

2.3.4 Aristobulus

Aristobulus, who describes Moses as legislator, inventor, engineering genius, and more, reports that "those who are able to think well marvel at his wisdom and at the divine spirit in accordance with which he has been proclaimed as a prophet also" (apud Eusebius, Praep. Ev. 8.10.4).[17]

2.3.5 The Exagoge

In the Exagoge of Ezekiel the Tragedian, lines 68-82, Moses relates a dream he has had in which he saw himself seated on a great throne in heaven, from which he

... ἐσεῖδον γῆν ἅπασαν ἔγκυκλον
καὶ ἔνερθε γαίας καὶ ἐξύπερθεν οὐρανοῦ
... beheld the entire circled earth,
Both beneath the earth and above the heaven" (77-78).[18]

In the following section (lines 83-89) Moses' father-in-law interprets the dream, saying,

καὶ αὐτὸς βραβεύσεις καὶ καθηγήσῃ βροτῶν
τὸ δ' εἰσθεᾶσθαι γῆν ὅλην τ' οἰκουμένην
καὶ τὰ ὑπένερθε καὶ ὑπὲρ οὐρανὸν θεοῦ·
ὄψει τά τ' ὄντα τά τε προτοῦ τά θ' ὕστερον.
And it is you who will judge and lead mortals
As you beheld the whole inhabited earth,

---

[15] Alexandrinus has προφῆται ἅγιοι; two Latin MSS omit ἅγιος.

[16] See below, pp. 52-63.

[17] Trans. A. Yarbro Collins, in The Old Testament Pseudepigrapha, ed. James H. Charlesworth, vol. 2, The Anchor Bible Reference Library (New York: Doubleday, 1985), 838.

[18] Text and trans. Carl R. Holladay, Fragments from Hellenistic Jewish Authors, vol. 2, Poets, Society of Biblical Literature Texts and Translations Pseudepigrapha Series, ed. James C. Vanderkam, Texts and Translations no. 30, Pseudepigrapha no. 12 (Atlanta: Scholars Press, 1989), 364-65.

The things beneath and the things above God's heaven,
So you will see things present, past, and future" (86-89).[19]

Gruen writes, "He takes Moses' vision of all things above and below Heaven as signifying ability to see into the past, present, and future. ... The symbolism connotes the prophetic powers that he could now exercise."[20] Additionally, Holladay points out that the verb translated "you will lead" (καθηγήση) may actually imply teaching or instruction, and "thus 'leader of mortals' may signify his role as preeminent prophet who provides inspired guidance."[21] Other aspects of this interesting scene, which obviously may imply more about Moses than prophetic ability alone, await more detailed discussion below.[22]

2.3.6 Views of Moses as Prophet Attested by Non-Jews

Non-Jewish sources given here may be guides to Jewish thinking as reliable as some of the Jewish literature already considered.

Porphyry attributes to Numenius of Apamea the statement, "the prophet (ὁ προφήτης) said that the spirit of god was borne over the water" (*De Antro Nymph.* 10).[23] Numenius had probably learned a great deal about Judaism in Apamea, which had a considerable Jewish population.[24] Perhaps for this reason, "Moses seems to have been considered by Numenius 'the Prophet' par excellence."[25]

In *Geography* 16.2.39 Strabo lists a number of prophets (οἱ μάντεις), including Moses, who "were held in so much honor that they were deemed worthy to be kings." For Strabo, "prophet" is apparently the more funda-

---

[19] I have slightly modified ibid., 366-67, who has in line 86 "judge and lead humankind."

[20] Erich S. Gruen, *Heritage and Hellenism: The Reinvention of Jewish Tradition*, Hellenistic Culture and Society, ed. Anthony W. Bulloch, et al., no. 30 (Berkeley: University of California Press, 1998), 134; also Richard Bauckham, "The Throne of God and the Worship of Jesus," in *The Jewish Roots of Christological Monotheism: Papers from the St. Andrews Conference on the Historical Origin of the Worship of Jesus*, ed. Carey C. Newman, James R. Davila, and Gladys S. Lewis, Supplements to the *Journal for the Study of Judaism*, ed. John J. Collins with Florentino García Martínez, vol. 63 (Leiden: Brill, 1999), 55.

[21] Holladay, *Fragments from Hellenistic Jewish Authors*, vol. 2, *Poets*, 448-49.

[22] See particularly pp. 90-102.

[23] Cited from John G. Gager, *Moses in Greco-Roman Paganism*, Society of Biblical Literature Monograph Series, ed. Robert A. Kraft, no. 16 (Nashville and New York: Abingdon Press, 1972), 65, who detects familiarity with the LXX.

[24] Menachem Stern, ed. and trans., *Greek and Latin Authors on Jews and Judaism Edited with Introductions, Translations, and Commentary*, vol. 2, *From Tacitus to Simplicitus*, Fontes and Res Judaicas Spectantes (Jerusalem: The Israel Academy of Sciences and Humanities, 1980), 207.

[25] Ibid., 206-207.

mental office of the two. Gager suggests "that a Jew, familiar with Greek and particularly Stoic philosophy, could have provided Strabo with the substance and perhaps even the actual form of his excursus on Moses" (cf. Philo, below). Strabo's ideas might represent elements of "a Hellenistic, perhaps apologetic, Jewish theology."[26]

2.3.7 The Assumption of Moses

The *Assumption of Moses* generally creates an atmosphere redolent of Moses as prophet,[27] and in one place calls Moses *divinum per orbem terrarum profetem* ("the divine prophet for the entire world," 11:16),[28] and *magnus nuntius ... intuens Omnipotentem orbem terrarum* ("the great messenger ... who could look at the Ruler of the whole world," 11:17), a description which recalls Exod. 33:11, Num. 12:7-8, and Deut. 34:10, where Moses is set apart from other prophets by his enjoyment of face-to-face knowledge of the Lord. Then in his farewell discourse in the *Assumption*, Moses foretells the whole of Israel's history, just as he might be thought to do in Deuteronomy 33.

A related role for Moses in the *Assumption* is "mediator." In *As. Mos.* 1:14 Moses describes himself as, "I who have been prepared from the beginning of the world to be the mediator of his covenant" (*arbiter testamenti illius*), which recalls the statement of Jer. 1:5 that before Jeremiah was formed in the womb God knew him and consecrated him to the prophetic office. *Assumption of Moses* 3:12 speaks of "commandments, which he mediated to us" (*mandata illius in quibus arbiter fuit nobis*). Both of

---

[26] Gager, *Moses in Greco-Roman Paganism*, 44-47; quotations from 47. On the derivation of Strabo's view of Moses, see further in Menachem Stern, ed. and trans., *Greek and Latin Authors on Jews and Judaism Edited with Introductions, Translations, and Commentary*, vol. 1, *From Herodotus to Plutarch*, Fontes and Res Judaicas Spectantes (Jerusalem: The Israel Academy of Sciences and Humanities, 1974), 264-67; Stern concludes, however, "it seems best to look for a pagan philosophical source, whatever it may be, for the chapters on Moses."

[27] See, e.g., 1.5, 14, 15(with 2.1-10.10), 3.11, 12, 11.16, and David Lenz Tiede, "The Figure of Moses in *The Testament of Moses*," in *Studies on the Testament of Moses: Seminar Papers*, ed. George W. E. Nickelsburg, Jr., Society of Biblical Literature Pseudepigrapha Group, Septuagint and Cognate Studies, no. 4 (Cambridge, Mass.: Society of Biblical Literature, 1973), 86-92, esp. 86-87: "He [the author] highlights those aspects of Moses' portrait which Jews of the Hasmonean-Herodian era who knew the biblical writings could recognize as pertaining to the office of prophet," 87.

[28] Text and trans., Johannes Tromp, ed. and trans., *The Assumption of Moses: A Critical Edition with Commentary*, Studia in Veteris Testamenti Pseudepigrapha, ed. A.-M. Denis and M. de Jonge, vol. 10 (Leiden: E. J. Brill, 1993), 22, 256 (on pp. 23 and 252 Tromp translates *per orbem terrarum* as "for this world," but this seems mistaken). The *Assumption of Moses* characterizes Moses in other ways, and it will accordingly be attended to in other contexts, notably pp. 188-90 and 204-205 below.

these statements and the specific mediatory function they describe recall Paul's reference to Moses as μεσίτης of the Law in Gal. 3:19.[29]

Excursus: The Scope of Moses' Prophetic Mission in the Assumption of Moses and in Jewish Thought of the First Century

Assumption of Moses 11:16 calls Moses:
divinum per orbem terrarum profetem
consummatum in saeculo doctorem.[30]

Closer consideration of this bit of text is justified on a number of counts. First, *Assumption of Moses* is one of a very few Jewish texts that are dated with confidence to the first Christian century.[31] This alone gives it a special place in the study of NT backgrounds. Second, the *Assumption of Moses* evidently originated in Palestine.[32] Even given the undoubted importance of the Jewish Diaspora for early Christian thought in general and for the New Testament in particular, Christianity was Palestinian Jewish at its birth. Any literary remains that share both the period and the milieu of the first Christians are self-evidently of great importance to the study of NT backgrounds, not least when treating a figure of the importance of Moses. Third, although the portrait of Moses found in *Assumption of Moses* shows connections with Greco-Roman culture and thought, it appears that the more important background is the Pentateuch.[33] This suggests that the *Assumption* can actually serve as a guide to how some Jews of the first century A.D. interpreted the Pentateuch, and specifically how they understood the portrayal of Moses therein. Fourth, the lines cited above are among the most specific characterizations of Moses found in this important work, alongside portions like *As. Mos.* 1:14 and 11:17. For a study such as the present one, then, interested in both the New Testament Moses and its Jewish context, some closer consideration is in order.

Generally speaking, the author of the *Assumption* in these lines characterizes the scope of the prophetic ministry of Moses. In the first line this is obvious, but *consummatus doctor* may have been intended as a further characterization of Moses, in his prophetic role, as the perfect teacher. Most likely it speaks of Moses specifically as the Lawgiver,[34] but in *The Assumption of Moses* this seems to have been a matter of prophecy.[35] Both lines then deal in some respect with the prophetic authority of Moses.

---

[29] That being said, one of the most important functions ascribed to Moses in the *Assumption* is another kind of mediation, to intercede for the people with God (11:10-11, 14, 17; 12:6).

[30] Tromp, *Assumption of Moses*, 22.

[31] Ibid., 116. The apparently precisely accurate references to the length of the reign of Herod the Great (*rex petulans*, 6:6), and to the relatively brief reigns of his children (6:7-8) point to a date early in the first century A.D., not long after the deposition of Archelaus in 6 A.D. (Two of Herod the Great's other children, Philip and Antipas, ruled not briefly but even longer than Herod himself did.)

[32] Tromp, *Assumption of Moses*, 107-109, 117-19.

[33] See William Horbury, "Moses and the Covenant in *The Assumption of Moses* and the Pentateuch," in *Covenant as Context*, ed. A. D. H. Mayes and R. B. Salters (Oxford: Clarendon Press, 2003), 203, drawing on 192, 193-94, 196-97, 202-203.

[34] Tromp, *Assumption of Moses*, 256.

[35] See 1:14, and p. 139 below.

It seems safe to take *per orbem terrarum* as a spatial characterization of Moses' prophetic office: Moses' authority runs everywhere. After 11:16 describes Moses as the prophet *per orbem terrarum*, 11:17 describes God as he who rules *orbem terrarum*. Moses' prophetic ministry is here coextensive with God's worldwide sovereignty, and is probably linked with it, perhaps through the medium of the Law. With this, compare Josephus's view of the Law, *Ap.* 2.284: ὥσπερ ὁ θεὸς διὰ παντὸς τοῦ κόσμου πεφοίτηκεν, οὕτως ὁ νόμος διὰ πάντων ἀνθρώπων βεβάδικεν; "As God permeates the universe, so the Law has found its way among all mankind." Philo, *Som.* 1.39 expresses a similar view. Also, in *As. Mos.* 1:14 Moses says that God prepared him to be a mediator of his covenant *ab initio orbis terrarum. Orbis terrarum* is the whole world in *Assumption of Moses*,[36] and for *Assumption of Moses* the whole world is the field of Moses' prophetic ministry. The universal importance of Moses' prophetic ministry is perhaps also behind the statement in 11:14, that the whole world is Moses' grave.[37]

This in turn does not seem too far from the roughly contemporary thought in Philo, *Virt.* 175 that "Our most holy Moses, who so dearly loved virtue and goodness and especially his fellow men, exhorts everyone everywhere (προτρέπει τοὺς πανταχοῦ πάντας) to pursue piety and justice, and offers to the repentant in honor of their victory the high rewards of membership in the best of commonwealths." The last clause makes it clear that for Philo Moses' exhortation extends to those not already Israelites. This would appear to be the view of *Assumption of Moses*, and of Josephus, all together constituting a fair sampling of first-century Jewish opinion. A Samaritan wedding contract, late but possibly preserving much older tradition, also lauds Moses as "leader of the entire world" (גביר כל העולם).[38]

Such a view finds precedent in the biblical literature. In Dan. 9:6 LXX it is said of the prophets that they have spoken "to our kings and our rulers and our fathers and to every nation of the world" (καὶ παντὶ ἔθνει ἐπὶ τῆς γῆς). The MT of this verse, it is true, only refers to "all the people of the land" (כל־עם הארץ), but this divergence only underscores the apparent intention of the LXX translators of Daniel to claim that the

---

[36] As in nearly any Latin text, e.g., Cicero, *Pro Sestio* 30.66, "Qui locus orbi terrae iam non erat alicui destinatus? ... Quae regio orave terrarum erat latior, in qua non regnum aliquod statueretur?", "What spot in the world was not already allotted to someone? ... What district or country in the world of any size was not made the seat of some kingdom?"; Virgil, *Aeneid* 1.233, "cunctus ob Italiam terrarum clauditur orbis?", "the whole world is barred for Italy's sake?"; further, Lewis and Short, under *orbis.* Cicero, *The Speeches: Pro Sestio and In Vatinium*, trans. R. Gardner, Loeb Classical Library (London: Heinemann, 1958); Virgil, *Eclogues, Georgics, Aeneid 1-6*, trans. H. Rushton Fairclough, rev. G. P. Goold, Loeb Classical Library (Cambridge, Mass.: Harvard University Press, 1999).

[37] See below, p. 205 n. 122.

[38] MS Firkovitch, Sam. X, 11 (1707), line 10, text, Reinhard Plummer with Abraham Tal, *Samaritan Marriage Contracts and Deeds of Divorce*, vol. 2 (Wiesbaden: Harrassowitz Verlag, 1997), 9; trans., 197. See also MS Firkovitch, Sam. X, 39 (1751), text, Plummer, vol. 2, 70; trans., 216. See also MS Firkovitch, Sam. X, 72, line 7, "all nations that cling to him will benefit," text, Plummer, vol. 2, 145, trans., 239.

Hebrew prophets had spoken to "every" nation (perhaps even via the LXX itself).[39] Compare further, already in the MT, Jer. 1:5: "I gave you a prophet to the nations," נָבִיא לַגּוֹיִם נְתַתִּיךָ (LXX: προφήτην εἰς ἔθνη τέθεικά σε). As D. L. Tiede observes, "As a prophet, the Moses of the TM shares many traits with his biblical predecessors."[40] In the context of Second Temple Jewish thought, someone like Moses might very easily be thought of as a prophet to the whole world, and the wording of *As. Mos.* 11:16 fits this view.

The expression *consummatum in saeculo doctorem* is more difficult. Tromp translates the *in saeculo* found here in two different ways. In his translation proper he renders it, "for this earth,"[41] so that the lines quoted above may appear to be a synonymous parallelism: "for the whole world/for this earth." In his commentary, however, he translates "for all time," an expression both freighted with deeper significance, and adding something more to the characterization of Moses, than the repetitive "for this earth."[42] The oversight that led to both alternatives being left unreconciled in Tromp's published work unfortunately leaves Tromp's final position uncertain but, on the other hand, serves as well as an explicit comment could do to show up the awkwardness of the expression *in saeculo*, which in *As. Mos.* 11:16 does not seem to comply perfectly with standard classical usage.[43]

One basic issue in deciding the meaning of *in saeculo* is the definition of *saeculum*. In the singular Lewis and Short offer the length of a man's life, or the length of a generation, but also the human race itself living in a period of such length. Ordinarily to refer to a much longer period, an "age," the word would occur in the plural. Thus at first glance the text under examination here seems to praise Moses as the great prophet of his generation. By combination of this line with *divinum per orbem terrarum projetem* Moses then is lauded as the greatest prophet and teacher in the world — of his day. This seems utterly inadequate, even ludicrous, when set in the context of the passage overall, where Moses is called, "the holy and sacred spirit, the worthy one before the Lord, the versatile and inscrutable lord of the word, the trusted one in everything, ... the great messenger" (11:16-17).

It is perhaps for this reason that Tromp opts in one place to translate *in saeculo* "for all time." This is a more satisfying rendering, one more in keeping with the tenor of the passage. It is difficult to justify lexically and grammatically, however. The rendering "for all time," or "to eternity," would perhaps better represent an accusative, *in saeculum* or *in saecula*, and not the ablative singular, *in saeculo*. The ablative singular expression might easily be translated "in his time," or "in his day," but once again this doesn't seem grand enough for the glowing context of *As. Mos.* 11:16-19.

The Latin text of the *Assumption of Moses* is most likely a translation of an earlier Greek composition.[44] In the present passage consideration of likely Greek precursors to *in saeculo* may be fruitful. Ordinarily, *saeculum* as a translation of αἰών would be

---

[39] The Theodotionic rendering follows the MT more closely than the LXX with καὶ πρὸς πάντα τὸν λαὸν γῆς.

[40] Tiede, "The Figure of Moses in *The Testament of Moses*," 88.

[41] Tromp, *Assumption of Moses*, 23, 252.

[42] Ibid., 256.

[43] The Latin of the *Assumption* overall is anything but classical, but is usually comprehensible.

[44] Tromp, *Assumption of Moses*, 79-85. A Semitic original preceding the Greek text is, however, unlikely, see Tromp, 81-85, 115-16.

late and ecclesiastical Latin, but of course *Assumption of Moses* as we have it is an ecclesiastical Latin text.[45] In the Vulgate the term *in saeculo* occurs rarely, and is usually modified. Thus, in Mark 10:30 it occurs as *in saeculo futuro*, and in Luke 18:30 as *in saeculo venturo*; in both places the critical Greek text has ἐν τῷ αἰῶνι τῷ ἐρχομένῳ. The expression *in hoc saeculo* occurs in 1 Cor. 3:18, Eph. 1:21, and Tit. 2:12, where the critical Greek text has similar expressions formed off αἰών, and the "age" is conceived along the same lines as in Mark 10:30 and Luke 18:30.

The expression *in hoc saeculo* also appears in the Vulgate Eccl. 9:6 where the LXX has εἰς τὸν αἰῶνα, "forever." The Vulgate Ecclesiastes, however, is probably a translation from the Hebrew and does not reflect a Greek Vorlage or Greek usage.[46] As it happens, the MT reads עוד לעולם, also "forever." Despite, however, what is read in the Greek and Hebrew texts, it seems impossible on contextual grounds to understand the *in hoc saeculo* of the Vulgate's Eccl. 9:6 as anything but "in the present age." It is nonetheless instructive for consideration of the Greek that lies behind *As. Mos.* 11:16 to see that an expression such as *in hoc saeculo* can (evidently) have translated language clearly speaking of perpetuity, or the end of the age, assuming that something like the MT's עוד לעולם lies behind the Vulgate here.

In all of these cases from the Vulgate, *in saeculo* appears to refer to an age or an epoch of the world, and not a generation, or the span of a man's life; the expressions in which it appears refer to the present world order, or that of the world to come. In all of these cases, however, *in saeculo* is modified by some other indicator of time or specificity.

Only once does the expression *in saeculo* appear in the Vulgate unmodified. Jerome's earliest version of the Psalter is his revision of the Old Latin on the basis of the Hexapla, now preserved as the Gallic Psalter. The version of Ps. 72:12 found there reads, *ecce ipsi peccatores et abundantes in saeculo obtinuerunt divitias* ("Behold, these are the sinners; and enjoying bounty in this world, they have acquired wealth"). Later Jerome prepared a fresh translation in which the verse says, *ecce ipsi impii et abundantes in saeculo multiplicaverunt divitias* ("Behold, these are the wicked; and indeed, enjoying bounty in this world, they multiplied riches").[47] The corresponding verse in the MT, Ps. 73:12, reads הנה־אלה רשעים ושלוי עולם השגו־חיל ("Behold, these are the wicked; continually at ease they increase their riches"), and the LXX of Ps. 72:12 reads, ἰδοὺ οὗτοι ἁμαρτωλοὶ καὶ εὐθηνοῦνται· εἰς τὸν αἰῶνα κατέσχον πλούτου ("Behold, these are sinners and they flourish; to the end they possess riches"). It may be impossible to know the precise *Vorlage* to either Vulgate tradition, but it is apparent that the Vulgate Psalters' *in saeculo* must translate something like either εἰς τὸν αἰῶνα or עולם, and must signify something like "while the age lasts," or "always." The usual expression in the Vulgate meaning "forever" is *in saecula*, but here the Vulgate seems to ratify the use of *in saeculo* with a meaning quite like it;

---

[45] Tromp, *Assumption of Moses*, 38 characterizes the Latin as both Vulgar and Late; The Latin vocabulary contains specimens of Christian usage that are definitely not known in classical Latin. Tromp, 38 gives words that are "used virtually exclusively by Christians," and words influenced by Christian usage. See further 39-41, 62, 84.

[46] Robert Weber, ed., *Biblia Sacra iuxta Vulgatem Versionem*, vol. 1, *Genesis-Psalmi* (Stuttgart: Württembergische Bibelanstalt, 1969), XXI.

[47] On the versions of the Psalter in the Vulgate see Weber, *Biblia Sacra iuxta Vulgatem Versionem*, 1.XXI.

where *in saecula (saeculorum)* means through all ages, *in saeculo* means to the end of the age (or where modified by *hoc* or some other adjective, the age in question).

Comparison of the presumed translation habits of *Assumption of Moses* and the Vulgate, being rather speculative, can only go so far. Nevertheless, the Vulgate serves at least as a rude guide to what sort of equivalencies between Latin and Greek were thought plausible in late, ecclesiastical Latin translation. It is indeed possible that a respected and influential work like the Vulgate could have acted as a guide to the translator of the *Assumption of Moses*. It is only a possibility, but it is not an unlikely one.

What seems established is that the most likely meaning of *in saeculo* in *As. Mos.* 11:16 is "in the present age" or, practically speaking, "always." The alternative, "in this generation," is technically possible, and perhaps more typical, but it is highly improbable in the eulogistic context of *As. Mos.* 11:16-17. Examination of the Vulgate shows that in ecclesiastical circles, where the Latin translation of *Assumption of Moses* probably was prepared, *in saeculo* could quite easily serve as a translation for Greek (and Hebrew) expressions denoting the end of the age.

In one place, as noted above, Tromp translates *per orbem terrarum* and *in saeculo* "for the entire world" and "for all time," but he concludes, "The universal validity of Moses' office expressed by these phrases is probably merely superlative and it is not intended to assert that Moses' teachings are, or should be, acknowledged by the gentiles."[48] In fact, these phrases are indeed very superlative, and probably constitute a claim that the Law and teaching of Moses enjoy authority at all times and in all places, and probably over all peoples, a claim for the authority of the Law not unheard of among Jews.

2.3.8 Moses as Prophet in Other Biblical Pseudepigrapha

Late in the first century A.D. writers still claim prophetic revelations for Moses, as in 4 Ezra 14:5, where it is said that on Mt. Sinai God told Moses "many wondrous things, and showed him the secrets of the times and declared to him the end of the times." From perhaps early in the second century A.D., 2 Bar. 59:4-8; 84:5 are similar. The *Biblical Antiquities* of Pseudo-Philo, 19:10-15, says much the same sort of revelation occurred just before Moses' death. In the *Martyrdom of Isaiah*, dating from before the end of the first century A.D., and perhaps (in the relevant section) from the late second century B.C., Belkira slanders Isaiah by accusing him of arrogantly saying, "I see more than Moses the prophet" (3:8).[49]

2.3.9 Philo

"Prophet" (mainly προφήτης but also θεοπρόπος) is one of the titles of Moses most prized by Philo.[50] He also calls Moses:

---

[48] Tromp, *Assumption of Moses*, 256.

[49] See M. A. Knibb, "Martyrdom and Ascension of Isaiah," in *The Old Testament Pseudepigrapha*, ed. James H. Charlesworth, vol. 2, The Anchor Bible Reference Library (New York: Doubleday, 1985), 149.

[50] προφήτης: *Leg. All.* 2.1; *Sac.* 130; *Gig.* 47, 56; *Quis Her.* 4, 262; *Fug.* 140; *Som.* 2.277; *Mos.* 1.57; 2.6, 76, 187, 209, 213, 246, 250, 257, 258, 262, 275, 278, 280, 284; *Dec.* 175; *Praem.* 123; *Mut.* 11; *Vit. Cont.* 87; *QG* 4.29; *QE* 2.43, 44, 46;

"the archprophet" (ἀρχιπροφήτης),⁵¹
"the revealer" (ἱεροφάντης),⁵²
"the revealer and prophet,"(ὁ ἱεροφάντης καὶ προφήτης Μωυσῆς)⁵³
"the most perfect prophet" (ὁ τελειοτάτος τῶν προφητῶν),⁵⁴
"a prophet of the highest quality" (προφήτης γέγονε δοκιμώτατος),⁵⁵
"the all-wise and prophet" (ὁ πανσόφος καὶ προφήτης),⁵⁶
"the prophetic word" (Μωυσῆς δὲ ὁ προφητικὸς λόγος)⁵⁷ or even
"the prophet-word" (ὁ προφήτης λόγος ὄνομα Μωυσῆς),⁵⁸
"the prophetic nature" (Μωυσῆς τὸ προφητικὸν γένος),⁵⁹
"an interpreter of God" (θεοφράδμονα),⁶⁰ and
"the theologian" (θεολόγος).⁶¹
Moses was entrusted with oracles from God,⁶² "sacred messages,"⁶³
"which he prophesied";⁶⁴ but even Moses' conjectures were "closely akin
to prophecies."⁶⁵

θεοπρόπος: *Ebr.* 85; *Conf.* 29; *Fug.* 138. See also *QG* 1.86; 4.27; *QE* 1.11; 2.44, 52.
Nature of prophecy in Philo: *Spec. Leg.* 1.65, with reference to *Mos.* 1.57, 175, 201,
210; 2.69, 246, 250, 258, 259, 263, 268, 270, 275, 278, and 280. Cf. on distinguishing
prophet from interpreter, *Mos.* 2.188, 191, 246, 250, 258, 259, 263, 270, 275, 278, 280.
Moses was both (*Mos.* 2.188-90; 269).
    ⁵¹ *Mut.* 103, 125; *Som.* 2.189; *QG* 4.8 (also the "archangel"); in *QG* 1.86 the first
prophet, or "protoprophet."
    ⁵² *Leg. All.* 3.151; *Sac.* 94; *Post.* 16, 164, 173; *Gig.* 54; *Quod Deus* 156; *Mig.* 14;
Som. 2.3, 29, 109; *Spec. Leg.* 1.41; 2.201; 4.177; *Virt.* 75, 163, 174. This term has to
do with the teaching of religious practices, and was used in connection with initiation
into the mysteries.
    ⁵³ *Leg. All.* 3.173; also *Dec.* 18.
    ⁵⁴ *Dec.* 175. Philo calls a canonical prophet (Zechariah) a disciple of Moses (τῶν
Μωυσέως ἑταίρων τις; *Conf.* 62); he also calls the psalmists disciples of Moses
(τῶν Μωυσέως γνωρίμων τις; *Conf.* 39).
    ⁵⁵ *Mos.* 2.187.
    ⁵⁶ *Gig.* 56.
    ⁵⁷ *Leg. All.* 3.43.
    ⁵⁸ *Cong.* 170; κατὰ τὰς τοῦ προφήτου λόγου Μωυσέως, *Mig.* 151. Cf. *Cong.*
40 where he is called "the holy word," (ὁ ἱερὸς ... λόγος).
    ⁵⁹ *Fug.* 147. Cf. *Mut.* (113 and) 120, and *QE* 2.20, where he is "the prophetic
mind."
    ⁶⁰ *Mos.* 2.269. Cf. *Spec. Leg.* 1.65; 4.49.
    ⁶¹ *Praem.* 53; *QG* 2.64; *QE* 2.37. One pagan writing, Pseudo-Galen's *Ad Gaurum*
11.1, calls Moses θεολόγος, where apparently it is synonymous with *mythologos*, a
sage whose knowledge of the gods is expressed in mythological form, Gager, *Moses in
Greco-Roman Paganism*, 74-75.
    ⁶² τὸ γε μὴν χρησθὲν τῷ πανσόφῳ Μωυσῆ λόγιον, *Post.* 28; λόγιόν ἐστι τοῦ-
το χρησθὲν τῷ προφήτῃ, *Gig.* 47; χρησμῳδουμένῳ, *Virt.* 55; also *Cher.* 124; *Mut.*
103, 113, 125; *Mos.* 1.175, 201; 2.69, 188-90, 259-60; *Praem.* 1.
    ⁶³ οἱ ἱεροί; *Spec. Leg.* 3.6.
    ⁶⁴ οὓς Μωυσῆς ἐθεσπίσθη, *Abr.* 262; see also *Mos.* 2.263.

H. A. Wolfson urges "the term 'prophet' is used by Philo not as something distinct from lawgiver and priest but rather as a general term under which lawgiver and priest are to be included."[66] For Philo, then, prophethood was the foundation of all of Moses' roles toward Israel, a position reminiscent of Strabo's treatment of kingship, including the kingship of Moses.[67]

2.3.10 Josephus

Josephus also regards Moses as a prophet, though he does not drive the point home like Philo.[68] In *Ant.* 2.327 and 5.20 he refers to Moses as a προφήτης, and records matters which Moses prophesied (προφητεύω, *Ant.* 4.320) or foretold (προεῖπε, *Ant.* 5.40, 69; cf. 5.39). Josephus concedes that as general Moses had a few who equaled him, "but as prophet none (προφήτης δὲ οἷος οὐκ ἄλλος), insomuch that in all his utterances one seemed to hear the speech of God" (*Ant.* 4.329). Therefore, Moses appoints his successor Joshua "to succeed him both in his prophetical functions and as commander-in-chief" (ταῖς προφητείαις καὶ στρατηγόν; *Ant.* 4.165) and so Joshua prophesies in the presence of Moses (*Ant.* 4.311).[69]

2.4 Moses as Prophet in Samaritan Literature

Given Samaritan adherence exclusively to the Pentateuch, the pre-eminence of Moses in Samaritan thought is not surprising. Moses is, for the Samaritans, the only true prophet.[70] Complete consideration of Moses as pro-

---

[65] αἱ τοιαῦται εἰκασίαι συγγενεῖς προφητείας εἰσίν; *Mos.* 2.264-65. To be sure, "the divine word assures every good man (ἀστεῖος) of the gift of prophecy," and "all those Moses describes as righteous (δίκαιος) he also brings forward as possessed and prophesying" (*Quis Her.* 259; see also *Spec. Leg.* 4.192). Cf. Wisd. 7:27.

[66] Harry Austryn Wolfson, *Philo: Foundations of Religious Philosophy in Judaism, Christianity, and Islam*, Structure and Growth of Philosophic Systems from Plato to Spinoza, II (Cambridge, Massachusetts: Harvard University Press, 1947), 2.17. See further discussion of Philo's conception of prophets and prophecy below pp. 132-33.

[67] In *Mos.* 2.16, 76, where he deals with him as priest, Philo still calls Moses prophet. Cf. *Praem.* 9.56; *Spec. Leg.* 4.36, 192; *Mos.* 2.50, 275.

[68] See Paul Spilsbury, *The Image of the Jew in Flavius Josephus' Paraphrase of the Bible*, Texte und Studien zum Antiken Judentum, ed. Martin Hengel and Peter Schäfer, no. 69 (Tübingen: J. C. B. Mohr [Paul Siebeck], 1998), 103-104, 105 on Josephus's description Moses' prophetic mediation.

[69] When Josephus, *Ap.* 1.37-39 writes of Moses as author of "the most remote and ancient history," he also notes, "the prophets alone had this privilege."

[70] See Meeks, ("Moses as King and Prophet in Samaritan Sources," chapter 5 in) *Prophet-King*, 216-57, esp. 220-27, 236-41, 256-57; John Macdonald, *The Theology of the Samaritans*, The New Testament Library, ed. Alan Richardson, C. F. D. Moule, and

phet in Samaritan thought would far exceed the needs of this study. "Enormous importance," J. E. Fossum writes, "is ... attached to Moses' prophethood."[71] For example, in *Memar Marqah* 1.9 God says to Moses, "Were it not for your prophethood, I would not have revealed myself."

One further quotation on Moses from Samaritan literature (from *Memar Marqah* 6.9) may illustrate the point:

This is the prophet whose prophethood (דנביותה נביה אהנו) is a treasure[72] which will not be removed from him as long as the world lasts — the father of wonders,[73] the store of miracles, the companion[74] of the covenants, the light of the two worlds, the sun of prophethood (נביותה שמש), like whom there is no prophet from the whole human race (דאדם בריו מכל נביא כוחה לא). The living listened to him, the dead feared him; heaven and earth did not disobey his words.[75]

2.5 Moses as Prophet in the Targums

All the Targums clarify and emphasize biblical intimations that Moses is a prophet.[76] So, for example, where the MT in Deut. 33:1 and Ps. 90:1 refers to Moses as "the man of God" (האלהים איש), in *Tg. Ps.-J.*, *Tg. Onq.*, *Tg. Neof.* and *Frg. Tg.*(V) to Deut. 33:1, and in *Tg. Ps.* 90:1, he is "Moses the prophet of the Lord" (דייי נביא משה *et var.*). *Targum Ps.-J.* and *Tg. Neof.* Deut. 32:1 pair as the "two prophets" (נביין תריין), "Moses the prophet and Isaiah the prophet (נבייא וישעייה נביה משה)."[77]

The targumic emphasis of a prophetic identity for Moses is especially visible in the Palestinian Targum, where, "el título [i.e. "prophet"] que con

---

Floyd V. Filson (London: SCM Press, 1964), 147-49; James Alan Montgomery, *The Samaritans, the Earliest Jewish Sect: Their History, Theology and Literature* (New York: Ktav Publishing House, 1968; reprinted from first edition, 1907), 225-30.

[71] Jarl E. Fossum, *The Name of God and the Angel of the Lord: Samaritan and Jewish Concepts of Intermediation and the Origin of Gnosticism*, WUNT, ed. Martin Hengel and Otfried Hofius, no. 36 (Tübingen: J. C. B. Mohr [Paul Siebeck], 1985), 111, see further, 87-88, 111-12, 122-23.

[72] Or סימן, "sign."

[73] Or, "He is the father of wonders," etc., as rendered in Macdonald, *Theology of the Samaritans*, 149.

[74] Or "lord," as rendered, ibid., 149.

[75] For more on Moses as (the great) prophet in *Memar Marqah* see Ferdinand Dexinger, "Die Moses-terminologie in Tibât Mârqe — Einige Beobachtungen," *Frankfurter Judaistische Beiträge* 25 (1998): 51, 55-58.

[76] See Ernest G. Clarke with Sue Magder, trans. *Targum Pseudo-Jonathan: Deuteronomy*, The Aramaic Bible: The Targums, ed. Martin McNamara, et al., vol. 5B (Edinburgh: T. & T. Clark, 1998), 97 n. 2.

[77] A popular coupling in rabbinic literature, see below.

tanta parquedad le concede la Biblia Hebrea es usual."[78] *Targum Neofiti* emphasizes that Moses is a prophet throughout Deuteronomy 32-33 (The Song and the Blessing of Moses) particularly. He is "Moses the prophet" (משה נבייה *et var.*) in *Tg. Neof.* Deut. 32:3, 4, 14 and 33:1, 7, 8, 12, 13, 18, 20, 21, 22, 23, 24.[79] Similarly, *Tg. Ps.-J.* Deut. 33: 8, 12 add משה נביא to the MT's simple אמר, while verses 13, 18, 20, 22, and 23 add משה נביא דה'.

As J. Ribera sums it up, the Targums' basic view of Moses is as the most exalted of prophets:

Moses possesses, like no one else, the Holy Spirit or spirit of prophecy. He can communicate it to others (FT(P) Ex. 2:12; PJ Num. 11:17, 25; TN mg., FT(P) Num. 11:26) and he can withhold it from them as well (PJ Ex. 33:16; PJ, TN Num. 11:28). ... His speech is, in a distinctive way, the prophetic word of Yahweh in which one can always trust (TN, PJ Ex. 14:31; TN, FT(P), FT(V) Ex. 19:9).[80]

In the MT, as well as in most other OT traditions, the prophetic powers of Moses might be thought diminished after the episode of Numbers 11, since in the MT and the traditions that follow the MT, God simply took of the prophetic spirit that was upon Moses and placed it upon the seventy elders (Num. 11:25). All the Targums avoid this potential embarrassment by expressly stating that, in the words of *Tg. Ps.-J.* Num. 11:25, before transferring any prophetic "spirit" to the elders, God first "increased some of the prophetic spirit that was on him" (ורבי מן רוח נבואה דעלוי), so that "Moses did not lack any" (ומשה לא חסיר מדעם; *Tg. Neof.* and *Tg. Onq.* Num. 11:25 similar), and thus preserve the full prophetic endowment of Moses intact.[81]

---

[78] Miguel Pérez Fernández, *Tradiciones Mesiánicas en el Targum Palestinense: Estudios Exegéticos*, Institución San Jerónimo, no. 12 (Valencia and Jerusalem: Institución San Jerónimo para la Investigación Bíblica, in collaboration with the Instituto Español Bíblico y Arqueológico [Casa de Santiago] de Jerusalén, 1981), 184, see 183-86. Josep Ribera, "Prophecy according to Targum Jonathan to the Prophets and the Palestinian Targum to the Pentateuch," trans. Fiona Ritchie, in *Targum Studies*, vol. 1, *Textual and Contextual Studies in the Pentateuchal Targums*, ed. Paul V. M. Flesher, South Florida Studies in the History of Judaism, ed. Jacob Neusner, et al., no. 55 (Atlanta, Georgia: Scholars Press, 1992), 68-69, agrees, citing *Tg. Neof.*, *Tg. Ps.-J.* Ex. 14:31, and *Tg. Neof.*, *Frg. Tg.*(P, V) Ex. 19:9. Ribera, 68 notes the addition to the name of Moses of the qualifier "the prophet" or "the prophet of Yahweh" in, e.g., *Tg. Ps.-J.* Ex. 6:27; *Tg. Neof.*, *Frg. Tg.*(V) Num. 11:26; *Frg. Tg.*(P) Num. 16:1; *Tg. Ps.-J.* Deut. 31:14; *Frg. Tg.*(P) Deut. 33:21, to which may be added *Tg. Ps.-J.* Lev. 24:12; Deut. 28:15.

[79] Also *Tg. Onq.* Deut. 33:21; *Onqelos* gives less emphasis to Moses' prophethood.

[80] Ribera, "Prophecy according to Targum Jonathan to the Prophets and the Palestinian Targum to the Pentateuch," 68-69.

[81] See comment by Israel Drazin, *Targum Onkelos to Numbers with English Translation of the Text with Analysis and Commentary* (U.S.A.: Ktav Publishing House, Cen-

2.6 Moses as Prophet in Rabbinic Literature

For the Rabbis, "prophet" became the dominant conception of Moses. In rabbinic literature, Moses is often called the "father of prophets," as in *Sifre* Deut. 306 (near the end): "Moses, the wisest of the wise, the greatest of the great, and the father of the prophets" (ואבי הנביאים).[82] *Midrash on Pss.* 18.11 on 18:7 includes Moses among "all the prophets" who speak of the distress of Israel.

Pesiqta Rabbati 4.2 preserves the remark attributed to R. Tanḥuma Berabbi, who confirms the identity of the delivering prophet of Hosea 12:14(13), "that prophet being Moses," and then goes on extensively to compare Moses and Elijah, the "two prophets" who arose out of the tribe of Levi. Moses and Elijah are especially frequently paired together, in rabbinic literature but also in earlier texts.[83]

Moses as prophet was also bracketed with Isaiah, as already noted in connection with the Targums.[84] The accusation against Isaiah in the *Martyrdom of Isaiah*, that he made himself equal with Moses the prophet, was also noted above.[85] *Deuteronomy Rabbah* 2(Vaethchanan).4, preserves a saying attributed to R. Joḥanan: "There are no greater prophets than Moses and Isaiah." In *Pesiq. R.* 4.3 an anonymous rabbi places Moses on par with Isaiah, by speaking of Isaiah "with whom God had spoken mouth to mouth, as He did to Moses."[86]

The Rabbis taught that Moses had received all the Torah on Sinai, both written and oral, and all later halakhic rulings.[87] Less well known is a similar tradition that extols "Moses who delivered all the prophecies of others with his own, with the result that all who prophesied later were inspired by the prophecy of Moses (*Exod. Rab.* 42.8)."[88]

---

ter for Judaic Studies University of Denver, and Society for Targumic Studies, 1998), 139, n. 40.

[82] Also in *Sifre Num.* 134 and *Lev. Rab.* 1.3. Elsewhere he is called "master of all prophets," *Midrash Tannaim* 213, ו., line 7, ממשה רבינו שהוא רבן שלכל הנביאים, and "foremost among prophets," *Midr. Pss.* 1.2 on 1:1. According to *b. Sot.* 13b, Moses, Aaron and Miriam were all three prophets.

[83] On Moses and Elijah as prophets, see further below, pp. 197-99.

[84] Above, p. 46.

[85] P. 43.

[86] Also *Midr. Pss.* 90.4 on 90:1, "R. Eleazar taught in the name of R. Jose ben Zimra: 'None of the prophets, as they uttered their prophecies, knew what they were prophesying, except Moses and Isaiah who did know.'" Cf. the targumic tradition, above.

[87] See below, p. 146 with n. 107.

[88] See *Sifre* Deut. 357. Cf. also the review by Josef M. Kastner, "Moses im Neuen Testament" (Th.D. Dissertation, Ludwig-Maximilians-Universität Munich, 1967), 84-87, Paul Billerbeck, *Kommentar zum Neuen Testament aus Talmud und Midrasch*, vol. 4 *Exkurse zu einzelnen Stellen des Neuen Testaments abhandlungen zur neutestamentliche Theo-*

Outside the New Testament, a great variety of sources either identify Moses as a great prophet, or describe him doing things that basically only a prophet was supposed to do. Philo, in particular, identifies Moses as the supreme prophet often and explicitly, and uses his name interchangeably with many prophetic titles (as well as titles associated with other roles). The writings of Josephus, and other literature either current or originating in the first century A.D., fill out the picture of Moses as prophet in Second Temple Judaism. The Targums identify Moses as a prophet with similar enthusiasm. The broad rabbinic tradition that identifies Moses as a prophet to whom God revealed the whole course of history implies the continuation of these views of Moses as a seer beyond the period when the New Testament was being written.

2.7 Moses as Prophet in the New Testament

The New Testament implies the prophetic status of Moses in various ways, and in a manner showing continuity with the expressions of regard for Moses reviewed above. His prophethood is fairly obvious in John 1:45 and 5:46, where Moses is said to have written of Jesus,[89] and in Acts 3:22-26 and 7:20-39, which cite Moses' prediction of a prophet like himself in Deut. 18:15-19 (as that text came to be understood).[90] Galatians 3:19 refers to Moses as the mediator of the Law. The important link between the prophethood of Moses and his role as mediator of the Law will become apparent in the discussion that follows, and more especially in Chapter Five, where the Jewish view of the role of Moses in the Lawgiving will receive special scrutiny.

2.7.1 Galatians 3:19 and Hebrews 8:5-6; 9:15, 19; and 12:21, 24

The Old Testament does not call Moses a mediator, but his mediatory role is clearly visible in Exod. 34:29-35. Jewish literature from the first cen-

---

logie und Archäologie, parts 1 and 2 (Munich: C. H. Beck'sche Verlagsbuchhandlung [Oskar Beck], 1928), 446-50 and many more texts cited by Louis Ginzberg, *The Legends of the Jews*, vol. 5 (Philadelphia: The Jewish Publication Society of America, 1925), 404 n. 68; ibid., *The Legends of the Jews*, vol. 6 (Philadelphia: The Jewish Publication Society of America, 1928), 142 n. 836 and 151 n. 902.

[89] On these verses see Kastner, "Moses im Neuen Testament," 274-75, who argues that John 1:45 actually implies that Moses exceeds the prophets.

[90] On the eschatological interpretation of this text, see below, pp. 85-86 with n. 28, 88-90.

tury, however, does call Moses a mediator, in so many words, as does the rabbinic literature later on.[91]

The mediation of Moses is explicitly mentioned only once in the New Testament, however, and there in passing, when Paul identifies Moses as the "mediator" (μεσίτης) of the Law (Gal. 3:19). Moses' mediation of the Law is implied, however, when Hebrews calls Jesus the mediator (μεσίτης) of the new covenant (Heb. 8:6; 9:15; 12:24). This implies a corresponding mediator of the old covenant, and indeed in the immediate context of each appearance of Jesus as the mediator of the new covenant, Moses also appears quite clearly mediating the old one (8:5; 9:19; 12:21 with v. 19), reinforcing the implication that Hebrews sees Moses as a mediator of the Law.[92]

It should be pointed out that, as shown by its application to Jesus in Hebrews, the title "mediator" need not be disparaging. In so far as it meant that someone had become the mouthpiece of God, it was clearly an honorific, as it is in 1 Tim. 2:5.

All these NT texts place the mediation of Moses in the context of the Lawgiving, which Chapter Five will examine specifically. Mediation, however, could embrace the functions of priest and king, as well as prophet and lawgiver. In the case of the mediation effected by Moses all these categories would apply, as the following chapters of the present study show.[93]

The two NT passages treated next, which cite Moses' prediction of a prophet like himself in Deut. 18:15-19, Acts 3:22-26 and Acts 7:20-39, cast Moses as a prophet both explicitly and implicitly (i.e., Moses predicted something — a successor for himself, and he characterized both his successor and himself as prophets). But these passages imply and characterize Moses' prophethood in other ways as well, which have not always been attended to.

---

[91] E.g. *LAB* 9.8, *mediator*; *y. Meg.* 74d.12, the Law was שניתנה על ידי סרסור ("given by the hand of a mediator"). *Pes. R. Kah.* 5 (2d ed. 2 vols. Edited by Bernard Mandelbaum [New York: The Jewish Theological Seminary of America, 1987], 1.83, line 13), "when they [Israel] had sinned, they could not look on the face of the mediator (פני הסרסור)." Further citations in Howard Jacobson, ed., *A Commentary on Pseudo-Philo's* Liber Antiquitatum Biblicarum *with Latin Text and English Translation*, Arbeiten zur Geschichte des antiken Judentums und des Urchristentums, ed. Martin Hengel, et al., no. 31 (Leiden: E. J. Brill, 1996), 1.418.

[92] Kastner, "Moses im Neuen Testament" thinks this practically exhausts what Hebrews makes of Moses. See his pp. 247-56 (esp. 249-50), 266-67.

[93] See Kastner, "Moses im Neuen Testament," 47, 80; A. Oepke, "μεσίτης," in *Theological Dictionary of the New Testament*, ed. Gerhard Kittel, trans. and ed. Geoffrey W. Bromiley, vol. 4, *Λ-Ν* (Grand Rapids: William B. Eerdmans, 1967), 599-602, 611-20.

2.7.2 Acts 3:21-26

Acts 3:22-26 is the closing section of Peter's sermon at the Portico of Solomon. Verse 22 quotes the words of Moses in Deut. 18:15, "The Lord shall raise up for you a prophet like me from your brethren; to him you shall give heed in everything he says to you" (προφήτην ὑμῖν ἀναστήσει κύριος ὁ θεὸς ὑμῶν ἐκ τῶν ἀδελφῶν ὡς ἐμέ· αὐτοῦ ἀκούσεσθε κατὰ πάντα ὅσα ἂν λαλήσῃ πρὸς ὑμᾶς). These words naturally are made out here as a prediction of Jesus.

The passage as a whole seems not only to parallel Moses with "a prophet" to come, but actually to name him as one of "the holy prophets" of old. Verse 21 ends with a reference to "all the things which God spoke by the mouth of his holy prophets from ancient time," πάντων ὧν ἐλάλησεν ὁ θεὸς διὰ στόματος τῶν ἁγίων ἀπ' αἰῶνος αὐτοῦ προφητῶν, which verse 22 follows immediately with Μωϋσῆς μὲν εἶπεν. The content of Moses' utterance, in verses 22-23, is a quotation combining Deut. 18:15-16a with either Deut. 18:19 or Lev. 23:29 (though influences that may derive from both are detectable).[94] Most translators find the particle μέν too weak to translate, but probably it carries its typical affirmative meaning and connects Moses with the preceding reference to "all the prophets."[95]

Besides the glance backward by the expression Μωϋσῆς μὲν εἶπεν of 3:22 to "the prophets" in 3:21 it is likely that μέν also correlates with καὶ πάντες δὲ οἱ προφῆται ἀπὸ Σαμουήλ in 3:24. The μέν ... καὶ δέ syntax which links verses 22 and 24 then makes the figure of Moses the pivot between the reference to "all the prophets" in verse 21 and the reference to Samuel and his successors in verse 24. Moses is both the first instance of

---

[94] The wording resembles, but does not match, LXX Deut. 18:15-16a. C. K. Barrett, *A Critical and Exegetical Commentary on the Acts of the Apostles*, vol. 1, *Preliminary Introduction and Commentary on Acts I-XIV*, The International Critical Commentary on the Holy Scriptures of the Old and New Testaments, ed. J. A. Emerton, C. E. B. Cranfield, and G. N. Stanton (Edinburgh: T. & T. Clark, 1994), 209 supposes Luke quoted the LXX from memory, see his discussion, 207-208. The same prophecy, attributed to Moses, is repeated in Acts 7:37 (cf. John 1:45), on which see Kastner, "Moses im Neuen Testament," 215-16. Acts 7:38 adds that Moses "received living oracles" (ὃς ἐδέξατο λόγια ζῶντα), see also 7:44.

[95] E. g., see Barrett, *Commentary on Acts*, 186, 210-11, though his comments on v. 24 make clear that he sees the overall drift of the passage to reckon Moses as one of the prophets; Ernst Haenchen, *The Acts of the Apostles: A Commentary*, trans. Bernard Noble and Gerald Shinn, under the supervision of Hugh Anderson, revised by R. McL. Wilson (Oxford: Basil Blackwell, 1971), 203 translates Μωϋσῆς μὲν εἶπεν, "Moses indeed said."

verse 21's "holy prophets," and a unique individual stationed at the head of their line as set out in verse 24.[96]

2.7.3 Acts 7:20-39

The second passage to imply Moses' prophethood, Acts 7:20-39, is part of the central section of the speech of Stephen. The Stephen narrative is one of the most important NT passages for contemporary views of Moses, and will be revisited later in this study. In the present passage, one element of the description of Moses, his τέρατα καὶ σημεῖα, invites detailed treatment here.[97]

2.7.3.1 Miracles as Prophetic Authentication in Second Temple Judaism

In the first century a broad swath of tradition associated prophets with miraculous signs.[98] Nearly every prophetic call in the Old Testament concluded with the provision of a sign (אוֹת) authenticating that call, for the people as well as for the prophet himself.[99]

---

[96] Kastner, "Moses im Neuen Testament," 179, concludes "Lk stellt Moses in die Reihe der Propheten."

[97] The suffering and rejection of Moses (Acts 7:24-25, 35, 39) are sometimes thought prophetic motifs (7:51-52). On the identification of Moses with the Isaianic suffering servant of Isaiah, see Davies, *Setting of the Sermon on the Mount*, 117.

[98] Ferdinand Hahn, *The Titles of Jesus in Christology: Their History in Early Christianity*, Lutterworth Library, ed. James Barr, et al. (London: Lutterworth Press, 1969), 378 traced the root of this expectation to the Old Testament. See also Morna D. Hooker, *The Signs of a Prophet: The Prophetic Actions of Jesus* (London: SCM Press, 1997), 5-6; Jepsen, *Nabi*, 208-10; Alfred Bertholet, *Deuteronomium*, Kurzer Hand-Commentar zum Alten Testament, ed. Karl Marti, vol. 5 (Freiburg i. B., Leipzig, and Tübingen: J. C. B. Mohr [Paul Siebeck], 1899), 42. Examine the presentations of Elijah: 1 Kings 17:17-24; Elisha: 2 Kings 4:32-7; 5:1-14; Isaiah: 2 Kings 20:7 (|| Isa. 38:21); 2 Kings 20:11 (|| Isa. 38:8). In 2 Kings 20:8 (cf. Is. 38:7) and Exod. 4:30-31 the authenticating sign (אוֹת; σημεῖον) is especially evident. John Barton, *Oracles of God: Perceptions of Ancient Prophecy in Israel after the Exile* (London: Darton, Longman and Todd, 1986), 99-101 presents a brief survey of prophets as men of power in the Old Testament and intertestamental literature. It is unnecessary to look to the Greco-Roman world for the motif, as does Bultmann who finds particularly in John the portrayal of Jesus in the style of a Hellenistic θεῖος ἀνήρ who persuades people to believe in him by working signs; see P. N. Anderson, *The Christology of the Fourth Gospel: Its Unity and Disunity in the Light of John 6*, WUNT/2, ed. M. Hengel and O. Hofius, no. 78 (Tübingen: J. C. B. Mohr [Paul Siebeck], 1996), 6, 35. A Jewish background is preferable.

[99] See p33 n. 4 above. Richter, *Die sogenannten vorprophetischen Berufungberichte* concludes his summation of the features that characterize the *Gattung* of the call of a prophet in the Old Testament by noting that "Von diesen Gliedern stellt nur das letzte (5) keinen Satz, sondern einen Begriff dar, *'ot* im Singular oder im Plural." N. Habel, "The Form and Significance of the Call Narratives," 319 notes, following his

Ben Sira emphasizes miracles in his tributes to prophetic heroes, though without an explicit focus on authentication. Besides the miracles of Moses, already considered,[100] note how it is said of Joshua, named in Ecclus. 46:1 as the successor to Moses in prophecies, that also "by his hand the sun was restrained" (ἐν χειρὶ αὐτοῦ ἐνεποδίσθη ὁ ἥλιος; 46:4). "Samuel, the prophet of the Lord" (46:9) called upon the Lord and "the Lord thundered from heaven" (46:17). In 48:2-5 Ben Sira recalls the miracles (θαυμάσια; 48:4) of Elijah. Then (in both the Greek and the Hebrew versions) he emphasizes Elisha's "signs" (מופתים and אתות; 48:12[101]) and "wonders" (נפלאות; τέρατα, θαυμάσια; 48:14), before mentioning, in 48:23, Isaiah's healing of Hezekiah, and how once again the sun was restrained.

E. Bammel concludes rightly that generally a miracle was a *conditio sine qua non* for prophets in the Jewish no less than the Hellenistic world.[102] The association of prophets and miracles was strong enough to make the performance of a miracle requisite as a sign for demonstrating the authenticity of the prophet and his message.[103] This connection will be demonstrated below.

2.7.3.2 Miracles as Prophetic Authentication in the New Testament

In the New Testament the connection between miracles and prophecy occurs frequently. The connection may be emphasized in Peter's Pentecost sermon, where the words, "and they shall prophesy" (καὶ προφητεύσουσιν), and, "[I will give] signs" (καὶ δώσω ... σημεῖα), not attested in

---

similar summation, that "the signs which the prophets received were also public credentials of their commission."

[100] See above, pp. 34-36.

[101] From a lacuna, which interrupts the second line of 48:12 in the Hebrew manuscript, which the Syriac completes as פי ש]נים אתות הר[בה (cited in Smend, *Weisheit des Jesus Sirach*, 1.56). The Greek diverges altogether here. Cf. on terminology *Sifre Deut.* 83: "אות refers to a phenomenon in the heavens. ... מופת to one on earth."

[102] E. Bammel, "'John did no miracle': John 10.41," in *Miracles: Cambridge Studies in Their Philosophy and History*, ed. C. F. D. Moule (London: A. R. Mowbray & Co., 1965), 181(-183). Bammel, 190-91 argues that in the immediately pre-Jamnian period, "a sign was considered decisive for the recognition of a prophet." Hahn, *Titles of Jesus in Christology*, 378-90 agrees. See further on the Herodian and post-Herodian periods William Horbury, *Jews and Christians in Contact and Controversy* (Edinburgh: T. &. T. Clark, 1998), 111-14. Later, Justin Martyr, *Dial.* 7.14-15, recalls with approval the testimony of an old man that the prophets "were also worthy to be believed because of the miracles (διὰ τὰς δυνάμεις) which they performed."

[103] Though *Assumption of Moses* presents Moses as a prophet without telling of miracles, it displays little interest in the Exodus story where they mainly occurred (Tiede, "Figure of Moses," 91). At Qumran, though "all traits are lacking which would call our attention to the eschatological Moses as a worker of miracles," this, Hahn, *Titles*, 362(-63) writes, is because at Qumran the eschatological prophet is no longer a prophet *per se*, but a teacher of Torah (and a sign is not required of a rabbi, 378).

the MT or LXX, are inserted together in the quotation from Joel 2:28-32 (Acts 2:18-19).[104] The two witnesses of Rev. 11:3-12 "prophesy" (προ-φητεύσουσιν, v. 3; cf. προφητείας αὐτῶν, v. 6) and have the power to work great miracles (v. 6).

A characteristic reaction to the wonders worked by Jesus was to accord him recognition as a prophet. After the raising of the widow of Nain's son, the people exclaim, "A great prophet has arisen among us!" (Luke 7:16).[105] On the basis of the sign of the multiplication of bread the people recognize Jesus as "the Prophet who is to come" (ὁ προφήτης ὁ ἐρχόμενος; John 6:14).[106] Here it is especially the Prophet like Moses who is in mind; this is implied by the fact that the sign is a Mosaic sort of sign, and especially by the discourse on bread that follows, which focuses on Moses and the manna of the Wilderness.

The admission, closely following the description of Jesus as a "prophet without honor" (προφήτης ἄτιμος), that "he could work no miracle" in Nazareth (Mark. 6:4-5; ‖ Matt. 13:57-58), and the recollection of the two disciples in Luke 24:19 of Jesus as "a prophet mighty in deed and word" (ἀνὴρ προφήτης δυνατὸς ἐν ἔργῳ καὶ λόγῳ), suggest, as G. Vermes has pointed out, that the terms "prophet" and "miracle-worker" were used synonymously by Jesus and his followers.[107]

---

[104] See Darrell L. Bock, *Proclamation from Prophecy and Pattern: Lucan Old Testament Christology*, Journal for the Study of the New Testament Supplement Series, ed. David Hill, publishing ed. David E. Orton, vol. 12 (Sheffield: JSOT Press, 1987), 159, 162-63.

[105] Oscar Cullmann, *The Christology of the New Testament*, 2d ed. (London: SCM Press, 1963), 30 argues on syntactical grounds that the remark of the crowd does not point to *the* eschatological Prophet, but simply makes Jesus out as a prophet. Hahn, *Titles of Jesus in Christology*, 379 demurs.

[106] See Meeks, *Prophet-King*, 90-91. Meeks, 164 says of the eschatological prophet in particular, "The performance of 'signs and wonders' must have been a fundamental characteristic of the mission of the prophet like Moses."

[107] Geza Vermes, *Jesus the Jew: A Historian's Reading of the Gospels* (London: William Collins Sons & Co., 1973), 89. Vermes, 89 also argues, however, that another view of prophecy, exemplified by Jesus' opponents in the Gospels, e.g. the Pharisaic host (Luke 7:39: "If this man were a prophet he would know ... that she is a sinner") and the servants of the high priest (Luke 22:64: "Prophesy, who hit you?"), held prophecy to be only an intellectual gift, the knowledge of secrets, with no miraculous element. However, while the Pharisaic host of Luke 7:39 certainly expects a prophet to know with whom he is eating, the notion that Jesus might be a prophet in the first place clearly derives from the preceding narrative, which includes the raising of the widow's son and the resulting acclaim of Jesus as "a great prophet" (Luke 7:11-16), which went out "all over Judea and in all the surrounding district" (7:17; see also 7:18-23). This pericope thus actually supports the attestation of a prophet by miracles. It is of course hopeless to attempt to deduce a philosophy of prophecy from the high priest's guards' one recorded taunt of Jesus.

2.7.3.3 The "Wonders and Signs" of Moses

In Acts 7:36, Stephen says of Moses, "this man performed wonders and signs" (ποιήσας τέρατα καὶ σημεῖα). These "wonders and signs" are specifically linked with the Exodus, although the statement may possibly also be connected with the earlier claim, in v. 22, that Moses generally "was powerful in his words and deeds" (ἦν δὲ δυνατὸς ἐν λόγοις καὶ ἔργοις αὐτοῦ — an expression which may even be a Lukanism for characterizing a prophet (see Luke 24:19, cf. Acts 2:22).[108]

The miracles of Moses were very widely celebrated in Jewish literature, from the biblical account of the Exodus[109] (cf. its commemoration in Ps. 105:27[110]) down through first-century A.D. compositions. Deuteronomy 34:10-12 states that since his death no prophet has arisen "like Moses, whom the Lord knew face to face, for all the signs and wonders" (לכל־ האתות והמופתים; ἐν πᾶσι τοῖς σημείοις καὶ τέρασιν) which the Lord sent him to perform in Egypt, "and for all the mighty power and for all the great terror which Moses performed in the sight of all Israel" (combining testimony to the equivalence of "prophet" and "wonder worker," while simultaneously establishing his "signs and wonders" as evidence specifically for Moses' exalted prophethood). References to his signs from Ben Sira and Wisdom were noted above.[111] Artapanus describes the plagues in general as the work of Moses,[112] while Philo is more scrupulous, and maintains the agency of Moses (or Aaron) in working miracles only where the biblical account so assigns it.[113] Josephus is most restrictive, limiting the

---

[108] See Darrell L. Bock, *Luke*, Baker Exegetical Commentary on the New Testament, ed. Moisés Silva, vol. 3(A&B) (Grand Rapids: Baker Books, 1996), 2.1912 and Barrett, *Commentary on Acts*, 1.356 on the NT usage of the (idiomatic?) combination "word and deed."

[109] E.g. Exod. 7:20; 8:1(EVV 8:5), 12(16); 9:22; 10:12; 14:16 (cf. 14:21), though Haenchen, 283 observes that in Exod. 7:3 it was God himself who promised to perform "many wonders and signs in the land of Egypt," implying that Acts breaks with Jewish tradition in assigning Moses responsibility for the miracles. If the "signs and wonders" of Acts are the signs of Moses' prophetic authentication, however, there is no conflict with tradition.

[110] "They [Moses and Aaron] performed [God's] wondrous acts (אתותיו) among them (following most translations, but the sense may be, "set words of his wonders," i.e., "announced."), and signs (ומפתים) in the land of Ham" (Ps. 105:27). The Targums and LXX maintain this way of speaking here and in the references of the previous note above.

[111] See above pp. 34-36.

[112] *Apud* Eusebius, *Praep. Ev.* 9.27.27-36.

[113] *Mos.* 1.97, 99, 103, 107, 113-14, 120, 126-27, 130, making three for Aaron, three for Moses, and one for them together, with the remainder effected by God without mediation.

miracles of Moses to his authenticating sign miracles.[114]   Likewise in the wilderness, for Josephus, Moses "trusted in God" (*Ant.* 2.329), who worked miracles (*Ant.* 3.18; 4.44-45).[115]   Pseudo-Philo emphasizes that it was God who worked all the miracles, signs, and wonders of the Exodus (*signa et prodigia*, *LAB* 9:7; *signa*, 9:10; 19:11; *mirabilia*, 12:2), through Moses. Likewise, in the *Exagoge* God works the signs and the plagues through Moses (120-151), though the Egyptian messenger reports that Moses himself performed signs and wonders (σημεῖα καὶ τεράτα; 224-28).[116]

Thus, while not every tradition maintains them in just the same way, Acts is in harmony with a broad cross-section of Jewish tradition in ascribing "wonders and signs" to Moses and, generally speaking, on the basis of material reviewed so far, this probably categorizes Moses as a prophet. Particularly within the context of a Lukan writing, it may be meant to do so.   Moreover, the application of the specific term "wonders and signs" may warrant yet firmer prophetic identification of Moses as a prophet.

2.7.3.4 "Signs" as Specifically the Authenticating Miracles of Prophets

Josephus tells of the so-called "sign prophets," all of whom were active between A.D. 44-70, and who claimed to be prophets (two, according to Josephus, in so many words, but all in some way or other) and promised to

---

[114] In the account of the plagues on Egypt Moses vanishes entirely, except as an occasional emissary to Pharaoh (*Ant.* 2.293-314).   Cf. Pharaoh's offence in behaving, "as though it were Moses and not [God] who was punishing Egypt on the Hebrews' behalf" (*Ant.* 2.302; also *Ant.* 2.294, 296, 300; 3.17, 86).   David Lenz Tiede, *The Charismatic Figure as Miracle Worker*, Society of Biblical Literature Dissertation Series, no. 1 (Missoula, Mont.: Society of Biblical Literature, 1972), 237, "One of the most telling features of Josephus' depiction is the clear reticence to describe his hero as a miracle worker. ... He idealizes Moses as a supreme sage ... while he steers clear of those parts of the tradition which would document Moses' elevated status on the basis of his reputation as a miracle worker"; see also 226-230.

[115] At the battle with the Amalekites (Exod. 17:8-13, *Ant.* 3.53), Josephus directs attention away from any supposed miraculous powers of Moses, 3.47-52, cf. *m. RH* 3.8.

[116] The Targum to 1 Sam. 12:6a seems concerned to clarify who did the miracles as well, as Samuel says, "It is the Lord who wrought mighty deeds through Moses and Aaron" (ואמר שמואל לעמא יוי דעבד גבורן על ידי משה ואהרן), where the MT has only ויאמר שמואל אל־העם יהוה אשר עשה את־משה ואת־אהרן, "It is the Lord who made Moses and Aaron," or possibly "the Lord sent Moses and Aaron," see Mary Rose D'Angelo, *Moses in the Letter to the Hebrews*, Society of Biblical Literature Dissertation Series, ed. Howard Clark Kee, no. 42 (Missoula, Montana: Scholars Press, 1979), 145-46. Kastner, "Moses im Neuen Testament," argues that the fifth Sibylline Oracle, lines 256-259, speaks of Moses as "the best of the Hebrews, who will one day cause the sun to stand, speaking with fair speech and holy lips."   The undoubtedly Christian origin of line 257, however, makes this a precarious identification.

perform miracles.[117] It is key to the discussion here to note that the promised miracles were evidently to have no other function than to authenticate the claim to be a prophet.[118] The testimony of Josephus is especially

---

[117] The list of six in Rebecca Gray, *Prophetic Figures in Late Second Temple Jewish Palestine: The Evidence from Josephus* (New York and Oxford: Oxford University Press, 1993), 112-23 seems nearly standard: 1) Theudas (*Ant.* 20.97-99; Acts 5:36; cf. Philo, *Mig.* 15); 2) a group of unnamed figures under Felix (*B.J.* 2.258-60; *Ant.* 20.167-68); 3) the Egyptian (*B.J.* 2.261-63; *Ant.* 20.169-72; Acts 21:38); 4) an unnamed figure under Festus (*Ant.* 20.188); 5) an unnamed figure who led his followers to the temple just before it was destroyed (*B.J.* 6.283-87); 6) Jonathan, a Sicarius refugee active in Cyrene after the war (*B.J.* 7.437-50; *Life* 424-25). Some would add: 7) the Samaritan under Pilate who promised to reveal the sacred vessels hidden by Moses on Mt. Gerizim (*Ant.* 18.85-87). All but the fourth mention the promise of either a sign or a miracle. Gray, 136-37 adduces strong evidence that the sign prophets clearly presented themselves as prophets, and were regarded as prophets by their followers.

[118] The present study is itself a kind of reminder that popular acceptance of the sign prophets as simply prophets would be hindered by any impression that these men patterned themselves not after prophets generally but after Moses specifically. Gray, *Prophetic Figures in Late Second Temple Jewish Palestine: The Evidence from Josephus*, refutes the two usual supports for connecting the sign prophets with Moses: 1) the interpretation of a wilderness motif as necessarily reminiscent of the Exodus (for which see her discussion, 117, and Martin Hengel, *The Zealots: Investigations into the Jewish Freedom Movement in the Period from Herod I until 70 A.D*, trans. David Smith [Edinburgh: T. & T. Clark, 1989], 249-53; see Glasson, *Moses in the Fourth Gospel*, 16-17 for discussion of the wide linkage made in Jewish tradition between eschatological deliverance and the wilderness, and below, pp. 196-98) and 2) the association of the sign prophets' "signs (and wonders)" with the Exodus miracles instead of, more correctly, with authentication miracles, which were in the first century probably judged to be common to all prophets, (Gray, 141-42). She concedes that in at least one case, Theudas, and perhaps in another, the Egyptian, the sign prophet did to some extent model himself on Moses. What she contests is an overgeneralization of all the sign prophets as "Mosaic." That being said, she may not give enough weight to the effects that wide popular expectations of a second Moses, and of a second "Exodus-like experience" would have had on 1) what the sign prophets would deem themselves to be communicating by their symbolic actions, and 2) how people would most naturally have perceived them. See Glasson, 20-21, 46-47 for some of the data on these expectations, especially as they are expressed in speculations about the renewal of the gift of manna. Micah 7:15; Isa. 48:21; 51:10; and Ezek. 20:34-38 are some notable OT passages which use the Exodus as a paradigm for later deliverance. It may be impossible to resist the imputation of at least some Mosaic overtones to what the sign prophets did. In any case, it cannot be proven that the sign prophets and their audiences had nothing of Moses in mind in what they were doing. What is urged forcefully by Gray is that the Moses motif alone is not the sole, or even the dominant, feature of the careers of the sign prophets, however much it may have colored them (contrast, e.g., the position of Kastner, "Moses im Neuen Testament," 71-73). Gray's arguments help establish the reference made here to the sign prophets for what would be "typical" for a prophet in the first century. Further, if the sign prophets are not fundamentally imitators of Mo-

interesting both because his accounts of the sign prophets certainly "give us some idea of what a prophetic figure in the first century would be expected to do"[119] (not least when set against the background of Jewish literature already surveyed here) and because in his writings the term σημεῖα seems, in the context of these claimants to the office of prophet, to have become a technical term.

R. Gray observes that even outside the accounts of the sign prophets Josephus uses the expression "signs" (σημεῖα) specifically to denote a prophet's "authenticating miracles" (as opposed to his "ordinary" miracles, if any). This distinction appears in his stories of several biblical prophets besides Moses, as well as in the narratives of Josephus's near contemporaries, the sign prophets.[120] This suggests that when used in connection with the activity of a prophet, σημεῖον functioned for Josephus as a *terminus technicus* denoting the authenticating miracle of a prophet. Gray contends that this refinement is original to Josephus.

Now actually this distinctive meaning of the word "sign" in Josephus's accounts appears rudimentarily in the biblical account of the call of Moses (and then persists in Josephus's retelling in *Antiquities*). There, Moses receives three signs (הָאֹתוֹת, σημεῖα; Exod. 4:9), which explicitly serve to persuade the people that he is sent from God. This occurs even after the Lord has declared, "I will stretch out my hand and strike Egypt with all my miracles (נִפְלְאֹתַי; LXX θαυμασίοις μου; Exod. 3:20)." Here already in the biblical account a distinction of some kind between signs and miracles is visible.

Because Josephus puts Moses at some distance from the plagues and the miracles of deliverance in the Exodus and Wilderness, in the *Antiquities* the three authenticating signs become the only miracles done by Moses (2.284, also 2.274, 287): Moses calls them, "the deeds done by me (τὰ ὑπ' ἐμοῦ πραττόμενα; *Ant.* 2.286). The authenticating function of these signs is clearly emphasized: in *Ant.* 2.274 God exhorts Moses "to use signs (σημείοις) to convince all men that thou art sent by me and doest all at my command," and in due course performance of the signs persuades the leading Hebrews (and even Moses himself) of Moses' divine commission (*Ant.* 2.275, 279-80, cf. 327).

While, as just noted, the Bible introduces the distinctive use of "signs," or at least could be supposed to do so, neither the MT nor the LXX consistently limit the use of "sign" to Moses' authenticating miracles; through-

---

ses, the parallels between them and Moses in Josephus may further serve as evidence for Josephus's conception of Moses as a prophet.

[119] Hooker, *Signs of a Prophet*, 13.

[120] Gray, *Prophetic Figures in Late Second Temple Jewish Palestine*, 128-32, see 123-24.

out both versions of the Old Testament, all the miracles of the whole Exodus narrative are "signs" or "signs and wonders,"[121] which is why Gray assigns the refinement in "signs" terminology to Josephus. Gray's observations are sound, but her theory of Josephan responsibility for the refinement in terminology may be too narrow. Note, in that regard, the following.

Philo, whom Gray does not examine, in his account of the Exodus calls the three authenticating miracles which God gives to Moses σημεῖα (*Mos.* 1.76), τέρατα (*Mos.* 1.90-91), and σημεῖα καὶ τέρατα (*Mos.* 1.95).[122] The plagues of Moses are not given any specific genre. Philo does not trace the career of any other prophet-like figure by which the comparison might be extended, but the usage in the passages dealing with Moses suggests that the distinction of authenticating signs from other miracles was known to Philo, and so is not unique to Josephus, which would imply that it is not his invention. This in turn might indicate that miraculous "signs" were especially associated with prophets among Jews earlier than Josephus, as far back as Philo perhaps, and certainly as far back as the period when the New Testament writings were forming.

Moreover, the refinement of OT nomenclature noted by Gray in Josephus, and which also appears in Philo, seems in evidence in the New Testament. M. D. Hooker observes that in every case in the Synoptic Gospels when Jesus is asked for a sign (σημεῖον), the demand follows *after* a miracle.[123] This suggests that the Evangelists are using the term in some special way, perhaps in the technical sense found in Josephus (of prophets generally) and Philo (of Moses).

According to both Paul and the Jesus of the Fourth Gospel, before they believe "Jews ask for a sign" (Ἰουδαῖοι σημεῖα αἰτοῦσιν; 1 Cor. 1:22; also John 4:48), a position that directly links signs with authentication.

Though sign terminology is not used, it is probably significant that to demonstrate his authority to forgive sins Jesus heals a man (Mark 2:1-12; Matt. 9:1-8; Luke 5:17-26). See that the point of what he does is explicitly not the performance of an act of mercy, which Jesus practically disavows (Mark 2:10; Matt. 9:6; Luke 5:24), but the proclamation of his standing as the emissary of God.

Mark 13:22 (‖ Matt. 24:24) predicts the appearance of false prophets who will attest themselves with "signs and wonders" (σημεῖα καὶ τέρατα). The beast of Rev. 13:11-17, referred to in Rev. 16:13; 19:20; and

---

[121] Ibid., 126; 203 n. 37.

[122] And θαυματουργήματα (*Mos.* 1.82).

[123] Hooker, *Signs of a Prophet*, 17-18; Matt. 12:2, 9, 14, 24, followed by 12:38 ‖ Luke 11:14-16; Mark 8:1-11‖ Matt. 15:29-16:1; see Hahn, *Titles of Jesus in Christology*, 378.

20:10 as "the false prophet" (ψευδοπροφήτης), performs "great signs" (σημεῖα μεγάλα; 13:13, 14), and, apparently because he has thus (falsely) attested himself, misleads many.[124]

Bammel observes that the statement in John 10:41, "While John performed no sign, yet everything John said ... was true," which clearly finds the absence from John's career of a confirming sign remarkable, "presupposes as normal a [positive] relationship between 'sign' (σημεῖον) and pronouncements."[125] One might refine this conclusion and say instead that the statement finds remarkable that John should have been a true prophet and yet never offered a sign to show it.

In the Fourth Gospel σημεῖα are actually sought from Jesus only twice. On one occasion, in 6:30, a crowd asks, "What then do you do for a sign (σημεῖον), that we may see and believe you?" The incident immediately follows the great miracle of the feeding in John 6:1-14. This miracle is itself taken for the authenticating σημεῖον of a prophet, as 6:14 nearly says in so many words when it relates that the people saw the σημεῖον which Jesus performed and thus concluded that he was the Prophet. Having already guessed that Jesus is a prophet on the basis of one sign, they ask for another (this time) avowedly authenticating sign to back it up.[126] Throughout this passage the authenticating function of a σημεῖον is to the fore, especially its role in authenticating a prophet.

The other occasion occurs at the end of John's Temple-cleansing narrative, when the Jews ask, "What sign (σημεῖον) do you show to us, seeing that you do these things?" (2:18). This is the only demand of Jesus for a sign recorded in all four Gospels which does not actually follow on the heels of one or more great miracles. It does, however, follow what Hooker has identified as a distinctively "prophetic action," in this case the cleansing of the Temple, which prompts the call for prophetic authenti-

---

[124] See further on σημεῖα as attestations for God's chosen envoys in the New Testament, Karl Heinrich Rengstorf, "σημεῖον κτλ.," in *Theological Dictionary of the New Testament*, ed. Gerhard Friedrich, trans. and ed. Geoffrey W. Bromiley, vol. 7, *Σ* (Grand Rapids: William B. Eerdmans, 1964), 230-32, 234-36, 243-44, 249-50, 258-60.

[125] Bammel, "'John did no miracle'," 188; 188-91 on miracles as prophetic attestation. Cf. the account of Hanina ben Dosa who, upon announcing a healing brought about through his prayer, was asked if he was a prophet (*b. Ber.* 34b; *y. Ber.* 9d).

[126] Hooker, *Signs of a Prophet*, 33, points to the "absurdity" of the demand for a sign. Her explanation is that the evangelist is using a literary device to highlight the fact that the crowd is seeing signs without understanding them — the "hard-hearted Jews" approach to the riddle posed by the account. But in light of Gray's work in Josephus, the comparable usage in Philo, and the wealth of very similar material in the four Gospels, a better explanation is a contemporary understanding of the specifically authenticating σημεῖα of a prophet. This also furnishes the account with yet another parallel with the narrative of Moses who authenticated himself with (not only one but) multiple signs.

cation in much the same way some more miraculous feat might do.[127] Note that in the Synoptic parallels to the cleansing the demand makes the request for authentication explicit: "By what authority are you doing these things, or who gave you this authority to do these things?" (Mark 11:27; || Matt. 21:23; Luke 20:2). These expressions demanding authentication are precisely equivalent to the Johannine request for a sign.

Elsewhere the Fourth Gospel itself explicitly connects σημεῖα with authentication and consequent belief.[128] In John 11:47-48 it is regarded as inevitable that people will believe in Jesus, owing to his many signs (πολλὰ σημεῖα).[129] P. N. Anderson writes, "For Mark, faith *precedes* miracles, while for John the primary purpose of Jesus' signs is to evoke faith in the audience. Thus, faith *follows* the signs in John."[130] On the basis of the above discussion Anderson's verdict on Mark might be reopened for discussion, but his assessment of the Fourth Gospel seems spot on, as other commentators have also observed.

All four Evangelists were clearly acquainted with the importance of σημεῖα for authenticating a prophet, and aware of a distinction, similar to that evidenced in Josephus (and in Philo), between great miracles, that accomplish deliverance of some kind, and authenticating signs.[131]

Apostles are the NT analogs to Israel's prophets — and so naturally they also attest themselves with miraculous σημεῖα. In Paul's own words, his ministry featured "the signs of an apostle (τὰ μὲν σημεῖα τοῦ ἀποστόλου) ... performed among you with all perseverance, by signs and won-

---

[127] Hooker, *Signs of a Prophet*, 18.

[128] John 3:2; 7:31 with 6:14. See Rengstorf, "σημεῖον κτλ.," 243-44.

[129] Cf. John 12:37.

[130] Anderson, *Christology of the Fourth Gospel*, 154.

[131] At least some groups of Jews seem to have believed that prophecy had ceased at some point since the construction of the second Temple. The key testimony is usually found in *t. Sot.* 13.2, along with 1 Macc. 4:44-46; 9:27; 14:41; for more extensive documentation and discussion, see Roger Beckwith, *The Old Testament Canon of the New Testament Church and Its Background in Early Judaism* (Grand Rapids: Eerdmans, 1985), 370-71; and Gray, *Prophetic Figures in Late Second Temple Jewish Palestine*, 7-34. Gray, 35-79, however, argues that this was certainly not the case with Josephus, who in fact seems to have regarded himself as a genuine prophet, as well as others of his day. What Josephus believed, according to Gray, is that prophecy had ceased to be of the same high caliber that it once was. Hooker, *Signs of a Prophet*, 6 argues that this was actually the general opinion of the time: "there was a nostalgic belief that there were no longer any prophets *like the prophets of old*." Richard A. Horsley and John S. Hanson, *Bandits, Prophets, and Messiahs: Popular Movements in the Time of Jesus*, New Voices in Biblical Studies, ed. Adela Yarbro Collins and John J. Collins (Minneapolis: Winston Press, 1985), 151-160 adduce evidence for prophetic activity in NT times among literate groups, and especially at the popular level; they say that the belief that prophecy had ceased arose, however, "from at least" the first century A.D. (146-47).

ders and miracles (σημείοις τε καὶ τέρασιν καὶ δυνάμεσιν; 2 Cor. 12:12;
also Rom. 15:18-19).[132] Hebrews 2:3-4 recalls how those who heard the
word of the gospel from the Lord "confirmed it to us ... by signs and wonders and by various miracles (σημείοις τε καὶ τέρασιν καὶ ποικίλαις
δυνάμεσιν)." Acts repeatedly makes the point that "many wonders and
signs (πολλά τε τέρατα καὶ σημεῖα) were taking place through the
apostles" (Acts 2:43, cf. 4:30; 15:12).

Finally, rabbinic discussion includes opinions that a prophet is attested
by a sign, despite the fact that in the rabbinic period the trend was to deny
the appeal to miracles.[133] A debate between Jeremiah and Hananiah assumes the value of signs to confirm a prophetic mandate:

אמר לו תן סימן לדבריך
א"ל אני מתנבא לרעה ואיני יכול ליתן סימן לדברי ...
ואתה מתנבא לטובה את הוא שאת הוא צריך ליתן סימן לדבריך
אמר לו לאו את הוא שאת צריך ליתן סימן לדבריך

He said to him, "give a sign for your words."
He said to him, "I prophesy for ill, and I am not able to give a sign for my
  words ...
but you prophesy for good, you are the one who ought to give a sign for your
  words."
He said to him, "No, you are the one who ought to give a sign for your words."
(y. Sanh. 11.7.3 [30b.46-50]).

In the next section of the Talmud the reflection appears, "And the prophet
who prophesied, if at the beginning he gave a sign or a wonder, they listen
to him, and if not, they do not listen to him,"

והנביא שנתנב' בתחילה
אם נתן אות ומופת שומעין לו
ואם לאו אין שומעין לו
(y. Sanh. 11.8.2[30c.47-48]).

2.7.3.5 Conclusion

The evidence surveyed here, especially the NT evidence, indicates that in
the first century miraculous σημεῖα were thought, in accordance with
Deut. 13:2-12, and as exemplified in the writings of Josephus and other
literature, to serve as the "authenticating miracles" of a prophet or similar
divine emissary. The Gospels and Acts most clearly demonstrate aware-
ness of this special function of signs, but the letters of Paul do as well, and
the notion of a wonder-working holy man (hasid) in rabbinic literature

---

[132] See 1 Cor. 2:4; 1 Thess. 1:5.
[133] E.g., Sifre Deut. 83-84 on Deut. 13:2-3.

seems to proceed directly from this older prophetic motif.[134] On this basis, ascription of miraculous signs to Moses would have conformed Moses to the prophet motif, bracketing him with the prophets. When the ascription is surrounded by other indications of prophetic status, as in Acts 7, the connection between the signs of Moses and the prophethood of Moses seems firm. The "wonders and signs" attributed to Moses in Acts 7:36 therefore add significantly to the fullness of the NT and first-century image of Moses as a prophet.

2.8 Conclusion

Both within and without the New Testament, a great variety of sources either identify Moses as a great prophet, or describe him doing things that only a prophet was supposed to do.[135]

In the context of ancient Judaism, Moses was not only one of the prophets, he was, as Philo puts it, "the archprophet" (ἀρχιπροφήτης), "the most perfect prophet" (ὁ τελειοτάτος τῶν προφητῶν). Josephus concedes that as general Moses had a few who equaled him, "but as prophet none" (προφήτης δὲ οἷος οὐκ ἄλλος; *Ant.* 4.329). Deuteronomy 18:15-19 became for Judaism the establishment of the institution of prophecy in Israel, specifically built on the foundation Moses provided.[136] Eventually the Rabbis were to teach that the prophecy of Moses encompassed all that was ever prophetically revealed.

None of this can really be surprising, given the quality of the biblical support such a conception enjoys. The closing words of the Pentateuch are devoted to a declaration of Moses' "archprophetic" greatness (and coincidentally incorporate the teaching on Moses' prophetic "signs and wonders" presented in this chapter).

The New Testament itself implies or assumes the prophethood of Moses in a handful of texts, and mentions it explicitly in Acts 3:22-26. Additionally, Moses receives the title of mediator in Gal. 3:19 in connection with his prophesying the Law. The NT texts that imply his prophethood emphasize the accuracy of his predictions, but the New Testament also includes the attribution to Moses of wonders and signs in Acts 7:36 (cf. Exod. 4:1-9).

---

[134] Vermes, *Jesus the Jew*, 89-90 urges strongly that wonder-working rabbis modeled themselves on prophets, or were so perceived by contemporaries.

[135] See above, p. 49, the summation of testimony outside the New Testament.

[136] On this, see below, pp. 86-87. Note as well that this does not mean Deut. 18:15 was not thought to have eschatological significance. If it were thought that a succession of prophets were promised, that succession might well have a most glorious conclusion.

Few Jews can have thought that even recognition as the greatest of all prophets could exhaust all that should be said about Moses. The office of the high priest was linked with prophethood,[137] and the combination of Moses' Levitic descent with his prophetic status would already suggest that he was a priest (cf. again John 11:51), even if his role in mediating before God for the people did not virtually demand it. The next chapter considers this Mosaic office along with the office of apostle, with which it is connected in the key NT text.

---

[137] E.g. in Deut. 33:8 (if Levi's "godly man" is the high priest), Philo *Spec. Leg.* 4.192, Josephus *Ant.* 3.192; 6.115, and John 11:51; these references point to Palestinian currency. Walter Grundmann, "The Decision of the Supreme Court to Put Jesus to Death (John 11:47-57) in Its Context: Tradition and Redaction in the Gospel of John," in *Jesus and the Politics of His Day*, ed. Ernst Bammel and C. F. D. Moule (Cambridge: Cambridge University Press, 1984), 305, claims it is especially so in Hellenistic Judaism.

Chapter 3

Moses As Priest and Apostle

Who can compare with Moses, the Servant of God,
the faithful one of His House?...
He was a holy priest in two sanctuaries.
—*Memar Marqah* 4.6

3.1 Introduction

As pointed out in the conclusion to the last chapter, the office of prophet
could often be accompanied by the office of priest, and also the office of
priest would tend to imply prophethood. One might argue that the distinction brought in by having separate chapters for priest and prophet is
artificial, and indeed in some cases it might be unjustified. Separate consideration of the two here is justified by the fact that however closely the
two functions are related, they are still distinctive enough often to be
named separately even when carried by the same individual, and by the
important fact that Moses appears to be one of these individuals.

Granted, the priesthood of Moses cannot be considered a prominent NT
theme. It appears to be implied only in Heb. 3:1-6. The scantiness of its
NT treatment is perhaps the product of a wider, contemporary hesitation to
fill the office with Moses (there were other, better-credentialed claimants
to archetypal high priesthood). On the other hand, the high priesthood of
Jesus is also treated in only one NT book, yet it was very important to the
early Church. Nor was the priesthood of Moses so inconceivable in the
first century that an allusion to it would be overlooked.

The same NT passage which implies the high priesthood of Moses apparently includes in the same breath the earliest extant allusion to Moses as
an apostle. The appearance of the titles "priest" and "apostle" together is
not entirely unprepared, since the Jewish priest could be seen as one sent
from God (see discussion below). In the New Testament and early Christian literature the term ἀπόστολος bears its now-familiar, exalted connotation[1] and its application to Jesus in Heb. 3:1 is clearly meant to extol

---

[1] Karl Heinrich Rengstorf, "ἀποστέλλω κτλ.," in *Theological Dictionary of the
New Testament*, ed. Gerhard Kittel, trans. and ed. Geoffrey W. Bromiley, vol. 1, *A-Γ*
(Grand Rapids: William B. Eerdmans, 1964), 408, 413.

him. Since Heb. 3:1-6 parallels Moses and Jesus, the evident intention of the author of Hebrews in that passage to glorify Jesus with the title heightens its interest for a study such as this, since the title that glorifies Jesus would seem also to glorify Moses.

3.2 The Priesthood of Moses

3.2.1 The Bible and Biblical Tradition

The priesthood of Moses is explicit only in one biblical text, Ps. 99:6 ("Moses and Aaron were among his priests"). It is apparent in the Pentateuch, however, that when Moses inaugurates the nation, he does so as the presiding priest.[2] The priesthood of Aaron, which Moses also inaugurated at that time, was evidently the delegated priesthood of Moses. While he lived, it was Moses who in the tabernacle (Exod. 25:22; Josephus, *Ant.* 3.212, 222) received the continuation of the Sinai oracles through an access to the divine presence that even exceeded the priestly privilege of Aaron and his successors (Lev. 16:2).[3] Judges 18:30, according to which the Danite priesthood claimed Mosaic lineage, would also suggest that Moses was a priest, and perhaps a priest superior to Aaron.

By the Herodian period the distinction between priests and "ordinary" Levites had worn down so that the terms were nearly interchangeable. Examples of the absence of distinction abound.[4] Concurrently the Levitical status of Moses had become greatly stressed.[5] The fact that Moses was

---

[2] Exod. 24:6; Lev. 8:30-9:24; H. L. Ellison, *The Centrality of the Messianic Idea for the Old Testament*, Tyndale Monographs (London: Tyndale Press, 1953), 17, "At the solemn conclusion of the Sinaitic covenant he is the priest (Ex. xxiv. 3-8). The twelve young men who kill the sacrificial oxen are merely the representatives of the people, for the sacrifices were normally killed not by the priest, but by the persons bringing the sacrifice. It is Moses who performs the priestly task of manipulating the blood. Equally it is Moses who consecrates Aaron and his sons to their priestly office. It is Moses who finds fault with Aaron when he does not carry out his tasks to the full (Lev. x. 16-20). Most significant of all, it is Moses, not Aaron, who passes on the high-priesthood from Aaron to Eleazar on Mount Hor. In other words, though after the consecration of Aaron Moses did not act as priest, he had only delegated the office"; see also Jacob Milgrom, *Leviticus 1-16: A New Translation with Introduction and Commentary*, The Anchor Bible, ed. W. F. Albright and D. N. Freedman, vol. 3 (New York: Doubleday, 1991), 555-58.

[3] William Horbury, "The Aaronic Priesthood in the Epistle to the Hebrews," *Journal for the Study of the New Testament* 19 (October 1983): 57, and John MacDonald, *The Theology of the Samaritans*, The New Testament Library, ed. Alan Richardson, C. F. D. Moule, and Floyd V. Filson (London: SCM Press, 1964), 153.

[4] Horbury, "The Aaronic Priesthood in the Epistle to the Hebrews," 50-54.

[5] MacDonald, *Theology of the Samaritans*, 153.

not only a Levite but Aaron's older brother as well must have supported the view that Moses, quite as much as Aaron, was a qualified priest.

In the first century all these pieces of Moses lore would have implied that Moses had functioned for his people as priest, just as the same material did in the rabbinic period (on which see below).

3.2.2 Graeco-Roman Writers

The description of Moses as an (Egyptian) priest crops up repeatedly in non-Jewish writings, starting with "pseudo-Manetho" (i.e., an interpolator in Manetho's work quoted as Manetho in Josephus, *Ap.* 1.250). This pseudo-Manetho, probably writing early in the first century A.D., equates Moses with a Heliopolitan priest of Osiris named Osarsiph.[6]

The description of Moses as either a disaffected or diseased Egyptian priest went on to become a common feature in Alexandrian expositions of Jewish history.[7] Strabo also describes Moses as an Egyptian priest who became dissatisfied with animal worship.[8] Pompeius Trogus alludes to Moses' priesthood with the statement that Arruas (=Aaron) succeeded him as priest of the Egyptian holy rites.[9] Lactantius Placidus may be the only pagan Latin to make Moses out as "priest of the Highest God," *Moyses, Dei summi antistes.*[10]

3.2.3 Philo

The priesthood of Moses is very important to Philo and, like prophethood, it is an important auxiliary to Moses' other offices.[11] Moses as high priest receives the divine instruction in all priestly duties,[12] builds and furnishes the sanctuary,[13] and appoints and instructs the priests.[14] Moses is explicitly stated to have functioned as high priest at the ratification of the covenant.[15] He also apparently officiated as priest during the installation of the Aaronic

---

[6] John G. Gager, *Moses in Greco-Roman Paganism*, SBL Monograph Series, ed. Robert A. Kraft, no. 16 (Nashville and New York: Abingdon Press, 1972), 116-18.

[7] Ibid., 121.

[8] Ibid., 38-39.

[9] Ibid., 54.

[10] Menachem Stern, ed. and trans., *Greek and Latin Authors on Jews and Judaism*, vol. 2, *From Tacitus to Simplicitus*, Fontes and Res Judaicas Spectantes (Jerusalem: The Israel Academy of Sciences and Humanities, 1980), 682, 685.

[11] *Sac.* 130; *Spec. Leg.* 4.192; *Mos.* 1.334; 2.2-7, 16, 76, 187, 292; *Praem.* 53, 56.

[12] *Mos.* 2.71.

[13] *Mos.* 2.71, 75.

[14] *Mos.* 2.141, 153.

[15] *Quis Her.* 182.

priesthood, as demonstrated by his manipulation of the blood of the sacrifices.[16]

The mediation of Moses, which, as seen in the last chapter, is prophetic, is at times also intercessory and priestly.[17] In *Mos.* 2.166, Moses takes the part of a mediator and reconciler (μεσίτης καὶ διαλλακτής) and of a protector and intercessor (ὁ κηδεμὼν καὶ παραιτητής) in the affair of the Golden Calf.

3.2.4 Josephus

The priesthood in Josephus is emphatically the possession of Aaron: no one, including Moses, is as qualified for the high priesthood (*Ant.* 2.210; 3.188-91, 307). In the dream announcing the birth of Moses and his great mission, Amram learns of another great privilege Moses will enjoy: "Furthermore, he shall have a brother [Aaron] so blessed as to hold my priesthood" (*Ant.* 2.210). The rebellion of Korah over the conferral of the priesthood of Aaron is one of the longer narratives in the *Antiquities*, and over and over therein it is emphasized that God's design was always for Aaron to have the high priesthood.[18] In noteworthy divergence from the biblical account, Eleazar receives the priestly attire directly from Aaron himself, and not from Moses (*Ant.* 4.83).

Despite Josephus's overriding emphasis on the Aaronic high priesthood, Moses still is shown carrying on the same priestly activity that other sources usually accord to him.[19] He sanctifies the new priests and tabernacle, sprinkling the blood (*Ant.* 3.197, 204-206). On other occasions, it is Moses who offers sacrifices (*Ant.* 2.269, 275, 349; 3.60; 4.101), or intercedes for the people (*Ant.* 3.22-23, 34, 310, 315; 4.194). Again, a first-century Jewish audience would automatically view these as priestly duties carried out by a leader with outstanding priestly credentials.

3.2.5 Pseudo-Philo

Pseudo-Philo's retelling of the Exodus story incorporates many of the same instances of priestly or mediating activity found in other first-century sources. So, in *LAB* 11.3 Moses sanctifies the people before Sinai, and in 13.1 he consecrates the priests. In *LAB* 11.15 and 12.8-10 Moses approaches

---

[16] *Mos.* 2.143-152; noticed by Harry Austryn Wolfson, *Philo: Foundations of Religious Philosophy in Judaism, Christianity, and Islam*, Structure and Growth of Philosophic Systems from Plato to Spinoza, II (Cambridge, Mass.: Harvard University Press, 1947), 2.338.

[17] See above, pp. 38-39, 49-50; Philo, *Plant.* 46; *Som.* 1.143; *Mos.* 1.128; 2.166.

[18] *Ant.* 4.15-16, 19, 23, 24, 26-33, 46, 58, 66.

[19] Paul Spilsbury, *The Image of the Jew in Flavius Josephus' Paraphrase of the Bible*, Texte und Studien zum Antiken Judentum, ed. Martin Hengel and Peter Schäfer, no. 69 (Tübingen: J. C. B. Mohr [Paul Siebeck], 1998), 104-105.

God to intercede for the people, and in 19.3 he makes atonement for their sins. *LAB* 51.6 introduces Ps. 99:6 (which would not otherwise appear in the *Biblical Antiquities*), the one biblical text to speak explicitly of Moses' priesthood, into Pseudo-Philo's rendition of the Song of Hannah.

3.2.6 Samaritan Literature

The Samaritans thought a great deal of Moses in terms of a priest. Two frequent Samaritan titles for Moses are "the Levite," and "the son of Amram," the former of which especially teaches his priesthood, and the latter of which calls his lineage to mind.[20] As to the duties of Aaron, Mac-Donald writes, "The Samaritans remind us frequently of the fact that [Moses] was a priest, though he functioned mainly as a prophet, leaving the priestly duties to his brother Aaron."[21] Here once again one finds the tradition that the Aaronic priesthood was only a delegation from Moses.

Memar Marqah 4.6.14-16 describes the priesthood of Moses in a way that rings of Heb. 3:1-6. He says:

Where is there the like of Moses, and who can compare with Moses, the Servant of God, the faithful one of His House (ומהימנה דביתה), who dwelt among the angels in the Sanctuary of the Unseen? ... He was a holy priest in two sanctuaries (הוהו כהן קדיש תרתי כנשאן).[22]

The idea of Moses as a priest not only on earth but in heaven is not uncommon in Samaritan texts. In a fourteenth-century Samaritan poem, the heavenly hosts address Moses by saying, "Begin, O priest; make proclamation!"[23] Moses as a heavenly priest also appears in a Samaritan *ketubah* (marriage document) where he is called, among many other things, "the priest of the angels."[24] *Ketuboth*, by virtue of their characteristically traditional and stylized language, are likely to preserve old ways of speaking. The antiquity of the wording of this one, (the manuscript dates from the eighteenth century), is indicated by the use of obsolete monetary units to assess the dowry, and more especially by the appearance of two Greek terms.[25]

---

[20] MacDonald, *Theology of the Samaritans*, 152-54.

[21] Ibid., 153.

[22] *Memar Marqah*, ed. John MacDonald, Beihefte zur Zeitschrift für die alttestamentliche Wissenschaft, ed. Georg Fohrer, no. 84 (Berlin: Alfred Töpelmann, 1963), text, vol. 1, 95 lines 2-4; trans. vol. 2, 155. Other resemblances between the Moses of Hebrews and that of the Samaritans in MacDonald, *Theology of the Samaritans*, 445.

[23] Quoted by Macdonald, *Theology of the Samaritans*, 175.

[24] John Bowman, trans. and ed., *Samaritan Documents Relating to Their History, Religion and Life*, Pittsburgh Original Texts and Translations Series, ed. Dikran Y. Hadidian, no. 2 (Pittsburgh: The Pickwick Press, 1977), 313, 318 n. 21.

[25] Ibid., 309-312. One term is "rhetor" (ibid., 318 n. 27), describing the groom; the second is not identified by Bowman. On the priesthood of Moses in Samaritanism, see

3.2.7 Rabbinic Literature

The Rabbis were interested in the same biblical data on Moses' priesthood that their predecessors had been. Many concluded specifically that Moses had been the presiding priest during the seven days' inauguration of the Aaronic priesthood.[26]

Some texts which address this week-long priesthood also maintain that Moses lost the priesthood to his brother.[27] Others, however, maintain that he continued as high priest for the rest of his life thereafter.[28] *Sifra* Shemini Mekhilta deMiluim on Psalm 99:6 affirms that Moses and Aaron were of equal merit in their priesthoods.

Thus, the only matter widely unresolved among the Rabbis regarding Moses' priesthood is whether it lasted his whole lifetime or ended with the accession of Aaron.[29] *Exod. Rab.* 37.1 sums up, "Our sages have said that Moses ministered as High Priest all the forty years that Israel was in the wilderness; but others hold that he only did so during the seven days of the consecration of the Tabernacle."[30] The Mosaic priesthood itself is (virtually) uncontested.

---

also James Alan Montgomery, *The Samaritans, the Earliest Jewish Sect: Their History, Theology and Literature*, intro. by Abraham S. Halkin (New York: Ktav Publishing House, 1968; reprint from 1st ed., 1907), 229-30 and Bowman, *Samaritan Documents*, 318 n. 21.

[26] E.g., *b. Zeb.* 101b on Lev. 8:29. The names of R. Eleazar b. Jose, R. Tanḥuma, R. Judah, and R. Ḥelbo recur over and over in such traditions, e.g., *Lev. Rab.* 11.6; *y. Yoma* 1.38b.46-48; 1.38b.76-1.38c.2; *Sifra* Shemini Mekhilta deMiluim; *b. Ta'anit* 11b; *Pesiq. Rab Kah.* 4.5; *Midr. Pss.* 99.4 on 99:6; *Exod. Rab.* 2.6. *Tg. Ps.-J.* Deut. 34:5 also allots him priesthood seven days.

[27] E.g., *Cant. Rab.* 1:7 § 3; *Exod. Rab.* 3.17.

[28] E.g., *Lev. Rab.* 11.6, and the same or very similar in *Pesiq. R.* 14.11; *Pesiq. Rab Kah.* 4.5; *Midr. Pss.* 99.4 on 99:6; *Exod. Rab.* 37.1; also *b. Zeb.* 102a and similar *Midr. Pss.* 18.22 on 18:27. Ps. 99:6 and 1 Chron. 23:13-14 are commonly appealed to.

[29] A few rabbinic opinions deny priesthood to Moses, e.g., *Gen. Rab.* 55.6 (but cf. *Exod. Rab.* 2.6); *Deut. Rab.* 2.7 on 3:24.

[30] More refs. in Louis Ginzberg, *The Legends of the Jews*, vol. 5 (Philadelphia: The Jewish Publication Society of America, 1925), 422 n. 139 and 419 n. 121.

3.3 The Apostleship of Moses

3.3.1 The Biblical Background

In the Old Testament, God "sends" Moses (וָאֶשְׁלָחֲךָ, ἀποστείλω σε; Exod. 3:10), who therefore says to the captive Israelites, "The God of your fathers has sent me (שְׁלָחַנִי) to you" (Exod. 3:13, 15; cf. 4:28).[31] In the Old Testament, however, no noun for one who is sent, such as שָׁלִיחַ or מַלְאָךְ, or ἀπόστολος or ἄγγελος, is used of Moses.[32]

3.3.2 Literature of Second Temple Judaism

Jewish evidence on Moses' apostleship through the end of the Second Temple period is very thin. J.-A. Bühner points out the fragment of Arta-panus in which God is called ὁ πέμψας αὐτόν that is, Moses.[33]

In the first century, Moses' "sentness" appears in Josephus' *Ant.* 2.274, where God exhorts Moses to "convince all men that thou art sent by me" (ὅτι πεμφθεὶς ὑπ' ἐμοῦ). Moses is termed the *magnus nuntius* in *As. Mos.* 11:17, which, while not the same as *apostolus*, still implies his divine mission.[34]

3.3.3 Samaritan Literature

According to J. Fossum, "The description of having been 'sent' by God and being God's 'Sent One' was a common way of representing Moses in

---

[31] See Jarl E. Fossum, *The Name of God and the Angel of the Lord: Samaritan and Jewish Concepts of Intermediation and the Origin of Gnosticism*, WUNT, ed. Martin Hengel and Otfried Hofius, no. 36 (Tübingen: J. C. B. Mohr [Paul Siebeck], 1995), 145. It is apparently on the basis of these verses that Geo Widengren asserts that "even in the O.T., Moses is looked upon as an Apostle, a Sent One" (*The Ascension of the Apostle and the Heavenly Book [King and Saviour III]*, Uppsala Universiteits Års-skrift, no. 7 [Uppsala: A. B. Lundequistska Bokhandeln, 1950], 47). Fossum points out the importance of "sentness" to prophets (which would include Moses) in the Old Testament, e.g. Judg. 6:8; Is. 6:8; 61:1; Ezek. 2:3; Jer. 1:7; Hag. 1:12; Zech. 2:12. See also Widengren, 31-34.

[32] In the LXX, ἀπόστολος is attested only once (and the text is in doubt), of the prophet Ahijah, at 3 βασ. 14:6, where the MT has שְׁלוּחַ. See Rengstorf, "ἀποστέλλω," 413.

[33] Jan-Adolf Bühner, *Der Gesandte und sein Weg im 4. Evangelium: Die kultur- und religionsgeschichtlichen Grundlagen der johanneischen Sendungschristologie sowie ihre traditionsgeschichtliche Entwicklung*, WUNT/2, ed. Martin Hengel, Joachim Jeremias, and Otto Michel, no. 2 (Tübingen: J. C. B. Mohr [Paul Siebeck], 1977), 299 citing Eusebius, *Praep. Ev.* 9.27.24.

[34] Cf. *As. Mos.* 10:2, where another *nuntius* may be depicted as an angel in heaven (but see Johannes Tromp, *The Assumption of Moses: A Critical Edition with Commentary*. Studia in Veteris Testamenti Pseudepigrapha, ed. A.-M. Denis and M. de Jonge, vol. 10 (Leiden: E. J. Brill, 1993), 229-31, against this idea).

Samaritanism."[35] Meeks observes occasional references to Moses as God's שליח both in the *Memar Marqah* and in the *Defter* (the liturgy).[36] Additionally, *Memar Marqah* 2.9 refers to the apostleship of Moses, either as an office he filled, or as a mandate he carried: "They believed in the True One and knew that the apostleship of Moses (שליחותה משה) was true." The difficulty in dating Samaritan traditions makes it hard to be certain how far back such language goes.

3.3.4 Rabbinic Literature

Perhaps the oldest, proper, (non-Christian) Jewish reference to Moses as an apostle comes in *Sifra* Behuqotai Pereq 8 (end), which says, "Moses had the merit of being made the שליח between Israel and their father in heaven." Here, however, it may be that Israel is the commissioning authority, not God.

Another reference, probably of similar antiquity, and in a context which depicts Moses as someone commissioned to bear the power and authority of the Lord, comes in one of the older *piyyuṭim*, "Ezel Moshe" (אזֶ[י]'ל משה), based on Exodus 14:30. Lines from this acrostic poem which identify Moses as "the apostle of the Creator of the Beginning" (אנה הוא שליחיה /דיוצר בראשית), or "the apostle of the King of Glory" (אנה הוא שליחיה דמלך הכבוד) are extant in two manuscripts from the Cairo Genizah,[37] but the base text to the poem (with these particular lines unfortu-

---

[35] Fossum, *Name of God*, 144.

[36] Wayne A. Meeks, *The Prophet-King: Moses Traditions and the Johannine Christology*, Supplements to *Novum Testamentum*, ed. W. C. van Unnik, et al., vol. 14 (Leiden: E. J. Brill, 1967), 226-27. Some of these and related texts are explored by Bühner, *Gesandte*, 302-306, and Fossum, *Name of God*, 144-45, who also considers, 146-49, the evidence for Moses as מלאך in Samaritanism.

[37] "Apostle of the Creator of the Beginning": Oxford Bodleian Ms. Heb. c. 74v, lines 34-35, and 75r, lines 6-7 in Michael L. Klein, *Genizah Manuscripts of Palestinian Targum to the Pentateuch* (Cincinnati: Hebrew Union College Press, 1986), 1.236-37. This shelfmark appears to be defective, as it lacks a numeral after "c." In the photograph in Klein the tag giving the shelfmark is cut off at the bottom, leaving only "MS Heb." Presumably, Klein worked from the photograph and the defect was not noticed. (The MS is cited as Ox. MS 2701/9 folios 63-64 in Joseph Yahalom, "Ezel Moshe — According to the Berlin Papyrus," *Tarbiz* 47, nos. 3-4 [Apr.-Sept. 1978]: 173-84 and Michael Sokoloff and Joseph Yahalom, *Jewish Palestinian Aramaic Poetry from Late Antiquity* [Jerusalem: Israel Academy of Sciences, 1999], 82, but this catalog number is also an error, since it belongs to the MS we cite next). "Apostle of the King of Glory": Oxford Bodleian Ms. Heb. e.25, folio 63v, line 15 (Klein, 1.238-39); in this MS, 64r, line 2, Moses cries, "The King of Kings has sent me" (שלחי; Klein, 1.238-39; Sokoloff and Yahalom cite — now correctly — catalog number Ox. MS 2701/9 folios 63-64).

nately lost in a lacuna) appears in a papyrus manuscript.[38] The presence of the *piyyuṭ* (in fragmentary form) on papyrus confirms that it goes back at least to the fourth century A.D.

Starting from here, a minor flowering of such language takes place in Jewish literature written in Semitic languages. Bühner surveys several rabbinic texts (mostly from later midrash but one as early as *Mekilta de-Rabbi Simeon ben Jochai*) where Moses is designated as God's שליח.[39] Eventually, the apostolate of Moses comes to form the background to the title of Mohammed as apostle.

In the Passover Haggadah, the liturgical function of which suggests its wording would conserve old traditions, appears the comment on Deut. 26:8, "'And the Lord brought us out of Egypt': not by means of an angel (מלאך), and not by means of a seraph (שרף), and not by means of the apostle (השליח)."[40] Fossum argues, "Since only the last term is determined by the article, the Apostle obviously is a special agent of God."[41] Intuitively, one supposes that "the Apostle" might be Moses, and Fossum adduces evidence that this text carries a very old tradition for referring to Moses as "the Apostle."[42]

3.4 The Priesthood and Apostleship of Moses in Hebrews 3:1-6

Hebrews 3:1-6, which opens a section running through Heb. 4:13, broadly concerned with Moses and his ministry, features the only explicit comparison in Hebrews between Jesus and Moses. Here Jesus is identified as ὁ ἀπόστολος καὶ ἀρχιερεὺς τῆς ὁμολογίας, "the Apostle and High Priest of our confession." The titles are linked by the common article, and

---

[38] Berlin Stadtmuseum P8498; published in Yahalom, "Ezel Moshe," 173-84, see Sokoloff and Yahalom, *Jewish Palestinian Aramaic Poetry*, 82-86.

[39] Bühner, *Gesandte*, 286-99; see Fossum, *Name of God*, 144-45; Widengren, *Ascension of the Apostle*, 47.

[40] Quoting from Fossum, *Name of God*, 147. Cf. Ησαι. 63:9, οὐ πρέσβυς οὐδὲ ἄγγελος, ἀλλ' αὐτὸς κύριος. Further, Judah Goldin, "Not by Means of an Angel and Not by Means of a Messenger," *Religions in Antiquity: Essays in Memory of Erwin Ramsdell Goodenough*, ed. Jacob Neusner, Studies in the History of Religion (Supplements to *Numen*), no. 14 (Leiden: E. J. Brill, 1968), 412-24.

[41] Fossum, *Name of God*, 147.

[42] Ibid., 147-48; cf. Jarl E. Fossum, *The Image of the Invisible God: Essays on the Influence of Jewish Mysticism on Early Christianity*, Novum Testamentum et Orbis Antiquus, ed. Max Küchler, with Gerd Theissen, no. 30 (Freiburg, Switzerland: Universitätsverlag Freiburg; Göttingen: Vandenhoeck & Ruprecht, 1995), 58-59.

the author probably meant to compound them into one grand title.[43] Moses is not similarly titled but when the author calls on his readers to "consider Jesus" as "apostle and high priest," and then draws their attention to Moses, the implication is that Moses was apostle and high priest as well.[44]

It is well to recall that the intent of Hebrews throughout is to portray Jesus as possessing the same glory as Moses, only more of it. Moses is not used in Hebrews as a foil, or even as a type for Jesus. The two are equivalent figures. J. Kastner has extensively documented this technique of Hebrews with regard to the figure of Moses.[45] In the argument of Hebrews Moses is "ein Gleichbild Christi."[46] In Heb. 3:1-6 particularly, Jesus transcends Moses only in that "Jesus ist in höherem Maße der δόξα gewürdigt worden als Moses. ... Moses und Jesus sind einer δόξα gewürdigt worden (ἠξίωται), die offenbar einer gemeinsam Quelle entspringt."[47]

P. R. Jones suggests that in Heb. 3:1-6 both Moses and Jesus are considered as apostles, distinguished in that role only as "servant" and "Son."[48] Neither the title "priest" nor "apostle" is applied to Jesus elsewhere in the New Testament (outside of Hebrews). Jesus is not called "apostle" again anywhere in early Christian literature, though his priesthood becomes very important. The unusualness of the two titles in the earliest christology (represented by NT texts), and the uniqueness to Hebrews of the title "apostle," might suggest that both terms are supplied in Heb. 3:1-6 in debt not to contemporary Christology but from a prior connection with the other individual named there, Moses.[49]

---

[43] William L. Lane, *Hebrews 1-8*, WBC, ed. David A. Hubbard and Glenn W. Barker, with Ralph P. Martin, vol. 47A (Dallas: Word Books, 1991), 75; Rengstorf, "ἀποστέλλω," 424.

[44] E. L. Allen, "Jesus and Moses in the New Testament," *The Expository Times* 67 (1955-1956): 105, argues that the author here has in mind a Christology that "comes near to equating Jesus with Moses."

[45] Josef M. Kastner, "Moses im Neuen Testament," (Th.D. Dissertation, Ludwig-Maximilians-Universität Munich, 1967), 236-67.

[46] Kastner, "Moses im Neuen Testament," 240.

[47] Ibid., 240-41, also 242 Kastner, however, does not see any priestly place for Moses in Hebrews, let alone an apostleship. Here as generally in the New Testament Kastner finds Moses a mediator only (see, e.g., 266-67, and 247-56 *passim*).

[48] Peter Rhea Jones, "The Figure of Moses as a Heuristic Device for Understanding the Pastoral Intent of Hebrews," *Review and Expositor* 76 (1979): 98; see Craig R. Koester, *Hebrews: A New Translation with Introduction and Commentary*, The Anchor Bible, ed. W. F. Albright and D. N. Freedman, vol. 36 (New York: Doubleday, 2001), 252-53. See above p. 33 n. 5 for references on Moses as God's servant. The possible royal imagery in Heb. 3:1-6 is taken up in the next chapter.

[49] See Jones, "Figure of Moses," 98, and Lane, *Hebrews 1-8*, 76. Lane, 75 points out, however, that the Fourth Gospel makes use of the conception of "the one sent" for Jesus without using the title ἀπόστολος. Other NT writings also call Jesus the one "sent" from God; see Koester, *Hebrews*, 243.

Fossum notices that Heb. 3:1-6 actually contains a number of epithets of Moses popular among the Samaritans. Like Jesus in Hebrews, Moses in Samaritanism is called "apostle" (of the Truth [i.e. of God])," "holy priest," "the faithful one of the house of God," God's "servant," "son of the house of God," and other, similar things many times. The titles occur together in the same contexts in Samaritan literature, even in the same sentences, just as they do in Heb. 3:1-6.[50] The correspondence is great enough to have led some scholars to postulate on that basis some kind of relationship between Hebrews and Samaritanism or Samaritan Christians.[51] It is possible, however, that the Samaritan texts preserve once-common ways of speaking about Moses as apostle and priest that have been incorporated into Hebrews from Jewish tradition independently of any direct Samaritan contribution.

This is suggested by the fact that other Jewish writers also speak of Moses in ways hauntingly similar to the language of Heb. 3:1-6. Compare, for example, Philo, *Det.* 160, who says that Moses erects the tabernacle in order that he might become "a perfect suppliant and servant of God" (ἱκέτης καὶ θεραπευτὴς ἔσεσθαι τέλειος θεοῦ). Here the tabernacle, God's house, is the place where Moses is God's servant (his priest) just as in Hebrews 3.[52]

Josephus also connects Moses' service to God with his work in the tabernacle: "Moses, for his part ... devoted himself solely to the service of God (τῇ τοῦ θεοῦ θεραπείᾳ). Desisting from further ascents of Sinai, he now entered the tabernacle and there received responses on all that he besought from God" (*Ant.* 3.212). Evidence for Jewish regard of Moses as a priest has already been reviewed above, but Hebrews appears to be one of many texts which interact with a familiar, perhaps even stock, Jewish image of Moses as a faithful, priestly "servant in God's house."

As in Samaritan thought, noted above, so among Jews it would not have been exceptional to link priesthood with the role of an apostle as Hebrews does. See, for example, Mal. 2:7, where the priest is the "messenger" (מלאך; ἄγγελος) of the Lord. *Assumption of Moses* 10:2 refers to a messenger, whose "hands are filled" (*Tunc implebuntur manus nuntii qui est in summo constitutus*). The "filling of the hands" is a standard technical expression for the consecration of a priest. The best explanation for this text is that *nuntius* is a translation of ἄγγελος, and that *Assumption of Moses* describes an individual who fuses these two roles, who is consecrated by God (*in summo*) as messenger and priest. The notion of a messenger (*nun-*

---

[50] Fossum, *Name of God*, 150-51.

[51] Discussion in Fossum, *Name of God*, 150-152. See also MacDonald, *Theology of the Samaritans*, 445.

[52] Cf. *QE* 2.105.

tius) involved here is not far from that of apostleship, and one of the titles for Moses in *Assumption of Moses* is *magnus nuntius*.[53]

From a later period, *Bavli Ned.* 35b-36a carries a debate in the *gemara* over whether or not priests are שלוחי דשמיא, "apostles of heaven," while *b. Kid.* 23b gives the opinion of R. Huna b. R. Joshua that, "The priests are apostles of the All-Merciful One" (נינהו הני כהני שלוחי דרחמנא). (The opinion was contested, but in the end the *gemara* accepts it.)

W. L. Lane asserts of Hebrews, "The writer's christology controls the development of the argument and the portrait of Moses."[54] This is also precisely the position of M. R. D'Angelo.[55] Given, however, the presence of themes in the extra-NT portrait of Moses which resonate so strongly with the ground on which Hebrews compares Moses and Jesus, it might rather be the reverse, that the writer's conception of Moses, or perhaps the conception of Moses among his readers, with which he has to contend, shapes his presentation of Christ.

3.5 Conclusion

The priesthood of Moses is taken for granted in rabbinic literature, probably on the basis of its solid biblical support, and the incidental and solitary manner in which the priesthood of Moses appears in the New Testament should not be assumed to indicate its unimportance to early Christians. Although Hebrews spends more time discussing the priesthoods of Aaron and Melchizedek, the priesthood of Moses actually provides the jumping-off point for that discussion, suggesting it had a higher profile than has generally been supposed.

The high priesthood of Moses seems connected with his apostolate in Hebrews 3:1-6, but also in Samaritan literature. The two motifs are also echoed in a variety of rabbinic traditions, often quite early ones, and the confluence of the New Testament, Samaritan literature, and rabbinic discussion suggests rather an old tradition along these lines. The evidence for an early ascription to Moses of both priesthood and apostleship in turn suggests that the depiction of Jesus in Heb. 3:1-6 as apostle and high priest is dependent on similar traditions about Moses, rather than the reverse.

The earliest extant specific reference to the apostleship of Moses seems to be in Hebrews 3, where he receives the title ἀπόστολος. In the same period he is probably also called ἄγγελος (tracing back from *nuntius* in

---

[53] See above, p. 38.

[54] Lane, *Hebrews 1-8*, 79.

[55] Mary Rose D'Angelo, *Moses in the Letter to the Hebrews*, Society of Biblical Literature Dissertation Series, ed. Howard Clark Kee, no. 42 (Missoula, Montana: Scholars Press, 1979), 2, 11-12.

As. Mos. 11:17), in a sense akin to that expressed by ἀπόστολος.[56] As seen here, however, his apostleship also appears explicitly in (other) Jewish writings, in colorful statements in rabbinic midrash, *piyyuṭim*, and probably the Passover Haggadah as well, where he is שליח, in the sense of an apostle of God. Prior to the New Testament the simple idea of "sentness" is certainly present in traditions about Moses, though a special title along that line does not seem to appear.

Jews had their own officials called "apostles,"[57] and although for Jews "apostle" seems, at least in the first century, to have been more a term than a title,[58] the use of such language suggests the possibility of a non-Christian Jewish background to Hebrews' application of the term to Moses. In the case of Heb. 3:1-6, of course, it is difficult to imagine that the title "apostle" was used of Moses (or of Jesus) without consciousness of the exalted importance of the title in Christian usage. At the same time the absence of further Christian references to Jesus as apostle suggests that the christological formulation in Hebrews must have derived not simply from Christian usage, but from older Jewish ideas about Moses, with whom Hebrews wished to compare Jesus. To the extent that Heb. 3:1-6 uses ἀπόστολος in the special sense arising in Christian circles (cf. Eph. 2:20), it amounts to a special, Christian-Jewish formulation of the functions of Moses and Jesus.

In the first century one might often see titles and offices constellated together in a single individual. In concluding the last chapter it was noted how the gift of prophecy could be linked with priesthood, but prophecy also suggested a claim to rule, or at least to lead. As Bammel puts it, "the proof a person has given of his prophetic status raises the expectation of a forthcoming political role."[59] As for the high priesthood, by the first century it had long been the senior political post in Palestine (*Ant.* 6.115), and

---

[56] But also see below, pp. 237-47 on Moses as an angel.

[57] According to Rengstorf, "ἀποστέλλω," 414, the Jewish שליח probably goes back to pre-exilic times (compare 2 Chron. 17:7-9 with Matt. 10:1-7; Luke 9:1-6, 10), and in the first century A.D. had become an institution, Rengstorf, 414-20. Cf. the caution against linking the Jewish and the Christian offices in Walter Schmithals, *The Office of Apostle in the Early Church*, trans. John E. Steely (London: SPCK, 1971), 98-110, and the review by William Horbury, *Journal of Theological Studies*, NS 23 (1972): 216-19 with additional bibliography.

[58] Rengstorf, "ἀποστέλλω," 418.

[59] Ernst Bammel, "The Feeding of the Multitude," in *Jesus and the Politics of His Day*, ed. E. Bammel and C. F. D. Moule (Cambridge: Cambridge University Press, 1984), 230-31. Cf. Richard A. Horsley, "Popular Prophetic Movements at the Time of Jesus: Their Principal Features and Social Origins," *Journal for the Study of the New Testament* 26 (Feb. 1986): 7-8.

under the Hasmoneans was combined with the king's office.[60] John Hyrcanus had combined in his person the offices of ruler, high priest, and prophet, a feat still celebrated by Josephus centuries later (*B.J.* 1.68; *Ant.*
13.299). Having already considered traditions concerning Moses as prophet, priest, and apostle, this study turns in the next chapter to Moses as
king.

---

[60] On the link of kingship and priesthood see E. R. Goodenough, *The Politics of
Philo Judaeus: Practice and Theory* (New Haven: Yale University Press, 1938), 97; see
also his *By Light, Light: The Mystic Gospel of Hellenistic Judaism* (New Haven, Conn.:
Yale University Press; reprint, Amsterdam: Philo Press, 1969), 189-91, and Philo, *QE*
2.105.

Chapter 4

Moses As King

Then a great, great-spirited king will rule the Hebrews,
One who has a name from sandy Egypt.
—*Eleventh Sibylline Oracle*

4.1 Introduction

In the ancient world, the offices of prophet and of priest were closely related to that of king. Divine commission, or "sentness," was an element of ancient kingship as well. In a sense, then, consideration of the Mosaic qualities reviewed so far lays the groundwork for considering at least one other. This chapter will consider evidence for a valuation of Moses as king in the New Testament, beginning first with biblical traditions and their ancient interpretation, then moving to other literature. The chapter will then examine what seem to be the key NT texts incorporating a view of Moses as king: the feeding narratives in Mark 6:34-44 and John 6:1-15, an expression from the speech of Stephen in Acts 7:35, and the Christology of Heb. 3:1-6.

4.2 Moses as King in Biblical Traditions

J. R. Porter argues that the whole Old Testament (particularly the Pentateuch and the Former Prophets) is shot through with Moses' royal status.[1] Though Porter's focus is on Israelite royal ideology, many of his observations about the portrayal of Moses are just as relevant to the Hellenistic period. A few individual OT texts call for attention here.

4.2.1 Exodus 4:20

Moses' kingship could be inferred from Exod. 4:20, which contains the suggestive reference to Moses taking the "staff of God" (מטה האלהים; ἡ ῥάβδος ἡ παρὰ τοῦ θεοῦ). Elsewhere in the OT מטה and ῥάβδος refer

---

[1] J. R. Porter, *Moses and Monarchy: A Study in the Biblical Tradition of Moses* (Oxford: Basil Blackwell, 1963).

to the scepter of a ruler,[2] and certainly in a later period the reference in
Exod. 4:20 was taken in that sense, e.g. in *Midr. Pss.* 21.2 on 21:2 where
the staff of Exod. 4:20 is identified as God's royal scepter, borne by his
viceroy, Moses.[3]

4.2.2 Deuteronomy 33:5

The OT text most relevant to Mosaic kingship, however, seems always to
have been Deut. 33:5. It reads:

Moses charged us with a law,
a possession for the assembly of Jacob.
ויהי a king in Jeshurun,
when the heads of the people are gathered.

It is the sole OT text that has been thought to name Moses king. At all
times, the critical interpretive question has been, what the meaning of ויהי
is.[4] The construction can be, and has been, pointed in more than one way,
and the attendant changes in aspectual and (by interpretation) temporal
reference alter the significance of the passage accordingly. Part of the difficulty, of course, is simply the blandness of the verb "to be," which always
holds out the possibility of an impersonal statement, which identifies no
one in particular as king.

4.2.2.1 The Masoretic Tradition

The context, however, of Deut. 33:5 suggests "Moses" as the subject of
ויהי, and if ויהי is pointed *waw*-consecutive, as the Masoretes thought,
"the obvious translation is 'he became king,' with reference to Moses who
has just been mentioned."[5] Aside from the fact that this would appear to
be the simplest, most straightforward way of reading the Hebrew, the
Masoretic tradition itself is a valuable witness to Jewish interpretation of

---

[2] E.g., Ezek. 19:11, 14; Ps. 110:2 for the former; Ψ 44(45):7 and 109(110):2 for the
latter; see H. Simian-Yofre, "מַטֶּה maṭṭeh," in *Theological Dictionary of the Old Testament*, ed. G. Johannes Botterweck, Helmer Ringgren, and Heinz-Josef Fabry, trans.
Douglas W. Stott, vol. 8, מֹר־לָכַד *lākad-mōr* (Grand Rapids: William B. Eerdmans,
1997), 243-44, 247-48.

[3] See also Wayne A. Meeks, *The Prophet-King: Moses Traditions and the Johannine Christology*, Supplements to *Novum Testamentum*, ed. W. C. van Unnik, et al.,
vol. 14 (Leiden: E. J. Brill, 1967), 188 for rabbinic traditions of Moses as God's viceroy.

[4] In poetic text the form would ordinarily be read as a simple *waw*-plus-verb (*wəqtl*,
וִיהִי), Peter C. Craigie, *The Book of Deuteronomy*, The New International Commentary
on the Old Testament, ed. R. K. Harrison (Grand Rapids: William B. Eerdmans, 1976),
392 n. 5, but such a rule as this must have been widely overlooked.

[5] Porter, *Moses and Monarchy*, 14, n. 35.

the older consonantal text. In the rabbinic period many agreed that Deut. 33:5 teaches the kingship of Moses.[6]

4.2.2.2 Targums

The Targums to this verse present at least two different traditions that all but state, "Moses was king in Israel."

The first is found in *Tg. Onq.* Deut. 33:4-5, which reads: "Moses gave us Torah, (and) delivered it as an inheritance to the congregation of Jacob. And he was the king in Israel (מלכא בישראל והוה), when the heads of the people were gathered with the tribes of Israel." While הוה can be an impersonal verb, O. Camponovo rightly argues that the particularly tight connection between verses 4 and 5 makes the naming of Moses as king here especially clear.[7]

The second, in *Tg. Ps.-J.* Deut. 33:5, is almost as clear: "And he was king in Israel (והוא הוה מלכא בישראל): when the chiefs of the people were gathered together, the tribes of Israel were obedient to him."[8] The Targum clarifies the verse with the masculine pronoun הוא, which rules out an impersonal sense for the verb הוה, as well as the subject "Law" (אורייתא from v. 4). If the context is any guide, the only starters for the identity of the king are Moses and God. To refer to the Lord, however, only by the pronoun הוא seems on general principles unlikely, while the subject of the preceding sentence is Moses. Moses must be seen as king here.[9] This Targum views Moses as a kingly figure elsewhere, which supports the idea that Moses is a king in Deut. 33:5. One chapter later, for

---

[6] *Lev. Rab.* (אמור) 31.4 (45c), *Lev. Rab.* (אמור) 32.2 (46d), *Midr. Pss.* 1.2 on Ps. 1:1 (which parallels David and Moses in such a way as to suggest that David reigned as heir to the throne of Moses); *Exod. Rab.* 52(פקודי).1 (81d); *Exod. Rab.* 48(ויקהל).4 (78c) (assigns Aaron priesthood, and Moses kingship); *Exod. Rab.* 2(שמות).6 (10c); *Num. Rab.* 15(בהעלותך).13 (66b); see further, Jeffrey H. Tigay, *Deuteronomy: The Traditional Hebrew Text with the New JPS Translation*, The JPS Torah Commentary, ed. Nahum M. Sarna, Chaim Potok, and (this volume) Jeffrey H. Tigay (Philadelphia and Jerusalem, The Jewish Publication Society, 1996), 407 n.43. See Meeks, *Prophet-King*, 186-90, esp. 188 on *Midrash Tannaim* 2.213, ה. line 11, which records a tradition calling Moses the king in Jeshurun: ד"א ויהי ביש' מלך זה משה רבינו.

[7] Odo Camponovo, *Königtum, Königsherrschaft und Reich Gottes in den frühjüdischen Schriften*, Orbis Biblicus et Orientalis, ed. Othmar Keel, with Erich Zenger and Albert de Pury, no. 58 (Freiburg, Switzerland: Universitätsverlag Freiburg; Göttingen: Vandenhoeck & Ruprecht, 1995), 413.

[8] Trans., J. W. Etheridge, *The Targums of Onkelos and Jonathan Ben Uzziel on the Pentateuch with the Fragments of the Jerusalem Targum: From the Chaldee*, vol. 2, *Leviticus, Numbers, and Deuteronomy* (New York: Ktav Publishing House, 1968 bound with vol. 1; first published 1865), 673.

[9] So also Camponovo, *Königtum, Königsherrschaft und Reich Gottes in den frühjüdischen Schriften*, 414.

example, *Tg. Ps.-J.* Deut. 34:5 tells that Moses has been honored with four crowns, law, priesthood, a good name, and "the crown of the kingdom."

None of the other extant Palestinian Targums of Deut. 33:5 indicate that Moses was king, but they do imply that they stem from such a tradition. Instead of saying something like מלכא והוה, *Tg. Neof.*, *Frg. Tg.*(V), and Cairo Genizah MS DD Deut. 33:5 all get away from the verb "to be" and use מלך ויקום (*et var.*), "and a king will arise." This unmistakably points to the appearance of some future king,[10] who would most naturally be a human ruler. W. Meeks points out that such a rendering "must have proceeded from a tradition that Yahweh was *not* the subject," it seeming unlikely that the kingship of the Lord would be set in some future day. As in the other traditions cited here, in each of these Targums the context of Deut. 33:5 still supplies only two possibilities for the identity of the king: Moses and God. That God is the expected king is unlikely on the grounds just noted. Meeks reasons that the Palestinian Targum tradition witnessed in these texts must at some stage have substituted a future king for Moses, quite possibly a king like Moses or Moses *redivivus* (again such a substitution would be hard to imagine if God originally had been seen as the king here).[11] Thus they indirectly witness to an older tradition which took the king of Deut. 33:5 to be Moses.

4.2.2.3 Greek Translations

The earliest interpretive tradition of the Hebrew text, the LXX, translates ויהי with ἔσται: καὶ ἔσται ἐν τῷ ἠγαπημένῳ ἄρχων.[12] The future tense makes the passage read like a messianic prophecy.[13] (The messiah might, however, be Moses or one like him.[14]) The only real alternative is some future kingship of God,[15] but the LXX renders the Hebrew מלך not

---

[10] See ibid., 413; also Martin McNamara, trans., *Targum Neofiti 1: Deuteronomy*, The Aramaic Bible: The Targums, ed. Kevin Cathcart, Michael Maher, and Martin McNamara, vol. 5A (Edinburgh: T. & T. Clark, 1997), 164 n. 17.

[11] Meeks, *Prophet-King*, 190. The idea of a returning Moses becomes more and more common in later Jewish apocalypse and midrash. See below, pp. 196-98.

[12] Alexandrinus and some minuscules omit ἄρχων.

[13] So, Camponovo, *Königtum, Königsherrschaft und Reich Gottes in den frühjüdischen Schriften*, 387.

[14] John William Wevers, *Notes on the Greek Text of Deuteronomy*, Society of Biblical Literature Septuagint and Cognate Studies Series, ed. Bernard A. Taylor, no. 39 (Atlanta: Scholars Press, 1995), 541 suggests that the LXX thinks of a kind of *Moses redivivus*. See further on notions of a returning Moses or a Moses-like eschatological figure, pp. 194-98 below.

[15] Moses is nowhere (else) in the Old Testament called a king but God frequently is (see the survey in Camponovo, *Königtum, Königsherrschaft und Reich Gottes in den frühjüdischen Schriften*, 72-126).

as βασιλεύς, but as ἄρχων, a relatively mild word, which would appear to make a divine reference less likely.[16]

It might be supposed that by using ἄρχων the LXX dispenses with kingship altogether in Δευτ. 33:5, whether of God or of man. Sometimes, however, ἄρχων was an acceptable substitute for βασιλεύς; the LXX, for example, uses ἄρχων for monarchs in the "Law of the King (MT: מלך)" of Deut. 17:14-20. Forbearing for now further analysis of the royal usage of ἄρχων, we can say at least that this aspect of the LXX rendering of Deut. 33:5 seems less favorable to a kingship specifically of God, and this combined with the future tense of ἔσται favors the sense of a messianic or Mosaic king.[17]

Theodotion and Symmachus on Deut. 33:5, however, apparently mean to say precisely that Moses was king. Their translations both read: καὶ ἦν ἐν τῷ εὐθεῖ βασιλεύς: "and he was king straightaway." Granted, in the Greek as in the Semitic versions, the use of the verb "to be" makes it impossible to be absolutely certain that a personal subject is intended, and these texts might have been read as impersonal statements, e.g., "there was a king just then." Aside from the strangeness of such a reading, however, there is no particular reason to pass over the name of Moses when it lies so near the verb for which it would serve as implied subject. Here, perhaps even more than in the MT, the most obvious sense is that Moses is the king in question. The evidence reviewed above that the Targums either associated Deut. 33:5 with Mosaic kingship or knew of traditions that did also suggests that these roughly contemporary Greek renderings referred to Moses as king as well.

4.2.2.4 Conclusion

The remarkable agreement of all extant Targum traditions in finding in Deut. 33:5 the expectation of a human king indicates how widespread interpretation along these lines was. Such interpretation, especially when so ubiquitous, is most consistent with the existence of an earlier interpretation which saw Moses as the king in question. This judgment is encouraged by the fact that this seems to be the actual position of *Onqelos* and *Pseudo-Jonathan* as they stand now. Moreover, although all Pentateuchal Targums as we have them are later than the New Testament, with reference to Deut. 33:5 they are seen to continue a line of interpretation which appears back in the third century B.C., in the LXX, and which turns up again in the revisions of the Greek text by Theodotion and Symmachus.

---

[16] Strongly on this point, Camponovo, *Königtum, Königsherrschaft und Reich Gottes in den frühjüdischen Schriften*, 387.

[17] The usage of ἄρχων is examined below, pp. 113-16 in connection with the instance of the term in Acts 7:35.

The affinity among all these witnesses suggests that an interpretation of Deut. 33:5 as concerned with a human king was probably current all along in Second Temple Judaism. As pointed out in the above discussion, such an interpretation would most naturally presuppose an interpretation that saw Moses as the king in question. This would appear to be the simplest solution to the meaning of many of the extant traditions of the text of Deut. 33:5.

4.2.3 Deuteronomy 18:15

Consideration of the promise of a Prophet like Moses at first seems out of place in the present chapter. The general linkage between prophecy and kingship, however, and the links made by Jews between this verse, the figure it might seem to predict, and the ruler of the Jews, turn Deut. 18:15 into a point of departure for talking about the kingship of Moses.

4.2.3.1 Prophets as Kings

The ancient link between prophecy and kingship has been noted here only in passing. In fact, the prophetic gift was often linked with kingship in the Ancient Near East,[18] while in Hellenism the ideal king enjoyed divine guidance and inspiration.[19] As noted in Chapter Two, Strabo lists a number of prophets (οἱ μάντεις) who "were deemed worthy to be kings, on the ground that they promulgated to us ordinances and amendments from the gods."[20] One of Strabo's prophet-kings was Moses, whose appearance in the list probably reflects the characterization of Moses as a prophet *cum* king by Strabo's Jewish sources, as well as a shared Jewish and Greco-Roman ideal of prophet-kings.[21]

Within Judaism the link between prophethood and kingship was just as strong as that in Hellenism generally, if not stronger.[22] Philo makes espe-

---

[18] Aage Bentzen, *King and Messiah*, Lutterworth Studies in Church and Bible (London: Lutterworth Press, 1955), 19, 50, 88 n. 13. Cf. the caution of Geza Vermes, *Jesus the Jew: A Historian's Reading of the Gospels* (London: William Collins Sons & Co., 1973), 137, with regard to Qumran. Vermes, 252 n. 31 finds only one example from Qumran in which the word 'Messiah' and the prophetic office seem to be connected (11QMelchizedek = 11Q13, dealing with the heavenly being, Melchizedek).

[19] Erwin R. Goodenough, *The Politics of Philo Judaeus: Practice and Theory* (New Haven: Yale University Press, 1938), 48-49. Prophecy may even have been a Jewish addition to the Greek philosophical concept of the ideal ruler, Roger Beckwith, *The Old Testament Canon of the New Testament Church and Its Background in Early Judaism* (Grand Rapids: William B. Eerdmans, 1985), 374; see further, Goodenough, 100.

[20] See above, pp. 37-38.

[21] On Strabo's sources, see above, p. 38 and n. 26.

[22] "Propheten können in der Tat auch als solche königliche Funktion haben," Klaus Berger, "Die königlichen Messiastraditionen des Neuen Testaments," *New Testament Studies* 20 (1974): 26.

cially clear that an important part of the nature of the ideal ruler is his endowment with the divine spirit, and his rank among the prophets.[23] The biblical background is strong as well, with both David and Saul either claiming or undergoing inspiration in contexts which closely link their prophesying with their kingship.[24] In the retelling of these tales by Josephus the connection is even more explicit,[25] and Josephus especially extols John Hyrcanus, who combined in himself the offices of ruler, high priest, and prophet.[26] The eschatological king of Is. 11:1-2 is characterized by endowment with the spirit of the Lord, and *T. Levi* 8.14-15, in the text as it stands now, predicts that a new king will arise and, with prophetic insight, will found a new priesthood. Perhaps with an ideal like this in mind Bar Kokhba's claim to be the Messiah was rejected, according to *b. San.* 93b, because it was found that he had to judge by sight, not by inspiration.

The narrative of David was naturally an ideal place to develop the concept of a prophet-king. The eulogy of David in 11Q5 (11QPs^a) col. 27 recalls that God "gave him a discerning and enlightened spirit" (line 4), and, mentioning the thousands of psalms and songs that David wrote, asserts that "all these he spoke in prophecy which had been given to him" (line 11). The New Testament also cites David as a prophet, as in Matt. 22:43, where he is a great king prophesying his own royal descendant, and in Acts 2:30, which flatly states, "he was a prophet."

The link between prophecy and kingship, a link that both Philo and Josephus major on, means that acknowledgment of Moses' great capacity as a prophet, while not determinative of royal status, would greatly facilitate it in the presence of other favorable indications, and would almost certainly become part of any kingly ideas Jews entertained about Moses.

4.2.3.2 A Prophet-King in Deuteronomy 18:15

Most modern scholars think Deut. 18:15 was used by Jews long before the Herodian period to legitimate a succession of prophets after Moses.[27] However, at least some Jewish sources from that period use the verse along the lines of its now-familiar, eschatological interpretation.[28] More

---

[23] *Virt.* 216-18, also *Praem.* 55.

[24] David: 2 Sam. 23:2; Saul: 1 Sam. 10:9-11; 11:6; 16:13-14; 19:23-24.

[25] *Ant.* 6.56 with 54, 57; 6.76, 165, 166.

[26] *B.J.* 1.68; *Ant.* 13.299. See Meeks, *Prophet-King*, 142-44 for an interesting connection Josephus seems to make between government and an office of "the prophet."

[27] Dale C. Allison, Jr., *The New Moses: A Matthean Typology* (Edinburgh: T. & T. Clark, 1993), 74, though not unanimously, see Rudolf Schnackenburg, *The Gospel According to St John*, vol. 2, *Commentary on Chapters 5-12*, trans. Cecily Hastings, et al., Herder's Theological Commentary on the New Testament, ed. Serafin de Ausejo, et al. (London: Burns and Oates, 1980), 19.

[28] Josef M. Kastner, "Moses im Neuen Testament" (Th.D. diss., Ludwig-Maximilians-Universität Munich, 1967), 66-74 mounts a strong defense of the position that

difficult is the proposition that the expected figure was also thought to be a king. In favor of this idea is the basic datum that the expected prophet would be like Moses, and Moses (as this chapter will demonstrate) was in late Second Temple Judaism widely regarded as a king.

4.2.3.2.1 Jewish Traditions of a Mosaic Prophet-King

Meeks argues on the basis of the haggadic traditions surrounding Deut. 18:15 that some first-century Jews held that verse to promise "a *succession of prophetic rulers* of Israel, beginning with Moses, passed on to Joshua, continuing in Samuel and, presumably, also found in the remaining great prophets of Israel, especially Jeremiah."[29]

Meeks's succession obviously had to begin with Moses and Joshua, and the procession thence to Samuel seems intuitive. It is interesting, however, that Meeks then looks to figures famed chiefly as prophets to fill out the rest of the "succession of prophetic rulers," for example, by adducing evidence that Jeremiah was seen as a ruler. The material on prophet-kings reviewed above suggests that proper rulers (i.e. the biblical kings) would be at least equally strong candidates. Meeks's "succession of prophetic rulers" might then be better viewed not as the line of prophets that Meeks suggests, but rather as a succession of rulers, headed by Moses and continuing through the judges (whom Meeks omits but who clearly fit the paradigm of inspired rulers) and Samuel, and then on to Saul and the kings of the Davidic dynasty. Such a succession would be fulfilled by a final prophetic messiah figure who would reprise the founding role of Moses as prophet-king.

The *Exagoge* of Ezekiel the Tragedian was already examined above in connection with its portrayal of Moses as a prophet.[30] It will be seen below that in that same passage the Tragedian also depicts Moses as a king. In fact the two functions are conferred upon Moses simultaneously.[31] The Tragedian may tell us nothing of the interpretation of Deut. 18:15 *per se*, but he does provide strong evidence, probably from the first century B.C., that Moses was seen carrying both the roles of prophet and king.

Jews in the NT era interpreted Deut. 18:15-19 eschatologically and looked for the appearance of an eschatological Prophet like Moses. See also his penetrating examination (61-66) of the portrayal in the Qumran literature of the End Time as a reprise of the time of Moses, and his contrasting review (96-104) of the lack of expectations of a prophet like Moses in the rabbinic literature (owing perhaps to Christian or Samaritan use of Deut. 18:15 in that way) at the same time that the End Time continued to be seen as a reprise of the time of Moses and Israel in the wilderness.

[29] Meeks, *Prophet-King*, 189, drawing on 143-45, 150-51, 179-81; see also Allison, *The New Moses: A Matthean Typology*, 74.

[30] See above, pp. 36-37.

[31] See below, pp. 90-91.

Philo, *Ebr.* 143 calls Samuel "the greatest of kings and prophets" (ὁ καὶ βασιλέων καὶ προφητῶν μέγιστος Σαμουήλ). Other Jewish lore of similar vintage links Samuel to Moses in this respect, while 1 Samuel 12:6-15 places Samuel in the Mosaic succession. Meeks reviews several traditions along the same lines as Philo's, for example the oracle given to Israel in Pseudo-Philo's *Biblical Antiquities* in which it is declared that Samuel "will rule over you and will prophesy" (*ipse principabitur in vobis et prophetabit*; *LAB* 49.7). Pseudo-Philo later specifically compares Samuel with Moses, in such a way that Samuel is cast almost as a new Moses (e.g., God says, "he is like my servant Moses," etc., *LAB* 53.2).[32]

Meeks also points to the tradition revealed by Josephus (*Ant.* 4.218), but evidently not derived from contemporary practice, of investing rulership in a prophet. This curious passage, wherein Josephus substitutes ὁ προφήτης for Deut. 17:9's שׁפט (LXX, ὁ κρίτης), suggests a holdover from earlier tradition, in which the prophetic and ruling offices were combined. Meeks suggests, with some plausibility, that the solution to this puzzle lies in a tradition that has its origin in the perception of Moses as combining these functions.[33]

It is worth mentioning again in connection with Josephus the great reverence he displays for John Hyrcanus, whom he lauds for his combination of the offices of prophet, priest and king (*B.J.* 1.68; *Ant.* 13.299). Meeks believes that Josephus sees the Hasmonean's gifts as unique, but J. C. H. Lebram urges that the threefold title of Hyrcanus "durch Zurückführung auf Mose sanktioniert werden."[34] The Hasmonean and priestly background of Josephus no doubt emboldened Josephus in his description of the great Hyrcanus, but may have also facilitated his employment of Moses as a model for such a description. K. Berger observes that it was "in levitischen Kreisen" that the portrait of Moses received its clearest royal messianic expression, able as it was to combine the priestly and the royal messiah on a prophetic foundation.[35]

---

[32] Meeks, *Prophet-King*, 150-51. Rabbinic literature also links Samuel and Moses as kings, see below, p. 107. See also below, p. 121, on Samuel as priest-king in Jewish tradition.

[33] Meeks, *Prophet-King*, 142.

[34] Meeks, *Prophet-King*, 144-45; Jürgen C. H. Lebram, "Der Idealstaat der Juden," in *Josephus-Studien: Untersuchungen zu Josephus, dem antiken Judentum, und dem Neuen Testament, Otto Michel zum 70. Geburtstag gewidmet*, ed. Otto Betz, Klaus Haacker, and Martin Hengel (Göttingen: Vandenhoeck & Ruprecht, 1974), 251.

[35] Berger, "Die königlichen Messiastraditionen des Neuen Testaments," 27-28

4.2.3.2.2 Samaritan Traditions of a Mosaic Prophet-King

The Samaritans, who took Deut. 18:15-19 as their key messianic passage,[36] expected a Moses-like eschatological prophet. This figure is the *Taheb* (תהב), the Restorer or the Returning One (deriving in an Aramaic-speaking period from the verb חוב, Heb. שוב).[37] The expectation of such an eschatological prophet is not specifically Samaritan, but an idea held in common with Jews as far back as the second century B.C.[38] Samaritans and Jews for some time remained able to interact with one another about such a prophetic figure.

An example is the Fourth Gospel's inclusion of the conversation between Jesus and the Samaritan woman about the Messiah. Note the Samaritan woman's description of "Messiah — he who is called Christ" in John 4:25: "He will declare all things to us." It is tempting to suppose that this characterization of the figure awaited by the Samaritans as Messiah and Christ (Μεσσίας, χριστός) and Revealer, reveals something of Samaritan eschatology in the first century A.D. Though the passage has been regarded as a reliable guide to Samaritan expectations,[39] embedded as it is in a Christian Gospel apparently intent on depicting Jesus as a prophet and king it is difficult to be certain how much the speech of the Samaritan woman reflects genuine Samaritan expectations, particularly when unexpounded use of two key Christian titles for Jesus is all that here implies that the expected prophet will also be a ruler.

Certainly in later Samaritan thought the Mosaic prophet was expected to be the eschatological ruler,[40] but the antiquity of this expectation of a prophet-king is difficult to determine. The association of the Taheb with kingship or a kingdom seems to appear in the fourth-century *Memar Marqah*.[41] John 4:25 indicates that Jews (and Christians) knew Samaritan expectations much earlier, and could at least coordinate them with their own royal messianism, but it would be difficult to draw firm conclusions about Samaritan royal messianism based on what is said about "the Messiah who is called Christ" in that passage, as already conceded.

A clearly royal Taheb appears only late, in Samaritan conceptions of the New Age (the *Rahuta*) that he ushers in. The New Age itself may have

---

[36] T. F. Glasson, *Moses in the Fourth Gospel*, Studies in Biblical Theology, ed. C. F. D. Moule, et al., no. 40 (London: SCM Press, 1963), 31-32.

[37] James Alan Montgomery, *The Samaritans, the Earliest Jewish Sect: Their History, Theology and Literature* (New York: Ktav Publishing House, 1968), 246-47; Ferdinand Dexinger, "Samaritan Eschatology," in *The Samaritans*, ed. Alan D. Crown (Tübingen: J. C. B. Mohr [Paul Siebeck], 1989), 268.

[38] Dexinger, "Samaritan Eschatology," 275.

[39] By, e.g., Montgomery, *The Samaritans, the Earliest Jewish Sect*, 243.

[40] Dexinger, "Samaritan Eschatology," 273-76, 279-81.

[41] Ibid., 279-80; Montgomery, *The Samaritans, the Earliest Jewish Sect*, 248.

been conceived as kingdom relatively early in Samaritan history,[42] but Deut. 18:15, 18 does not seem to have been connected with this kingdom at an early stage, which, again, argues against an early conception of the prophetic Taheb as a king.[43]

Besides traditions centering on the Taheb and Deut. 18:15, other traditions combined Moses' prophetic greatness with an apparently royal status. Samaritan marriage contracts, which probably preserve much older traditions, refer to the appearance of Moses with the words, "And the star of the Prophet arose (וזרח כוכב הנבי), the owner of the Day of Horeb."[44] Given the Samaritan reliance on the Pentateuch, the application to a figure of the epithet "star" would most likely carry overtones of Num. 24:17, a text with clear royal implications. Here Moses is portrayed as a prophet and king, which once more suggests that the prophet like Moses might also be thought a king.[45]

4.2.3.2.3 Conclusion

Deuteronomy 18:15 is concerned with prophethood like the prophethood of Moses. First of all of course, this will have been taken to refer to the intimacy of Moses and God, to the fact that God spoke to the prophet Moses face to face (Num. 12:6-8).

But Moses was more than a prophet, and a number of traditions specifically combine the roles of prophet and king in association with him, so that he could be viewed as the archetypal prophet and ruler. This supposition is strengthened by the fact that the non-eschatological successors of Moses were often seen as prophets and rulers.

If Deut. 18:15 was thought to speak of an eschatological figure (as it was in both Jewish and Samaritan circles), and that figure were expected to fulfill the role of Moses, he would also be anticipated as a prophet-king, if not even more. D. Bock writes:

---

[42] Dexinger, "Samaritan Eschatology," 279.

[43] Ibid., 280.

[44] BL Or 12375c (1907?) line 6, text, Reinhard Plummer, *Samaritan Marriage Contracts and Deeds of Divorce*, vol. 1 (Wiesbaden: Otto Harrassowitz, 1993), 161; trans., Plummer, *Samaritan Marriage Contracts and Deeds of Divorce*, vol. 2, with Abraham Tal (Wiesbaden: Harrassowitz Verlag, 1997), 185; Smithsonian Institution II (1838) line 6, text, Plummer, vol. 1, 205; trans., vol. 2, 243.

[45] The connection of the prophecy of the star in Num. 24:17 with both Moses and the Taheb has long been noted, see John MacDonald, *The Theology of the Samaritans*, The New Testament Library, ed. Alan Richardson, C. F. D. Moule, and Floyd V. Filson (London: SCM Press, 1964), 160, 195, 363, 430.

The belief in the prophet like Moses who was a prophet-king was widespread in Judaism, especially alongside the expectation that the messianic times would parallel the Mosaic times. It was combined with a view of him as prophet-lawgiver.[46]

The inclusion of the role of lawgiver in the picture adds to the Mosaic "likeness" of the Prophet like Moses, whose likeness to Moses consists in his fulfillment of the station of Moses over Israel. Bock says correctly, "It is the combination of ruler-prophet that distinguishes the prophet *like Moses* from other prophets."[47]

All the traditions just reviewed here, whether eschatological or historical in focus, and whether specifically grounded in Deut. 18:15 or associated with Moses on other grounds, are further evidence for the Jewish conception, on the basis of biblical traditions, of Moses and his successors as kings.

4.3 Moses as King in Second Temple Period Literature

While the biblical traditions, and literature dependent on them, provided important support for the idea of Moses as king, the strongest affirmations of Moses' kingship come in literature only implicitly dependent on such traditions. Investigation of the biblical traditions about Moses' kingship has already involved examination of literature from the Second Temple period and later. This and subsequent sections will examine such evidence more closely.

4.3.1 The Exagoge of Ezekiel the Tragedian

The Tragedian is an important witness to portrayal of Moses as king by, or before, the Herodian period.[48] In one scene (lines 68-89), Moses dreams of a great throne (θρόνος) on the peak of Mt. Sinai (68). On it Moses sees a "man" (φώς) with a crown (διάδημα) and scepter (μέγα σκῆπ-

---

[46] Darrell L. Bock, *Proclamation from Prophecy and Pattern: Lucan Old Testament Christology*, Journal for the Study of the New Testament Supplement Series, ed. David Hill, vol. 12 (Sheffield: JSOT Press, 1987), 193.

[47] Ibid.

[48] On a late second century B.C. date see Howard Jacobson, ed. and trans., *The Exagoge of Ezekiel* (Cambridge: Cambridge University Press, 1983), 5-13; cf. Carl R. Holladay, *Poets*, vol. 2 of *Fragments from Hellenistic Jewish Authors*, Society of Biblical Literature Texts and Translations Pseudepigrapha Series, ed. James C. Vanderkam, Texts and Translations no. 30, Pseudepigrapha no. 12 (Atlanta: Scholars Press, 1989), 308-312. Rick Van De Water, "Moses' Exaltation: Pre-Christian?," *Journal for the Study of the Pseudepigrapha* 21 (2000): 59-69 now dates the drama late in the first century A.D.; see the response by William Horbury, *Messianism Among Jews and Christians: Twelve Biblical and Historical Studies* (London and New York: T. & T. Clark, 2003), 66-68.

τρον; 70-71).[49] On Moses' approach, the man hands over to Moses the crown, scepter, and throne, and then withdraws (καὶ αὐτὸς ἐκ θρόνων χωρίζεται; 74-76). From the throne Moses beholds the entire world, and a host of stars does obeisance to him (77-81).[50]

4.3.1.1 Divine Moses or Royal Moses?

The undoubted highlight of the passage is clearly the moment when the figure on the throne gives his place entirely over to Moses. The pointed royal symbolism may be taken to establish that Moses is depicted as a surrogate ruler for God, a divine king. But how divine is the divine king? Is it Ezekiel's intent not merely to portray Moses as (even a very grand) king but as a god? Solutions may be bracketed into alternatives, one that emphasizes the divine aspect of Moses' surrogacy for God, and one that does not.

The former position is represented by P. van der Horst, who believes that the scene "certainly implies a deification of Moses."[51] Much of the debate over this position has to do with controversy over the suitability of language of "deification" in a monotheistic context like Judaism.[52] It can probably be taken for granted that hardly anyone in antiquity would have wanted to suggest that Moses[53] had taken God's place in heaven and

---

[49] Text and translation for *Exagogē*, Holladay, *Poets*, 362-371. On the φώς see Erich S. Gruen, *Heritage and Hellenism: The Reinvention of Jewish Tradition*, Hellenistic Culture and Society, ed. Anthony W. Bulloch, et al., no. 30 (Berkeley: University of California Press, 1998), 132.

[50] Text and trans. Carl R. Holladay, *Fragments from Hellenistic Jewish Authors*, vol. 2, *Poets*, Society of Biblical Literature Texts and Translations Pseudepigrapha Series, ed. James C. Vanderkam, Texts and Translations no. 30, Pseudepigrapha no. 12 (Atlanta: Scholars Press, 1989), 362-65.

[51] P. van der Horst, "Moses' Throne Vision in Ezekiel the Dramatist," *Journal of Jewish Studies* 34 (1983): 25. See, sympathetic but against, Martin Hengel, *Studies in Early Christology* (Edinburgh: T. & T. Clark, 1995), 190-91). Also see discussion by Larry W. Hurtado, *One God, One Lord: Early Christian Devotion and Ancient Jewish Monotheism* (London: SCM Press, 1988), 57-59. C. R. A. Morray-Jones, "Transformational Mysticism in the Apocalyptic-Merkabah Tradition," *Journal of Jewish Studies* 43, no. 1 (1992): 16 on the other hand, thinks the φώς is a demiurgic "heavenly man," which would alter the significance of the dream significantly.

[52] Even the term "monotheism" itself is controversial and needs defining when employed in the context of Second Temple Judaism; see John J. Collins, "Jewish Monotheism and Christian Theology," in *Aspects of Monotheism: How God Is One*, ed. Hershel Shanks and Jack Meinhardt (Washington, D.C.: Biblical Archaeology Society, 1997), 82-94 and Charles A. Gieschen, *Angelomorphic Christology: Antecedents and Early Evidence*, Arbeiten zur Geschichte des Antiken Judentums und des Urchristentums, ed. Martin Hengel, et al., no. 42 (Leiden: Brill, 1998), 30.

[53] Or any other king whether non-Jew, Goodenough, *The Politics of Philo Judaeus: Practice and Theory*, 98-99, or Jew, 110.

become a rival Lord of the Universe (and a key problem for interpreters of the scene is that this seems to be what is depicted). But it was entirely plausible in the ancient world to speak of deification, or of divinization, on a more relative scale. In the Greco-Roman world divine status of some kind could be ascribed to nearly anyone who transcended the mundane norms of ordinary existence.[54] It was a regular feature of ruler cult in the Greco-Roman world to hold that a king possessed divine rank as a kind of "god to the nation."[55] The sentiment of the Greco-Roman tradition is exemplified by Horace, writing of Augustus, "Dread Jove in Thunder speaks his just domain; On Earth a present God shall Caesar reign."[56]

Many scholars have argued that among Jews as well it was possible to think of divinity as a sliding scale with God at the top, and featuring numbers of other beings holding intermediate positions beneath.[57] On this view, Jewish monotheism meant not so much an ascription of divinity to God alone as an establishment of which divine being was to be worshipped.[58] Jews could conceive of rulers, for example, as divine in some sense (witness the text under consideration here, also Ps. 110:1 and its handling in the New Testament,[59] Exod. 4:16; 7:1 and their treatment in Philo, etc.).[60]

---

[54] Not necessarily without controversy; see below, p. 246 with n. 175.

[55] Goodenough, *The Politics of Philo Judaeus: Practice and Theory*, 26-27; James D. G. Dunn, *Christology in the Making: A New Testament Inquiry into the Origins of the Doctrine of the Incarnation*, 2d ed. (London: SCM Press, 1989), 16; especially in the Roman principate, D. E. Aune, "The Problem of the Genre of the Gospels: A Critique of C. H. Talbert's *What Is a Gospel?*," in *Gospel Perspectives: Studies of History and Tradition in the Four Gospels*, vol. 2, ed. R. T. France and David Wenham (Sheffield: JSOT Press, 1981), 31.

[56] *Od.* 3.5.1-3, trans. Philip Francis, quoted in William Horbury, *Jewish Messianism and the Cult of Christ* (London: SCM Press, 1998), 73, more examples, 73-74. Cf. *Gen. Rab.* 79.8, on Gen. 33:20.

[57] See n. 52 above and the bibliography in Richard Bauckham, *God Crucified: Monotheism and Christology in the New Testament*, Didsbury Lectures, 1996 (Carlisle, Cumbria: Paternoster Press, 1998), 3 n. 3.

[58] See Adela Yarbro Collins, "The Worship of Jesus and the Imperial Cult," in *The Jewish Roots of Christological Monotheism: Papers from the St. Andrews Conference on the Historical Origin of the Worship of Jesus*, ed. Carey C. Newman, James R. Davila, and Gladys S. Lewis, Supplements to the *Journal for the Study of Judaism*, ed. John J. Collins with Florentino García Martínez, vol. 63 (Leiden: Brill, 1999), 235-36; cf. the contrasting Richard Bauckham, "The Throne of God and the Worship of Jesus," in the same volume, 45-47, who lays greater stress on the unique identity of God, but detects that identity in his unique roles as Creator and Lord. Bauckham, 48-51 agrees Jews conceived of other divine beings but these did not impinge on God's uniqueness in Jewish thought; see also below on men as angels in Jewish thought, pp. 238-245.

[59] On Ps. 110:1 see Hengel, *Studies in Early Christology*, 133-225, esp. 149, 155-57, 171, 172-75, 181-203, 225. Jacobson, *The* Exagoge *of Ezekiel*, 90 points out the similarity between the dream scene and Ps. 110:1-3.

[60] On the divinization of Moses see below, pp. 229-47.

The divinity of Moses, of course, would enjoy the Scriptural warrant that he became god to both Aaron and Pharaoh, in references (Exod. 4:16; 7:1) used in other traditions to focus especially on the divinity of Moses.[61] For Philo these texts became a springboard for speaking of Moses as "god *and* king of the whole nation" (ὅλου τοῦ ἔθνους θεὸς καὶ βασιλεύς; *Mos.* 1.158). The question of the Tragedian's intent in depicting Moses as he does cannot be decided then solely on *a priori* grounds concerning what was or was not in bounds for late Second Temple Judaism. In principle, it is possible that the dream depicts Moses entering heaven to become God's divinized vice-regent.

The alternative interpretation of the dream, however, minimizes the deification of Moses in the passage under consideration, or considers it entirely symbolic of the role Moses was thought to have played as an earthly king. Richard Bauckham is an advocate of this position, which holds that Ezekiel merely meant to depict Moses taking God's place over the realm of Israel.[62] This position is related to his scheme for the Jewish conception of divinity, which tends to eliminate the notion of intermediate divinity, and locate true divinity exclusively in God.[63] Bauckham argues that the dream represents the Tragedian's exegesis of Exod. 4:16 and 7:1 as cases where the word "God" is "a metaphor for Moses' rule over Israel and his inspired knowledge. ... As God is in relation to the cosmos, so Moses will be in relation to Israel."[64]

Jews employed the concept of the divine king who rules on earth as heaven's viceroy.[65] This tendency actually increases throughout the post-

---

[61] See below, pp. 230-32, 236, 239-40, 246-47, 257.

[62] Richard Bauckham, "The Throne of God and the Worship of Jesus," in *The Jewish Roots of Christological Monotheism: Papers from the St. Andrews Conference on the Historical Origin of the Worship of Jesus*, ed. Carey C. Newman, James R. Davila, and Gladys S. Lewis, Supplements to the *Journal for the Study of Judaism*, ed. John J. Collins with Florentino García Martínez, vol. 63 (Leiden: Brill, 1999), 57.

[63] Bauckham, *God Crucified*, 3-4. See further below.

[64] Bauckham, "The Throne of God and the Worship of Jesus," 56-57.

[65] On OT background, see Hengel, *Studies in Early Christology*, 175-89; Bentzen, *King and Messiah*, 19; Sigmund Mowinckel, "General Oriental and Specific Israelite Elements in the Israelite Conception of the Sacral Kingdom," in *The Sacral Kingship: Contributions to the Central Theme of the VIIIth International Congress for the History of Religions*, Studies in the History of Religions (Supplements to *NVMEN*), no. 4 (Leiden: E. J. Brill, 1959), 286 (who in surveying OT kingship ideology coincidentally repeats many of the dream's symbols); and S. Aalen, "'Reign' and 'House' in the Kingdom of God in the Gospels," *New Testament Studies* 8 (1961-1962): 216 and 233. On Hellenistic Judaism, Goodenough, *The Politics of Philo Judaeus: Practice and Theory*, 58; Dunn, *Christology in the Making*, 17 and 274, n. 32; J. A. Emerton, "Some New Testament Notes," *Journal of Theological Studies*, NS, 11 (1960): 329-32.

exilic and Second Temple periods.[66] According to this alternative, Ezekiel did not mean to describe a deified Moses, but only "draped Moses in the emblems of royal power that would resonate with those who lived in the era of the great monarchies."[67]

A variant of this position, advocated by L. W. Hurtado, takes the *Exagoge* to portray Moses as God's vice-regent not only over Israel, but over all creation. Despite what this might seem to imply, Hurtado also avoids ascription of divine status to Moses in the *Exagoge*.[68]

4.3.1.2 The Ascent of Moses

Attention on the dream naturally focuses on the royal regalia, but the question of whether Moses acquires divinity is perhaps as strongly affected by the subtle notice that Moses "approached" God. The Tragedian times Moses' rise to vice-regency for God with the Sinai ascent. That Moses ascended into heaven when he went up Mount Sinai to receive the Law became a staple of rabbinic lore,[69] and it appears in literature of the first century, most notably Philo.[70] Philo duplicates the scene in a midrash on Exod. 7:1 (and 20:21), writing, as noted above, that Moses "was named god and king (θεὸς καὶ βασιλεύς) of the whole nation" (*Mos.* 1.158) at the time when he entered into the darkness where God was, presumably on Mount Sinai.[71]

---

[66] Aalen, "'Reign' and 'House' in the Kingdom of God in the Gospels," 216-17. The New Testament, which (except for Revelation) pushes aside the kingship of God in favor of God as Father, is actually a notable contrast (see Aalen, 217, 218-219).

[67] Gruen, *Heritage and Hellenism: The Reinvention of Jewish Tradition*, 134; see Goodenough, *The Politics of Philo Judaeus: Practice and Theory*, 90, 98-100; Jacobson, *The* Exagoge *of Ezekiel*, 96-97; Meeks, "Moses as God and King," in *Religions in Antiquity: Essays in Memory of Erwin Ramsdell Goodenough*, ed. Jacob Neusner, Studies in the History of Religions (Supplements to *Numen*), no. 14 (Leiden: E. J. Brill, 1968), 359.

[68] Technically, he reserves judgment on the matter, *One God, One Lord: Early Christian Devotion and Ancient Jewish Monotheism*, 58, but he seems to incline to the view that in the *Exagoge* Moses becomes God's human surrogate; see, for example, p. 152 n. 40, in reply to van der Horst's "exaggerated" claim, "The seating of Moses on the throne need imply nothing more than the appointment of Moses as ruler (perhaps cosmic ruler) on God's behalf."

[69] Key literature is set out by Meeks, *Prophet-King*, 205-209.

[70] On which see Meeks, *Prophet-King*, 122-25 (Philo), 142 (Josephus), 156-59 (pseudepigrapha). But it does not appear in the New Testament itself (or else it would receive more attention in this study). Even John says nothing of the ascent and descent of Moses, despite the potentially useful contrast with the descent and ascent of the Son. Of course, the contrast may be implied all the same.

[71] See Meeks, "Moses as God and King," 355. Jacobson, *The* Exagoge *of Ezekiel*, 94 points out the affinity between the dream and Philo's description of Moses' rise to kingship.

The precise attitude of the Tragedian to any traditions of his time that at Moses' ascent of Sinai he entered heaven is a matter of dispute.[72] At a minimum he betrays knowledge of such traditions, as Jacobson points out,[73] and he gives no indication that he disapproves of them. And while the implications of Moses' ascent into heaven are not self-evident, they are at least potentially quite glorious.

The Moses of the *Exagoge* dreams not only of his ascent into heaven, but of his enthronement there. The closest parallel to Ezekiel's enthronement of Moses may be the Enochic ascent traditions that appear in the Similitudes of Enoch, which are roughly contemporary with the *Exagoge*, wherein Enoch (the Elect One) is enthroned on the throne of God (1 Enoch 51:3; 61:8; 62:5; 69:29).[74] These traditions come to full flower in 3 Enoch, a much later text,[75] where Enoch's ascent into heaven results in his being transformed into a being of immense size and fantastic attributes (3 Enoch 9:1-5; 48C:5-7); in the context of 3 Enoch this indicates his transformation into an angel.[76] The 3 Enochic tradition is powerfully suggestive, but clearly the nearest parallel from the Moses traditions (the *Exagoge* dream) is nowhere close in content to these late Enochic developments. The descriptions of the Enoch figure in the Similitudes are closer in content and period of origin, but among the traditions about the ascent of Moses the *Exagoge* is still essentially unique in its notion of the enthronement of Moses in God's own throne.[77]

---

[72] See brief survey in Hurtado, *One God, One Lord: Early Christian Devotion and Ancient Jewish Monotheism*, 58-59.

[73] Jacobson, *The* Exagoge *of Ezekiel*, 90.

[74] Hengel, *Studies in Early Christology*, 185 offers a variant of 55:4 as well. It has been conjectured that 62:2 may also have God seating the Elect One in his throne, though no MS supports this, see E. Isaac, "1 (Ethiopic Apocalypse of) Enoch," in *Old Testament Pseudepigrapha*, ed. J. H. Charlesworth, vol. 1 (New York: Doubleday, 1983), 43 n. 62c.

[75] Fifth or sixth century A.D., according to P. Alexander, "3 (Hebrew Apocalypse of) Enoch," in *Old Testament Pseudepigrapha*, ed. J. H. Charlesworth, vol. 1 (New York: Doubleday, 1983), 229, but the question is vexed and it may be later, see his pp. 225-29. 3 Enoch develops traditions also found in some earlier rabbinic texts, see Hengel, *Studies in Early Christology*, 192.

[76] Alexander, "3 Enoch," 263 n. 9c, see Hengel, *Studies in Early Christology*, 193. After this, Enoch is given "a throne like the throne of glory" opposite to the throne of God (3 Enoch 10:2; 48C:8), and given authority over the angels, apart from the eight great princes "who are called YHWH by the name of their King" (10:3-4). Apparently by reason of this limitation on his power Enoch/Metatron is dubbed "the lesser YHWH" (3 Enoch 12:5; 48C:7; 48D:1.90). His status is angelic.

[77] Hengel, *Studies in Early Christology*, 196(-97), confesses that adducing evidence for a heavenly enthronement of Moses is "most difficult." The nearest thing to an allusion to it is the already very late midrash of *Deut. Rab.* 11.10. See Hengel, 197 n. 185 and the discussion on 197-201. He concludes that there are no traditions about Moses

Rabbinic traditions include some reflections on the themes that occupied Philo, and may have occupied Ezekiel Tragicus. Meeks identifies the "coronation on Sinai" motif in *Pesiqta de Rav Kahana*, which interprets the expression "Moses, the man of God" (מֹשֶׁה אִישׁ הָאֱלֹהִים) in Deut. 33:1 as, "A man when he ascended on high; a god when he descended below." Meeks interprets, "Thus it was in heaven that Moses was made 'god' (and therefore king), which meant that Moses ... was crowned ... as the heavenly King's earthly vice-regent."[78] Despite Meeks' placement of the word "god" in scare quotes, and his insistence that Moses remained "earthly," he immediately goes on to interpret the passage in *Pesiqta* as implying that Moses "became imbued in some sense with God's fiery substance," etc. or, in other words, became divinized. Meeks himself calls attention to *Midr. Pss.* 90.1: "When a mortal goes up to the Holy One, blessed be He, who is pure fire, and whose ministers are fire — and Moses did go up to Him — he is a man. But after he comes down, he is called God." *Deuteronomy Rab.* 11.4 (which Meeks also adduces and which debates several possible implications of Deut. 33:1) seems in touch with a similar tradition when it says, "When he went up to heaven he was a man. And in which respect was he a man? Compared with the angels who are made entirely of fire. But when he came down from heaven he was as God."[79]

Meeks's interpretation of Moses' ascent into heaven in the *Pesiqta* results in his being made God's emissary on earth, and nothing more. His majesty then is earthly, not heavenly. On the face of it, however, the teaching of the *Pesiqta* is remarkably laudatory of Moses, and bears a striking resemblance to the Greco-Roman view of divine kings, i.e., it appears to call Moses a present god on earth.

Other rabbinic traditions also have Moses partake of God's power or glory. Meeks assesses a stream of Jewish and Samaritan tradition which associated the shining face (קֵרַן עוֹר) of Moses in Exod. 34:29-35 with a "crown of light," and thence with God's own crown which Moses was permitted to use.[80] These traditions would appear to support the idea of a Moses who enjoys the delegated authority of God. This, as has already

---

to compare with those about Enoch/Metatron. The Tragedian's account of the enthronement of Moses in heaven appears unique in that respect.

[78] Meeks, *Prophet-King*, 195 cites *Pesiq. Rab Kah.* Piska 32, p. 198b of the Buber edition. This corresponds to the Mandelbaum edition, 443 line 6 (Appendix I on Deut. 33:1, § 9). A variety of interpretations of this expression are listed in *Midr. Pss.* 90.5.

[79] *Deut. Rab.* 11 is rich in such speculations about Moses.

[80] Meeks, "Moses as God and King," 361-65. The interpretation found in *Pesiqta de Rav Kahana* defends its reading of Deut. 33:1 from this passage. See Louis Ginzberg, *The Legends of the Jews*, vol. 6 (Philadelphia: The Jewish Publication Society of America, 1928), 166 n. 965 for other rabbinic references to the (near-) divinization of Moses.

been noticed here, could be construed as a kind of divinization, but could equally support the idea of an earthly vice-regency.

Some rabbinic traditions compare Moses with God along the lines of kingship. *Midrash Pss.* 21:2, like Philo, interprets Exod. 7:1 to mean that God made Moses his vice-regent. Meeks argues that a homily occurring in *Tanḥuma* Buber, Numbers, Parashah בהעלתך, 15 (Seder IV [Bamidbar], 51-52) and repeated in *Num. Rab.* 15.13, suggests that Moses was thought to share the kingship of God.[81] Meeks gives the gist of the homily's conclusion: "As God the supreme king made Moses 'god,' [in Exod. 7:1] so also he made him 'king.'" Meeks claims that the core of the *Tanḥuma* homily is the same as Philo's midrash on Exod. 7:1 from *Mos.* 1.155-58; both take the statement of Exod. 7:1, "I have made you a god to Pharaoh," to mean that God made Moses "king" as well, since "king" is one of the attributes of "God."[82] In all these texts, be it noted, "king" and "god" are correlative, not alternative, designations.

4.3.1.3 Divinity and Divinization

For the status Moses acquires in his dream in the *Exagoge* there seem to be three possibilities. Either 1) Moses is God's designated ruler of Israel and merely wears the divine trappings of Hellenistic kingship, or 2) Moses is appointed king of Israel but, along lines similar to Greco-Roman ideals of kingship, is thereby also promoted to earthly divine status, or else 3) Moses is purely and simply raised to divine standing, with the rights and privileges appertaining thereto, including rulership, whether of Israel or the world.

The debate as reviewed thus far would appear to involve a good deal of question begging. Is the scepter in the dream of Moses in the *Exagoge* the scepter of God as king (i.e. of Israel), or of God as the supreme being? The same question applies to the crown and to the throne. But the most obvious questions outstanding are simply, "What constitutes 'divinity'?" and in light of that, "What would constitute 'divinization'?"

In the past few years scholars have been sharpening the tools for assessing claims for the divinity of figures in Jewish thought and literature.

4.3.1.3.1 Criteria for Ascription of Divinity: R. Bauckham

One set of criteria, that of Bauckham, has received particular attention, and has already been noted here. He finds that "the overwhelming tendency in Second Temple Judaism was to depict God as absolutely unique, to differentiate God as completely as possible from all other reality, and to under-

---

[81] Meeks, "Moses as God and King," 356-57.

[82] Ibid., 357. Meeks, 357-59 also identifies Samaritan traditions along very similar lines. *Tanḥuma* Buber Exodus, Parashah 2(Wa'era).1 on Exodus 6:2-3 preserves rabbinic traditions linking the terms "god" and "ruler."

stand the exclusive worship of God as marking, in religious practice, the
absolute distinction between God and all creatures."[83] Having defined "divinity" as something pertaining exclusively to God, Bauckham characterizes it as consisting:

especially in that God is sole Creator and sole Supreme Ruler of all things. ... It is intrinsic to the divine identity, intrinsic to who God is, that God is sole Creator and sole
Ruler of all things. These are not mere functions that can be delegated to creatures.[84]

Bauckham acknowledges that Second Temple Jews maintained some less
strict ideas making God out as the chief of a divine hierarchy, but he maintains that "such traces are in fact only rarely and weakly discernible, and
can be usually be seen to have been subordinated and neutralized by the
dominant tendency."[85] Elsewhere he writes, "In his sovereignty over the
universe and history, however, God, of course, employs servants, especially the myriads of angels. Here the dominant image is of God as the great
emperor ruling the cosmos as his kingdom," etc.[86] One might ask, if divinity is a matter of function (creation and rule), then would not God's employment of ministers mean that these ministers acquire some kind of derivative divinity? Perhaps even as Romans might think of the divinity of
Caesar?

Bauckham goes on to say:

In Second Temple Judaism, then, the throne of God in the highest heaven became a key
symbol of monotheism, representative of one of the essential characteristics definitive
of the divine identity. While a few traces of other enthroned figures associated with
God's rule can be found, the subordination of such figures to God's rule is almost
always stressed.[87]

Again, is it not an expression of divinity, even on Bauckham's definition of
divinity, that "other enthroned figures" can be associated with God's "intrinsic" function of ruling the cosmos?

Bauckham's positions on the nature of divinity in Jewish thought might
seem to set his position on the throne vision in the *Exagoge* in jeopardy.
Bauckham, however, understands Moses' dream in that text as figurative,
specifically as a figurative exegesis of Exod. 7:1, where God says to Moses, "I will make you God (to Pharaoh)."[88] In the dream, "The *image* of
Moses as God is interpreted to *signify* that Moses will be a king and a pro-

---

[83] Bauckham, "The Throne of God and the Worship of Jesus," 48.

[84] Ibid., 48; also Bauckham, *God Crucified*, 9-13.

[85] Bauckham, "The Throne of God and the Worship of Jesus," 48.

[86] Bauckham, *God Crucified*, 12.

[87] Bauckham, "The Throne of God and the Worship of Jesus," 53.

[88] Ibid., 55-57.

phet. ... The dream depicts Moses quite literally as God, but the meaning of the dream is not its literal meaning."[89]

Nevertheless, Bauckham has championed the view that for Jews God is "identified by his distinctive activities and personal characteristics."[90] Were we left to our own devices in interpreting the dream it would indeed be difficult to resist the implication that Moses has indeed been deified, as van der Horst urges. Bauckham himself acknowledges this.[91]

4.3.1.3.2 Criteria for Ascription of Divinity: C. A. Gieschen

Partially in response to Bauckham, a larger set of five "Criteria for Divinity" is proposed by C. A. Gieschen.[92] These consist of relatively straightforward sets of language or imagery that Gieschen derives from the ancient sources. Briefly, they are: 1) the "divine position criterion," which asks if a figure is "positioned with or near God or his throne" (such a position would indicate divine status); 2) the "divine appearance criterion," which takes possession of "physical characteristics of God's visible form" as evidence of divine status; 3) the "divine function criterion," which asks if a given figure is seen to carry out acts or actions "typically ascribed to God," and takes such acts as indicators of divine status; 4) the "divine name criterion," which holds that a figure who possesses the divine name shares in "the very authority and essence" of God; 5) the "divine veneration criterion," which takes veneration of a given figure as evidence that a figure shares in divine honors.

Gieschen explicitly finds that Moses dreams of himself fulfilling the first criterion,[93] but one could take the dream to indicate the third and fifth as well, depending on the interpretive decision taken on the significance of the stars and Moses' ability to number them. The difficulty here is that one must almost assume what is to be proved. The decision on what the stars represent almost dictates what the dream depicts, since if they are angelic beings, Moses would appear most likely to have acquired divine majesty, but if they are the Israelites then his majesty might be more mundane. One could reason in the opposite direction as well, and interpret the stars in the dream on the basis of conclusions taken on the significance of the throne and regalia. The aggregate impression of all the elements of the dream, as already noted, is undoubtedly extremely impressive.

---

[89] Ibid., 57.

[90] Ibid., 45.

[91] Ibid., 55("the extravagant exaltation of Moses to the throne of the universe in the dream")-56.

[92] Gieschen, *Angelomorphic Christology: Antecedents and Early Evidence*, 30-33.

[93] Ibid., 31 n. 17, 88.

Gieschen's own position is quite clear. He finds that in the dream Moses "is enthroned and worshipped as a monarch over all creation."[94] There is, he writes:

no doubt that Moses will not merely stand by God and assist; he will sit on God's throne in order to rule. Furthermore, worship by the angelic hosts after the enthronement demonstrates the significance of what is being proposed: a human being exalted to God's throne and receiving the adoration due to God.[95]

Again, such an argument may prove too much. Gieschen himself is sensitive to the fact that veneration of figures (held to be divine) other than God was not seen by Jews as a substitute for the veneration of God.[96] On Gieschen's reading this would seem to be what the Tragedian depicts.

4.3.1.4 Raguel's Interpretation of the Dream

Using the criteria for divinity proposed by Bauckham, the divinity of Moses in the dream seems nearly assured. Using those formulated by Gieschen, Moses' divinity is clearly possible, though key elements of such an interpretation may assume what is to be proved. The safest place to look for guidance on the question is the *Exagoge* itself.

The lines following the recitation of the dream by Moses provide Moses' father-in-law's interpretation of the dream, an interpretation which confirms that Ezekiel depicts Moses dreaming fundamentally of his entry into kingship on Mount Sinai. Raguel implies that he will live to see the dream fulfilled, saying:

ζῴην δ', ὅταν σοι ταῦτα συμβαί<ν>η ποτέ.
ἆρά γε μέγαν τιν' ἐξαναστήσεις θρόνον
καὶ αὐτὸς βραβεύσεις καὶ καθηγήση βροτῶν

---

[94] Ibid., 163. He expressly aligns his view (pp. 164-65) with that of P. van der Horst. In the same place he also cites W. Meeks, *Prophet-King*, 148-49 in support of deification of Moses in the *Exagoge* dream, but this is in fact exactly the opposite of what Meeks says. On the pages cited, Meeks is clear that Moses' panoramic vision of heaven and earth is "a symbol of Moses' prophetic office." Meeks writes, "It is apparent that Moses' kingship — one might even say 'divine kingship' — and the closely related office of prophecy were taken for granted by Ezekiel and his audience. ... The lines of Ezekiel that have been preserved do not reveal how he may have portrayed the fulfillment of the Sinai vision — how Moses 'set up a mighty throne' and practiced the gift of prophecy. ... Ezekiel may safely be taken as a witness to traditions of the second century B.C. that God gave to Moses unique powers as king and prophet." Meeks actually supports the view opposite to that of Gieschen and van der Horst.

[95] Gieschen, *Angelomorphic Christology*, 164.

[96] Ibid., 33-36.

Might I live until the time when these things happen to you.
You will raise up a great throne (θρόνου)
And it is you who will judge and lead mortals (βροτῶν)[97] (84-86).

Raguel implies that the events the dream prefigures could happen in his lifetime, and in the context of the play the suggestion to the audience must be that they will (i.e., that Raguel lived to see Moses become king).[98] The dream then becomes a prophecy of the greatness to which Moses will attain in his lifetime.

The fact that it is "mortals" that Moses will judge and lead is possibly of critical importance. On one hand it might be thought to distinguish Moses in his new role from the mortal men he rules. But in rabbinic lore of the ascent of Moses into heaven, and in the tales of Enoch's ascent and glorification, a key motif is the reaction of the angels,[99] and the assignment to the human interloper in heaven of privileges and prerogatives over the angels (e.g. 1 Enoch 55:4; 61:8). That Moses is assigned the rule of mortals may place him on a different trajectory from the exalted human of Enochic lore who is transformed into an angelic figure. While stars, such as occur in the dream of Moses, were commonly used as metaphorical representations of angels,[100] they certainly could also represent the people of Israel.[101] Jacobson probably only errs in the extremity of his certainty when he claims, "when the stars fall before Moses one can scarcely not think of Joseph's dream in Genesis (37.9).[102] Jacobson backs his analysis with a very plausible comparison between the contents of the dream and the Herodotean scheme of dreams that presage a ruler's rise to power.[103] Taking

---

[97] Always plural, βροτοί is one of the Tragedian's favorite words for men or humans. Text and trans., Holladay, *Fragments from Hellenistic Jewish Authors*, vol. 2, *Poets*, 366-67

[98] Raguel's wish could possibly indicate another possibility, that what is envisaged is the messianic age with Moses reigning as the eschatological king. The possibility is intriguing, not least because Moses is shown in his dream in the twin roles of prophet and king so persuasively associated with him by Meeks in *The Prophet King*, who also shows how John describes Jesus in the same way. In the absence of some clearer indication by Ezekiel, however, it remains only a tantalizing possibility.

[99] Actually, in 1 Enoch 51:4 the angels rejoice at the enthronement of the Elect One.

[100] See Hurtado, *One God, One Lord: Early Christian Devotion and Ancient Jewish Monotheism*, 59.

[101] Ibid., 59, though Hurtado is inclined to see them as angels here.

[102] Jacobson, *The* Exagoge *of Ezekiel*, 92.

[103] Ibid., 93, 95-97.

this line the dream does not depict Moses as God (*pace* Bauckham), but only as a king.[104]

Raguel's interpretation leaves no doubt what the Tragedian's basic intent was. The implications of this passage of the *Exagoge* for the prophetic ministry of Moses were considered in Chapter Two, including the possible teaching role indicated by "you will lead (καθηγήσῃ) mortals";[105] the royal implications are much more obvious. This leaves open the question whether Ezekiel meant Moses to be seen as divine *in his capacity* as king, that is, as a divine king, perhaps along the lines of Greco-Roman royal ideology. Viewers of the play may well have been caught up in the divinity of the imagery and thought of Moses as a present god of Israel, along the lines of a Caesar (or a Pharaoh). Philo's decision that at Sinai Moses was made both god and king over Israel illustrates that it is certainly possible to have the cake and eat it too. The precise question of whether Moses was thought of as a divine being or even a god will be taken up in a later portion of this study, but the basic thrust of the passage under consideration here seems to be that Moses was king, necessarily of Israel, possibly (in the grandiose scheme of the Tragedian) of the world.[106]

4.3.1.5 Conclusion

The throne Moses ascends in the *Exagoge* dream is the throne of a king. The location of the throne on Mt. Sinai, combined with the implication that Raguel lived to see the dream's fulfillment, suggest that Moses became king at the Sinai convocation, where the nation was inaugurated. The divine summons to the throne echoes the biblical summons to Moses to ascend the mountain, but is additionally the sort of call that any king claimed to possess. The expansive dominion which Moses appears to inherit is likewise the scope of authority (whether realized or not) to which an ideal king claimed the right. Ezekiel the Tragedian here witnesses to a view of Moses as king.

4.3.2 The Eleventh Sibylline Oracle

The eleventh book of the Sibylline Oracles calls Moses a king (in the same sentence in which God is a great lord or potentate [ἄναξ]).[107] Lines 35-40 deal with Egypt and the Exodus:

---

[104] The Tragedian may also apply the "adopted son" conception of the king to Moses when, in line 100, not long after the dream, God addresses Moses as "my child" (ὦ παῖ). In Hellenism, divine sonship was a typical royal boast.

[105] Pp. 36-37 above. Meeks, *Prophet-King*, 147-49 highlights the passage as an instance of Moses the Prophet-King.

[106] See below on the divinization of Moses, pp. 229-45.

[107] J. J. Collins, trans. "Sibylline Oracles," in *The Old Testament Pseudepigrapha*, ed. James H. Charlesworth, vol. 1, *Apocalyptic Literature and Testaments*, The Anchor

35 Then when the people of twelve tribes, bidden by the Immortal,
36 leave the fruitful plain of destruction
37 and God himself, the prince (ἄναξ), gives a law to men,
38 then a great, great-spirited[108] king (βασιλεύς)will rule the Hebrews,
39 one who has a name from sandy Egypt,
40 a man falsely thought to have Thebes as his homeland.[109]

Moses is here the king of Israel. In fact, here it is his sole attribute. His kingship was probably taken enough for granted that the writer could expect his readers to understand the reference to Moses without having to name him.

4.3.3 Views of Moses as King Attested by Non-Jews

As mentioned earlier, Strabo regarded Moses as a prophet-king.[110] Writing about the turn of the era, in his *Historiae Philippicae*, Pompeius Trogus assigns Moses only the role of leader (*dux*; *apud* Justin, epitome of *Historiae Philippicae*, Book 36, 1.13),[111] though he says that Moses' supposed son Arruas was made king (*rex*; 36, 1.16).[112] The only ancient pagan writer to call Moses a king is the writer known as Pseudacro, who calls him *Moyses, rex Iudeorum, cuius legibus reguntur* ("Moses, king of the Jews, by whose laws they are ruled").[113] This evidence is so scanty it is difficult to say whether it actively reflects Jewish thinking, though it is certainly consonant with it

4.3.4 Philo

Philo has already been drawn into the discussion above. In his biography of Moses, kingship is the main category for discussion: the entire first book

---

Bible Reference Library (New York: Doubleday, 1983), 432 describes the eleventh Sibylline oracle as being clearly Egyptian Jewish and (more tentatively) dateable to the turn of the era (after summarizing the controversy on the question of dating). See his earlier discussion in *The Sibylline Oracles of Egyptian Judaism*, SBL Dissertation Series, no. 13 (Missoula, Mont.: Society of Biblical Literature, 1974), 180 n. 108.

[108] μεγάθυμος; i.e., "high-minded," "mettlesome."

[109] Greek, Joh. Geffcken, ed., *Die Oracula Sibyllina*, Die griechischen christlichen Schriftsteller der ersten drei Jahrhunderte (Leipzig: J. C. Hinrichs'sche Buchhandlung, 1902), 175-78; translation, Collins, "Sibylline Oracles," 434-35.

[110] See above, p. 84.

[111] Menachem Stern, ed. and trans., *Greek and Latin Authors on Jews and Judaism Edited with Introductions, Translations, and Commentary*, vol. 1, *From Herodotus to Plutarch*, Fontes and Res Judaicas Spectantes (Jerusalem: The Israel Academy of Sciences and Humanities, 1974), dating, 332, text 335, translation 337.

[112] Ibid., text, 336, translation, 338.

[113] Menachem Stern, ed. and trans., *Greek and Latin Authors on Jews and Judaism Edited with Introductions, Translations, and Commentary*, vol. 2, *From Tacitus to Simplicitus*, Fontes and Res Judaicas Spectantes (Jerusalem: The Israel Academy of Sciences and Humanities, 1980), 656. Pseudacro cannot be reliably dated.

of *De Vita Mosis* aims to depict Moses as king (*Mos.* 1.334).[114] The second book deals with "allied and consequent matters" (*Mos.* 2.1), i.e., that
he was philosopher, lawgiver, high priest, prophet (*Mos.* 2.2): all roles recognized as requisite to proper kingship.[115] For Philo, Moses is "the truly
perfect ruler" (ὁ τελειοτάτος ἡγεμών; *Mos.* 2.187; also *Virt.* 54, 70;
Praem. 54).[116]

4.3.5 Josephus

Meeks claims that Josephus was "strongly opposed" to monarchy,[117]
though in fact Josephus has no trouble using royal terminology to narrate
the annals of the OT kings,[118] and he calls the Hasmoneans kings.[119] But
while Josephus undoubtedly appreciates Moses as a leader (ὁ ἡγεμών),[120]
not once does he call him a king.

This reluctance is made remarkable by the fact that, as Meeks observes,
"the functions which Josephus attributes to Moses were so naturally associated with kingship."[121] The picture of Moses in Josephus resembles the
description by Diotogenes of the three-fold task of the ruler: he must act as

---

[114] See Erwin R. Goodenough, *By Light, Light: The Mystic Gospel of Hellenistic Judaism* (New Haven, Connecticut: Yale University Press, 1935; reprint, Amsterdam: Philo Press, 1969), 181. The people are his subjects (οἱ ἀρχομένοι, *Mos.* 1.151; *Praem.* 54; οἱ ὑπηκόοι, *Virt.* 57, 72).

[115] Goodenough, *By Light, Light: The Mystic Gospel of Hellenistic Judaism*, 188. Goodenough, 181-98 carefully explores how Philo shows Moses to fulfill the ideals of royal perfection. See also Meeks, *Prophet-King*, 107-17. Outside the *Vita Mosis*, *Praem.* 53-55, and *Spec. Leg.* 4.176, the kingship *per se* of Moses goes totally un- remarked, and references to him as a ruler of any kind are few outside the *Vita*; Meeks, *Prophet-King*, 117 n. 2 lists three, to which may be added *Virt.* 63, 70, 72. See also *Virt.* 58, and on Moses' care for the people in general terms, *Praem.* 77 (cf. *Virt.* 54).

[116] His good character justified his accession, *Mos.* 1.148-49. Goodenough, *The Politics of Philo Judaeus: Practice and Theory*, 50 makes much of this conformity to the Hellenistic ideal of a king. Both Philo (*Praem.* 54; *Mos.* 2.67; cf. *Mos.* 2.142) and Josephus (*Ap.* 2.159) have Moses ruling by popular acclaim, another Hellenistic royal ideal (Goodenough, "The Political Philosophy of Hellenistic Kingship," in *Yale Clas- sical Studies*, ed. Austin M. Harmon, vol. 1 [New Haven: Yale University Press, 1928], 90), along with simultaneous divine appointment, which Moses also enjoys, according to Philo, *Praem.* 54; *Mos.* 1.148; 2.3; *Virt.* 63; and *Tg. Ps.-J.* Deut. 34:5.

[117] Meeks, *Prophet-King*, 135; see Paul Spilsbury, *The Image of the Jew in Flavius Josephus' Paraphrase of the Bible*, Texte und Studien zum Antiken Judentum, ed. Martin Hengel and Peter Schäfer, no. 69 (Tübingen: J. C. B. Mohr [Paul Siebeck], 1998), 137, 160-85.

[118] *Antiquities* 6-10, *passim.*

[119] *Ant.* 13.301, 306, 320, 398, 403, 405-407, 409.

[120] *Ant.* 4.11.

[121] Meeks, *Prophet-King*, 134; see Spilsbury, *The Image of the Jew in Flavius Jose- phus' Paraphrase of the Bible*, 137.

military leader and as supreme judge, and he must worship the gods.[122]
For Josephus, Moses is "the best of generals, the sagest of counselors, and
the most conscientious of guardians";[123] as shown in the previous chapter,
he carries out some important priestly tasks;[124] he is the supreme judge;[125]
he (or his administration) is a great ἀρχή;[126] and like Simon the Hasmonean (*Ant.* 13.228) "he rules" (ἦρξε; *Ant.* 4.327); but he is never βασιλεύς.

The explanation for Josephus's reticence on Moses' kingship, ironically,
may lie in his appreciation of Moses. According to Josephus, Moses
spurned monarchy in favor of theocracy, in which all rule and authority
was vested with God (θεοκρατίαν ἀπέδειξε τὸ πολίτευμα, θεῷ τὴν
ἀρχὴν καὶ τὸ κράτος ἀναθείς; *Ap.* 2.165), and theocracy was realized
through the rule of a priest (*Ap.* 2.194).[127] Even the legend the Rabbis tell,
e.g. in *Exod. Rab.* (שמות) 1.26, wherein the child Moses "used to take the
crown of Pharaoh and place it upon his own head, as he was destined to do
when he became great," appears in Josephus in a form which makes Moses

---

[122] *Apud* Stobaeus 4.7.61, cited by Goodenough, *The Politics of Philo Judaeus:
Practice and Theory*, 97. See too Philo's appraisal of the ideal king in *Plant.* 90, 92,
and Goodenough, "The Political Philosophy of Hellenistic Kingship," 90-91.

[123] *Ap.* 2.158, similarly *Ant.* 3.66, 68, 98; 4.312. Meeks, *Prophet-King*, 133 lists
places where Josephus calls Moses στρατηγός, to which add *Ant.* 3.11, 12, and see
further Spilsbury, *The Image of the Jew in Flavius Josephus' Paraphrase of the Bible*,
95-99. The term can refer to a senior civil official (as in *Ant.* 13.265, of the practor)
and Meeks, *Prophet-King*, 134 seems to favor this with regard to Moses in Josephus; it
fits well in *Ant.* 3.2, 102. But more frequently Josephus uses it to designate a military
commander, whether Moses or someone else (*Ap.* 2.157-58; *Ant.* 2.268; 3.47, 50, 59;
4.82, 159, etc.), while Josephus regularly styles the whole Israelite nation in the wilderness as an army (see *Ant.* 3.5, 70-71; 4.9, 76, 82, 85, 100, 106, 116, 122; 5.16, 38), and
Moses behaves like a general (*Ant.* 3.50-51).

[124] Included with those mentioned in the last chapter is Moses' role as intercessor
(see above, p. 68), which is a role for a king, Goodenough, *The Politics of Philo Judaeus: Practice and Theory*, 119.

[125] *Ant.* 3.66-72.

[126] *Ant.* 4.194 (in subordination to God, *B.J.* 5.383-386; *Ant.* 2.268).

[127] Also *Ap.* 2.158-59; H. St. J. Thackeray, in *Josephus, The Life, Against Apion*,
Loeb Classical Library (Cambridge, Mass. and London: Harvard University Press,
1926), 358 n. a believes the term θεοκρατία was Josephus's invention. The same thing
is called ἀριστοκρατία in *Ant.* 4.223-24. See also Josephus's negative appraisal of
tyranny (τυραννίς; *Ant.* 4.16, 22; 5.338-339; also 4.146; 19.172-84). Priestly rule, according to Josephus, was the Jewish tradition (*Ant.* 4.223-24; 14.41); see Clemens Thoma, "The High Priesthood in the Judgment of Josephus," in *Josephus, the Bible, and
History*, ed. Louis H. Feldman and Gohei Hata (Leiden: E. J. Brill, 1989), 200-202.
Philo also has Agrippa I remark that his ancestors were both kings (βασιλεῖς) and
high priests (ἀρχιερεῖς), but that they considered their priesthood far superior to their
kingship (*Leg.* 278). "King" (βασιλεύς) was a style preferred by certain brigand
leaders (e.g. *Ant.* 17.285, c.f. *B.J.* 2.35).

despise royal dignity, not aspire to it. In Josephus's version, Pharaoh sets the crown on Moses' head himself, "But Moses tore it off and flung it on the ground ... and trampled it underfoot" (*Ant.* 2.233).

4.3.6 Justus of Tiberias

A chronicle by Justus of Tiberias is described in the *Bibliotheca* of Photius (33.6b.23-7.a5) as, *A Chronicle of the Jewish Kings* (Ἰούστου Τιβεριέως Ἰουδαίων Βασιλέων τῶν ἐν τοῖς στέμμασιν).[128] Photius describes it as beginning from Moses and carrying on through to the death of Agrippa II, the last of the Jewish kings (ἄρχεται δὲ τῆς ἱστορίας ἀπὸ Μωϋσέως, καταλήγει δὲ ἕως τελευτῆς Ἀγρίππα τοῦ ἑβδόμου μὲν τῶν ἀπὸ τῆς οἰκίας Ἡρῴδου, ὑστάτου δὲ ἐν τοῖς Ἰουδαίων βασιλεῦσιν). The implication is that Justus considered Moses, like Agrippa II, a king of the Jews.[129]

4.4 Moses as King in Rabbinic Literature

Evidence for consideration of Moses as king in the Targums was incorporated into the examination of the biblical traditions above. By comparison with the evidence that the Targums viewed Moses as a prophet, the evidence for his kingship was comparatively scanty.

The rabbinic literature more strongly perpetuates the tradition of Moses as king. Most opinions involve Deut. 33:5, and so were surveyed above.

Additional rabbinic references include *Sifre* Deut. 357, where, having been told that he may not enter the land, Moses negotiates, "If I may not enter it a king (מלך) I will enter it a commoner."[130]

---

[128] On the historical Justus see Josephus, *Vit.* 36, 40; also Emil Schürer, *The History of the Jewish People in the Age of Jesus Christ (175 BC-AD 135)*, revised by Geza Vermes, Fergus Millar, and Martin Goodman (Edinburgh: T. & T. Clark, 1986), vol. 3, pt. 1, 546. For introduction to his *oeuvre*, see Carl R. Holladay, ed., *Historians*, vol. 1 of *Fragments from Hellenistic Jewish Authors*, Society of Biblical Literature Texts and Translations Pseudepigrapha Series, ed. Harold W. Attridge, Texts and Translations no. 20, Pseudepigrapha no. 10 (Chico, California: Scholars Press, 1983), 371-72; for Greek text of the relevant segment of the *Bibliotheca* of Photius, see Holladay, 375 n. 17.

[129] Cf. the similar, though far less clear, case for Demetrius the Chronographer's *On the Kings of Judaea*, which includes treatment of Moses and the Exodus; see P. M. Fraser, *Ptolemaic Alexandria*, vol. 1, *Text* (Oxford: Clarendon Press, 1972; reprint, 1984), 690-94.

[130] I have modified the translation by Reuven Hammer, *Sifre: A Tannaitic Commentary on the Book of Deuteronomy* (New Haven and London: Yale University Press, 1986), 380.

In light of other rabbinic statements about Moses, *Mek. de-Rabbi Ishmael* 4.10-11 probably also points to an early rabbinic tradition of Moses as a kingly figure: "*And When Moses' Father-in-Law Saw*, etc. What did he see? He saw him behaving like a king (כמלך) who sits on his throne while all the people around him stand" (Ex. 18:14).

In *Pesiq. Rab Kah.* 1.7, R. Aha described the throne of Solomon by comparing it to the seat of Moses, which suggests similar dignity.[131] Midrash *Tanhuma* Buber, Exodus, Parashah 10 (Wayyaqhel).5 on Exodus 35:30 reflects a tradition, also appearing in *b. Zeb.* 102a, assigning priesthood to Aaron and kingship to Moses, and *Midr. Pss.* on Psalm 1:3 suggests a likeness between Moses and Samuel: "For you find. ... The one became king, and the other became king."

The extremely evocative early evidence on Moses' kingship from Ezekiel the Tragedian is complemented by somewhat later and more explicit evidence to the same effect. In every period it is apparent that there were those who viewed Moses as king, probably reflecting a continuous tradition. Such a tradition could have been sustained by a need to make sense of the biblical texts, and certainly one reasonable interpretation of texts like Deut. 33:5 and Exod. 7:1, an interpretation regularly put forward, was that Moses was king of Israel. The Targums and the rabbinic literature both show this, along with earlier literature. The convictions of Philo concerning the kingship of Moses are abundantly clear. They are plainly echoed in the eleventh Sibylline Oracle; and they are probably paralleled in different ways in Justus of Tiberias and Josephus, while they find precedent in yet older material, such as the *Exagoge*, and the reading tradition finally preserved by the Masoretes. Indubitably, one of the images of Moses treasured by the first century A.D. was that of him as a king, as the New Testament itself also shows.

4.5 Moses as King in the New Testament

4.5.1 Mark 6:34-44 and John 6:1-15

Ancient Judaism looked for deliverance in the form of a second Exodus. This included the expected repetition of the blessings of the Exodus, among the most prominent and significant of which was the provision of food.[132] At the feeding of 5000 in John 6 the people quickly connect the

---

[131] That is, like the seat of Moses it had a round top (1 Kings 10:19).

[132] 2 Baruch 29:8; *Mek.* 5.63-65 on Exod. 16:25; *Eccl. Rab.* 1.9; *Tanhuma* Buber 4(Beshallah).21 on Exodus 16:4; 4(Beshallah).24, part 5 (end), on Exod. 16:19-20; see

provision of bread with the provision of manna in the wilderness. The narratives of the feeding are likely to be connected at some basic level with Moses and the story of the Exodus.

4.5.1.1 Mark 6:34-44

Several details of the Markan account suggest a portrayal of something corresponding to the Exodus under Moses, and J. Marcus argues that the feeding story and its context are actually saturated with allusions to the Exodus.[133] For example, the feeding itself is three times (6:31, 32, 35) said to have occurred in a deserted place, and the note that the people were organized into fifties and hundreds might possibly recall Moses marshaling the people (Exod. 18:21, 25).[134]

4.5.1.1.1 Sheep Without a Shepherd

Of special interest is the statement in Mark 6:34 that the people were like sheep without a shepherd. A nearly identical expression occurs at Num. 27:17 (in connection with the death of Moses and the choice of his successor). Given the likely significance of the feeding itself, these words in Mark could easily recall the loss of the leadership of Moses. Jesus' immediate response was not, "he took charge of them," but that "he began to teach them" (6:34). This reaction strengthens the connection with Moses, the teacher of Israel. The obvious implication, however, is that the people had no leader.

Nearly the same expression is also found at 1 Kings 22:17 ‖ 2 Chron. 18:16 (at the death of King Ahab the people were "like sheep which have no shepherd"),[135] while Ezekiel 34:23-24 explicitly identifies the shepherd

---

further, Glasson, *Moses in the Fourth Gospel*, 45-47. See further on the Second Exodus below, pp. 198-99, 280.

[133] Joel Marcus, *Mark 1-8: A New Translation with Introduction and Commentary*, The Anchor Bible, ed. William Foxwell Albright and David Noel Freedman, vol. 27 (New York: Doubleday, 2000), 381, 385, 389-90, 411. Cf. Robert H. Gundry, *Mark: A Commentary on His Apology for the Cross* (Grand Rapids: William B. Eerdmans, 1993), 328.

[134] These, and the connection with Num. 27:17 in the next paragraph below, are noted by Larry W. Hurtado, *Mark*, New International Biblical Commentary, New Testament ed., W. Ward Gasque (Peabody, Massachusetts: Hendrickson, 1989), 100. On the numbering of the people, see Marcus, *Mark 1-8*, 408 and compare 1QS 2.21; CD 13.1; see refs. in Gundry, *Mark: A Commentary on His Apology for the Cross*, 325. Kastner, "Moses im Neuen Testament," 117-18 finds the Markan arrangement of the people into hundreds and fifties a distinct allusion to the Wilderness generation, but finds little other allusion to Moses traditions. Mark 6:39 might allude to Ps. 23:2; Dale C. Allison, Jr., "Psalm 23(22) in Early Christianity: A Suggestion," *Irish Biblical Studies* 5 (July 1983): 134-36 suggests further allusions to Psalm 23 (but note the cautions of Gundry, *Mark: A Commentary on His Apology for the Cross*, 328).

[135] Cf. also Ezek. 34:8; Zech. 10:2; 13:7 and Jdt. 11:19.

of Israel as David the Prince.[136] The association of kingship generally with the tasks of the shepherd is very old, and very enduring in Eastern thought. Israel associated kingship with the tasks of the shepherd before the Greek period,[137] so that Goodenough even argues that Judaism enriched Greek shepherd-king ideology.[138] At any rate, the idea long remained influential in both Greek and Jewish thinking.[139]

In Mark, Montefiore writes, "The phrase ['sheep without a shepherd'] means, according to Old Testament usage ... 'an army without a general, a nation without a national leader.'"[140] Hurtado further surmises, "Immediately following the episode about 'King' Herod, this account [Mark's] suggests that Jesus is the rightful king and the true leader of Israel."[141] The conclusion that the need of proper kingship is at issue in Mark[142] is corroborated by the explicitly royal ideas in the Johannine presentation of the same event (on which see below), while the response of Jesus (teaching, not ruling) is again evocative of Moses.

The link between shepherds and kings has special applicability to Moses. The Pentateuch gives Moses a background as a herdsman and implies that he was Israel's shepherd (Num. 27:16-20), as does Isa. 63:11. J. Kastner argues that "the great shepherd of the sheep" of Heb. 13:20 is a reference

---

[136] Note the proximity of Ezek. 34:8; E. Bammel, "The Feeding of the Multitude," in *Jesus and the Politics of His Day*, ed. Ernst Bammel and C. F. D. Moule (Cambridge: Cambridge University Press, 1984), 217 argues that Ezekiel 34 is itself an interpretation of Num. 27:17 in Davidic terms.

[137] Mowinckel, "General Oriental and Specific Israelite Elements in the Israelite Conception of the Sacral Kingdom," 288; see also J. Jeremias, "ποιμήν κτλ.," in *Theological Dictionary of the New Testament*, ed. Gerhard Friedrich, trans. and ed. Geoffrey W. Bromiley, vol. 6, *Πε-Ρ* (Grand Rapids: Wm. B. Eerdmans, 1968), 486-88, and a text ca. 2000 B.C. in James B. Pritchard, ed., *Ancient Near Eastern Texts Relating to the Old Testament*, trans. W. F. Albright, et al. (Princeton, New Jersey: Princeton University Press, 1950), 443. No ruling OT king is ever called a shepherd, but the Lord's charge to David in 2 Sam. 5:2 ‖ 1 Chron. 11:2 couples the two functions, and the motif recurs in Ps. 78:71-72; see John F. X. Sheehan, "Feed My Lambs," *Scripture* 16 (1964): 21-27. The people of Israel are often compared to a flock: 2 Sam. 24:17 ‖ 1 Chron. 21:17; Ps. 77:20[MT 21]; 78:52; Jer. 31:10; Ezekiel 34 throughout, esp. vv. 5, 31; Zech. 10:2.

[138] Goodenough, *The Politics of Philo Judaeus: Practice and Theory*, 94-95.

[139] E.g. *Iliad* 1.263; 2.243. Philo links the rule of kings with shepherding (*Jos.* 2-3; *Mos.* 1.61-62; *Quod Omn. Prob.* 30-31). See Goodenough, *The Politics of Philo Judaeus: Practice and Theory*, 45-46. Raymond E. Brown, *The Gospel According to John (xiii-xxi)*, The Anchor Bible, ed. William Foxwell Albright and David Noel Freedman, vol. 29A (Garden City, New York: Doubleday and Co., 1970), 1113-16 traces the motif of the shepherd as authority figure into NT times. See also *Midr. Pss.* 78 §21.

[140] Hugh Montefiore, "Revolt in the Desert? (Mark VI.30ff)," *New Testament Studies* 8 (1961-1962): 136.

[141] Hurtado, *Mark*, 100.

[142] Thus Montefiore, "Revolt in the Desert? (Mark VI.30ff)," 136.

to Moses in Is. 63:11.[143] Philo treats Moses as a shepherd-become-king in *Mos.* 1.60. In the rabbinic literature extensive links between Moses and David as shepherds and as kings appear.[144] The figure of Moses is fully part of the Jewish shepherd-king myth.

In saying, in a context rich in other allusions to the Exodus, that the people were "like sheep without a shepherd," the text seems to allude to needs both for a true king and for Moses.

4.5.1.1.2 A Mosaic King

Marcus argues that the Markan passage "strengthens the impression that Jesus is both the Davidic Messiah and a Mosaic figure."[145] Curiously, Marcus identifies no Davidic elements in the text, while at the same time he detects many Mosaic elements.[146] The present chapter has demonstrated that Jews often thought of Moses as a king, while the Markan pericope points to Moses in the same role. The gathering of people in a desert(ed) place recalls not only the Exodus, but also numerous (some explicitly royalist) messianic movements of the period.[147] The Markan passage might therefore better be said to link Jesus to a royal Mosaic figure than to "both the Davidic Messiah and a Mosaic figure," as Marcus seems simply to assume. There is no Davidic messiah to be found here, only a true Mosaic king or, to paraphrase Marcus, a Mosaic messiah figure. The people, when described as "sheep without a shepherd," especially in a context with so many other Mosaic connotations, are described as standing in need of their true, Mosaic king.[148]

4.5.1.2 John 6:1-15

John seems to indulge in none of the pointed symbolism (sheep, shepherds, Exodus imagery) found in Mark's account. Jesus ascends a mountain, but

---

[143] Kastner, "Moses im Neuen Testament," 265-66.

[144] *B. Suk.* 52b; *Exod. Rab.* 2(שמות).2; *Exod. Rab.* 2(שמות).3 connect both David and Moses as kings with shepherding. Also, in *Midr. Pss.* 77 §3 on 77:12 and *Midr. Pss.* 78 §17 on 78:52 (discussing Ezek. 34:31), Israel is a flock led by Moses and Aaron. See further on Moses as shepherd, Louis Ginzberg, *The Legends of the Jews*, vol. 5 (Philadelphia: The Jewish Publication Society of America, 1925), 130 n. 142; 414 n. 109.

[145] Marcus, *Mark 1-8*, 406.

[146] Ibid., 406, 417, 419.

[147] E.g. the Egyptian (*B.J.* 2.262; Acts 21:38), Jonathan the Sicarius (*B.J.* 7.438), some unnamed leaders (*B.J.* 2.259; *Ant.* 20.167); cf. Matt. 24:24-26. Montefiore, "Revolt in the Desert? (Mark VI.30ff)," 135-41 argues that Mark 6:30-47 is another such account.

[148] To the extent that Ezekiel 34 stands behind the pericope, David the Prince (Ezek. 34:23-24) also stands behind it. Within the passage, however, all the allusions seem to run toward Moses and the Exodus, and this must be judged the dominant motif.

only uses the height to observe the crowd. John notes that "there was much grass in the place" where Jesus commanded that the people lie down, but this does not sustain the allusion to (the pastoral) Psalm 23 found by some commentators.

More promising is E. Bammel's suggestion that the mountain of John's story is the mountain of Ezekiel 34 (Ezek. 34:13-14 especially), a parallel which might also be extended to the feature of lying down on green grass (Ezek. 34:14). The link is favored by the possible connection between Ezekiel 34, in which Israel is a flock in need of a good shepherd, and the Markan account just reviewed.[149] Partly on that basis, reflections on Ezekiel 34 seem likely to have formed part of the tradition John knew rather than to have been part of the design of his own presentation.[150]

The interest of John's feeding account for this study lies in that where Mark employs suggestion, John employs assertion, but still points to a Mosaic king. For Meeks, this is the passage which finally establishes the link in the Fourth Gospel between the prophet like Moses and kingship.[151]

In John, the revelation of the significance of the feeding is left until the end of the pericope when the people, perceiving what has happened, acclaim Jesus as "the Prophet who is to come." There can be little doubt what prophet is meant.[152] The discourse (John 6:26-59) which follows revolves around the manna in the wilderness and its significance, with 6:32 mentioning Moses by name. The "Prophet who is coming into the world" in 6:14 is the prophet like Moses, a "well-known eschatological figure,"[153] who was expected in fulfillment of Deut. 18:15. Where Mark only suggests (though strongly) that the feeding miracle is the act of a Mosaic figure, John makes it explicit.

What follows this recognition in John complements the royal symbolism of Mark with narrative action. Once the people recognized Jesus as the expected Prophet, John 6:15 continues, "Jesus *therefore* knew that they were about to come and seize him to make him king (βασιλέα)."[154] The

---

[149] See above, pp. 108-109.

[150] Bammel, "The Feeding of the Multitude," 217, 220, who notes the unelaborated condition of these references as signs of the appearance of original tradition.

[151] Meeks, *Prophet-King*, 87-99, esp. 98-99.

[152] Despite efforts to forge a connection with Elisha's feeding miracle in 2 Kings 4:42-44, e.g., Ernst Haenchen, *John 1: A Commentary on the Gospel of John Chapters 1-6*, trans. Robert W. Funk, ed. Robert W. Funk with Ulrich Busse, Hermeneia — A Critical and Historical Commentary on the Bible, ed. Frank Moore Cross, Helmut Koester, et al. (Philadelphia: Fortress Press, 1984), 271-72; Schnackenburg, *The Gospel According to St John*, vol. 2, *Commentary on Chapters 5-12*, 15-16.

[153] Meeks, *Prophet-King*, 90; see also 21-25.

[154] Meeks, therefore, holds that Jesus is here designated "prophet-king," in the mold of Moses. This is disputed by Rudolf Schnackenburg, *Jesus in the Gospels: A Biblical Christology*, trans. O. C. Dean, Jr. (Louisville, Kentucky: Westminster John Knox

apparent "fit" of the two elements — the Prophet like Moses and kingship — in the narrative urges the kingly rank of Moses in current thinking.[155] The account can hardly remain coherent if Moses and his expected successor were not seen as kings.

For Meeks, the intention of the crowd to make Jesus king "is revealed to the reader only by the indirect device of Jesus' supernatural knowledge."[156] This implies that the crowd's reaction is a surprising one. If, however, the author and his readers (and Jesus) understood Moses to have been a king, and therefore knew the Prophet like Moses to be a kingly figure, then the crowd's reaction is entirely expected, and Jesus' perception quite natural. Meeks here has not read the account in the full light of contemporary views of Moses as king, views which, oddly enough, he is writing generally to emphasize.

4.5.1.3 Conclusion

Many scholars agree that if John was not either dependent on, or familiar with, Mark, then both evangelists drew independently on a common core of tradition.[157] Perhaps the references in John to the mountain and to the

---

Press, 1995), 72-73, who holds that the two designations remain distinguished. See also Marinus de Jonge, "Jesus as Prophet and King in the Fourth Gospel," *Ephemerides Theologicae Lovaniensis* 49, no. 1 (May 1973): 160-77 and Bammel, "The Feeding of the Multitude," 217.

[155] Cf. also the change of address between John 6:25 and 6:34.

[156] Meeks, *Prophet-King*, 89.

[157] For the latter, Meeks, *Prophet-King*, 91. C. K. Barrett, *The Gospel According to St John: An Introduction with Commentary and Notes on the Greek Text*, 2d ed. (London: SPCK, 1978), 43-45 argues for Johannine dependency on canonical Mark; he is rebutted by Leon Morris, *The Gospel according to John*, rev. ed., The New International Commentary on the New Testament, ed. Gordon D. Fee (Grand Rapids: William B. Eerdmans, 1995), 44-45. B. Lindars, *The Gospel of John*, New Century Bible, ed. R. E. Clements and M. Black (London: Oliphants, 1972), 237-38 argues that John used a more primitive version of the same tradition that appears in Mark and Matthew. P. Gardner-Smith, *Saint John and the Synoptic Gospels* (Cambridge: The University Press, 1938), 27-33, P. N. Anderson, *The Christology of the Fourth Gospel: Its Unity and Disunity in the Light of John 6*, WUNT/2, ed. Martin Hengel and Otfried Hofius, no. 78 (Tübingen: J. C. B. Mohr [Paul Siebeck], 1996), 97-103, and Edwin D. Johnston, "The Johannine Version of the Feeding of the Five Thousand — An Independent Tradition?," *New Testament Studies* 8 (1961-1962): 151-54 emphasize the independence of John, e.g., "The Johannine version of the feeding and the sea crossing is radically distinctive, as contrasted to parallel accounts in Mark 6 and 8, and this distinctiveness extends both to matters of detail and interpretation. The distinctiveness of John 6:1-24 is especially striking given its high degree of sequential and linguistic correlation with the Marcan tradition. Therefore, John's independent account will be analyzed as the evangelist's reflection upon (dialogue with) his tradition," Anderson, 170. Older bibliography in Werner Georg Kümmel, *Introduction to the New Testament*, rev. ed., trans. Howard Clark Kee (London: SCM Press, 1975), 200-204.

grass are remnants brought forward from that portion of the tradition more fully expressed in Mark. Perhaps the hasty departures of Jesus and the disciples in Mark are somehow connected with the situation described in John 6:14-15, as both Bammel and J. A. T. Robinson argue.[158] In any case, each evangelist appears to find the tradition recognizing in Jesus a royalty that is Mosaic. Mark and John both attest the conception of Moses as king. The presence of such strongly complementary details in their accounts of the feeding probably throws the connection between Moses and kingship back to the early first century A.D.

4.5.2 Titles of Moses in Acts 7:35

Moses is identified explicitly as Israel's sovereign in the New Testament in Acts 7:35, where Stephen affirms of Moses: τοῦτον ὁ θεὸς ἄρχοντα καὶ λυτρωτὴν ἀπέσταλκεν ("God has sent this ruler and redeemer"). In this section it will be argued, first, that this nomenclature fits within a milieu that saw Moses as king, and second, that it also actively implies Moses' kingship.

4.5.2.1 Ἄρχων

The term ἄρχων is employed with a broad range of meaning in Hellenistic Greek, and has clear upward potential in Jewish usage.[159] The clearest, most dramatic evidence, from the Greek Ezekiel, suggests not only that ἄρχων was thought appropriate for the most exalted rank of ruler, but perhaps (for the translators of Ezekiel at least) only for the most exalted rank.[160] In the Greek version of Ezekiel, ἄρχων is used of kings, as in Ἰεζεκ. 34:24 of the eschatological David (MT: נשׂיא), in Ἰεζεκ. 28:2 and 12 of the king of Tyre (MT: נגיד and מלך), and in Ἰεζεκ. 7:27; 12:10, 12 of the king in Jerusalem. In Ἰεζεκ. 37:22 the Lord promises one day to reunite Israel in one βασιλεία — under one ἄρχων (MT: מלך). In Ἰεζεκ. 37:24, 25 this eschatological ruler is identified as David, but where the MT calls David "king" (מלך), the LXX reads ὁ δοῦλός μου Δαυιδ ἄρχων.

---

[158] Bammel, "The Feeding of the Multitude," 223-24; J. A. T. Robinson, "'His Witness is True': A Test of the Johannine Claim," in *Jesus and the Politics of His Day*, ed. Ernst Bammel and C. F. D. Moule (Cambridge: Cambridge University Press, 1984), 463-64.

[159] According to Hatch and Redpath, in the LXX ἄρχων translates thirty-six different Hebrew expressions; see also Gerhard Delling, "ἄρχω κτλ.," in *Theological Dictionary of the New Testament*, ed. Gerhard Kittel, trans. and ed. Geoffrey W. Bromiley, vol. 4, *Α-Γ* (Grand Rapids: Wm. B. Eerdmans, 1964), 488-489. It is among the titles applied to Moses by Philo (*Mos.* 2.214, 226, 235, 260).

[160] All foreign kings are ἄρχων, and in the MT are נשׂיא. Aristocrats or officials in the LXX are ἀφηγούμενοι. See Ἰεζεκ. 26:16; 27:21; 30:13; 32:29; 38:2-3; 39:1, 18; cf. Ἰεζεκ. 21:17, 30; 22:6.

The Greek version of Ezekiel is a key witness to this usage but not the sole one. Beyond Ezekiel, Balaam discerns in Israel the shout of a מלך in Num. 23:21, but the glories of ἀρχόντων in the LXX version. In Γεν. 49:10 the Judahite, and probably messianic, king is the ἄρχων.[161] As noted before, the LXX translators turn the מלך in Deut. 33:5 into an eschatological (and almost certainly therefore messianic) ἄρχων, while the מלך of Israel becomes an ἄρχων in Δευτ. 17:14-20 (the Law of the King) and 28:36 (Aquila, Symmachus, and Theodotion all later returned in these places to explicitly royal terminology[162]). A. Rofé observes that, apart from four references in Genesis,[163] whenever in the LXX Pentateuch a king of Israel is mentioned his title consistently is ἄρχων. Rofé believes the phenomenon goes back to pre-LXX tradition, concluding that the Hebrew Vorlage of the Greek Pentateuch contained a recension in which all Israelite kings were denominated princes.[164]

The change in terminology may have had any of several motivations, such as that the translators had no wish needlessly to arouse the jealous suspicions of their Ptolemaic rulers, or that among the Jews the title "king" had for some reason come to be reserved exclusively to God.[165] The important point to notice is that Jews were self-consciously using ἄρχων as the title for their supreme ruler, even for the eschatological David.

Philo, it is true, happily describes Moses as βασιλεύς. Philo, however, is interested in the kingship of Moses primarily for its payoff in the world of ideas, not politics. Even if Philo were inclined to restrict kingship to

---

[161] See further, Horbury, *Jewish Messianism and the Cult of Christ*, 48-49, 178-79 n. 35.

[162] See Cécile Dogniez and Marguerite Harl, *Le Deutéronome: Traduction du texte grec de la Septante, Introduction et Notes*, vol. 5 in *La Bible d'Alexandrie*, ed. Marguerite Harl (Paris: Les Éditions du Cerf, 1992), 225. The LXX Deuteronomy uses βασιλεύς only of heathen kings (and not always of them), Camponovo, *Königtum, Königsherrschaft und Reich Gottes in den frühjüdischen Schriften*, 387.

[163] Abraham is a βασιλεύς παρὰ θεοῦ in Γεν. 23:6; βασιλεῖς will come forth from Abraham (Γεν. 17:6, 16) and from Jacob (Γεν. 35:11), and a βασιλέα reigns in Israel (Γεν. 36:31). Additionally, Ψ. 104:15 (following the MT Ps. 105:15) calls Abraham, Isaac and Jacob χριστοί.

[164] Alexander Rofé, "Qumranic Paraphrases, the Greek Deuteronomy and the Late History of the Biblical נשיא," *Textus* 14 (1988): 170.

[165] I.e., "king of Israel"; Gentile rulers may still appear as king in the LXX. For discussion on possible motives for the changes here, and also in the LXX of Ezekiel 34 and 37, see Dogniez and Harl, *Deutéronome*, 225; in favor of the latter, see Rofé, "Qumranic Paraphrases, the Greek Deuteronomy and the Late History of the Biblical נשיא," 172-73. Richard A. Freund, "From Kings to Archons: Jewish Political Ethics and Kingship Passages in the LXX," *Scandinavian Journal of the Old Testament* (1990, part 2): 62-71, critiqued by Horbury, *Jewish Messianism and the Cult of Christ*, 179 n. 35, suggests a change in Jewish political theory.

God, for such a person as Moses, who shared with the Self-Existent even the title "god," the title "king" was nothing to scruple at.

Again, however, the phenomenon is not limited to the Greek tradition. Rofé postulates a Vorlage to LXX Ezekiel which, like the one he suspects for the Pentateuch, regards kings as princes.[166] Indeed, the tendency is apparent even in the MT of Ezekiel.[167] This suggests that not only ἄρχων but also נשיא was being used of kings. The explanations offered for the LXX usage of ἄρχων would naturally apply to Semitic terminology as well; in fact, if the religious and sociological explanations for the LXX nomenclature are correct they predict equivalent changes in Semitic usage.

It comes as no surprise then that Meeks observes the Qumran texts "avoid altogether the term 'king' as a designation for the royal 'Messiah of Israel.'"[168] Rofé calls attention to CD 5.1-2 where the Law of the King is made the Law of the נשיא. Concerning Deut. 17:17, "He should not multiply wives to himself," it is said, "And about the prince (הנשיא) it is written." Moreover, David the king *par excellence* is then made the exemplary נשיא,[169] and so נשיא becomes David's royal title.[170] The "scepter" of Num. 24:17, widely understood as a messianic passage,[171] is in CD 7:19-20, "the prince of the whole congregation" (נשיא כל העדה). In 1QSb 5.20 again the נשיא העדה appears, who will establish the kingdom (מלכות) for his people (5.21), who carries a scepter (5.24, 27) and is viewed as a world ruler (5.22-28) — a king under the title נשיא.[172] The use of "prince" for "king" in Semitic sources thus corroborates the view that, for many Jews, נשיא and ἄρχων were the highest rank of ruler.

Corroboration from a later date comes from Bar Kokhba, who takes the title "prince of Israel" (נשיא ישראל), as shown on numerous manuscripts

---

[166] Rofé, "Qumranic Paraphrases, the Greek Deuteronomy and the Late History of the Biblical נשיא," 172-73.

[167] The only difference is that the MT does not restrict נשיא to kings as the LXX does ἄρχων.

[168] Meeks, *Prophet-King*, 21; for details see 165-68.

[169] Rofé, "Qumranic Paraphrases, the Greek Deuteronomy and the Late History of the Biblical נשיא," 170.

[170] Also, the leader of the Sons of Light in their battle against the Sons of Darkness is called the נשיא in 1QM 5.1, as is the leader of The Ten Thousand in 1QM 3.16. The commanders of the twelve tribes, whose names are written on his shield, are also called נשיאים in 1QM 3.3, 15. See H. Niehr, "נָשִׂיא nāśî'," *Theologisches Wörterbuch zum Neuen Testament*, ed. G. Johannes Botterweck, Helmer Ringgren, and Heinz-Josef Fabry, vol. 4, מרד־עזב (Stuttgart: W. Kohlhammer, 1986), 656 on interchange at Qumran between נשיא and שר.

[171] Horbury, *Jewish Messianism and the Cult of Christ*, 44-45.

[172] More references from Qumran material in Rofé, "Qumranic Paraphrases, the Greek Deuteronomy and the Late History of the Biblical נשיא," 173.

and coins from his reign.[173] At the same time, the application to him of the prophecy of Num. 24:17 indicates that he was regarded even with this title as the messianic king.[174] Eusebius knows about this (*H.E.* 4.6.2), and a *baraitha* in the name of Simeon b. Yohai claims that Aqiba applied this verse to Bar Kokhba and considered him מלכא משיחא (*y. Taan.* 68d.48-51).[175]

Thus, it appears that the description of Moses in Acts 7 as ἄρχων may support an appreciation of him as king. To speak of him as ἄρχων and not as βασιλεύς no more downgrades his rank than it does that of David, or of the Messiah. (The LXX translation of Deut. 33:5, considered above, needs to be appreciated in the same light.) The importance of the title ἄρχων in Acts 7:35 is suggested not only by contemporary usage, but also by its repetition in the speech of Stephen, by the specific reminder that Moses obtained this distinction by God's appointment (a king's boast, incidentally), by the loftiness of the passage overall,[176] and by the coupling of this title with the term λυτρωτής.

---

[173] See, among the Murabb‘ât papyri, Document no. 24: Col. B, lines 2-3, 9-10; col. C, lines 2-3, 8-9; col. D, lines 2-3; col. E, lines 2-3; col. F, line 3; col. G; col. I, line 1; "Letter no. 1," col. 1, line 1 (in Y. Yadin, "Expedition D," *Israel Exploration Journal* 11, nos. 1-2 [The Expedition to the Judean Desert, 1960] [1961]: 41 and more fully as P. Yadin 54 in Yigael Yadin, et al., eds., *The Documents from the Bar Kokhba Period in the Cave of Letters: Hebrew, Aramaic, and Nabatean-Aramaic Papyri*, Judean Desert Studies [Jerusalem: Israel Exploration Society, Hebrew University Institute of Archaeology, Israel Museum Shrine of the Book, 2002], 305-308); P. Yadin 42 (a lease agreement), line 1, in Yadin, et al., *Documents from the Bar Kokhba Period in the Cave of Letters*, 142-49; and coins from the first year of his revolt in Ya‘akov Meshorer, *Jewish Coins of the Second Temple Period*, trans. by I. H. Levine (Tel-Aviv: Am Hassefer, 1967), 94, 159-160, with plate XXI.

[174] *Pace* Yigael Yadin, et al., "Bar-Kokhba's Title," in *Documents from the Bar Kokhba Period in the Cave of Letters*, 369-72.

[175] See Horbury, *Jewish Messianism and the Cult of Christ*, 92.

[176] Gustav Stählin, *Die Apostelgeschichte*, Das Neue Testament Deutsch, ed. Paul Althaus and Gerhard Friedrich, no. 5 (Göttingen: Vandenhoeck & Ruprecht, 1966), 109 describes Acts 7:35-38 as a kind of Moses-hymn, of the same sort as the Christ-hymn of Col. 1:13-20, which served as a kind of confession of Moses. See discussion in C. K. Barrett, *A Critical and Exegetical Commentary on the Acts of the Apostles*, vol. 1, *Preliminary Introduction and Commentary on Acts I-XIV*, The International Critical Commentary on the Holy Scriptures of the Old and New Testaments, ed. J. A. Emerton, C. E. B. Cranfield, and G. N. Stanton (Edinburgh: T. & T. Clark, 1994) 362-63.

4.5.2.2 Λυτρωτής

In its sole NT appearance, λυτρωτής displaces δικαστής in a quotation of Exod. 2:14. The substitution seems pointed.[177] In Jewish thought Moses remained the archetypal deliverer,[178] and among non-Jews, "two events of Moses' career form the core of practically every pagan account of Moses — his leadership of the exodus from Egypt and his status as the lawgiver of the Jews."[179]

The related epithet Σωτήρ recurs in Hellenistic dynasties. The role of deliverer was part of Hellenistic royal ideology, and part of a monarch's claim to the throne.[180]

Kingly deliverance is important in Jewish thought as well. 1QM 11.1-8 conceives of divine deliverance as given through kings. Philo assumed the concept, according to Goodenough, and "in the section on the Roman emperor it will appear that Philo knew and used that title (Σωτήρ; *Flac.*

---

[177] Contrast Acts 7:27, 35a. A saving judge is also found in *Tg. Is.* 19:20. Barrett, *Commentary on Acts*, 1.363, on the other hand, seems to suggest that δικαστής was dropped from Acts 7:35b because it was too lofty.

[178] "'Erloser' (Übersetzung: 'Befreier' — Ps. 18:15 LXX; 77:35 LXX) Luke 24:21," Gottfried Schille, *Die Apostelgeschichte des Lukas*, Theologischer Handkommentar zum Neuen Testament, ed. Erich Fascher, Joachim Rohde and Christian Wolff, no. 5 (Berlin. Evangelische Verlagsanstalt, 1983), 183; also F. Büchsel, "λύω κτλ.," *Theological Dictionary of the New Testament*, ed. Gerhard Kittel, trans. and ed. Geoffrey W. Bromiley, vol. 4, *Λ-Ν* (Grand Rapids: Wm. B. Eerdmans, 1967), 351. God is λυτρωτής in Ψ. 18:15; 77:35, but many human deliverers appear in biblical traditions, e.g. in Is. 19:20; 59:20; 62:11; Obad. 21. In Judges the leaders are sometimes called saviors, e.g. Judg. 2:18; 3:9, 15, 31; 6:14; 10:1; 13:5. See also *Tg. Is.* 19:20; 46:13; 59:20. Moses is a redeemer in, e.g., Heb. 3:16; Exod. 32:7 (cf. 19:5; 20:2), with 32:11 and the concluding 32:14; see also discussion in Scott J. Hafemann, *Paul, Moses, and the History of Israel: The Letter/Spirit Contrast and the Argument from Scripture in 2 Corinthians 3*, WUNT, ed. Martin Hengel and Otfried Hofius, no. 81 (Tübingen: J. C. B. Mohr [Paul Siebeck], 1995), 199-201. In *Tg. Ps.-J.* Exod. 6:16 Moses and Aaron are "the redeemers of Israel," and a familiar midrashic refrain is, "As the first redeemer (Moses), so the final (or second) redeemer (Messiah)," *Eccl. Rab.* 1.28 on 1:9 and many other references listed in J. Jeremias, "Μωυσῆς," in *Theological Dictionary of the New Testament*, ed. Gerhard Kittel, trans. and ed. Geoffrey W. Bromiley, vol. 4, *Λ-Ν* (Grand Rapids: Wm. B. Eerdmans, 1967), 860-63.

[179] John G. Gager, *Moses in Greco-Roman Paganism*, Society of Biblical Literature Monograph Series, ed. Robert A. Kraft, no. 16 (Nashville and New York: Abingdon Press, 1972), 21.

[180] See Gerhard Friedrich, "εὐαγγελίζομαι κτλ.," in *Theological Dictionary of the New Testament*, ed. Gerhard Friedrich, trans. and ed. Geoffrey W. Bromiley, vol. 2, *Δ-Η* (Grand Rapids: Wm. B. Eerdmans, 1964), 724 and Wilfred L. Knox, *Some Hellenistic Elements in Primitive Christianity*, The Schweich Lectures of the British Academy, 1942 (London: Oxford University Press, 1944), 37 with n. 3. Moses appears in such a role in Josephus *Ant.* 4.312. Cf. Bock, *Proclamation from Prophecy and Pattern: Lucan Old Testament Christology*, 78.

74, 126; *Leg.* 22), while God as ruler is Savior and Benefactor throughout his writings (e.g. *Opif.* 169; *Leg. All.* 2.56)."[181]

While not by itself determinative of royal status, the obviously deliberate addition of λυτρωτής to the titles ἄρχων and δικαστής in Acts 7:35 adds to the overall *gravitas* of the passage and heightens the exaltation of Moses in a manner certainly consistent with a view of him as king.

4.5.2.3 Conclusion

The apologetic function of Stephen's speech suggests an appeal to acknowledged tradition rather than a fresh departure in thinking about Moses. This is true whether the speech is conceived of as a first-century Jewish oration or simply interpreted in its present context as a specimen of Christian apologia.[182] Even if a precise identification of provenance is unattainable, there is no reason not to expect that the speech carefully exploits, and thereby witnesses to, authentic Jewish opinion about Moses.

4.5.3 Moses as a King in God's House in Hebrews 3:1-6

In the previous chapter this study already considered Heb. 3:1-6 with reference to Moses as priest and apostle. This, however, should not be taken to exhaust the significance for Moses of this text, which also seems to harbor allusions to his kingship. To be a priest would not rule out being a king, nor would being a king rule out being a priest: Moses and John Hyrcanus have already been noted as holders of multiple offices in the writings of Philo and Josephus respectively. Note also Philo, *QE* 2.105, "The early kings were at the same time high priests who by their acts showed that those who rule over others should themselves be servants in ministering to God." In Hebrews itself Melchizedek is "king of Salem, priest of the Most High God" (7:1), while Jesus is "a high priest who has taken his seat at the right hand of the throne of the Majesty in heaven" (8:1).[183]

---

[181] Goodenough, *The Politics of Philo Judaeus*, 97; he adds, God's rule is always saving (σωτηρίως; e.g. *Conf.* 98; *Abr.* 70; *Jos.* 149; *Dec.* 60, 155; *Praem.* 34).

[182] Barrett, *Commentary on the Acts of the Apostles*, vol. 1, 338 maintains that Stephen's speech is most probably a pre-Christian Hellenist-Jewish sermon; William Manson, *The Epistle to the Hebrews: An Historical and Theological Reconsideration*, The Baird Lecture, 1949 (London: Hodder and Staughton, 1951), 27, "a written document of some kind."

[183] See further, James Hamilton Charlesworth, *The Old Testament Pseudepigrapha and the New Testament: Prolegomena for the Study of Christian Origins*, Society for New Testament Studies Monograph Series, ed. G. N. Stanton, vol. 54 (Cambridge: Cambridge University Press, 1985), 84; cf. H. Anderson, "The Jewish Antecedents of the Christology in Hebrews," in *The Messiah: Developments in Earliest Judaism and Christianity*, ed. James H. Charlesworth, et al. (Minneapolis: Fortress Press, 1992), 530.

In Heb. 3:2 it is said of Moses that he was faithful in all God's house (ἐν ὅλῳ τῷ οἴκῳ αὐτοῦ). Heb. 3:5 further explains, "Moses was faithful in all God's house as a servant (ὡς θεράπων)." Two elements tie these thoughts to concepts of kingship: Moses' status as a "servant" of God, and his faithful service in God's "house."

4.5.3.1 Moses as Servant

"Servant," of course, is a fairly bland term, with connotations that depend much more on the context in which the word appears than on the word itself. In the Hellenistic period the conception of the king as the special servant of God was important, but naturally God could have other kinds of servants as well. Moses especially is the "servant of God," notably in Num. 12:7-8 (verses quoted in Heb. 3:2, 5), where servanthood is connected with his role as a prophet.[184] In Chapter Three the special conception of the priest, and especially of Moses as priest, as a "servant in God's house" came into discussion in connection with the same passage in Hebrews. In a text as complex as Heb. 3:1-6, in which a figure as grand as Moses is given no explicit identification other than "servant" (one of the most important titles of Moses in the Pentateuch), it may be impossible to disentangle the different strands of meaning gathered up in that one term.

Thus, it may not be realistic to expect to distill a single significance out of the reference to Moses as servant in Heb. 3:1-6. To choose between "priest" and "king" seems particularly unnecessary, since Hebrews itself so clearly holds out the possibility of priest-kings. In light of all of this, perhaps the conclusions of the previous chapter about the priestly and apostolic Mosaic servant of Heb. 3:1-6 should be amended to include the kingliness of the servant as well.[185]

4.5.3.2 God's House

The term "servant," with its inherent plasticity, is one thing, but the last chapter of the present study only stopped just short of declaring the "house" of Heb. 3:1-6 to be God's tabernacle (although the best evidence supporting this equation was Samaritan, not Jewish), and a tabernacle is not a palace. Pausing only for another hasty appeal to the high priest Jesus, who both sits beside the throne of heaven (Heb. 8:1) and ministers in the sanctuary and in the true tabernacle (Heb. 8:2), we leave this awkward objection to one side momentarily.

---

[184] See above, p. 33 n. 5. W. D. Davies, *The Setting of the Sermon on the Mount* (Cambridge: The University Press, 1964), 39 observed in connection with different material, "It has become clear that the concepts of the Messiah and the Servant of the Lord . . . were probably fused . . . in pre-Christian Judaism, with the figure of Moses."

[185] And see above on similarly combined roles in the Josephan portrait of John Hyrcanus, pp. 78, 85, 87.

4.5.3.2.1 Kingdom as Locality

While the concept of the king as a special servant of God can be traced back into Judaism prior to the New Testament, the concept of the kingdom of God as a place is less evident.[186] Jesus seems to have made a fresh departure in this regard by giving the kingdom of God a strong, local flavor in his teachings.[187] "The kingdom of God [in the teaching of Jesus] ... is to be understood as a community, a house, an area where the goods of salvation are available and received."[188] Jesus' teaching about the kingdom and its nature subsequently become fundamental to the NT view of the kingdom of God, with likely ramifications for Hebrews.[189] Aalen singles out 1 Chron. 17:14 as a key launch point for the NT notion of a local kingdom, a verse which also plays a key role in Heb. 3:1-6.[190]

4.5.3.2.2 God's House as Kingdom and Temple

Hebrews 3:1-6 is ordinarily considered an interpretation of Num. 12:7, based on its apparent quotation of that verse in 3:2. God's "house" in Num. 12:7, and therefore in Heb. 3:2 as well, is usually regarded either as the Temple or the tabernacle, or as something like God's "affairs," or perhaps Israel itself. Aalen, however, asserts that Heb. 3:2 treats not only Num. 12:7 but also the prophecy of Nathan in 1 Chron. 17:4-14,[191] where God's house is at times the Temple, but at other times David's kingdom and dynasty.[192] This insight opens the way for detecting a wave of double-entendres in Hebrews involving a "house," the kingdom-temple where God is served by a prophet-priest-king.

---

[186] Aalen, "'Reign' and 'House' in the Kingdom of God in the Gospels," 220 asserts, "the thought that the kingdom of God is an area into which one enters cannot be documented from Jewish texts at all. ... [Of the few texts employing ἐν or ב with βασι-λεία or מלכות] only in 1 Chron. 17:14 may perhaps the translation 'in the kingdom' be the adequate one."

[187] Ibid., 220, 227-31.

[188] Ibid., 222-23; see also 228-29.

[189] Ibid., 240.

[190] Ibid., 220, 233-34. Only *Tg.* 1 Chron. 17:14 and 1 Enoch 41:1-2 join the Gospels in combining "kingdom" with the idea of a dwelling place (Aalen, "'Reign' and 'House' in the Kingdom of God in the Gospels," 239) though Aalen, 235 also traces the thread through the Qumran writings.

[191] || 2 Sam. 7:5-16; note that 2 Sam. 7:14 is quoted in Heb. 1:5b; see Aalen, "'Reign' and 'House' in the Kingdom of God in the Gospels," 236.

[192] Cf. 1 Chron. 17:4-5, 12 and vv. 10, 14. Mary Rose D'Angelo, *Moses in the Letter to the Hebrews*, Society of Biblical Literature Dissertation Series, ed. Howard Clark Kee, no. 42 (Missoula, Montana: Scholars Press, 1979), 69 denies that Heb. 3:2 quotes Num. 12:7 at all but only alludes to it as it quotes the LXX 1 Chron. 17:14; see her argument, pp. 72-76. She does (76), however, see Num. 12:7 quoted in Heb. 3:5, though with another simultaneous reference to 1 Chron. 17:14.

Aalen finds the connection with Hebrews clearest in the Chronicles Targum, which inserts the word "faithful (sure)" (מְהֵימָן) into 1 Chron. 17:14 to describe the heir of David's throne,[193] but the links between Hebrews and Chronicles appear in the MT as well: David's descendant is settled in God's house in 1 Chron. 17:14, and Heb. 3:2, 5 describes Moses as faithful in God's house; in 1 Chron. 17:13 David's descendant is called God's son, while Heb. 3:6 describes Christ as a faithful Son; and in 1 Chron. 17:12 the Davidite is given the task of building God's house, while Heb. 3:3 implies that Jesus is the builder of God's house.[194] A further connection is suggested by the fact that in Hebrews both God and Christ build the house (Heb. 3:3-4): both God and the descendant of David build a house according to 1 Chron. 17:10, 12.[195] D'Angelo observes in Hebrews the accommodation of Moses to the Davidic Messiah,[196] and the many links between the texts in Hebrews and Chronicles just reviewed help suggest that Hebrews applies 1 Chron. 17:12-14, a text associating God's house both with David's kingdom and the Temple, to Moses.

As noted earlier, 1 Chron. 17:14 may launch the notion of "house" as the place where God rules, but it is the Targums that apply the principle in interpreting the MT. While in the MT of 2 Samuel 7 "house" and "kingdom" seem to be separate things, the Targums to 2 Sam. 7:11‖1 Chron. 17:10, "the Lord declares to you that the Lord will make you a house," substitute מלכו for the MT's בית. Another example appears in 1 Sam. 2:35, a verse speaking of the boy Samuel: "I will build him a sure house, and he shall go in and out before my anointed for ever." Here also the Targum has מלכו instead of בית, perhaps reflecting a view of Samuel as a king as well as a priest.[197]

All this suggests that "house" in Heb. 3:1-6 may have a much wealthier connotation than what is usually assigned to it, e.g., "universe,"[198] "sanctuary,"[199] "people (of God)."[200] D'Angelo, depending on 1 Sam. 2:35,

---

[193] This term (as πιστός) is also found in Hebrews 3:1-6 describing Moses and Jesus, and is one of the key words used to link the Hebrews passage to Num. 12:7.

[194] Aalen, "'Reign' and 'House' in the Kingdom of God in the Gospels," 236. D'Angelo, *Moses in the Letter to the Hebrews*, 72-73 determines that the links remain even if the author used the LXX.

[195] Another of Aalen's insights, "'Reign' and 'House' in the Kingdom of God in the Gospels," 236-37. The two Chronicles verses appear to speak of David's kingdom or household, and of the Temple, respectively.

[196] D'Angelo, *Moses in the Letter to the Hebrews*, 146.

[197] Aalen, "'Reign' and 'House' in the Kingdom of God in the Gospels," 234.

[198] As in *Tg. Neof.* Num. 12:7.

[199] As often in the Old Testament and in the context of Num. 12:7.

[200] As in *Tg. Onq.* Num. 12:7; Aalen, "'Reign' and 'House' in the Kingdom of God in the Gospels," 237 takes this option. Craig R. Koester, *Hebrews: A New Translation with Introduction and Commentary*, The Anchor Bible, ed. William Foxwell Albright

achieves a synthesis of the latter two and thinks "house" refers specifically to a priestly community.[201]   Strikingly, none of these views attends to the royal implication of "house" in the texts that Hebrews draws on, nor to the evidence that Moses was seen as both a king and a priest, vitally important information in the context of an allusion to 1 Chronicles 17. The detailed use of the Chronicles passage by Hebrews strongly suggests that Heb. 3:1-6 employs "house" not with regard to Temple service alone, but with an eye to the rule of God through the legitimate priestly king.

4.5.3.3 Conclusion

Aalen's work points to a way of reading Heb. 3:1-6 that makes use of elements of the passage that are often overlooked. Aalen reveals a special meaning for the term, "house," and demonstrates that this special meaning derives from the OT texts to which Hebrews turns at this point. The use Hebrews makes of 1 Chron. 17:12-14 indicates that the author not only recognized the kingly undertones in his cross-reference, but desired to exploit them. The "house/kingdom" theology of Hebrews ties the book in with the general NT presentation of the kingdom of God, adding another reason to accept Aalen's direction here. Its coherence both with the wider NT view of "kingdom" and with Jewish exegesis of the specific OT text(s) involved commends the conclusion that in Heb. 3:1-6 Moses is conceived as the (apostolic) priest-king servant whose service in God's "house" is taken over and fulfilled by the apostolic, priest-king son, Jesus.

4.6 Conclusion

In OT and Jewish thought, God is uniquely and specially king of his people. Yet, having God as king is not incompatible with having a human monarch, and many looked back on Moses as an early human king of Israel. The Old Testament suggested it, and its interpretation confirmed it. A wide cross-section of literature carries the tradition, or interacts with the idea.

The New Testament bears the marks of its first-century context in all these respects, including the recognition of Moses as king. His kingship is

---

and David Noel Freedman, vol. 36 (New York: Doubleday, 2001), 245-46 lists these three options.

[201] D'Angelo, *Moses in the Letter to the Hebrews*, 84-89. Cf. "the kingdom of the congregation of Zion" of *Tg. Isa.* 37:22. D'Angelo draws support from 1 Sam. 2:30-35, which she regards as "deeply involved" with the Nathan oracle, D'Angelo, 69. D'Angelo goes on later (142-49) to find four themes packed into Hebrews's use of "house": heaven and its angels, creation, the tabernacle, and the people, "all" of which "must in some way be operative in the argument" of Heb. 3:1-6, (147), see also 163-64.

more often assumed than stated, though Acts 7:35 may provide such a statement, and the feeding narratives of John and Mark are nearly incomprehensible without a conception of Moses as king. To these can be added Heb. 3:1-6, a passage perhaps even more densely packed with christological significance than interpreters have generally recognized. Intricate allusions to various OT and targumic texts found there can perhaps only be satisfied by the involvement of the priest-king Moses. In all these passages the best, or perhaps the only, sense that can be made depends on Moses being recognized both by author and by reader as king.

The first three chapters of the present study have focused on (more or less) familiar impressions of Moses. The fact that this cluster of essentially staple titles, "Prophet," "Priest," "King," and "Apostle" (less usual but not outlandish), can be illustrated from the New Testament itself gives a strong preliminary impression of the great prestige of the figure of Moses. Moreover, all of these titles describe the role of someone standing between man and God, which recalls a fifth important title subsumed within the discussion, "Mediator." The following chapter will give a fresh appraisal to another familiar element of the picture of Moses, his role in lawgiving.

Chapter 5

Moses as Lawgiver

I purpose to write the life of Moses,
whom some describe as the legislator of the Jews.
—Philo, *De Vita Mosis*, 1.1

5.1 Introduction

At the core of practically every Gentile account of Moses lies his role as lawgiver to the Jews.[1] Though lawgiving was important both to Greeks and to Romans, the emphasis must have originated from Jewish conceptions, a supposition borne out by the Jewish sources in which the provision of laws by Moses is consistently highlighted. Examples of this include the writings of Philo, whose usual title for Moses is "Lawgiver" (νομοθέτης),[2] Josephus, who uses the term of Moses extensively as well,[3] and the *Assumption of Moses*, which also praises Moses as a lawgiver.[4]

All Jews, it can safely be said, saw Moses as a lawgiver, but how they characterized the role of Moses in the lawgiving is less clear. Was he a

---

[1] John G. Gager, *Moses in Greco-Roman Paganism*, Society of Biblical Literature Monograph Series, ed. Robert A. Kraft, no. 16 (Nashville and New York: Abingdon Press, 1972), 21-22, **25**, **76**, see 91.

[2] *Leg. All.* 2.14; *Sac.* 72; *Post.* 47, 133; *Det.* 105; *Gig.* 19; *Quod Deus* 21, 23, 52, 61, 67, 94; *Agr.* 27, 84, 86, 144; *Conf.* 135; *Quis Her.* 163, 292; *Cong.* 44; *Fug.* 120; *Som.* 2.4; *Mos.* 1.128, 162; *Spec. Leg.* 2.132, 239; *Quod Omn. Prob.* 29, 68; *Aet.* 19; "most holy lawgiver" (ὁ ἱερώτατος νομοθέτης; *Spec. Leg.* 1.15); "the great and wise lawgiver" (ὁ πάντα μεγάλος καὶ σοφὸς νομοθέτης; *Ebr.* 1).

[3] *Ap.* 2.154, 156, 186, 209, 237, 279, 290; *Ant.* 1.15, 18, 95, 240; 3.180; 4.322; 5.401; *legislator* (*Ap.* 2.75); "the giver of laws" (νομοθετήσαντος; *Ap.* 2.145). Cf. "the legislation of Moses" (ἡ Μωυσέος νομοθεσία; *Ant.* 6.93).

[4] With the words *consummatum in saeculo doctorem* (11:16), if, as Tromp argues, *docere* is a verb which is especially used with regard to the law, and "*doctor* simply the name of a profession, namely the study and the instruction of the law," Johannes Tromp, ed. and trans., *The Assumption of Moses: A Critical Edition with Commentary*, Studia in Veteris Testamenti Pseudepigrapha, ed. A.-M. Denis and M. de Jonge, vol. 10 (Leiden: E. J. Brill, 1993), 256 and 195.

legislator or a prophet?[5] It is not now — and was not then — a trivial distinction. Philo remarks on controversy in his day over "whether what he [Moses] told them came from his own reasoning powers or was learnt from some supernatural source" (*Hyp.* 6.9). Elsewhere he reports debate over what grade to assign to Moses, "whom some describe as the legislator of the Jews (νομοθέτης τῶν Ἰουδαίων), others as the interpreter of the Holy Laws (ἑρμηνεύς νόμων ἱερῶν; *Mos.* 1.1)"; in other words, some Jews thought of Moses as the one who laid down the Law, while others saw him more as a prophet, who taught and interpreted the Law that came from heaven.[6]

The controversies reported by Philo imply that other Jewish sources, particularly those contemporary with Philo, should also witness to these divergent views of the role of Moses in the Lawgiving. Yet even fuller scholarly treatments of Jewish views of the Lawgiving seem to regard the place of Moses in it as too obvious for close examination, so that this potentially dynamic aspect of ancient Judaism has been left relatively neglected. What follows here attempts to rectify this omission.

5.2 Old Testament Traditions of Moses as Lawgiver

As might be expected given the diverse views witnessed by Philo, the Old Testament can be construed to support conceptions of Moses as either prophet or legislator.

5.2.1 Deuteronomy

For example, in one sense Deuteronomy clearly implies the prominence of Moses as a legislator. Moses' first address in that book (Deut. 1:6-4:40) maintains at least a theoretical distinction between the words of Moses and the words of the Lord in the Law — but with both carrying authority. Note the particularly clear distinction in Deut. 4:13-14 between the Lord's covenant, "which He commanded you to perform, the Ten Commandments," (עשרת הדברים) and "the statutes and judgments" (חקים ומשפטים), which the Lord commanded Moses at that time to teach. This distinction is carried through in Moses' second address (Deut. 5:1-28:68), where both the Ten Commandments and the "statutes and judgments"

---

[5] In the discussion to follow, "legislator" refers to someone possessing personal authority to make laws, and "prophet" explicitly to a mediator of overt divine commandments. Related vocabulary is used accordingly.

[6] The typical role of a prophet, at least by rabbinic times, but also in the Old Testament.

(הַחֻקִּים וְהַמִּשְׁפָּטִים; 12:1) are proclaimed, again apparently setting forth Moses as one who imparts a second set of laws.

Of this second address R. Polzin observes, "Whereas Moses quotes the Ten Commandments of the Lord in direct discourse (Deut. 5:6-21) — that is, God is allowed to speak to the Israelites directly — in the law code of chapters 12-28 it is Moses who speaks directly to the Israelites concerning 'the statutes and judgments'."[7] The differentiation of voices serves to promote the personal authority of Moses, because laws that appear as his own get packaged into a single authoritative code alongside the commandments spoken by the Lord himself.

While this distinction seems to make a legislator of Moses, the composition of Deuteronomy also tends to strengthen the prophetic nature of Moses' share of the Lawgiving. In the same second Mosaic address, where the distinction between the voice of God and the voice of Moses generally holds, so that the discourse stands on the authority of two speakers, at certain points the identity of the speaker becomes uncertain. At first in these verses Moses speaks, when suddenly it appears as though a direct address from the Lord has broken in, and then just as suddenly the voice of Moses returns (Deut. 7:4, 11:13-15; 28:20). As Polzin realizes, "the effect of the law code's composition, therefore, is to show us that the authoritative status of the Mosaic voice is *almost* indistinguishable from the voice of God."[8]

On one hand, the legislative authority of Moses seems established with the ascription to him of "statutes and judgments" that seem to stand apart from the laws that God delivers himself. On the other, a blurring of voice (and authority) in that Mosaic legislation, in which the human voice becomes swallowed up in the divine, points to a more prophetic ideal, in which Moses' voice is really God's voice.

The ambiguity of Deuteronomy is perhaps reflected in the mixed traditions on the Lawgiving that it inspired. *Targum Onq.* Deut. 4:13-14, for example, completely separates the Ten Commandments from the post-Decalogue legislation, which apparently has been devolved entirely to Moses.[9]

---

[7] Robert Polzin, "Deuteronomy," in *The Literary Guide to the Bible*, ed. Robert Alter and Frank Kermode (London: William Collins & Sons, 1987), 95-96.

[8] Ibid., 96; see Judah Goldin, "Not by Means of an Angel and Not by Means of a Messenger," in *Religions in Antiquity: Essays in Memory of Erwin Ramsdell Goodenough*, ed. Jacob Neusner, Studies in the History of Religion (Supplements to *Numen*), no. 14 (Leiden: E. J. Brill, 1968), 423; see also Kevin J. Vanhoozer, *Is There a Meaning in This Text?: The Bible, the Reader and the Morality of Biblical Knowledge* (Grand Rapids, Mich.: Zondervan, 1998), 176.

[9] *Targum Neofiti 1* on that passage is equally clear. Cf. also the Vulgate of Deut. 4:13-14.

In the LXX of Deut. 33:3d-4, by contrast, all the Law Moses commanded consisted simply of what he had received from God.[10]

5.2.2 Other Old Testament Texts

Outside Deuteronomy, while many OT texts refer to the "Law of Moses," or "the law Moses commanded," and give the impression that the commands really originated with Moses,[11] other traditions want to make clear that Moses was only passing on the Law, not making it.

The Chronicler uses especially clear language along these lines. For example, in Neh. 8:14 the regulations for the Feast of Booths are found in "what the Lord commanded by the hand of Moses" (אשר צוה יהוה ביד־ משה; ᾧ ἐνετείλατο κύριος τῷ Μωυσῇ); and in 2 Chron. 35:6 the Passover regulations are called "the word of the Lord by the hand of Moses" (דבר־יהוה ביד־משה; ὁ λόγος κυρίου διὰ χειρὸς Μωυσῆ).[12] The role of Moses is carefully circumscribed.

Malachi 3:22(4:4) makes clear where the Law came from, by apparently overturning the division of labor laid out in Deut. 4:13-14. It says: "Remember the Law of Moses my servant (תורת משה עבדי), which I commanded him in Horeb for all Israel: statutes and judgments" (חקים ומשפטים).[13]

The Greek versions of Daniel suggest thinking that puts Moses even further from the Law. In the prayer of Daniel chapter 9, the Theodontionic text of verse 10 speaks of God's Law, "which you gave in the presence of Moses and us through your servants the prophets" (ᾧ ἔδωκας ἐνώπιον

---

[10] As interpreted, e.g., by Philo, *Migr.* 130. In the MT the connection between receiving and commanding is not made.

[11] E.g., Josh. 1:7, אשר צוך משה התורה, ἐνετείλατό σοι Μωυσῆς; the same again, Josh. 8:31, 33, 35 (LXX 9:2b, 2d, 2f); 2 Kings 18:12; 21:8.

[12] The emphasis on mediation is yet stronger in the parallel to 2 Chron. 35:6, 1 Esdr. 1:6, which speaks of τὸ πρόσταγμα τοῦ κυρίου τὸ δοθὲν τῷ Μωυσῇ; see also 1 Esdr. 9:39, κομίσαι τὸν νόμον Μωυσέως τὸν παραδοθέντα ὑπὸ τοῦ κυρίου θεοῦ Ισραηλ (contrast Neh. 8:1), and Scott J. Hafemann, "Moses in the Apocrypha and Pseudepigrapha: A Survey," *Journal for the Study of the Pseudepigrapha* 7 (1990): 80-81. Neh. 1:7, 8; 9:14; 10:29; and 1 Kings 8:56 also emphasize the merely mediating role of Moses. To be fair, Ezra, Nehemiah, and Chronicles use a tremendous variety of expressions for the Law, on which see H. G. M. Williamson, "History," in *It Is Written: Scripture Citing Scripture: Essays in Honour of Barnabas Lindars, SSF*, ed. D. A. Carson and H. G. M. Williamson (Cambridge: Cambridge University Press, 1988), 25, making it precarious to formulate an implied view of Moses on the basis only of selected texts.

[13] "The terms [used here in Malachi] 'law, statutes and judgments,' and 'Horeb') are characteristically deuteronomic," John Day, "Prophecy," in *It Is Written: Scripture Citing Scripture: Essays in Honour of Barnabas Lindars, SSF*, ed. D. A. Carson and H. G. M. Williamson (Cambridge: Cambridge University Press, 1988), 40.

Μωσῆ καὶ ἡμῶν διὰ τῶν παίδων σου τῶν προφητῶν). The standard LXX version is similar, except that the Law becomes the laws "which he (God) set before us by the hands of his servants the prophets" (οἷς ἔδωκεν κατὰ πρόσωπον ἡμῶν ἐν χερσὶ τῶν δούλων αὐτοῦ τῶν προφητῶν). No mention is made of Moses at all.

5.2.3 A Law of Moses and a Law of God

Despite the way writers like the Chronicler and Malachi smooth the whole Law into one divine legislation, Jews clearly preserved the "Two Laws" idea inherited from the Old Testament. Philo is especially consistent in representing the statutes of Deuteronomy as commands and charges of Moses.[14] Even non-Jews (e.g. Strabo, *Geography* 16.2.39 and Tacitus, *Histories* 5.4-5) have heard about two different strata of legislation in the Law, though they attribute the one to Moses and the other to his later corrupters.

The Christian distinction between the "two Laws" occurs early enough to imply it was present in, and inherited from, contemporary Judaism. The *Didaskalia*, to name but one example, makes a great point of distinguishing the eternal and edifying Ten Words from the worthless Second Legislation, from which the Christian is freed.[15]

5.3 Moses as Lawgiver in Literature of Second Temple Judaism

5.3.1 Ben Sira

Ecclesiasticus 24:23 is not extant in Hebrew, but the Greek text names the Law as βίβλος διαθήκης θεοῦ ὑψίστου, νόμον ὃν ἐνετείλατο ἡμῖν Μωυσῆς, "the book of the covenant of the Most High God, the law that Moses commanded us as an inheritance for the congregations of Jacob." This verse should be seen in the context of the Siracidean emphasis on the prophetic nature of the Lawgiving, noted in Chapter Two.[16]

The same verse may hint in the direction of Law as prophecy when in its latter part it duplicates Δευτ. 33:5. As seen above, the LXX here teaches that Moses only commanded what he received,[17] so that Ben Sira effectively cites the Torah itself as his authority for casting Moses as a prophet in the giving of the Law.

---

[14] E.g., *Agr.* 84, 86, 172; *Quis Her.* 13, 49; *Som.* 2.263.
[15] E.g. 1.6; 2.5; 6.16-17; cf. 6.18,19.
[16] Pp. 34-36.
[17] P. 127.

5.3.2 The Letter of Aristeas

The author of *Aristeas* writes (partly) to engender Gentile appreciation for the Jewish Law and customs. The opening section of the letter mentions "the God who appointed them their Law" (15), probably referring to the ultimate authority behind the Law (which always was ultimately held to be sanctioned by God, no matter how Moses' role was conceived). An entire section (130-171), however, is devoted to a defense of the methods of the Lawgiver, ostensibly given by Eleazar the high priest.

"Moïse apparaît dans cette apologie comme le premier des législateurs, ayant fixé point par point les principes de la piété et de la justice: l'unité de Dieu, l'inanité des idoles, le châtiment inévitable des péchés."[18] Eleazar mentions no oracles. Instead, "Moses enacted this legislation" (ἐνομοθέ-τει ταῦτα Μωϋσῆς; 144), "in his wisdom ... and being endowed by God for the knowledge of universal truths" (139). It is not a case of inspiration but of (divinely endowed but nonetheless) native abilities. Here, "Moses himself is the author of the Law."[19] "Aristeas" in this respect seems to resemble his fellow Alexandrians, Aristobulus, who considers the Law "the personal achievement of Moses,"[20] and Philo (on whom see below). M. Hadas rightly observes that Moses seems here analogous to Greek civic founders like Solon or Lycurgus.[21]

Several other individual texts in the same section depict Moses going about the business of issuing commands and making wise laws (e.g. 131, 133, 142). God's role is simply to equip the Lawgiver to do his work. S. Hafemann notices "the incredible authority which is vested in Moses. Moses does not derive his status from the law; the law derives its status from Moses!"[22] (This, incidentally, is the exact opposite of the eventual rabbinic view.) Hadas also suggests that rather than Moses gaining his status from the Law, Aristeas and Alexandrian Jews generally "may have regarded the Law merely as another illustration of the greatness of the national hero."[23]

---

[18] Geza Vermes, "La figure de Moïse au tournant des deux Testaments," *Cahiers Sioniens* 8, nos. 2, 3, and 4 (*Moïse: L'homme de l'alliance*, 1954): 65.

[19] Hafemann, "Moses in the Apocrypha and Pseudepigrapha: A Survey," 87.

[20] John M. G. Barclay, *Jews in the Mediterranean Diaspora from Alexander to Trajan (323 BCE-117 CE)* (Edinburgh: T. & T. Clark, 1996), 150. See Fragment 2, *Praep. Ev.* 8.10.3 and Fragment 3, *Praep. Ev.* 13.12.3.

[21] Moses Hadas, ed. and trans., *Aristeas to Philocrates (Letter of Aristeas)*, Dropsie College Edition, Jewish Apocryphal Literature, ed. Solomon Zeitlin, et al. (New York: Harper & Bros., 1951), 63.

[22] Hafemann, "Moses in the Apocrypha and Pseudepigrapha: A Survey," 87-88.

[23] Hadas, *Aristeas to Philocrates*, 63, Moses being the one individual conceived of as "the exemplar and bearer" of the whole Jewish national tradition, along the lines of Greek historiography of Near-Eastern peoples, e.g. Semiramis and the Assyrians, Ninus and the Babylonians, Sesostris and the Egyptians, Manes and the Phrygians.

5.3.3 Views of Moses as Lawgiver Attested in Non-Jewish Literature

In probably the earliest reference to Moses in pagan Greek literature (in his early-third century B.C. *Aegyptiaca*), Hecataeus presents an extensive account of Moses' legislative activity, in which all the laws conform to standard Greek models.[24] Hecataeus's statement that Moses heard all of his laws from God and then spoke them to the Jews is probably a paraphrase of a summary formula "transmitted to him orally by Jewish acquaintances in Alexandria."[25] Therefore, in all probability Hecataeus witnesses to at least one segment of Jewish thinking in his day that saw the role of Moses in the Lawgiving as that of a prophet.

Much the same is Strabo. In his survey of prominent lawgivers (*Geog.* 16.2.38-39), he covers both proper lawgivers (e.g. Lycurgus) and those prophets (μάντεις) who function as lawgivers. As already noted in Chapter Two, he classes Moses in the latter category: "He is pictured as an archetype of the religious and prophetic lawgiver."[26] Gager, drawing on A. D. Nock and others, defends the suggestion first made by Schürer that Strabo's source for information about Moses was (ultimately) Hellenistic Jewish.[27]

Most non-Jewish writers, however, simply attribute the laws to Moses himself, often with no reference to divinity at all. Juvenal mocks the Jews, who "keep the law which Moses handed down in his secret tome" (*Satire* 14.100-104). Others mention the divine attribution of the Law as a Mosaic ruse to win its acceptance. This is the view in the first century B.C. of Diodorus the Sicilian, *Bibliotheca Historica* 58,[28] and perhaps the view of Galen in the second century A.D. as well.[29]

---

[24] Gager, *Moses in Greco-Roman Paganism*, 26 (on dating), 31-34; see pp. 28-29 above.

[25] Ibid., 32. Indications are that he relies generally on Greek-speaking Jewish sources in Egypt for his account of Moses and the Law, 32-34, 37.

[26] Ibid., 43, and see above, pp. 37-38.

[27] Emil Schürer, *The History of the Jewish People in the Age of Jesus Christ (175 BC-AD 135)*, rev. and ed. Geza Vermes, Fergus Millar, and Martin Goodman, vol. 3.1 (Edinburgh: T. & T. Clark, 1986), 154. See Gager, *Moses in Greco-Roman Paganism*, 47.

[28] See Menachem Stern, ed. and trans., *Greek and Latin Authors on Jews and Judaism Edited with Introductions, Translations, and Commentary*, vol. 1, *From Herodotus to Plutarch*, Fontes and Res Judaicas Spectantes (Jerusalem: The Israel Academy of Sciences and Humanities, 1974), 167, 171-72.

[29] Galen: "Moses, who framed the laws for the tribe of the Jews, since it is his method in his books to write without offering proofs, saying 'God commanded, God spoke,'" *On Hippocrates' Anatomy*. The passage, preserved only in Arabic, is quoted by Gager, *Moses in Greco-Roman Paganism*, 88 who cites from R. Walzer, *Galen on Jews and Christians* (1949), 10-11. Galen, too, probably had his Jewish sources, Gager, 91.

5.3.4 Qumran

Moses' role in the Lawgiving appears not to be a matter of explicit discussion in the Qumran texts, but some light is shed on it in CD 6.4-7, where the well of Num. 21:18 and the staff (מחוקק) with which it is dug are viewed as the Law (התורה) and the Interpreter of the Law (דורש התורה) respectively. The title מחוקק became attached to Moses in a variety of Jewish (and Samaritan) literature.[30]

Here it is interesting that the Damascus Document thinks of the מחוקק as an "interpreter" of law. N. Wieder inadvertently captures the implication of most interest here when he writes of this figure, "Like Moses of old, the primary task of the second Moses was to act as *doresh ha-torah*, as the authoritative teacher and exponent of the Torah."[31]   G. Vermes agrees, "Dans ce contexte palestinien ... il apparaît que le *Meḥoqqéq*, Interprète de la Torah, docteur suprême de la Communauté et chef de son exode ... est vraiment représenté comme un 'nouveau Moïse.'"[32]   Both scholars seem implicitly to recognize that the Damascus Document views both the old Moses and the "new Moses" as interpreters and teachers of the Law (handed down from God), not makers or givers of it. This places both figures firmly within the prophetic ideal.

This observation of the prophetic role the Damascus Document assigns to Moses in the Lawgiving comports with the distinction in Deuteronomy between those sections in which God speaks directly and those in which Moses speaks in his own right, already noticed above and observed in the Damascus Document as well. A good example from the latter is CD 19.22 which introduces Deut. 32:33, from the Song of Moses, with "God said" (though this verse comes in a section written [Deut. 32:20] as the speech of the Lord),[33] while a few verses later in CD 19.26-27, Deut. 7:8 and 9:5 are "what Moses said to Israel" (אשר אמר משה לישראל).[34] An apparent nonconformity to this pattern comes in CD 5.8-9, which introduces Lev. 18:13 with "Moses said," but here an attentive reader of the biblical text

---

[30] While *Tg. Onq.*, *Ps.-J.*, *Neof.*, *Frg. Tg.*(P,V) Deut. 33:21, and *Sifre* 355 (Finkelstein, p. 417, line 14, 418 lines 1-2) on that verse do not repeat the term מחוקק, they all expound the חלקת מחוקק of the MT as the burial plot of Moses, and clearly mean to make Moses the מחוקק. See also Naphtali Wieder, "The 'Law-Interpreter' of the Sect of the Dead Sea Scrolls: The Second Moses," *Journal of Jewish Studies* 4, no. 4 (1953): 158-175 161.

[31] Wieder, "The 'Law-Interpreter' of the Sect of the Dead Sea Scrolls: The Second Moses," 172; see further, Gert Jeremias, *Der Lehrer der Gerechtigkeit*, Studien zur Umwelt des Neuen Testaments, ed. Karl Georg Kuhn, vol. 2 (Göttingen: Vandenhoeck & Ruprecht, 1963), 273-75.

[32] Vermes, "La figure de Moïse au tournant des deux Testaments," 81-82.

[33] As also CD 8.9.

[34] As also CD 8.14.

may have noticed that Lev. 18:1-3 nests the words of the Lord inside an oration by Moses dictated to him by the Lord. The exception may merely prove the rule.

Damascus Document 5.21-6.1 seems also to allude to Moses' role as intermediary in the giving of the Decalogue, calling them "God's precepts (given) through the hand of Moses and also of the holy anointed ones" (מצות אל ביד משה וגם במשיחו הקודש), especially if the משיחו הקודש are the angels held in some traditions to have passed the stone tablets from God to Moses (Gal. 3:19; Acts 7:38). Similarly, the statement in 1QS 1.2-3, that the Instructor ought to do as God "commanded by the hand of Moses and by the hand of all his servants the prophets" (צוה ביד מושה וביד כול עבדיו הנביאים), both sets Moses apart as special and seems to suggest that the Lawgiving was a prophetic message merely mediated by him like any other prophetic oracle.

In possible conflict with this assessment is the reference in CD 15.8-9 to "the covenant which Moses established with Israel, the covenant to revert to the law of Moses" (הברית אשר כרת משה עם ישראל את הברית [לשֹ]וב] אל תורת משה again in 15.12; 16.2, 5). Elsewhere in Damascus Document the covenant is "the covenant with the forefathers" (ברית ראשנים, CD 1.4, 4.9), "the covenant with the fathers," (ברית האבות, 8.18), and God's covenant (ברית אל) that he established with Israel forever (הקים אל את בריתו לישראל עד עולם, CD 3.11, 13).[35] The "covenant which Moses established" in CD 15.8-9 is probably merely then the covenant which Moses mediated.

5.3.5 Philo

Philo's thinking on the Lawgiving, particularly regarding the connection between prophecy and lawgiving, is deeply nuanced. The gift of prophecy, for Philo, embraces all Moses' other functions, including lawgiving, so that he even calls Moses ὁ προφήτης τῶν νόμων (*Virt.* 51, also *Spec. Leg.* 2.104), but that does not mean that he considered all the Law to have been

---

[35] The majority of the covenant language in Damascus Document appears to be related to the biblical, Mosaic covenant. Little effort is made to distinguish any new, sectarian covenant from the covenant: kept by the patriarchs (CD 3.1-4; 4.9) but not by Jacob's sons nor by the Israelites in Egypt (CD 3.4-7), the covenant the curses of which fall on its violators (CD 1.17), the vengeance of which is carried out by the sword (CD 1.17-18), God's covenant that he established with Israel forever (CD 3.13; 4.9). Damascus Document 2.2 might seem to introduce a new covenant, but need not do so, especially when the "covenant of conversion" (CD 19.16) has violators written about in Deut. 32:33 (CD 19.21-22; cf. 8.9), something that seems to make "covenant of conversion" another name for the Deuteronomic covenant. The burden of Damascus Document seems to be a call to submission to the Mosaic covenant, not the promulgation of another alternative, and so again Moses is magnified.

strictly "revealed" to Moses, even if he did consider all the Law to carry divine sanction (*Hyp.* 6.8-9).[36]

For Philo, prophecy functions in three modes, all of which involve divine influence over the prophet, perhaps merely an endowment with special insight (*Mos.* 2.190), but only one of which involves "divine possession in virtue of which he is chiefly and in the strict sense considered a prophet" (ἐνθουσιῶδες ... καθ' ὃ μάλιστα καὶ κυρίως νενόμισται προφήτης; *Mos.* 2.191).[37] Since the latter Philo regards as only occasionally true even of a prophet,[38] the prophetic element of the lawgiving could merely amount to the conferral upon Moses of a special measure of divine wisdom. Thus Philo writes: "This is Moses, who, ... with a wisdom given by divine inspiration, received the art of legislation and prophecy alike" (οὗτός ἐστι Μωυσῆς ... ὁ νομοθετικὴν ὁμοῦ καὶ προφητείαν ἐνθουσιώδη καὶ θεοφορήτῳ σοφία λαβών; *Cong.* 132). Here Philo distinguishes fully inspired prophecy, which is a divine gift, from true legislation, which is an art, albeit an art performed in dependence on divine wisdom.

Undoubtedly, Philo considered Moses, his overarching prophethood and constant divine supervision notwithstanding, to have exercised in some respect personal and even independent authority in the making of the Law. For Philo, "All things written in the sacred books are oracles (χρησμοί) delivered through Moses"[39] — but some are "more especially his" (τὰ ἰδιαίτερα; *Mos.* 2.188). The cleavage falls between "the heads which sum up the particular laws,"[40] the Ten Commandments, which "God judged fit to deliver in His own person alone without employing any other," and others which he delivered "through His prophet Moses" (διὰ προφήτου Μωυσέως; *Dec.* 18; see also 20, 46; *Praem.* 2).[41]

---

[36] See above, p. 45.

[37] Cf. Rudolf Meyer, "προφήτης κτλ.," in *Theological Dictionary of the New Testament*, ed. Gerhard Friedrich, trans. and ed. Geoffrey W. Bromiley, vol. 6, *Πε-Ρ* (Grand Rapids: William B. Eerdmans, 1968, reprint, 1988), 822.

[38] See *QE* 3.9 and 2.29, which calls Moses "the prophetic mind" and then goes on, "for when the prophetic mind becomes divinely inspired and filled with God," etc.

[39] The books are sacred writings (ἱεραὶ γραφαί; *Mos.* 2.84; see also *Post.* 158; *Mos.* 2.15).

[40] *Spec. Leg.* 3.125; see *Dec.* 18; τὰ δέκα λογία; *Spec. Leg.* 4.132. All the particular laws which Moses expressed (διηρμήνευσε; *Spec. Leg.* 4.132; with this meaning cf. *Mig.* 73; *Jos.* 189; *Spec. Leg.* 2.256; *Vit. Cont.* 31; *Leg.* 353) are dependent on the ten heads (*Virt.* 80-81), and are truly divine (ἀληθῶς θεῖοι; *Mos.* 2.12), since even his own laws Moses "composed under God's guidance" (συνέγραψεν ὑφηγησαμένου θεοῦ; *Mos.* 2.11).

[41] In *QE* 2.42 the Decalogue is called "the true Law," which could not be written with human hands but which God must put down himself.

In the Lawgiving according to Philo, Moses legislates (νομοθετεῖ),[42] handing down laws on his own authority, or in his own name.[43] He allots the Levites the priesthood by "the prerogative of one beloved of God" (τῇ <τοῦ> θεοφιλοῦς περιουσίᾳ).[44] Moses is "the lawgiving word" (θεσμοθέτης λόγος Μωυσῆς),[45] and "the framer of the laws" (ὁ τοὺς νόμους διαταξάμενος).[46] The creation account is "the dogma of Moses" (τὸ δὲ δόγμα τοῦτο Μωυσέως ἐστίν; Op. 25). Even the Decalogue is at least once described as Moses' composition: "Moses wrote up (Μωυσῆς ἀναγέγραφεν) the holy and divine law in ten words altogether."[47] Other laws also, attributed in the Pentateuch to God's direct speech, Philo attributes to Moses. For example, God's demand for offerings in Num. 28:2 becomes "the most sacred ordinance of Moses" (τὸ ἱερώτατον Μωυσέως γράμμα).[48]

Moses freely "conditions" (ὁριζόμενος) his laws.[49] Philo gives various reasons for Moses' rulings, often nothing to do with divine will. For example, Moses, in Philo's view, commands as he is minded to do (Gig. 32), or according to what seems reasonable (Fug. 65).[50] "Our lawgiver," Philo writes in one place, was motivated by "indignation" (ἀγανάκτησις; Spec. Leg. 3.42). His prohibition of disclosing the shame of parents is given reasonable grounds, not divine sanction (Fug. 193). Moses exempts mere misintent from penalty on the basis of his own personal sense of propriety (Mut. 243). The Sabbath itself was established owing to "a great and marvelous achievement which the lawgiver had in view" (πρὸς ἔργου μεγάλου καὶ θαυμαστοῦ τινος ᾠήθη δεῖν ὁ νομοθέτης ; Hyp. 7.11; see

---

[42] Virt. 125; e.g. 82-124.

[43] E.g. esp. Cher. 87; Det. 103; Quod Deus 127; Plant. 62; Fug. 53-54, 185-86, 193; Spec. Leg. 4.120, 126, 194; Virt. 80-83, 87-88, 125; Hyp. 6.8-9; also, Leg. All. 3.22, 32-33; Sac. 72, 97; Gig. 32-33; Quod Deus 6, 60, 88; Agr. 84, 86, 145, 172; Conf. 192-93; Quis Her. 13, 120, 239; Congr. 89-90, 92, 94, 120; Fug. 83-84; Som. 2.263; Spec. Leg. 4.55, 116, 119; Virt. 201.

[44] Plant. 62-63.

[45] Mig. 23.

[46] Virt. 201.

[47] Cong. 120, present author's translation. This may simply refer to the fact that the whole Law is based on the Decalogue, see n. 40 above. Interestingly, Philo's De Vita Mosis makes no mention of the Sinai revelation.

[48] Quod Deus 6; Som. 1.92-93, 95. The words of God in narrative portions of Genesis and Exodus are also attributed to Moses (e.g. φησι Μωυσῆς; Quis Her. 296; also Conf. 192-93; Mut. 168). Moses, not God, rebukes Cain in Gen. 4:7 (Mut. 195). Note also the curious QE 1.1 where in the Armenian text the Exodus commences at the command of Moses, or at "the voice of the man" (aṛ aṛn zain), Questions and Answers on Exodus, trans. Ralph Marcus, Loeb Classical Library, Philo, Supplement 2 (Cambridge, Mass.: Harvard University Press; London: William Heinemann, 1953), 6 n. d.

[49] Sac. 97.

[50] For a general example, Quod Deus 67.

Cher. 87). Although Moses "prophesied" the laws (ὁ τοὺς νόμους ἡμῖν προφητεύσας) yet he explicitly was "also moved by that habitual kindliness which he aims at infusing into every part of the legislation" (καὶ τῆς συνήθους φιλανθρωπίας, ἣν ἅπαντι μέρει τῆς νομοθεσίας συνυφαίνειν; *Spec. Leg.* 2.104; cf. *Mig.* 23-24). Philo views Moses not merely as the mediator of the Law but as the genius behind it.

By the first century the Torah was widely regarded as an ideal πολι-τεία,[51] and for Philo, Moses is the author (ὁ εἰσηγητής) of the holy commonwealth (ἡ ἱερὰ πολιτεία, *Spec. Leg.* 4.120; also *Virt.* 87), which incidentally he also calls the commonwealth of Moses (ἡ κατὰ Μωυσέα πολιτεία, *Spec. Leg.* 4.55).[52] Moses "rejected (ἐκμυσαξάμενος)," "prohibited (ἐκώλυσε)," etc. various forms of wedlock on grounds of their unacceptability to "a commonwealth free from reproach" (πολιτείας ἀνεπι-λήπτου; *Spec. Leg.* 3.24, 26). He detested persons and forbade judicial practices which he judged inimical to the ideal commonwealth (*Spec. Leg.* 3.167-68). In such a role, Moses as lawgiver conforms to a Greco-Roman model of lawgiving. His laws are directly comparable with those of other legislators,[53] some of whom opposed him (*Mos.* 1.2), but others of whom copied him (*Spec. Leg.* 4.61).[54] Even the more or less divine origin of his laws does not set Moses totally apart from the rest, since for Philo God is the fountain of laws for all lawgivers.[55]

Philosophical considerations frequently prompt Moses' rulings, for example, on bloodshed (*Leg. All.* 3.32). Moses instituted the six-day work week and the Sabbath day out of love of virtue and honor of the number Seven (*Op.* 128), and all sorts of other provisions for life and worship are ordered according to important numbers.[56] This philosophical feature of the portrait of Moses translated particularly well across ethnic lines into Greco-Roman Moses lore.[57]

Moses is a τεχνίτης (*Cher.* 53, 55) of the Law. Moses' skill is shown in his beginning his lawbook with a history (*Mos.* 1.45, 47-48), which he

---

[51] Nils Alstrup Dahl, *Das Volk Gottes: Eine Untersuchung zum kirchenbewusstsein des Urchristentums*, Skrifter Utgitt Av Det Norske Videnskaps-Akademi I Oslo, II. Hist.-Filos. Klasse, 1941, no. 2 (Oslo: Jacob Dybwad, 1941), 98. *QE* 2.42 likens the Law to the law of a great city.

[52] Also *Spec. Leg.* 3.51; cf. ἡ κατὰ τοὺς νόμους πολιτεία, *Spec. Leg.* 1.63.

[53] *Op.* 1-2; though he clearly was the best, *Mos.* 2.12.

[54] Josephus also claims that the legislation of Moses was copied by the Greeks, by Plato in particular (*Ap.* 2.257, 281), and knows the Law of Moses as a πολιτεία (*Ant.* 3.84, 322; 4.193, 312). Further references from Philo and Josephus on the Law as πο-λιτεία in Dahl, *Das Volk Gottes: Eine Untersuchung zum kirchenbewusstsein des Urchristentums*, 98.

[55] *Sac.* 131 with *Fug.* 66.

[56] *Congr.* 89-90, 92, 94; *Mig.* 202-203; *Fug.* 185.

[57] Gager, *Moses in Greco-Roman Paganism*, 91.

crafted carefully according to principles of his own choosing.[58] He choo-
ses his words in Gen. 6:7 to serve as an elementary lesson (*Quod Deus* 52),
and in Gen. 11:5 to help his pupils learn (*Conf.* 134-35). Moses says not
"God said" or "God spoke" (παρατετήρηται δὲ ἄκρως τὸ μὴ "εἶπεν" ἢ
"ἐλάλησεν") but "a voice of God came to him" (φωνὴ θεοῦ ἐγένετο
πρὸς αὐτόν) in order to connote just the right nuance of revelation (*Quis
Her.* 67). Names of people (*Cong.* 25, 43; *Quis Her.* 128) and places
(*Som.* 1.14-15) are given at his discretion as well: Moses "is in the habit of
using names that are perfectly apt and expressive" (*Agr.* 2), i.e., are not
revealed. To sum up, "Für Philon, mehr als für jeden vergleichbaren jüd.
oder chr. Theologen, ist Mose der *Verfasser* der Tora und kann als solcher
auch Lob erhalten."[59]

5.3.6 Josephus

It is difficult to reduce the statements of Josephus to a consistent position
on Moses and the Lawgiving, because while he expresses nearly the full
range of Philo's ideas, he puts them in such terms that it is difficult to harmonize them all. Philo's subtlety allows him to have Moses both a prophet
of the Law and a legislator for the people. With Josephus it is hard to find
the same coherence in what can appear as an incomplete fusion of two very
alien traditions, one, possibly characterizable as Pharisaic/rabbinic, which
severely limits Moses' role to simple mediation, and the other, rather "Philonic," which magnifies his role to one of active legislation.

Josephus follows other Jewish traditions already seen here in distinguishing the Decalogue, which the people heard "from God himself" (ἀκροα-
σάμενον αὐτοῦ τοῦ θεοῦ; *Ant.* 3.93), from the laws which came after-
ward, when "they besought him to bring them laws also from God (καὶ νόμους αὐτοῖς παρὰ τοῦ θεοῦ κομίζειν). And he both established these
laws and in after times indicated how they should act in all circumstances"
(*Ant.* 3.93-94).

Despite the distinction between two sets of laws, it can be seen that
both have for Josephus a divine origin. They are distinguished really only
by the former set being unmediated, and the latter mediated. As Spilsbury

---

[58] *Leg. All.* 2.15-16; *Det.* 105; *Virt.* 201; *Som.* 1.221; cf. also *Leg. All.* 3.96; *Mut.*
187; *Som.* 1.34, 76.

[59] Folker Siegert, *Philon von Alexandrien: Über die Gottesbezeichnung "wohltätig
verzehrendes Feuer" (*de Deo): Rückübersetzung des Fragments aus dem Armenischen,
deutsche Übersetzung und Kommentar*, WUNT, ed. Joachim Jeremias and Otto Michel,
no. 46 (Tübingen: J. C. B. Mohr [Paul Siebeck], 1988), 46 n. 21, see also 114. See also
Yehoshua Amir, ("Mose als Verfasser der Tora bei Philon,") *Die hellenistische Gestalt
des Judentums bei Philon von Alexandrien*, Forschungen zum jüdisch-christlichen
Dialog, ed. Yehuda Aschkenasy and Heinz Kremers, vol. 5 (Neukirchen-Vluyn: Neukirchener Verlag, 1983), 77-106.

points out, "Josephus does not allow the idea of Moses as lawgiver to detract from the status of the laws as the gift of God."[60] In *Ant.* 3.85-87, which prefaces the scene just noted above, Moses urges the Israelites not to despise his words as though they were addressed to them by a human speaker, and professes that God had first spoken them to him: "For it is not Moses, son of Amram and Jochabad, but He who constrained the Nile to flow for your sake a blood-red stream, [etc.] who favors you with these commandments, using me for interpreter (ὑμῖν τούτους χαρίζεται τοὺς λόγους δι' ἑρμηνέως ἐμοῦ)." Note that the commandments here are not the Decalogue, which the people hear directly from God (*Ant.* 3.89-93), but the subsequent laws often credited to Moses in Jewish tradition. Elsewhere, Josephus repeats that all the laws, even those commanded by Moses, came from God,[61] and in his final address to the people Moses warns them not to neglect the laws, which were begotten by God himself (*Ant.* 4.318-319).

Aspects of Josephus's view of the Lawgiving resemble the teaching of the Rabbis (see below), particularly his "dictation theory" of the Law.[62] In *Ant.* 3.84 Moses, referring to the laws he is about to begin teaching, says that God "has dictated for you a blissful [way of] life and an ordered constitution" (καὶ βίον τε ὑμῖν εὐδαίμονα καὶ πολιτείας κόσμον ὑπαγορεύσας). The mode of mediation in this statement is open to interpretation, but another is clearer, when Moses later recalls, "I have compiled for you, at the dictation of God, laws and a constitution" (συνέθηκα ὑμῖν καὶ νόμους ὑπαγορεύσαντός μοι τοῦ θεοῦ καὶ πολιτείαν; *Ant.* 4.193-94). According to *Ant.* 3.99-101, besides the stone tablets with the Ten Commandments, the whole national constitution, as well as the plan for the tabernacle, were revealed to Moses during his forty-day sojourn on Sinai (and this sounds very rabbinic indeed).[63]

For Josephus, again as for the Rabbis, the laws are believed to be a gift of God, the product of instruction Moses received.[64] "To this very day," Josephus writes, "the writings left by Moses have such authority that even

---

[60] Paul Spilsbury, *The Image of the Jew in Flavius Josephus' Paraphrase of the Bible*, Texte und Studien zum Antiken Judentum, ed. Martin Hengel and Peter Schäfer, no. 69 (Tübingen: J. C. B. Mohr [Paul Siebeck], 1998), 102, see 102-103.

[61] *Ant.* 3.317, 319, followed by 3.320.

[62] Wayne A. Meeks, *The Prophet-King: Moses Traditions and the Johannine Christology*, Supplements to *Novum Testamentum*, ed. W. C. van Unnik, et al., vol. 14 (Leiden: E. J. Brill, 1967), 132 n. 4 also thinks that "the rabbinic view is known to Josephus." On the Rabbis, see below, pp. 144-48.

[63] Josephus also credits the preparation of the Pentateuchal histories to Moses' prophetic endowments (*Ap.* 1.38-41), as does Philo, *Praem.* 1, though, as seen above, in not quite the same way.

[64] *Ant.* 3.222-23.

our enemies admit that our constitution was established by God himself, through the agency of Moses" (ὁμολογεῖν ὅτι τὴν πολιτείαν ἡμῖν ὁ καταστησάμενός ἐστι θεὸς διὰ Μωυσέος; *Ant.* 3.322). Moses' "agency," as elsewhere in Josephus, is distinctively passive. This comes out again in another place when Moses is "recounting all that he had done for the people's salvation in war and peace, in compiling laws and in cooperating to procure for them an ordered constitution ..." (νόμους τε συντιθεὶς καὶ τὸν τῆς πολιτείας κόσμον συμπορίζων; *Ant.* 4.312). Here again, Moses "compiles" the Laws, he does not legislate them.

And yet Josephus, like Philo, at times describes Moses as having complete discretion over the content of the laws.[65] Some laws Moses transmitted (παρέδωκεν), but others he devised (ahead of time; προενόησεν; *Ant.* 3.280). Moses did not merely mediate these laws, he "ordained" (διέταξε; *Ant.* 4.[205], 308) them.

Like Philo, Josephus describes Moses' personal concerns playing a part in the framing of the laws. His humanity is seen in the measures he took to give a gracious welcome to aliens.[66] Moses forbade the making of images "out of contempt for a practice profitable neither to God nor man" (*tamquam causam neque deo neque hominibus utilem despiciens*; *Ap.* 2.75). Moses set the festival calendar, starting with the month in which "he brought the Hebrews out of Egypt" (ἐξ Αἰγύπτου τοὺς Ἑβραίους προαγαγών; *Ant.* 1.81). In his role as legislator (νομοθέτης) Moses was the people's "best guide and counselor" (ἄριστος ἡγεμὼν καὶ σύμβουλος),[67] which also suggests Moses' personal involvement in legislating for them.

Like Philo, Josephus is alive to the philosophical refinement of Moses' laws. He notes that Moses, before legislating for others, first studied the nature of God in order to imitate the best of all models in making his laws (*Ant.* 1.18-19). This is an ambition that Philo praises in a ruler. For Josephus, the lawmaking work of Moses could be viewed simply as the study and interpretation of nature (φυσιολογεῖν; *Ant.* 1.34).

Perhaps surprisingly, it is Josephus, not Philo, who says that the νομοθέτης was a divine man (θεῖος ἀνήρ; *Ant.* 3.180). The apparent divinity of the Law caused Moses to be ranked higher than his own human nature (*Ant.* 3.320).

---

[65] *Ap.* 2.167-174; *Ant.* 3.266-68.
[66] *Ap.* 2.209-210.
[67] *Ap.* 2.156.

It is difficult to know how to reconcile the two pictures. Josephus uses language that almost seems borrowed from Philo,[68] which makes Moses an apparently independent agent, or at least a genuine contributor, in the Lawgiving. And yet, in his clearest statements, Josephus is emphatic that the Law comes strictly from God. He is hardly outdone by the Rabbis in his description of Moses as something like a scribe, taking down heavenly decrees. One hesitates to condemn apparent incoherence, but perhaps the solution lies in the generally unpolished condition of the *Antiquities*, which may on that account imperfectly blend Josephus's personal (Pharisaic?) convictions about the Law with the apologetic statement that he hoped to make for the Jewish history and constitution (*Ant.* 1.5). In a work so large and composed in such difficult circumstances, the author perhaps never managed to merge the two axes into one.

5.3.7 *The* Assumption of Moses

Perhaps the *Assumption of Moses* also fits the "Pharisaic/rabbinic" paradigm of the lawgiving that seems to appear in parts of the work of Josephus.[69] The characterization of Moses as "the mediator of God's covenant" (*arbiter testamenti illius*; *As. Mos.* 1:14), and the delicate description of Moses' Law as, "his (God's?) commandments, which he mediated to us" (*mandata illius in quibus arbiter fuit nobis*; *As. Mos.* 3:12),[70] both with their emphasis on mediation rather than creativity, certainly fit better there than with a view like Philo's.

5.3.8 *Conclusion*

For the moment it seems best to conclude simply that the sources on Second Temple Judaism witness two divergent lines of thinking, each strong and clear. The tradition that saw in Moses a personal authority figure seems to have older support, but, as the works of Josephus, the *Assumption of Moses*, and the reports of Philo make clear, another opinion that made rather less of Moses had come up strongly by the Herodian period. The Targums, while necessarily classed separately from sources definitely from the first century A.D., should probably be added to these witnesses for a fuller picture.

---

[68] H. St. J. Thackeray, in *Josephus, Jewish Antiquities*, vol. 1, *Books I-III*, Loeb Classical Library (Cambridge, Mass. and London: Harvard University Press, 1926), xii-xiii, thinks Josephus may depend on Philo.

[69] On its origin, Tromp, *The Assumption of Moses*, 107-109, 118-19.

[70] As Tromp, *The Assumption of Moses*, 173 n. 4 reads it, "*Illius* refers to God"; see Tromp, 44, his grammatical note 59 (not note 60).

5.4 Moses as Lawgiver in the Targums

Earlier the Targums on Deut. 4:13-14 were noted for distinguishing between the Lord's own unmediated Ten Commandments, and the other
laws, which Moses wrote.[71] It should be said that this appears to be an
exceptional position within the Targums; all the Pentateuchal Targums,
both *Targum Onqelos* and the Targums from the Palestinian tradition, generally emphasize the prophetic character of Moses (see Chapter Two),
and minimize any idea of his independence in lawmaking.[72] The Targums
(and Samaritan tradition) bestow on Moses the title מחוקק, which, as
noted above, in CD 6.7 is identified with "the interpreter of the Law."[73]

J. Ribera observes in the Palestinian Targums "an intimate relationship
between the Giver of Torah and the prophet, [i.e.] between Torah and Prophecy."[74] Ribera notes the frequency with which the Palestinian Targums
refer to "Moses, the Prophet and Scribe of Israel" (משה נבייא סופריהון
דישראל, *et var.*).[75] The epithet "great scribe" is appended to the name of
Moses in *Tg. Cant.* 1:2; 2:4; 3:3; *Tg. Pss.* 62:12,[76] and *Tg. Onq.* Deut.
33:21 (משה ספרא רבא דישראל; *et var.*). "Scribe" need not be thought
equivalent to "clerk" or "secretary"; recall the great authority of Ezra (derived, to be sure, from the Law he received). Nonetheless, given the other
options available, the title seems to put Moses in a more passive role in the
Lawgiving.

The Law is not something Moses commands, but something received
from heaven that then becomes the subject of his teaching. *Targum Onq.*
Deut. 33:4 replaces the MT's "Moses commanded us (צוה־לנו) a Torah"
with the more passive "Moses gave us (יהב־לנו) Torah" (the rabbinic literature generally rejects even that formulation as too active [see below]).
Targum Ps.-J. Deut. 34:5 comes closer to a rabbinic view when it teaches
that Moses carried off the Law from high heaven.

---

[71] See above, pp. 126-27.

[72] See above, pp. 46-47.

[73] See above, pp. 131-32.

[74] Josep Ribera, "Prophecy according to Targum Jonathan to the Prophets and the
Palestinian Targum to the Pentateuch," trans. Fiona Ritchie, in *Targum Studies*, vol. 1,
Textual and Contextual Studies in the Pentateuchal Targums, ed. Paul V. M. Flesher,
South Florida Studies in the History of Judaism, ed. Jacob Neusner, et al., no. 55 (At-
lanta, Georgia: Scholars Press, 1992), 68; see also 73.

[75] Ibid., 68, citing *Tg. Neof.*, *Ps.-J.* Gen. 27:29; *Frg. Tg.*(V) Num. 11:26; 24:9; *Frg.
Tg.*(P, V) Deut. 33:21. To these can be added *Tg. Neof.*, *Tg. Ps.-J.* Deut. 33:21.

[76] These citations provided by Israel Drazin, trans., *Targum Onkelos to Deuteronomy: An English Translation of the Text with Analysis and Commentary (Based on A.
Sperber's Edition)* (*N.p.* [USA]: Ktav Publishing House, 1982), 309 n. 85.

Targum Ps.-J. Lev. 24:12; Num. 9:8; 15:34; 27:5 and *Frg. Tg.* Lev. 24:12(P, V); Num. 9:8(V) all recall the famous "four legal decisions" that Moses rendered outside the proper proclamation of the Law, "which came before Moses the prophet, and he judged them according to the Holy Memra."[77] In other words, not even these post-Sinai cases were left to Moses' discretion, but were handled through fresh prophetic revelation.

In all of these targumic passages Moses is also called the "Master of Israel" (משה רבהון דישראל), because he instructed the Sanhedrin of Israel. The teaching function of prophets, with special reference to Torah, is familiar from *m. Ab.* 1.1, and "certainly the most characteristic prophetic mission of Moses is, according to the PT, the teaching of the Torah."[78] This in turn harmonizes with the rabbinic conviction that teachers of the Law are the heirs of the prophetic spirit.[79] The usual rabbinic title for Moses, "Moses our master"(משה רבינו), has come into use in the Targums as well (though it is not yet routine) suggesting that his teaching role was seen in the model of the rabbinic academies.[80]

The witness of the Targums is not univocal. Nonetheless, while witnessing to a certain diversity of opinion (cf. the traditions centered on Deut. 4:13-14, reviewed earlier), the Targums generally attest a view of Moses akin to what became normal in the rabbinic period, a view that held him a recipient, not a maker, of the Law.

5.5 Moses as Lawgiver in Samaritan Literature

Samaritans, like Jews, treasured views of Moses as a legislator (הנומיק, from ὁ νόμικος),[81] though from their strong emphasis on the function of

---

[77] *Frg. Tg.* Num. 15:34(V); 27:5(V); *Tg. Onq.* Lev. 24:12; Num. 9:8; 15:34-35; 27:5 recall the need for additional revelation without mentioning Moses specifically. See below, p. 146 n. 107.

[78] "[I.e., teaching it] (PJ Num. 26:11; TN, FT(P), FT(V) Deut. 30:12, and TJ Mic. 4:4[*sic*; 6:4]), explaining it, adopting [*sic*] it (PJ, FT(V) Lev. 22:27; FT(P), FT(V) Deut. 32:3), and judging the cases that derive from it (PJ Gen. 14:7; PJ, FT(P) Lev. 24:12; PJ Num. 2:10; 9:8; 15:34; 27:5)," Ribera, "Prophecy according to Targum Jonathan to the Prophets and the Palestinian Targum to the Pentateuch," 69. Teaching and interpreting Torah are also characteristic of prophets in Targum Jonathan to the Prophets, Ribera, 64.

[79] Ibid., 71-72; Meyer, "προφήτης," 817-18.

[80] See below, pp. 147-48, 154-55. In the MT of Num. 11:28 Joshua calls Moses אדני משה, this is carried forward in *Targums Onqelos, Pseudo-Jonathan*, and *Neofiti* as רי[ר]בוני משה. The amplified title משה רבהון דישראל also appears in *Tg. Ps.-J.* Num. 3:3; Deut. 9:19; and 34:5(twice).

[81] See, e.g., MS Firkovitch, Sam. X, 8, line 8, in Reinhard Plummer, *Samaritan Marriage Contracts and Deeds of Divorce*, vol. 1 (Wiesbaden: Otto Harrassowitz,

Moses as a prophet one might deduce a diminished place for the personal authority of Moses in the Law.[82]

And indeed, the Law, as Samaritans conceived it, had a strongly supernatural origin. It was absolutely divine. "The Law came forth from the very essence of God, was detached from the fire of deity."[83] The origin of the Tables of the Law in particular is as divine as in rabbinic writings. God wrote the Tables and gave them to Moses with his own hand (no angelic intermediaries). In one respect only does the Samaritan conception fall short of the rabbinic outlook: the Law does not seem to be regarded as pre-existent.[84]

Even so, the Law is imbued with the personal authority of Moses. The Law may be absolutely heavenly but Moses has a heavenly origin too, having been with God before the creation of the world.[85] Many texts view Moses acting as intermediary in the Lawgiving,[86] but the Law in these instances is the Decalogue. Beyond the Decalogue Moses was no simple messenger. Nor was he merely inspired, like a prophet. Instead Moses expounds the Ten Words into the complete Torah on his personal authority as the incarnation of the primordial light of the world. MacDonald sums up, "It is fitting, strangely enough, to think of this corpus as Moses' legislation, in its expanded form, rather than God's directly, for Moses had the capacity as incarnate Logos to proclaim what was to be."[87] Thus the high Samaritan view of the Law is in some sense balanced by an equally high view of Moses.

The Samaritans also seem to reflect the Deuteronomic distinction between two sets of laws in the Torah: as regards the Decalogue, Moses is a prophet of the Law; but as regards the "statutes and judgments," Moses is completely authoritative as a legislator, and his authority in these matters is as full as God's in the Ten Commandments.

1993), 176 (text), and *idem*, with Abraham Tal, *Samaritan Marriage Contracts and Deeds of Divorce*, vol. 2 (Wiesbaden: Harrassowitz Verlag, 1997), 194 (translation) and n. 115; MS Firkovitch, Sam. X, 61, line 6, Plummer, vol. 2, 119 (text) and 232 (trans.); MS Sassoon 725 (1848), line 9, text, Plummer, vol. 1, 209; trans., Plummer, vol. 2, 244.

[82] See above, pp. 45-46.

[83] James Alan Montgomery, *The Samaritans, The Earliest Jewish Sect: Their History, Theology and Literature* (New York: Ktav Publishing House, 1907), 232.

[84] Ibid., 233.

[85] See below, pp. 212-13, 236-37.

[86] See, e.g., Plummer, *Samaritan Marriage Contracts and Deeds of Divorce*, vol. 2, 184-255, *passim*.

[87] John MacDonald, *The Theology of the Samaritans*, The New Testament Library, ed. Alan Richardson, C. F. D. Moule, and Floyd V. Filson (London: SCM Press, 1964), 201.

5.6 Moses as Lawgiver in Rabbinic Literature

Rabbinic literature attests a decisive change in the Jewish appraisal of the role of Moses in the Lawgiving, the culmination of a trend perhaps beginning to appear in Josephus, and coming into blossom in the Targums. More consistently than their predecessors the Rabbis denied Moses the title "law giver" since God alone *gave* Torah, while Moses was involved only as a courier and an explainer.[88] Moses had no role in composing the Law, something which also sets the Rabbis off from Philo: "Die Heilige Schrift beim Zitieren zugleich zu loben, ist eine Eigenart Philons. Den Autoren des NT oder den Rabbinen wäre es wohl anmaßend erschienen, Gottes Wort als 'sehr vernünftig' oder 'wohlbegründet' zu empfehlen."[89]

This attitude toward Moses is matched by a parallel change in attitude toward the Law, which was increasingly regarded as a supernatural, direct expression of God himself, along the same lines that Wisdom or the Logos had been in earlier traditions. The Law often was not thought of as the product of composition. Rather, God "created" it in the primordial time.[90]

5.6.1 Notable Relics of Earlier Usage

Despite this general rule, in the rabbinic literature a few significant traces of Moses as a dynamic, authoritative legislator still lurk. This mostly occurs in texts that are thought to incorporate some of the earliest rabbinic traditions. *'Abot. R. N.* 2.3 describes Moses adding "a third day [of purification] for them of his own accord." Lest what is happening elude the reader, the account explains, "Moses was not willing to tell it to Israel in the manner in which the Holy One, blessed be He, spoke to him"! So Moses asserts his legislative autonomy to the extent that he alters divine direc-

---

[88] Meeks, *The Prophet-King: Moses Traditions and the Johannine Christology*, 132, citing in turn, Renée Bloch, "Quelques aspects de la figure de Moïse dans la tradition rabbinique," *Cahiers Sioniens* 8, nos. 2, 3, and 4 (*Moïse: L'homme de l'alliance*, 1954): 139-40; see also Amir, *Die hellenistische Gestalt des Judentums bei Philon von Alexandrien*, 77-79. The paradigm is laid out in *Ab. R. Nat.* 1.2. On the overall weakness of Moses in rabbinic literature, and derivation of Moses' authority strictly from the divine origin of what he says, see Hafemann, "Moses in the Apocrypha and Pseudepigrapha: A Survey," 85-89.

[89] Siegert, *Philon von Alexandrien: Über die Gottesbezeichnung "wohltätig verzehrendes Feuer"* (de Deo), 46, "To praise the Holy Scriptures at the same time as quoting them, is a peculiarity of Philo. To the authors of the NT or to the Rabbis it would have appeared presumptuous to commend God's Word as 'reasonable' or 'wellfounded.'" He cites *Mut.* 51, *Congr.* 137, *QG* 2.45, 62; 4.1, 2; *QE* 1.23; 2.38.

[90] See Roy A. Stewart, *Rabbinic Theology: An Introductory Study* (Edinburgh and London: Oliver and Boyd, 1961), 34-39. In broad agreement with the position taken here, see also Josef M. Kastner, "Moses im Neuen Testament" (Th.D. diss., Ludwig-Maximilians-Universität Munich, 1967), 81-84.

tives according to his own agenda. The passage goes on to mention other things "which Moses did of his own accord."[91]

Bills of marriage and divorce also preserve the earlier exaltation of Moses.[92] The phrase, "in accordance with the laws (כדין) of Moses and Israel," "appears in almost every known Jewish Aramaic and Hebrew marriage contract."[93] Likewise, the words, "according to the law of Moses and of Israel" (כדת משה וישראל), form the conclusion to the rabbinic bill of divorce.[94] The antiquity of the formulation in this context is suggested by *m. Yad.* 4.8, which mentions the citation of "the name of the ruler together with the name of Moses" in the bill of divorce.[95] The conservative tendency of such traditional and stylized documents as marriage and divorce papers helps explain the prominent appearance of Moses in them even down to a relatively late period.

5.6.2 General Rabbinic Usage

Without glossing over these important exceptions, one may still say that in the rabbinic period Moses generally is no longer seen as a legislator responsible for laws in his own right.

The Torah becomes known as "the Torah of Moses" not because Moses is its author, but as a reward for his humble response to the honor of having received it,[96] or because "he devoted himself with his whole soul to the Torah and [so] it is named after him,"[97] or because "whenever a man suffers for a cause, it is called by his name."[98] And so, "because Moses went on high and there meditated forty days and forty nights, almost dying for its sake, the Written Law came to be called after Moses."[99]

---

[91] Cf. *b. Shab.* 87a; *b. Yeb.* 62a.

[92] See above, pp. 3, 69.

[93] David Instone-Brewer, "1 Corinthians 7 in the Light of the Jewish Greek and Aramaic Marriage and Divorce Papyri," *Tyndale Bulletin* 52, no. 1 (2001): 105. "Some early versions have 'laws of Moses and the Judaeans,'" 105 n. 17, see 107. Instone-Brewer, 105 n. 17 even adduces Tob. 6:13; 7:12 (κατὰ τὴν κρίσιν τῆς βίβλου Μωυσέως), though here the law of levirate marriage seems to be in view.

[94] Note possible first-century example in Instone-Brewer, "1 Corinthians 7 in the Light of the Jewish Greek and Aramaic Marriage and Divorce Papyri," 113 n. 43.

[95] Ludwig Blau, *Die jüdische Ehescheidung und der jüdische Scheidebrief: Eine historische Untersuchung*, part two (Budapest: In conjunction with *Jahresbericht der Landes-Rabbinerschule in Budapest für das Schuljahr 1910-1911*, 1912; reprint, Westmead, Farnborough, Hants., England: Gregg International Publishers, 1970), 49.

[96] *B. Shab.* 89a.

[97] *Mekilta de Rabbi Ishmael*, Shirata 1, and same again in *Exod. Rab.* 30.4 and *Num. Rab.* 12.9. He "all but gave his life" for it, *Pesiq. R.* 5.2.

[98] *Midr. Pss.* 30 §4, applied specifically to Moses and the Law.

[99] *Midr. Pss.* 1 §16.

For the Rabbis it is inappropriate to speak of Moses making the smallest contribution to the Law. In the rabbinic literature, as in the Targums (generally), Moses functions strictly as God's mouthpiece.[100] *Bavli Sanh.* 99a condemns anyone who should claim that even a single verse of Torah was uttered not by God but by Moses himself. "Wer irgendein Wort der Tora Mose zuschreibt, hat damit ihren göttlichen Charakter überhaupt geleugnet."[101] The usual rabbinic view is expressed in *b. Mak.* 23b by R. Simlai, who teaches that all six hundred and thirteen precepts of the Law were received by Moses from God.[102] The only real variation in the traditions is in the manner in which the Law came to be written down: *Gen. Rab.* 8.8 depicts Moses writing the creation account in God's presence, as he is directed. Another haggadic tradition finds God himself writing out the whole Torah word-for-word.[103]

In another well-represented tradition, the Law, far from being the work of Moses, existed before Creation. The tradition that the Law was at least as old as the world goes back as far as *LAB* 32:7. *'Abot R. Nat.* 31.3 (29a ‎ה-ו,ב) records, "R. Eliezer the son of R. Jose the Galilean said: Nine hundred and seventy-four generations before the creation of the world the Torah was already written."[104] Many other early texts seem to assume the

---

[100] *Tg. Cant* 1:1; "God who gave us a law through Moses" = *b. Sot.* 13b; see also *Tg. Pss.* 68:19; *Gen. Rab.* 6.5; these refs. cited along with others Drazin, *Targum Onkelos to Deuteronomy*, 295 n. 17; see also Louis Ginzberg, *The Legends of the Jews*, vol. 3, trans. Paul Radin (Philadelphia: The Jewish Publication Society of America, 1911), 87.

[101] "Whoever attributes any word of the Torah to Moses has entirely denied its divine character," Amir, *Die hellenistische Gestalt des Judentums bei Philon von Alexandrien*, 69.

[102] Similarly, *b. Yoma* 4a; *b. Shab.* 88b; *Exod. Rab.* 41.6; *Cant. Rab.* 1.2 §2; see Ginzberg, *Legends of the Jews*, vol. 3, 81 (unfortunately he provides no reference note).

[103] A haggadah in *b. Sanh.* 111a describes Moses coming upon God writing Exod. 34:6 specifically; cf. *Exod. Rab.* 47.2 on Exod. 34:27. *'Abot. R. N.* 2.3 includes Ex. 22:19 (EVV 22:20) on the tablets which had been inscribed since creation. The implication is that God wrote out the whole Pentateuch.

[104] The same opinion is recorded in *b. Shab.* 88b; *Eccl. Rab.* 1:15 §2; 4:3 §1; similarly, *Mid. Pss.* 72.6; *Pirqe R. El.* 3; *Lev. Rab.* 19.1 ‖ *Cant. Rab.* 5.11 §1. Louis Ginzberg, *The Legends of the Jews*, vol. 5 (Philadelphia: The Jewish Publication Society of America, 1925), 132-33, n. 2 cautions, however, that the version of the tradition holding that the Torah was written down before the creation of the world "is a comparatively recent presentation" of the haggadah, which in its original form "has nothing to do with the doctrine of the pre-existence of the Torah." Elsewhere the Torah pre-exists only in the mind of God, e.g. *Midr. Pss.* 90.12; 93.3. See John T. Townsend, trans., *Midrash Tanḥuma: Translated into English (S. Buber Recension)*, vol. 2: *Exodus and Leviticus* (Hoboken, New Jersey: Ktav Publishing House, 1997), 109 n. 59 and Ginzberg, *Legends of the Jews*, vol. 5, 4 n. 5 and 132-33 n. 2 for many more references.

pre-existence of Torah.[105] Sometimes the Rabbis even gave the Law a kind of independence from God, let alone from Moses. According to an opinion in *b. AZ* 3b God sits and occupies himself with the Torah for the first three hours of each day. [106]

That Moses received the entire Torah intact from God, even already written down, is consonant with the later Jewish emphasis on the inspiration of the text, as opposed to the inspiration of the writers or speakers of the text. For Philo, inspiration is primarily a matter of the influence of the Spirit of God over chosen individuals (as seen especially in his description of prophecy in *Mos.* 2.188-91), and for him Moses functions as such a person, always under greater or lesser influence of the Spirit. This, on the whole, is the idea of inspiration that was carried forward among Christians. In rabbinic writings the locus of inspiration came to be found in texts, as Judaism adverted to formulae like אמר הכתוב ("what is written says"). Of course in the rabbinic period especially the oral traditions were committed to writing — and rabbinic tradition holds that all these texts were given simultaneously and completely to Moses on Mount Sinai.[107]

It is commonly asserted in rabbinic literature (often using Ps. 68:19) that in his ascent of Mt. Sinai Moses entered into heaven for an audience before God; many *haggadoth* describe in detail the ascent and how Moses received the Torah there.[108] An ascent to heaven fits the image of prophetic mediation, and increases the grandeur of Moses the prophet, just as it shrinks the place for Moses as a legislator: Moses cannot really be said to enact laws that he merely collects and then hands on, and the more vivid

---

[105] Both world and man are created for the sake of Torah (*m. 'Aboth* 2:8; cf. *b. Ber.* 6b bottom), and in *Sifre Deut.* 48 on 11:22, *m. 'Aboth* 3.15, *Gen. Rab.* 1.1 on 1:1, and *Pirqe R. El.* 3 the Torah was God's instrument or his consultant at Creation. According to *Pes. R. Kah.* 5, Abraham was shown the Torah, which implies its existence before Sinai at least.

[106] A hyperbolic praise of Torah study, but nonetheless a striking formulation, especially in light of other views of Torah expressed in the rabbinic writings.

[107] Etan Levine, *The Aramaic Version of the Bible: Contents and Context*, Beiheft zur Zeitschrift für die alttestamentliche Wissenschaft, ed. Otto Kaiser, no. 174 (Berlin: Walter de Gruyter, 1988), 75. The Pentateuch itself names four episodes after the Sinai revelation wherein Moses received additional juridical revelations: Lev. 24:10-23, Num. 9:6-14; 15:32-36; 27:1-11; see above, p. 140. Moses' reception of the oral law on Sinai appears in *Sifra* Behuqotai Pereq 8(end); *m. Pe'ah* 2:6; *m. 'Ed.* 8:7; *m. Yad.* 4:3; *b. San.* 99a, and is the implication of the chain of authoritative tradition described in the opening of *m. 'Abot*; see Levine, 143. Eventually, rabbinic lore uniformly held that Moses received not merely the biblical Torah, but also all the oral law that followed from it, Mishnah, halakah, Talmud, etc; see *y. Peah* 17a.58-60, *Eccl. Rab.* 1.10 §1; 5.8 §2; *Exod. Rab.* 47.1. on Exod. 34:27; *Lev. (Vayyiqra) Rab.* 22.1, paralleled in *Tanḥuma* Buber, Exodus, 9(Ki-Tissa).17 (Exodus 34:27, Part 1).

[108] *'Abot. R. N.* 2.3; *Exod. Rab.* 47.5; *b. Shab.* 88b; 89a; *b. Sanh.* 111a; *b. B.M.* 86b; *b. Yoma* 4a; *Exod. Rab.* 28.1(end).

and glorious his act of mediation appears, the more thin and anemic his role as legislator becomes.

The Rabbis do not even seem to regard Moses as somehow uniquely qualified to be the Lawgiver, again in distinction from their predecessors. In *b. Sanh.* 21b, R. Jose teaches that in lawgiving Moses was no different than Ezra, and that if Moses had not preceded him, Ezra would have been worthy to receive the Torah. Ezra, of course, was another colossus from antiquity, and a sort of lawgiver,[109] but Moses elsewhere (*Sifre* Deut. 357) is also bracketed with other Jewish teachers who "led Israel" — e.g., Hillel, Johanan b. Zakkai, Aqiba. As reported in *b. Ber.* 32a, R. Eleazar taught that Moses had no special greatness of his own, but only a temporary endowment for Israel's sake.[110] In the same *gemara* Eleazar also teaches that Moses spoke insolently toward heaven. Nor were other rabbis averse on occasion to criticizing Moses for his quick temper[111] or to stating that he had erred.[112]

Rabbinic willingness to think of Moses as merely one of many great teachers prepares one for Rashi's claim that the name of Moses was used as a title, an honorific that could be applied to any distinguished scholar, as when Rav Safra addresses Rava with the words, משה שפיר קאמרת ("[By?] Moses! Are you speaking correctly?") in *b. Sukk.* 39a and *b. Shab.* 101b.[113] In *y. Meg.* 75c.4 and *b. Ḥul.* 93a, rabbis also appear to speak to each other as ומשה. This again implies that Moses was regarded as a great, maybe the greatest, teacher of the Torah, a senior colleague of the Rabbis, but not, as earlier generations seemed to think, a uniquely authoritative lawgiver.

When they give Moses a title, the rabbinic sources generally speak of him as "Moses our master" (משה רבינו), the teacher of the Torah par ex-

---

[109] Thought in one tradition (4 Ezra 14:19-48) actually to have been the second writer of the Torah — though once more by rote mediation of what had already been written.

[110] "R. Eleazar said: The Holy One, blessed be He, said to Moses: 'Moses, descend from thy greatness. Have I at all given to thee greatness save for the sake of Israel? And now Israel have sinned; then why do I want thee?' Straightway Moses became powerless and he had no strength to speak."

[111] *B. Pes.* 66b; *b. Sot.* 13b.

[112] *B. Zeb.* 101a; see further, Louis Jacobs, "Moses (Rabbinic View)," *Encyclopaedia Judaica*, ed. Cecil Roth, et al., vol. 12 (Jerusalem: Keter Publishing House, 1972), 394.

[113] Or it may be that "Moses" was used as an oath or exclamation; according to Rashi this is what the same three words mean in *b. Beṣ* 38b, Jacobs, "Moses (Rabbinic view)," 394-95; Jacobs claims that it was widely accepted in the Middle Ages that the name "Moses" was sometimes given to scholars as a title of honor.

cellence.[114] It may be debatable whether giving Moses the title of a teacher implies that he is not a lawmaker, but the title seems to appear at a time when the estimation of Moses has been thoroughly revised in that direction, and calls to mind a prophet or the leader of a school rather than a νομοθέτης. As already noted above, teaching and interpreting the Law were seen as prophetic roles in the rabbinic period and earlier.[115]

Other titles given to Moses in rabbinic literature generally reinforce the impression that his role is strictly that of a mediator. For example, *b. Sot.* 13b calls Moses, Aaron, and Miriam prophets (נביאים), but then calls Moses only "the great scribe of Israel" (משה ספרא רבה דישראל), just as the Targums do. The *piyyuṭ* "אזל משה", noted in Chapter Two, which dubs Moses "apostle" (שליחא) is perhaps another witness to the new estimation of Moses, which saw him essentially as an emissary.[116]

In an earlier day, OT references to the laws of Moses, as well as the whole thrust of the book of Deuteronomy, had provided fertile ground for viewing Moses as a lawgiver or a lawmaker in his own right. By the first century, as evidenced by Philo, Josephus, and others, this viewpoint had fully flowered though it apparently was never unchallenged. In a subsequent era the emphasis on God as author of the laws waxed sufficiently to throw Moses' standing as a legislator into eclipse. Though Moses remained greatly honored in post-Second Temple Judaism, as demonstrated by rabbinic literature surveyed here and in the other chapters of this study, he did not remain so highly honored as a lawgiver, or, perhaps one should say, as a lawmaker.

---

[114] Jacobs, "Moses (Rabbinic View)," 394; see Ginzberg, *Legends of the Jews,* vol. 5, 403 n. 68; Scott J. Hafemann, *Paul, Moses, and the History of Israel: The Letter/ Spirit Contrast and the Argument from Scripture in 2 Corinthians 3,* WUNT, ed. Martin Hengel and Otfried Hofius, no. 81 (Tübingen: J. C. B. Mohr [Paul Siebeck], 1995), 84. This title, however, is entirely absent from the Mishnah. Neumark (cited in Jacobs, 394) offers the unlikely conjecture that its absence there is a conscious anti-Christian attempt to avoid giving Moses a title given to Jesus (Acts 2:36). More likely the absence of the title is a consequence of the fact that Moses generally appears little in the Mishnah; perhaps the only significant reference to him comes in *m. RH* 3:8, which cautions that the hands of Moses did not in themselves have any effect on the fortunes of Israel in the battle with Amalek, but rather it was the rise and fall of Israel's reverence toward God. Moses' one important mishnaic appearance serves to guard against undue reverence of him.

[115] See above, pp. 131, 141.

[116] None of this means that rabbinic thought utterly abased Moses. Moses was very great, he just did not have authority over the Law.

5.7 Moses as Lawgiver in the New Testament

The New Testament presents a varied view of Moses' lawgiving, consonant with what has been seen in other sources of the period. Readers generally have considered Moses in the New Testament simply as a foil for one of several more perfect Christian phenomena, for example as a type of Christ, of the Church, or of the apostle Paul. Perhaps as a result the very positive depictions of Moses as an authoritative lawmaker that occur there have been relatively neglected. The following sections highlight material in several NT corpora that directs attention to Moses in his lawmaking capacity.

5.7.1 The Synoptic Gospels

5.7.1.1 The Law of Divorce

The debate over divorce in Mark 10:2-12 echoes the impression found in the writings of Philo and Josephus of Moses as the father of his country, enacting appropriate laws at his own discretion. The question of the will of God is almost absent, save in the implied plan for marriage (10:6-9) that Moses seems to have altered.

In Mark 10:3, in reply to questions posed over the lawfulness of divorce, Jesus asks the Pharisees, "What did Moses command (ἐνετείλατο) you?" The Pharisees reply in 10:4, "Moses permitted (ἐπέτρεψεν) a man to write a certificate of divorce." J. Kastner correctly sees the exchange "zielen ungenauerweise nicht auf Moses als Mittler des Gesetzes ab; es entsteht dadurch der Eindruck, als habe Moses relativ unabhängig verfügt, was geboten und was erlaubt sei."[117] Both parties to the debate tacitly acknowledge the authority of Moses, and place Moses in the role of a legislator creating an exception to God's own general rule about marriage, laid out in 10:6-9.[118]

Jesus' further rebuttal to the Pharisees only deepens the impression that Moses was regarded as an independently creative lawmaker who could respond authoritatively to the exigencies with which he was confronted; in Mark 10:5 Jesus replies that it was "because of your hardness of heart that he wrote you this commandment (ἔγραψεν ὑμῖν τὴν ἐντολὴν ταύτην)."

---

[117] Kastner, "Moses im Neuen Testament," 343 n. 151.

[118] Kastner, "Moses im Neuen Testament," 138 is wide of the mark when he regards the opposition between 10:4 and 10:6-9 as an internal contradiction between two commandments of Moses, which Jesus has the authority to resolve. The passage clearly sets what Moses permitted in opposition to the original design of God. This conclusion actually coheres with Kastner's overall view, 141, "Gegenüber der 'Notverordnung' des Moses macht er [Jesus] den ursprünglichen Schöpferwillen geltend, der eine Auflösung der Ehe durch Mensche ausschloß."

The citation of Moses' motivation for prescribing laws resembles the Philonic conception of the Lawgiving, which was often controlled by Moses' own sensibilities. In this pericope the Pharisees and Jesus both give an impression of the publishing of the Law as a very human event.[119] It is Moses, not God, who is confronted with the hard hearts of the people, and it is Moses who responds with a new commandment.

The version of the debate given in Matt. 19:3-9 varies the composition of the story but nonetheless again presents Moses as a legislator responding to a need and not merely as an intermediary passing on a code. The imputation of authority to Moses is, if anything, stronger since it is so much clearer that it is the divine plan for marriage that Moses assumes authority to amend.

In Matt. 19:3-6 Jesus opens with remarks focusing on God's Creation-design for marriage, a feature of the debate which in Mark appears only as an aside. This makes it all the more remarkable that the Pharisees recall that "Moses commanded (ἐνετείλατο) to give her a certificate and divorce her." Where Mark's Pharisees refer to what Moses "permitted," in Matthew's revision they view the divorce ordinance as a Mosaic "command" which creates an exception to God's own design.[120] In Matthew also, Jesus explains this Mosaic provision by reference to the Israelites' hard hearts. The implication once again is that Moses acted on his own initiative, as seemed best to him, in the situation as he found it.

Both passages seem to present Moses overruling God, so that Moses and God appear as something like a binary source of the Law, with Moses making independent contributions which, if they do not overturn divine promulgations, seem at least to join with them as equally authoritative.

5.7.1.2 The Fifth Commandment

Jesus introduces the Fifth Commandment with the words Μωϋσῆς γὰρ εἶπεν in Mark 7:10. As seen above, the Rabbis generally took care to show that the Law came from God; this was doubly so not only for the Rabbis but also for Josephus, Philo, and nearly everyone else with regard to the Decalogue, which was sometimes thought to have been delivered to Israel virtually without mediation, the people hearing for themselves the voice speaking from the mountain. Mark here witnesses to a manner of speaking which implied a greater Mosaic role (the parallel in Matt. 15:4

---

[119] Ibid., 137, "Daß Moses mit dieser Bestimmung die Scheidung der Frau von ihrem Mann erlaubt hat, leugnet Jesus nicht. ... Jesus um dieses Gebot sehr wohl weiß und darum auch die Argumentation der Pharisäer ernst nimmt."

[120] In Mark 10:3 Jesus, not the Pharisees, refers to what "Moses commanded."

corrects the wording to ὁ γὰρ θεὸς εἶπεν) in the delivery of the Ten Commandments.[121]

It is hardly ever, of course, a question of choosing either solely divine authorship of the Law or solely Mosaic. In the Markan context the Fifth Commandment, which Μωϋσῆς εἶπεν, is still Jesus' exemplary "commandment of God" (ἡ ἐντολὴ τοῦ θεοῦ; 7:9), which can be contrasted to the tradition of men. The text betrays no tension over referring to what "Moses said" as the commandment of God and probably no (Jewish or Christian) author surveyed in this chapter would fail to view the whole Law of Moses as the commandments of God.

Philo, in *Hyp.* 6.8-9, which was cited at the beginning of this chapter as evidence for the division of Jewish opinion on the precise role of Moses in the Lawgiving, also makes this point: "They held it all to come from God (τοῦτο ἅπαν εἰς τὸν θεὸν ἀναγεῖν) and ... would endure to die a thousand deaths sooner than accept anything contrary to the laws and customs which [Moses] had ordained (ἢ τοῖς ἐκείνου νόμοις καὶ ἔθεσιν ἐναντία πεισθῆναι)."

The question is over how much importance is ceded to Moses. Already in this chapter it has emerged that some Jews saw in Moses a figure who did not merely mediate the Law, but cooperated in its provision. The binary relationship between God and Moses in the Lawgiving which that suggests will be especially important in Chapter Seven below, on Moses as the focus of Jewish loyalty. Here in Mark 7:6-13 one notes the opposition between 1) the commandment of God, and 2) the tradition of men, terms which apparently find suitable equivalents in the parallel 1′) "Moses said," and 2′) "but you say."

5.7.1.3 The Law of Levirate Marriage

In Mark 12:19 (∥ Luke 20:28), in the discussion of the woman married in turn to seven brothers, the Sadducees inquire regarding the law of levirate marriage which "Moses wrote for us" (Μωϋσῆς ἔγραψεν ἡμῖν). In Matt. 22:24 they refer to the same commandment as simply what "Moses said" (Μωϋσῆς εἶπεν). These expressions should be included among those that describe even the contributions of Moses to the Law as an immutable norm.[122]

---

[121] Kastner, "Moses im Neuen Testament," 136 finds in this only that Jesus "in Moses den authentischen Mittler der Offenbarungen Gottes erkennt," but perhaps this does not go far enough.

[122] So also Kastner, "Moses im Neuen Testament," 139; cf. Francois Bovon, "La figure de Moïse dans l'oeuvre de Luc," in *La figure de Moïse: Ecriture et relectures*, by Robert Martin-Achard, et al., Publications de la Faculté de Théologie de l'Université de Genève, no. 1 (Geneva: Labor et Fides, 1978), 51, "comme *norme* immuable." This is one of just a few texts that Matthew-scholar D. Allison cites when he writes, "Moses

In Mark 12:26 the reply of Jesus on the question cites the book of Moses (ἡ βίβλος Μωϋσέως), a neutral and formulaic expression with regard to the authority behind the Torah, and in Matt. 22:31 Jesus appeals to "that which was spoken to you by God (τὸ ῥηθὲν ὑμῖν ὑπὸ θεοῦ)," leaving Moses entirely out of consideration. Neither of these statements reveals much about what anyone thought of Moses, though Matthew may imply that Moses is not to be regarded as more than a mediator, as he did also with regard to the Fifth Commandment.

In the Lukan version, however, the tradition of Mark is corrected in the opposite direction to Matthew, as Jesus replies, "But that the dead are raised, even Moses showed, in the [passage of the burning] bush (καὶ Μωϋσῆς ἐμήνυσεν ἐπὶ τῆς βάτου), where it says 'the Lord the God of Abraham'," etc. (Luke 20:37). This should be recognized as part of a general Lukan emphasis on the authority of Moses in the Torah (on which see further below).[123]

5.7.1.4 The Leper's Offering

In Mark 1:44 (‖ Matt 8:4; Luke 5:14), Jesus orders the healed leper to go to the priest and "bring the things Moses commanded for a witness to them" (ἃ προσέταξεν Μωϋσῆς, εἰς μαρτύριον αὐτοῖς). Kastner points out that the words ἃ προσέταξεν Μωϋσῆς are derived from both identical and similar formulas that are used in the LXX. The formula "betont nicht so sehr die Mittleraufgabe als vielmehr die Autoritat des Moses."[124] Kastner maintains, somewhat perplexingly, that the Law is still seen as mediated by Moses, but that Moses insists on the performance of the laws he mediated on the basis of his own personal authority.[125] In any case, the denotation of commandments as "the things Moses commanded" ipso facto suggests the authority of Moses. Kastner's observation regarding the formulaic wording used serves further to tighten up the connection.

The words εἰς μαρτύριον αὐτοῖς are usually believed to explain the intention of Jesus in giving his instruction (complications set in over what exactly is being "witnessed" to). Another possibility, however, is that they

---

was for Judaism the personification of authority, its living definition. To him was given the Torah, and 'Moses says' was interchangeable with 'Scripture says' and with 'God says.' Given this, is it coincidence that the theme of Jesus' authority frequently coincides with Matthew's Moses typology?," *The New Moses: A Matthean Typology* (Edinburgh: T. & T. Clark, 1993), 276.

[123] Kastner, "Moses im Neuen Testament," 139, "Dadurch führt Lk Moses selbst als Zeugen für die Auferstehung der Toten an, um zu sagen, daß die Behauptung der Sadduzäer im Widerspruch zu Moses stehe."

[124] Kastner, "Moses im Neuen Testament," 135.

[125] Reminding one that Kastner is at all times concerned to show Moses as principally a great mediator.

represent the intentions of Moses. Within this minority view, C. E. B. Cranfield suggests two possible meanings for εἰς μαρτύριον αὐτοῖς, on which the following points are based.[126]

First, εἰς μαρτύριον αὐτοῖς might be equivalent to "for a statute for Israel." Cranfield argues that the Old Testament often refers to laws or the Law as עדות, particularly in poetic texts.[127] If this option is preferred, εἰς μαρτύριον αὐτοῖς underlines another instance where a commandment in the Law appears as the work of Moses.

Alternatively, εἰς μαρτύριον αὐτοῖς could indicate that the requirements really were intended by Moses as some sort of testimony to Israel. A reference to the intentions of Moses may go back to a tradition on which Mark drew, or may reflect Mark's own redactional emphasis. The phrase betrays a high view of Moses the lawgiver by involving Moses' intentions in the framing of the laws.

Cranfield only entertains the possibility that the passage draws attention to Moses' intentions as a legislator. The tone of the other Markan passages considered above, however, suggests that Mark here again depicts the Law as partly the product of Moses' considerations.

5.7.1.5 The Seat of Moses

In Matt 23:2-3a, Jesus says, "The scribes and the Pharisees have seated themselves in the chair (καθέδρα) of Moses, therefore all that they tell you, do and observe."

The expression "Seat of Moses" has exasperated many commentators, though most think that somewhere behind it is an actual chair of some kind.[128] Old synagogues excavated at Ḥammath-by-Tiberias, Chorazin, and Delos contain isolated stone chairs which have been the subject of

---

[126] C. E. B. Cranfield, *The Gospel According to Saint Mark*, rev. ed., Cambridge Greek Testament Commentary, ed. C. F. D. Moule (Cambridge: Cambridge University Press, 1972), 95. (Cranfield himself interprets the phrase as an expression of Jesus' intentions.)

[127] Cranfield notes Ps. 81:4-5 (MT 81:5-6) where עדות is parallel with חוק (there, as generally, the LXX translates עדות with μαρτύριον). It is, however, unlikely that the two terms in the psalm would be read as synonyms — rather, עדות probably would suggest that the "feast day" (the psalm deals with the ordination of a certain יום חגנו [MT Ps. 81:4]) served as a reminder. The parallelism between עדות and חוק is probably not synonymous, but additive. (This would weaken Cranfield's argument here.)

[128] W. D. Davies and Dale Allison, *A Critical and Exegetical Commentary on the Gospel According to Saint Matthew*, vol. 3, *Commentary on Matthew 19-28*, The International Critical Commentary on the Holy Scriptures of the Old and New Testaments, ed. J. A. Emerton, C. E. B. Cranfield, and G. N. Stanton (Edinburgh: T. & T. Clark, 1997), 268 provide four possibilities, "between which it is impossible to decide."

warm speculation in connection with Matt. 23:2.[129]   It is commonly
thought that these were reserved for synagogue presidents. E. L. Sukenik
freely identifies them as the "Seat of Moses" of Matt. 23:2,[130] but a firm
identification has not so far been possible since no inscriptional evidence
has been found.

The term "Seat of Moses" itself remains extant solely in the New Testament until the fifth-century compilation *Pesiqta de Rab Kahana*, according
to which the fourth-century Palestinian R. Aḥa described the appearance of
the throne of Solomon (in 1 Kings 10:19) by saying it had a round top like
the seat of Moses (דמשה קתדרא כהדא; *Pesiq. Rab Kah.* 1.7). The implication is that the Seat of Moses was by the talumudic period in Palestine a
recognized piece of furniture.

The gap between Jesus and R. Aḥa may be narrowed by a handful of
other traditions, probably to be dated to the second, third and fourth centuries, featuring, not specially named "Seats of Moses," but prominent chairs
in the synagogue reserved for especially eminent teachers or leaders. For
example, R. Eliezer b. Hyrcanus, in the second century A.D., had a stone
chair reserved for him as a teacher of Jewish law.[131] R. Huna, teaching in
the third century A.D. in the name of R. Jose, reports that whenever a
learned man from Jerusalem visited a city of the Diaspora they gave him a
קתדרא in which to sit.[132] *Yerushalmi Sukk.* 5.1, 55a.75 tells of seventy
golden *cathedrae* (זהב של קתידראות שבעים) reserved for the elders in
the synagogue of Alexandria, apparently prior to its destruction by Trajan
early in the second century A.D.[133] All of these special chairs are associated with rabbinic authority.[134]

Of course, "Seat of Moses" need not necessarily refer to a chair and
could, by metaphor, refer directly to the teaching authority of Moses,
which his successors took up.[135] (This was the usual interpretation before

---

[129] Key bibliography is summarized by Kenneth G. C. Newport, "A Note on 'the
Seat of Moses'," *Andrews University Seminary Studies* 28, no. 1 (1990): 53-58.

[130] E. L. Sukenik, *Ancient Synagogues in Palestine and Greece*, The Schweich Lectures of the British Academy, 1930 (London: Published for the British Academy by Oxford University Press, 1934), 57-59.

[131] *Cant. Rab.* 1.3 §1.

[132] *Lam. Rab.* 1.1 §4.

[133] These are not solitary seats, but that does not detract from their interest as specially honorable seats for synagogue leaders.

[134] Such seats may have prompted the midrashic description of Joseph occupying a
stone seat while engaged in the judgment of his brothers (*Gen. Rab.* 93.7).

[135] I. Renov, "The Seat of Moses," *Israel Exploration Journal* 5, no. 4 (1955): 266
thinks there was a real chair, but that its point was to symbolize the authority of Jewish
legal scholars (262); Jesus' words acknowledge "the leading role these scholars played
in the Jewish world of his time" (266). Cecil Roth, "The 'Chair of Moses' and Its
Survivals," *Palestine Exploration Quarterly* (July-October 1949): 110 argues that the

archaeology offered an alternative.[136]) Such a derivation of authority from Moses is the burden of *m. 'Aboth* 1. The term "Seat of Moses" suggests that a teacher could be viewed as a "vicar" of Moses.

The chair, if there was one, need not necessarily have been located in a synagogue; Davies and Allison suggest that Jesus means that the scribes and Pharisees run Moses' "school." [137] As seen above, "teacher of Torah" was one of the Rabbis' favorite conceptions of Moses, and he was thought of in some respects simply as their most senior colleague. The "seat of Moses," then, might refer to the authority of those who taught the Law and its interpretation, perhaps in the *beth midrash*.[138]

Whether or not there was in Jesus' day an actual item of furniture called the Seat of Moses, prominent spiritual leaders and teachers of Torah, according to Matt. 23:2, could be described as being seated in the same seat as Moses or in the chair that Moses endowed. In doing so they acquired the authority of Moses, authority which — to judge from the words of Jesus in Matt. 23:3 — was unquestionable. Moses is envisioned as a figure who commanded obedience, and in whose name others now do the same, with either legislative or interpretive authority. As already seen, both these were roles associated with Moses in contemporary Jewish tradition.

5.7.1.6 Conclusion

This section has reviewed the main Synoptic Gospel texts on Moses and the Law. All of them reveal or are coherent with conceptions of a very strong, authoritative Moses who had a dynamic role in the making of the Law.[139] Certain additional texts from the Gospel of Luke contribute fur-

---

"seats of Moses" were stands for the Torah itself, making "sit in the seat of Moses" an idiom for arrogance. Renov, 266 refutes the Torah stand speculation, but the suggestion of an idiom is intriguing.

[136] Roth, "The 'Chair of Moses' and Its Survivals," 100-101.

[137] Davies and Allison, *Commentary on the Gospel According to Saint Matthew*, vol. 3, 268.

[138] Davies and Allison, ibid., 270 assign Matt. 23:2-3 to pre-Matthean tradition. The earliest reference to the *beth midrash* occurs in the Geniza fragments of Ben Sira, 51:23. The existence of the Greek parallel indicates that the Hebrew text is correspondingly old (early second century B.C.; the Greek translation was made sometime after 132 B.C.). Ben Sira may use the expression metaphorically but this is no argument against the existence of *batei midrash* from which he drew the metaphor; see discussion and bibliography in James K. Aitken, "Hebrew Study In Ben Sira's *Beth Midrash*," in *Hebrew Study from Ezra to Ben-Yehuda*, ed. William Horbury (Edinburgh: T. & T. Clark, 1999), 27-28, esp. n. 6.

[139] Kastner, "Moses im Neuen Testament," 140-41, summing up his treatment of the passages just reviewed here, "Die Wendungen 'Moses hat verordnet' [etc.] aus dem Munde Jesu und der jüdischen Diskussionsgegner legen ein beredtes Zeugnis darüber ab, wie sehr für die frühe Zeit des Christentums die Autorität des Moses als eines Ge-

ther toward this impression. Consideration of these will be taken up in discussion of Luke and Acts.

5.7.2 Luke-Acts

Luke's Gospel was included with the other Synoptic Gospels, but deserves
a reprise since Luke-Acts as a corpus seems to have an especially well-
developed sense of the importance of Moses. As already seen above, Luke
presents Moses as an author and a lawmaker, yet the overall thrust of his
presentation seems to set Moses in relation to the prophets, specifically as
the leading prophet. Luke's special focus on Moses is probably traceable
to the author, or at least to the special traditions he brings to his work.[140]

In the New Testament, only in Luke-Acts is appeal is made to "Moses
and the prophets." One example occurs in Luke 16:29, 31, at the climax of
the parable about Lazarus and the rich man (L source). There, Abraham
tells the tormented rich man that his still-living kin "have Moses and the
Prophets" (ἔχουσι Μωϋσέα καὶ τοὺς προφήτας) to listen to. Contrast
Q, only a few verses earlier, where it is the Law and the Prophets that are
proclaimed (Luke 16:16 ‖ Matt. 11:13). In Luke 24:27 (again L), when
the resurrected Jesus meets the two disciples on the way to Emmaus, he
explains everything to do with himself in the Scriptures, "beginning with
Moses and with all the prophets" (ἀρξάμενος ἀπὸ Μωϋσέως καὶ ἀπὸ
πάντων τῶν προφητῶν). The only other NT use of this pairing is in the
declaration of Paul to Agrippa of "what the Prophets and Moses said was
going to take place" (τε οἱ προφῆται ἐλάλησαν μελλόντων γίνεσθαι
καὶ Μωϋσῆς) in relation to the Christ (Acts 26:22-23).

It is tempting to regard "Moses" in these texts as simply a reference to
"the Law of Moses." Yet in each of these passages the focus is on the twin
testimonies or witnesses of Moses and the prophets, suggesting a parity of
some kind between authoritative figures. In the Acts text the concern is
explicitly with what Moses spoke (ἐλάλησαν). The implication may be
that in one corpus the prophets speak, and in the other Moses speaks.

Evidently, Luke (or the L source) simply prefers to cite Moses rather
than the Law. The Lukan "Moses-consciousness" also appears in Luke's
preference to cite specifically the "Law of Moses" rather than simply the

---

setzgebers feststand." Of the synoptic Evangelists Matthew is the weakest on the authority of Moses, and the clearest on his role as a mediator. Cf. Kastner, 165.

[140] On the presentation of Moses as a prophet in Luke-Acts see above, pp. 51-63.
The verdict of Kastner, "Moses im Neuen Testament," 178, "Daß Moses als Übermittler
der Gesetzesoffenbarungen fungierte und nicht als Gesetzgeber, wird dabei nicht näher
erörtert, sondern stillschweigend vorausgesetzt," is close to the mark, but he overlooks
his own observations on texts like Luke 5:14 and 20:37, which portray Moses as an authority indeed.

"Law," as elsewhere generally in the New Testament.[141] This, however, only brings Moses onto the stage; the characterization of Moses' role vis-à-vis the Law in Luke-Acts requires further investigation.

The controversy with the Sadducees about the resurrection was already noted above.[142] As recorded in Mark 12:26, Jesus inquires, "Have you not read in the book of Moses, in the [passage of the burning] bush, how God spoke to him, saying, 'I am the God of Abraham ..., etc.?'" In the parallel Luke 20:37, however, Moses jumps into the foreground as a theologian. There Jesus says, "But that the dead are raised, even Moses showed (καὶ Μωϋσῆς ἐμήνυσεν), in the [passage of the burning] bush, where he calls the Lord the God of Abraham ...". Here Moses knows about the resurrection of the dead and communicates his teaching through a meticulous selection of words. The attribution of this kind of wordsmithing to Moses is nearly Philonic.

In many places Acts seems conscious of Moses as the genius behind the law, or at least behind the "ceremonial" law. In Acts 15:21 James's defense of the propriety of the Jerusalem Decree consists of a reminder that "Moses has in every city those who preach him (Μωϋσῆς γὰρ ἐκ γενεῶν ἀρχαίων κατὰ πόλιν τοὺς κηρύσσοντας αὐτὸν ἔχει)." The sentiment seems to be offered as a consolation to the "lawkeeping party" in the group, and certainly implies that Moses was responsible for that portion of the Law which the Council determined not to demand of the Gentiles. No real harm, James is saying, will be done if circumcision ("the custom of Moses," Acts 15:1) is not required of Gentile Christians since Moses will be honored as usual among Jews. Not only is God's agency behind the Law passed over, in fact it is claimed that those who would enjoin the Law (of Moses) on Gentiles are actually "putting God to the test" (τί πειρά-ζετε τὸν θεόν; 15:10). God appears here not as the giver of the Law, but only as the one who sets Moses' law aside for the Gentiles.[143]

The same idea about Moses recurs in Acts 21:21, where to teach Jews not to circumcise is to teach apostasy from Moses (ἀποστασία ἀπὸ Μωϋσέως). Circumcision, be it noted, is among the few provisions in the Pentateuch not very easily laid at Moses' door (cf. John 7:22) but Acts strongly connects it with him.[144]

The Mosaic authority behind the Law is implied in the Acts passages just mentioned, but occurs almost explicitly in Acts 6:11, 14, where Stephen is accused of speaking "blasphemous words against Moses and God" (ῥήματα βλάσφημα εἰς Μωϋσῆν καὶ τὸν θεόν). False witnesses accuse

---

[141] Luke 2:22; Acts 13:39; 15:5; 28:23.
[142] See above, pp. 151-52.
[143] See further, below, pp. 221-22.
[144] See further, below, pp. 222, 253-54.

him of teaching that Jesus would destroy the Temple "and alter the customs which Moses handed down to us" (τὰ ἔθη ἃ παρέδωκεν ἡμῖν Μωϋσῆς). Note that this is a repetition of the same two charges from 6:13, where the "customs" of Moses are termed "Law." Again the divine authorship of the Law falls almost completely into the background.[145] The prestige of the Law is the prestige of Moses.[146]

God as a revealer to Moses occurs only in Acts 7:44, and there very obliquely, as the one who directed Moses to make the tabernacle "according to the pattern which he had seen" (κατὰ τὸν τύπον ὃν ἑωράκει). Compare Heb. 8:5, where the divine passives are preserved in the quotation of Exod. 25:40, so that Moses builds according to the pattern he was shown (κατὰ τὸν τύπον τὸν δειχθέντα σοι ἐν τῷ ὄρει, sc. by God). Acts moves Moses into a less passive role.

Overall, Luke shows a greater interest in Moses than the other Synoptic Evangelists, and his interest appears to be in Moses as an individual personality, not merely as a cipher for the Law. Despite the unquestionable link Luke makes between Moses and the prophets, he also seems keen that Moses should be seen in much more glorious way than the prophets. A context like Luke-Acts, which suggests that setting aside circumcision might offend (not God but) Moses (Acts 15:21), and which makes blasphemy an offense that can be committed against God and Moses in tandem (Acts 6:11, 14), throws the ascription to Moses of the Laws and customs into sharpest relief.[147] Luke-Acts seems, even more than the other Synoptic Gospels, to have a high estimate of Moses and to see Moses as the genius behind the Law.

5.7.3 The Fourth Gospel

The situation in the Fourth Gospel is more complex than that in the Synoptics. The Fourth Gospel seems to critique a popular Jewish view of Moses by portraying a conflict between that view and the way Jesus (or perhaps the narrator) wanted Moses to be estimated.[148] This conflict probably represents a genuine range of opinion about Moses among Jews of the first

---

[145] See further, below, p. 253.

[146] All of this going rather against the judgment of Kastner, "Moses im Neuen Testament," 178, who concludes of Luke-Acts that "Moses als Übermittler der Gesetzesoffenbarungen fungierte und nicht als Gesetzgeber."

[147] Recall that the customs, i.e., the oral law, were soon to be regarded just as much Torah as the Mosaic code itself.

[148] In John, the crowds seem to cherish an extremely high view of Moses in general, not just with respect to the Lawgiving. See, e.g., John 6:31-32, citing Ps. 78:24 but ignoring its assignment of the provision of manna to God.

century.[149] Four texts from the Fourth Gospel will be examined here: John 1:17; 5:46-47; 7:16-24; and 8:2-6.

5.7.3.1 John 7:16-24 and 5:45-47

John 7:16-24 is the most extensive passage on Moses as Lawgiver in the Fourth Gospel. It begins (John 7:16-18) with perhaps the clearest endorsement in the Gospel of prophetic, as opposed to personally authoritative, teaching, an important theme throughout the Gospel. When Jesus says, "My teaching is not mine, but his who sent me," he sets himself apart both from anyone who teaches on his own authority and from those, like the Rabbis, whose authority is derived from a chain of tradition. "The one who speaks from himself" (ὁ ἀφ᾽ ἑαυτοῦ λαλῶν, 7:18) is clearly disparaged. When immediately after this beginning Jesus asks (in 7:19), "Did not Moses give you a law?" (Οὐ Μωϋσῆς δέδωκεν ὑμῖν τὸν νόμον;), it could be implied that Moses gave laws, in Johannine parlance, "from himself."

As the present chapter has already shown, this would not be such an exceptional view, and elsewhere in the Fourth Gospel (5:45-47) Jesus suggests that the writings of Moses are regarded as expressions of Moses' own authority. The Jews put their hope in Moses (Μωϋσῆς, εἰς ὃν ὑμεῖς ἠλπίκατε), Jesus says. They evidently do not really believe him though, "because he wrote of me (περὶ γὰρ ἐμοῦ ἐκεῖνος ἔγραψεν). Here the appeal is to the authority and trustworthiness of Moses himself, though again in Fourth Gospel it is better to speak on God's authority than on one's own.

Returning to John 7:19, the suggestion that Moses gave laws on his own account is reinforced in 7:22 where in nearly the same words as in 7:19 Jesus names the law of circumcision as a specific law which Moses enjoined (Μωϋσῆς δέδωκεν ὑμῖν τὴν περιτομήν). The authority of this law is unquestionable: it is "the Law of Moses" which must not be broken (verse 23: ἵνα μὴ λυθῇ ὁ νόμος Μωϋσέως), even, as in this case, when it conflicts with a portion of the Decalogue.[150] The reference to the unbreakable

---

[149] Recall again the words of Philo, in the Introduction to the present Chapter. All the Gospels are valuable as witnesses not only to the teaching of Jesus and the responses of his hearers, but also to the outlooks of their respective authors. Telling them apart is another matter, and little effort is expended here in trying to do so.

[150] The discussion in John 7:16-24 assumes familiarity with the problem of keeping the requirement to circumcise newborn boys on the eighth day when the birth has occurred on a Sabbath. Such a case would oblige the circumcision to take place eight days later, (by inclusive reckoning) on the following Sabbath. According to *m. Ned.* 3:11, "R. Jose says: Great is circumcision which overrides even the rigour of the Sabbath. R. Joshua b. Karha says: Great is circumcision which even for the sake of Moses, the righteous, was not suspended so much as an hour." This seems clear enough: Cir-

law of Moses recalls the authority of teaching that comes from the "seat of Moses" in Matt. 23:2-3, teaching which must be obeyed.

Though many commentators have concluded that the διὰ τοῦτο which begins John 7:22 should be attached to the preceding verb, giving θαυμά-ζετε διὰ τοῦτο, i.e. they were amazed at the work Jesus had done,[151] the phrase more likely links to the following clause, as in most English versions, giving "For this [reason] Moses gave you circumcision (διὰ τοῦτο Μωϋσῆς δέδωκεν ὑμῖν τὴν περιτομήν)." This reading would recall the many occasions in Philo where the enactment of laws is related to the aims of Moses,[152] and further support the view of Moses as legislator here in John.

The entire discussion assumes that Moses is responsible for the law of circumcision. The "correction" of the law's pedigree, which is inserted in v. 22: "not that it is from Moses, but from the fathers (οὐχ ὅτι ἐκ τοῦ Μωϋσέως ἐστὶν ἀλλ' ἐκ τῶν πατέρων)," however, cautions against that view. The reason for the correction is no longer clear, though possibly it is intended as a justification for prioritizing the law of circumcision over the Fourth Commandment on the grounds of its greater antiquity.[153] In any case, the parenthesis opposes inflation of the importance of Moses as a legislator by pointing out that the commandment of Moses was not his at all but was inherited from the Patriarchs.

---

cumcision is to take place on schedule, regardless of any other calendrical obligations that may coincide. Further, *m. Shab.* 18:3-19:4 contains detailed provisions for circumcision on or around the Sabbath. But then in *m. Shab.* 19:5 adjustments to the eight-day rule are given to allow circumcision to be put off, either for a birth at the very end of a day, or for a birth from which the eighth day is a Sabbath or festival. As so often in the rabbinic materials, the case is left unresolved.

[151] Defended by Bernhard Weiss, *Das Johannes-Evangelium*, 6th ed., Kritisch-exegetischer Kommentar über das Neue Testament, 9th ed. (Göttingen: Vandenhoeck & Ruprecht, 1902), 245; see also M.-J. LaGrange, *Évangile selon Saint Jean*, 2d ed., Études Bibliques (Paris: Librairie Victor LeCoffre, 1925), 206; J. H. Bernard, *A Critical and Exegetical Commentary on the Gospel According to St. John*, ed. A. H. McNeile, 2 vols., The International Critical Commentary (Edinburgh: T. & T. Clark, 1928; reprint, 1942), 263; J. N. Sanders, *A Commentary on the Gospel according to St. John*, ed. and completed by B. A. Mastin, Black's New Testament Commentaries, ed. Henry Chadwick (London: Adam & Charles Black, 1968), 207 n. 2.

[152] In all its fourteen other occurrences in John διὰ τοῦτο falls at the beginning of its clause; see C. K. Barrett, *The Gospel According to St John: An Introduction with Commentary and Notes on the Greek Text*, 2d ed. (London: SPCK, 1978), 319; D A. Carson, *The Gospel According to John* (Leicester: Inter-Varsity Press; Grand Rapids: Wm. B. Eerdmans, 1991), 314. Barnabas Lindars, *The Gospel of John*, New Century Bible, ed. Ronald E. Clements and Matthew Black (London: Oliphants, 1972), 290 has it in this text referring both directions.

[153] Cf. Gal. 3:17.

In the text as it now stands the explanation in v. 22 of "why Moses gave circumcision" both cautions against attributing circumcision to Moses and attests the apparently common view that saw Moses as the party responsible for a rite that is also elsewhere (Acts 15:1) called "the tradition of Moses," and here is "the law of Moses" (vv. 19, 23).

5.7.3.2 John 8:2-6

The Fourth Gospel's account of the woman caught in adultery deserves to be noticed here. The pericope is almost undoubtedly secondary, yet still quite early, and it probably testifies to the Jewish view of Moses in the first century.

The scribes and Pharisees press Jesus with the reminder, "Now in the Law Moses commanded us to stone such women" (ἐν δὲ τῷ νόμῳ ἡμῖν Μωϋσῆς ἐνετείλατο τὰς τοιαύτας λιθάζειν). The intent is to force a dilemma on Jesus, for the sake of which the command should stem from the highest possible authority; the higher the authority behind the command the sharper the horns of the dilemma. In this passage that high authority is Moses.

5.7.3.3 John 1:17a

John 1:17a, "The Law was given through Moses" (ὁ νόμος διὰ Μωϋσέως ἐδόθη), seems to portray the Law as prophecy, not legislation, although as just seen the Fourth Gospel goes on to speak of Moses as lawgiver in terms just as impressive as the other Gospels. Not even the most exalted (Jewish) portrait of Moses as lawgiver, however, relinquishes the idea that the laws are God's, whether God revealed them to Moses directly or equipped Moses to make them on his own.[154] Moreover, the link between authority and mediation is a special theme of the Fourth Gospel, and John 1:17 may present the view of its author when it upholds this ideal for both Jesus and Moses. When at its outset the Fourth Gospel compares Jesus and Moses as mediators, the role is seen as exhaustive for neither.

5.7.3.4 Conclusion

The indications in the Fourth Gospel are not as clear as those in the Synoptics and Luke-Acts. Nonetheless, the evidence that appears is for a view of Moses as an authority in the giving of the Law, not just a messenger. The Fourth Gospel, like the other three, stands closer to what appears to be the contemporary, more blended, view of Moses as a prophet and lawgiver, or perhaps as an inspired lawmaker, than it does to that which emerged in the rabbinic period, which saw Moses strictly as a mediator. In some respect, the Law in the Fourth Gospel carries the authority of Moses personally.

---

[154] Compare the view of Philo, p. 151 above.

This coheres well with the Johannine presentation of Moses as a focus of loyalty for Jews, which will be taken up in Chapter Seven of this study.

5.7.4 Paul

"Strictly," M. D. Hooker writes, "Moses does not belong to Paul's scheme. He appears, of course, because he is the mediator of the Jewish Law and cannot be ignored."[155] In fact, Paul typically ignores the mediator, and refers to the Law directly.[156] Paul, like the Rabbis, may have preferred not to think of the Law as something Moses wrote but rather to focus on its divine origin, and its nearly hypostatic independence. As Paul was a Pharisee, it is not surprising to find in his thought elements of what later became part of established rabbinic Judaism.

5.7.4.1 Paul on the Law

Paul's treatment of the Law seems to be another case of the New Testament yielding the earliest references to what eventually became widespread Jewish custom. This is true for several of Paul's methods.

5.7.4.1.1 Citations of the Law

For example, in 1 Cor. 14:21, the citation of Isa. 28:11 with the words, "in the Law it is written," is still best explained as Paul's adoption of what became the custom of referring to the whole Old Testament as the Law.[157] (The next earliest firm evidence for the practice appears in the Babylonian Talmud.[158]) In 1 Cor. 14:34, Paul (or a very early glossator) also provides

---

[155] Morna D. Hooker, "Paul and 'Covenantal Nomism'," in *Paul and Paulinism: Essays in Honour of C. K. Barrett*, ed. M. D. Hooker and S. G. Wilson (London: SPCK, 1982), 56. The paucity of Paul's references to Moses is particularly striking in light of his numerous references to the Law, and also in light of his citation formulae for the other Scriptures, which involve the author's names. Of course, C. K. Barrett, *From First Adam to Last: A Study in Pauline Theology* (London: Adam & Charles Black, 1962), 46 thinks that Moses' nine Pauline mentions are a significantly large number. Everything is relative. On Pauline citation formulae, see below, n. 174.

[156] Also, he compares Christ with Adam, not Moses, a move which deletes the most obvious reason for Paul to discuss Moses in his surviving letters.

[157] Rom. 3:19 and John 10:34 also point in this direction, Gordon D. Fee, *The First Epistle to the Corinthians*, The New International Commentary on the New Testament, ed. F. F. Bruce (Grand Rapids: William B. Eerdmans, 1987), 679 n. 19.

[158] See Herman L. Strack and Paul Billerbeck, *Kommentar zum Neuen Testament aus Talmud und Midrasch*, vol. 3, *Die Briefe des Neuen Testaments und die Offenbarung Johannis* (Munich: C. H. Beck'sche Verlagsbuchhandlung [Oskar Beck], 1926), 462-63 and further 15; vol. 2, *Das Evangelium nach Markus, Lukas, und Johannes und die Apostelgeschichte* (1924), 542-43. *Tanḥuma* Buber, Exodus, 5(Yitro).8 (Exodus 19:1, Part 2) states, "The Torah (in the sense of Scripture) is threefold: Torah, Prophets, and Writings"; *Midr. Pss.* 78:1 explicitly argues that the Prophets and the

probably the earliest instance of the use of "Law" to refer to the oral traditions,[159] a custom which became widespread alongside rabbinic teaching about the delivery of both the written Law and all its later developments at Sinai as "Torah."[160] Similarly, Paul's relative "neglect" of Moses in his lengthy discussions of the Law may stem from a contemporary pattern of thought about the Law, perhaps the beginnings of a Pharisaic consensus on the Lawgiving that eventually gave rise to the rabbinic conception of Moses as purely a mediator.

Psalms are to be considered Torah, and implies that Proverbs is also. Contrast Luke 24:44; Acts 13:38-39; 28:23; *y. Meg.* 70b.60.

[159] The "Law" in 1 Cor. 14:34 is widely taken to be Gen. 3:16. S. Aalen, "A Rabbinic Formula in I Cor. 14,34," in *Studia Evangelica*, vol. 2, *Papers Presented to the Second International Congress on New Testament Studies Held at Christ Church, Oxford, 1961*, part I, *The New Testament Scriptures*, ed. F. L. Cross, Texte und Untersuchungen zur Geschichte der altchristlichen Literatur, vol. 87 (Berlin: Akademie-Verlag, 1964), 522-523 argues that the prohibition on women speaking must derive from the written Torah, though he does not cite a specific text. He explains Paul's statement as a rabbinic אִיסוּר אוֹרַיְיתָא, a prohibition often found in the biblical text explicitly, but which sometimes "is contained in the text of the Bible only by implication; in other words it has to be deduced," 524. This, however, sounds a great deal like an appeal to tradition, and not to the written Torah. Max Küchler, *Schweigen, Schmuck und Schleier: Drei neutestamentliche Vorschriften zur Verdrängung der Frauen auf dem Hintergrund einer frauenfeindlichen Exegese des Alten Testaments im antiken Judentum*, Novum Testamentum et Orbis Antiquus, ed. Max Küchler with Gerd Theissen, no. 1 (Freiburg, Switzerland: Universitätsverlag; Göttingen: Vandenhoeck & Ruprecht, 1986) argues first (58-60) that the author of 1 Cor. 14:34c must have had a tradition founded on the written Law in mind, and then goes on (60-63) to argue specifically for Gen. 3:16. His argument, however, is closely linked with citations from the Talmud and Targums, and he himself judges the argument from Gen. 3:16, which he attributes to the author, as "[die] ungenügenden alttestamentliche Schriftbasis den notwendigen Zuschuss an Argumentationskraft," 62, and goes on, "Der Verweis auf 'das Gesetz' in 1Kor 14,34c, um die Unterordnung der Frau unter den Mann in Schweigen der Frauen vor den Männern biblisch zu begründen, muss deshalb als unzutreffender exegetischer Versucht gewertet werden," 63. This conclusion, ironically, once again rather supports the view that a tradition is in view, just one with biblical support. See *Ap.* 2.200-201 where Josephus apparently also uses νόμος to refer to tradition, and touching on the very same issue of the need for women to be submissive. On this passage, and Philo, *Hyp.* 7.3, which includes the submission of women in discussion of the Jewish νόμοι (6.8; also called πολίτευμα, νομοθεσία in the introductory *Praep. Ev.* 8.5.11), see Küchler, *Schweigen*, 58-59.

[160] See above, p. 146 with n. 107.

5.7.4.1.2 Hypostasis of the Law

In another, less certain, foreshadowing of later rabbinic tendencies, Paul verges at times on hypostatizing the Law.[161] Inquiry into this question is complicated by the fact that Paul seems willing, like the Rabbis, to use ὁ νόμος to refer to the entire Bible, and to use ἡ γραφή to refer to the Law. So in Rom. 9:17, the statement "Scripture says to Pharaoh" (λέγει γὰρ ἡ γραφὴ τῷ Φαραώ) introduces words (of the Lord) quoted from Exod. 9:16. In Gal. 3:8 Paul writes of Gen. 12:3 that "Scripture preached to Abraham" (ἡ γραφὴ ... προευηγγελίσατο τῷ Ἀβραάμ). To these add Gal. 4:30 where λέγει ἡ γραφή introduces Gen. 21:10. Only in Rom. 10:11 does the expression λέγει ἡ γραφή introduce a non-Pentateuchal text, Isa. 28:16. Clearly, for Paul νόμος and γραφή are interchangeable terms. This is most concisely demonstrated in Gal. 3:22-23, which introduces ἡ γραφή and ὁ νόμος apparently as synonyms: Paul says both "Scripture shut up all men under sin" (συνέκλεισεν ἡ γραφὴ τὰ πάντα ὑπὸ ἁμαρτίαν; v. 22), and "we were kept in the Law's custody" (ὑπὸ νόμον ἐφρουρούμεθα; v. 23).

The evidence for Pauline hypostasis of ὁ νόμος is if anything slightly weaker than that for his hypostasis of ἡ γραφή. The only potentially hypostatic use of νόμος (with reference to the Pentateuch) is in Rom. 7:7, where Paul writes, "the Law said (ὁ νόμος ἔλεγεν), 'You shall not covet.'" In Rom. 3:19 Paul says that the Law speaks (λέγει and λαλεῖ) though here, most likely, "Law" refers back to the preceding *catena* of texts from the Prophets and the Writings.

Traces of the hypostasis of the Law appear in rabbinic literature, as in the *haggadoth* in which the book of Deuteronomy prostrates itself before God to protest at Solomon's behavior, or in which individual letters speak before God.[162] Regarding hypostasis of the Law, however, Paul is actually better paralleled by Philo, who refers to the Law, though not to Scripture, giving commands,[163] teaching,[164] testifying,[165] detesting infanticides,[166] dis-

---

[161] The notion of "the hypostatized Law" in Paul is not conclusively demonstrated, or perhaps even demonstrable (see W. Gutbrod, "νόμος," in *Theological Dictionary of the New Testament*, ed. Gerhard Kittel, trans. and ed. Geoffrey W. Bromiley, vol. 4, *Λ-Ν* [Grand Rapids: Wm. B. Eerdmans, 1967], 1070). Nonetheless, at least some Pauline references to the Law use language very suggestive of the Law as a distinct entity.

[162] *Y. Sanh.* 20c.48-50 ‖ *Lev. Rab.* 19.2(26a.19-21); *Cant. Rab.* 5:11 §3-4(31.11-18).

[163] In Deuteronomy, *Post.* 89.

[164] *Post.* 80, 102.

[165] In Deut. 32:15, *Post.* 121. *Post.* 122 goes on to mention Moses "also testifying," in Num. 14:9, as if Moses and the Law were complementary voices.

[166] *Spec. Leg.* 3.119.

allowing,[167] exhorting,[168] ruling on unclean animals,[169] and telling stories.[170] The law itself "lays down rules," commanding and forbidding.[171] In *Spec. Leg.* 4.213-217 there is even a speech by Law speaking in the first person of its commands, such as Sabbath observance.

The evidence for hypostasis in Paul is too confused to allow confident conclusions to be drawn about Paul's exact position on that subject, and its implications for his position on Moses with regard to the Law. Moreover, Philo, who seems to parallel Paul closely in his tendency to hypostatize the Law, at the same time gives enormous credit to Moses in the composition of the Law, as observed above. This serves as a warning against drawing hasty conclusions about Paul's thinking on Moses from the limited and uncertain evidence on available on Paul's notions of hypostasis.

It is clear, however, that Paul sometimes speaks of the Law (or of the Scripture) as an independent or hypostatic entity. This custom seems more consistent with the rabbinic, or even with the Philonic, conception of the Law as an independent authority than with the idea of the Law as the collected statutes of Moses, and therefore may show Paul inclining toward what later became the general rabbinic view of the lawgiving as prophecy.

Paul also attaches great importance to the Law while at the same time usually leaving Moses entirely out of the picture, whether as mediator or as legislator. This too could suggest that Paul viewed the Law as a free-standing authority, or at least as bearing an authority independent of Moses.

5.7.4.2 Paul's Citations of Moses

Paul, however, twice mentions Moses by name in citation formulae that connect him with the Lawgiving. Romans 10:19 introduces an utterance, attributed in Deut 32:21 to the Lord, with "Moses says" (Μωϋσῆς λέγει). Since the text quoted is from Deuteronomy, though, the attribution to Moses is not so remarkable.

Romans 10:5, however, cites Lev. 18:5, also attributed to the Lord, with "Moses writes (Μωϋσῆς γὰρ γράφει)." But since only a particularly radical rabbinic view denied that Moses was involved even in reducing the Law to writing, this citation too is not very remarkable. Additionally, in its original setting Lev. 18:5 is prefaced with the command in Lev. 18:2

---

[167] οὐδε ... ἐᾷ; *Post.* 94.
[168] *Spec. Leg.* 3.182.
[169] *Agr.* 131.
[170] *Det.* 159; *Post.* 96.
[171] *Virt.* 18-19.

for Moses to speak to the people of Israel. It may then only be natural to introduce a quotation from that passage with an attribution to Moses.[172]

Paul's two citation formulae connecting Moses with the Law cannot of themselves prove any Pauline position on Moses resembling that argued above from the Gospels,[173] nor on the other hand are they sufficient to label him particularly "rabbinic" in outlook, though Rom. 9:15 might suggest the special prophetic status of Moses, if τῷ Μωϋσεῖ γὰρ λέγει means "the Lord (not Scripture) says to Moses."[174] Romans 10:5 shows that Paul understood Moses to have been involved in committing the Law to writing, which at least separates him from the most extreme rabbinic view, while Paul's sole reference to "the Law of Moses" (ἐν γὰρ τῷ Μωϋσέως νόμῳ γέγραπται; 1 Cor. 9:9) quotes Deuteronomy (Deut. 25:4),[175] where contemporary Jewish thought tended to see the authority of Moses most. Romans 10:19 (with 10:20), however, seems to make Deuteronomy a distinctly prophetic message. Put all together, Paul's citations of Moses do little to suggest that Paul saw the Law as a combination of divine and Mosaic legislation, let alone that he saw Moses as an authoritative legislator, and are rather better suited to a view of the Law as prophecy.

---

[172] Michel Quesnel, "La figure de Moïse en Romains 9-11," *New Testament Studies* 49 (July 2003): 329-331 points out, however, that Rom. 10:5-8 places Moses in dialogue with "Righteousness of faith." What Moses wrote concerning "la justice qui vient de la loi," is opposed to "le discours de la Justice (qui vient) de la foi," 331. Quesnel sees the passage depicting Moses as a legislator or redactor, in a kind of opposition to what Quesnel, 331-33 sees as the depiction of Moses as a prophet in Rom. 10:19-21.

[173] But see the remark of Thrall below.

[174] Paul generally uses a variety of citation formulae for Scripture, though his favorite is the simple "it is written." Where he does attribute a saying, he follows no obvious pattern. Besides those just noted, Rom. 9:27, 29; 10:16, 21-22 all credit Isaiah. In 2 Cor. 6:16-17 Paul attributes Lev. 26:11, Exod. 37:27, and Is. 52:11 to God; attribution to the Lord is also implied in Rom. 9:15, where Exod. 33:19 is introduced with τῷ Μωϋσεῖ γὰρ λέγει (or does he mean "Scripture says"?), and in Rom. 9:25-27, of Hos. 2:1, 25. In Rom. 4:6; 11:9 Paul attributes to David Pss. 31(EV 32):1; 68:23. Kastner, "Moses im Neuen Testament," 182 believes Rom. 9:15, τῷ Μωϋσεῖ γὰρ λέγει, is the only clear statement in Paul's writings that Moses himself received words from God; Kastner, 183 suggests that there is an implied contrast with Rom. 9:17, in which it is (merely) the Scriptures that speak to Pharaoh. Romans 5:13-14 only nods at the connection between Moses and the coming of the Law. For a tabulation of all of Paul's OT quotations and their citation formulae, see D. Moody Smith, "The Pauline Literature," in *It Is Written: Scripture Citing Scripture: Essays in Honour of Barnabas Lindars, SSF*, ed. D. A. Carson and H. G. M. Williamson (Cambridge: Cambridge University Press, 1988), 267-71.

[175] More often Paul modifies "Law" with "of God"; Rom. 7:22, 25; 8:7.

5.7.4.3 Second Corinthians 3

In 2 Cor. 3:14-15 Paul parallels, apparently synonymously,[176] "at the reading of the old covenant" (ἐπὶ τῇ ἀναγνώσει τῆς παλαιᾶς διαθήκης) with "whenever Moses is read" (ἡνίκα ἂν ἀναγινώσκηται Μωϋσῆς). Here "Moses" stands for "covenant of Moses," that is, the Law.[177] Thrall argues from this text back to the citation formulae of Rom. 10:5 and 19 just reviewed to show that Moses "is seen as writing and uttering the passages from the Pentateuch which are quoted there [in Romans], just as here he is the lawgiver whose utterances in the whole Pentateuch are read in the synagogue."[178]

That Moses appears in 2 Corinthians 3 in the context of the Lawgiving is evident from the many reminders of the Sinai Lawgiving therein: the stone tablets (3:3, 7), the covenant (3:6, 14), the engraved letters (3:7) with the condemnation and death they bring (3:6, 7, 9),[179] and the midrash on Exodus 34:29-35, with its feature of the glowing face of Moses, are all clearly connected with the reception of the Law by Moses.

Thrall's conclusion about Moses "uttering" the Pentateuchal laws suggests that she sees more in Paul's attitude toward Moses than this study has so far allowed. The Rabbis, who emphasized that Moses received the Law, would be uncomfortable with such a formulation, which comes near to saying that Moses issued the laws, and, as shown above, the Romans texts by themselves cannot support that claim, outside perhaps of Deuteronomy. In rabbinic literature Moses is not "seen as writing" the Law, at least not in any authorial capacity. Indisputably, no other Pauline text places Moses in a lawgiving capacity like 2 Cor. 3:14-15 does, but the precise function of Moses in that capacity may not be that of a legislative au-

---

[176] So Margaret E. Thrall, *A Critical and Exegetical Commentary on the Second Epistle to the Corinthians*, vol. 1, *Introduction and Commentary on II Corinthians I-VII*, The International Critical Commentary on the Holy Scriptures of the Old and New Testaments, ed. J. A. Emerton, C. E. B. Cranfield, and G. N. Stanton (Edinburgh: T. & T. Clark, 1994), 267.

[177] See Victor Paul Furnish, *II Corinthians: Translated with Introduction, Notes, and Commentary*, The Anchor Bible, ed. William Foxwell Albright and David Noel Freedman, vol. 32A (Garden City, N.Y.: Doubleday & Co., 1984), 210; cf. Acts 15:21. The tempting suggestion by J.-F. Collange, *Énigmes de la deuxième épître de Paul aux Corinthiens: Étude exégetique de 2 Cor. 12:14-7:4*, Society for New Testament Studies Monograph Series, ed. Matthew Black, no. 18 (Cambridge: The University Press, 1972), 100 that "'Lire Moïse', c'est interpréter sa vie et son oeuvre, ce que les adversaires de Paul font, mais font mal," is dismissed by Furnish, and by Thrall, *Commentary on the Second Epistle to the Corinthians*, vol. 1, 267.

[178] Thrall, *Commentary on the Second Epistle to the Corinthians*, vol. 1, 267.

[179] Cf. Rom. 7:9-10; Gal. 3:10. "To kill had now become the function of the law," Thrall, *Commentary on the Second Epistle to the Corinthians*, vol. 1, 236; see also 241, 249.

thority (see below), and so a query should be set against Thrall's extrapolation to the Romans citation formulae, which are themselves clearly unable to support such a conception of Moses.

5.7.4.3.1 Moses the Mediator of the Law

The question is whether 2 Corinthians 3 makes Moses an authority in himself or only a mediator. This is where Thrall's conclusion about Paul thinking of Moses writing and uttering the laws seems overstated. Galatians 3:19 shows that Paul thought of Moses as a mediator of the Law, and perhaps not even as a very exalted one, since in that verse his contact is not with God himself but only with the angels,[180] who themselves were also (a yet higher class of) mediators.[181] The citations from Romans just reviewed also make the best sense if at least the non-Deuteronomic portion of the Law was thought by Paul to be the product of mediation only. In 2 Corinthians 3, a Pauline view of Moses as essentially a mediator or messenger may help to explain how Paul the apostle is able so easily to place Moses and himself on the same plane.

The most persuasive proposal for the background of 2 Corinthian 3 is Thrall's:

> The natural way of reading 3.7-11 is to see it as a comparison and contrast between non-Christian Judaism and Christianity. ... If Paul is reacting to criticism, it must come originally from non-Christian Jews who have compared him to his disadvantage with the glorious figure of Moses, and drawn the conclusion that his alleged new covenant must be totally inauthentic, since he lacks the splendour of the mediator of the Sinai-covenant.[182]

---

[180] A probably pejorative point, contrasting with Abraham's personal contact with God (Gal. 3:8, 16) and with the Christian gospel, Hans Dieter Betz, *Galatians: A Commentary on Paul's Letter to the Churches in Galatia*, Hermeneia: A Critical and Historical Commentary on the Bible, New Testament Editorial Board, Helmut Koester, et al. (Philadelphia: Fortress Press, 1979), 168. Cf. Acts 7:38. Note also that Gal. 3:19 does not make "the Mediator" a title for Moses, but only describes his role. Kastner, "Moses im Neuen Testament," 182 offers the possibility that Moses is further disparaged by the apparent independence of the angels, so that in the case of Moses one may not even be confident that what was mediated represents the will of God: "Dadurch aber reduziert er die Bedeutung des mosaischen Mittlertums. Denn im Hintergrund seiner Argumentation steht die Behauptung, daß die in relativer Selbständigkeit handelnden Engel dem Mittler Moses schwerlich im Gesetz die authentische Willensäußerung Gottes mitgeteilt haben konnten." On Gal. 3:19 see above, pp. 49-50.

[181] Paul may give Moses even less credit than the Rabbis. Barrett, *From First Adam to Last*, 61-62 observes, "Moses was to the Rabbis ... the mediator, in the sense of intercessor and advocate. In contrast with this, Moses takes for Paul the character of a postman or telephone operator — an astounding reversal."

[182] Thrall, *Commentary on the Second Epistle to the Corinthians*, vol. 1, 247-48. Ralph P. Martin, *2 Corinthians*, Word Biblical Commentary, ed. David A. Hubbard and

Moses appears because others have already compared him with Paul, and Paul responds not by denigrating Moses but by praising him, by agreeing with his detractors that the ministry of Moses was indeed glorious.[183] He defends his apostolate not by comparing himself with Moses directly, but by "contrasting in the verses following 2 Cor. 3:1-3 the work of Moses and his own work as a Minister of Christ."[184] Since he parallels himself with Moses, to make little of him would be counterproductive.[185] Instead, Paul gives Moses glory but as the minister of Christ naturally assumes "that he himself is no less a distinguished person."[186] "He is daring enough to think of himself as a second Moses, with a superior glory in his heart, in the presence of which the glory on Moses' face after communing with God on Sinai is but a fading ray."[187] Paul's view of Moses here is obviously quite high. In fact, the strength of Paul's argument depends on the glory of Moses.

Glenn W. Barker, New Testament Editor, Ralph P. Martin, vol. 40 (Waco, Texas: Word Books, 1986), 64 suggests that Paul is countering a Jewish or Christian apologetic on Moses' behalf. Approaches by Schulz and Georgi, proposing Corinthian opponents with a too-exalted view of Moss, are critiqued by Furnish, *II Corinthians*, 242-45. Some have been inclined to see all of 3:7-18 as a unified section, even comprising, or based on, a preformed document, see Martin, *2 Corinthians*, 58-60 (and 65-66 on the suggestion that 3:12-18 is basically a preformed midrash, of either Jewish or Jewish-Christian origin); Hafemann, *Paul, Moses, and the History of Israel*, 189 discusses the seminal theory of H. Windisch, *Der Zweite Korintherbrief*, 9th ed., Meyer Kommentar, vol. 6 [1924; reissued, ed. G. Strecker, 1970]), that the whole of 3:7-18 is a Christian midrash on Exod. 34:29-35, but see thorough discussion by Hafemann, 255-62, who rejects the idea of midrash in the passage altogether, 456-57; Thrall, *Commentary on the Second Epistle to the Corinthians*, vol. 1, 246-47 is also extremely skeptical of "the theory of the reshaping of an existing exegetical tradition." Even were the preformed document theories accepted the idea hardly need govern exegesis of the passage (see Thrall, 246-47, 251-52, 258-59, 266, 267-68, 276, 288-90), since the final product in any case is Paul's.

[183] Barrett, *From First Adam to Last*, 50, 52 thinks the passage "glorifies Moses," though it is "a paradoxical glorification," colored by Paul's new faith, "which points to the meaning Paul found in the law of which Moses was the mediator."

[184] W. D. Davies, *Paul and Rabbinic Judaism: Some Rabbinic Elements in Pauline Theology*, 4th ed. (Philadelphia: Fortress Press, 1980), 225-26.

[185] See Thrall, *Commentary on the Second Epistle to the Corinthians*, vol. 1, 237. Paul Démann, "Moïse et la Loi dans la pensée de Saint Paul," *Cahiers Sioniens* 8, nos. 2, 3, and 4 (*Moïse: L'homme de l'alliance*, 1954): 197 believes that Paul, "n'entend nullement diminuer Moïse."

[186] Davies, *Paul and Rabbinic Judaism*, 148.

[187] R. H. Strachan, *The Second Epistle of Paul to the Corinthians*, The Moffatt New Testament Commentary, ed. James Moffatt (London: Hodder and Stoughton, 1935), xxxv; further, 86, "In comparing the gospel he preached with the religion of the Old Testament, Paul assumes that he himself is a person no less distinguished than Moses (4:6); a claim that must have appeared to his opponents extraordinarily audacious."

In 2 Cor. 3:6 Paul characterizes himself as a "servant of a new covenant" (on which see below). Paul finds much in his ministry to parallel with that of Moses, with the caveat that Paul clearly believes that both his new covenant (3:8-9), and his ministry of it (3:12-18), are superior to those of Moses, and therefore the glory he derives from them is superior as well. It would hardly make sense for Paul, defending his ministry, to introduce a comparison with a person and ministry which outclassed him. Therefore, when in 2 Cor. 3:4-5 Paul emphasizes that his confidence in ministry is through Christ, "not that we are adequate in ourselves to consider anything as [coming] from ourselves,"[188] it seems reasonable to suppose that Paul must have viewed Moses similarly, as someone whose message and confidence did not come from himself.

Astonished by such boldness on the apostle's part to compare himself favorably with Moses, A. Menzies asserts "how little Paul was of a Jew when he wrote this letter; the passage is one which no one could like who had any reverence for the Jewish law or its lawgiver."[189] This may fairly represent the respect Jews maintained for Moses, but it misunderstands Paul's comparison, which was not meant to question the glory of Moses, but rather to affirm the glory they each derive from their ministries.

The sharp end of Paul's argument is that the glory of Moses was derivative from the covenant he ministered, and it is here the Paul comes out ahead. It is hardly necessary to explain Paul's move here by resorting to an anti-Jewish Paul; in the (incidentally, clearly Jewish) rabbinic material surveyed above, an opinion of Moses as a glorious, though strictly mediating, figure was ascendant. One thinks also of the *piyyut*, "אַזְ[יִ]ן לְ מֹשֶׁה," which dubs Moses the "apostle of the king of glory" (שליחיה דמלך הכבוד).[190] The post is a glorious one, and yet the glory is clearly derived from the one represented, which is how Paul understood both his apostolate and the ministry of Moses. It is therefore no slight to Moses to make him out as a mediator, just as it is no humiliation for Paul to admit that he too is a mediator.

The stone tablets, to which Paul repeatedly adverts in 2 Cor. 3:2, 7, recall that the Law (the Decalogue, anyway) was written down by God and only delivered by Moses (Exod. 31:18; 32:15-16; 34:1). Moses' shining face, which is so emphasized in Paul's remarks, is the aspect of the Pentateuchal account of the Lawgiving that most recalls the tradition of Moses'

---

[188] That this is the sense of the Greek is argued by Thrall, *Commentary on the Second Epistle to the Corinthians*, vol. 1, 229-30.

[189] Allan Menzies, *The Second Epistle of the Apostle Paul to the Corinthians: Introduction, Text, English Translation and Notes* (London: Macmillan and Co., 1912), 23.

[190] See above, pp. 72-73.

heavenly ascent, an element of the Lawgiving which, as noted above in discussion of rabbinic literature, leads to a conception of Moses as a messenger of the Law, not a maker of the Law. Galatians 3:19 has already been noticed in this regard: the angelic ordination of the Law mentioned in that text is a well documented element of rabbinic haggadah, indicating that Paul's conception of the Lawgiving and of Moses' role in it is not (from a rabbinic standpoint) particularly unusual or idiosyncratic.[191]

5.7.4.3.2 Moses the Διάκονος of the Old Covenant

There is a further indication that Paul views Moses strictly as the prophetic mediator of the Law. It is commonly assumed that the primary meaning of διάκονος is "servant." Thrall, however, cites the work of J. N. Collins, which shows that

> the underlying idea of the διακον- terminology is that of being a 'go-between', of acting in an 'in-between' capacity. ... In the present context, where Paul has been speaking about the proclamation of the gospel, he will term himself διάκονος because he sees himself (as in 1 Cor. 3.5) as an intermediary who is charged with a message from God, i.e., the message of the new covenant which he transmits through his preaching.[192]

This is an extremely important observation because 2 Corinthians 3 is the one Pauline passage from which it could be argued that Paul viewed Moses as truly a lawmaker, and not merely a mediator. Indeed, as noted above, Thrall attempts to derive such an impression from this passage and to influence the reading of the Romans citation formulae accordingly. Surely the reverse is more likely. That is, the many other texts which suggest that Paul was already much like the Rabbis in viewing Moses as essentially a mediator of a heavenly, nearly hypostatic, Law suggest that in 2 Corinthians 3 he would view Moses in that way as well.

In 2 Corinthians 3 Paul takes but one title to himself: διάκονοι καινῆς διαθήκης (3:6). Through the work of Collins it emerges that this description reflects not firstly subservience, but mediation. That Paul's one clear self-designation in paralleling his own ministry with that of Moses should be that of the mediator of the new covenant surely indicates that this was also his view of the activity of Moses in the promulgation of the old covenant.[193] The interchange between "the old covenant" and "Moses" in 2 Cor. 3:14-15 is safeguarded from misconstrual (i.e. as implying that Moses was truly the author of the Law) both by the overall aim of the passage,

---

[191] See above, pp. 49-50.

[192] Ibid., 231, citing J. N. Collins, *Diakonia*, 73-191, 195-98. See also Thrall, *Commentary on the Second Epistle to the Corinthians*, vol. 1, 241.

[193] And cf. Eph. 3:6-7, where Paul is διάκονος of the gospel, and Rom. 15:8 where Christ is a διάκονος of the truth to the circumcision.

which is to defend Paul's ministry as superior to Moses' (and Paul was not
the author of the gospel), and by Collins's insight into the function of the
διακον- word group: that it denotes mediation, a meaning completely in
harmony with Paul's other treatments of Moses.[194] Accordingly, in 2 Cor.
3:14-15, "Moses" stands not simply for the covenant Moses wrote, but for
"the covenant mediated by Moses."

5.7.4.4 Conclusion

Despite the limited extent of the Pauline corpus, it seems safe to assert that
Paul's assessment of Moses as a Lawgiver leaned toward that of a mediator. The Law was given by God, and owes its existence to divine intent,
or maybe to its own divine nature. While perhaps it cannot be claimed that
Paul rules out Mosaic lawgiving which is not entirely prophetic, he makes
no place for it, except possibly in Deuteronomy.

Paul's writings contain antecedents both for the personification of the
Law and for the primarily mediating role of Moses in the Lawgiving, both
of which became important themes in rabbinic teaching. It is interesting to
find both in such a small space. The similarities that appear between Paul's
writings and the rabbinic materials, along with Paul's avowed Pharisaic
background, suggest that he was an early representative of the rabbinic line
of thinking that Moses as lawgiver was not a lawmaker, but a prophetic
mediator.

To say that Paul viewed Moses as a mediator is not to say that Moses
was utterly insignificant to Paul. The emphasis on the glory of Moses in 2
Corinthians 3 itself suggests the contrary. A certain paucity of Pauline references to Moses may suggest, as Hooker concludes, that Moses is not
"part of Paul's scheme," but he nevertheless plays a key role in the brief
Pauline corpus, not least as a type for the ministry of Paul himself.

5.8 Conclusion

Ancient Judaism presents a rich and varied view of the Lawgiving, something which has tended to be overlooked. The New Testament is in that
regard convincingly Jewish, with its essentially dual perspective on the role
of Moses in the Lawgiving perfectly matching the perspective of contemporary Judaism, both as assessed by Philo and as it emerges from the sources themselves. The traditions seem to break cleanly into two main
streams, one of which saw Moses principally as a transmitter, and the other
as a maker, of the Law.

---

[194] Indeed, the Law in 2 Corinthians 3, as elsewhere in Paul's writings, is arguably
a more active figure than Moses is.

The New Testament, like contemporary Judaism generally, resists conformity in the matter of Moses as Lawgiver, though it mostly gives him a
very prominent role. The Rabbis, by contrast, were careful to keep clear
that God was the author of the Law, and Moses merely his scribe or, in the
case of the Oral Law, a repeater. The relative uniformity of rabbinic opinion in comparison with the variety of NT expression and with the ambi-
valence of Josephus suggests that at some later period it became more important to assert the simple divine authorship of the Torah, or perhaps that
the party which had viewed Moses chiefly as a scribe gained complete dominance after the first century A.D.

The Synoptic Gospels contain traditions which ascribe a great deal of
authority to Moses personally. This is most pronounced in Luke, which
with Acts shows the most uninhibited propensity to locate the authority
behind the Law in Moses himself, but even Matthew, which tends to emphasize divine authority in the Law includes the extremely suggestive remark about the "seat of Moses."

John's Gospel is unique in the New Testament, and perhaps in Jewish
literature, for the way it portrays conflict over how Moses ought to be
viewed. The narrator, and the narrator's Jesus, apparently view Moses as
essentially a mediator. But the Gospel also attests a "popular view," which
apparently both the Evangelist and Jesus oppose, which locates in Moses
not only the power to work wonders (the manna), but also the authority of
the Law he gave. The Gospel shows that Jews were prone to think of Moses' lawgiving activities in ways that put a good deal more emphasis on
Moses than might now be assumed. For them, Moses was not a simple
functionary or mere mediator, but a legislator.

Paul's outlook, on the other hand, seems nearly the opposite of that of
Luke-Acts. The Law is a topic particularly well-treated in his extant writings, yet Moses himself apparently was not a figure with whom Paul felt
he needed to contend. The brevity and occasional nature of Paul's epistles
make it hard to make sweeping claims about the significance of Moses' absence, however, especially while two texts do indeed strongly connect Moses with the Law as its mediator (2 Corinthians 3; Gal. 3:19). The emphasis on Moses' role as mediator of the Law, however, combined with Paul's
silence about Moses as a figure of authority, seem to bracket Paul's view
of Moses more with that of the Rabbis than with that of his fellow NT
authors. For them, but not for Paul, Moses appears as the bearer of independent personal authority.

As 2 Corinthians 3 and the *Assumption of Moses* show, even a view
conceiving Moses (only) as a mediator could still make of him a glorious
figure. This serves as a reminder that the two streams of tradition traced
here are not reducible to something as simple as one for, and the other

against, high esteem for Moses. Both could think quite a lot of Moses; it is
the precise role of Moses that distinguishes them.

Chapter 6

Baptism into Moses

All our fathers were baptized into Moses in the cloud and in the sea.
—Paul, First Corinthians 10:2

6.1 Introduction

Most agree that the midrash of 1 Cor. 10:1-11 represents a tradition (whether Jewish or Christian) inherited by Paul.[1] One element of the opening typology of that midrash (10:1-4), however, almost everyone assigns to the apostle himself: the baptism into Moses. A few lump this in with the rest of the tradition that Paul is believed to have inherited from,[2] or held in common with,[3] other Christians, by far the governing consensus is that

---

[1] C. K. Barrett, *From First Adam to Last: A Study in Pauline Theology* (London: Adam & Charles Black, 1962), 49 argues a Jewish origin, while Hans Lietzmann, *An die Korinther I/II*, expanded ed., Handbuch zum Neuen Testament, ed. Günther Bornkamm, vol. 9 (Tübingen: J. C. B. Mohr [Paul Siebeck], 1949), 44 specifies Hellenistic Judaism. Georg Braumann, *Vorpaulinische christliche Taufverkündigung bei Paulus*, Beiträge zur Wissenschaft vom Alten und Neuen Testament, 5th series, ed. K. H. Rengstorf and Leonhard Rost, vol. 2 (Stuttgart: W. Kohlhammer, 1962), 18-20 nominates 2 Esdr. 19:9-20 as the background. C. J. A. Hickling, "Paul's Use of Exodus in the Corinthian Correspondence," in *The Corinthian Correspondence*, ed. R. Bieringer, Bibliotheca Ephemeridum Theologicarum Lovaniensum, no. 125 (Leuven-Louvain: Leuven University Press, 1996), 367-76 hypothesizes that this passage and 2 Cor. 3:12-16 are linked either as parts of a common topos in Jewish interpretation, or "a collection of Christian midrashim on passages from Exodus" (p. 372). Wayne A. Meeks, "'And Rose Up to Play': Midrash and Paraenesis in 1 Corinthians 10:1-22," *Journal for the Study of the New Testament* 16 (1982): 65-66 detects a pre-Pauline Christian homily, similarly Richard L. Jeske, "The Rock was Christ: The Ecclesiology of 1 Corinthians 10," in *Kirche: Festschrift für Günther Bornkamm zum 75. Geburtstag*, ed. Dieter Lührmann and Georg Strecker (Tübingen: J. C. B. Mohr [Paul Siebeck], 1980), 247. Gordon D. Fee, *The First Epistle to the Corinthians*, The New International Commentary on the New Testament, ed. F. F. Bruce (Grand Rapids: William B. Eerdmans, 1987), 442 n. 5, thinks it not impossible that Paul composed the midrash himself; see also his 443 nn. 9, 10.

[2] So Meeks, "'And Rose Up to Play': Midrash and Paraenesis in 1 Corinthians 10:1-22," 65-66.

[3] So Jeske, "The Rock was Christ: The Ecclesiology of 1 Corinthians 10," 246-247.

Paul coined the expression "baptized into Moses" by analogy with his doctrine of baptism into Christ.[4]

This chapter will argue, by contrast, that the typology of 1 Cor.
10:1-4 could reasonably have arisen from pre-Pauline Judaism, and will explain
the baptism into Moses of 1 Cor. 10:2, in which Moses appears as a unifying, incorporative figure for Israel,[5] not by derivation from Christian baptism into Christ, but by suggesting that Jews in Paul's day thought of Moses as a spiritual, unifying figure, into whom Jews could be thought, and
perhaps were thought, to be baptized, and that this conception of Moses is
the basis for Paul's expression.

The claim that baptism into Moses is nothing more than a Pauline invention based on Christian teaching about Christ stands essentially on an *argu-*

---

[4] J. Héring, *La première épître de saint Paul aux Corinthiens*, Commentaire du
Nouveau Testament, ed. P. Bonnard, et al., no. 7 (Paris: Delachaux & Niestlé, 1949),
78 says "l'expression εἰς Μωϋσῆν = *en Moise* ne peut s'expliquer par le judaïsme;
l'apôtre l'a formée par analogie à εἰς Χριστόν." Likewise, Paul Démann, "Moïse et la
Loi dans la pensée de Saint Paul," *Cahiers Sioniens* 8, nos. 2, 3, and 4 (*Moïse:
L'homme de l'alliance*, 1954): 193-94; G. R. Beasley-Murray, *Baptism in the New Testament* (London: Macmillian & Co.; New York: St. Martin's Press, 1962), 185; Rudolf
Schnackenburg, *Baptism in the Thought of St. Paul: A Study in Pauline Theology*,
trans. G. R. Beasley-Murray (Oxford: Basil Blackwell, 1964), 93; C. K. Barrett, *A Critical and Exegetical Commentary on the Acts of the Apostles*, vol. 1, *Preliminary Introduction and Commentary on Acts I-XIV*, The International Critical Commentary on the
Holy Scriptures of the Old and New Testaments, ed. J. A. Emerton, C. E. B. Cranfield,
and G. N. Stanton (Edinburgh: T. & T. Clark, 1994), 363; *idem*, *From First Adam to
Last*, 49-50; Fee, *The First Epistle to the Corinthians*, 445; Richard B. Hays, *First Corinthians*, Interpretation: A Bible Commentary for Teaching and Preaching, ed. James
Luther Mays, Patrick D. Miller, and Paul J. Achtemeier (Louisville, Kent.: John Knox
Press, 1997), 160; James D. G. Dunn, *Christology in the Making: A New Testament Inquiry into the Origins of the Doctrine of the Incarnation*, 2d ed. (London: SCM Press,
1989), 448; *idem*, *Baptism in the Holy Spirit: A Re-examination of the New Testament
Teaching on the Gift of the Spirit in relation to Pentecostalism Today*, Studies in Biblical Theology, 2d series, ed. C. F. D. Moule, et al., no. 15 (London: SCM Press, 1970),
112; Archibald Robertson and Alfred Plummer, *A Critical and Exegetical Commentary
on the First Epistle of St Paul to the Corinthians*, 2d ed., The International Critical
Commentary on the Holy Scriptures of the Old and New Testaments, ed. Samuel Rolles
Driver, Alfred Plummer, and Charles Augustus Briggs (Edinburgh: T. & T. Clark,
1914, reprint, 1929), 200; R. St John Parry, *The First Epistle of Paul the Apostle to the
Corinthians*, 2d ed., Cambridge Greek Testament for Schools and Colleges (Cambridge: The University Press, 1926, reprint 1937), 145; Josef M. Kastner, "Moses im
Neuen Testament," (Th.D. Dissertation, Ludwig-Maximilians-Universität Munich,
1967), 188-89.

[5] The generation of the Exodus and wilderness could be held paradigmatic for all
later generations; Jer. 2:1-7 addresses all the families of Israel as though they were in
the wilderness; cf. Heb. 6:9-10.

mentum ex silentio: the notion of baptism into Moses is nowhere else to be found in Jewish sources. This is an impressive amount of silence.

Still, "baptism into Moses" would be a peculiar invention for Paul. For one thing, it coheres poorly with his usual treatment of Moses. As J. Jeremias observes, Paul — uniquely in the New Testament — uses Moses as a type not for the Messiah, but for the community; 1 Cor. 10:1-2, where Paul uses Moses/Messiah typology, is the only exception to this rule.[6] The singular exception constituted by 1 Cor. 10:2, the fact that Paul betrays no awkwardness there as he departs from his customary usage, and the peculiarity of the typology of 1 Cor. 10:1-4 in general within the Pauline corpus have led some to suspect that at least some of the ideas in these verses are borrowed from material already familiar to Paul and his readers.[7]

In the twentieth century possibly only one scholar goes so far as to assert, "Paul certainly did not invent the idea that the passage of the Red Sea was baptism *into Moses*. Here is indeed a survival from his earlier thought ways." E. R. Goodenough's evidence comes from the Dura-Europos synagogue, in which one of the paintings, he believes, depicts the baptism into Moses, along with the elements of baptism associated with it in 1 Cor. 10:2 (the cloud and the sea), as part of the story of the Exodus.[8]

Of course, the Exodus was an important focus of reflection for Christians as well as Jews, through its importance in OT literature as well as contemporary Jewish tradition.[9] Paul, on other occasions than 1 Corinthians 10, connects baptism and the Lord's Supper with the Exodus, which might suggest that reflection along that line circulated in the early

---

[6] Joachim Jeremias, "Μωυσῆς," in *Theological Dictionary of the New Testament*, ed. Gerhard Kittel, trans. and ed. Geoffrey W. Bromiley, vol. 4, *Λ-Ν* (Grand Rapids: Wm. B. Eerdmans, 1967), 869-70; though he finds other Pauline texts where the typology is alluded to. His mature view remained much the same, see "Paulus als Hillelit," in *Neotestamentica et Semitica: Studies in Honour of Matthew Black*, ed. E. Earle Ellis and Max Wilcox (Edinburgh: T. & T. Clark, 1969), 91. Cf. Barrett, *From First Adam to Last*, 65.

[7] E.g., Jeske, "The Rock was Christ: The Ecclesiology of 1 Corinthians 10," 246-247 argues, "The words οὐ θέλω ὑμᾶς ἀγνοεῖν in 10,1 are used ... by Paul to introduce traditional material (1 Thess 4,13; cf. 1 Cor 12,1; 2 Cor 1,8; Rom 1,13; 11,25)." But cf. E. Earle Ellis, "Traditions in 1 Corinthians," *New Testament Studies* 32 (1986): 490-91 and Fee, *The First Epistle to the Corinthians*, 443 on this point.

[8] Erwin R. Goodenough, *Jewish Symbols in the Greco-Roman Period*, Bollingen Series, no 37, vol. 10 (New York: Pantheon Books, 1964), 135; see below pp. 215-17.

[9] See, e.g., R. E. Nixon, *The Exodus in the New Testament*, Tyndale Monographs (London: The Tyndale Press, 1962); Harald Sahlin, "The New Exodus of Salvation according to St Paul," in *The Root of the Vine: Essays in Biblical Theology*, Anton Fridrichsen, et al. (London: Dacre Press, 1953), 81-95; E. Earle Ellis, *Paul's Use of the Old Testament* (Edinburgh: Oliver and Boyd, 1957), 131-33; W. D. Davies, *Torah in the Messianic Age and/or the Age to Come*, Journal of Biblical Literature Monograph Series, ed. Ralph Marcus, vol. 7 (Philadelphia: Society of Biblical Literature, 1952), 7.

Church;[10] the typology of 1 Cor. 10:1-4 could be borrowed from that background.[11] This general background, however, would not automatically bring forth a conception like baptism into Moses. The rest of this chapter will examine aspects of Jewish belief that might provide more specific support.

6.2 Background Provided by Concepts of Baptism

6.2.1 Jewish Proselyte Baptism

Jews were regularly baptizing proselytes early in the second century A.D., and it is apparent from the New Testament itself that at least some Jews were baptizing early in the first century. Developments in Jewish baptistic practice in between, however, are far from clear, though it is generally accepted that the emergence of proper proselyte baptism among Jews occurred sometime in the first century. Since Jewish proselyte baptism is of the greatest interest in investigating a text like 1 Cor. 10:2, aspects of the debate concerning it will be explored here.

6.2.1.1 Antiquity of Jewish Proselyte Baptism

By the mishnaic period the process by which a man was made a proselyte was threefold: circumcision, immersion in water, and the presentation of an offering in the Temple.[12] After A.D. 70, with the suspension of the requirement of an offering, baptism was thus the only rite of passage applicable to all converts (female as well as male).

Jewish proselyte baptism was thus firmly institutionalized by the second century, but opinion is divided on how much further back the practice

---

[10] Ellis, *Paul's Use of the Old Testament*, 133-34; the connection is often merely implicit.

[11] See Jeremias, "Μωυσῆς," 868-69.

[12] *Sifre* Num. 108 on Num. 15:15. Paul P. Levertoff, trans., *Midrash Sifre on Numbers: Selections from Early Rabbinic Scriptural Interpretations*, Translations of Early Documents, Series 3: Rabbinic Texts (London: Society for Promoting Christian Knowledge, 1926), 92 argues that the ruling goes back to a much earlier date than Judah the Prince. See also George Foote Moore, *Judaism in the First Centuries of the Christian Era: The Age of the Tannaim*, vol. 1 (Cambridge, Mass.: Harvard University Press, 1927), 331. By the Talmudic period a fourth element, acceptance of the Torah, had been added; see *b. Yeb.* 47a-b, *b. Ger.* 1:4, and Shaye J. D. Cohen, *The Beginnings of Jewishness: Boundaries, Varieties, Uncertainties*, Hellenistic Culture and Society, ed. Anthony W. Bulloch, et al., no. 31 (Berkeley and Los Angeles: University of California Press, 1999), 218-19.

goes.[13] Scholars generally accepted the priority of Christian baptism until in the early part of the twentieth century many came to the opposite view, that Jewish proselyte baptism predated its Christian counterpart. A. Oepke sets out the basic position: "It is hardly conceivable that the Jewish ritual should be adopted at a time when baptism had become an established religious practice in Christianity. ... Proselyte baptism must have preceded Christian baptism."[14]

A more recent advocate of the same opinion, L. H. Schiffman, in 1981 (and with but slight revision in 1985) held more specifically that it is "certain" that immersion was part of the conversion ceremony of the Schools of Shammai and Hillel, and that such immersion must date from before the time of John the Baptist and the rise of Christian baptism.[15] The starting

---

[13] "A much-debated question," Cohen, *The Beginnings of Jewishness*, 222-23, with guide to key literature in the debate. H. H. Rowley, "Jewish Proselyte Baptism and the Baptism of John," *Hebrew Union College Annual* 15 (1940): 313-20 surveys the debate in first part of the twentieth century to 1940, and its key elements. On the principal non-rabbinic witnesses (Epict. *Diss.* 2.9.21 and *Sib. Or.* 4.165) see Martin Goodman, *Mission and Conversion: Proselytizing in the Religious History of the Roman Empire* (Oxford: Clarendon Press, 1994), 67-68; the relevant rabbinical passages, which apparently chronicle debates in the Schools of Shammai and Hillel, are *m. Pes.* 8.8 (= *m. Ed.* 5.2); *t. Pes.* 7.13; *y. Pes.* 8.36b.31; *b. Pes.* 92a; *b. Yeb.* 46a. On these see Herman L. Strack and Paul Billerbeck, *Kommentar zum Neuen Testament aus Talmud und Midrasch*, vol. 1, *Das Evangelium nach Matthäus* (Munich: C. H. Beck'sche Verlagsbuchhandlung [Oskar Beck], 1922), 102-13.

[14] Albrecht Oepke, "βάπτω κτλ.," in *Theological Dictionary of the New Testament*, ed. Gerhard Kittel, trans. and ed. Geoffrey W. Bromiley, vol. 1, *Α-Γ* (Grand Rapids: William B. Eerdmans, 1964[German, 1932]), 535. Rowley, "Jewish Proselyte Baptism and the Baptism of John," 313-314 (see also 320) is nearly identical, adding that the Jewish rite preceded the time of Jesus; with this Billerbeck, *Kommentar zum Neuen Testament aus Talmud und Midrasch*, vol. 1, 103 concurs; see also Joachim Jeremias, "Proselytentaufe und Neues Testament," *Theologische Zeitschrift* 5 (1949): 418-28, and "Der Ursprung der Johannestaufe," *Zeitschrift für die Neutestamentliche Wissenschaft* 28 (1929): 313, 319. More guardedly, George Foote Moore, *Judaism in the First Centuries of the Christian Era: The Age of the Tannaim*, vol. 3 (Cambridge, Mass.: Harvard University Press, 1930), 109-10 N. 102 (to vol. 1, p. 333) only goes so far as to grant that Hillelite-Shammaite debate over baptism pre-dates the fall of Jerusalem, while F. Gavin, *The Jewish Antecedents of the Christian Sacraments* (London: Society for Promoting Christian Knowledge, 1928), 31-32 and Emil Schürer, *The History of the Jewish People in the Age of Jesus Christ (175 BC-AD 135)*, vol. 3.1, rev. Geza Vermes, Fergus Millar, and Martin Goodman (Edinburgh: T. & T. Clark, 1986), 174 with n. 89 only locate proselyte baptism's development somewhere in the first century.

[15] Lawrence H. Schiffman, "At the Crossroads: Tannaitic Perspectives on the Jewish-Christian Schism," in *Jewish and Christian Self-Definition*, vol. 2, *Aspects of Judaism in the Graeco-Roman Period*, ed. E. P. Sanders with A. I. Baumgarten and Alan Mendelson (Philadelphia: Fortress Press, 1981), 130 = idem, *Who Was a Jew?: Rabbinic and Halakhic Perspectives on the Jewish Christian Schism* (Hoboken, N.J.: Ktav Publishing House, 1985), 28.

point for his case (and for all discussion on the subject) is *m. Pes.* 8.8, which records a debate about immersion between the two schools (examined more closely below). Schiffman concedes only that he "cannot prove that immersion was a *sine qua non* for conversion before the early first century C.E."[16]

Other scholars, however, recently have swung back to the older position. K. Rudolph allows a "striking interest in baptist practices" among Jews in the first century, but only on a sectarian basis.[17] Wider proselyte baptism, according to Rudolph, only began to establish itself among Jews late in the first century, "as a reaction against Christian baptism" (precisely what Oepke urges is unthinkable!).[18] S. J. D. Cohen holds that the baptism associated with conversion in the Hillelite-Shammaite debates, which Schiffman and others have considered key pointers to early proselyte baptism, is only the ordinary, Jewish washing of purification. Cohen urges that Jewish purificatory washings and initiatory washings must be kept strictly distinguished (see further below); thus a washing that was purificatory cannot in his view have been an initiatory proselyte baptism.[19]

Cohen's treatment of the key *m. Pes.* 8.8, in which the Shammaites insist that a proselyte must undergo immersion before approaching the Temple to take part in Passover, is perhaps the best modern argument for the priority of Christian proselyte baptism. The Mishnah reads:

The School of Shammai say: If a man became a proselyte on the day before Passover he may immerse himself and consume (טובל ואוכל) his Passover-offering in the evening. And the School of Hillel say: He that separates himself from his uncircumcision is as one that separates himself from a grave.[20]

---

[16] Schiffman, "At the Crossroads," 131 (also 133-34) = *idem, Who Was a Jew?*, 29-30.

[17] Kurt Rudolph, "The Baptist Sects," in *The Cambridge History of Judaism*, vol. 3, *The Early Roman Period*, ed. William Horbury, W. D. Davies, and John Sturdy (Cambridge: Cambridge University Press, 1999), 481.

[18] Ibid., 482. Lester L. Grabbe, *Judaic Religion in the Second Temple Period: Belief and Practice from the Exile to Yavneh* (London and New York: Routledge, 2000), 295-96 is very similar, and places Jewish proselyte baptism after 70 A.D., citing the absence of evidence from before that date and the silence of Josephus.

[19] Shaye J. D. Cohen, "The Rabbinic Conversion Ceremony," *Journal of Jewish Studies* 41 (1990): 194 n. 46. This article, heavily revised, is reproduced in Chapter 7 of Cohen's *The Beginnings of Jewishness*, 198-238, where Cohen, 222 with n. 56 specifically challenges the interpretations of Billerbeck, Schürer (revised), and Schiffman, and treats the material used by Oepke as well.

[20] I.e., he is unclean and needs to be sprinkled on the third and seventh days following before he becomes clean, Herbert Danby, *The Mishnah: Translated from the Hebrew with Introduction and Brief Explanatory Notes* (London: Oxford University Press, 1933; reprint, 1959), 148 and n. 4. Hebrew text from Philip Blackman, *Mishnayoth*, vol. 2, *Order Moed*, 2d ed. (New York: The Judaica Press, 1963), 208, and see n. 7.

Cohen works out that there are just four possible explanations for the Jewish immersion requirement that appears in the Mishnah: "(1) the immersion is 'proselyte baptism'; (2) the immersion is the statutory immersion required of all those about to enter the temple; (3) the immersion is to purify the convert of impurity; (4) [Cohen's choice] the immersion marks a change in the convert's status vis-à-vis the temple cult."[21]

Cohen's four options seem to cover the realistic possibilities for the purpose of the immersion being debated. The trouble is that they are not mutually exclusive; Cohen only thinks so because he is already persuaded that a purificatory washing will not have been seen as initiatory, and so he brackets out (1) "proselyte baptism" as though it were an option clearly unlike the others, but while the other options are not proselyte baptisms *per se*, all would have clear, and perhaps primarily, initiatory functions in the context of the proselyte's first sacrifice (Temple sacrifice, as noted above, being the final act of the conversion process). Thus option (3) would actually seem a strong candidate for a form of proselyte baptism. Why Cohen believes as momentous an occasion as option (4) is not to be deemed a proselyte baptism is not at all clear, beyond Cohen's position that a washing that was purificatory will not have been seen as initiatory.

Mishnah Pes. 8.8 itself makes plain that it is an immersion of proselytes that is under dispute, and all of Cohen's suggestions for the significance of the immersion have, or could have, strong initiatory connotations in such a setting. Far from closing the door on the idea of proselyte baptism, Cohen seems inadvertently to have established that no matter how one looks at it, the proselyte washing the Shammaites were concerned about was in some way initiatory for the proselyte, and thus quite liable to have constituted a proselyte baptism of some kind, in the pre-Christian era.

On top of such difficulties comes the proposal by Schiffman that rather than being either initiatory or purificatory, Jewish proselyte baptism was probably always seen as combining both functions.[22] This seems a much more realistic approach than Cohen's forced dichotomy between purification and initiation. As pointed out earlier, Cohen's argument for classifying the immersion of *m. Pes.* 8.8 as non-initiatory assumes this distinc-

---

[21] Shaye J. D. Cohen, "Is 'Proselyte Baptism' Mentioned in the Mishnah?: The Interpretation of *m. Pesahim* 8.8 (= *m. Eduyot* 5.2)," in *Pursuing the Text: Studies in Honor of Ben Zion Wacholder on the Occasion of his Seventieth Birthday*, ed. John C. Reeves and John Kampen, Journal for the Study of the Old Testament Supplement Series, ed. David J. A. Klines and Philip R. Davies, no. 184 (Sheffield: Sheffield Academic Press, 1994), 281. Cohen's position is given on p. 286.

[22] Schiffman, *Who Was a Jew?*, 26. Cf. Oepke, "βάπτω κτλ.," 536, "Probably even earlier than the middle of the 1st century A.D., and under the influence of the many women proselytes who could not be circumcised, the existing washing of proselytes came to have the significance of an independent rite of reception."

tion. But this is tantamount to assuming what is to be proved. If Cohen's dichotomy is mistaken, his argument that the immersion in the Mishnah cannot have been initiatory because it was purificatory is also mistaken.[23]

Debate on this subject often seems to focus on when Jewish proselyte baptism became "officially" established. This, however, would likely represent a late stage in the ascendancy of the rite. Justice would be done to the rabbinic evidence of a Hillelite-Shammaite debate over baptism (in *m. Pes.* 8.8 and elsewhere) if it were merely postulated that in the pre-Christian period the first washing of a convert was receiving at least tacit acknowledgment as an initiatory rite, while even on conservative estimates *á la* Cohen, official establishment of proselyte baptism was not to be long in coming. On the basis of the representative arguments reviewed here, it seems reasonable to maintain that some form or another of Jewish proselyte baptism predated the similar Christian practice.

Further, while official Jewish establishment of proselyte baptism may have come late, for Christians, who were well-accustomed to the idea that the "true Israel" was entered by baptism, even inconsistent Jewish baptism of proselytes would appear as the counterpart to Christian baptism, that is as a climactic initiatory rite, of which "baptism into Moses" might seem a rather obvious description. If Jewish proselyte baptism had acquired any recognition at all, Paul's readers can hardly have failed to make the connection.

Other reasons can also be adduced for linking the baptism into Moses with the baptism of Jewish proselytes.

6.2.1.2 Biblical Basis for Jewish Proselyte Baptism

Jeremias claims not only that proselyte baptism was common Jewish practice early in the first century A.D., but that the practice had already acquired a specific biblical and traditional basis. According to Jeremias, the Jews grounded the baptism of proselytes in the notion that the Wilderness Generation had undergone a proselyte baptism before joining the Sinai covenant.[24] Such an idea would stand a strong chance of being recalled by the expression "baptism into Moses," especially given the importance of the Exodus narrative in 1 Corinthians 10:1-11 generally.

---

[23] Actually, all four of Cohen's possibilities probably represent genuine aspects of proselyte baptism.

[24] Jeremias, "Der Ursprung der Johannestaufe," 316-19; on 319 he specifically argues that the connection predates the conversion of Paul, ca. A.D. 33; Jeremias, "Μωυσῆς" (1942), 867, 870. Jeremias is followed by Oepke, "βάπτω κτλ.," 536; Andrew Bandstra, "Interpretation in 1 Corinthians 10:1-11," *Calvin Theological Journal* 6, no. 1 (April 1971): 6-7; Richard N. Longenecker, *Biblical Exegesis in the Apostolic Period* (Grand Rapids: William B. Eerdmans, 1975), 118-19 virtually quotes Bandstra.

The problem is that there is just no evidence for widespread teaching along the lines that Jeremias suggests. Lietzmann presses the case against Jeremias (chiefly) on the grounds that the rabbinic tradition went on to struggle for scriptural justification for proselyte baptism, betraying no memory of an earlier solution (certainly not one with Hillelite prestige behind it).[25] Despite, however, the lack of direct testimony to a basis for proselyte baptism such as Jeremias envisages, a number of indirect arguments suggest that Jeremias is on the right track.

C. K. Barrett offers support for Jeremias' position that a pre-Pauline, Palestinian midrash linked proselyte baptism to the Exodus on two grounds. First, he observes that Paul seems to feel no need to explain what he means in 1 Cor. 10:2. As Barrett observes, "this is not a very strong point," though not for the reasons he gives.[26] The real problem is that the background which Paul evidently assumes will make his meaning clear could consist of any of a variety of things besides knowledge of a baptistic Exodus tradition. Nevertheless, perhaps the most plausible background is such a tradition, which would make the same link Paul does between baptism and the Exodus.

Second, Barrett considers the middle voice of the verb "to baptize" (preferring, with many other scholars, the middle ἐβαπτίσαντο to the passive ἐβαπτίσθησαν adopted in critical editions) to refer to a "Jewish baptism."[27] The passive voice is a natural fit with Christian baptismal practice, but Jewish baptism was self-administered and for it one used the middle voice,[28] since "the middle voice of βαπτίζω is never synonymous with the passive but stresses the action, or at least the volition, of the person baptized."[29] The middle voice of ἐβαπτίσαντο thus suggests that "baptism into Moses" is meant to refer to a Jewish baptism of some kind, since if it were an expression formed by analogy with Christian baptism the passive

---

[25] Lietzmann, *Korinther I/II*, 181; Karl-Heinrich Ostmeyer, *Taufe und Typos: Elemente und Theologie der Tauftypologien in 1. Korinther 10 und 1. Petrus 3*, WUNT, 2d series, ed. Martin Hengel and Otfried Hofius, no. 118 (Tübingen: J. C. B. Mohr [Paul Siebeck], 2000), 86-87 is also skeptical.

[26] Barrett, *From First Adam to Last*, 49 refers to Paul's style of argument, which, Barrett holds, may assume too much of the knowledge of his readers.

[27] E.g., on the text, G. Zuntz, *The Text of the Epistles: A Disquisition upon the Corpus Paulinum*, Schweich Lectures of the British Academy, 1946 (London: Oxford University Press for the British Academy, 1953), 234, a minority (Metzger and Wikgren) of the UBS committee (Bruce Metzger, *A Textual Commentary on the Greek New Testament: A Companion Volume to the* United Bible Societies' Greek New Testament, 4th rev. ed., 2d ed. [Stuttgart: German Bible Society and United Bible Societies, 1994], 493), and Fee, *The First Epistle to the Corinthians*, 441 n. 2.

[28] Metzger, *A Textual Commentary on the Greek New Testament*, 493, and Barrett, *From First Adam to Last*, 48-49.

[29] Zuntz, *The Text of the Epistles: A Disquisition upon the* Corpus Paulinum, 234.

voice would be more natural (as the editors of the critical text seem to have realized[30]). This strengthens the case that Paul has a Jewish rite in mind in 1 Cor. 10:2, one connected with the Exodus traditions he employs in 1 Corinthians 10. This might indeed suggest Jewish proselyte baptism, perhaps even proselyte baptism based on Exodus traditions.

More can be said in support of the thesis of Jeremias. While extant rabbinic tradition betrays no explicit link between the Exodus and proselyte *baptism*, it is known that Jews linked the Exodus with proselyte *conversion* more generally, a link which could naturally foster the deduction of a baptism in the Exodus narrative.[31] With that in mind, it becomes significant both that several Jewish traditions regard those who passed through the Red Sea as subsequently inspired,[32] and that Christians from the earliest days associated the reception of the Spirit with baptism. This might imply that the crossing of the sea was also regarded as a baptism in which the Jewish "converts" of the Exodus were endowed with the Spirit. Such a tradition would support a view of the Red Sea crossing as a type of proselyte baptism, giving proselyte baptism the exegetical basis that Jeremias argues it had. The Jewish and the Christian conceptions can be completely paralleled if it is supposed that the water of Christian baptism was analogous to the water of the Jewish baptismal, which in turn was an antitype of the water of the Red Sea.

Finally, Paul (elsewhere) clearly associates Christian baptism with the Exodus (as noted above). A prior Jewish tradition such as Jeremias postulates could stand behind that association, a similar Jewish proselyte baptism, and the notion of baptism into Moses in 1 Cor. 10:2.

6.2.1.3 Conclusion

The likelihood that Jews were (to an extent, at least) practicing initiatory, or proselyte, baptism, together with Jewish traditions linking the Exodus with proselytism and (if Jeremias is right) with baptism *per se* as well, suggests that a mid-first century A.D. reference to "baptism into Moses," particularly one occurring in a passage that is focused simultaneously on the

---

[30] The majority of the committee were persuaded to accept the passive voice by Paul's normal usage, which of course deals with Christian baptism, Metzger, *A Textual Commentary on the Greek New Testament*, 493.

[31] Note, in Εξοδ. 22:20 the Israelites are said to be προσήλυτοι ἐν γῇ Αἰγύπτῳ.

[32] Philo, *Vit. Cont.* 87; Wisd. 10:20-21 with 7:22; 9:17; cf. Eph. 1:17; *Mek.* Beshallaḥ 7.161-62 on Exod. 14:31; *Mek.* Shirata 1.87-90 on Exod. 15:1; *m. Sot.* 5.4; *t. Sot.* 6.2. See William Horbury, "Septuagintal and New Testament Conceptions of the Church," in *A Vision for the Church: Studies in Early Christian Ecclesiology in Honour of J. P. M. Sweet*, ed. Markus Bockmuehl and Michael B. Thompson (Edinburgh: T. & T. Clark, 1997), 6-7.

Exodus and on life as a convert (or proselyte?),[33] would readily have been understood as a reference to Jewish proselyte baptism. The question then becomes, what does such an expression say about what Jewish proselyte baptism was thought to do and, more specifically, what part was Moses thought to play in it?

6.2.2 Baptism into Christ

The background to the "baptism into Moses" likely includes the Jewish material adduced above, but undeniably includes Christian proselyte baptism, which was well known to Paul and his readers. It is possible, then, to imagine that the expression "baptism into Moses" (if it were not common coin among Jews) might have been a less ambiguous expression for Christians (whether Jewish or Gentile) than for Jews, both because Christians might have been better prepared to see Jewish proselyte baptism as initiatory, and because Christians knew the similar expression "baptism into Christ." Unfortunately, the meaning of βαπτίζεσθαι εἰς among Christians remains the object of spirited discussion.[34]

6.2.2.1 The Idiom of "Baptism Into"

It is often contended that, at least for Paul, "baptism into" was essentially a shortened form of "baptism into the name,"[35] which seems in turn to have been a technical idiom in Hellenistic commerce ('to the account'), denoting a relationship of belonging to someone.[36]

Others emphasize the incorporative, spiritual relationship which a less idiomatic interpretation of "baptism into" seems to involve. In key passages the language of baptism seems to demand this (Rom. 6:3; 1 Cor. 12:13; Gal. 3:27).[37]

---

[33] The theme, with regard to eating in pagan temples, of 1 Cor. 8-10.

[34] On the grammatico-syntactical issues involved see M. J. Harris, "Prepositions and Theology in the Greek New Testament," in *The New International Dictionary of New Testament Theology*, ed. Colin Brown, trans. G. H. Boobyer, et al., vol. 3 (Exeter: Paternoster, 1978), 1207-11.

[35] E.g. Schnackenburg, *Baptism in the Thought of St. Paul*, 21-26.

[36] Oepke, "βάπτω κτλ.," 539 (with special reference to 1 Cor. 10:2); G. R. Beasley-Murray, "Baptism," in *Dictionary of Paul and His Letters*, ed. Gerald F. Hawthorne, Ralph P. Martin, and Daniel G. Reid (Downers Grove, Illinois: InterVarsity Press, 1993), 60-61; Schnackenburg, *Baptism in the Thought of St. Paul*, 22-23, adding that this explains 1 Cor. 10:2, where baptism is a "sign of adherence to Moses"; and bibliography in Dunn, *Baptism in the Holy Spirit*, 117 n. 5. Dunn, 117-18 supposes that the commercial element in the expression of "a change in ownership" would be especially to the fore in a commercial city like Corinth.

[37] Dunn, *Baptism in the Holy Spirit*, 109, 112; *idem*, *The Theology of Paul the Apostle* (Edinburgh: T. & T. Clark, 1998), 405, similarly, Joseph A. Fitzmyer, *Paul and*

An unwieldy combination of these two themes of ownership and personal union is sometimes attempted. Thus, for Barrett, "baptism is *into* Christ: that is, into his possession and under his authority, so as to be incorporated into him and to share in him the transference from the old age of sin and death into the new age of resurrection."[38]

In any case, "baptism into" seems to involve striking up a personal relationship. Whether the relationship is commercial or mystical, this is much easier to conceive if the person "into" or "toward" whom baptism occurs is not just some dead man. Even on the view according to which "baptism into" refers to a mere change in ownership, the practice is practically impossible to account for if the person in whose interest the baptism occurs is not an ongoing, living person. Christ was conceived as a spiritual presence,[39] and only when Christ is such a presence or living person, in which or with whom one could somehow participate, could "baptism into Christ" hope to make much sense.

6.2.2.2 Parallel between Baptism into Moses and Baptism into Christ

So striking and important is Paul's use of the idea of baptism into Christ, it is nearly impossible not to link with it the expression of 1 Cor. 10:2. Most writers resist the implication of baptismal participation with Moses, but it must be noted that they tend to take this position on general principles, not on an exegetical basis. For example, G. R. Beasley-Murray admits the basic similarity of 1 Cor. 10:2 with Gal. 3:26-27 and Rom. 6:3,[40] but balks that Paul "can scarcely be said to mean 'into Moses.'"[41] G. Braumann similarly deems the notion of "mystical union" with Moses unworthy of consideration.[42]

As βαπτίζω in the New Testament is already a technical term of Christian initiation, however, it is likely that "baptism into Moses" must be interpreted in light of Christian usage.[43] Scholars have (generally unsuccessfully) attempted compromise solutions, with "baptism into Moses" repre-

---

His Theology: A Brief Sketch, 2d ed. (Englewood Cliffs, N.J.: Prentice Hall, 1989), 86, 87, 89.

[38] Barrett, *From First Adam to Last*, 50.

[39] W. D. Davies, *Paul and Rabbinic Judaism: Some Rabbinic Elements in Pauline Theology*, 4th ed. (Philadelphia: Fortress Press, 1980), 225-26.

[40] Beasley-Murray, *Baptism in the New Testament*, 128-29; Schnackenburg, *Baptism in the Thought of St. Paul*, 92-93, and Simon J. Kistemaker, *Exposition of the First Epistle to the Corinthians*, New Testament Commentary (Grand Rapids: Baker Books, 1993), 323 also support this connection.

[41] Beasley-Murray, *Baptism in the New Testament*, 128.

[42] Braumann, *Vorpaulinische christliche Taufverkündigung bei Paulus*, 20.

[43] Fee, *The First Epistle to the Corinthians*, 445 n. 2; Dunn, *Baptism in the Holy Spirit*, 129-130.

senting initiation into the community created by Moses,[44] or allegiance to Moses.[45] R. Schnackenburg's overall position on the meaning of βαπτίζω εἰς in Paul is taken partly because he is confident that βαπτίζεσθαι εἰς Μωϋσῆν must set a person into "a particular relationship of belonging" to Moses (and nothing more).[46] E. Best adopts the curious position that Moses was held to have represented Christ in the Exodus, so that the baptism into Moses was a true baptism, but it was a baptism not into Moses but into Christ.[47] Barrett accepts the implication that, for Paul, "Israelites were in a sense incorporated into him [Moses]."[48] As with baptism into Christ, so with baptism into Moses, Barrett prefers to lose as few of the available nuances as possible in his final assessment: "His people are baptized into him, so as to become one with him, his property, and his obedient subjects and devotees."[49]

6.2.2.3 Conclusion

Viewed against the backdrop of contemporary Christian ideas about baptism and Christian usage of the construction βαπτίζω εἰς, 1 Cor. 10:2 seems to depict Moses as an incorporating, unifying figure for his people, a candidate for mystical participation.

So far, this chapter has examined the "baptism" half of "baptism into Moses," and concluded that "baptism" is best interpreted mystically, with reference to initiation into Judaism, probably with reference to Jewish proselyte baptism. What is needed now is an assessment of the evidence for a Jewish conception of Moses as a spiritual, unifying figure, capable of supporting this conception. The second half of this chapter undertakes this investigation.

6.3 Background Provided by First-Century Conceptions of Moses

The wide recognition accorded to Moses in the Greco-Roman world means that even if the "baptism" in 1 Cor. 10:2 were strictly a Christian invention

---

[44] Lewis B. Smedes, *All Things Made New: A Theology of Man's Union with Christ* (Grand Rapids: William B. Eerdmans, 1970), 145.

[45] Jeske, "The Rock was Christ: The Ecclesiology of 1 Corinthians 10," 247.

[46] Schnackenburg, *Baptism in the Thought of St. Paul*, 23.

[47] Ernest Best, *One Body in Christ: A Study in the Relationship of the Church to Christ in the Epistles of the Apostle Paul* (London: SPCK, 1955), 72, citing Edwards, *First Corinthians*, 4th ed. (London: Hodder & Staughton, 1903), *ad loc.*

[48] Barrett, *From First Adam to Last*, 50.

[49] Barrett, *From First Adam to Last*, 54; see above, p. 186.

(which seems unlikely), Paul's deployment of the idea of "baptism into Moses" would still have to interact with a going conception of Moses, which would necessarily both shape his expression and provide guidelines for its interpretation. The question of the identity of Moses in Corinth is too often neglected in discussion of 1 Cor. 10:2. But there was a Corinthian conception of Moses, and Paul knew it, meaning it is likely to be crucial to his intended meaning.

Hypothetically, "baptism into Moses" could derive from nothing more than a contemporary estimation of Moses which made him suitable for comparison with Christ. The existence of very early Moses Christologies, traces of which have been detected in the New Testament,[50] shows that Moses was, in fact, found suitable for such comparison. Barrett also suggests the existence of early Christian (pre-Pauline) material exalting Moses directly (he names both 1 Cor. 10:1-4 and the oration in Acts 7:35-40 as examples).[51]

Beside these reasonable surmises, explicit evidence emerges from the ancient sources for viewing Moses as a spirit, or a similarly glorified personage, capable of a unifying, or perhaps even incorporative, relationship with his followers.

6.3.1 The Assumption of Moses

In the first century the idea that people are essentially embodied spirits, and that the human spirit is at least potentially immortal, was widespread.[52] Moses in particular was thought of as possessing an especially great spirit.

In *As. Mos.* 11:16-19 Joshua describes Moses as "the holy and sacred spirit (*S[anctu]m et sacrum spiritum*),[53] the worthy one before the Lord, the manifold and inscrutable lord of the word (*multiplicem et inconpraehensibilem dominum verbi*)." Moses is then both a "holy and sacred spirit," and "*inconpraehensibilis*," which, Tromp notes, "is a characteristic

---

[50] See below, pp. 260-70.

[51] Barrett, *Commentary on the Acts of the Apostles*, vol. 1, 362-63.

[52] Philo, *Gig.* 34; Ps.-Phocylides, *Sentences* 107-108; 1QH 11.21; CD 5.11; 7.3-4; 1 Cor. 14:14-15, 32; D. E. Aune, "The Problem of the Genre of the Gospels: A Critique of C. H. Talbert's *What Is a Gospel?*," in *Gospel Perspectives: Studies of History and Tradition in the Four Gospels*, vol. 2, ed. R. T. France and David Wenham (Sheffield: JSOT Press, 1981), 27; also Mark 3:11; 8:33; John 6:70.

[53] The manuscript reads *esse SEMET sacrum spiritum*, which makes no sense. Tromp's conjecture rests on the slight alteration of SEMET into SCM ET, in which SCM is understood as an abbreviation of *sanctum*, Johannes Tromp, ed., *The Assumption of Moses: A Critical Edition with Commentary*, Studia in Veteris Testamenti Pseudepigrapha, ed. A.-M. Denis and M. de Jonge, vol. 10 (Leiden: E. J. Brill, 1993), 254 n. 1, see also 196.

connected with deities and spirits."[54] Both ascriptions highlight Moses' transcendent nature.

Tromp believes that the "spirit" of *As. Mos.* 11:16 is not the holy spirit of Moses, but the Holy Spirit of God, of which Moses is "the embodiment" while he lives, but which at his death will simply be transferred to Joshua. "Therefore," Tromp concludes, "the laudations of Moses in 11:16 are in reality a description of the spirit of God, which dwelled in Moses during his lifetime."[55]

Tromp's position throws the extremely exalted manner in which Moses is described into sharp relief. The context in *Assumption of Moses*, how-ever, equates the spirit of 11:16 with "the worthy one *before* the Lord," "the trusted one in everything," and, decisively, "Moses, the great messen-ger" (11:17). Never is it indicated that the *sanctus et sacer spiritus* only indwelled Moses. Rather, it is Moses.[56]

In *As. Mos.* 1:15 and 10:14, Moses refers to his own death, which implies that in the (lost) ending of the story he dies. "The idea of [Moses'] death," however, "was not incompatible with the idea of the assumption of his soul into heaven,"[57] and Tromp argues for a reconstruction of the lost ending of *Assumption of Moses* which details the assumption of Moses' spirit to a glorified heavenly existence.[58] Tromp surveys a number of rele-vant texts, including the tradition preserved in Clement of Alexandria of a "double Moses," one which went with the angels, and the other which was buried.[59] The *Assumption of Moses* might have ended with the assumption "of a spiritual component of Moses' person (something like an ethereal, glorified, spiritual body, or perhaps his spirit or soul)," with the burial of his body undertaken by the archangel Michael (from the ostensible frag-ment in Jude 9).[60]

Chief among Joshua's concerns in *As. Mos.* 11:16-19 is that with the passing of "the holy and sacred spirit" Israel would lack for an intercessor before God. On the basis of Moses' reply to Joshua, in *As. Mos.* 12:6, D. L. Tiede suggests that the author may have believed that Moses' interces-

---

[54] Tromp, *Assumption of Moses*, 255.

[55] Ibid., 252.

[56] Cf. the τὸ πνεῦμα τὸ ἅγιον that is Daniel in Σουσ. 45 θ. Cf. also the way Philo describes the spirit of God indwelling Moses, below. Tromp's analysis fits Philo well.

[57] Tromp, *Assumption of Moses*, 283.

[58] Ibid., 270-85, esp. 281-85, see also 101, 115. "In post-mortem ascension myths ... it was often the soul which was thought to ascend to the heavens unencumbered by a mortal body," Aune, "The Problem of the Genre of the Gospels," 27.

[59] *Stromateis* 6.132.2 cited in Tromp, *Assumption of Moses*, 283. The same idea oc-curs in Origen, *In Jesu Nave* 2.1, see Tromp, 284.

[60] Tromp, *Assumption of Moses*, 285. See Tromp, 270-85 on Jude 9 and the lost ending of *Assumption of Moses*.

sory role did not end with his natural life.[61]   The verse in question is in
particularly rough condition in the manuscript.   The reconstructed text is
[*Dominu*]*s me constituit pro eis et pro peccatis eorum <ut orarem> et
in<pr>ecare<r> pro eis* ("The Lord has appointed me for them and for
their sins, that I should pray and supplicate for them").[62]   Moses appears to
be reassuring Joshua that he will continue to care for Israel from beyond
the grave.[63]

Moses in the *Assumption of Moses* has, or is, a great and holy spirit.   In
life he is a prophet whose ministry spans the whole world,[64] and after death
he remains intimately concerned with and active on behalf of his people.
With its date anchored firmly in the early first century A.D.,[65] *Assumption
of Moses* provides solid evidence of a conception of Moses which well
supports an impression of him as a universal, spiritual figure.   The presence
of such a conception in the milieu of Judaism by the time of Paul's writing
to the Corinthians would easily support the idea of Moses as a suitably incorporating figure for baptism.   Such a view of Moses also resonates with
the depiction of Moses in 2 Cor. 3:15, which implies that Moses continues
somehow to be present whenever his Law is read.

6.3.2 Pseudo-Philo

Pseudo-Philo is clear that the fate of Moses is to die and be buried,[66] but
LAB 19.16 sees Moses transfigured prior to his death to a "state of glory"
(*et mutata est effigies eius in gloria*) and, after he dies "in glory" (*et mortuus est in gloria*), an expression wherein F. J. Murphy finds Moses' pas-

---

[61] David Lenz Tiede, "The Figure of Moses in *The Testament of Moses*," in *Studies
on the Testament of Moses: Seminar Papers*, ed. George W. E. Nickelsburg, Jr., Society of Biblical Literature Pseudepigrapha Group, Septuagint and Cognate Studies, no. 4.
(Cambridge, Mass.: Society of Biblical Literature, 1973), 89.

[62] See Tromp, *Assumption of Moses*, 265 on how lacunae in the text are filled out.
Wayne A. Meeks, *The Prophet-King: Moses Traditions and the Johannine Christology*,
Supplements to *Novum Testamentum*, ed. W. C. van Unnik, et al., vol. 14 (Leiden: E. J.
Brill, 1967), 160-61 follows basically the same translation.   Jeremiah seems to take a
similar *post mortem* role in 2 Macc. 15:14.

[63] But see Tromp, *Assumption of Moses*, 265. See below pp. 204-205 for more on
the death of Moses in *Assumption of Moses*.

[64] See excursus above, pp. 39-43.

[65] On the theory of George W. E. Nickelsburg, Jr., "An Antiochan Date for the Testament of Moses," in *Studies on the Testament of Moses*, ed. George W. E. Nickelsburg, Jr., Septuagint and Cognate Studies, no. 4 (Cambridge, Mass.: Society of Biblical
Literature, 1973), 33-37, which builds on the hypothesis of Licht (see Nickelsburg,
"Introduction," same volume, 6), even earlier; cf. above, p. 5 n. 2.

[66] *LAB* 19.5-6; cf. 19.2; God tells Moses that he will rest where he is buried "until I
visit the world," 19.12.

sage to a higher plane of existence,[67] God buries him "in a high place as a light for the entire world" (*super excelsam terram et in lumine totius orbis*).[68]

In *LAB* chapter 9 God announces that Moses "will serve me forever" (*mihi serviet in eternum*; 9.7).[69] As if to underscore the point, God also tells Miriam in a dream that her brother "will exercise leadership always" (*et ipse ducatum eius aget semper*, 9.10). Thus Pseudo-Philo, though without a great deal of elaboration, depicts Moses having or being given qualities which transcend the limitations of ordinary mortal life.[70]

6.3.3 Philo

A discussion of Moses as spirit in Jewish thought might seem inevitably to run to Philo, and Philo's reputation is one of such profligate hyperbole that one almost expects him to make more of Moses than could possibly be thought to reflect Judaism outside of Philo's own mind. Yet Philo is very careful to circumscribe the greatness of Moses, especially by comparison with the greatness of God, and he cagily prevents his readers from drawing too grand conclusions about Moses' spirit and spirituality. And as mentioned earlier, Philo's value as a window into Jewish thought (and life) is greater than is often acknowledged.[71]

6.3.3.1 The Mortality of Moses

In *Gig.* 19-23 Philo opens an extended discussion of the spirit of God (πνεῦμα θεῖον).[72] In *Gig.* 23 Philo says that this spirit is "the pure knowledge in which every wise man naturally shares." He then more plainly defines that spirit (τὸ πνεῦμα θεῖον) with reference to Bezalel: "[God] 'filled him with the divine spirit (ἐνέπλησεν αὐτὸν πνεύματος θείου), with wisdom, understanding, and knowledge to devise in every work' (Ἐξοδ. 31:2-

---

[67] Frederick J. Murphy, *Pseudo-Philo: Rewriting the Bible* (New York and Oxford: Oxford University Press, 1993), 94.

[68] Jacobson's translation, adopted here, is contended; see Howard Jacobson, *A Commentary on Pseudo-Philo's* Liber Antiquitatum Biblicarum *with Latin Text and English Translation*, Arbeiten zur Geschichte des antiken Judentums und des Urchristentums, ed. Martin Hengel, et al., no. 31 (Leiden: E. J. Brill, 1996), 2.657-58; D. J. Harrington, trans., "Pseudo-Philo," in *The Old Testament Pseudepigrapha*, ed. James H. Charlesworth, vol. 2, The Anchor Bible Reference Library (New York: Doubleday, 1985), 328.

[69] Something that is said in *Biblical Antiquities* only of Moses, Murphy, *Pseudo-Philo: Rewriting the Bible*, 57, 58.

[70] See below, pp. 203-204, for more on the death of Moses according to Pseudo-Philo.

[71] See above, pp. 5-6.

[72] Deriving from Ἐξοδ. 31:2-3, cited in *Gig.* 23. The same Philonic passage establishes a kind of equivalence between πνεῦμα θεῖον and πνεῦμα θεοῦ, derived from the citation in *Gig*, 22 of Γεν. 1:2.

3). In these words we have suggested to us *a definition of what the divine spirit is (*τὸ τί ἐστι πνεῦμα θεῖον)" (emphasis added). The τὸ πνεῦμα θεῖον, according to this passage, is an endowment of wisdom, understanding, and knowledge from God.

Philo immediately follows the "definition" of τὸ πνεῦμα θεῖον by adding, "Such is the spirit of Moses (τοιοῦτόν ἐστι καὶ τὸ Μωυσέως πνεῦμα; *Gig.* 24)." For Philo, the τὸ πνεῦμα θεῖον of Moses is not Moses' own soul, but the τὸ πνεῦμα θεῖον of *Gig.* 23, which is "wisdom, understanding, and knowledge" received from God.[73] Thinking of Num. 11:17, where God distributes from Moses' spirit among the seventy elders, Philo explains further:

> If, then, it were Moses' own spirit (πνεῦμα), or the spirit of some other created being (γενητός), which was according to God's purpose to be distributed to that great number of disciples, it would indeed be shredded into so many pieces, and thus lessened. But as it is, the spirit which is on him is the wise, the divine (τὸ θεῖον), the excellent spirit, ... which though it be shared with others or added to others suffers no diminution in understanding and knowledge and wisdom (*Gig.* 26-27).

Philo here clearly distinguishes Moses' own (created) spirit from the divine spirit, which is uncreated and omnipresent. "Moses' own spirit," it is clearly implied, is of an entirely different order, and indeed in *Virt.* 62 Moses is made to speak of his own beginning (his creation) long after the creation of the world, again implying his mortality. A little later, Moses distinguishes all human leaders including himself from God, since they lack "the essential attribute of eternality" (*Virt.* 65).[74]

What distinguishes Moses then is not his own nature but his long indwelling by this divine spirit. According to *Dec.* 175, when God selected Moses he "filled him with the divine spirit (καὶ ἀναπλήσας ἐνθέου πνεύματος)," a condition in which Moses persisted for the rest of his life.[75] So Philo writes, "He then has ever the divine spirit (τὸ θεῖον πνεῦμα) at his side ... but from those others, as I have said, it quickly separates itself" (*Gig.* 55; also 19-20, 53), after also saying, "Thus may the divine spirit of wisdom (τὸ σοφίας πνεῦμα θεῖον) ... long, long abide with us, since He did thus abide with Moses the wise" (*Gig.* 47).

Moses' distinctive endowment with God's spirit does not transmute his mortality, which, for example, still thwarts his desire clearly to behold God (*Mut.* 7-8). The same quality of being "born into mortality" (εἰς τὴν θνητὴν γένεσιν) prevented his learning the true divine name (*Mut.* 13). In the end, Moses dies like any other mortal and is buried (*Mos.* 2.290, 292).

---

[73] Cf. *Fug.* 186.

[74] Cf. Josephus, *Ant.* 3.320 where the Law, "being believed to come from God, caused this man to be ranked higher than his own nature (τῆς αὐτοῦ φύσεως)."

[75] Paralleled in *Mos.* 2.67, 69; see *Mos.* 2.264-65; cf. Is. 63:11-12.

6.3.3.2 The Divinity of Moses

Philo thus has no doubt about Moses' mortality, but nonetheless the quality of Moses' mortal nature is clearly of a higher grade than normal. His was a "great nature" (μεγάλη φύσις) and a gifted soul (εὐφυὴς ψυχή; *Mos.* 1.22). In *Mos.* 1.27 the Israelites find "the mind which dwelt in his body" so exceptional that they debated "whether it was human or divine or a mixture of both." The aggregate description of Moses becomes reminiscent of that of Solomon in Wisdom of Solomon who, though he was a good soul placed in an undefiled body (8:19-20) and perfect among men (9:6), yet prayed for Wisdom (Philo's πνεῦμα θεῖον; 9:4).[76]

Philo also views Moses, at least after his death, as in some way an exalted being, engaged in important, *post mortem*, spiritual activity. In *Mos.* 2.40, Philo says that readers of the Septuagint regard its translators not as translators but as prophets and priests, "whose sincerity and singleness of thought has enabled them to go hand in hand with the purest of spirits, the spirit of Moses (τὸ Μωυσέως καθαρωτάτο πνεῦμα)." In this instance it apparently is not the divine spirit resting on Moses which is active, but the spirit of Moses itself, going hand in hand with those who, as his prophets, translate the Law.

Similar ideas may only be hinted at in *Sac.* 8, where Moses is spoken of as one who transcended his natural order and came to stand with God. Philo connects this predicate of Moses, drawn from Deut 5·31 and the ascent of Sinai, to the translation of Moses at his death when Moses was drawn to God. Philo in *Sac.* 9 even describes Moses as "a loan to the earthly sphere," referring not to Moses' pre-existence but to his fate at death, which was to be translated to immortality and taken to the higher sphere. According to *Mos.* 2.288, at the end of Moses' life God "resolved his twofold nature of soul and body (σῶμα καὶ ψυχήν) into a single unity, transforming his whole being into mind (εἰς νοῦν)."[77]

E. R. Goodenough even thinks he has identified a prayer addressed to Moses as "an active and present power" in *Som.* 1.164-65.[78] Moses is not named in the prayer, which is addressed to ὦ ἱεροφάντα, but though Goodenough does not explain his view one surmises that he sees Moses in the ἱεροφάντης, which is one of the titles that Philo applies to Moses

[76] Wilfred L. Knox, *St Paul and the Church of the Gentiles* (Cambridge: Cambridge University Press, 1939), 78 suggests that Solomon is here viewed as a perfect spiritual being.

[77] At which time once more the divine spirit fell upon him (καταπνευσθείς) and he prophesied (*Mos.* 2.290, see 288). See more on Philo's view of the death of Moses below, pp. 201-202.

[78] Erwin R. Goodenough, *By Light, Light: The Mystic Gospel of Hellenistic Judaism* (New Haven, Conn.: Yale University Press, 1935; reprint, Amsterdam: Philo Press, 1969), 233.

from time to time.[79] In fact, aside from one application to Jeremiah (*Cher.*
49), whenever Philo applies the term to an individual he applies it to Moses, never to God or to the Logos or one of God's powers. On that basis
one might argue that Philo's unmodified use of the term in *Som.* 1.164
necessarily refers to Moses. As to the "prayer," perhaps it is more probably only a rhetorical address to Moses, for example as the author of the
Law.[80] Even if the passage is not pressed as a prayer *per se* it still says
something about the status of Moses that he could be addressed in this
way. Josephus may similarly treat Moses as an "authorial presence" when
he says that even "now (νῦν)," "there is not a Hebrew who does not, just
as if [Moses] were present and ready to punish any breach of discipline,
obey the laws he laid down" (ἔστι γοῦν οὐδεὶς Ἑβραίων, ὃς οὐχὶ καθάπερ παρόντος αὐτοῦ καὶ κολάσαντος ἂν ἀκουσμῇ πειθαρχεῖ τοῖς
ὑπ᾽ αὐτοῦ νομοθετηθεῖσι; *Ant.* 3.317).[81]

6.3.3.3 Conclusion

Philo is careful to avoid giving the impression that Moses was a being of
the same order as God, and in one place even makes the case for his mortality and dependence on God. But at the same time he clearly thinks of
Moses as a mortal of a different order than other mortals.[82]

   Not all scholars would want to leap from Philo of Alexandria to other
spheres of Jewish thinking. Jeremias, who is second perhaps only to
Goodenough in the height of his appraisal of Moses in the first century,
cautions, "To summarise, it is plain that the Moses of the NT has nothing
whatever to do with either the hero of the Moses romance or the ideal sage
of Philo."[83] In this case, however, a good deal of kinship has emerged between the two portraits, the Philonic, and one (from Pseudo-Philo and the
Assumption of Moses) which can be characterized as Palestinian. In both,
Moses appears as a transcendent and glorious figure, particularly after
death, and as a figure with strong "spiritual" overtones.

6.3.4 The Transfiguration

The Transfiguration account has vexed interpreters of the Bible for centuries, largely because it is presented in the Synoptic Gospels with essentially no accompanying explanation or interpretation. Ironically, the very

---

[79] See p. 44 above.

[80] Meeks, *Prophet-King*, 125 n. 3 replies to Goodenough, calling the Philonic passage, "rhetorical, though admittedly the language is strong."

[81] Cf. *Ap.* 2.277; thence 2.216, 269, 271.

[82] Cf. Howard M. Teeple, *The Mosaic Eschatological Prophet*, Journal of Biblical
Literature Monograph Series, vol. 10 (Philadelphia: Society of Biblical Literature,
1957), 38, "Philo did not fully deify Moses, but he came very close to it."

[83] Jeremias, "Μωυσῆς," 866.

absence of explanatory remarks suggests that the account was comprehensible and meaningful to those who first circulated it. On this basis then, it seems safe to assume that the appearance of Moses (and Elijah) at the Transfiguration in some way reflects the existing Jewish religious background of the early Christian community. The fact that the account names three followers of Jesus as witnesses, all of whom remained well known and active in the early Palestinian Church where the account would have first circulated, also points toward a background in the Jewish context of Jesus and his movement.[84] In other words, the Transfiguration is cast in the idiom of Palestinian Judaism.

On that basis the account of the Transfiguration may be the strongest NT evidence that Jews were prepared to view Moses as a supernaturally active figure. The impression given of Moses coheres well with the notion of him as a figure alive and active in heaven, and some notion like this must underlie the account, however Peter and his companions would have expressed their views on the matter.

6.3.4.1 The Availability of Moses

Discussion of the "idiom" of the Transfiguration easily becomes involved in questions regarding the antiquity and prevalence of Jewish belief in the physical ascent of Moses. For the sake of present discussion, however, it is unnecessary to prove that Moses was thought to have been taken alive into heaven.[85] In Jewish belief it was possible for heroes of faith to return to life and interact with the living regardless of whether they were thought to have escaped death, especially in an eschatological context.[86] This might sometimes explicitly involve resurrection.[87] A belief that Moses

---

[84] See Christopher Rowland, *The Open Heaven: A Study of Apocalyptic in Judaism and Early Christianity* (London: SPCK, 1982), 502 n. 47.

[85] In agreement, Kastner, "Moses im Neuen Testament," 95.

[86] Kastner, "Moses im Neuen Testament," 123.

[87] Generally: Is. 26:19; Job 42:17 LXX; 4 Ezra 4:41-42; 7:28; 13:52; 2 Bar. 21:23-24; specifically, John the Baptist (Matt. 14:2; Mark 6:14-16; 8:28; Luke 9:19); the prophets (Luke 9:19; Sir. 49:10; Job: Job 42:17 LXX); Samuel (1 Sam. 28:12-19); Daniel (Dan. 12:13); Josiah (2 Bar. 66:6); heroes of old (Dan. 12:2); the patriarchs (1 Enoch 70:4; *T. Sim.* 6:7; *T. Jud.* 25; *T. Zeb.* 10; *T. Ben.* 10:6-7; 2 Bar. 21:24; Justin, *Dial.* 45); the martyrs (2 Macc. 7:9, 11, 14, 23; 14:46; cf. 12:43-45; 1 Enoch 90:33; *T. Jud.* 25:4); David (*y. Ber.* 5a.10-12; *b. Meg.* 18a; *b. Chag.* 14a); Hezekiah (*y. Sot.* 24c.29-31 = *y. AZ* 42c.42-44; *b. Ber.* 28b; cf. Justin, *Dial.* 4, 67, 83, 85). See Paul Volz, *Die Eschatologie der jüdischen Gemeinde im neutestamentlichen Zeitalter: Nach den Quellen der rabbinischen, apokalyptischen und apokryphen Literatur* (Hildesheim: Georg Olms Verlagsbuchhandlung, 1966), 206-207, 229-32, 235-38. The belief in resurrection generally coheres with this as well. This point would become more significant on the (unlikely) supposition that the account of the Transfiguration is a displaced resur-

might have escaped ordinary death could have played a role in the Transfiguration, but is not crucial to the account.

The impression given by the Transfiguration, that Moses was somehow
available to his people, is enhanced by his pairing with Elijah. While the
Transfiguration is unusual in its depiction of Moses as personally available,
Elijah was often thought to visit[88] or be available for consultation.[89] Elijah
may also be a help in time of need.[90]

Even without ruling on the evidence for a Jewish belief in the living assumption of Moses, the Transfiguration may be taken at face value as evidence merely for a Jewish belief in the availability of Moses, and concomi-
tantly as evidence for viewing Moses as a divine or similarly glorified figure. A figure thought to be existing in a glorified state, and to be available for consultation or assistance, might easily be judged to be in some
sort of mystical communion with his followers, which is the argument being pursued here.

While it may not be vital to that argument, evidence for Jewish views of
the ascent or the death of Moses is clearly relevant not only to the assessment of the appearance of Moses in the Transfiguration but also to the
understanding of his place in the New Testament generally, and the place
of the New Testament in Jewish literature of the first century. Such evidence might also help correlate Jewish views of Moses with Christian
views of Christ. Further consideration of the end of Moses is therefore
appropriate here.

6.3.4.2 The Ascent of Moses

Undoubtedly traditions that Moses escaped death existed, though dating
their emergence is not easy, and the evidence for them is thin.[91] *Sifre* 357

---

rection account. Moses then becomes a risen Moses, flanking a risen Messiah and a similarly glorified Elijah.

[88] E. g., *b. BQ* 60b.

[89] E. g., *y. Terum.* 46b.54; *b. BM* 59b. Though in *b. Men.* 29b Moses has a vision in
which he appears on the 8th row of Aqiba's academy (and does not understand Aqiba's
teaching).

[90] Matt. 27:47; *b. AZ* 17b. In *Eccl. Rab.* 4.1 §1 Elijah is a heavenly advocate. See
further Volz, *Die Eschatologie der jüdischen Gemeinde im neutestamentlichen
Zeitalter*, 195.

[91] Kastner, "Moses im Neuen Testament," 94, calls the evidence "spärlich," but
concludes "daß die Himmelfahrt des Moses wohl hier und dort gelehrt wurde." Jarl E.
Fossum, *The Name of God and the Angel of the Lord: Samaritan and Jewish Concepts
of Intermediation and the Origin of Gnosticism*, WUNT, ed. Martin Hengel and Otfried
Hofius, no. 36 (Tübingen: J. C. B. Mohr [Paul Siebeck], 1985), 134 writes, "In view of
the fact that there are so few rabbinic witnesses to this tradition, it would seem that its
origin must be sought outside main stream Judaism," Fossum, 134-36 goes on to sug-

and *Midrash Tannaim* on Deut. 34:5, apparently relying ultimately on the same source, both report the same series of traditions regarding that verse and the death of Moses, a series which concludes, "Others say, our master Moses never died, and he stands and serves on high" (וויש אומ׳ משה רבינו לא מת אלא עומד ומשרת למעלן).[92] The clear implication is that Moses was thought by some to have been received bodily into heaven.

This twice-repeated tradition of an ascended Moses serving in the heavenly sanctuary is completely singular in rabbinic Judaism.[93] Something like it might be assumed, however, in the tradition that Moses will return with Elijah at the end of the age, reported in *Deut. Rab.* 10.1, and attributed to Johanan ben Zakkai in *Deut. Rab.* 3.17.[94] T. F. Glasson argues for a first-century origin for this tradition, wherein God says to Moses "In the time to come, when I send them Elijah the prophet, you will both come at one time."[95] The same sort of tradition may be reflected in the two witnesses of Rev. 11:1-6, who bear characteristics somewhat reminiscent of Moses and Elijah. That the more usual eschatological combination with Elijah is Enoch[96] suggests again a latent conception of Moses as having been taken up into heaven, ready to return.[97]

The expectation of Moses is distinctly absent in the New Testament[98] by contrast, for example, with a quite lively expectation of the return of Eli-

---

gest that the origin of the tradition of the bodily rapture of Moses may have been lay teachings in Samaria.

[92] *Midrash Tannaim* (Hoffman), 224, ה. line 10, repeated again in *b. Soṭ.* 13b.

[93] Elsewhere, Michael or Metatron perform such functions, Klaus Von Haacker and Peter Schäfer, "Nachbiblische Traditionen vom Tod des Mose," in *Josephus-Studien: Untersuchungen zu Josephus dem antiken Judentum und dem Neuen Testament: Otto Michel zum 70. Geburtstag gewidmet*, ed. Otto Betz, Klaus Haacker, and Martin Hengel (Göttingen: Vandenhoeck & Ruprecht, 1974), 171.

[94] See further Volz, *Die Eschatologie der jüdischen Gemeinde im neutestamentlichen Zeitalter*, 197.

[95] T. F. Glasson, *Moses in the Fourth Gospel*, Studies in Biblical Theology, ed. C. F. D. Moule, et al., no. 40 (London: SCM Press, 1963), 27. From an early date Elijah and Moses came be seen as peers. It may be that in the Synoptic Gospel accounts of the Transfiguration, Moses appears with Elijah simply as a great prophet. *Pesiq. R.* 4.2 extensively compares Moses and Elijah, the "two prophets" who arose out of the tribe of Levi. On parallels between the OT traditions of Moses and Elijah, see Kastner, "Moses im Neuen Testament," 30-32.

[96] Ibid., 174 n. 52.

[97] In *b. Suk.* 5a, R. Jose claims that neither Moses nor Elijah ever ascended to heaven, but that both God and men kept always to their appointed realms (see also *Exod. Rab.* 28.1). Knox, *St Paul and the Church of the Gentiles*, 102 claims that later rabbinical Judaism came to view ascent traditions with suspicion, perhaps through conflict with Christianity.

[98] Though there is Jewish evidence outside the New Testament, see Volz, *Die Eschatologie der jüdischen Gemeinde im neutestamentlichen Zeitalter*, 194-95.

jah, warranted always by Mal. 3:23.[99] But it seems at least plausible that the appearance of Moses and Elijah in the Transfiguration is an expression of the hope eventually expressed in *Deuteronomy Rabbah*, that Moses and Elijah would return in "the time to come," i.e., the end of the age, even if such a hope was not a dominant theme among Jews of the first century A.D.[100]

In a hope apparently distinct from his eschatological pairing with Elijah, at least some Jews seem to have looked for Moses to return and join Messiah at the head of the people (*Tg. Neof.* Exod. 12:42), so that the last days could be conceived of as "eine Rückkehr der Mosezeit."[101] A similar inference may be drawn from *Frg. Tg.*(P) Exod. 15:18, with the tradition, "When the world will reach its fixed time to be redeemed, ... Moses will go forth from the wilderness, and the King Messiah will go forth from Rome."[102] Once more, the New Testament does not explicitly witness to hopes such as these. Even so, eventually some Jews connected the appearance of Messiah with the reappearance of Moses, something at least potentially relevant to the scene at the Transfiguration.

Hopes that Moses might return to lead the Wilderness Generation out of exile into blessing may be of special relevance to the Lukan version of the Transfiguration, wherein Moses and Elijah discuss with Jesus the "exodus"

---

[99] E.g., Mark 9:11; Matt. 17:10; Mark 6:14-15. "Die drei Elemente Himmelfahrt, Wiederkunft und endzeitliche Aufgabe, die sich in den Eliastraditionen ohne jede Schwerigkeit nachweisen lassen, find sich in der Überlieferung der Mosesgeshichte nur andeuteutungsweise," Kastner, "Moses im Neuen Testament," 123, see also 125; Elijah is the forerunner of Messiah in 1 Enoch 90.31; 4 Esdr. 4(6).26; 1 Macc. 2:58; Sir. 48:9. Other texts teach the rapture of Ezra (4 Ezra 14:9, 50) and Baruch (2 Bar. 48:30; 76:2) to return at the end of the age (2 Bar. 13:3; 25:1; perhaps 4 Ezra 7:28 and 13:52). For more on the extensive evidence for the expectation of Elijah in Jewish literature see Volz, *Die Eschatologie der jüdischen Gemeinde im neutestamentlichen Zeitalter*, 195-97.

[100] Haacker and Schäfer, "Nachbiblische Traditionen vom Tod des Mose," 174. On Jewish ideas of the role of Moses at the end of the age, see Billerbeck, *Kommentar zum Neuen Testament aus Talmud und Midrasch*, vol. 1, 757-58.

[101] Nils Alstrup Dahl, *Das Volk Gottes: Eine Untersuchung zum kirchenbewusstsein des Urchristentums*, Skrifter Utgitt Av Det Norske Videnskaps-Akademi I Oslo, II. Hist.-Filos. Klasse, 1941, no. 2 (Oslo: Jacob Dybwad, 1941), 39. Development of this idea continued into the rabbinic period. E.g., Is. 53:12 was applied to Moses (*b. Sot.* 14a); see P. M. Casey, *From Jewish Prophet to Gentile God: The Origins and Development of New Testament Christology* (Cambridge: James Clarke & Co.; Louisville, Kent.: Westminster/John Knox Press, 1991), 83-84. 2 Bar. 59:1 only teaches the appearance of a Moses-like messiah, see Kastner, "Moses im Neuen Testament," 48. For extensive parallels in rabbinic literature between the *Moseszeit* and the *Heilszeit*, see Kastner, 98-104. See further above, p. 57 n. 118 and below, pp. 261-62, 268, 280, 286.

[102] Trans., Michael L. Klein, *The Fragment-Targums of the Pentateuch According to Their Extant Sources*, vol. 2 (Rome: Biblical Institute Press, 1980), 48.

(ἔξοδος), which he is about to accomplish in Jerusalem. The word chosen is too fraught with meaning not to be significant in this context: the "exodus" of Jesus is both his death and the deliverance he would accomplish for his people by that death. The participation of Moses in the discussion recalls the Exodus from Egypt,[103] but quite possibly also calls up Jewish beliefs about the return of Moses as a partner with Messiah to lead the Wilderness Generation into blessing.[104]

The appearance of an explicit tradition of an ascended Moses in both *Sifre* and *Midrash Tannaim* seems to place it securely in the tannaitic period. At a minimum it represents the fruition of lines of thinking that appear in Philo, Josephus, the New Testament, and elsewhere concerning the glorious state of Moses at and after his death (seen above and to be considered again presently). The appearance of Moses on the Mount of Transfiguration would cohere with such a view of a glorified and ascended Moses. Although the dominant view at all times was that Moses had died and been buried (see discussion below), at least some Jews by the tannaitic period had thought differently.[105]

6.3.4.3 The Glorious Death of Moses

Even though evidence for the precise view the Moses had ascended alive into heaven only appears in the tannaitic period, speculation along that line seems to have taken place earlier. Jeremias points out, however, both how limited the evidence for such ideas is, and how it seems to place any such speculations outside Palestine in the first century A.D.. Further, such speculations must at all times have been modulated by the testimony of Deuteronomy 34 that Moses had died and been buried.[106]

---

[103] It is by no means indefensible to claim that in Luke's version of the Transfiguration there is a deliberate allusion to the Exodus. "There appears to be a striking reference to 2 Peter 1:15 in Irenaeus's citation of an earlier writer ... to the effect that after the death (*exodos*) of Peter and Paul, Mark, the interpreter of Peter, wrote down the gospel message which Peter used to preach. Not only is the content of these two sayings similar; so is the form. ἔξοδος, used absolutely with the meaning "death," appears to be restricted to Luke 9:31, 2 Peter 1:15 and this passage in Irenaeus," E. M. B. Green, *2 Peter Reconsidered*, Tyndale Monographs (London: Tyndale Press, 1960), 8. (In n. 2 on that page Green notes that in late Greek ἔξοδος with the genitive commonly refers to death, e.g. ἔξοδος τοῦ βίου.)

[104] These beliefs, however, seem to be connected with belief in a future resurrection, in which Moses would rise from his grave in the wilderness to lead the likewise risen Wilderness Generation onward. In the first century, Pseudo-Philo (19:12) expressly links the resurrection of Moses with that of the fathers.

[105] "Die Mehrzahl der spätjudischen Schriftsteller an einem leiblichen Tod des Moses festhalten," Kastner, "Moses im Neuen Testament," 93.

[106] Jeremias, "Μωυσῆς," 854-55.

6.3.4.3.1 Josephus

Perhaps the most important evidence is thought to come from Josephus. According to *Ant.* 4.326, while Moses spoke with Joshua and Eleazar on the summit of Mt. Abaris,[107] a cloud suddenly descended upon him (undoubtedly signifying the presence of the Lord, cf. *Ant.* 3.79-80) and he disappeared into a certain chasm, or cave (ἀφανίζεται κατά τινος φάραγγος). In this account, though paraphrastic as usual, Josephus still may be said generally to conform to the MT, in which Moses dies (שם וימת משה; Deut. 34:5). God then buries him in a valley (ויקבר אתו בגי) and no one knows where the his grave is (Deut. 34:6). The "chasm" or perhaps "cave" (φάραγξ) into which Josephus has Moses vanish seems to correspond well enough to the גי that is the biblical gravesite of Moses, and the cloud and the sudden disappearance seem a suitable device for bringing about the desired conclusion without having to go into irreverent details about God physically handling a dead body.[108]

For comparison, in the LXX, Moses dies (ἐτελεύτησεν) and the burial by God is apparently implied by the reverent use of the plural verb with no expressed subject (καὶ ἔθαψαν αὐτὸν ἐν Γαὶ).[109] Again no one sees where his tomb is (οὐκ οἶδεν οὐδεὶς τὴν ταφὴν αὐτοῦ). The Targums are divided on the burial, with *Onqelos* and *Pseudo-Jonathan* using the singular form וקבר and the *Fragment Targum* (V), *Neofiti*, and the Cairo Genizah Oxford Bodleian MS Heb. e 43, folio 65r using the plural form וקברו. All the Targums agree that Moses was buried in a hollow, or valley (בחילתא, *et var.*), seeming to split the difference between the MT גי and the φάραγξ of the tradition represented by Josephus. The early strata of the rabbinic literature, however, are often categorical that God himself buried Moses (*m. Sot.* 1.9, בגיא; *t. Sot.* 4.8, בנחלת בני גד (in a field in Gad); *Mek.* בשלח 1.119, בגיא).[110]

---

[107] Pseudo-Philo makes the same switch, from Deuteronomy's Mt. Nebo to Mt. Abarim (*LAB* 19.8).

[108] The device of the cloud is not uncommon, but generally it is the instrument by which the person is caught upward (e.g. Acts 1:9; Livy, *Ab Urbe Condita* 1.16.1 of Romulus; Dion. Hal. *Ant.* 2.56.2 also of Romulus and *Ant.* 1.77.2 of a manifestation of a god. Tertullian, *Apol.* 21 compares the ascension of Jesus to that of Romulus, tying those cloud/ascension motifs together. Josephus, however, seems merely to have borrowed the cloud motif as a way of dressing the biblical account of Moses' divine burial for non-Jewish sensibilities, and not in order to describe an ascension of Moses. See, for an assessment more favorable to ascension in Josephus, Haacker and Schäfer, "Nachbiblische Traditionen vom Tod des Mose," 149 n. 8.

[109] I.e., to avoid the anthropomorphism involved in God burying a body, see Cécile Dogniez and Marguerite Harl, *Le Deutéronome: Traduction du texte grec de la Septante, Introduction et Notes*, La Bible d'Alexandrie, ed. Marguerite Harl, vol. 5 (Paris: Les Éditions du Cerf, 1992), 355-56.

[110] See also below, p. 205.

The position of Josephus himself is clear if the verb τελευτάω carries its usual meaning. Josephus concludes his account by saying, like the LXX, that Moses died (ἐτελεύτησε), having lived (ἐβίωσε) one hundred and twenty years (*Ant.* 4.327). "Such," he writes, " was the end of Moses" (τὸ μὲν κατὰ Μωυσῆν τέλος; *Ant.* 4.331).

Scholars have wondered, however, if Josephus indicates his openness to an alternative view which saw Moses raptured into heaven. After describing the disappearance into the φάραγξ, Josephus says, "But he has written of himself in the sacred books that he died, for fear lest they should venture to say that by reason of his surpassing virtue he had gone back to the Deity." A thin argument can be made that when Josephus says "But he has written of himself (γέγραφε δ' αὐτὸν) that he died" he means to suggest the opposite was actually the case, and that Moses did not really die. The weak adversative δέ, however, does not suggest that the statement in question presents a contrary view and, as already seen here, Josephus really cannot be supposed to hold any other view than that Moses died and was buried.

It may also be supposed, however, that Josephus here opposes an alternative view held by others. Since all the statements found in Josephus's version fit the Pentateuchal account rather well, it would be difficult to describe any supposed Jewish contention that Moses did not die by working backward from Josephus alone. The question then, assuming Josephus knew of an alternative, is how to characterize such a view.

6.3.4.3.2 Philo

In this connection it will be noted that Philo, with whose work Josephus seems to have been familiar and upon whom he at times seems to rely,[111] writes of the end of Moses' life as "a pilgrimage from earth to heaven" (*Mos.* 2.288). Philo writes that before the end God "resolved his twofold nature of soul and body into a single unity, transforming his whole being into mind, pure as the sunlight" (εἰς νοῦν ἡλιοειδέστατον; *Mos.* 2.288), and Moses in that glorified state uttered his final prophecies concerning the tribes of Israel (cf. Deuteronomy 33). Then, having uttered his last oracles, and already being exalted (ἤδη γὰρ ἀναλαμβανόμενος), he prophesied the story of his own death (τὰ ὡς ἐπὶ θανόντι ἑαυτῷ), how he died, before he died (ὡς ἐτελεύτησε μήπω τελευτήσας), how he was buried with none present (ὡς ἐτάφη μηδενὸς παρόντος) by immortal powers (ἀθανάτοις δυνάμεσιν; note plural, and the contrast between the deathless powers and the dying Moses), how his tomb has never been seen by men, and how the nation mourned his passing (*Mos.* 2.291). "Such,"

---

[111] See above, p. 139 n. 68.

Philo writes, "was the life and such the end of Moses" (Τοιοῦτος μὲν ὁ βίος, τοιαύτη δὲ καὶ ἡ τελευτὴ ... Μωυσέως; *Mos.* 2.292).

Josephus seems to follow Philo in attributing the account of Moses' death to Moses' own prophecy concerning it, but he may find the idea that Moses embarked on a pilgrimage to heaven more distasteful, particularly in the absence of a clear reference to the burial of Moses' body. It is possible that Josephus is reacting to this account, or to other ones like it.

Philo also discusses the death of Moses in *De Virtutibus*, starting at paragraph 51, where he describes Moses as the supreme exemplification of φιλανθρωπίας. Here he relates that Moses, when his life neared its end, announced, "with a face beaming with the gladness of his soul" (reminiscent of the shining of his face whenever he emerged from the presence of God), "The time has come for me to depart (ἀπαλλάττεσθαι) from the life of the body" (*Virt.* 67-68).[112] Moses then began the passage from mortal existence to immortal life,[113] and became aware of the disuniting of the elements of which he was composed, as his body was stripped away from his soul (*Virt.* 76). In this condition he renders his final prophecies over the tribes. Philo then embarks on a long discourse on the laws and never returns to describe the close of Moses' life. Nonetheless, it appears evident that here again is the familiar tableau of the glorification of Moses prior to his death, the delivery of especially inspired messages, and then the departure of Moses' soul, i.e. his death.[114]

Philo's overall position, like Josephus's, seems to conform to the biblical account. It is noteworthy, however, that the one point of embellishment concerns a kind of striking glorification of Moses prior to his demise. The importance of this feature of the story as a clue to the meaning of Josephus's words protecting the mortal nature of Moses is amplified when virtually the same embellishment is found in the retelling of the same episode in Pseudo-Philo's *Biblical Antiquities*, often thought to have a provenance similar to the traditions carried forward by Josephus (see below), and in the Similitudes of Enoch. It seems likely that Josephus would have known one or more of these traditions, in addition to the works of Philo.

6.3.4.3.3 The Similitudes of Enoch

A combination of glorification and subsequent death remarkably similar to that of Philo's account of the end of Moses seems to be presented in the Similitudes of Enoch, ordinarily thought to come from an entirely different

---

[112] In *Virt.* 73 he is imprisoned in "a corruptible body" (σῶμα φθαρτόν).

[113] Philo in this context specifically denies to Moses the divine power (θεία δύναμις) of insight into the character of men (*Virt.* 54), and instead has him turn to God who surveys the invisible soul (*Virt.* 57).

[114] On this passage, see Goodenough, *By Light, Light*, 196-97.

background than that of Philo. In the midst of an extended allegory of the people of Israel as a flock of sheep, one sheep, representing Moses, is turned into a man (אנוש והוא אתהפך דן [א]מר[א]; 1 Enoch 89:36),[115] possibly representing transformation into an angel.[116] This sheep clearly stands for Moses. After building the tabernacle, "that sheep which led them, which had become a man, separated from them and fell asleep" (1 Enoch 89.38), that is, died.[117] Here again, Moses is marvelously glorified prior to his death.

6.3.4.3.4 Pseudo-Philo

In Pseudo-Philo's account of the end of Moses, Moses says to the people, "Behold, I am to lie with my fathers and will be gathered unto my people" (*LAB* 19.2).[118] Later, God repeats, "Behold, you go to lie with your fathers" (*LAB* 19.6). Then, after Moses prays saying, "Behold, I have completed the time of my life, I have completed 120 years" (*LAB* 19.8), God says to Moses:

I will take you from here and lay you down to sleep with your fathers, and I will give you rest in your resting place and bury you in peace. All the angels will mourn over you, and the heavenly hosts will grieve. But no angel nor man will know your sepulchre in which you will be buried. You will rest in it until I visit the world. I will raise up you and your fathers from the earth in which you sleep" (*LAB* 19.12).

When God buries Moses there is mourning in heaven (*LAB* 19.16; which implies that Moses is not there). The account closes with the notice that God buried Moses with his own hands, "in a high place as a light for the entire world" (*super excelsam terram et in lumine totius orbis*; *LAB* 19.16). This account hews very much to the biblical version of the tale,

---

[115] Text, 4QEn[e] 4.10, J. T. Milik, ed., with Matthew Black, *The Books of Enoch: Aramaic Fragments of Qumrân Cave 4* (Oxford: Clarendon Press, 1976), 205.

[116] "In this apocalyptic allegory ... angels are anthropomorphic and humans zoomorphic. Moses' transformation is thus an angelization," Crispin H. T. Fletcher-Louis, "4Q374: A Discourse on the Sinai Tradition: The Deification of Moses and Early Christology," *Dead Sea Discoveries* 3 (1996): 243.

[117] Trans., Michael A. Knibb, with Edward Ullendorff, *The Ethiopic Book of Enoch: A New Translation in the Light of the Dead Sea Fragments*, vol. 2, *Introduction, Translation and Commentary* (Oxford: Clarendon Press, 1978), 206. Similarly, "fut separée d'elles et s'endormit," François Martin, et al., *Le Livre d'Hénoch traduit sur le texte Éthiopien*, Documents pour l'Étude de la Bible, ed. François Martin, Les Apocryphes de l'Ancien Testament (Paris: Letouzey et Ané, 1906; reprint, Paris: Archè, 1996), 211; "trennte sich von ihnen und entschlief," Joh. Fleming and L. Radermacher, *Das Buch Henoch*, Die Griechischen Christlichen Schriftsteller der ersten drei jahrhunderte, (Leipzig: J. C. Hinrichs'sche Buchhandlung, 1901), 113; "withdrew from them and fell asleep," R. H. Charles, *The Book of Enoch*, Translations of Early Documents, Series 1, Palestinian Jewish Texts (Pre-Rabbinic) (London: SPCK, 1921), 119.

[118] On the death of Moses in Pseudo-Philo, see above, pp. 190-91.

with the deviations that the grave of Moses is seen as high, instead of low or in a cave, and that Moses' tomb is a kind of light to the world. This curious statement by Pseudo-Philo about the grave of Moses is probably a sign of contact with Greco-Roman traditions, according to which, due to their great and lasting achievements for posterity, the whole world is the grave of great men.[119]

Despite these categorical descriptions of mortality and death, Pseudo-Philo writes that Moses at the very end of his life "was filled with understanding and his appearance was changed to a state of glory; and he died in glory (*et mutata est effigies eius in gloria et mortuus est in gloria*; *LAB* 19.16)," words that recall Philo's description of the physical transformation and endowment with special insight that came upon Moses at his final prophecy. The glorification of Moses before he dies represents an important affinity between the usually sober narrative of Pseudo-Philo and the glorious colorings applied to the story of Moses' death in some of the other versions seen here, providing a link between the death of Moses as described by Philo, Pseudo-Philo, and the Similitudes.

The common features in these accounts of glorious appearance and prophetic knowledge are also a fair characterization of Moses as he appears in the Transfiguration, especially in the Lukan version wherein the conversation of Jesus and Moses (and Elijah, if Elijah is not altogether in the background for Luke[120]) centers on the future, specifically the ἔξοδος of Jesus. Here again appears the combination of glorified appearance and inspired prophecy.

6.3.4.3.5 The Assumption of Moses

Another source for Jewish interpretation of the death of Moses about the time of the New Testament is the *Assumption of Moses*. In *As. Mos.* 10:12 Moses refers to the time "from my death, my removal" (*enim a morte, receptione mea*), and says "I will go to the resting place of my fathers" (*ego autem ad dormitionem patrum meorum eram*; 10:14). *Assumption of Moses* even reports that Moses wept at the thought (11:2), and Joshua comments on the bitterness of Moses' speech, full of tears and sighs (*plena lacrimis et gemitibus*) because he is going away. *Assumption of Moses* next recalls not only the biblical account, but also traces of the embellishments that appear in the other accounts surveyed here, such as the supernatural agents of Moses' burial, and the entire world serving for his tomb, as Joshua asks:

---

[119] See below, n. 122.

[120] Luke, like John, displays special interest both in Samaritans and in Moses; the appearance of the one theme alongside the other is noteworthy, given the Samaritan emphasis on Moses.

What place will receive you, or what will be the monument on your grave (*quod erit monumentum sepultrae*), or who, being human, will dare to carry your body from one place to another? For all who die when their time has come have a grave in the earth. But your grave extends from the East to the West, and from the North to the extreme South. The entire world is your grave (*omnis orbis terrarum sepulcrum est tuum*; 11:5-8).[121]

Less prosaically, Joshua refers to Moses as "the holy and sacred spirit" (*sanctum et sacrum spiritum*; 11:16), an evocative appellation that (as already noted above) at least emphasizes Moses' qualifications to take on a mystical role over his people after his death.[122] But despite the *Assumption of Moses'* undoubtedly glorious description of Moses, his work, and his death, the death of Moses remains a mortal ending to a mortal life.[123]

6.3.4.3.6 Targumic and Rabbinic Tradition

The rabbinic traditions have already been referred to above.[124] Generally it upholds the line that Moses died, though again both his death and his grave were glorious. *Targum Onq.* Deut. 34:7 teaches that at his death the face of Moses still shone with the radiance of his meetings with God.[125] In the late *Midrash Peṭirat Moshe*, Samael, the angel of death is too frightened of Moses to take his soul and he must ask Moses to yield it.[126] Moses refuses, and in an ensuing struggle puts Samael to flight. In the end, God himself attends to the matter, and summons the soul of Moses to come out. The soul of Moses still refuses, owing to the greatness of the body of Moses. At last, promised a place in glory beneath the Throne of Glory, the soul of Moses negotiates its departure from Moses. The Midrash again holds fast to the death of Moses.

6.3.4.3.7 Conclusion

All of the accounts surveyed here appear at least to intend to harmonize with the reading of Deuteronomy, whether in the MT or in the Targums and LXX. At the same time, there appears a willingness to tell the story in

---

[121] To reckon the whole world as the grave of Moses is to remark on his reputation and influence. In his funeral oration in the *Peloponnesian War*, Pericles says, "the whole earth is the sepulchre of famous men" (2.43). This is so because their story is not only graven on stone over their native earth, but lives on far away, woven into other men's lives.

[122] See above, pp. 188-90.

[123] As also Kastner, "Moses im Neuen Testament," 47.

[124] See above, p. 200.

[125] *Deuteronomy. Rab.* 11.3 and 11.10 repeat similar traditions. *Deuteronomy Rab.* 11 contains many hagiographical embellishments of the death of Moses.

[126] A German translation of the relevant passage, from MS Paris 710, fol. 123r-124r, is given in Haacker and Schäfer, "Nachbiblische Traditionen vom Tod des Mose," 168-70.

such a way as to call up echoes of the glorious departures of the heroes of Greco-Roman lore.

The points of contact among these retellings of the death of Moses are obvious. What is especially interesting is the consistency. The extant first century A.D. Jewish tradition is remarkably uniform in what it says about the death of Moses: Moses dies, yes, but he dies gloriously, with prophecy on his lips, often with the promise of *post mortem* activity on behalf of his people, and his burial is supernatural. The most radical first-century text of all those reviewed here seems to be the Transfiguration account of the Synoptic Gospels, because it is here that Moses actually appears as an active figure *post mortem eium*. In the Transfiguration Moses makes good on the great things augured by his manner of passing in all the other accounts.

Accordingly, it is apparent that the portrayal of Moses in the Transfiguration is not a radical departure from typical Jewish conceptions of Moses. Rather, the way for the conception of such an appearance by Moses was prepared across a broad spectrum of Jewish thought. The most plausible background for the appearance of Moses in the Transfiguration is supplied by the apparent fact that a wide cross-section of Jews, perhaps even "normative Jews," believed rather uniformly that his passing had been of a supernatural character and that in his last moments he had been endowed with special glory and deep prophetic insights. In the context of Jewish belief in the persistence (in some fashion) of even the ordinary mortal soul, such a figure would be a prime candidate for visitation and consultation such as occurs in the Transfiguration. Such a figure might well also be a candidate for mystical participation with his followers everywhere.[127]

6.3.5 The Corinthian Conception of Moses

Moses was unquestionably the most widely known Jewish figure in Greek and Roman culture. Not to put too fine a point on it, he was famous. He would have been recognized in Corinth as the colossus he appears to be in the Jewish writings that survive from that day.

Chapter Seven of the present study opens with an abbreviated résumé of the numerous superlatives piled onto Moses in literature aimed at Jewish and Gentile audiences alike, stemming both from the intellectual elite and from the common people. The Corinthian church should be supposed to have absorbed lore of this kind. Not only as participants in Hellenistic life and thought, but also as converts and catechumens, the Corinthians should

---

[127] Samaritan literature agrees that Moses was glorified but places him at rest in his grave with no active role, Haacker and Schäfer, "Nachbiblische Traditionen vom Tod des Mose," 164

be presumed to have as thorough an acquaintance with what people thought and said about Moses as Paul the scholar and former Pharisee did.

The Corinthian impression of Moses would have been anything but prosaic. Rather, it likely included magical and mystical elements known to have been associated with Moses in antiquity.[128] W. B. Badke estimates the Corinthian background on Moses so highly that he reckons in 1 Cor. 10:2 Moses would have come across to Paul's readers as a mystery god.[129] As already suggested above, the grandeur of the Corinthian conception of Moses may be hinted at by the mere fact that in 1 Cor. 10:2 Paul uses language about Moses that elsewhere he reserves for Christ.[130]

6.4 Conclusion

This chapter has explored the possibility that we have in the baptism into Moses of 1 Cor. 10:2 not just risqué rhetoric, but an echo of a Jewish piety which saw in Moses a unifying and spiritual figure for Jews. Goodenough puts forward a comparable view, but he relies almost exclusively on Philo for evidence and applies it only to his Mystic Judaism construct. As shown here, however, evidence for such a view of Moses arises not just in Philo, and not only in Alexandrian literature, but also in texts generally thought to have a Palestinian provenance, such as Josephus, the *Assumption of Moses*, the *Biblical Antiquities* of Pseudo-Philo, the sources of the Synoptic Gospels, and in the writings of Paul. This is accompanied by other evidence which strongly suggests that there was extant in Paul's day a Jewish rite, probably involving the baptism of proselytes, which could easily wear the label, "baptism into Moses."

Many, though not all, commentators have rightly recognized that "baptism into Moses" would have been interpreted (by Paul and his readers) in the same terms as the contemporary "baptism into Christ," but commentators too readily assume that the concept of baptism into Moses is in-

---

[128] See below, p. 212. Richard A. Horsley, "'How can some of you say that there is no resurrection of the dead?': Spiritual Elitism in Corinth," *Novum Testamentum* 20 (1978): 227 suggests that Paul's handling of the midrashic material implies that all the elements mentioned in 1 Cor. 10:1-4, including the baptism into Moses, were "some sort of quasi-magical soteriological symbols for the Corinthians." See John G. Gager, *Moses in Greco-Roman Paganism*, Society of Biblical Literature Monograph Series, ed. Robert A. Kraft, no. 16 (Nashville and New York: Abingdon Press, 1972), 159, 162.

[129] William B. Badke, "Baptised into Moses — Baptised into Christ: A Study in Doctrinal Development," *The Evangelical Quarterly* 88, no. 1 (1988): 27.

[130] *Pace* Fee, *The First Epistle to the Corinthians*, 445 n. 19. That Paul in the first instance is saying something about Christ and Christians does not mean that something important about Moses is not assumed by his teaching. See above, pp. 185-87.

debted to no other background than the Christian expression. It seems almost impossible, however, that the expression should neither arise from, nor be understood in light of, what was widely said and thought about Moses. The contemporary Mosaic background against which the expression would appear suggests that 1 Cor. 10:2 should be read as one more statement of the elevated standing of Moses, specifically as indicating that Moses was thought in some way to continue to stand as head over the Jewish people.

It would appear that an estimation of Moses as an incorporative figure for Jews that turns up in other Jewish literature has also found expression in the New Testament. The findings of this chapter thus even suggest, against the majority of scholars, that Paul's doctrine of baptism into Christ may be indebted to the baptism into Moses, and not the other way round.

Chapter 7

Moses the Focus of Jewish Loyalty

In a similar fashion it is acknowledged that before now faith has been placed in men:
"for the people believed in God and Moses his servant."
—Eustathius of Sebaste[1]

7.1 Introduction

In the rabbinic period, the Torah itself, independent of any mediator and sometimes even personified, to some extent seems to put Moses as Law-giver into eclipse. In the Second Temple period, however, a great deal of authority was still generally ascribed to Moses, and in consequence the status of Moses and the status of his Law were more positively linked. The idea that even the oral law had been revealed at Sinai (*Jubilees*, to cite one source, includes a good deal of haggadic and halakhic material which it locates in a revelation to Moses on Mount Sinai) meant that Moses stood behind even the most current *halakhoth* of the given day, with attendant implications for the relevance of Moses in day-to-day life.[2]

Meanwhile, one consequence of the growth of the Diaspora was that the keeping of the Law, as opposed to, say, attendance at a national Temple, became the fundamental mark of Jewishness.[3] J. M. G. Barclay observes that for Philo, the Jewish people are "defined less in genealogical terms than by reference to their common 'constitution,' the holy πολιτεία of

---

[1] Quoted by Basil the Great, *De Spiritu Sancto* 14.31.

[2] On the revelation of the oral law to Moses, see above, p. 146.

[3] See Yehoshua Amir, *Die hellenistische Gestalt des Judentums bei Philon von Alexandrien*, Forschungen zum jüdisch-christlichen Dialog, ed. Yehuda Aschkenasy and Heinz Kremers, vol. 5 (Neukirchen-Vluyn: Neukirchener Verlag, 1983), 78; on Philo's similar view, see John M. G. Barclay, *Jews in the Mediterranean Diaspora from Alexander to Trajan (323 BCE-117 CE)* (Edinburgh: T. & T. Clark, 1996), 173; Augustine, *Contra Faustum Manichaeum*, 13, reports, "The Jewish people ... never gave up serving its law, by which it is distinguished from the rest of the nations and peoples (*quo a caeteris gentibus populisque distinguitur*); see further, Ephraim E. Urbach, *The Sages: Their Concepts and Beliefs*, trans. Israel Abrahams, Publications of the Perry Foundation in the Hebrew University of Jerusalem (Jerusalem: Magnes Press, The Hebrew University, 1979), 524-25 and Josef M. Kastner, "Moses im Neuen Testament," Th.D. Dissertation, Ludwig-Maximilians-Universität Munich, 1967), 223.

Moses."[4] P. Spilsbury points to the invocation in Josephus of "a specifically law-based piety" as the basis for the Jewish community. Moses for Josephus, says Spilsbury, was the great lawgiver and the Jews are specifically the people who adhere to those laws.[5] As the Law increasingly became the one really distinctive thing about all Jews, so the position of Moses equally increased in importance.[6] Moses became in Second Temple Judaism the most important of a very few figures whose legacy was central and emblematic to every Jewish community.[7]

Although this chapter represents yet another fresh departure in outlining the NT Moses, it relies on the background provided by the rest of this study, and on the impression created by the full portrait of Moses. For the sake of that full portrait, this introduction includes a brief review of some of the extraordinary things said of Moses in Second Temple Judaism, many of which have not been touched on in this study until now.

7.1.1 The Greatness of Moses

In Acts 7:22 Stephen pauses in his narrative of Moses' life to mention his great learning and his "mighty words and deeds." Although this study has not focused on the Moses *haggadoth*, the glimpses of them that appear in Acts 7:17-44 (loaded with allusions to hagiographic Moses lore[8]), 2 Tim. 3:8, and Jude 9 indicate that the early Christians knew them, and undoubtedly legends about Moses contributed to his greatness for them as for other Jews.

Jews of the Second Temple period attributed many feats of wisdom and strength to Moses that make no appearance in the Old Testament. Eupolemos tells that Moses was the first wise man and that he invented writing.[9] Artapanus relates that Moses (as Musaeus) taught Orpheus; he invented boats, devices for masonry, the Egyptian arms, implements for drawing water, and, to cap it all, philosophy. He also organized the Egyptian

---

[4] Barclay, *Jews in the Mediterranean Diaspora*, 173.

[5] Paul Spilsbury, *The Image of the Jew in Flavius Josephus' Paraphrase of the Bible*, Texte und Studien zum Antiken Judentum, ed. Martin Hengel and Peter Schäfer, no. 69 (Tübingen: J. C. B. Mohr [Paul Siebeck], 1998), 110, see also 127-29, 145.

[6] P. M. Casey, *From Jewish Prophet to Gentile God: The Origins and Development of New Testament Christology* (Cambridge: James Clarke & Co.; Louisville, Kent.: Westminster/John Knox Press, 1991), 83.

[7] And to at least one para-Jewish community, such as the Samaritans.

[8] See Kastner, "Moses im Neuen Testament," 203-220.

[9] Cited in Eusebius, *Praep. Ev.* 9.26.1. Almost exactly the same thing is said of Enoch, e.g. Jub. 4:17.

government and, perhaps bizarrely, its religion.[10] Josephus similarly boasts that the Greek philosophers followed Moses.[11]

Literature of this kind often is deemed to have been written for its appeal to non-Jews. It may be more accurate to view it as written for its appeal to non-Jewish culture, of which Jews were often satisfied partakers. Thus Artapanus, Barclay suggests, wrote both as "a proud Egyptian and a self-conscious Jew."[12] The writings of Artapanus, et al. may best be conceived as Hellenistic Jews' own retellings of the story of Moses as the great Hellenistic statesman and *savant* that the founder of the Jewish nation and constitution naturally would be. Such a view of Moses would have apologetic value both within and without the Jewish community,[13] while reflecting a genuine Hellenistic Jewish perspective. The origins of these amplifications clearly lie long before the Herodian period, but they appear to be the direct forebears of the similar accounts which were told and retold in the time of Jesus and the apostles.

The stories told go beyond the intellectual and political achievements of Moses. Legends and amplifications grew up concerning miraculous or portentous events surrounding his birth (which may be reflected in Acts 7:20).[14] His death too was portentous and wonderful, according to a variety of sources, such as Josephus (*Ant.* 4.326), the *Assumption of Moses* (11:8), and Pseudo-Philo (*LAB* 19.16).[15] The glory of his departure, as al-

---

[10] Cited in Eusebius, *Praep. Ev.* 9.27.4. Presumably, claiming Moses as the founder of Egyptian society and culture was a direct counter to typical Egyptian slurs of Moses as a renegade from the same. Crispin H. T. Fletcher-Louis, "4Q374: A Discourse on the Sinai Tradition: The Deification of Moses and Early Christology," *Dead Sea Discoveries* 3 (1996): 243-45 argues (with questionable success) that Artapanus meant to portray Moses as divine in an episode where, during a nocturnal visit to Pharaoh's chambers, Moses speaks the name of God and so causes Pharaoh to fall down dumb, but then takes hold of Pharaoh and revives him. See n. 13 below.

[11] *Ap.* 2.281, also 2.168.

[12] Barclay, *Jews in the Mediterranean Diaspora*, 132.

[13] Victor Tcherikover, "Jewish Apologetic Literature Reconsidered," *Eos* 48, no. 3 (1956): 169-93 insists that the works of the Alexandrian Jewish apologists were written for the Jewish community. Erich S. Gruen, *Heritage and Hellenism: The Reinvention of Jewish Tradition*, Hellenistic Culture and Society, ed. Anthony W. Bulloch, et al., no. 30 (Berkeley: University of California Press, 1998), 155-60 finds Artapanus a whimsical, humorous writer, who gleefully places Moses at the center of all important Gentile institutions — knowing he will fool no one but that nonetheless he and his fellow Jews will be amused by the joke; cf. Wilfred L. Knox, *St Paul and the Church of the Gentiles* (Cambridge: Cambridge University Press, 1939), 112, "it [i.e. extravagant apologetics] was not intended to be taken seriously."

[14] E.g., Pseudo-Philo declares that he was born circumcised (*LAB* 9.13) after his sister received an oracle predicting his future greatness (9.10).

[15] These and other accounts of Moses' passing reviewed above, pp. 189-92, 199-206.

ready argued here, would appear to be the best explanation for his appearance in the Transfiguration accounts of the Synoptic Gospels, accounts which must also reflect Jewish perceptions of Moses as a glorious, heavenly figure.[16]

The Synoptic repetition of the Transfiguration account attests the importance of Moses among Jews and Jewish Christians of the first century. Luke, in keeping with his general interest in Moses, clearly prioritizes Moses, as shown by his displacement of the name of Elijah to second place (Luke 9:30), and the note that Moses (and Elijah) discussed with Jesus the "exodus" (ἔξοδος; 9:31) he would soon accomplish in Jerusalem. The importance of Moses must be inferred in Mark and Matthew, which clearly prioritize Elijah in the account itself, and then focus on Elijah in the discourse that follows (in Matt. 17:9-13 and Mark 9:9-13).[17] Given the clear expectations expressed in these very Gospels concerning the return of Elijah the mere fact that Moses appears on the mountain at all suggests his importance (i.e., given the emphasis on the expectation of Elijah, why not Elijah alone?).

The writings of Jewish apologists and other intellectuals will have been influential across a wide spectrum of society, but reflect most reliably the views of the learned. The writings of ordinary people, however, reveal a view of Moses that is, if anything, even grander, as T. Savage observes:

His name occurs repeatedly in magical recipes and formulae where it ensures the efficacy of charms and the prevention of evil. It appears as well on magical amulets, for similar reasons. The popularity of Moses seems to stem from his unique knowledge of the divine name which he received on Sinai, a knowledge which many believed empowered him to perform his extraordinary deeds. ... No other name in antiquity was more revered for its wonder-working powers.[18]

As noted in the discussion of the likely view of Moses in Corinth, Moses was famous, in both the Jewish and Gentile worlds, as an ancient master of lore and as a living, mystical power.[19] It was thus not merely learned writers with apologetical axes to grind who had glorious things to say about Moses. Moses was popularly extolled as well.

Samaritan beliefs about Moses can resemble a doctrine of his pre-existence, though generally only in terms of his priority in the order of

---

[16] On this see discussion above, pp. 194-206.

[17] Margaret Pamment, "Moses and Elijah in the Story of the Transfiguration," *Expository Times* 92 (1980-81): 338.

[18] Timothy B. Savage, *Power through Weakness: Paul's Understanding of the Christian Ministry in 2 Corinthians*, Society for New Testament Studies Monograph Series, ed. Margaret E. Thrall, no. 86 (Cambridge: Cambridge University Press, 1996), 107, with documentation noted.

[19] See above, pp. 206-207.

Creation, or his pre-determined role in the divine plan.[20]   Such a foreordained mission is ascribed to Moses in Jewish literature in *As. Mos.* 1.14,
where Moses says, "He has devised and invented me, I who have been prepared from the beginning of the world (*ab initio orbis terrarum praepa-
ratus sum*) to be the mediator of his covenant."[21]   If Moses' pre-existence
is at least under consideration in the first century A.D., as seen in Chapter
Six his later existence is clearly very exalted, in literature stemming from
both Palestine and the Jewish Diaspora.[22]

The sheer number of offices and abilities ascribed to Moses, including
the ones noted in the previous chapters of this study, adds significantly to
his glory.   The accumulation of offices was itself an important Jewish

---

[20] E. g, MSS Firkovitch, Sam. X, 48 (1775), line 9 "standing at the mystery of the
creation" (דלנסתר בראשית עמד), text, Reinhard Plummer with Abraham Tal, *Samaritan Marriage Contracts and Deeds of Divorce*, vol. 2 (Wiesbaden: Harrassowitz Verlag, 1997), 91, trans., ibid., 224 and MS Sassoon 725 (1848), line 10, text, Reinhard
Plummer, *Samaritan Marriage Contracts and Deeds of Divorce*, vol. 1 (Wiesbaden:
Otto Harrassowitz, 1993), 209; trans., Plummer, vol. 2, 244.   See also above, p. 142.
The difficulty of dating Samaritan sources is severe, and it has been noticed that these
beliefs show signs of derivation from Muslim legends of Mohammed; see James Alan
Montgomery, *The Samaritans: The Earliest Jewish Sect: Their History, Theology, and
Literature* (New York: Ktav Publishing House, 1968), 227 29; John MacDonald, *The
Theology of the Samaritans*, The New Testament Library, ed. Alan Richardson, C. F.
D. Moule, and Floyd V. Filson (London: SCM Press, 1964), 162-65; James D. G.
Dunn, *Christology in the Making: A New Testament Inquiry into the Origins of the
Doctrine of the Incarnation*, 2d ed. (London: SCM Press, 1989), 71.   Perhaps the ab-
sence of Moses from the seven pre-existent things of rabbinic Judaism (*Pirqe R. El.* 3)
shows this to be a late, or at least non-Jewish, development.

[21] David Lenz Tiede, "The Figure of Moses in *The Testament of Moses*," in *Studies
on the Testament of Moses: Seminar Papers*, ed. George W. E. Nickelsburg, Jr., Society of Biblical Literature Pseudepigrapha Group, Septuagint and Cognate Studies, no. 4
(Cambridge, Mass.: Society of Biblical Literature, 1973), 90 convincingly argues that
this text speaks of God's comprehensive plan, including Moses (see *As. Mos.* 12.4, 6-
7), rather than true Mosaic pre-existence: "The author of *TM* is primarily interested in
affirming that God had already designated a mediator of his covenant before he had actually created anything.   God's plan [not Moses] is primordial."   See, in agreement, J.
Priest, trans., "The Assumption of Moses," in *The Old Testament Pseudepigrapha*, ed.
James H. Charlesworth, vol. 2, The Anchor Bible Reference Library (New York: Doubleday, 1985), 922-23, "It seems dubious that the text can bear the weight of claiming
pre-existence for Moses as a *person*. ... It seems wiser simply to say that our author,
consistent with his thorough determinism, stated that Moses' *role* had been decreed
from the beginning of the world."   See also, Dunn, *Christology in the Making*, 71;
Johannes Tromp, *The Assumption of Moses: A Critical Edition with Commentary*, Studia in Veteris Testamenti Pseuepigrapha, ed. A.-M. Denis and M. De Jonge, vol. 10
(Leiden: E. J. Brill, 1993), 143; Jer. 1:5; Gal. 1:15.

[22] See above, pp. 188-99.

ideal,[23] praised by Josephus in figures like John Hyrcanus (*B.J.* 1.68) and the other Hasmonean rulers. Philo extols "Moses, king, lawgiver, high priest, prophet" (*Mos.* 2.292, repeating 2.3, 6, 187).[24] In any other figure, Philo would criticize such a combination of offices,[25] and even of Moses he grants that "why it is fitting that they should all be combined in the same person needs explanation (*Mos.* 2.3)," an admission that only heightens the impression made by the titles he heaps on Moses.[26]

That Philo makes of Moses a towering, epic figure is therefore likely to be less a product of Philo's own fertile creativity and more a product of already widespread Jewish thinking.[27] His ὁ πάντα μέγας Μωυσῆς,[28] who "exemplified his philosophical creed by his daily actions,"[29] recalls the Renaissance man-like achievements claimed for Moses by Artapanus. Philo never runs short of honorifics for Moses. Expressions like "most perfect Moses" (ὁ τελειότατος Μωυσῆς),[30] "most-admirable Moses" (ὁ θαυμασιώτατος Μωυσῆς),[31] "holiest Moses" (ὁ ἱερώτατος Μωυσῆς),[32] "the most flawless witness Moses" (μάρτυς ἀψευδέστατος Μωυσῆς),[33] "the best-beloved by God Moses" (Μωυσῆς ὁ θεοφιλέστατος),[34] and "friend

---

[23] E. Bammel, "The Feeding of the Multitude," in *Jesus and the Politics of His Day*, ed. Ernst Bammel and C. F. D. Moule (Cambridge: Cambridge University Press, 1984), 230; see further Erwin R. Goodenough, *By Light, Light: The Mystic Gospel of Hellenistic Judaism* (New Haven, Conn.: Yale University Press, 1935; reprint, Amsterdam: Philo Press, 1969), 190, idem, *The Politics of Philo Judaeus: Practice and Theory* (New Haven: Yale University Press, 1938), 97-98, and Harry Austryn Wolfson, *Philo: Foundations of Religious Philosophy in Judaism, Christianity, and Islam*, Structure and Growth of Philosophic Systems from Plato to Spinoza, II (Cambridge, Mass.: Harvard University Press, 1947), 2.17.

[24] *Praem.* 53 adds θεολόγος. See also *Sac.* 130. On multiple offices see above, pp. 77-78.

[25] See *Virt.* 54 and Wolfson, *Philo*, 2.339.

[26] Rudolf Meyer, "προφήτης κτλ.," in *Theological Dictionary of the New Testament*, ed. Gerhard Friedrich, trans. and ed. Geoffrey W. Bromiley, vol. 6, *Πε-Ρ* (Grand Rapids: William B. Eerdmans, 1968, reprint, 1988), 826 observes the criticism such accumulation attracts in 1QS 9.7-11, and notices that Bar Kokhba, by contrast, made no effort to amalgamate offices, being accompanied by a high priest, Eleazar, with Aqiba effectively functioning as his prophet.

[27] Larry W. Hurtado, *One God, One Lord: Early Christian Devotion and Ancient Jewish Monotheism* (London: SCM Press, 1988), 51: "The glorification of Old Testament patriarchs is standard fare in post-exilic Judaism. ... Especially Moses."

[28] *Mos.* 2.211.

[29] *Mos.* 1.29.

[30] *Det.* 132; *Ebr.* 94 — of all the patriarchs the most dear to God.

[31] *Ebr.* 210.

[32] *Leg. All.* 3.185; *Cher.* 45; *Det.* 135; *Agr.* 85; *Plant.* 86, 168; *Spec. Leg.* 2.59; 4.95; *Abr.* 181; *Mut.* 30.

[33] *Det.* 138.

[34] *Mig.* 67; *Spec. Leg.* 1.41.

of God" (ὁ θεοφιλός)[35] ring false, or perhaps just nauseous, unless supported by the general concurrence of a wider Jewish public. Even if not everyone would put it in quite the same way, Philo must have been at least in harmony with his Jewish confreres when he wrote that Moses was "the greatest and most perfect of men" (ἀνδρὸς τὰ πάντα μεγίστου καὶ τελειοτάτου),[36] who in the functions of king, lawgiver, high priest and prophet "won the highest place" (ἐν ἑκάστῳ τὰ πρωτεῖα ἠνέγκατο).[37]

The preceding chapters illustrate the dominance of Moses in ancient Judaism and in the milieu of the New Testament. Many other luminaries were held in high regard in ancient Judaism, as can be seen in Ben Sira's "Hymn of the Ancestors" (Sir. 44-50), in the Hall of Faith of Hebrews chapter 11, in the heroes cited by Mattathias in 1 Macc. 2:51-60, and in the apocalyptic works bearing the great names of Enoch, Elijah, and others, but no other figure achieved the standing of Moses, whose fame lapped over into the Gentile world coupled with numerous great deeds and worthy achievements. As J. Jeremias said of the Second Temple Period, "Moses is for later Judaism the most important figure in salvation history."[38]

7.1.2 The Centrality of Moses Illustrated at Dura-Europos

The centrality and greatness of Moses are (literally) well illustrated by the murals in the synagogue of Dura-Europos.[39] Aside from the singularly prominent, iconic quality of the images of Moses (no other figure is painted in such large scale), the manner in which Moses is depicted, particularly in the scenes of the Exodus proper, has excited comment. Moses in these frames, as well as in the scene depicting the provision of water in the Wilderness, is portrayed towering over the other, much smaller, surroun-

---

[35] *Sac.* 77.

[36] *Mos.* 1.1.

[37] *Mos.* 2.3.

[38] Joachim Jeremias, "Μωυσῆς," in *Theological Dictionary of the New Testament*, ed. Gerhard Kittel, trans. and ed. Geoffrey W. Bromiley, vol. 4, *Λ-Ν* (Grand Rapids: Wm. B. Eerdmans, 1967), 849.

[39] Though they date from A.D. 244/45 at the earliest, Joseph Gutmann, ed., *The Dura-Europos Synagogue: A Re-evaluation (1932-1992)*, South Florida Studies in the History of Judaism, ed. Jacob Neusner, et al., no. 25 (Atlanta: Scholars Press, 1992), x. The synagogue was (re-)built at that time, and the city then fell to the Sasanian Persians in either A.D. 256 or 257, Comte du Mesnil du Buisson, *Les peintures de la synagogue de Doura-Europos, 245-256 après J.-C.*, Scripta Pontificii Instituti Biblici, no. 86 (Rome: Pontifical Biblical Institute, 1939), 9. Clark Hopkins, *The Discovery of Dura-Europos*, ed. Bernard Goldman (New Haven and London: Yale University Press, 1979), 142 notes several *dipinti* written on the paintings in the Persian of Mesopotamia (some distance away) recording visitations and viewings, several of which include a day and month in the year A.D. 253/54, indicating that the paintings were complete by that time, and already of considerable repute.

ding figures. This may be nothing more than a way of highlighting the main focus of each picture,[40] a depiction of "Moses and a cast of thousands."[41] The viewer is reminded, though, of the way that a king towers over ordinary people like a colossus in the royal portraiture of Egypt and the Ancient Near East.

Speaking of colossi, in the tableau at Dura the famous staff which Moses carries is not a smooth wand or rod, but a stubby, somewhat knobby baton. Goodenough argues that it was meant to be a club, and in one painting Moses is indeed shown wielding it over his head, possibly like a truncheon (though the pictorial context rather suggests a magic wand or scepter). Goodenough argues on this basis, and from the assertion that in Greek mythology only Heracles and Theseus carry such a club, that the artist intended Moses to be understood as "the Jewish Theseus-Heracles."[42]

Whatever the merits of this specific suggestion, the murals clearly show that Moses was the most important figure depicted in the synagogue. Even details of his life, such as his infancy, merited generous coverage. The only individual "portraits" among the paintings are four iconic images of Moses, ranged above the Torah niche on the west wall of the synagogue, in the four wing-panels which flank the reredos.[43] The same wall, apparently the front wall of the assembly room, features on either side of the "icons" fur-

---

[40] Erwin R. Goodenough, *Jewish Symbols in the Greco-Roman Period*, Bollingen Series, no 37, vol. 10 (New York: Pantheon Books, 1964), 119 points out that "the artist at Dura always represented the especial protagonists thus large," citing the instances of Moses, Samuel, Ezekiel, and others.

[41] Goodenough, *Jewish Symbols*, vol. 10, 119-20 wants to suggest that a measure of divinity was implied, but allows that a firm conclusion cannot be taken in this regard.

[42] Ibid., (120-)121. His position is seconded by Jacob Neusner, "Judaism at Dura-Europos," in *The Dura-Europos Synagogue: A Re-evaluation (1932-1992)*, ed. Joseph Gutmann, South Florida Studies in the History of Judaism, ed. Jacob Neusner, et al., no. 25 (Atlanta: Scholars Press, 1992), 170, but it is difficult to know that such clear implications were intended by the artist — or artists: du Mesnil du Buisson, *Les peintures de la synagogue de Doura-Europos*, 40 points out that no one of the depictions of the staff/club is like another, moreover, in two of the scenes, that of the provision of water, and the final (leftmost) scene of the Exodus tableau, the staff is clearly an afterthought painted in after the scenes had been completed. Hopkins, *The Discovery of Dura-Europos*, 142-43 emphasizes the new artistic departure for Jews which the murals represent, which suggests that the murals may well represent a more "adventurous" creative undertaking, and perhaps not "typical" Jewish thought.

[43] Erwin R. Goodenough, *Jewish Symbols in the Greco-Roman Period*, Bollingen Series, no 37, vol. 9 (New York: Pantheon Books, 1964), 110-21 argues all four portray Moses. He is seconded by Michael Avi-Yonah, "Goodenough's Evaluation of the Dura Paintings: A Critique," in *The Dura-Europos Synagogue: A Re-evaluation (1932-1992)*, ed. Joseph Gutmann, South Florida Studies in the History of Judaism, ed. Jacob Neusner, et al., no. 25 (Atlanta: Scholars Press, 1992), 119.

ther images of Moses, in scenes from the Exodus itself across the top register of paintings, and across the middle and lower registers in depictions of Moses as an infant and of Moses providing water in the desert.

Moses thus dominates the front wall of the synagogue, in both the quantity and the quality of his images. While the murals appear by contemporary standards to have been regarded as exceptional works of art, they are painted in a communal building and therefore can be expected in some respect to reflect the outlook of that community. C. K. Barrett thinks the paintings illustrate the tendency of Jews to make of Moses a divine, cult figure,[44] and they certainly illustrate the centrality of Moses to Judaism, particularly given that "synagogues that deviated notably from 'normative' standards often suffered iconoclastic defacement."[45]

The impression of Moses that one gains from the murals of Dura is approximately the one normally associated with the Alexandrian Philo. Such an estimation of Moses, if it hadn't been further attested, might have been supposed to have died out. Instead, it turns out still somehow to have been relevant three centuries later in Syria.

The foregoing discussion helps to flesh out the greatness of the Jewish conception of Moses in the Herodian period. This, combined with the view of Moses gained in Chapter Six, which argued that Jews saw Moses not only as an impressive historical figure but as someone still actively engaged with them as a leader, yields the impression of Moses as someone vested with supernatural greatness and crowned with superhuman accomplishments. The impression of Moses as such a figure is a good starting point for this chapter's focus: the Jewish treatment of Moses as a personal focus of their loyalty and even of their trust.

7.2 Jews as Disciples of Moses

7.2.1 John 9:28

In John 9:28 some Pharisees say to the man born blind, "You are [Jesus'] disciple, but we are disciples of Moses (ἡμεῖς δὲ τοῦ Μωϋσέως ἐσμὲν μαθηταί)." On the supposition that Jewish views are authentically reflec-

---

[44] C. K. Barrett, *From First Adam to Last: A Study in Pauline Theology* (London: Adam & Charles Black, 1962), 54; he thinks the paintings relevant to the New Testament, 2 Corinthians 3 specifically. See above, p. 177.

[45] Wayne A. Meeks, *The Prophet-King: Moses Traditions and the Johannine Christology*, Supplements to *Novum Testamentum*, ed. W. C. van Unnik, et al., vol. 14 (Leiden: E. J. Brill, 1967), 21 n. 2.

ted, the statement invites a number of plausible inferences regarding the "disciples of Moses."

Most likely, "we are disciples of Moses" is a statement of Jewish self-identity (i.e., is synonymous with "we are true Jews"). The claim to discipleship may further imply that Moses could be viewed as a founder of a school, with his adherents viewed as his pupils (or as the pupils of the heirs of his position, which recalls the likely implication of the "seat of Moses" in Matt 23:2).[46] As noted already, in the Targums and rabbinic writings Moses could often be addressed as master, as in the common phrase, *Moshe Rabbenu*.[47] It is also possible that a narrower, more sectarian, connotation may be involved in John 9:28, reflecting the idea that the Pharisees and the followers of Jesus could be seen as members of rival schools, with the Pharisees claiming Moses as their founder.

Despite debate over the origins of the Fourth Gospel, the familiarity of the author with Judaism and the compatibility of the Gospel with Jewish thought are widely conceded. Of course one cannot rule out the possibility that the expression "disciples of Moses" arises here because the author made it up for the occasion to contrast with the more familiar "disciples of Jesus." Yet the frequent occurrence of very similar expressions in Philo (see below), as well as the appearance of the expression תלמידיו של משה in a *baraita* of *b. Yoma* 4a (where interestingly the disciples of Moses, as in John 9:28, seem expressly to be the Pharisees[48]) both show that such an assumption is unnecessary; and the evident insights into Judaism of the Fourth Gospel suggest that even if the precise terminology of John 9:28 were of Christian origin, the conception of Moses — and the conception of his Jewish disciples — which lie behind the terminology need not be.[49]

---

[46] On the seat of Moses, see above, pp. 153-55.

[47] See above, pp. 141, 147-48.

[48] ושני תלמידי חכמים מתלמידיו של משה לאפוקי צדוקין ("and two scholars of the disciples of Moses, to the exclusion of Sadducees").

[49] Jews are exhorted to be disciples of other ancestral figures, e.g., Aaron (*m. 'Abot* 1.12; מִתַּלְמִידָיו שֶׁל אַהֲרֹן), and Abraham (*m. 'Abot* 5.19; מִתַּלְמִידָיו שֶׁל אַבְרָהָם, contrasted with "disciples of Balaam"). Billerbeck thinks the disciples of Abraham and Balaam here are Jews and Christians, which suggests that Abraham and Jesus (= Balaam) appear as focuses of loyalty, and provides a close parallel to the reading of John 9:28 urged here, Herman L. Strack and Paul Billerbeck. *Kommentar zum Neuen Testament aus Talmud und Midrasch*, vol. 2, *Das Evangelium nach Markus, Lukas, und Johannes und die Apostelgeschichte*, (Munich: C. H. Beck'sche Verlagsbuchhandlung [Oskar Beck], 1924), 535. When *Tg. Ps.-J.* Num. 3:3 refers to "the sons of Aaron, the priests, disciples of Moses, lord of Israel (תלמידיא דמשה רבהון דישראל)" on the other hand, Moses seems to be regarded as the first priest, and the priests coming after are truly his disciples, but as priests, and not necessarily as Jews.

7.2.2 Philo

Philo designates Jews generally as "pupils" of Moses (φοιτηταὶ or γνώ-ριμοι Μωυσέως).[50] They are his γνώριμοι because they learn from him (*Det.* 86). To be a φοιτητής of Moses is to "have often heard from his prophetic lips those most holy and godly instructions" (*Spec. Leg.* 2.256).

Noteworthy Jews are often so to Philo because of their singular discipleship. Among all the "associates" (ὁμιληταί) of Moses, his "true followers" (φοιτηταὶ γνήσιοι) are those who from their earliest years have been "trained in his excellent institutions" (*Spec. Leg.* 2.88). The Therapeutae garner Philo's special praise as "the pupils (γνώριμοι) of Moses trained from their earliest years to love the truth" (*Vit. Cont.* 63), and "those who have dedicated their own life and themselves to knowledge and the contemplation of the verities of nature, following the truly sacred instructions of the prophet Moses" (*Vit. Cont.* 64). Solomon,[51] the psalmists of Pss. 30(31),[52] 36,[53] and 65(64),[54] and Zechariah[55] are all likewise named as followers of Moses.

Philo also refers to his readers as "you initiated" (ὧ μύσται; *Cher.* 48), and to what they learn as "holy mysteries indeed" (ἱερὰ ὄντως μυστήρια; *Cher.* 48). Goodenough's theory, derived almost exclusively from Philonic texts, that Hellenistic Judaism had evolved into the Jewish Mystery, has not had much success, partly because of Philo's own manifest contempt for the mysteries themselves. Possibly a widespread conception of Judaism as discipleship after Moses provides a better paradigm for understanding Philo's use of mystery terminology than Goodenough's theory.

Thus it would be as a leader of disciples that Moses is a ἱεροφάντης.[56] This term may refer either to one who expounds sacred things[57] or to an initiating priest. For Philo, Moses, "the keeper and guardian of the mysteries of the Existent One" (*Plant.* 26), fulfills both functions toward Jews, and not only in the past, but in an ongoing sense as well.[58]

First, as to initiation, Philo envisions Moses still taking an active part in the induction of "multitudes of disciples (Μυρίους δὲ τῶν γνωρίμων)

---

[50] *Conf.* 135; *Quis Her.* 81; *Mos.* 2.205; *Spec. Leg.* 1.345. Γνώριμος basically means "acquaintance," but Liddell-Scott list "pupil" as well, and that seems to fit very well in these contexts.

[51] *Cong.* 177, φοιτητής.

[52] *Conf.* 39, γνώριμος.

[53] "A member indeed of Moses' fellowship" (ὁ τοῦ Μωυσέως δὴ θιασώτης; *Plant.* 39).

[54] "One of Moses' company" (τις τῶν ἑταίρων Μωυσέως; *Som.* 2.245).

[55] "One of the associates of Moses" (τῶν Μωυσέως ἑταίρων τι; *Conf.* 62).

[56] *Leg. All.* 3.151; *Spec. Leg.* 1.41; *Quod Deus* 156, see above, pp. 44, 193-94.

[57] As it clearly functions, for example, in *Gig.* 54; *Leg. All.* 3.151.

[58] Moses, too, had his initiation at Sinai; *Leg. All.* 3.100(-102); also *Gig.* 54.

whom he has "anointed," (ἤλειψεν; *Hyp.* 11.1 — in this case the multitudes of the Essenes). The activity of Moses envisioned here, incidentally,
recalls the "baptism into Moses" of 1 Cor. 10:2. In both cases, Moses appears as a figure still vital for the induction of followers into his company,
with attendant implications for Jewish self-identity and "ecclesiology."

Second, as an expositor of sacred truths Moses gathers people who wish
to convert from sin to a blameless life, and initiates them into his mysteries
by instructing them.[59] He is "the ἱεροφάντης and teacher of divine
rites."[60] Speaking autobiographically, Philo says, "I myself was initiated
under (or "by,") Moses the God-beloved into the greater mysteries" (καὶ
γὰρ ἐγὼ παρὰ Μωυσεῖ τῷ θεοφιλεῖ μυηθεὶς τὰ μεγάλα μυστήρια;
Cher. 49).[61]

7.2.3 Conclusion

The characterization of Jews as followers of Moses was a favorite expression of Philo, but scholars (often wrongly) categorize Philo as an aberrant,
esoteric Jew, and disregard him as a source for more popular Judaism.
John 9:28 provides important confirmation of the currency of the expression "disciple of Moses" in non-"Philonic" first-century Judaism (conce-
ding that Philo uses two different terms [γνώριμος, φοιτητής] for "disciple" and John yet a third [μαθητής]).

John 9:28 is, however, clearer than Philo in its implication of "Moses-
discipleship" to Jewish practice, both because the expression "disciples of
Moses" occurs in narrative text, not philosophical meditation, and because
the notion is explicitly compared with being a disciple of Jesus, clearly both
a known quantity in the early Church and a defining mark of Christians.
The implication is that just as to be a Christian is to be a disciple of Jesus,
so to be a Jew is to be a disciple of Moses. M.-É Boismard calls this statement by the Jews "their profession of faith,"[62] and W. Meeks titles his exegesis of John 9:28-29, "Moses as the Center of Jewish Piety."[63] John 9:28
seems to attest a first-century Jewish self-conception as disciples of Moses,
and of Moses as the central figure of Jewish allegiance.

---

[59] *Virt.* 178; cf. *Praem.* 120-21.

[60] *Gig.* 54.

[61] Goodenough, *By Light, Light,* 231. Moses is Philo's greatest, but not sole, ἱεροφάντης. Jeremiah, like Moses, is also enlightened (μύστης ἐστίν; *Cher.* 49) and like
Moses is "a worthy minister (ἱεροφάντης ἱκανός) of the holy secrets" (*Cher.* 49).

[62] M.-É Boismard, *Moses or Jesus: An Essay in Johannine Christology,* trans. B. T.
Viviano, Bibliotheca Ephemeridum Theologicarum Lovaniensum LXXXIV-A (Louvain: Leuven University Press, 1993), 22.

[63] Meeks, *The Prophet-King,* 292.

7.3 Moses as a Personal Focus of Loyalty

Chapter Five of the present study stressed the fact that in many texts both within and without the New Testament the authority of Moses seems to derive from himself rather than being mediated from above. Such a distinction between possessing great authority and merely mediating that authority may naturally be clearer in principle than in practice, and with both Moses and the biblical prophets the distinction was sometimes blurred. Nonetheless, the great personal authority of Moses shines through in many, many places.

The extent to which the Law's authority is seen to derive from both Moses and God in the New Testament and other Jewish writings suggests that the NT writers and other Jews of their time were acquainted with a bipolar authority behind the Torah. This in turn suggests that Jews saw themselves living in submission not only to God, but also to Moses. This could probably still be the case even if Moses were seen only as God's mediator, but Moses as an independent authority would have a more personal right to submission.

The fifth chapter of this study noted that in Luke-Acts generally the Law appears as an expression of the authority of Moses.[64] In fact, Luke-Acts repeatedly frames the Jewish faith in terms of commitment to Moses, and, like the Fourth Gospel, portrays a Jewish attitude toward Moses that shows resemblance to the attitude Christians in the New Testament are called to have toward Christ.

7.3.1 The Custom of Moses in Acts 15:1

Acts 15:1 makes circumcision the "custom of Moses" (τὸ ἔθος τῷ Μωϋσέως).[65] In this expression Moses is associated with the most important marker of Jewish identity, which in the Pentateuch seems to be associated more with Abraham, and of which Moses himself does not even seem a very regular practitioner (Exod. 4:24-26).[66]

As early as 1 Maccabees "circumcision" is seen to sum up Jewish identity and its masking is equated with loss of that identity. Thus one reads, "they removed the marks of circumcision and abandoned the holy covenant and joined with the Gentiles (ἐποίησαν ἑαυτοῖς ἀκροβυστίας καὶ ἀπέστησαν ἀπὸ διαθήκης ἁγίας καὶ ἐζευγίσθησαν τοῖς ἔθνεσιν; 1:15)."

---

[64] See above, pp. 156-58.

[65] Cf. John 7:22-23, pp. 157, 159-60 above.

[66] Though in Lev. 12:1-3, God does pass the command to Moses that males shall be circumcised.

The New Testament witnesses especially abundantly to the centrality of circumcision to Jewish identity. Many texts use "circumcision" and "uncircumcision" as synonyms for "Jew" and "Gentile."[67] "Circumcision" sums up the aims of those who enjoined observance of the Law on Gentile Christians.[68] Circumcision is repeatedly put forward as the one really essential element to Jewish observance and self-identification, the *sine qua non* of membership in the Jewish people.[69]

The central, all-embracing importance of circumcision in the rabbinic literature is likewise readily apparent,[70] so that:

in many respects, indeed, circumcision can be seen as constitutive of the identity of Israel. ... more than a central component of Jewish identity, it represents the exclusive covenant between the Almighty and Abraham (hence Israel).[71]

The fact that circumcision according to the Pentateuch is from Abraham (obviously himself no insignificant figure), strengthens the interest of the New Testament twice (Acts 15:1; John 7:22-23) referring to it as from Moses. To characterize circumcision as the "custom of Moses" focuses the one essential marker of Jewish identity on Moses, and makes Moses the reference point of Jewish allegiance.

7.3.2 Preaching Moses in Acts 15:21

The same centrality of Moses is again illustrated in Acts 15:21 where James justifies the decision not to bind Gentile Christians to the Law with the observation that "Moses from ancient generations has in every city those who preach him" (Μωϋσῆς γὰρ ἐκ γενεῶν ἀρχαίων κατὰ πόλιν τοὺς κηρύσσαντες αὐτόν).[72]

The second portion of the verse continues, "since he is read in the synagogues every Sabbath" (ἔχει ἐν ταῖς συναγωγαῖς κατὰ πᾶν σάββατον ἀναγινωσκόμενος); that is, "Moses" is "read" in the sense that an author is read when his book is.

It is not surprising that recitation of passages from the Law should be referred to as "reading Moses," but it is significant that, in a book about the preaching of Christ,[73] the theme of this activity should be summed up as "preaching Moses." "Cette phrase étonnante," observes Bovon, "mani-

---

[67] Acts 10:45; 11:2; Gal. 2:7, 9, 12; Eph. 2:11; Col. 3:11; 4:11; Tit. 1:10.

[68] Acts 15:1, 5; Gal. 2:3.

[69] Acts 16:3; 21:21; Gal. 5:2-3.

[70] See Sacha Stern, *Jewish Identity in Early Rabbinic Writings*, Arbeiten zur Geschichte des antiken Judentums und des Urchristentums, ed. Martin Hengel, et al. (Leiden: E. J. Brill, 1994), 63; a key text is *b. Ned.* 32a.

[71] Ibid., 64.

[72] See above, p. 157.

[73] 8:5, κηρύσσειν Χριστόν; 9:20; 19:13, κηρύσσειν Ἰησοῦν.

feste comme vivantes l'oeuvre et, dans une certaine mesure, la personne de Moïse."[74] Actually, while this phrase alone might only put forward the liveliness of Moses "in a certain measure," in the context of Herodian Judaism, wherein Moses was thought to be very much alive, the phrase "preaching Moses" speaks of Moses as a living focus of Jewish allegiance and self-identity.

This feature of the portrait of Moses coheres well with the impression of Moses gained in Chapter Five of this study, that of a leader and lawgiver of great personal authority. It also coheres well with the image of Moses that emerged in Chapter Six, of Moses as still an active leader for his people. Against such a backdrop, the two texts from Acts just considered suggest that Moses was not only an authority figure for Jews, but a personal overseer of Jewish life.

7.3.3 Oversight by Moses in Josephus

This in turn draws attention to the characterization of Jewish life by Josephus as a life under the watchful eye of Moses: "Certainly there is not a Hebrew who does not, just as if he [Moses] were still there (καθάπερ παρόντος αὐτοῦ) and ready to punish him for any breach of discipline, obey the laws laid down by Moses, even though in violating them he could escape detection" (*Ant.* 3.317).[75] Josephus overlooks the watchful eye of God. Rather, Jews live as if Moses were watching them (recall the image of Moses as a prophet-king surveying his realm in the *Exagoge*[76]).

Deference to the personal authority of Moses also appears in a passage in the Slavonic Additions to *The Jewish War*, "The Appeal of the Rabbis Judah and Matthias Quoting Previous Examples of Heroism" (which in the Slavonic version replaces the less full oration of *B.J.* 1.650):

Easy it is to die for the law of (our) fathers. ... Forward, ye Jewish men! Now is the time to play the man. We will show what reverence we have for the law of Moses, in order that our people may not be put to shame, in order that we may not offend our lawgiver.[77]

This text implies that to fail to show reverence to the law of Moses is to offend Moses himself.

---

[74] Francois Bovon, "La figure de Moïse dans l'oeuvre de Luc," in *La figure de Moïse: Ecriture et relectures*, by Robert Martin-Achard, et al., Publications de la Faculté de Théologie de l'Université de Genève, no. 1 (Geneva: Labor et Fides, 1978), 49.

[75] On this text see also above, p. 194.

[76] See above, pp. 36-37, 100-102.

[77] Josephus, *The Jewish War, Books V-VII*, trans. H. St. J. Thackeray, Loeb Classical Library (London: William Heinemann; Cambridge, Mass.: Harvard University Press, 1928), 445.

7.3.4 Oversight by Moses in the Fourth Gospel

In John 5:45, Jesus describes Moses as an active, dynamic figure, saying, "Do not think that I will accuse you before the Father; the one who accuses you is Moses, in whom you have set your hope (μὴ δοκεῖτε ὅτι ἐγὼ κατηγορήσω ὑμῶν πρὸς τὸν πατέρα· ἔστιν ὁ κατηγορῶν ὑμῶν Μωϋσῆς, εἰς ὃν ὑμεῖς ἠλπίκατε)." A case for metonymy of "Moses" for "Moses' Law," or the "Scriptures," here could be supported from 5:39, where Jesus claims that the Jews (5:18) believe eternal life is found in the Scriptures, which at suggests at least the possibility that in 5:45 the accuser is also the Scriptures or the Law. As S. Harstine points out, however, "Moses' name does not function in the Fourth Gospel as a metonym for the Law. Moses is presented as the historical figure responsible for the Law."[78] So rather than Moses' Law, it is Moses himself who accuses the Jews, according to Jesus, just as it is in Moses himself that the Jews set their hope.

It can be startling to find figures in the New Testament placing Moses in such a position, yet the abundance of Jewish material testifying to a supernatural conception of Moses at in the Second Temple period, much of which has been examined in the present study, makes a reference to the personal activity of Moses with regard to the Jews less surprising than it might otherwise be. As a result, Jesus' words, which parallel his own activity with that of Moses, seem not to require a great deal of interpretation: Jesus himself will not need to accuse the Jews, because Moses himself accuses them.

The image of Moses accusing wayward Jews recalls Josephus's image of Moses always standing ready to punish any breach of discipline among the people (just reviewed), as well as an (exceptional) rabbinic haggadah in which Moses accuses Israel.[79] The Jesus of the Fourth Gospel is appealing to just such a conception of Moses in the rebuke of his interlocutors here, while he subverts the popular Jewish hope in Moses as their great advocate in heaven. As Meeks puts it, "The full irony of this taunt becomes clear only when it is recalled that in almost every circle of Judaism and in Samaritanism Moses was regarded as the primary *defender* (συνήγορος, παράκλητος) of Israel before God."[80]

---

[78] Stan Harstine, *Moses as a Character in the Fourth Gospel: A Study of Ancient Reading Techniques*, Journal for the Study of the New Testament Supplement Series, no. 229, ed. Stanley E. Porter, et al. (Sheffield: Sheffield Academic Press, 2002), 95; see pp. 44, 58-59, 65-69.

[79] *Exod. Rab.* 47.9, "Moses likewise indicted Israel," etc.

[80] Meeks, *The Prophet-King*, 294; for literature see Rudolf Schnackenburg, *The Gospel According to St John*, vol. 2: *Commentary on Chapters 5-12*, trans. Cecily Hastings, et al., Herder's Theological Commentary on the New Testament, ed. Serafin de

Jeremias argues that the accusations attributed to Moses are set in the eschatological future, as shown by the future tense given to Jesus' (non-) accusation: "Do not think that I will accuse (κατηγορήσω) you."[81] R. Schnackenburg points out, however, that the future tense in κατηγορήσω need point no further ahead than to Jesus' departure to the Father,[82] which, again, would suggest that Jesus, in his characteristic (Johannine) heavenly role as the Christians' advocate before the Father (1 John 2:1), was a kind of counterpart to Moses, (in Johannine thought) the heavenly accuser of the Jews.[83]

7.3.5 Conclusion

Acts 15:21 exalts Moses by making of him someone who is preached, and by making the preaching of Moses central to the weekly synagogue service. This places Moses at the center of Jewish faith and life, and suggests that he is not merely a hallowed memory but a vital figure attracting loyalty from his followers, expressed in Acts 15:1 through assiduous practice of his custom, the very custom which goes furthest toward establishing Jewish identity. The necessity of honoring Moses and keeping his custom highlights the strength with which Jewish life focused on Moses. The remarks of Josephus illustrate the extent to which Moses personally was thought to attend to the obedience and submission of his people to his instructions.

The Fourth Gospel picks up the Jewish conviction of the caring oversight of Moses and subverts it, paralleling the advocacy of Christ for Christians not with the heavenly advocacy of Moses for Jews, but with Mosaic accusations against them. The power of this rhetorical maneuver rises from the vigor with which the Jewish belief in the advocacy of Moses was held. All these texts demonstrate the liveliness in the first century of the impression of Moses as an active overseer for Jews and a focus of Jewish loyalty.

Ausejo, et al. (London: Burns and Oates, 1980), 128-29. *Eccl. Rab.* 4.1 §1 presents Elijah as the heavenly advocate.

[81] Jeremias, "Μωυσῆς," 867 nn. 216, 217.

[82] Schnackenburg, *The Gospel According to St John*, vol. 2, 471 n. 144.

[83] In the parallel to this passage found in Egerton Papyrus no. 2 Moses clearly delivers his accusations in the present, conforming to this interpretation. See Fragment 1 verso, lines 10-14 (cf. line 18) in H. Idris Bell and T. C. Skeat, eds., *Fragments of an Unknown Gospel and Other Early Christian Papyri* (London: The British Museum, 1935), 9.

7.4 Blasphemy of Moses

The view of Moses as leader and personal focus of the Jewish religious community comports well with what might otherwise be the surprising charge of "blasphemy against Moses." Acts 6:11 relates how Stephen's opponents induced men to say that they had heard him "speak blasphemous words against Moses and God" (ῥήματα βλάσφημα εἰς Μωϋσῆν καὶ τὸν θεόν).[84]

7.4.1 Joint Sins against Moses and God

It is striking not simply to encounter the notion of blasphemy toward Moses, but to find Μωϋσῆν and τὸν θεόν governed by the same preposition, as if Moses and God were thought to be offended jointly by the same blasphemous words. No other biblical text links Moses and God in quite this way, though Exod 14:31 (see below) and several others present a parallel link of a similar kind.[85]

S. Loewenstamm, for example, notices how the account of the rebellion at Massah and Meribah (Exod. 17:1-7) "greatly emphasizes the unity between God and Moses" in receiving the people's dissatisfaction.[86] Moses asks the people, "Why do you quarrel with me? Why do you test the Lord'?" (Exod. 17:2; מַה־תְּרִיבוּן עִמָּדִי מַה־תְּנַסּוּן אֶת־יְהוָה; Tί λοιδορεῖσθέ μοι, καί τί πειράζετε κύριον;). Other texts present similar parallels to the phraseology of Acts 6:11, for example Exod. 10:16, where Pharaoh confesses to sinning against God and Moses (חָטָאתִי לַיהוָה אֱלֹהֵיכֶם וְלָכֶם; Ἡμάρτηκα ἐναντίον κυρίου τοῦ θεοῦ ὑμῶν καὶ εἰς ὑμᾶς).

Acts 6:11 best of all recalls Num. 21:5, the incident of the fiery serpents, where "the people spoke against God and Moses" (וַיְדַבֵּר הָעָם

---

[84] The charges are recast in 6:14 as speaking against the Temple and threatening that the customs of handed down by Moses would be altered. C. K. Barrett, *A Critical and Exegetical Commentary on the Acts of the Apostles*, vol. 1, *Preliminary Introduction and Commentary on Acts I-XIV*, The International Critical Commentary on the Holy Scriptures of the Old and New Testaments, ed. J. A. Emerton, C. E. B. Cranfield, and G. N. Stanton (Edinburgh: T. & T. Clark, 1994), 319 theorizes that the two sets of charges come from what were originally two sources for the narrative, which Luke has combined.

[85] Kastner, "Moses im Neuen Testament," 222 assumes that here "Moses" is synonymous with "Law of Moses." This is a possibility, but the syntax of the statement, the immediate context of the passage, and the existence of contemporary literature clearly holding Moses personally as liable to blasphemy (see below), all make the idea of blasphemy of Moses in Acts 6:11 a real prospect, and one quite coherent with contemporary Jewish thought.

[86] Samuel E. Loewenstamm, "The Death of Moses," in *Studies on the Testament of Abraham*, ed. George W. E. Nickelsburg, Jr., Septuagint and Cognate Studies, ed. Harry M. Orlinsky, no 6 (Missoula, Montana: Scholars Press, 1972), 189-90.

ובמשה באלהים; καὶ κατελάλει ὁ λαὸς πρὸς τὸν θεὸν καὶ κατὰ Μωυσῆ). When the people confess this in Num. 21:7, they repeat, "We have sinned, because we have spoken against the Lord and against you" (ובך ביהוה כי־דברנו חטאנו; Ἡμάρτομεν ὅτι κατελαλήσαμεν κατὰ τοῦ κυρίου καὶ κατὰ σοῦ).[87]

Josephus, in *Ant.* 3.298, presents Moses and God as co-recipients of disrespect or hostility from the people in the matter of the provision of meat in Numbers 11. Josephus has Moses say, "God and I though vilified by you will not cease our efforts on your behalf (ὁ θεός κἀγὼ καίτοι κακῶς ἀκούοντες πρὸς ὑμῶν οὐκ ἂν ἀποσταίημεν κάμνοντες ὑπὲρ ὑμῶν)." *Antiquities* 3.21, which reads in part, "lest in flinging those stones at him [Moses] they should be thought to be pronouncing sentence upon God" (μὴ δι᾽ ὧνπερ αὐτὸν βάλλουσι λίθων τοῦ θεοῦ κατακρίνειν νομισθῶσιν), may also so closely bind Moses and God together that joint offense against both is possible.

7.4.2 Blasphemy of Moses in Acts 6:11

The verb βλασφημέω, with the related terms βλασφημία and βλάσφημος, has a broader range of meaning than simply, "speak irreverently of divinity." Luke-Acts uses "blasphemy" mainly of slander or abuse of Jesus,[88] as well as of hostility to the Christian message,[89] or, on the lips of the Ephesian town clerk, impiety towards Diana.[90] Once, in Luke 5:21, it has its special meaning of irreverence toward God when Jesus is accused of blasphemy for forgiving sins.

---

[87] The LXX of all four verses and the Targums here (and elsewhere) make the distinction between sinning against Moses and sinning against God clear, generally through the use of different prepositions to govern each. See *Tg. Onq.*, *Tg. Neof.*, *Tg. Ps.-J.* Num. 21:5, 7; see too Israel Drazin, *Targum Onkelos to Numbers: An English Translation of the Text with Analysis and Commentary (Based on the A. Sperber and A. Berliner Edition)* (*N.p.* [USA]: Ktav Publishing House, the Center for Judaic Studies of the University of Denver, and the Society for Targumic Studies, 1982), 209 n. 16, who refers to the Targums of Gen. 50:20; Exod. 14:31; 20:16; 23:11; Num. 20:3; 21:7; 32:22; on the LXX, see John William Wevers, *Notes on the Greek Text of Numbers*, Society of Biblical Literature Septuagint and Cognate Studies Series, ed. Bernard A. Taylor, no. 46 (Atlanta: Scholars Press, 1998), 341 and also idem., *Notes on the Greek Text of Exodus*, Society of Biblical Literature Septuagint and Cognate Studies Series, ed. Claude E. Cox, no. 30 (Atlanta: Scholars Press, 1990), 154, on Exod. 10:16, "Sinning 'against Yahweh' is quite different from sinning 'against you.'" He notes that the distinction does not appear in the Peshitta or Vulgate.

[88] Luke 12:10 (perhaps against the Holy Spirit, but cf. Mark. 3:28]; Luke 22:65; 23:39; Acts 18:6?; 26:11 (here perhaps against God).

[89] Acts 13:45; 18:6?.

[90] Acts 19:37.

In Acts 6:11 it is particularly the idea of ῥήματα βλάσφημα being spoken of the paired "Moses and God" that suggests that somehow Moses can be blasphemed *in the same way* that God can be blasphemed. It is thus context and background more than vocabulary that is critical.[91]

The frequent description of the disparagement of Jesus as "blasphemy" suggests that "blasphemy of Moses" might be viewed as a similar kind of offense. There must be more than coincidence in the facts both that the charge against Stephen echoes Luke's description of Jewish abuse of Jesus and that Moses is given titles in Acts 7:35 (ἄρχων καὶ λυτρωτής) which serve "as an echoing variation of the titles of Jesus [ἀρχηγὸς καὶ σωτήρ] in Acts 5:31 (cf. also Lk. 24:21)."[92]

7.4.3 Blasphemy of Moses in Josephus

Josephus provides a remarkable parallel to the charge of blasphemy brought in Acts 6:11. He reports of the Essenes that, "After God they hold most in awe the name of their lawgiver, any blasphemer of whom is punished with death (σέβας δὲ μέγα παρ᾽ αὐτοῖς μετὰ τὸν θεὸν τοὔνομα τοῦ νομοθέτου, κἂν βλασφημήσῃ τις εἰς τοῦτον, κολάζεται θανάτῳ; *B.J.* 2.145)."

Both texts link reverence for Moses with reverence for God. In Acts 6:11 the blasphemy is dual, which in a way is easier to understand. Josephus's Essenes, by apparent contrast, punish blasphemers of Moses alone with death. Again, it is not the vocabulary of "blasphemy" that is decisive for meaning, but rather the link between blasphemy of God and blasphemy of Moses. The penalty also implies the severity of the crime (though it is true that Josephus's Essenes are not exactly sparing in their use of capital punishment; *B.J.* 2.143).[93]

Blasphemy against Moses appears again in the same discussion of the Essenes. Josephus relates how the Romans attempted to induce Essenes captured during the Revolt to blaspheme Moses: "Racked and twisted,

---

[91] It is interesting that Stephen defends himself on the charge of blaspheming Moses (Acts 6:11) in part with extensive praise of Moses (Moses takes up twenty-five of the fifty-two verses of Stephen's oration). Marcel Simon, *St Stephen and the Hellenists in the Primitive Church* (London: Longmans, Green and Co., 1958), 44-45 observes, "To be stressed is the considerable length of development dedicated to Moses. ... The setting and meaning of the speech ... can be described as 'Moseocentric.'"

[92] James D. G. Dunn, *The Acts of the Apostles*, Epworth Commentaries, ed. Ivor H. Jones (Peterborough, England: Epworth Press, 1996), 94. See Luke Timothy Johnson, *The Acts of the Apostles*, Sacra Pagina Series, ed. Daniel J. Harrington, vol. 5 (Collegeville, Minn.: The Liturgical Press, 1992), 129.

[93] Josephus himself is an enthusiast for harsh punishments, see his boast, *Ap.* 2.215, "The penalty for most offenses against the Law is death," also 216-17 ("instant death"), 262-72, esp., 272, 278 292.

burnt and broken, and made to pass through every instrument of torture, in order to induce them to blaspheme their lawgiver (ἵν᾽ ἢ βλασφημήσωσιν τὸν νομοθέτην ἢ φάγωσίν τι τῶν ἀσυνήθων) or to eat some forbidden thing, they refused to yield to either demand" (*B.J.* 2.152).[94]

The test of forbidden food is a standard emblem of Jewish faithfulness,[95] here paralleled with a test of blaspheming Moses, as if speaking ill of Moses were a similar litmus test of faithfulness. This passage in Josephus suggests not only that Moses remained someone liable to being blasphemed, but that to do so would be an instant betrayal of one's Jewishness.[96]

7.4.4 Conclusion

The charges of blasphemy against Moses in Acts 6:11 and the linked offenses against Moses and God (often in that order) in that text and in other Christian and Jewish literature, highlight Moses as someone who in some sense is seen to stand alongside God as a focus of Jewish loyalty, and conversely as someone who is offended with God by disloyal behavior or speech. The "blasphemy" against Moses of which Stephen is accused need not automatically be interpreted as "slander of a divine being," but the linkage between God and Moses in Acts 6:11 serves to indicate the magnitude of the offense, and the passages cited here from Josephus confirm the seriousness among Jews of blaspheming the Lawgiver.

7.5 Moses as a Divine Being

Even without assuming that an expression like "blasphemy of Moses" means all that it conceivably could mean, the existence of such an idea calls attention to the sometimes very exalted terms in which Moses was described. Chapter Four of this study noticed how the writer of Acts 7:35 made a point of describing Moses as a deliverer (λυτρώτης). As noted there, this could be a royal role, but among Jews to deliver or save was not only royal but divine.[97] The link between the two is highlighted by Philo

---

[94] 2 Esdr. (4 Ezra) 7:89 recalls those who "withstood danger every hour, that they might keep the law of the Lawgiver. The Lawgiver's identity is uncertain, with arguments in favor of both Moses and of God, see Michael Edward Stone, *Fourth Ezra: A Commentary on the Book of Fourth Ezra*, ed. Frank Moore Cross, Hermeneia — A Critical and Historical Commentary on the Bible, Old Testament Editorial Board, Frank Moore Cross, et al. (Minneapolis: Fortress Press, 1990), 243.

[95] Dan. 1:8-16; 1 Macc. 1:48, 62-63; 2 Macc. 6:18-26; 7:1-9, 42.

[96] Cf. above, pp. 221-22.

[97] See above, pp, 117-18, and Darrell L. Bock, *Proclamation from Prophecy and Pattern: Lucan Old Testament Christology*, Journal for the Study of the New Testament Supplement Series, ed. David Hill, vol. 12 (Sheffield: JSOT Press, 1987), 78.

who, in addition to the many honorifics he gives Moses ending in -ατος, says that Moses was named "god *and* king (θεὸς καὶ βασιλεύς; *Mos.* 1.158), an expression which was also introduced into discussion of Moses' kingship, and which comes into further discussion below.[98]

Chapter Six introduced into discussion numerous texts describing Moses, not only in life but especially at and after his death, as a glorified figure, a spiritual figure, one thought to be active on behalf of his people from beyond the grave. The Transfiguration in particular appears to confirm such a view of Moses among the early Christians, and certainly implies it among Jews of the same period.[99]

The question of blasphemy of Moses now draws attention specifically to the ascription of divinity to Moses in Philo and other sources, a large number of which take Exod. 7:1 as their starting point, indicating widespread exegetical tradition along such lines.[100]

7.5.1 Moses as God

7.5.1.1 Moses as "God" in Philo

In back of Philo's assessment of Moses as "god (and king)" lies Exod. 7:1, where God makes Moses god to Pharaoh (נתתיך אלהים לפרעה; δέδωκά σε θεὸν Φαραω), and very probably also Exod. 4:16, where Moses is set up "as God" (תהיה־לו לאלהים; αὐτῷ ἔσῃ τὰ πρὸς τὸν θεόν) to Aaron, who in turn becomes as Moses' mouth to the people.

Philo explains Exod. 7:1 in various, related ways. In one of the clearest exegeses, Philo explains that Moses is "god" to Pharaoh because he is wise whereas Pharaoh is a fool (*Mut.* 128).[101]

In another place, Philo explains quite specifically that when Moses was appointed "a god unto Pharaoh,"

he did not become such in reality, but only by a convention is supposed to be such. ... The wise man is said to be a god to the foolish man, but ... in reality he is not God. ... But when the wise man is compared with Him that *is*, he will be found to be a man of

---

[98] See above, pp. 93-94, 102, 104, and Wayne A. Meeks, "Moses as God and King," in *Religions in Antiquity: Essays in Memory of Erwin Ramsdell Goodenough*, ed. Jacob Neusner, Studies in the History of Religions (Supplements to *Numen*), no. 14 (Leiden: E. J. Brill, 1968), 355.

[99] See above, pp. 194-206, 211-12.

[100] Josephus is omitted from the following discussion. On the unlikelihood that Moses as θεῖος ἀνήρ in *Ant.* 3.180 is anything more than "divinely inspired," see Spilsbury, *The Image of the Jew in Flavius Josephus' Paraphrase of the Bible*, 107-110.

[101] And again in *Leg. All.* 1.40; *Sac.* 9-10; *Mig.* 69 with 84, and briefly *Som.* 2.189. *Mut.* 129 goes on to specify that Moses' "divine" role is to intercede before God on Pharaoh's behalf; see *Mos.* 1.155-58.

God; but when with a foolish man, he will turn out to be conceived of as a god, in men's ideas and imagination, not in view of truth and actuality (*Det.* 161-62).[102]

As J. D. G. Dunn correctly concludes

[Philo] is ... quite clear that Ex. 4.16 and 7.1 ascribe deity to Moses only in a relative sense, of Moses in relation to Aaron and Pharaoh, of a wise man in relation to a foolish man ... and the overall impression is that he deliberately refrained from interpreting the two Exodus passages literally.[103]

This important qualification should not obscure the fact that Philo's opinion of Moses remains high; "divine" language was not used lightly. At other points in this study other aspects of the Philonic Moses have emerged, which place the additional title of "god" in a very exalted setting when applied to Moses. However the ascription should be qualified, it should not be glossed over that, for Philo, Moses is a divine figure.

Philo bears this out. Besides the more common type of explanation just noted, Philo also explains Exod. 7:1 as an assignment of authority to Moses: "god," like "lord," is for Philo a designation not for the Deity (ὁ ὢν, who cannot be truly named) but for one of his powers.[104] For Moses to be called "god," then, speaks not of his essential being but of his elevation to divine office. *Mut.* 19-22 makes clear that when the Lord makes Moses God to Pharaoh, he assigns one of his powers to Moses with relation to Pharaoh.

Both sets of Jewish criteria for divinity discussed earlier in this study include "divine function" (C. A. Gieschen's term) as one key indicator of divine status. For R. Bauckham divine function is the sole criterion, broken down into "creating" and "ruling."[105]

Bauckham's criteria happen to correspond precisely to Philo's denomination of the two principal powers of God. In one place, Philo ranks the creative power θεός third alongside the ruling power κύριος among the seven powers of God, behind the Logos from which they both spring and

---

[102] Elsewhere Philo describes Moses "as having passed from a man into a god, though, indeed, a god to men, not to the different parts of nature, thus leaving to the Father of all the place of King and God of gods" (*Quod Omnis Prob.* 43-44). As this text implies, "there are thus a whole range of beings that can be called θεοί: certain men, heavenly bodies, angels, divine powers"; see D. T. Runia, "God and Man in Philo of Alexandria," *Journal of Theological Studies*, NS 39, part 1 (April 1988): 56.

[103] Dunn, *Christology in the Making*, 19; likewise Runia, "God and Man in Philo of Alexandria," 63, 71. Compare *Tanḥuma* Buber on Exodus, Parashah 2(Wa'era).9 on Exod. 7:1, "You are a god only to Pharaoh."

[104] See Henry Chadwick, *The Church in Ancient Society from Galilee to Gregory the Great* (Oxford: Oxford University Press, 2001), 33.

[105] See above, pp. 97-100.

the Speaker of the Logos (*QE* 2.68).[106] Elsewhere God's two chief powers are named "God" and "Lord" (*QG* 1.57; 2.16). On Bauckham's description of divinity Philo's language seems especially clear about the divinity given to Moses in Exod. 7:1.

Philo remains a stauch monotheist. He makes clear that only the Un-created truly rules (μόνος δ' ὁ ἀγένητος ἀψευδῶς ἡγεμών), and that none who is created is truly a lord (κύριος γὰρ γενητὸς πρὸς ἀλήθειαν οὐδείς; *Mut.* 22). Also, as pointed out above, Philo carefully circum-scribes the glory of Moses.[107] Even so, as observed in that discussion, Philo's praise of Moses' exalted nature is effusive, and the impression given in the texts being considered here, that Moses even received a dele-gated divine status, must be considered in that light. Moses may have a mortal nature, but nonetheless the delegation of divine power to Moses in Exod. 7:1 truly sets him apart from other men and gives him a share of divinity.[108]

7.5.1.2 Moses as "God" in a Qumran Text

While some texts, the writings of Philo and the *Exagoge* of Ezekiel Tragi-cus particularly, depict the elevation of Moses to a divine kingship or to divine standing in connection with kingship, in other settings the kingship element is relatively neglected, making the texts in question witnesses to a belief in the simple divinization of Moses. Some of these texts have the additional value of rooting the divinization of Moses outside Alexandrian literature. This applies not only to Ecclus. 45:2, discussed below, but also to material extant only at Qumran.

Thus 4Q374, frag. 2, col. 2, gives what seems to be a description of the deification of Moses at Sinai and its effect on the Israelites:[109]

6) and he made him like a God over the powerful ones, and a cause of reel[ing] (?) for Pharaoh [...]

([...]ויתננו לאלוהים על אדירים ומחיג[ה] לפרעה עב[ן)

7) melted, and their hearts trembled, and [th]eir entrails dissolved. [But] he had pity with [...]

8) and when he let his face shine for them for healing, they strengthened [their] hearts again.

(ובהאירו פנו אליהם למרפא ויגבירו לב[ם] עוד)

---

[106] The Greek terms are attested in the fragment, see Ralph Marcus, *Questions and Answers on Exodus*, Philo Supplement 2, Loeb Classical Library (Cambridge, Mass.: Harvard University Press; London: William Heinemann, 1953), 256.

[107] See above, pp. 191-94.

[108] See above on criteria for divinity, pp. 98-100.

[109] See Fletcher-Louis, "4Q374: A Discourse on the Sinai Tradition: The Deifica-tion of Moses and Early Christology," 238-40, 252. Throughout this article, Fletcher-Louis is not terribly precise in his use of similar but distinct terms like "angelization," "divinization," and "deification."

As C. H. T. Fletcher-Louis argues, this is probably another midrash on Exod. 7:1, ratifying its assignment to Moses of the title "god."[110]

7.5.1.3 Moses as "God" in Pseudo-Orpheus

The textual history of Pseudo-Orpheus is complex, but one recension of the poem, which appears in its entirety in Eusebius, *Praep. Ev.* 13.12.5 (who quotes it from Aristobulus), can be dated to anytime in the mid-second to late first centuries B.C.[111] This dating is supported by its similarities with Ezekiel the Tragedian and Sirach.[112]

In this recension, known as the "Mosaic" recension because of its overall tendency to emphasize Moses,"[113] new lines appear (bracketed here) by which the redactor has oriented toward Moses older material describing a certain "Chaldean," who, as presented in a previous recension, had been more vaguely reminiscent of Moses or perhaps of Abraham.[114]

21	Αὐτὸν δ' οὐχ ὁρόω· περὶ γὰρ νέφος ἐστήρικται
25	Λοιπὸν ἐμοί· 'στᾶσιν δὲ δεκάπτυχον ἀνθρώποισιν.
26	Οὐ γάρ κέν τις ἴδοι θνητῶν μερόπων κραίνοντα,
27	Εἰ μὴ μουνογενής τις ἀπορρὼξ φύλου ἄνωθεν
28	Χαλδαίων· ἴδρις γὰρ ἔην ἄστροιο προείης
29	Καὶ σφαίρης κίνημ' ἀμφὶ χθόνα ὡς περιτέλλει
30	Κυκλοτερὲς ἐν ἴσῳ, κατὰ δὲ σφέτερον κνώδακα.
31	Πνεύματα δ' ἡνιοχεῖ περί τ' ἠέρα καὶ περὶ χεῦμα
32	Νάματος· ἐκφαίνει δὲ πυρὸς σέλας ἰφιγενίηου.
33	Αὐτὸς δὴ μέγαν αὖθις ἐπ' οὐρανὸν ἐστήρικται
34	Χρυσέῳ εἰνὶ θρόνῳ· γαίη δ' ὑπὸ ποσσὶ βέβηκε·

---

[110] Fletcher-Louis, "4Q374: A Discourse on the Sinai Tradition," 239; also see his *All the Glory of Adam: Liturgical Anthropology in the Dead Sea Scrolls*, Studies on the Texts of the Desert of Judah, edited by F. García Martínez with P. W. Flint, vol. 42 (Leiden: E. J. Brill, 2002), 136-41.

[111] Carl R. Holladay, *Orphica*, vol. 4 of *Fragments from Hellenistic Jewish Authors*, Society of Biblical Literature Texts and Translations Pseudepigrapha Series, ed. James C. Vanderkam, Texts and Translations no. 40, Pseudepigrapha no. 14 (Atlanta: Scholars Press, 1996), 63-66. While its precise age remains controversial, this recension is generally agreed to pre-date the New Testament. On textual witnesses, see Holladay, 44-45. The poem, attributed to Orpheus by Aristobulus, is cited by Eusebius as a unified piece in *Praep. Ev.* 13.12.5, and in certain portions in 13.13.50-51, 53-54.

[112] See Holladay, *Orphica*, 63-66.

[113] See Holladay, ibid., 45.

[114] In favor of the latter, Clement of Alexandria, *Stromateis* 5.14.123.2, who quotes that earlier recension, see Holladay, *Orphica*, 50, 119. Valckenaer, however, thinks Clement was mistaken, and that the "Chaldean" section (lines 27-30) always (i.e. even in earlier recensions, which lacked lines 25-26, 41-42) referred to Moses (L. C. Valckenaer, *Diatribe de Aristobulo Judaeo; philosopho peripatetico Alexandrino*, ed. J. Luzac [Leiden: S. & J. Luchtmans, 1806], 11-16, 73-85; reprinted in T. Gaisford, *Eusebii Pamphili Evangelicae Praeparationis Libri XV*, vol. 4 (Oxford: Oxford University Press, 1843), 351-56, 406-407, and cited in Holladay, *Orphica*, 50.

35   Χεῖρα δὲ δεξιτερὴν ἐπὶ τέρμασιν ὠκεανοῖο
36   Ἐκτέτακεν· ὀρέων δὲ τρέμει βάσις ἔνδοθι θυμῷ
38   Οὐδὲ φέρειν δύναται κρατερὸν μένος. ἔστι δὲ πάντως
39   Αὐτὸς ἐπουράνιος καὶ ἐπὶ χθονὶ πάντα τελευτᾷ,
40   Ἀρχὴν αὐτὸς ἔχων καὶ μέσσον ἠδὲ τελευτήν,
41   Ὡς λόγος ἀρχαίων, ὡς ὑλογενὴς διέταξεν,
42   Ἐκ θεόθεν γνώμῃσι λαβὼν κατὰ δίπλακα θεσμόν.
43   Ἄλλως οὐ θεμιτὸν δὲ λέγειν· τρομέω δέ γε γυῖα,
44   Ἐν νόῳ· ἐξ ὑπάτου κραίνει περὶ πάντ᾽ ἐνὶ τάξει.
45   Ὦ τέκνον, σὺ δὲ σοῖσι <νόοις πέλας ἴσθι ἐς αὐτόν, >
46   <Μηδ᾽ ἀπόδος> μάλ᾽ ἐπικρατέων στέρνοις <θεοφήμην>.

21   But I do not see him [God]; for around him a cloud has been fixed
22-24 [*omitted in this recension*]
25   Remaining in my way; and it stands tenfold for other men.
26   For no one among mortals could see the ruler of men,
27   Except a certain person, a unique figure, by descent an offshoot
28   Of the Chaldean race; for he was expert in following the sun's course
29   And the movement of the spheres around the earth, as it rotates
30   In a circle regularly, all on their respective axes.
31   And the winds he drives around both air and stream
32   Of water. And he brings forth a flame of mighty fire. [115]
33   He indeed is firmly established hereafter over the vast heaven
34   On a golden throne, and earth stands under his feet.
35   And he stretches out his right hand upon the extremities
36   Of the ocean; and the mountain base trembles from within with rage
37   [*omitted in this recension*]
38   And it is not possible to endure his mighty force. But in every way
39   He himself is heavenly, and on earth brings all things to completion,
40   Since he controls their beginning, as well as their middle and end,
41   As a word of the ancients, as one born in the undergrowth proclaimed
42   Having received God's ancient teaching in statements on the two-tablet law.
43   Now to say anything other than this is not allowed, indeed I shudder
44   At the very thought; from on high he rules over everything in order.
45   O child, be near to him in your thoughts,
46   And do not abandon this divine message, but rather preserve it in your heart. [116]

Starting in line 31 there is either a change of subject, from the "Chaldean" to God or another heavenly being (such as the sun, which might represent God), or else an abrupt change of tone, from describing the Chaldean's great learning to extolling his rule over the natural world. The

---

[115] Or (line 32) "Of the stream. A comet makes manifest these events — he had a mighty birth," M. Lafargue, trans. "Orphica," in *The Old Testament Pseudepigrapha*, ed. James H. Charlesworth, vol. 2, The Anchor Bible Reference Library (New York: Doubleday, 1985), 799-800.

[116] Text and translation prepared by Holladay, *Orphica*, 194-95; Underline: new material, not found in previous recensions. "< >" encloses text supplied from a later, Christian recension, see Holladay, 49, 60.

Chaldean seems to be described in terms befitting a celestial being, and is exalted to a heavenly throne (33-34). That is, in this recension, Moses may be portrayed in celestial terms, enthroned in heaven.[117]

The section begins and ends with reasonably clear statements about Moses, who seems to appear here as the one person who could see God (lines 26-27, recalling Num. 33:12-34:8),[118] and who received the Law (line 42), and teaches the right way to think about God (lines 31-40). He is also an expert in astronomy (lines 28-30), recalling widespread description of Moses as a great sage, and perhaps also the ability of the enthroned Moses to survey and number the stars in the *Exagoge* vision.[119] The best parallels to the presentation of Moses here come from Philo. He affirms, "Moses was by race a Chaldean (Μωυσῆς γένος μέν ἐστι Χαλδαῖος; *Mos.* 1.5)." Philo also relates that inhabitants of the neighboring countries taught Moses "the Chaldean science of the heavenly bodies" (τὴν τῶν οὐρανίων Χαλδαϊκὴν ἐπιστήμην; *Mos*; 1.23), in which he gained yet further expertise from the Egyptians, "who give special attention to astrology (μαθηματικὴν ἐν τοῖς μάλιστα ἐπιτηδευόντων; *Mos.* 1.24)."

It seems reasonable, then, to suppose that the "Mosaic recension" of Pseudo-Orpheus speaks of Moses in the selection quoted here. But a caution is set against against seeing the poem as a description of an apotheosis of Moses by the fact that Moses actually seems to appear as a witness to the heavenly vision in lines 41 and 42. M. Lafargue accordingly inclines to the position that the poem only describes Moses' vision of the divine, introduced in line 26, and not his own apotheosis.[120] If correct, this position would still not militate against the idea that what Moses saw was a vision his own elevation, along the lines of the throne vision in the *Exagoge* of Ezekiel.

C. R. Holladay believes that this redaction of Pseudo-Orpheus is the product of an incomplete insertion of Moses material into an existing paean of God, perhaps conceptualized as the disk of the sun, which ascribes to God the rule of nature and a heavenly enthronement.[121] His theory of an incomplete redaction is reflected in the ambiguity of his translation, quoted above. Holladay notes that line 26, which makes explicit reference to God as "the ruler of all men," is redactional material that actually removes some of the ambiguity in the passage by making it easier for the reader to think of God as the subject in line 31. Holladay argues therefore that the inten-

---

[117] See, e.g. Lafargue, "Orphica," 796-97, 799-800; Fletcher-Louis, *All the Glory of Adam*, 137-38.

[118] Cf. above, p. 34, on the intimacy of God and Moses.

[119] On the vision, see above, pp.36-37, 90-91.

[120] Lafargue, "Orphica," 796-97.

[121] Holladay, *Orphica*, 210-11.

tion of lines 31-40 of the poem, even in this redaction, is to glorify God, not Moses.

The present examination has done no more than review highlights of this difficult but vivid passage. It should be pointed out that evaluation of this text has not always proceeded in the full light of all that was actually said about Moses in the ancient world. The sorts of things that were said of Moses, as reviewed in this study, show how easily the description of the heavenly being in lines 31-40 of the Orphic poem could be thought to apply to Moses, either during the ascension of Sinai or following his death.

Both the density of the Orphic text and the unresolved condition of the debate concerning it serve as a caution against overzealous interpretation. It seems possible, however, that the redactor meant to leave the text describing the divinization of Moses. The wide range of other texts in which traces of the divinization of Moses appear means that even the possibility is worth noticing here.

7.5.1.4 Moses as "God" in Rabbinic Literature

In rabbinic writings the notion of the deification of Moses is clearest in a clutch of passages which interpret מֹשֶׁה אִישׁ הָאֱלֹהִים (from Deut. 33:1), as Meeks says, "against all rules of syntax," as "Moses, man and god: A man, when he ascended on high; a god, when he descended" (בשעה, אִישׁ, שעלה למרום. אלהים, בשעה שירד למטה).[122] This rabbinic exegesis, Meeks judges, must be a relic of the older tradition, also expressed in Samaritan literature and in Philo, that at the ascension of Mount Sinai Moses received both the name of God and a share in the functions which that name entailed.[123]

7.5.1.5 Moses as "God" in Samaritan Literature

This emerges with great clarity in Samaritan imagery.[124] Meeks observes that in the early Samaritan sources the vice-regency of Moses is directly connected with the implications of the report of Exod. 7:1 that he was called "god."[125] In Samaritan literature at the ascension of Sinai Moses is "crowned" with the name Elohim (always, and never YHWH, which is "the name which God revealed to him"),[126] and sharing God's name means

---

[122] Meeks, "Moses as God and King," 361 on the syntax; text here quoted from *Pesiq. Rab Kah.* Appendix 1 (Deut. 33:1) §9 (Buber ed., chap. 32, 198b). Cf. *Midr. Pss.* 90.5. On Moses' ascent of Sinai and its implications, see also above, pp. 94-97.

[123] Meeks, "Moses as God and King," 361.

[124] Ibid., 357-59.

[125] Ibid., 359.

[126] Ibid., 360.

sharing his function and status. Indeed, Samaritan tradition often regarded Moses' ascension of Mount Sinai as a kind of deification.[127]

In another tradition, Moses is the incarnation of the primordial "light" of Creation. In consequence, he is regarded as the first thing that God created.[128] Subsequent creation was done for the sake of Moses.[129] Moses himself, or "the light," had no active role in producing creation, but worked in it and sustained it.[130] "Since the world was created from and of that light, it was dependent on Moses; without him it could not have come into being, and without him it could not continue to exist (cf. John 1.3-4)."[131] "Moses was *light from light*, in the sense that he is in essence light, of the light of God, who issued from that light into the darkness of the material world."[132] From the primordial light came also the (pre-existent) spirit of the prophets, the spirit that finally was fully manifested in Moses.[133]

7.5.2 Divine Beings Denominated as Both "Gods" and "Angels"

In the late Second Temple Period, Greek and Hebrew terms which we can translate "god" and "angel" were for many Jews essentially interchangeable.[134] This former flexibility is at least partly explained by the fact that the category "angel" did not become firmly linked with its now-traditional meaning until relatively late. Fundamentally, both מלאך and ἄγγελος simply mean "messenger," and in Second Temple Judaism the cloud of heavenly beings around God, or between God and man, went by a number of rather non-descriptive titles ("watchers," "holy ones," etc.), which might be interchanged with one another or with the generic "gods."

---

[127] Ibid., 359-60. See also Jarl E. Fossum, *The Name of God and the Angel of the Lord: Samaritan and Jewish Concepts of Intermediation and the Origin of Gnosticism*, WUNT, ed. Martin Hengel and Otfried Hofius, no. 36 (Tübingen: J. C. B. Mohr [Paul Siebeck], 1985), 111-12: "he possesses a share in God's nature, " 112.

[128] John Bowman, "Samaritan Studies," *Bulletin of the John Rylands Library* 40 (1957-1958): 302-303; Montgomery, *The Samaritans: The Earliest Jewish Sect*, 226.

[129] Bowman, "Samaritan Studies," 302-303; Montgomery, *The Samaritans: The Earliest Jewish Sect*, 226.

[130] Bowman, "Samaritan Studies," 306.

[131] MacDonald, *The Theology of the Samaritans*, 170.

[132] Ibid.

[133] As already observed above, p. 213 n. 20, scholars have noted similarities of this with the Muslim legend of Mohammed, but Bowman, "Samaritan Studies," 304 n. 1 reckons that the question of originality is still open. On pre-existence of Moses, see also above, pp. 142 and 212-13.

[134] J. A. Emerton, "Some New Testament Notes," *Journal of Theological Studies*, NS, 11 (1960): 330.

The Dead Sea Scrolls in particular may frequently speak of angels as
אלים, for example in the Songs of the Sabbath Sacrifice (4Q400-405).[135]
11Q13 (11QMelch) col. 2, lines 10-12 appears to call both an eschatological Melchizedek, and the heavenly court around him, אלהים.[136]

Also, in the Peshitta of Psalm 82 verses 1a and 6 translate אלהים as
אלהא and אלהין respectively, much as one might expect. But verse 1b
translates אלהים as מלאכא, and verse 1a gives מלאכא as the translation of
אל. J. Emerton believes this phenomenon probably testifies to a Jewish
interpretation of the psalm that deemed the same divine beings to be either
gods or angels, in other words which held the two terms to be interchangeable.[137]

7.5.3 Great Men as Angels in Jewish Literature, especially at Qumran

This means that in many Jewish writings one may speak not only of divinization but also of "angelization" of human beings. Numerous Qumran
texts speak of the community of the sect sharing in the worship of the
angels, as members evidently experienced a merging of heaven and earth.[138]
4Q400 (4QShirShabb[a]) 1.1-20 is especially rich in these connections,
blending the earthly and angelic communities (e.g. lines 2-3, "[he has
established] the most holy ones among the eternal holy ones" [(יסד)
בקדושי עד קדושי קדושים]). The further step that may be called angelization may occur in 1QH[a] 11.21-22, which speaks of the depraved spirit of
one fashioned out of dust (a human being) being purified to join an ever-
lasting community (the covenant), and entering into communion with the
host of holy ones and the sons of heaven (the angels).[139] Clearly, one can
read in these lines a fellowship between men and angels that does not
include outright angelization. On the other hand, these texts could suggest

---

[135] See, with examples, Emerton, ibid., 330-31. To these add 4Q400 (4QShir-
Shabb[a]) frag. 1, 1.2, frag. 2, line 2, line 3, and line 5 (the last reference, however, is
sometimes thought to refer to members of the community and its leader, as is also [the
badly damaged] 4Q401 [4QShirShabb[b]] frag. 11); see also 4Q401 (4QShirShabb[b]) frag.
14. Helmer Ringgren, *The Faith of Qumran: Theology of the Dead Sea Scrolls*, trans.
Emilie T. Sander, ed. James H. Charlesworth, Christian Origins Library (New York:
Crossroads, 1995), 84, concludes, "*'Elîm* most probably then is to be taken [in 1QH
10.8] as 'divine beings.'"

[136] See Jarl E. Fossum, *The Image of the Invisible God: Essays on the Influence of
Jewish Mysticism on Early Christianity*, Novum Testamentum et Orbis Antiquus, ed.
Max Küchler, with Gerd Theissen, no. 30 (Freiburg, Switzerland: Universitätsverlag
Freiburg; Göttingen: Vandenhoeck & Ruprecht, 1995), 5-6.

[137] Emerton, "Some New Testament Notes," 331. A similar interpretation of the
psalm is found in Origen, see Emerton, 331-32.

[138] Fletcher-Louis, "4Q374: A Discourse on the Sinai Tradition," 240; Ringgren,
The Faith of Qumran: Theology of the Dead Sea Scrolls, 84-86, 127-28, 136.

[139] Thanks go to Paul Swarup for these references.

such a thing, and other texts show that such ideas were in the air in late Second Temple Judaism.

The *Visions of Amram* speaks of angelization, and may parallel it with divinization in the same sentence. The human in question is either Moses or Aaron, with a final decision on that question made impossible by the fragmentary state of the evidence (to be considered presently). The full title of the work, as preserved in 4Q543 (4QVisions of Amramᵃ ar), frag. 1, lines 1-2, is, "Copy of the writing of the words of the vision of 'Amram, son of Qahat, son of Levi. All that he revealed to his sons (לבנוהי) and what he advised them in [the day of his death]."[140] Immediately the text goes on to describe what appears to be the arrangement and celebration of the wedding of Amram's daughter, Miriam.

4Q545 (4QVisions of Amramᶜ ar) preserves in one fragment (frag. 1a. col. 1) occasionally damaged text from the beginning of *Visions of Amram* through to the lines of real interest here. These commence at the end of the wedding, in line 7:[141]

7) Then, when

8) the [d]ays of the feast were completed, he sent and called Aaron, his son. [H]e was [...] years old]

9) [... and said] to him: Call my son Malachiyah ... from the house of ([...] ואמר] לה קרי לברי למלאכיה א ... מן ביה)

10) [...] ... above, called him.

11) [...] I

12) [...] my father

13) [...] from

14) [...] your word

15) [and we will give you ... for e]ver,

16) [and we will give you wisdom ...] it will be added

17) [to you ... you will be God, and an]gel of God (אל ומ[ן]לאך)

18) [you will be called ... you will do in] this [land,]

19) [and a judge ... and when] your name.[142]

---

[140] These lines are supplemented from 4Q545 frag. 1a i, col. 1, lines 1-2, as edited by Émile Puech, ed., *Qumrân Grotte 4 XXII: Textes Araméens, première partie, 4Q529-549*, Discoveries in the Judaean Desert, ed. Emanuel Tov, vol. 31, edited with James Vanderkam and Monica Brady (Oxford: Clarendon Press, 2001), 292, 333 (frag. 1, lines 1-2 as edited by Florentino García Martínez and Eibert J. C. Tigchelaar, eds., *The Dead Sea Scrolls Study Edition*, vol. 2, 4Q274-11Q31 [Leiden: Brill, 1998], 1085); trans. García Martínez and Tigchelaar, 1085.

[141] In García Martínez and Tigchelaar, *The Dead Sea Scrolls*, vol. 2, 1088-89. In Puech, *Qumrân Grotte 4 XXII*, 292, begin at line 8.

[142] Text and trans. from García Martínez and Tigchelaar, *The Dead Sea Scrolls*, vol. 2, 1088-89 who denominate this frag. 1, col. 1.

The text peters out in that manuscript, but the part of the ending most crucial here can be supplied from 4Q543 (4QVisions of Amram[a] ar), frag. 2a-b:[143]

4) [...] you will be God, and an angel of God you will be call[ed ...]

([... אל תהוה ומלאך אל התקר]ה [...])

5) [...] you will do in this land, and a judge [...]

([...] תעבד בארעא דא ודין [...])

6) [...] And when your name for all [...]

7) [...] for etern[al] generations [...]

8) [...] ... you will do [...]

9) [...] Isra[el ...].[144]

Translating the crucial lines this way, 4Q545 gives the name Malachiyah to an individual "who will be god and called an angel of God." This person would logically be Moses, who does not otherwise appear in the extant remains of the passage, but who would be expected to appear somewhere on the basis of the statement of 4Q543 frag. 1a line 2 (just cited), which says that Amram addressed his "sons" (לבנוהי). A similar name for Moses is attested in *LAB* 9.16, where "Moses" is the name given to the boy by Pharaoh's daughter, while his mother Jochabad calls him "Melchiel," for which Malachiyah is a possible analogue. The name Melchiel may even be suggested as an alternative for Malachiyah in *Visions of Amram* itself, 4Q543, frag. 2.a-b, line 4: "and an angel of God (ומלאך אל =? ומלאכאל) you will be called."[145]

The fact that *Visions of Amram* starts by saying that Amram addressed both his sons (Aaron and ?Malachiyah), the possibility of an allusion to Exod. 7:1 where Moses is "a god to Pharaoh," the reference to activity "in this land," i.e. Egypt, and an apparent reference to being a judge (4Q543, frag. 2a-b, line 5), all point toward Moses, which would suggest that *Visions of Amram* here describes what can be called an angelization of Moses. That this description occurs in an Aramaic document preserved in multiple copies at Qumran implies that the text represents a popular assessment of Moses, nicely complementing the opinions of the erudite Greek, Philo.

Such an interpretation of the evidence of *Visions of Amram*, however attractive from the standpoint of this study, has its difficulties. É. Puech understands the text much differently. In particular, he understands מלאכיה not as the proper name Malachiyah, but as a simple plural, "mes-

---

[143] As published by Puech, *Qumrân Grotte 4 XXII*, 294; García Martínez and Tigchelaar, *The Dead Sea Scrolls*, vol. 2, 1084-85 publish this as fragment 3.

[144] This is the translation by García Martínez and Tigchelaar, *The Dead Sea Scrolls*, vol. 2, 1085.

[145] Denominated by García Martínez and Tigchelaar, *The Dead Sea Scrolls*, vol. 2, 1084-85, frag. 3 line 1. In the MS מלאך with final ך is clearly a separate word.

sengers" (the word ends in ה in place of the expected א, but this would not be the only such irregularity in this manuscript and poses no real obstacle to his view).[146]

Perhaps more importantly, he reads 4Q545 frag. 1a, col. 1, line 9 with two important differences (plus others). Where García Martínez and Tigchelaar read:

[... ואמר] לה קרי לברי למלאכיה א . . . . מן בית],

Puech reads:

[עשרי]ן [אמר] לה קרי לי ברי למלאכיה אחיכון מן בית.

First, in place of קרי לברי Puech claims, "La lecture קרי לי ברי est assurée."[147] The former reading makes it almost certain that the ל of both לברי and למלאכיה is the ל of direct object, and accordingly "my son" and "Malachiyah" are parallel; thus Malachiyah must be Amram's other son, or Moses, whom Aaron is dispatched to call. On Puech's reading, however, ברי is spoken in direct address to Aaron, and מלאכיה therefore, no longer standing in apposition to ברי, is not *necessarily* Amram's son (though he still might be). The difference in readings is a matter of conjectural word lengths and letter sizes, since whatever immediately followed the relevant ל in the MS, whether the ב of ברי or a י and then a space, has been completely obliterated.[148] Puech's guess does look to be slightly more likely.

Puech's second decision, however, to replace the last lacuna with אחיכון, is far more conjectural, despite Puech's claims regarding traces of letters.[149] The manuscript in this spot is nearly obliterated and it seems questionable whether אחיכון, "your brothers" really has any stronger claim to be the correct reading than אחיך, "your brother," i.e., Moses.[150]

Thus Puech translates line 9, "Et il lui dit, 'Appelle-moi, mon fils, les messagers, vos frères, de la maison.'" The main difference this makes, from the point of view of this study, is that it suggests no entry of Moses on the scene to be the subject of the apparent allusions to Moses in the text to follow (which were pointed out just above) including the features that suggest angelization or divinization.

Moreover, Puech deems the first אל of 4Q543 frag. 2a-b, line 4 to be the *nomen rectum* of an expression parallel to מלאך אל. He writes, with

---

[146] See Puech, *Qumrân Grotte 4 XXII*, 333. Puech does not acknowledge the possibility of מלאכיה as a proper name.

[147] Ibid., 336, L. 9. This is a drastic overstatement, but Puech, in contrast to García Martínez and Tigchelaar, at least indicates that the letters in question here, י and ב, are only represented by traces. García Martínez and Tigchelaar, *The Dead Sea Scrolls*, vol. 2, 1088 give no sign of the lacuna (formed by the edge of the manuscript crossing the line of text).

[148] See the photograph, Puech, *Qumrân Grotte 4 XXII*, plate 19.

[149] Ibid., 335, "L. 9."

[150] Examine ibid., 335 and plate 19.

specific reference to García Martínez and Tigchelaar, "On ne peut certaine-
ment comprendre 'you will be God'," and prefers instead "you will be בחיר
אל, the "elect of God."[151] The lacuna at the head of the line is complete,
however, and, since consequently there is no way to tell what text preceded the אל in question, there is no way to judge the merit of Puech's
conjecture (or, granted, that of García Martínez and Tigchelaar's).

It may admittedly be far-fetched to link the name Malachiyah in *Visions
of Amram*, through Pseudo-Philo's Melchiel, to Moses (though this connection is supported by the Mosaic characterization of the figure in
4Q543), and the fact is that Aaron, like Moses, could be very highly ap-
praised in Second Temple Judaism. At the end of the day, faced with manuscripts in such poor condition, particularly the large lacuna after 4Q545,
frag. 1a, col. 1, lines 9-10, all that can be said with assurance is that the
Visions of Amram describes the angelization of one of Amram's sons,
either Moses or Aaron.

The possibility that the angelization of Aaron might actually be what is
meant calls attention to the importance that was attached to Aaron, which
in some ways resembled that given to Moses. Ecclesiasticus 45:2 makes
Moses equal to "the holy ones" (ἅγιοι), which, as will be seen shortly,
probably refers to the angels (or the gods), but according to Ecclus. 45:6
Aaron too was exalted as an ἅγιον (Heb.: [כמוהו] קדוש וירם).

Aaron specifically, or the high priest generally, is exalted in other
Second Temple literature as well.[152] Note, for example, Philo's treatment
of the high priest, whom he describes as "a being whose nature is midway
between <man and> God, less than God, superior to man" (μεθόριός τις
θεοῦ <καὶ ἀνθρώπου> φύσις, τοῦ μὲν ἐλάττοων, ἀνθρώπου δὲ
κρείττων; *Som.* 2.188).[153] According to Hecataeus of Abdera, the high
priest is called ἄγγελος τῶν τοῦ θεοῦ προσταγμάτων ("messenger of
the commandments of God"), and when he speaks the Jews fall to the

---

[151] Puech, *Qumrân Grotte 4 XXII*, 295-96, "L. 4," with 296 n. 7. Unfortunately, the
only evidence he cites turns out to be a reading he has supplied in the corresponding lacuna of 4Q545, on p. 334.

[152] See William Horbury, *Jewish Messianism and the Cult of Christ* (London: SCM
Press, 1998), 55-56, and idem., "The Aaronic Priesthood in the Epistle to the Hebrews," *Journal for the Study of the New Testament* 19 (October 1983): 45. On the cosmic importance of the high priest in Josephus, see Clemens Thoma, "The High Priesthood in the Judgment of Josephus," in *Josephus, the Bible, and History*, ed. Louis H.
Feldman and Gohei Hata (Leiden: E. J. Brill, 1989), 202-204. On priestly angelomor-
phism in the Dead Sea Scrolls, see Fletcher-Louis, *All the Glory of Adam*, 150-221,
who concludes, 187-89, that the *Visions of Amram* MSS examined here indeed describe
a divinized Aaron.

[153] See Knox, *St Paul and the Church of the Gentiles*, 34 ("[In Philo] the figure of
the High Priest has replaced Zeus."), 86.

ground and προσκυνεῖν him.[154] Wisdom 18:22-25 describes Aaron's robes in such a way that Aaron appears as the Logos,[155] and Mal. 2:7 describes the priest as the messenger (מלאך) of the Lord of Hosts. In a sense, the case for Jewish divinization of Moses is incomplete without acknowledgment of a similar though less-pronounced tradition with regard to Aaron (or his successors). If Puech is right, this is what appears in *Visions of Amram*.

Such traditions about Aaron detract nothing from Moses (or indeed from the thesis of the present chapter), but merely reflect the dual constitution of Israel. Treatment of the two brothers often went hand in hand and, to the extent that Moses was seen as greater than Aaron, the glory of Aaron redounds to Moses' credit as well.

In later Jewish literature the notion of great men being transformed into angels occurs with some abundance. Enoch, who was sometimes said to have been transformed into the angel Metatron, is well known in this regard,[156] but other figures receive similar treatment. In some literature Adam started out as an angel.[157] Several midrashim teach that "the righteous will, like Enoch-Metatron, become like or superior to the angels,"[158] and the idea that the reception of heavenly visions involves transformation of the visionary into an angelic being occurs in several places in apocalyptic literature.[159] With this compare Matt. 22:30, "in the resurrection ... they are like the angels in heaven." C. R. A. Morray-Jones argues:

there are good grounds for believing that some first- and second-century rabbis attempted to suppress an early tradition of the ascent into heaven of an exceptionally righteous

---

[154] *Aegyptiaca* 5-6, apud Diodorus Siculus, *Bibliotheca*, 40.3, cited here from Menachem Stern, ed. and trans., *Greek and Latin Authors on Jews and Judaism Edited with Introductions, Translations, and Commentary*, vol. 1, *From Herodotus to Plutarch*, Fontes and Res Judaicas Spectantes (Jerusalem: The Israel Academy of Sciences and Humanities, 1974), 27.

[155] See Goodenough, *By Light, Light*, 275-76; Knox, *St Paul and the Church of the Gentiles*, 33-34.

[156] Enoch says " I was enlarged and increased in size until I matched the world in length and breadth (3 Enoch 9:2; also 15:1-2). See C. R. A. Morray-Jones, "Transformational Mysticism in the Apocalyptic-Merkabah Tradition," *Journal of Jewish Studies* 43, no. 1 (1992): 10-11, and Hurtado, *One God, One Lord: Early Christian Devotion and Ancient Jewish Monotheism*, 55-56 on the relevant passages in 3 Enoch. See also above, pp. 95-96.

[157] Morray-Jones, "Transformational Mysticism in the Apocalyptic-Merkabah Tradition," 16-17. Rabbinic sources state that Adam's body was so large it filled the universe, while they also contain the tradition that Adam was like God or one of the angels.

[158] Morray-Jones, "Transformational Mysticism," 17-19.

[159] Ibid., 22-28; the phenomenon extends into Christian sources.

man or men who ... became in some way associated or identified with the Angel of the
LORD.[160]

A number of other passages have been suggested as witnessing the
angelization of great and good humans.[161] Not all are equally transparent,
but some of the clearest involve Moses.

7.5.4 Moses as an Angelic Being

The Greek text of Ecclus. 45:2 says that God "made him [Moses] equal in
glory to the holy ones" (ὡμοίωσεν αὐτὸν δόξῃ ἁγίων), i.e., the angels.[162] The text in the only extant Hebrew manuscript of these verses[163] is
obscure just at the critical line from verse 2, but Fletcher-Louis concludes
from the extant fragment, אלהי[...], that the Greek ἁγίων translates
אלהים. The Hebrew version appears to have made Moses equal to God or
the gods (i.e., אלהים), while "the Greek clearly understood the Hebrew as
a reference to an angelic, and in that sense divine, state of existence."[164]
The context, as so often in such descriptions of Moses, is again Mount
Sinai.[165]

1 Enoch 89:36 has already been examined in connection with the glorious death of Moses.[166] In this verse, the sheep (Moses) who leads the
other sheep (Israel) is transformed into a man at the point in the allegory
corresponding to the Sinai revelation. Fletcher-Louis argues, "In this apocalyptic allegory ... angels are anthropomorphic and humans zoomorphic.
Moses' transformation is thus an angelization,"[167] which is as much to say
that Moses is portrayed being raised to divine status.

Fletcher-Louis also calls attention to 4Q377, fragment 1, recto, column
2, lines 10-11, which, in the midst of a description of the mediation of the

---

[160] Ibid., 14.

[161] Citing more from Qumran, and throwing in some harmonious references from
Josephus, Fletcher-Louis, "4Q374: A Discourse on the Sinai Tradition: The Deification
of Moses and Early Christology," 240-42, see also 246-47.

[162] Angels are called "holy ones" often in Qumran literature as well, Ringgren, *The
Faith of Qumran: Theology of the Dead Sea Scrolls*, 83.

[163] Genizah MS B.

[164] Fletcher-Louis, "4Q374: A Discourse on the Sinai Tradition," 243. On Ecclus.
45:2 and other Jewish texts using ἅγιοι to denote angels, see Hurtado, *One God, One
Lord*, 56-57, and 150 n. 26.

[165] Crispin H. T. Fletcher-Louis, "The Revelation of the Son of Man: The Genre,
History of Religions Context and the Meaning of the Transfiguration," in *Auferstehung-Resurrection*, ed. Friedrich Avemarie and Hermann Lichtenberger, WUNT, ed.
Martin Hengel and Otfried Hofius, vol. 135 (Tübingen: J. C. B. Mohr [Paul Siebeck],
2001), 251.

[166] See above, pp. 202-203.

[167] Fletcher-Louis, "4Q374: A Discourse on the Sinai Tradition," 241.

Law at Mount Sinai, describes Moses the man of God (ומושה איש האלוהים) speaking as an angel from his mouth (כמלאך ידבר מפיהי).[168]

In Samaritan thought as well, "Moses not only was assimilated to the angels; it is stated that he actually attained angelic nature or mode of being."[169] That is to say, he was made into "a divine or angelic being."[170] In a hymn by Marqah, Moses is described as "the Elohim who is from mankind," giving him a divine name shared by angels.[171] Also, as noted above in Chapter Three, in a Samaritan *ketubah* Moses is called "the priest of the angels," and *Memar Marqah* 4.6 likewise describes Moses, "who dwelt among the angels in the Sanctuary of the Unseen," as "a holy priest in two sanctuaries." Marriage contracts (of the sixteenth and eighteenth centuries, but probably preserving older tradition) call Moses "the teacher of the living (beings), and the priest of the angels (ספרון דחייה: וכהן מלאכיה)."[172]

Various rabbinic texts also portray Moses after his death in a manner resembling the ministering angels in heaven, though without saying specifically that an angel is what he became.[173]

7.5.5 Conclusion

In the Hellenistic period, many would have considered any human to possess a soul which partook in some measure of the divine,[174] and the title and honors of a god could be granted to anyone who seemed to have a special divinity that transcended the ordinary standard of human exis-

---

[168] Fletcher-Louis, "The Revelation of the Son of Man," 252, *All the Glory of Adam*, 141-48. "As" is a tricky word to interpret: James Vanderkam and M. Brady, "[4Q]377: 4QApocryphal Pentateuch B," in *Wadi Daliyeh II and Qumran Cave 4 XXVIII*, ed. Douglas M. Gropp and Moshe Bernstein, et al., Discoveries in the Judaean Desert, ed. Emanuel Tov, vol. 28 (Oxford: Clarendon Press, 2001), 216 conclude here, "Moses is here compared to an angel/messenger; he is not actually said to be one." The expression, "a man a god" recalls Deut. 33:11 and its exegesis in rabbinic literature, noted above, see pp. 96-97 and pp. 235-36.

[169] Fossum, *The Name of God and the Angel of the Lord*, 123.

[170] Ibid., 124.

[171] Ibid., 124, quoting from A. E. Cowley, ed., *The Samaritan Liturgy* (Oxford, 1909), 55 line 5. See also Morray-Jones, "Transformational Mysticism," 13.

[172] MS Firkovitch, Sam. X, 1 (1510/1511), line 15, text, Plummer, *Samaritan Marriage Contracts and Deeds of Divorce*, vol. 1, 164; trans., Plummer with Tal, *Samaritan Marriage Contracts and Deeds of Divorce*, vol. 2, 187; MS Firkovitch, Sam. X, 58 (1794-1795), line 8, text, Plummer with Tal, vol. 2 (Wiesbaden: Harrassowitz Verlag, 1997), 113, trans., ibid., 231, and see p. 69 above.

[173] Fossum, *The Name of God and the Angel of the Lord*, 130-32.

[174] See Knox, *St Paul and the Church of the Gentiles*, 72-75.

tence.[175] Among non-Jews not only emperors and kings were honored as gods, but also conquering generals and even high imperial officials.

Even among Jews it was acceptable to speak of men as "gods," or "angels," which amounts to the same thing. As pointed out above, Jewish monotheism may have meant not so much an ascription of divinity to God alone as an establishment of which divine being was to be worshipped, with the Lord conceived of at the top of a pyramid of divine beings.[176]

The *Visions of Amram* may attest a divine estimation of either Moses or of Aaron, but in either case shows that Jews of the late Second Temple Period could think of the divinization of great men. The Jewish criteria of divinity assembled by Bauckham and Gieschen both seem to confirm that various Jewish traditions esteemed Moses as divine. Even if Jews held that only God himself possesses essential divinity, Jewish literature describes Moses (and other figures) as possessing or being delegated aspects of that divinity, or measures of it. Billerbeck, after reviewing biblical passages including Exod. 4:16; 7:1 and Ps. 82:6 and rabbinic comments on them concludes, "Diesen Stellen darf man entnehmen, daß die Bezeichnung eines Menschen als 'Gott' für das jüdische Empfinden gerade nichts Unerhörtes war ... nur durfte sich der Betreffende nicht selbst die Bezeichnung beilegen."[177] There is no *a priori* reason to neglect such strong indications as we have that at least in some circles Moses was regarded as a divine being, an angel, or a "god."

These indications show that Philo's declaration that Moses "was named both god and king of the whole nation (*Mos.* 1.158)" is not just a Philonic eccentricity.[178] The distinction between "god" and "king" in the remark implies that it cannot adequately be treated only as a reference to divine kingship, although Philo certainly makes use of that model in describing Moses. For Philo, Moses inherits one of God's own powers.[179] Rather

---

[175] The impression should not be given that the title "god" was so common in Greco-Roman circles as to be mere commonplace: Apollonius was thrown on the defensive when given the title, and various authors objected to such strong language; see Horbury, *Jewish Messianism and the Cult of Christ*, 72-74.

[176] See above, p. 92. See also Knox, *St Paul and the Church of the Gentiles*, 44 ("Nor was Judaism ... always strict in its adherence to the limits of Jewish monotheism")-53.

[177] "One ought to conclude from these references, that the designation of a man as 'god' was nothing really outrageous for Jewish sentiment ... only the person in question ought not give himself the title," Strack and Billerbeck, *Kommentar zum Neuen Testament aus Talmud und Midrasch*, vol. 2, 465.

[178] See above, pp. 229-32.

[179] Philo was comfortable with the idea that exceptional men could share God's qualities, as in *Virt.* 177, where he says "absolute sinlessness belongs to God alone, or possibly to a divine man" (τὸ μὲν γὰρ μηδὲν συνόλως ἁμαρτεῖν ἴδιον θεοῦ τάχα δὲ καὶ θείου ἀνδρός).

than being a one-off remark, Philo's reference to Moses as "both god and king" seems to give particularly vivid expression to an opinion of Moses which circulated widely among Jews of his day, helped always by the remarkable statements of Exod. 4:16 and 7:1 that Moses had been made god.

Without the backdrop provided by contemporary Jewish thought, the reference in Acts 6:11 to blasphemy of God and Moses seems nearly inexplicable, both because Moses would seem incapable of being blasphemed in the same way that God is, and because, ironically, on that basis it would seem a bit blasphemous to suggest that he could be. After taking into consideration the conception of Moses which was in play at the time, however, the charges of Acts 6:11 seem almost straightforward. It is, however, of great interest that the New Testament of all literature should provide such a strong formulation of the idea of a divine Moses.

In Acts 6:11 Moses and God appear as joint objects of blasphemy. The next section will examine texts which speak of Jewish faith in Moses. The two conceptions together are powerful testimony to a very exalted view of Moses, one which comfortably found a place for him near to God and at the center of Jewish life and practice.

7.6 Jewish Faith in Moses

7.6.1. Moses and Jesus as Objects of Faith

The language used in John 5:46-47 points to comparability between Moses and Jesus, as personal objects of faith. Jesus says, "For if you believed Moses, you would believe Me; for he wrote of Me. But if you do not believe his writings, how will you believe My words?" Jesus distinguishes faith in Moses from faith in Moses' writings, a distinction made unmistakable by the personal activity of Moses himself described in the preceding verse.[180] Jesus thinks his hearers ought both to believe in what Moses wrote, and to trust Moses personally.[181]

The formula implicit in the Johannine saying is paralleled in Samaritan marriage contracts, which exhort, "Let us believe in Moses and in his

---

[180] Schnackenburg, "The Notion of Faith," in *The Gospel According to St John*, vol. 1: *Introduction and Commentary on 1-4*, trans. Kevin Smyth, Herder's Theological Commentary on the New Testament, ed. Serafin de Ausejo, et al. (London: Burns and Oates, 1968), 562 argues that "Johannine faith is always referred to witnesses and testimony," that is, to persons and their words.

[181] In agreement, see Harstine, *Moses as a Character in the Fourth Gospel*, 58-60. Consider also the argument that the witness in John 5:32 is Moses, in Peter F. Ellis, *The Genius of John: A Composition-Critical Commentary on the Fourth Gospel* (Collegeville, Minn.: Liturgical Press, 1984), 93-94.

book" (במשה ובכתבו נאמן).[182] Another such contract urges, "Happy is
the one who believes in him (טובי מן בו יימן) and walks on the path of
his law."[183] Yet another exhorts, "Let us bow down and believe this faithful messenger" (נרכן קנומן ונאמן: בזה השליח המימן).[184]

The implications of the likeness between Christian belief in Jesus and
Jewish belief in Moses for the Jewish conception of Moses are usually
passed over by commentators, but deserve exploration.

7.6.2 Biblical Background

"Faith in Moses" can at first sound like a Christian's idea of Judaism. Exodus 14:31, however, pairs the Lord and Moses as the objects of Israel's
belief: "The people feared the Lord, and they believed in the Lord and in
his servant Moses (ויאמינו ביהוה ובמשה עבדו; ἐπίστευσεν τῷ θεῷ καὶ
Μωυσῆ τῷ θεράποντι αὐτοῦ)."[185]

Moses also occasionally appears in the Pentateuch less as a mediator for
God than as his assistant or co-worker; Loewenstamm's observation of the
way Moses and God might be jointly offended in the Pentateuch was noted
above.[186] He also detects a joint ministry of Moses and God in the accounts of Massah and Meribah (Exod. 17:1-7) and Meribat Kadesh (Num.
20:1-15), where "an act of Moses replaces direct Divine action."[187]

7.6.3 The Targums

This pairing was not always easily digested, and the Targums witness to a
desire to guard against such a (mis)understanding. *Targum Onq.* Exod.
14:31 amends, "The people feared the Lord. They believed in the Memra
of the Lord and in the prophecy of Moses (ובנביות משה), his servant."
The same insertion of "the prophecy of" is also found in *Tg. Ps.-J.*, *Tg.
Neof.*, *Frg.-Tg.*(P), and Genizah Targum MS PP Exod. 14:31.[188] One

---

[182] MS Smithsonian 1 (1809), text: Plummer, *Samaritan Marriage Contracts and
Deeds of Divorce*, vol. 1, 193; trans.: Plummer with Tal, *Samaritan Marriage Contracts and Deeds of Divorce*, vol. 2, 233. MS Firkovitch, Sam. X, 72 (1829), line 10,
text: Plummer and Tal, vol. 2, 145, trans.: ibid., 239. Cf. MS Firkovitch, Sam. X, 71
(1829), line 8, "Let us believe in him and in his allegiance" (נאמן בה ובימנותה), text:
Plummer with Tal, vol. 2, 143, trans.: ibid., 238.

[183] MS Firkovitch, Sam. X, 91 (1835), line 5, text: Plummer with Tal, *Samaritan
Marriage Contracts and Deeds of Divorce*, vol. 2, 150; trans.: ibid., 241.

[184] MS Girton College (1905), line 12, text: Plummer, *Samaritan Marriage Contracts and Deeds of Divorce*, vol. 1, 224; trans.: Plummer with Tal, *Samaritan Marriage Contracts and Deeds of Divorce*, vol. 2, 250.

[185] Cf. Matt. 27:54. A similar coupling in Acts 6:11 refers to blasphemy of God and
Moses, see above, pp. 227-28.

[186] P. 226.

[187] Loewenstamm, "The Death of Moses," 189.

[188] MS PP folio 7 (4r), ll. 18-19.

might (and apparently some did) infer from the MT that faith could be placed in Moses personally, a possibility the Targums are eager to rule out by saying explicitly that it was only in his prophecy that the people believed.[189]

The targumic emendations almost certainly represent an effort to put an end to or foreclose inappropriate esteem for Moses, based on Exod. 14:31.[190] The MT of Exod. 14:31 blandly tells of belief in Moses, and all the Targums deflect that belief away from Moses and safely onto his prophecy, which has the effect of placing the belief in question in God alone. The fact that all the Targums make this change either suggests that Jews generally did not think of Moses as someone in whom to believe, or else it points to "faith in Moses" being identified as a problem rather early, at least before the Targums reached their extant form. The fact that John 5:45-47 speaks of Jews both believing in Moses and setting their hope in him speaks in favor of the latter possibility.

7.6.4 The Greek Old Testament

In fact, the implications of the MT were apparently embraced well before the turn of the era. The LXX translates Exod. 14:31 simply, ἐπίστευσαν τῷ θεῷ καὶ Μωυσῇ τῷ θεράποντι αὐτοῦ.

Not only does the LXX not share targumic concern over the idea of the Israelites believing in Moses, it actually appears to encourage it. The LXX of Exod. 4:1-9 adds "in you" (σοί), referring to Moses, after "believe" in verses 5, 8, and 9. True, even in the MT Moses starts off by asking, "What if they will not believe me?" (וְהֵן לֹא־יַאֲמִינוּ לִי; 4:1), but the effect of the LXX insertions is to give a sense not found in the MT that Moses himself,

---

[189] Bernard Grossfeld, *The Targum Onqelos to Exodus: Translated, with Apparatus and Notes*, The Aramaic Bible: The Targums, ed. Kevin Cathcart, Michael Maher, and Martin McNamara, vol. 7 (Edinburgh: T. & T. Clark, 1988), 40 n. 13. But cf. *Tg. 2 Chron.* 20:20, "Put your trust in the Memra of the Lord, your God, put your trust in his Law, put your trust in his prophets (בנביאוהי)," which preserves the MT's implication that the Lord's prophets (בנביאיו) themselves are objects of faith. Aberbach claims that the insertion in the Pentateuchal Targums was necessitated by the impossibility in Judaism of "believing" in a human being since "belief" is reserved for God alone (cited from personal correspondence by Israel Drazin, *Targum Onkelos to Exodus: An English Translation of the Text with Analysis and Commentary (Based on the A. Sperber and A. Berliner Edition)* [N.p. (USA): Ktav Publishing House, 1990], 148 n. 37). This claim is apparently denied by John 5:45-47.

[190] *Pace* Drazin, *Targum Onkelos to Exodus*, 148 n. 37, who says that the Targums meant merely "to clarify what it was about Moses that the people believed," and concludes that no excessive exaltation of Moses was feared. The problem, however, is that the MT has the people believing in Moses *tout court*. The Targums do not merely tell what about Moses was believed, they substitute something else besides Moses to be believed in.

and not merely the revelations he claims from God (v. 5), is an appropriate object of Israelite faith.

7.6.5 Josephus

Josephus's *Ant.* 3.298 was already mentioned above for its depiction of Moses as being jointly offended with God by the people's rebellion.[191] In the same scene, Josephus omits the biblical story of Moses' appeal to God on the people's behalf, instead simply having Moses promise, "God and I ... will never cease our efforts on your behalf" (ὁ θεός κἀγὼ ... οὐκ ἂν ἀποσταίημεν κάμνοντες ὑπὲρ ὑμῶν), and immediately "the camp was filled with quails" (*Ant.* 3.298).[192] The passage depicts God and Moses functioning as (an exasperated) team, not as a master and his emissary as in the biblical version. Josephus also gives to Joshua words that seem to place the promises of God and the predictions of Moses side by side as twin grounds for assurance of Israel's future (*Ant.* 5.39-40), again making both God and Moses appropriate objects of trust.

7.6.6 Rabbinic Literature

The results of the examination of rabbinic literature on Moses as Lawgiver might (rightly) be taken to imply that the Rabbis betray little interest in Moses as an object of belief.[193] The concept did not utterly vanish among them, however, and appears for example in the *Mekilta de-Rabbi Ishmael* on Exodus 14:31, where having faith in Moses is the same as having faith in God (and speech against God is speech against Moses, and *vice versa*).[194] Moses in Jewish literature, both early and late, thus shares with God his role as provider and as object of Israelite faith.

7.6.7 Samaritan Thought

"Perhaps the most striking difference between the Samaritan traditions and those of Rabbinic Judaism," W. Meeks writes, "is the existence of a 'Samaritan creed' of which one essential element is 'belief in Moses.'"[195]

Generally speaking, Samaritans appear to have put a greater emphasis on belief than did Jews, at least as Jews are represented in the rabbinic writings. Samaritan literature gives extensive evidence for creedal formulas, for which Jewish literature provides no real parallel.[196] J. Bowman writes, "Samaritanism did not present a blueprint for every action in life,

---

[191] P. 227.

[192] Though cf. 3.5-21.

[193] See above, pp. 143-48.

[194] See discussion in Meeks, *The Prophet-King*, 239-40.

[195] Ibid., 238.

[196] Bowman, "Samaritan Studies," 302, 309-310.

but a blueprint for belief. ... Samaritanism stressed works ... but faith was equally stressed."[197]

In many places in Samaritan liturgy and theology (mainly in the *Memar Marqah*) Moses appears alongside God in a two-member formula of belief. Elsewhere belief in God and belief in Moses lead lists of four or five cardinal points of Samaritan belief.[198] This suggests that Samaritanism has long worked with a two-member focus of faith, God and Moses, much resembling the "confession of faith" appearing in Exod. 14:31. MacDonald acknowledges that Exod. 14:31 probably lies at the root of the Samaritan "two-member" creed,[199] but he nonetheless believes that the development of the creed itself depends on Christian influence.[200]

Meeks acknowledges that MacDonald's hypothesis of Christian influence in back of the Samaritan creed has a *prima facie* attractiveness,[201] but while he takes MacDonald's point about the formulation of the Samaritan creed, he rejects MacDonald's confidence that Samaritan belief in Moses is itself the product of Christian influence. Instead, Meeks suggests an older, Jewish root, for which he draws chiefly on the *Mekilta* passage just cited. Without taking on the burden of showing where exactly the Samaritan ideas came from, he urges that early derivation from Jewish thinking is a possibility not simply to be dismissed.[202] The LXX as just discussed obviously supports the possibility of an old Jewish teaching about faith in Moses, and much of the discussion undertaken in the present chapter adds further to its plausibility.

Bowman insists that the Samaritan creeds are very old and though he does not propose a precise date he notes that they appear in a Samaritan prayer that appears to pre-date the destruction of their Mt. Gerizim temple in the second century B.C.[203] It seems clear that the oldest Samaritan literature contains creed-like statements prioritizing faith in God, but closely associating faith in God with faith in Moses, and these statements in some form reach back into the Second Temple period. Given the plausibility of a Jewish background or a parallel Jewish development to these Samaritan

---

[197] Ibid., 309.

[198] Generally, belief in God, Moses, Torah, Mount Gerizim, and sometimes the Day of Vengeance and Retribution, Bowman, "Samaritan Studies," 310.

[199] MacDonald, *The Theology of the Samaritans*, 53 and 51 n.1, "Ex. 14.31, which in itself could have provided the first creed."

[200] MacDonald, *The Theology of the Samaritans*, 52-53, 150-51.

[201] Meeks, *The Prophet-King*, 239.

[202] Ibid., 238-40.

[203] Bowman, "Samaritan Studies," 309-311. See also Jarl Fossum, "Sects and Movements," in *The Samaritans*, ed. Alan D. Crown (Tübingen: J. C. B. Mohr ([Paul Siebeck], 1989), 324.

beliefs, the Samaritan evidence suggests strongly that Jews in the pre-Christian era thought of Moses as in some sense a focus of faith and trust.

7.6.8 Christian Thought

The interpretation which in Exod. 14:31 saw faith being placed both in God and in Moses even appears in Christian writing. Eustathius of Sebaste, who debated baptism with Basil of Caesarea in the mid-fourth century A.D., compared faith in Moses with baptism into Moses. His point was that Basil was misguided to exalt the Holy Spirit merely because baptism is sometimes in his name, because baptism had also taken place into Moses, and yet he is only a man. His argument, as cited by Basil, goes on:

In a similar fashion it is acknowledged that before now faith has been placed in men (ὁμοίως δὲ καὶ ἡ πίστις ὁμολογεῖται ἤδη καὶ εἰς ἀνθρώπους γεγενῆσθαι): 'for the people believed in God and Moses his servant.' Therefore, it is asked, why do you exalt and magnify the Holy Spirit so far above creation, on the basis of faith and baptism, when the same have before now also been testified of men?[204]

7.6.9 Conclusion

The Fourth Gospel only contains the clearest description of Moses as the object of Jewish faith. A broad range of Jewish material, starting with Exod. 14:31, seems to place Moses in this position, while the LXX underscores it with its insertions of "in you" in the discussion of the faith of Israel in Exodus 4. The Targums demonstrate that not all Jews agreed on this point, yet their unanimous opposition looks tendentious in the presence of indicators that at least some Jews did think of Moses in this way.

Both Samaritans and Christians know of Moses as someone in whom faith can be placed, and their source for this conception is almost certain to be Judaism. The Samaritan conception almost certainly was taken up long before the Herodian period, which suggests a stream of tradition regarding faith in Moses reaching well back into the Second Temple period. One hesitates to depend on hypothesized Jewish reaction to Christianity, but it is not inconceivable that the Targums and rabbinic writings reflect a reaction against earlier Jewish dabblings in the idea of faith in Moses, which was sparked by the problem of similar Christian teaching about faith in Christ.

In any case, John 5:45-47 harmonizes with a broad range of Jewish (and other) material in speaking of Moses as an object of Jewish faith. Jews in that passage appear self-consciously to believe in Moses in a way that

---

[204] *De Spiritu Sancto* 14.31(beginning); trans. Michael A. G. Haykin, "'In the Cloud and in the Sea': Basil of Caesarea and the Exegesis of 1 Cor 10:2," *Vigiliae Christianae* 40 (1986): 137.

appears to be comparable to Christian belief in Jesus. These verses also interact with the Jewish view that Moses is Israel's advocate and defender in a way that seems to view Moses as currently active. This suggests that the writer of the Fourth Gospel may have thought of Moses as the leader of the Jewish "church," and possibly as a cosmic or spiritual figure, and in both respects would have been relying on, and reflecting, Jewish ideas about Moses.

7.7 Acts 21:21 and Apostasy from Moses

Luke-Acts, which more explicitly than any other NT corpus views the Law as a personal expression of the authority of Moses,[205] is also the only NT material — the only material anywhere — to speak of "apostasy from Moses," (ἀποστασία ἀπὸ Μωϋσέως; Acts 21:21).[206] Not in the first place a "religious" concept, ἀποστασία is rebellion against a leader. More overtly than any other passage, Acts 21:21 seems to assume Moses as the focus of Jewish loyalty, a personal center of allegiance for the Jewish people.[207]

In that verse, James reports the charge of apostasy from Moses as an allegation of those suspicious of Paul's ministry in the Diaspora. Some Jerusalem Christians, perhaps on the basis of reports by the "Jews of Asia" in 21:27, suspect Paul of teaching Jews to leave off Jewish practice and Jewish identity in their conversion to Christ, specifically, of telling Jews no longer to circumcise their children, nor to maintain the customs (λέγων μὴ περιτέμνειν αὐτοὺς τὰ τέκνα μηδὲ τοῖς ἔθεσιν περιπατεῖν).

As already noted above, Acts 15:1, 5 makes circumcision the central and definitive rite of Jewish identity and strongly links it with Moses.[208] This link is only strengthened, not created, in Acts 21:21, where to leave off circumcision is to commit apostasy from Moses.[209] Further, the "cus-

---

[205] See above, pp. 156-58.

[206] Though Josephus should be noted for the grave implications he gives to cases of στάσις against Moses, Spilsbury, *The Image of the Jew in Flavius Josephus' Paraphrase of the Bible*, 135-37.

[207] As above with Acts 6:11, Kastner, "Moses im Neuen Testament," 222 simply assumes that the apostasy is from the "Law of Moses," that "Moses" is a synonym for "the books of the Torah."

[208] See above, pp. 157, 221-222; cf. 159-61.

[209] C. K. Barrett, *A Critical and Exegetical Commentary on the Acts of the Apostles*, vol. 2, *Introduction and Commentary on Acts XV-XXVIII*, The International Critical Commentary on the Holy Scriptures of the Old and New Testaments, ed. J. A. Emerton, C. E. B. Cranfield, and G. N. Stanton (Edinburgh: T. & T. Clark, 1998), 1008.

toms" that Acts 21:21 connects with circumcision are quite likely the "customs Moses handed down" (τὰ ἔθη ἃ παρέδωκεν ἡμῖν Μωϋσῆς) of Acts
6:14. In Acts 6:11-14, merely to suggest the alteration of these customs is
tantamount to blasphemy of Moses.[210] It is reasonable to suppose that the
conception of Moses in Acts 21:21, as a personal focus of Jewish loyalty,
is the same as that which influenced the other two Acts passages.

In fact the charges leveled against Paul in Acts 21:21 "have a strong
resemblance to those brought against Stephen in Acts 6:13-14."[211] This
resemblance is strengthened if the charges cried out by the mob against
Paul in Acts 21:28, οὗτός ἐστιν ὁ ἄνθρωπος ὁ κατὰ τοῦ λαοῦ καὶ τοῦ
νόμου καὶ τοῦ τόπου τούτου πάντας πανταχῇ διδάσκων, are meant
to amplify the intimations of James in 21:21 concerning Paul's supposed
attitude toward Moses, circumcision, and the customs, as seems likely to
be the case. Then both Paul and Stephen stand accused of teaching
"against the law and against this place," and of teaching disregard for the
customs of Moses and for Moses himself. The parallel can be deepened by
the natural step of setting apostasy from Moses in Acts 21:21 side by side
with speaking blasphemy against Moses in Acts 6:11. In either case Moses
appears as a personal focus of (supposed) irreverence and disloyalty.

Earlier, this chapter examined depictions of Moses and God as joint objects of faith and joint objects of blasphemy.[212] The concept of apostasy
"from Moses," which coheres so well with these other conceived disposi-
tions toward Moses, seems to suggest a third idea, Moses and God as joint
objects of allegiance.

P. Spilsbury notices something of this kind in Josephus's narrative of
events following Moses' prohibition of entry to the promised land. Whereas Num. 14:44 says that the Israelites disregarded warnings against entering the Land without God's support, Josephus charges them with imagi-
ning that "even without his [Moses'!] support they could by themselves defeat their enemies" (δίχα τῆς παρ' ἐκείνου προθυμίας κρατήσειν αὐτοὶ
τῶν πολεμίων νομίζοντες; *Ant.* 4.1). The point is clarified when the
people are depicted setting out for battle "scorning the arrogance of Moses
and in reliance upon God (τῆς ἀλαζονείας αὐτοῦ καταγνόντες καὶ τῷ
θεῷ πιστεύσαντες; 4.5),"and "claiming God as their leader and without
waiting for any concurrence on the part of their legislator (τὸν θεὸν προ-
στησάμενοι στρατηγὸν ἀλλ' οὐχὶ τὴν παρὰ τοῦ νομοθέτου συν-
εργίαν περιμένοντες; 4.6)." In a startling revision of the biblical reason
for the disaster at Kadesh, Josephus assigns the problem not simply to the
hubris of the people in disobeying God, but to the fact that they claimed

---

[210] See above, pp. 226-28 with n. 84.
[211] Johnson, *The Acts of the Apostles*, 375.
[212] Above, blasphemy, pp. 226-29; faith, 247-53.

God as their commander (a role usually filled by Moses) and gave no thought for the cooperation of their lawgiver.[213] The end of the episode sees the people "having once more committed themselves to him — for they understood that without his vigilance they could never prosper" (καὶ τοῦ πλήθους ἐπιτρέψαντος ἑαυτὸ πάλιν ἐκείνῳ, συνῆκε γὰρ δίχα τῆς αὐτοῦ προνοίας οὐ δυνησόμενον ἐρρῶσθαι τοῖς πράγμασιν; 4.10).

By no means is the problem of defiance of God's will absent from the affair as Josephus tells it: the scene opens with Israelite disregard of "the prohibition of God" (κωλύοντος τοῦ θεοῦ; 4.1) and the battle ends with the recognition that the defeat was on account of having gone into battle without God's assent (4.8). But Josephus has revised the whole account to turn Moses into another locus of authority over the people, and the reason for the disaster is the insubordination of the people toward both Moses and God, not toward God alone.

Spilsbury's assessment is that Josephus shows the people to have "distinguished between obedience to Moses and obedience to God. This is a position which Josephus quite clearly presents as false. ... The implication is that Moses' assent is equal to God's."[214] Put slightly differently, in Josephus's version of the story obedience to Moses is just as important as obedience to God. The two are really complementary priorities, and obedience to Moses is essential to maintaining God's favor.[215]

This is echoed in another Acts passage besides those just examined. In Acts 7:35, Stephen recalls the attitude of the Jewish ancestors toward Moses: "Moses whom they disowned ... God sent to be both a ruler and a deliverer."[216] With these words Stephen rebukes not the ancestors' distrust of God, but their disloyal repudiation of Moses.

Likewise in Acts 7:39, remembering the Israelite rejection of the Law, Stephen recalls, "our fathers were unwilling to be obedient to him [Moses], but repudiated him." The offense of the people was in turning away from Moses; God then turned away from them (7:42). This recalls Spilsbury's assessment of the evidence from Josephus, that the key to right standing with God is right standing with Moses. In all these texts, from Acts and from Josephus, Moses is depicted as the leader of something like the Jewish "church," who deserves loyalty from his followers.

---

[213] "It is astonishing that Josephus should choose this particular section of the biblical narrative to make a point about Moses' authority," Spilsbury, *The Image of the Jew in Flavius Josephus' Paraphrase of the Bible*, 133; see 133-34.

[214] Ibid., 134(-35).

[215] So here on the latter point , Spilsbury, ibid., 135.

[216] Acts 7:35 was considered above, pp. 113-18.

Barrett argues that the perfect ἀπεστάλκεν of Acts 7:35 expresses the
thought that Moses continued to be a ruler and redeemer for his people.[217]
This idea recalls Philo's way of characterizing the ministry of Moses, which
often seems to imply that his rule still goes on. For example, *Spec. Leg.*
4.66, by using the present tense of the verb προστατέω, implies that Moses presides over his people through his instruction even now. This recalls
the "spiritual" quality ascribed to Moses in some quarters, which was examined in Chapter Six in connection with the idea that Moses somehow
unifies his people in himself. Such conceptions, in connection with ideas of
Moses' divinity, would help explain how to leave Judaism could also be
conceptualized as to forsake, or to apostatize from, Moses.

7.8 Conclusion

Philo as a matter of course characterizes Jews as disciples of Moses. This
way of thinking survived in the Talmud, but John 9:28 provides an important non-Philonic, first-century instance of such a way of thinking about
Moses. The evidence for Jews viewing themselves as disciples of Moses is
not terribly strong, but in combination with other aspects of the figure of
Moses even isolated remarks, as in John 9:28, take on heightened significance.

In Acts 15:1 and 15:21 Moses again appears as a central focus of Judaism, being read and preached in synagogues, and having the central rite
of Jewish identity placed under his name. This ties in with the discoveries
of Chapter Five of this study about the authority Moses was thought to
wield. Acts 21:21 most clearly establishes Moses as the focus of Jewish
loyalty, by describing him as the one rebelled against by those who forsake
Judaism.

Perhaps the single most evocative NT text reviewed here was Acts 6:11,
where it appeared that Moses was also someone who could be blasphemed,
much as God could be blasphemed. This turned attention to other texts
which place Moses in a similar position, either by suggesting that he could
be blasphemed, or by suggesting that he was like God, or both. The implicit demand of Acts 6:11 of due reverence for Moses harmonizes not only
with Josephus' descriptions of the harsh punishments that awaited those
(Essenes) who did not render it, but also with the extensive ascriptions of
divine status to Moses from a variety of Jewish circles, including Philo and
Alexandrian sources, Qumran, and the Rabbis.

The notion of faith in Moses, or of Moses as someone to be believed in,
is relatively well attested, starting as it does from explicit biblical state-

---

[217] Barrett, *Commentary on the Acts of the Apostles*, vol. 1, 364.

ments, and surviving in a variety of traditions before and after the first century. The remarks in John 5:45-47 about belief in, and hope in, Moses fit well into this pattern and recall the contemporary evidence in Josephus that Moses could be thought of as a coordinate focus of trust, along with God. In the John passage, Jewish faith in Moses is paralleled with Christian faith in Jesus. Thus, Jews believed in Moses, hoped in Moses, and submitted to Moses.

The sheer scale of the accumulation of offices and functions to Moses noticed in this study, references to Moses as (some kind of) a divine or angelic figure, the ascription to Moses of disciples, comprising either all Jews or especially devout groups of them, and the description of Moses as an effective overseer and personal authority over the Jews, all seem to work together to establish Moses as a personal focus for Jewish allegiance, an allegiance which is deemed to be broken by apostates from Judaism.

The murals in the synagogue at Dura may have fostered such feeling among congregants there, as well as visually representing teaching along those lines; the iconic portraits of Moses which dominate the front wall of the synagogue recall the description of a synagogue service in Acts 5:21 as a time when Moses was preached, while their position on either side of the Torah niche recalls Bultmann's suggestion (commenting on 2 Cor. 3:14) about "die Verlesung der παλαιὰ διαθήκη ... nämlich im Synagogen-gottesdienst, in dem Mose ja immer präsent ist."[218] The ascription to Moses of the title "god," which apparently took place in more than one Jewish setting, and which could always find support in Exod. 4:16 and 7:1 would naturally qualify Moses as a suitable focus for such loyalty.

At least some of the NT writers either knew Jewish communities where Moses took on such a role, or came from one themselves. In fact, the NT writings provide some of the clearest characterizations of the role of Moses as something like the head of the Jewish church. Such a description of Moses may even be viewed as the summation, or the final implication, of the material surveyed in this study.

---

[218] Rudolf Bultmann, *Der zweite Brief an die Korinther*, ed. Erich Dinkler, Kritisch-exegetischer Kommentar über das Neue Testament, ed. Ferdinand Hahn (Göttingen: Vandenhoeck & Ruprecht, 1976), 89.

Chapter 8

Points of Contact with Christology

And they sang the song of Moses, the bondservant of God, and the song of the Lamb.
—Revelation 15:3

8.1 Introduction

At various points throughout the preceding chapters, this study has noted the at times remarkable congruence between aspects of the NT Moses and the NT Christ. This chapter will attempt to make a more coherent assessment of this congruence. In such a short space it will be impossible to answer all the questions which naturally arise from the appearance of these parallels. But if the various threads can be gathered together it may be possible at least to see the sorts of questions that need to be pursued in further research.

Toward this end, this chapter will probe the modern secondary literature most important for Moses Christology. This will set the stage for setting out the main connections suggested by this study between ancient conceptions of Moses and early conceptions of Christ.

8.2 Mosaic Christology in Modern Research

Most NT scholars concede the influence of Moses on the New Testament, particularly on NT Christology, at some level. The recognition is by no means universal, however, and some important christological studies skip Moses almost entirely.[1] Even recent studies by *P. Fredriksen* (1988), and *M. de Jonge* (1977, 1998), two scholars with special interest in the Jewish background to the New Testament, give no place to Moses.[2] If complete

---

[1] E.g., Frank J. Matera, *New Testament Christology* (Louisville, Kent.: Westminster John Knox Press, 1999).

[2] Paula Fredriksen, *From Jesus to Christ: The Origins of the New Testament Images of Jesus* (New Haven, Conn. and London: Yale University Press, 1988); Marinus de Jonge, *God's Final Envoy: Early Christology and Jesus' Own View of His Mission* (Grand Rapids and Cambridge: William B. Eerdmans, 1998); his *Jesus, Stranger from Heaven and Son of God: Jesus Christ and the Christians in Johannine Perspective*, ed.

silence implies anything, de Jonge (1998) finds nothing of Moses in "the earliest Christian response to Jesus."[3]

Early in the twentieth century, doing Christology by titles was in vogue. But even the fifty-five christological titles identified by *V. Taylor* (1953) fail to introduce Moses into discussion (not even under the heading, "Prophet; the Prophet").[4] In fact, among the drawbacks of doing Christology by titles is the near guarantee that Moses will slip through unnoticed.[5]

Early Christology is often studied as prophetic Christology. Ordinarily, however, prophetic Christology is built on the promise of a prophet like Moses in Deut. 18:15-19, so that the figure of Moses is automatically introduced into the equation.[6] While *O. Cullmann* (1957), however, considers Jesus as a prophetic Christ, he specifically *distances* his treatment of the Eschatological Prophet from a Mosaic figure in favor of an Elianic interpretation ("Vor allem aber wird die Rückkehr *Elias* erwartet"[7]).

F. C. Burkitt (1913) draws attention to the resemblance between Christian eschatological expectations in the Synoptic Gospels and those of the *Assumption of Moses*, and so finds a rather distant link between the Gospels and Moses traditions.[8] *C. F. Evans* (1955) thinks Luke in particular knew the pseudepigraphic work.[9] *P. M. Casey* (1991) mentions scattered parallels between Moses and Jesus, but suggests no important causal link

---

and trans. John E. Steely, Society of Biblical Literature Sources for Biblical Study, ed. Wayne A. Meeks, no. 11 (Missoula, Mont.: Scholars Press, 1977) interacts extensively with Meeks's work on the Mosaic prophet-king (e.g., 51-69), but minimizes Moses (e.g., 58).

[3] In its single reference to the promise of Deut. 18:15-18, Marinus De Jonge, *Christology in Context: The Earliest Christian Responses to Jesus* (Philadelphia: The Westminster Press, 1998), 106 steers the significance of the text away from a Mosaic figure.

[4] Vincent Taylor, *The Names of Jesus* (London: Macmillan and Co., 1953), 15.

[5] See the critique of title-oriented approaches by Darrell L. Bock, *Proclamation from Prophecy and Pattern: Lucan Old Testament Christology*, Journal for the Study of the New Testament Supplement Series, ed. David Hill, publishing ed. David E. Orton, vol. 12 (Sheffield: JSOT Press, 1987), 152.

[6] As granted by Oscar Cullmann, *The Christology of the New Testament*, 2d ed. (London: SCM Press, 1963), 37.

[7] Oscar Cullmann, *Die Christologie des Neuen Testaments* (Tübingen: J. C. B. Mohr [Paul Siebeck], 1957), 16. Cullmann stresses that the concept of prophet was an important part of Christology only briefly, with only the Fourth Gospel and the first (Jewish-Christian) part of Acts still maintaining prophetic Christology in the New Testament, and only the former being specially concerned to contrast Jesus with Moses, see idem., *The Christology of the New Testament*, 2d ed., 37-38, and below, pp 263-64.

[8] F. Crawford Burkitt, *Jewish and Christian Apocalypses*, The Schweich Lectures, 1913 (London: Oxford University Press, 1914), 40.

[9] C. F. Evans, "The Central Section of St. Luke's Gospel," *Studies in the Gospels: Essays in Memory of R. H. Lightfoot*, ed. D. E. Nineham (Oxford: Basil Blackwell, 1955), 39-42.

and develops no christological implications of the Moses figure.[10] In support of his argument that angelic categories were an important resource in the formation of early Christology,[11] C. H. T. *Fletcher-Louis* (1997) suggests (the angelomorphic) Moses as one of several prototypes for angelomorphic Christology.[12] These and many other christological studies postulate the influence of the figure or the narrative of Moses in only the most general way.

Sometimes the influence of Moses is descried in the broad background of a given NT presentation of Jesus. *W. D. Davies* (1964) searches the Gospel of Matthew for a New Exodus, or a New Moses (he regards the two as interchangeable).[13]   Davies's conclusions regarding Moses in Matthew are very restrained: "Matthew has been shown to reveal the influence of the New Exodus and New Moses motif, but this has not been allowed to dictate his presentation of the Gospel to any serious degree."[14]

C. F. Evans (1955), referred to above, suggests that the central section of the Gospel of Luke is designed to read as a second Deuteronomy.[15] This would suggest attendant characterization of Jesus as a second Moses, but Evans's thesis, somewhat like Davies's, is based only on parallel narratives, on "resemblances of subject matter and wording" between the Gospel and the Pentateuch.[16] The only specific function of Moses that Evans mentions in passing is his prophetic office.[17]

E. L. Allen (1956), something of a pioneer among modern scholars in this regard, suggests more specific and greater influence by the figure of Moses. He detects in many NT texts signs of early Moses Christologies, which suggests that the first Christians explicitly drew on Moses traditions

---

[10] P. M. Casey, *From Jewish Prophet to Gentile God: The Origins and Development of New Testament Christology* (Cambridge: James Clarke & Co.; Louisville, Kent.: Westminster/John Knox Press, 1991), 81-82, 83.

[11] Crispin H. T. Fletcher-Louis, *Luke-Acts: Angels, Christology and Soteriology*, WUNT, 2d series, ed. Martin Hengel and Otfried Hofius, vol. 94 (Tübingen: J. C. B. Mohr [Paul Siebeck], 1997), 251. Nils Alstrup Dahl, *Jesus the Christ: The Historical Origins of Christological Doctrine*, ed. Donald H. Juel (Minneapolis: Fortress Press, 1991), 120 vigorously supports this approach.

[12] Fletcher-Louis, *Luke-Acts: Angels, Christology and Soteriology*, 173-83, see also 47-48 on the deification of Moses, and in this study, pp. 229-37, 243-45. Fletcher-Louis bases his angelomorphic Moses in large part on material also surveyed in this study.

[13] W. D. Davies, *The Setting of the Sermon on the Mount* (Cambridge: The University Press, 1964).

[14] Ibid., 106-107.

[15] Evans, "The Central Section of St. Luke's Gospel," 37-53. esp. 42(-51).

[16] Ibid., 50. See the critique by Josef M. Kastner, "Moses im Neuen Testament" (Th.D. diss., Ludwig-Maximilians-Universität Munich, 1967), 176-77.

[17] Evans, "The Central Section of St. Luke's Gospel," 51.

for describing Christ. Allen believes, however, that even in the apostolic period Moses Christology was already going into eclipse behind other sorts of christological thought.[18]

Allen claims to identify two main sorts of Moses Christology, "Servant-Christology" and Mosaic "Prophet-Christology." On closer inspection, though, his is a distinction without a difference. All Moses Christology for Allen is really just prophet Christology. Here Allen may reflect the tendency among NT scholars, noted in the Introduction to this study, to view Moses simply as a prophet. Despite partaking in this common attenuation of the Mosaic motif, Allen can be credited with having pointed to specific instances of the influence of the figure of Moses on Christology across the breadth of the New Testament, and so to having led the way for other scholars to pay greater attention to such influence.

Many writers echo Allen's observation about an early Mosaic Christology behind one portion or another of the New Testament. *F. Hahn* (1963) agrees:

Die Vorstellung von Jesus als dem neuen Mose hat ... im Neuen Testament vielfältige Spuren hinterlassen. Zwar kommt ihr in den meisten Zusammenhängen nur eine untergeordnete Stellung zu, aber es legt sich der Schluß nahe, daß es eine alte, ehemals dominierende Anschauung gewesen sein muß.[19]

Hahn, however, like Allen, thinks of this as strictly a prophetic Christology.[20]

J. Mánek's thesis (1957) on Luke's Christology is that, "For Luke it is very important to construct a positive relation between Moses and Jesus."[21] In fact, "In Luke's conception Jesus is obviously and purposely the new Moses."[22] In a stimulating departure from the usual, the positive relation between the two figures consists in leadership of their people: "Moses is the leader of the Exodus — Jesus is the leader of the Exodus.

---

[18] E. L. Allen, "Jesus and Moses in the New Testament," *The Expository Times* 67 (1955-1956): 104-106.

[19] Ferdinand Hahn, *Christologische Hoheitstitel: Ihre Geschichte im frühen Christentum*, Forschungen zur Religion und Literatur des Alten und Neuen Testamentes, ed. Ernst Käsemann and Ernst Würthwein, no. 83 (Göttingen: Vandenhoeck & Ruprecht, 1963), 404, "The conception of Jesus as the new Moses ... has left behind it manifold traces in the New Testament. Though indeed, in most contexts, its role is only minor, the conclusion is easily drawn that it is an old view, which at an earlier stage dominated the scene."

[20] See Ferdinand Hahn, *The Titles of Jesus in Christology: Their History in Early Christianity*, trans. Harold Knight and George Ogg, Lutterworth Library, ed. James Barr, et al. (London: Lutterworth Press, 1969), 372-88.

[21] Jindřich Mánek, "The New Exodus in the Books of Luke," *Novum Testamentum* 2 (1957): 20.

[22] Ibid., 21.

That which Moses and Jesus have in common Luke expresses with the verb, '*exagó*.'"[23] Mánek, however, with so many others, strives mainly to parallel the narratives of Moses and Jesus,[24] and does not tease out specific functions of Moses and Jesus in the leadership of their respective "Exoduses," and, despite his intriguing proposal about leadership, Mánek seems partial to the usual prophetic Moses motif.[25]

J. Dunn (1989) is another who accepts an early prophetic Christology. He grants that Jesus was indeed believed in as the prophet like Moses, but finds in the ascription simply a recognition of Jesus' especially rich endowment with the Spirit:[26] Jesus is the prophet like Moses because he is greatly inspired, not because he is like Moses.[27]

Dunn's dichotomy is problematic in light of the findings in the second chapter of this study; the paradigmatic nature of the prophethood of Moses seen there suggests how easily an exceptional prophet would recall the archprophet Moses. On that basis, the rich endowment with God's Spirit that Jesus was held to have would seem likely, even necessarily, to call up at least comparison with Moses. Further, while Moses' endowment with prophetic spirit was indeed legendary, it is unlikely that in the first century this was all that the title "prophet like Moses" was thought to entail, as others have recognized (see below).[28]

Nevertheless, most of those who accept a NT "Moses Christology" connected with the concept of the Eschatological Prophet grant no further significance to the Moses paradigm. *Hahn* (1963), for example, already mentioned above, discusses Jesus as the New Moses entirely within the scheme of the Eschatological Prophet (which he sees as a fully Mosaic figure).[29] *R. N. Longenecker* (1970) brings the term "Mosaic Messiah" into discussion of messianism, but for him this potentially royal term still refers only to an expected prophet,[30] and, in Christology, to the Jewish-Christian con-

---

[23] Ibid., 20 and 10; Luke 9:31 specifies that in the Transfiguration Moses and Elijah spoke with Jesus about the ἔξοδος which he would accomplish.

[24] E.g., ibid., 15-20, 22.

[25] E.g., ibid., 9, 14.

[26] James D. G. Dunn, *Christology in the Making: A New Testament Inquiry into the Origins of the Doctrine of the Incarnation*, 2d ed. (London: SCM Press, 1989), 138-41.

[27] Echoed by M.-É. Boismard, *Moses or Jesus: An Essay in Johannine Christology*, trans. B. T. Viviano, Bibliotheca Ephemeridum Theologicarum Lovaniensum LXXXIV-A (Louvain: Leuven University Press, 1993), 39-40. Dunn minimizes the importance of Moses in Christology generally.

[28] See also above, pp. 89-90; John 6:14.

[29] Hahn, *The Titles of Jesus in Christology: Their History in Early Christianity*, 190.

[30] Richard N. Longenecker, *The Christology of Early Jewish Christianity*, Studies in Biblical Theology, 2d series, ed. C. F. D. Moule, et al., no. 17 (London: SCM Press, 1970), 33-34.

sciousness that Jesus was that Mosaic prophet.[31] The Moses typology *R. Schnackenburg* (1993) finds in the Gospels (and Acts) also deals exclusively with the notion of Jesus as the prophet like Moses.[32]

G. Vermes (1973) considers Moses to have been one of the chief prototypes for the Messiah in the days of the first Christians, but for him Moses represents only a prophetic ideal, and he sees a connection between Christology and Moses only in this respect; moreover, prophetic Christology is not uniquely Mosaic, since in Vermes's view it is also indebted to Elijah.[33] Likewise, among the "Messianic prototypes" identified by *N. A. Dahl* (1992; kings, high priests, and prophets) Moses plays a strictly prophetic part — and he isn't even the sole type, again being supplemented by prophetic successors like Joshua and Elijah.[34]

Most christological discussion seems to have been little affected by *H. M. Teeple*'s summary (1957) of the first century A.D. portrait of Moses. He makes, as noted in the Introduction to this study, a particularly strong attempt, since he recognizes the ruling, lawgiving, and priestly functions of Moses in Jewish lore, as well as his prophetic role.[35] Moreover, he connects the ruling and the lawgiving of Moses with the expected messianic functions of the Eschatological Prophet as prophet-king and prophet-lawgiver.[36]

Teeple, however, does not put the whole package together, and link Moses himself with Christology. Discussion of Christology in his work is limited mainly to showing how writers in the Gospels and Acts (and later Christian literature) wove narratival allusions to Moses into the stories of Jesus.[37] His discussion of Christology, somewhat paradoxically, includes no NT portrayals of Jesus as a prophet (which in his judgment is the paramount feature of Moses).

In a manner somewhat reminiscent of Cullmann, Teeple claims that Jesus viewed himself as an Eschatological Prophet but not as a Mosaic Pro-

---

[31] Ibid., 35-37.

[32] Rudolf Schnackenburg, *Jesus in the Gospels: A Biblical Christology*, trans. O. C. Dean, Jr. (Louisville, Kent.: Westminster John Knox Press, 1995), 13.

[33] Geza Vermes, *Jesus the Jew: A Historian's Reading of the Gospels* (London: William Collins Sons & Co., 1973), 94-98. He speculates, 98, that the description of Jesus as a "prophet (like Moses)" only lost favor owing to "a plethora in Palestine of pseudo-prophets" contemporaneous with the formation of primitive Christian thought.

[34] Nils Alstrup Dahl, "Messianic Ideas and the Crucifixion of Jesus," revised by D. H. Juel, in *The Messiah: Developments in Earliest Judaism and Christianity*, ed. James H. Charlesworth (Minneapolis: Fortress Press, 1992), 400-401.

[35] But see critique above, pp. 12-13.

[36] Howard M. Teeple, *The Mosaic Eschatological Prophet*, Journal of Biblical Literature Monograph Series, vol. 10 (Philadelphia: Society of Biblical Literature, 1957), 102-110, 110-15.

[37] Ibid., 100.

phet. Teeple maintains the distinction between a Mosaic figure and an eschatological Prophet figure from the thought of Jesus himself right down into early Christology, which he says was strongly influenced by expectations of an eschatological Prophet, but only weakly by the figure of Moses.[38] In sum, he rejects the idea of an early portrait of Christ meaningfully influenced by the figure of Moses.

R. H. Fuller (1965), perhaps picking up the trail of Moses where Teeple left it, believes not only that Jesus saw himself as an eschatological prophet[39] but also urges that both the earliest Church and Jesus himself interpreted Jesus' earthly ministry explicitly in terms of the Mosaic Servant-Prophet.[40]

Fuller judges that in Jewish thought of the first century the final Mosaic prophet was already sinking to the status of a mere forerunner, as at Qumran, or being subsumed into the Davidic Messiah, as in the rabbinic literature and most NT Christology.[41] This implies that any Mosaic Christology must have arisen early, probably with Jesus himself. And Fuller believes this is "precisely what Jesus had implied about himself throughout his ministry."[42]

In distinction to some others, Fuller completely identifies prophet Christology with Moses Christology. In his treatment evidence for one is evidence for the other. Fuller's analysis however, like many others, stops with the prophetic roles of Christ and Moses though Fuller, like Teeple, hints that the prophetic role may involve both rule and redemption.[43]

The Th.D. dissertation of *J. Kastner*, "Moses im Neuen Testament" (1967), was reviewed in the Introduction to the present study.[44] As noted there, in the portion of his study devoted to the New Testament Kastner

---

[38] Ibid., 115-21.

[39] Reginald H. Fuller, *The Foundations of New Testament Christology*, Lutterworth Library, ed. James Barr, et al. (London: Lutterworth Press, 1965), 125-131, 167.

[40] Ibid., 47, 119, 125, 128-30, esp. 167-69. Fuller, 167-73 judges the Mosaic Servant and Mosaic Prophet concepts to have been joined in earliest Palestinian Christology, as shown for example by the combination of Deut. 18:15-19 with Isa. 52:13 and 53:11 in Acts 3:12-26; see too Bock, *Proclamation from Prophecy and Pattern*, 115-116, and on Acts 3, 197. This expansion of Moses typology to include "servant" greatly broadens the number of potential allusions to Moses to be detected in the New Testament. This is expanded still further through the argument that often where the Gospels describe Jesus as "son," υἱός, the earlier Palestinian tradition had described him as "servant," עֶבֶד, Fuller, 170.

[41] Ibid., 47.

[42] Fuller, *The Foundations of New Testament Christology*, 173.

[43] Ibid., 168-69.

[44] Josef M. Kastner, "Moses im Neuen Testament" (Th.D. diss., Ludwig-Maximilians-Universität Munich, 1967). See above, pp. 18-20.

explores the use of Moses motifs in the NT presentation of Christ. His concern throughout is with typology.

Accordingly, the typical thrust of his attack in the Synoptic Gospels (and later also in John and Hebrews) is the "Parallelisierung der Jesusgeschichte mit der Mosesüberlieferung,"[45] as unfolded in Part One of his study. Examples include his investigations of the portrayal of John the Baptist, the Temptation narratives, the call of the disciples, and the several feeding narratives.[46]

In the Synoptic Gospels, Kastner is concerned to show how Jesus was presented as a New Moses (again, through the Evangelists' use of typological allusions to the career of Moses).[47] Kastner devotes special sections to Matthew with this aim,[48] and to Luke,[49] with a view to unearthing Moses typology that draws on the narrative of Moses in biblical tradition and elsewhere. Along the way, Kastner makes special contributions to understanding how Matthew and Luke have strengthened the Mosaic elements in the Temptation narrative,[50] and to understanding the significance of the appearance of Moses in the Transfiguration.[51]

In his separate treatment of the book of Acts Kastner provides detailed exegesis of the portion of Stephen's speech dealing with Moses, tying it in with legendary lore from Second Temple Jewish literature and from rabbinic *haggadoth*, and highlighting Moses typology relevant to Luke's Christology.[52] In this section, Kastner particularly highlights the Lukan portrayal of Jesus as a prophet like Moses.

In the Fourth Gospel, as was just mentioned, Kastner is chiefly concerned with using the Moses lore discussed in Part One of his book to explore Moses typology in the Johannine presentation of Jesus. This typology is again mainly derived from the narrative of the career of Moses, in both its biblical and its hagiographical forms.

Kastner explores the Pauline literature with a view mainly to how Paul employs Moses as a reference point in salvation history and as a source of typology for Christ and the Christian community.[53] In Hebrews also, Kastner examines the way Moses serves as the model for description of Christ and the community.[54] Kastner finds that Hebrews presents Moses almost

---

[45] Ibid., 112. Cf. 140-43, and *passim*.
[46] Ibid., 109, 110-14, 114-16, 116-18.
[47] Ibid., 112.
[48] Ibid., 143-71.
[49] Ibid., 172-79.
[50] Ibid., 112-14.
[51] Ibid., 118-30.
[52] Ibid., 203-220.
[53] E.g., ibid., 200-201.
[54] Ibid., 262-63.

exclusively as a glorious mediator, for the sake of proclaiming the even more glorious mediator, Jesus.[55]

Given his wide-ranging investigation of the Second Temple Jewish portrait of Moses, Kastner's Moses Christology is surprisingly narrow. His focus is precisely on "Die Vorstellung von Jesus als der Erfüllung des weissagenden Mosestypos."[56] For Kastner the New Testament authors handle and depict Moses almost exclusively as a mediator.[57] No matter how highly Kastner may appraise a NT writer's esteem for Moses, the role of Moses remains firmly prophetic, and Moses Christology is prophet Christology.

In what at first appears a move toward a bolder synthesis, *M.-É. Boismard* (1993) argues that in the Fourth Gospel the titles "the Prophet" and "the Christ" have become very closely related terms.[58] But rather than finding in them a unified reflection of Moses, Boismard connects the Christ motif of John's Christology with Samaritan-influenced allusions to Joseph [*sic!*] as king.[59] Like many scholars of the Synoptic Gospels, Boismard finds Jesus in the Fourth Gospel linked to Moses mainly through narrative parallels, specifically: 1) Jesus is God's emissary;[60] 2) Jesus speaks with God's words;[61] 3) Jesus authenticates his work with (three) signs;[62] 4) the words of Jesus set before his hearers a choice for life or death.[63] Boismard pays scant attention to the functions of Moses (or of Jesus), however, focusing instead on narratival allusion. Moreover, with kingship assigned to

---

[55] Ibid., 240-41, 243 ("Der Autor 'braucht' die relativ hohe Würde des Moses"), 247-56, 266-67.

[56] Ibid., 308. See above, pp. 19-20.

[57] E.g., as in Hebrews, noted above. In John, Moses is Mittler des Gesetzes (271, 287).

[58] The nature of this relationship does not seem to be made particularly clear, to judge by the variety of incompatible expressions for it which appear (at any rate, in this translation): M.-É. Boismard, *Moses or Jesus: An Essay in Johannine Christology*, trans. B. T. Viviano, Bibliotheca Ephemeridum Theologicarum Lovaniensum LXXXIV-A (Louvain: Leuven University Press, 1993), 8: "equivalent"; 29-30: "parallel," "link"; 32-33: "blended."

[59] Boismard, *Moses or Jesus: An Essay in Johannine Christology*, 32-38.

[60] Ibid., 59-61.

[61] Ibid., 61-62.

[62] Ibid., 55-58, 62-65; as noted earlier in this study (pp. 56-62), authentication through the working of signs is a common prophetic motif in the first century, see esp. Rebecca Gray, *Prophetic Figures in Late Second Temple Jewish Palestine: The Evidence from Josephus* (New York and Oxford: Oxford University Press, 1993), 123-33. Boismard, 58 proposes that only the first three of John's signs are numbered in reference to the three signs done by Moses in Exod. 3:1-9.

[63] Boismard, *Moses or Jesus: An Essay in Johannine Christology*, 65-66. The parallel is upset to an extent, through Boismard's observation (93, 98) that in John 1:1-17 while Moses is the transmitter of what God told him, Jesus is God himself.

a Joseph tradition, Moses is once again portrayed as a prophet, and Mosaic Christology is essentially prophet Christology.

All of these treatments, even Teeple's wide-ranging study, allow only for a prophetic Christology in connection with Moses, and sometimes that connection is quite remote. Some scholars, however, have taken discussion of the figure of Moses beyond the usual prophetic paradigm and the Christology connected with that figure has moved forward as well.

D. Allison's *The New Moses* (1993) illuminates aspects of Moses' portrait beyond prophethood, such as kingship and deliverance. Allison's treatment resembles that of many of his predecessors in that it discovers NT Mosaic typology primarily in narratival allusions to Moses (in Matthew's Gospel). Like Teeple, Allison seems content to argue simply that Moses typology *exists*; i.e., the significance of that typology is not drawn out. Thus he devotes just two pages to Matthean Christology, within which he discusses a very broad range of contact between the narratives of Moses and Jesus without going into any depth concerning the significance of that contact. He writes:

Both Moses and Jesus were many things, and they occupied several common offices. Moses was the paradigmatic prophet-king, the Messiah's model, a worker of miracles, the giver of Torah, the mediator for Israel, and a suffering servant. And Jesus was similarly a suffering servant, the mediator for Israel, the giver of Torah, a worker of miracles, the Mosaic Messiah, and the eschatological prophet-king.[64]

Even after such a promising set of recognitions, Allison argues only that Matthew correlates the Messiah to Moses mostly in order to make Jesus, like Moses, the full bearer of God's authority — which is the prophetic motif once more.[65] Allison's study, while rich in narrative parallels between Moses and Jesus in Matthew, does not go on to suggest the broad Mosaic basis for early Christology that those narrative parallels might be taken to imply.

D. Bock (1987) finds Luke-Acts presenting Christ under two schemes: Messiah, for Bock a distinctly Davidic title,[66] and Servant,[67] which also turns out to be Davidic.[68] According to Bock, the christological key to

---

[64] Dale C. Allison, Jr., *The New Moses: A Matthean Typology* (Edinburgh: T. & T. Clark, 1993), 275.

[65] Ibid., 277.

[66] Darrell L. Bock, *Proclamation from Prophecy and Pattern: Lucan Old Testament Christology*, Journal for the Study of the New Testament Supplement Series, ed. David Hill, publishing ed. David E. Orton, vol. 12 (Sheffield: JSOT Press, 1987), 55, 61-74, 119, but esp. 81, 88-89, and 148.

[67] Ibid., 82, 87.

[68] Ibid., 203, 207, 209.

Luke is his presentation of Jesus as the combined Servant-Messiah.[69] Though Bock notes Lukan allusions to prophet Christology, such as the performance of signs and the proclamation and effecting of deliverance,[70] in the Gospel especially the fused Davidic Servant-Messiah theme is dominant.[71]

Despite his insistence that, for Luke, "Jesus is the Davidic Messiah,"[72] Bock finds in Luke's Gospel the ideas of a new Exodus and of the prophet like Moses.[73] It is in Acts, however, that Moses Christology comes to real prominence in Bock's assessment, particularly in Acts 3:22-23 and 7:35-38, where the prophethood of Moses is emphasized. In his recognition of Mosaic Prophet Christology in these Acts passages Bock has plenty of company, but he differs from other scholars in his handling of it because he continues to hew to the Servant-Messiah motif he takes as the key to Luke's Christology overall. Thus, where other writers make the category of "prophet" so vague and flexible that it can embrace anything a NT writer may be supposed to have made of Moses, Bock calls up the remembrance that Moses specifically "functioned *both* as a national leader *and* as a prophet," that is, as a Messiah and a Servant, to explain the christological function of Moses in Acts 3 and 7.[74]

Bock observes of Deut. 18:15-19 in Acts 3:22 that "it is the combination of ruler-prophet that distinguishes the prophet *like Moses* from other prophets."[75] He then goes on to expand the Mosaic ambit further to include "prophet-lawgiver,"[76] and — tellingly — observes how closely the resulting composite Mosaic image resembles the image of the Davidic Servant-Messiah he detects in Luke's Gospel.[77] Bock does not go so far as to inquire how far this Mosaic image is capable of carrying the burden of his Davidic Servant-Messiah construct, but his own conclusions suggest that it would be worth looking into.

In Acts 7, as in Acts 3, Bock again finds the functions of Moses as national leader and as prophet both to be crucial. Thus, in Acts 7:35-38

---

[69] Ibid., 7-9, also 87, 88-89, 104-105, 110, 115, 138. Bock, 151 specifically identifies "the determination that Messiah-Servant is the fundamental Lucan christological category" as "a major contribution" of his study.

[70] Ibid., 143.

[71] Ibid., 148.

[72] Ibid., 93.

[73] Ibid., 114-15.

[74] Ibid., 193.

[75] Ibid., 193, "The belief in the prophet like Moses who was a prophet-king was widespread in Judaism, especially alongside the expectation that the messianic times would parallel the Mosaic times. It was combined with a view of him as prophet-lawgiver."

[76] Ibid., 193.

[77] Ibid., 194, i.e., the "regal Messiah."

Moses is a doer of signs, a giver of living oracles, a bringer of a decisive revelation from God, and a deliverer.

Bock's Mosaic Christology, by contrast with that of other NT scholars, is correspondingly full:

> What makes Jesus a prophet *like Moses* is that he combines *all* these elements [doing of signs, giving living oracles, bringing a new and decisive revelation from God, working deliverance] into *one* person as Moses did. ... Jesus is proclaimed from prophecy and pattern to be the prophet like Moses, a prophetic figure who delivers the nation like a king would.[78]

Bock finds in Luke-Acts a quite substantial Moses Christology based on a Moses who resembles in breadth the one discovered by the present study.

Bock's NT work is confined to Luke-Acts, however, and in his discussion of Moses, though not of Christ, "prophet" remains the ruling category, despite some promising insights into how the prophet idea may be inflected by ruling and lawgiving. Additionally, even within Luke-Acts Moses is depicted in ways that are not taken into account in Bock's presentation, suggesting that Bock himself might have taken his Moses Christology a bit further.

Nonetheless it is obvious that Bock's work represents a tremendous advance on most other investigations of Moses Christology in the New Testament. This is so because Bock has a deeper appreciation of the stature of Moses in the first century than many NT scholars do, and because he worked in a NT corpus so noted for its emphasis on Moses that even Bock's commitment to Davidic Christology must take Moses into account.

The most important contribution to the elucidation of Mosaic christological thought remains the work of *W. Meeks*.[79] As already highlighted in the Introduction to the present study, his *The Prophet-King* (1967) concluded that:

> the Johannine traditions were shaped, at least in part, by interaction between a Christian community and a hostile Jewish community whose piety accorded very great importance to Moses and the Sinai theophany.[80]

He further concludes:

> It has been demonstrated to a high degree of probability that the depiction of Jesus as prophet and king in the Fourth Gospel owes much to traditions which the church inherited from the Moses piety.[81]

---

[78] Ibid. 221.

[79] Wayne A. Meeks, *The Prophet-King: Moses Traditions and the Johannine Christology*, Supplements to *Novum Testamentum*, ed. W. C. van Unnik, et al., vol. 14 (Leiden: E. J. Brill, 1967).

[80] Ibid., 318.

[81] Ibid., 318-19, see 1.

Meeks acknowledges a greater importance for Moses in Second Temple Judaism than many other writers, and he views this Moses as influential in early Christology. Meeks does not argue that the Fourth Evangelist sought to depict Jesus as a "New Moses." Rather, the Evangelist means for those familiar with the traditions about Moses to recognize that Jesus fulfills Moses' functions — for Meeks, prophet and king — in a superior and exclusive way.[82]

In some respects, Meeks's work could be characterized as the application to NT studies of the groundbreaking study of Philo by *E. R. Goodenough*, to whom Meeks acknowledges his debt.[83] Meeks specifically credits Goodenough with arguing for the existence of a Moses-centered piety in Judaism, a theory which Meeks's work corroborates by extending it beyond the Hellenized Diaspora Jews Goodenough tried to focus on to Palestinian, "normative" Judaism.[84] Goodenough ventured to say very little about Christianity, and certainly did not explore the ramifications of his "mystic Moses" ideas for Christology,[85] seeming to regard Christian thought as a parallel development to his Mystic Judaism.[86] In Christology, then, Meeks has taken Goodenough's ideas another definite step forward, though only in study of the Fourth Gospel.

8.3 Implications of This Study for New Testament Christology

Despite the important advances made in studies such as those of Teeple, Bock, Allison, and Meeks, it would appear that no NT Christology has adequately allowed for the likely impact of the figure of Moses on NT conceptions of Christ. This is so in part because no NT Christology has worked with a figure of Moses of the proper dimensions. The Jewish conception of Moses' relationship to Israel, which is likely to be of salient importance with regard to any Mosaic Christology, has been left largely unelucidated. Most treatments of Moses in NT Christology are in fact extremely attenuated, with those scholars who are interested in Moses at all generally attending only to the Pentateuchal narrative of Moses, and usually only the prophetic motif, while failing to take note of other elements of

---

[82] Ibid., 319.

[83] Ibid., 101, and 100-75 *passim*.

[84] Ibid., 287 n. 1, though see Erwin R. Goodenough, *By Light, Light: The Mystic Gospel of Hellenistic Judaism* (New Haven, Conn.: Yale University Press, 1935; reprint, Amsterdam: Philo Press, 1969), 265-77.

[85] Goodenough, *By Light, Light*, 9, but note 197, 234.

[86] Ibid., 2.

the Moses portrait in the Second Temple period, even those appearing in the New Testament itself.[87]

When then it is also argued, quite reasonably, that "prophet" was early on deemed inadequate to express what Christians wanted to say about Christ, Moses (as only a prophet) becomes irrelevant to the development of Christology, and can be left to one side.[88] Addressing this problematic situation has been one of the goals of this study.

8.4 Moses and Christ in the New Testament

In light of what has just been said, this section will consider some likely connections between the NT Moses and the NT Christ. This is not intended to be a comprehensive study, but the principal connections noticed in the foregoing chapters will be reviewed and some suggestions for further study will be offered.

8.4.1 Moses and Christ as Prophet

As seen in the review earlier in this chapter, this is the one Mosaic theme which receives regular attention in NT studies. Even frequent consideration is not necessarily thorough consideration, however, and the common recognition that Jesus was hailed as the "Prophet like Moses" is not often colored with the recognition of just how greatly the prophethood of Moses was esteemed.

All four Gospels agree that during his ministry at least some people thought of Jesus as a prophet (or as "The [Eschatological] Prophet"),[89] with Luke especially rich in this respect, and John not far behind. The characterization of Jesus as "a prophet mighty in deed and word" by some of his closer followers in Luke 24:19 recalls remarks by Jesus about himself in Luke 4:16-30 and 13:31-35, as well as the public judgments recor-

---

[87] Excepting the many scriptural and legendary details of Moses' life that NT writers may have taken up in an effort to create Moses typologies. Renée Bloch, "Quelques aspects de la figure de Moïse dans la tradition rabbinique," *Cahiers Sioniens* 8, nos. 2, 3, and 4 (*Moïse: L'homme de l'alliance*, 1954): 164-66, for example, observes the apparent efforts of Matthew to construct his infancy narrative in the spirit of the legends about the birth of Moses found in midrashic tradition. Such parallels between the stories of Moses and Jesus may point toward the general importance of Moses for Christology, but they do not shed much light on precisely how Moses was characterized and how that characterization impacted Christology.

[88] See a typical example of the process in James D. G. Dunn, *The Acts of the Apostles*, Epworth Commentaries, ed. Ivor H. Jones (Peterborough, England: Epworth Press, 1996), 47.

[89] Cullmann, *The Christology of the New Testament*, 36-37; Vermes, *Jesus the Jew*, 87-89.

ded in Luke 7:16, 39; 9:9, 18-19; and Acts 10:38-39.[90]   Despite their testimony regarding what people said about Jesus, it is not clear that all the Evangelists themselves favored the title "prophet" for him, though Luke must have, and John seems to have done so in some respect.[91]

While it is debatable whether the prophethood of Christ was necessarily seen in connection with the prophethood of Moses,[92] almost invariably the NT passages which speak of Moses as a prophet speak christologically of Jesus as well. Additionally, a text like Acts 3:22-23 would seem to insist that the prophethood of Jesus was connected precisely with the prophethood of Moses.   John 6:14 also, when exegeted along the lines laid out above in Chapter Four, makes the Mosaic quality of the prophethood ascribed to Jesus reasonably clear.[93]   In addition, the general preeminence of Moses over all other prophets marks him out as the prophetic archetype. Anyone seen as holding an eschatological prophetic office, which is without doubt how Christians saw the prophethood of Jesus, would be compared with Moses, and if found genuine would be likened to Moses.   The prophethood of Jesus in the New Testament thus appears both explicitly and implicitly to be a Mosaic prophethood (if also more than that).

8.4.2 Moses and Christ as Apostle and Priest

The priesthood of Jesus is a major NT theme, though only because the one book in which it appears is itself a major contributor to NT theology. Undoubtedly the major type in Hebrews for the priesthood of Jesus is Melchizedek, and yet when the theme of Jesus' high priesthood first appears the comparison is with Moses. The very dominance of the Melchizedekian and Aaronic priesthoods in the succeeding discussion highlights the appearance of Moses in Heb. 3:1-6, as if the discussion of priesthood could not properly begin without him. A great deal of the relationship between the priesthoods of Melchizedek and Aaron has been worked out, but what of the priesthood of Moses and the priesthood of Jesus? Has Jesus abolished the royal priesthood of Moses referred to in Heb. 3:1-6, or has he inherited and fulfilled it? More research is needed here.

The ideal of a Mosaic priest-king may be pertinent to other christological passages, such as Luke 20:42-43. Bock explains the priestly refe-

---

[90] Darrell L. Bock, *Luke*, vol. 2, *9:51-24:53*, Baker Exegetical Commentary on the New Testament, ed. Moisés Silva, vol. 3B (Grand Rapids: Baker Books, 1996), 1912.

[91] See Cullmann, *The Christology of the New Testament*, 37; Cullmann, 38 and Vermes, *Jesus the Jew*, 97 agree that the concept was not long an important part of Christology; Cullmann, 37 notes that the latter part of Acts and the NT epistles do not apply the concept of the Prophet to Jesus at all.

[92] E.g., the position of Cullmann above, p. 259.

[93] See p. 110-12. Recall also the attestation by signs and wonders, Luke. 24:19; Acts 2:22; 7:36.

rence that appears there, in the midst of royal imagery, by appeal to "the Jebusite ancestry of the Jerusalem kingship."[94] The royal priesthood of Moses may provide a more satisfactory explanation, particularly given the strong Mosaic flavor of Lukan Christology and the high appraisal of Moses evident in Luke-Acts.

The discovery that Moses was known as an apostle of God in a scattering of literature outside Hebrews, some of which (i.e., some Samaritan traditions) bears a strong resemblance to Heb. 3:1-6, suggests that Moses possessed unique qualifications to serve as the template for the apostolic, priestly, and royal Christology of that passage (neither Aaron nor Melchizedek is called an apostle in Hebrews). P. R. Jones, who urges that Hebrews actually has Moses in mind as the type for all of its Christology, calls for further investigation of the apostle Christology of Hebrews, and of the Gospel of John as well.[95] It would appear that a Mosaic christological scheme would accommodate apostle Christology well, and perhaps better than any other could do, since Second Temple period and later Jewish accounts of Moses so strongly characterize him as one who was sent or as an "apostle" outright.

8.4.3 Moses and Christ as King

In NT Christology before Meeks's work it had been customary to treat eschatological kingship as Davidic, without reference to the kingship of Moses.[96] Meeks observes, "New Testament scholarship has been almost unanimous: the King of Israel is assumed to be equivalent to *Messiah ben David*."[97] More than thirty years after Meeks wrote, his assessment still rings true, but the findings of this study can be added to those of others, especially including Meeks, in calling this view into question.

Certainly part of the problem is simply that scholars continue not to appreciate the kingliness of the figure of Moses in Second Temple Judaism,

---

[94] Bock, *Proclamation from Prophecy and Pattern*, 129.

[95] Peter Rhea Jones, "The Figure of Moses as a Heuristic Device for Understanding the Pastoral Intent of Hebrews," *Review and Expositor* 76 (1979): 105 n. 21.

[96] E.g., Fuller, see above, p. 264. Meeks by no means succeeded in overthrowing the old paradigm. Stefan Schreiber's *Gesalbter und König: Titel und Konzeptionen der königlichen Gesalbtenerwartung in frühjüdischen und urchristlichen Schriften*, Beihefte zur Zeitschrift für die neutestamentliche Wissenschaft und die Kunde der älteren Kirche, ed. Michael Wolter, vol. 105 (Berlin: Walter de Gruyter, 2000) (554 pages), a nearly exhaustive study of royal messianism in the period of interest here, even while emphasizing diversity in Jewish kingship conceptions gives almost no treatment to the subject of Moses as king or to royal Mosaic messianism (pp. 193, 195[Philo], 199, 269-74[Philo], 397-99, 402, and esp. 428). Cf. also Bock's Davidic Servant-Messiah, above, pp. 267-69.

[97] Meeks, *The Prophet-King*, 20, also 17, "It is commonly assumed that the term 'king' refers to the Messiah, the Son of David."

and consequently miss the royal potential of Mosaic Christology.[98]   An older example is Bultmann, who, purely on the grounds that Moses was not seen as a king, rejects the idea of a Mosaic prophet-king in John 6:14 (a passage that almost makes no sense without such an idea).[99]   The obtuseness of many students of the New Testament on this score is ironic given that the New Testament is apparently our best source on the subject of royal Mosaic messianism: faced elsewhere with "a near dearth of earlier materials" comparing Moses and the Messiah, Allison finds in the New Testament considerable evidence for Jewish expectation of an eschatological Mosaic king.[100]

In fact, as noted in Chapter Four, it was possible in the first century A.D. to think of Moses at the head of a long line of Israelite kings, which included David as successor to Moses.[101]   Through its greater antiquity, the Mosaic kingship could be thought more exalted than the Davidic.   In such a climate of thought, even pronounced Davidic messianism would be completely compatible with royal Mosaic messianism.   The two need not be seen as mutually exclusive.[102]

NT passages like the feeding narratives in John and Mark seem to present Jesus within a royal Mosaic Christology.   In Mark 6:34 (|| Matt. 9:36), the expression "sheep without a shepherd" recalls the appearance of the same expression in the ordination of Joshua as leader (Num. 27:17), while in John 6:14-15 the link with a royal Moses is expressed in the crowd's monarchist reaction to the "Prophet" Jesus and in the Mosaic theme of the discourse which follows.   Kingship appears always to have been fundamental to the Christian view of Jesus, and the (likely, as shown here) derivation of this feature at least partly from the kingship of Moses, which need not entail any concomitant diminishment of the importance of the

---

[98] Allison, *The New Moses*, 85-90 discusses the general problem of assessing a pre-rabbinic view of Messiah as a Mosaic figure.

[99] Rudolf Bultmann, *Das Evangelium des Johannes*, 11th ed. (2d ed. by Bultmann), Kritisch-exegetischer Kommentar über das Neue Testament, part 2, 11th ed. (Göttingen: Vandenhoeck & Ruprecht, 1950), 158 n. 2, "Schwerlich darf man unter dem 'Propheten' den wiederkehrenden Mose verstehen."

[100] Allison, *The New Moses*, 87. Jarl E. Fossum, *The Name of God and the Angel of the Lord: Samaritan and Jewish Concepts of Intermediation and the Origin of Gnosticism*, WUNT, ed. Martin Hengel and Otfried Hofius, no. 36 (Tübingen: J. C. B. Mohr [Paul Siebeck], 1985), 62-67 reviews the cases of Samaritan messianic pretenders who presented themselves as Mosaic figures. These of course would have nothing to do with Davidic pretensions.

[101] See above, pp. 86-87.

[102] Klaus Berger, "Die königlichen Messiastraditionen des Neuen Testaments," *New Testament Studies* 20 (1974): 22-28 notes the importance of the traditions about Moses as king for the messianic title "King of the Jews."

Davidic tradition, has yet to be taken consistently into account in christo-logical research.

8.4.4 Moses and Christ as Lawgiver

Chapter Five of this study showed the personal authority of Moses in the New Testament to make laws. The exercise of personal authority, espe-cially authority with respect to the Law, represents another convergence between the portraits of Jesus and Moses which, through underestimation of Moses, has not been properly investigated.

The analogy between the lawmaking of Moses and the lawmaking of Jesus is frequently adduced only at the level of literary criticism, in connec-tion with Moses typology, as is said to occur in the narrative setting of the Sermon on the Mount, or in the construction of the Gospel of Matthew, sometimes held to fall into a five-fold division analogous to the Pentateuch. While scholars have often attended to these and other narratival parallels between Moses and Jesus, the resemblance between the two figures in the actual exercise of authority has not been so well-explored,[103] in large part because until now the manner in which Moses is said to have exercised his authority has not been a central focus of study, particularly in the New Testament.[104]

Often in the same Gospel passages where Moses appears to have pos-sessed authority to adjust observance of the Law, Jesus is also shown to possess the same authority.[105] Elsewhere, Jesus appears to set forth alto-gether new laws, but this also turns out to be a feature of the authority of Moses. Scholars usually chalk up the astonishment that Jesus' lawbreak-ing/lawmaking behavior excites from his hearers to the wholly unpre-cedented nature of his actions, when in fact Jesus' activity in making and amending laws should be seen as precedented (solely) by Moses, and the astonishment of onlookers as a sign that Mosaic Christology is in play at some level. The wonder-struck marveling of the people is best explained as a reaction to Jesus' display of Moses-like authority, not merely shock at what would otherwise be mere audacity or impudence.

---

[103] Kastner, "Moses im Neuen Testament," 306, for example, misses this point be-cause, despite his overarching concern to show that the NT authors employ Moses as a glorious model for Christ (see e.g., 232, 240, 242-43), not an inglorious type, he holds that the authority of Jesus over the Law is something that distinguishes him from Mo-ses. In fact, the authority of Jesus over the Law is one of the most strikingly Mosaic motifs of early Christology.

[104] One small exception is T. F. Glasson, *Moses in the Fourth Gospel*, Studies in Biblical Theology, ed. C. F. D. Moule, et al., no. 40 (London: SCM Press, 1963), 77, who relates Deut. 33:3d-4a, "[Everyone] receives of thy words. Moses charged us with a law," to John 17:8, "Words I have given unto them ... they have received them."

[105] E.g., Mark 7:10-15 || Matt. 15:3-11; Mark 10:2-12 || Matt. 19:3-11.

Jews would obviously see Moses as someone who would champion the Law that he delivered, and yet in the New Testament he is said to have altered the Law (e.g. of marriage) as he saw fit, to accommodate arising exigencies. Jesus' standing as a "new Moses" helps explain the paradoxical way that he defends the Law, endorsing the most detailed observance of it while at the same time freely employing (Mosaic) authority both to make and to amend it.[106] Matthew implies that the authority of Jesus in this respect is greater even that that of those who sit in the seat of Moses.[107]

The Lawgiving element of Moses Christology persisted into the second century A.D. in the Christian comparison of the teaching activity of Jesus to the Mosaic Lawgiving. The view is not mentioned as such in the New Testament, but Christians in the second century certainly taught that Jesus had delivered a new Law, and early Christian sarcophagi feature the *traditio legis* motif, which depicts Jesus standing on a mountain (or being otherwise elevated) handing down the scroll of his heavenly "new Law" to Peter and Paul, who stand on either side.[108] Extant remains of this kind go back to the fourth century A.D.[109] but these relatively late artifacts carry forward older Jewish ideas of a two-fold accession to authority, and a two-fold witness to revelation, which happen frequently to be embedded in traditions about the succession to Moses.[110] The presence of these older ideals suggests a related Christian *traditio legis* tradition much older than the extant artifacts, dependent on similar ideas about Moses.

---

[106] See the examples in Helmut Merkel, "The Opposition between Jesus and Judaism," in *Jesus and the Politics of His Day*, ed. Ernst Bammel and C. F. D. Moule (Cambridge: Cambridge University Press, 1984), 138-42.

[107] Matt. 7:29; 23:2.

[108] Berger, "Die königlichen Messiastraditionen des Neuen Testaments," 104. The motif is pictorial, but the contents of the scroll are suggested by parallel literary motifs, see Berger, 109-112.

[109] Peter Franke, "Traditio Legis und Petrusprimat," *Vigiliae Christianae* 26 (1972): 270; William Horbury, "Old Testament Interpretation in the Writings of the Church Fathers," in *Mikra: Text, Translation, Reading and Interpretation of the Hebrew Bible in Ancient Judaism and Early Christianity*, ed. Martin Jan Mulder, Compendia Rerum Iudaicarum ad Novum Testamentum, ed. W. J. Burgers, H. Sysling, and P. J. Tomson, Section Two, The Literature of the Jewish People in the Period of the Second Temple and the Talmud, Volume 1 (Assen and Maastricht: Van Gorcum; Philadelphia: Fortress Press, 1988), 757.

[110] E.g., Moses, Eleazar and Joshua in *Ant.* 4.323-26; 1Q22(*1QWords of Moses*).11-12; cf. on other figures *Jub.* 31.21-23; Paral. Jer. 9:2p; see Berger, "Die königlichen Messiastraditionen des Neuen Testaments," 114-16, 117-18. For Christian analogues, see Berger, 116-18.

8.4.5 Baptism into Moses and Baptism into Christ

At present, the significance of Paul's reference to "baptism into Moses" remains an unsettled question, while the theory that it is a back-formation from Christian "baptism into Christ" remains comfortably dominant among scholars. That theory, however, derives in large part from presuppositions that this study shows to be precarious, if not unfounded, such as the assumption that Moses was not thought of in a way that would make sense of "baptism into Moses," or that Jewish proselyte baptism clearly postdates Christian baptism.

To the contrary, as Chapter Six of this study showed, it is far from clear that Jewish proselyte baptism postdated Christian baptism. Its institutionalization may be relatively late, but well before it came to be an officially recognized step in conversion, Jewish baptism of converts would have been practiced widely enough to be recognizable as the baptism of conversion to Judaism, and so be connected with Paul's "baptism into Moses."

Chapter Six also showed that Moses could quite easily be contemplated in a spiritual or semi-spiritual sense quite similar to that in which Christ came to be viewed. Baptism into Moses would therefore be comprehensible in the same way that baptism into Christ was, as entry into a relationship (however characterized) with a living person. This by itself does not demand that "baptism into Moses" was understood by Paul, or by anyone else, as describing an ontological reality, but it does indicate that "baptism into Moses" could be conceived as describing an ontological reality. There is no reason to assume that the one thing that "baptism into Moses" cannot describe is a relationship with a living Moses.

It appears that it may easily be the case that Jewish proselyte baptism, combined with a conception of the unifying figure of Moses, could have informed Paul's theology of baptism and of the unity of the church in Christ, rather than the (usually assumed) reverse. Christ himself may have come to be conceived of as spirit in a sense prepared for by a similar conception of Moses. Outside this study, apparently only Goodenough has proposed such a development. His proposal has been generally ignored, perhaps through his nearly total reliance on Philo; this study seeks to relieve that difficulty.

8.4.6 Moses and Jesus as Focuses of Loyalty

Most suggestive of all the motifs in this study is the placement of Moses at the center of the Jewish faith. It appears that Jews can have thought of their loyalty, hope, and faith being given in some fashion both to God and to Moses. The vitality of this idea in the first century, as witnessed by the New Testament and other sources, may suggest something of how the early Christians found the way to a settlement between their monotheism and their devotion to Christ. An analogue may appear in 1QpHab 8.2-3, which praises faith in the Teacher of Righteousness (ואמנתם במורה הצדק), a figure that Meeks urges bears many traits acquired from Moses traditions.[111]

The Church is certainly modeled (at least partly) on Israel. The concept of the people of God expressing loyalty to Christ, and in some sense being found in Christ and enjoying his presence when they meet together, finds a close parallel in the similar concept of the people of God living in loyalty to Moses, in some sense being baptized into Moses, and enjoying his presence when they meet as a community. It is remarkable that the body of literature that teaches the former also assumes the latter.

Observations like these raise questions about Jewish and Christian self-identify, and how Christians came to be divided from Jews. If Jews could frame their identity in terms of commitment to Moses, one wonders how Jewish a Jewish Christian could really feel himself to be. Does the Fourth Evangelist believe that the discipleship of Moses in John 9:28 only entails the discipleship of Jesus, or does he actually think that the two are mutually exclusive? If Jesus and Moses were seen in such similar terms, how early did loyalties to Jesus and to Moses come to be seen as competing, or even antithetical commitments? How might research into these questions, in the light of this study, modify our understanding of what constituted a Jew in the eyes of the ancient Judaism, or a Jewish-Christian in the eyes of the early Church or of Paul?

J. R. Davila asks, in his introduction to the volume he and others edit on the Jewish roots of christological monotheism:

How did the man Jesus come to be worshipped as a divine being by communities who nevertheless regarded themselves as monotheists? What were the historical and cultural factors that caused the worship of Jesus to make sense to some people in the first century C.E.?[112]

The volume he introduces is filled with learned essays on these and related questions, and the present study holds out no pretensions of having revolutionized the study of christological monotheism at a stroke. Nonetheless, it seems likely that Davila's questions can be at least partially addressed on ground prepared by this study, on the basis of attitudes toward Moses in the Judaism in which Christianity took root.

---

[111] Meeks, *The Prophet-King*, 169-70, 240.

[112] James R. Davila, "Of Methodology, Monotheism and Metatron: Introductory Reflections on Divine Mediators and the Origins of the Worship of Jesus," in *The Jewish Roots of Christological Monotheism: Papers from the St. Andrews Conference on the Historical Origin of the Worship of Jesus*, ed. Carey C. Newman, James R. Davila, and Gladys S. Lewis, Supplements to the *Journal for the Study of Judaism*, ed. John J. Collins with Florentino García Martínez, vol. 63 (Leiden: Brill, 1999), 3.

8.4.6 Conclusion

While early Christology need not have been exclusively Mosaic, no other figure in Jewish lore incorporated so fully the concepts which became important in NT Christology, and so gave precedent for coherently uniting diverse, and at times potentially baffling, christological attributes. First-century Christians clearly spoke about Jesus in the same way that, as Jews, they had been accustomed to speak about Moses.[113] This turns out to be true in so many key areas that it seems likely that the portrait of Moses provided Christians with a kind of norm for the claims they were prepared to make about Christ. As Christians sought to establish Jesus in the same pivotal position that Jews ascribed to Moses, they found in Moses a template for describing the kind of figure they believed Christ to be.

8.5 Jesus as a Mosaic Messiah

8.5.1 Implications of This Study

The survey of scholarship undertaken above demonstrates how commonly it has been noticed that NT Christology includes Moses Christology, and that Moses Christology must have been especially important for the Christology of the first Christians.

The same survey, however, demonstrates how assessment of early Christology has been handicapped both through certain stereotyped ways of evaluating the Jewish conception of Moses, and through the consequent persuasion that Moses Christology can adequately be summed up as prophet Christology. Mosaic Prophet Christology, as the result often becomes formulated, is then quickly deemed subordinate to the christological formulations that became most highly prized by the end of the first century A.D., which involve motifs such as Christ as king, and Christ as the focus of Christian allegiance and faith.

By contrast, the above survey of points of contact between the NT Moses and NT Christology indicates that Moses is actually a very plausible type of Christ in a number of key respects. Each individual instance is suggestive, but it is the aggregate which becomes compelling, as Bock also recognizes.[114] The impression left by so many overlaps between the NT Moses and the NT Christ is that Moses was a recognized proto-messianic

---

[113] Christian literature continued to preserve a correspondingly broad impression of Moses, as for example *Apost. Const.* 6.19, which calls him "Moses, lawgiver as well as high priest and prophet and king."

[114] Above, p. 269.

figure, while Jesus in turn was recognized among the first Christians as a Mosaic messiah.

This conclusion comports well with the ample evidence for Mosaic messianism current in the time of Christ and in the rest of the first century A.D. Already in the pre-Christian era the Exodus from Egypt was seen as a prototype for future redemption, and most scholars have supported the idea that a Jewish messianism incorporating Moses motifs went along with such a scheme.[115] Expectations of a "new Moses" seem to be attested in a broad cross-section of literature including the Qumran texts,[116] Jose-

---

[115] Miguel Pérez Fernández, *Tradiciones Mesiánicas en el Targum Palestinense: Estudios Exegéticos*, Institución San Jerónimo, no. 12 (Valencia and Jerusalem: Institución San Jerónimo para la Investigación Bíblica, in collaboration with the Instituto Español Bíblico y Arqueológico [Casa de Santiago] de Jerusalén, 1981), 192-207, and Geza Vermes, "La figure de Moïse au tournant des deux Testaments," *Cahiers Sioniens* 8, nos. 2, 3, and 4 (*Moïse: L'homme de l'alliance*, 1954): 78-85 trace Mosaic and Exodus motifs in Jewish messianic literature. See Bloch, "Quelques aspects de la figure de Moïse dans la tradition rabbinique," 127-38, 163 on Palestinian traditions about the sufferings of Moses and of the Messiah, on which see also Ernst Haenchen, *The Acts of the Apostles: A Commentary*, trans. Bernard Noble and Gerald Shinn, supervised by Hugh Anderson, rev. and updated by R. McL. Wilson (Oxford: Basil Blackwell, 1971), 282. Joachim Jeremias, "Μωυσῆς," in *Theological Dictionary of the New Testament*, ed. Gerhard Kittel, trans. and ed. Geoffrey W. Bromiley, vol. 4, *Λ-Ν* (Grand Rapids: Wm. B. Eerdmans, 1967), 857-64 assembles a mass of relevant material. On Mosaic messianism more generally, see Teeple, *The Mosaic Eschatological Prophet*, 43-58; Bloch, "Quelques aspects," 149-161; Hahn, *The Titles of Jesus in Christology*, 357-62; Vermes, *Jesus the Jew*, 97-98; Longenecker, *The Christology of Early Jewish Christianity*, 33; Pérez Fernández, *Tradiciones Mesiánicas*, 183-209; William Horbury, *Jewish Messianism and the Cult of Christ* (London: SCM Press, 1998), 31, and see above, pp. 198-99.

[116] Naphtali Wieder, "The 'Law-Interpreter' of the Sect of the Dead Sea Scrolls: The Second Moses," *Journal of Jewish Studies* 4, no. 4 (1953): 167-72 especially on the Teacher of Righteousness; on Wieder see, approvingly, Scott J. Hafemann, *Paul, Moses, and the History of Israel: The Letter/Spirit Contrast and the Argument from Scripture in 2 Corinthians 3*, WUNT, ed. Martin Hengel and Otfried Hofius, no. 81 (Tübingen: J. C. B. Mohr [Paul Siebeck], 1995), 67, and with a fuller critique and endorsement, Gert Jeremias, *Der Lehrer der Gerechtigkeit*, Studien zur Umwelt des Neuen Testaments, ed. Karl Georg Kuhn, vol. 2 (Göttingen: Vandenhoeck & Ruprecht, 1963), 273-75. Robert Banks, "The Eschatological Role of Law in Pre- and Post-Christian Jewish Thought," in *Reconciliation and Hope: New Testament Essays on Atonement and Eschatology presented to L. L. Morris on his 60th Birthday*, ed. Robert Banks (Exeter: Paternoster Press, 1974), 180 sees the Teacher of Righteousness of the Damascus Document not as a "second Moses," but as an Elianic "law-interpreter," apparently because Banks overlooks the stream of tradition which saw in Moses an interpreter and teacher of the Law.

phus,[117] Philo,[118] and the Targums and rabbinic literature.[119] The New Testament also attests such expectations, linked with views of Jesus as messiah.[120]

It is not being suggested here that Jewish messianic expectations were solely Mosaic; there were apparently a multiplicity of messianisms in ancient Judaism, and all of these coexisted and interacted in various ways in different groups and at different times. Mosaic and Davidic expectations, for example, would be entirely compatible with each other, and could even cohere in the same figure. The Mosaic strand of Jewish messianism, however, has not received the attention it appears to deserve. What is true of assessments of Jewish messianism also holds for early Christology.

N. A. Dahl correctly remarks, "The development of early Christology did not follow any single line, and the language used drew upon many and diverse sources."[121] Thus he rightly cautions against assumptions that any one figure (even a figure like Moses) accounts for all christological categories. Nonetheless, while early Christology may not have followed any

---

[117] *Ant.* 20.97 (Theudas).

[118] Although P. Borgen, "'There Shall Come Forth a Man': Reflections on Messianic Ideas in Philo," in *The Messiah: Developments in Earliest Judaism and Christianity*, ed. James H. Charlesworth (Minneapolis: Fortress Press, 1992) rejects the idea that Philo entertained notions of an eschatological "new Moses," he does find, 353, that for Philo "eschatology means the realization of the universal aspect of Moses' kingship." The coming messianic ruler is "an emperor who, on the basis of the exodus, will continue Moses' work and bring it to its complete fulfillment"; see further, 361.

[119] Pérez Fernández, *Tradiciones Mesiánicas en el Targum Palestinense*, 188-92, citing *Tg. Cant.* 4:5; 7:3; *Tg. Lam.* 2:2; *Cant. Rab.* 2.9.3; *Eccl. Rab.* 1.28, "The Second Redeemer is like the First Redeemer," etc.; cf. *Exod. Rab.* 1.26; *Ruth Rab.* 5.6. Moses appears in rabbinic haggadah as a returning figure, see Naphtali Wieder, *The Judean Scrolls and Karaism*, East and West Library (London: Horovitz Publishing Company, 1962), 8 n. 14, 46; Teeple, *The Mosaic Eschatological Prophet*, 41-48, shows that Moses as a character remains very much alive in rabbinic thought.

[120] Longenecker, *The Christology of Early Jewish Christianity*, 33. The links are not always recognized; e.g., Jesus' prophetic signs fit a Mosaic paradigm (see Luke 24:19; Acts 2:22; 7:36), and the feeding narratives are strongly laced with Mosaic messianic flavor (see above, pp. 107-113). The titles that Moses is given in Acts 7:35 seem to serve "as an echoing variation of the titles of Jesus" in Acts 3:15; 5:31 and Luke 24:21, Dunn, *The Acts of the Apostles*, 94; see Luke Timothy Johnson, *The Acts of the Apostles*, Sacra Pagina Series, ed. Daniel J. Harrington, vol. 5 (Collegeville, Minn.: The Liturgical Press, 1992), 129, and above pp. 113-18.

[121] Dahl, "Messianic Ideas and the Crucifixion of Jesus," 396. Similarly, W. D. Davies, "Jewish Sources of Matthew's Messianism," in *The Messiah: Developments in Earliest Judaism and Christianity*, ed. James H. Charlesworth (Minneapolis: Fortress Press, 1992), 506-507 cautions that the varied elements of Judaism which contribute to (Matthean) Christology (among which he includes a messianic "Greater Moses") are ultimately inseparable, being intermingled and expressed as an integrated whole, not a collection of discrete themes.

single line some lines were more important than others; among the types of Christ evidently recognized by Christians, Moses is qualitatively superior to others in at least two ways, each alluded to before but repeated here for emphasis.

First, perhaps the most important finding of this study for NT Christology is to have noticed how many diverse and important christological functions *appear together in one figure* in pre-Christian Judaism. While not every element of early Christology can be drawn from the NT Moses,[122] most of the major categories can. This represents a significant contribution to christological research, which usually draws various elements of Christology piecemeal from a number of antecedent figures without reference to any single figure which might have shown how they could all be united. Moses accomplishes this.

Second, figures like David, Melchizedek, or Elijah notwithstanding, among the types of Christ evidently recognized by Christians Moses stands out by the degree to which what are often regarded as special elements of Christology find counterparts in him. The special authority of Christ for example, particularly with regard to the Law, finds a precedent in Moses that no other figure could provide. In Jewish tradition, while the pattern of binary leadership of the people through a partnership between God and a human appears in the case of the Davidic (especially eschatological) king, it is found emphatically, and in full flower, perhaps only with Jesus (as Christ) and Moses, and Moses is the only named Jewish figure that can be adduced as an antecedent for this feature as it is applied to Christ. The mystical, spiritual relationship between the people and their human leader, sometimes expressed in the language of baptism, is also apparent in Jewish circles with regard to Moses and Israel, as it is in Christianity with Jesus and the Church, and here again the motif may be fully expressed only in these two figures.[123]

---

[122] E.g., perhaps the "Son of Man" sayings — but it is interesting that in the Old Testament Moses appears as "the man Moses" (Num. 12:3) and "Moses the man of God" (e.g. Deut. 33:1; 1 Chron. 23:14; 2 Chron. 30:16; Ezra 3:2; Ps. 90:1)." On the possible overlap of "man" titles with the semantic range of "Son of Man," and the messianic implications of both, see William Horbury, "The Messianic Associations of 'The Son of Man'," *Journal of Theological Studies*, NS 36, no. 1 (April 1985): 38, 48-52, idem, *Jewish Messianism and the Cult of Christ*, 43; Geza Vermes, *Scripture and Tradition in Judaism: Haggadic Studies*, Studia Post-Biblica, ed. P. A. H. de Boer, vol. 4 (Leiden: E. J. Brill, 1961), 56-66; Taylor, *The Names of Jesus*, 25-27.

[123] Here too, the Isaianic Branch appears to bear traces of the idea; see Horbury, *Jewish Messianism and the Cult of Christ*, 91-92.

8.5.2 Further Mosaic Antecedents for Christology

Only those aspects of the figure of Moses that actually appear in the New Testament can with certainty be placed in the thought world of its writers, and those features of Moses actually mentioned by the NT writers are clear favorites to be those that mattered most to them. The elements of the portrait of Moses of greatest interest for the study of Christology are necessarily then those that arise from the New Testament Moses.

The fullness of the overlap between Moses and Christ could of course be filled out dramatically by drawing on ideas about Moses not included in the New Testament Moses. In fact, the role of Moses as a type not just for individual elements of Christology but precisely for the union of so many disparate soteriological and messianic elements makes even the enumeration of possible further points of contact interesting, if only because it heightens the sense, already acquired from the New Testament Moses, that the figure of Moses was uniquely qualified in Judaism of the Herodian period to unite a range of roles associated with eschatological and supernatural figures. A few such possible further points of contact can be sketched.

8.5.2.1 Pre-existence

The present study noted evidence, primarily Samaritan evidence, for the belief that Moses enjoyed some fashion of pre-existence.[124] As explained before, Samaritans regarded Moses as pre-existent in the sense that he was first in the order of Creation. Moses was sometimes reckoned a perfect incarnation of the primordial light, the first thing that God's *fiat* brought forth. Another form of pre-existence ascribed to Moses in Samaritan beliefs is the sense of his pre-determined role in the world. This, however, is itself an expression of the revelatory and illuminatory role of light, which Moses was held to incarnate. It is an essential part of the Samaritan conception of Moses, then, that he is regarded as the incarnation of the primordial light, and in that way was really, and not merely ideally, pre-existent.

Neither the ontological pre-existence of Moses nor his primordial creation appear to be supported in the literature of Second Temple Judaism (and he is absent from the seven pre-existent things of rabbinic Judaism [*Pirqe R. El.* 3]), though pre-existence in the sense of foreordination is clearly associated with him. A foreordained mission is ascribed to Moses in *As. Mos.* 1.14, where Moses says, God "devised and invented me, I who have been prepared from the beginning of the world to be the mediator of his covenant (*excogitavit et invenit me qui ab initio orbis terrarum prae-*

---

[124] See above, pp. 212-13 and 237.

paratus sum ut sim arbiter testamenti illius)."[125] As granted earlier, this statement appears to cohere best with similar ideas in Jer. 1:5 and Gal. 1:15, and like these texts seems to speak of a pre-existent divine plan for God's special servant.[126]

Inclusion in a divine plan, however, is an important element of Jewish teachings about pre-existence, and one with relevance to Christology. Some NT passages speak of Christ's pre-existence in terms that suggest his unqualified transcendence, as with the full protological pre-existence implied by John,[127] and perhaps also by Phil. 2:6[128] and Gal. 4:4-6, and for the Church the doctrine of the pre-existence of Christ rapidly became a way of speaking of his divine essence, but in the New Testament itself many passages are content with speaking only of Christ's ante-mundane existence, or God's foreordination of his mission.[129] For such statements as these the sorts of things said about Moses provide clear antecedent.

That such teaching about Christ was so widespread among Christians may actually support the argument that Samaritan teaching about Moses' pre-existence springs from some older teaching about Moses once held in common with Jews. For the NT teaching of Christ's pre-existence, contemporary ideas of the pre-existence of Moses provide a better parallel than might at first be supposed.

8.5.2.2 Afterlife

From pre-existence one could turn to afterlife. True, in the description of the actual ends of their lives there could hardly be a greater disparity between Jesus and Moses. M. Hengel draws the contrast:

Jesus died miserably, with a wordless cry, the death of a cursed one. In contrast, according to the widespread legend, Moses was either transported to heaven without dying or God himself took the soul from the mouth of this friend of God (Ex. 33.11) without the

---

[125] Cf. the description of the Son of Man in 1 Enoch 48:2-7.

[126] See above, p. 213 n. 21.

[127] R. G. Hamerton-Kelly, *Pre-existence, Wisdom, and the Son of Man: A Study of the Idea of Pre-existence in the New Testament*, Society for New Testament Studies Monograph Series, ed. Matthew Black and R. McL. Wilson, no. 21 (Cambridge: The University Press, 1973), 203.

[128] Ibid., 168 and Martin Hengel, "Präexistenz bei Paulus?," in *Jesus Christus als die Mitte der Schrift: Studien zur Hermeneutik des Evangeliums*, ed. Christof Landmesser, Hans-Joachim Eckstein, and Hermann Lichtenberger, Beihefte zur Zeitschrift für die neutestamentliche Wissenschaft und die Kunde der älteren Kirche, ed. Erich Gräßer, no. 86 (Berlin and New York: Walter de Gruyter, 1997), 488-91. Cf. also the suggested identification of Jesus with the Wisdom of God in Matt. 8:20; 23:34-36, 37-39; Luke 9:58; 13:34-35, see Hamerton-Kelly, 35-36, 67-71, 101-102.

[129] E.g., the Son of Man sayings (on which see Hamerton-Kelly, *Pre-existence, Wisdom, and the Son of Man*, 29-46, 57-67, 79-83), Gal. 3:19-20; 4:4-6 And they continued to be read in this way, see Horbury, *Jewish Messianism and the Cult of Christ*, 88.

pangs of death, "as with a kiss". The gulf between the Jewish legends of the end of Moses and the death of Jesus could not be deeper here. Furthermore, Moses' attempt to ask forgiveness for his people after the sin of the Golden Calf, throwing his life into the balance, is rejected, whereas Jesus gives his life as "a ransom for the many."[130]

Some aspects of Christology even the figure of Moses does not embrace.

With regard to *post mortem* existence, however, the parallels between Moses and Jesus become astonishingly close. As observed at various places in the present study, Moses was thought to be active in heaven on behalf of his people as an advocate, as an intercessor, and as a vigilant overseer.[131] He was thought to have partaken (in some manner or other) of a divine nature.[132] All of these features of the life after death of Moses provide noteworthy antecedent for aspects of the work of the ascended Christ, and suggest that commentators have erred who have found in such things unique and completely unprecedented Christian contributions to messianism and Christology.

8.5.2.3 Session

Among the most astonishing features of the doctrine of the risen Christ is the *sessio ad dextram*. It is a very early ingredient to Christian doctrine, with the expression "seated at the right hand of the Father" going back at least to pre-Johannine Christology.[133] Hengel asks:

My question is how the earliest congregation could persistently venture to make the *unheard of* claim that Jesus of Nazareth, the crucified Messiah, not only was resurrected from the dead by God — there are occasional reports of the resurrection of individuals in Judaism and in late antiquity — but also that he was exalted to his right hand, that is, to become his companion on the throne.[134]

Hengel's point about the combination of crucifixion and exaltation is well-taken. But as seen already in this study, it is not necessary to wait for the full flower of Enochic speculations to find God sharing his throne with a human. Before the turn of the era, in the *Exagoge* of Ezekiel, that image has already emerged.[135] The Tragedian seems to have meant the scene as a (provocative indeed) assertion of royalty, but there is no denying the impact of a scene which depicts God himself vacating his throne for Moses. Descriptions of God merely sharing his throne seem relatively conservative

---

[130] Martin Hengel, *The Four Gospels and the One Gospel of Jesus Christ: An Investigation of the Collection and Origin of the Canonical Gospels* (London: SCM Press, 2000), 159-60.

[131] Pp. 223-24.

[132] Pp. 229-47.

[133] Martin Hengel, *Studies in Early Christology* (Edinburgh: T. & T. Clark, 1995), 122.

[134] Ibid., 134.

[135] See above, pp. 90-94.

by contrast. If it is conceded that the death of Jesus was from the beginning an extraordinary wrinkle in ordinary Jewish messianic expectations, the session of the risen Christ represents a return to what can be considered a Mosaic model.

One further note concerns the parallel eschatologies of Moses and Christ. As noted above, both figures are thought to have accomplished a kind of Exodus, and the followers of both are thought to live presently in a kind of exile from their promised destinies. Both figures are expected by their followers to return and lead their people into the age of blessing, of which the period when they personally led their followers is thought to have been a foretaste.[136] Once more, at the very climax of their work vis-à-vis their people, the ministries of Moses and Jesus converge.

The connections just traced out here are gauzy, not possessing anything like the substance of the overlap between Moses and Jesus detected in the main body of the present study. The evidence is much thinner, and the similarities not as clear. These connections suggest, however, that there might be more to Jesus as a Mosaic Messiah than readily meets the eye. These further connections lie, as it were, just off stage, and by being found there they help to substantiate what has been found on stage. Especially they suggest that the figure of Moses, even more than already suspected, provided a nearly comprehensive model for the elaboration of early Christology, more comprehensive than any other figure in Judaism of the Herodian Period.

8.6 Mosaic Ecclesiology

All of the functions of Moses discussed in this study are specifically functions toward Israel, so that in characterizing Moses this study has to some extent characterized the way his relationship with Israel was conceived, and in so doing has helped to illuminate Jewish self-conception in the Second Temple Period. This in turn has important implications for ecclesiology, the Church having inherited its constitution in large part from Judaism. Once attention has been focused on Jesus as a Mosaic figure, renewed interest rises, for example, in the parallel between Jesus' twelve apostles and the twelve princes of the tribes who served under Moses (Num. 1:4, 16-17; Matt. 19:28) as possibly an intentional modeling of Jesus' followers on the twelve tribes.[137] The parallel between baptism into

---

[136] See above, pp. 197-98.

[137] Treated extensively by William Horbury, "The Twelve and the Phylarchs," *New Testament Studies* 32 (1986): 503-527, esp. 503-509, 520-26. Horbury, 525 urges on this basis that by selecting twelve subordinates Jesus declared messianic pretensions.

Moses and baptism into Christ suggests another resemblance between Jewish and Christian ecclesiology.

Scholars of the development of Christian ecclesiology have generally neglected the importance of the Jewish precedent for uniting their congregation(s) around a human figure as well as around God himself.[138] Just as Paul did not introduce *de novo* the idea of entry into the covenant by grace, but only adapted it for what he saw as the new dispensation introduced by the gospel, so Jesus and the Church did not create from nothing the idea that God's people could be constituted around simultaneous devotion and trust both in God and in his human, or more than human, mediator. While scholars have not always gone so far as to say that such Christian ideas were pure invention, the lines of development have not been well picked out. This study suggests that Moses could have provided the model for viewing Christ as the head of the Church. By implication, the constitution of the Church as the congregation of those with faith in Christ would be modeled on the similar constitution of Israel as the followers of Moses.

8.7 Conclusion

This study suggests that Judaism in the first century had a superhuman leader, who was held to function in a manner strongly analogous to the way in which Christ subsequently was thought to head the Church. The similarity is so extensive that it is difficult to resist the implication that early Christians in thinking about Christ must consciously have drawn on the figure of Moses in a fuller, more coherent way than has heretofore been acknowledged. No other figure of Jewish lore provided so many opportunities for comparison or derivation. It now appears that all the key concepts of Christology, including the more "spiritual" dimensions of high Christology, can be derived from Jewish roots.

Meeks observes, "Certain traditions about Moses provided for the Fourth Gospel ... the figure who combines in one person both royal and prophetic honor and functions."[139] It has been shown here that Moses provided an even more comprehensive figure than that. Throughout the New Testament a full range of Mosaic motifs occur, all of which can be

---

[138] William Horbury, "Septuagintal and New Testament Conceptions of the Church," in *A Vision for the Church: Studies in Early Christian Ecclesiology in Honour of J. P. M. Sweet*, ed. Markus Bockmuehl and Michael B. Thompson (Edinburgh: T. & T. Clark, 1997), 5-6, 8 notes the importance of Moses as a focus of faith, though without quite bringing out the extent to which Moses seems to have been the focus of loyalty in the Second Temple period. He observes rightly the important precedent provided by traditions of congregational belief in Moses for NT conceptions of the Church.

[139] Meeks, *The Prophet-King*, 29.

connected with Jesus, often in the same passages. Essentially, what Meeks
argued for the Fourth Gospel is argued here for the New Testament: Moses was a large and luminous figure who stood at the center of Jewish identity and piety. Christians, in marking out their claims for Christ and, in
some cases, consciously posing Christ as the heir to the claims of preeminence made for Moses, borrowed expressions and ideas from the notions
made available to them from the Moses portrait. Meeks concluded that
"the depiction of Jesus as prophet and king in the Fourth Gospel owes
much to traditions which the church inherited from the Moses piety."[140]
What Meeks claimed for only the Fourth Gospel, and only with regard to
two christological motifs, extends much further.

---

[140] Ibid., 318-19.

Chapter 9

Conclusion

This study assessed the various ways the New Testament, viewed in the context of ancient Judaism, characterizes the relationship of Moses to Israel and to the Jewish people. The study contributes to the study of ancient Jewish and early Christian belief. In particular, this study suggests Moses had a greater place both in Jewish life and in the formation of early Christology than scholars have generally believed.

9.1 Review

Chapter Two examined the conception of Moses as prophet. All kinds of ancient Jewish literature, including the New Testament, emphasized the prophetic role of Moses; Moses was many things, but he was all the rest because he was first God's chosen mediator. Along with the New Testament's explicit statements of his prophethood, among which may be included the identification of Jesus as a prophet like Moses, Moses' prophethood is indicated by the parallels between NT and other accounts of Moses and contemporary prophetic ideals. For example, the miracles worked by Moses, which undoubtedly served in earlier times to confirm his credentials as God's emissary, seem likely in the first century A.D. to have been read as distinctively prophetic acts. Moses was not just a prophet, but the greatest prophet, and his prophethood is closely connected with his office as ruler of the nation.

Chapter Three focused on two relatively minor (in the New Testament, that is) aspects of Moses that are twinned in a single text, Heb. 3:1-6. Since the priesthood of Moses receives substantial attention in material outside the New Testament, its sole NT appearance can safely be taken as a ratification of this common view of Moses by at least a portion of the Christian community. By contrast, the New Testament appears to be the earliest witness to a somewhat less common view of Moses as apostle. The heightened importance of the title "apostle" among Christians, combined with the majestic resonance of the term in Heb. 3:1-6, makes the attribution one to take seriously, especially when subsequent Jewish literature then takes up the same idea. Both titles underline the mediating role of Moses in the relationship between God and the community.

Chapter Four turned to the kingship of Moses. Many traditions in the first century A.D. supported a view of Moses as the leader of Israel, while Jews in the Second Temple period generally, including first-century writers such as Philo, clearly thought of Moses as a king. Many passages in such writers seem to partake of specifically Hellenistic ideals of kingship in describing Moses. Finally, several NT passages both imply the kingship of Moses as they stand, and receive their most satisfying interpretations in a context in which Moses was viewed as a king, reinforcing the impression that kingship was a consistently important part of the conception of Moses in the time they were written.

Whereas some elements of the NT portrait of Moses in previous chapters had to be sifted from the evidence, Chapter Five found in the New Testament clearly expressed views of Moses as a lawgiver. The clarity of these views is, however, balanced by their variety; Paul seems to view Moses the Lawgiver as a mere functionary, but the Evangelists attest opinions that seem compatible even with Philo's accolades of Moses as the real composer of the Law. The Synoptic Gospels in particular seem to assume that Moses is an authoritative legislator, so much so that debates over the Law recorded in the Gospels appear incoherent if some such view of Moses was *not* current. At the same time, these debates make clear that such an exalted view of Moses must have been controversial. The Fourth Gospel in particular, more than other NT literature, communicates a sense of controversy among Jews over the precise nature of Moses' function in the Lawgiving and as leader of Israel.

The New Testament is in this respect shown to conform to the wider Judaism of its day. By contrast with the plurality of views found in the New Testament and in contemporary literature, some of which seem to take Moses for the real authority behind the Law, the Rabbis as a rule keep clear that God was the author of the Law, and Moses merely a (glorious) functionary. The relative uniformity of rabbinic opinion on the prophetic nature of the Lawgiving suggests that it became important at some period later than the New Testament to assert more forcefully the simple divine authorship of the Law.

Chapter Six urged that the baptism into Moses of 1 Cor. 10:2 should be viewed not as a hypothetical foil to Christian baptism, but as the echo of a strain of Jewish piety that saw in Moses a unifying and spiritual figure. To interpret "baptism into Moses" as mere rhetoric is unsatisfying on a number of counts. Meanwhile evidence abounds from the first century A.D. for ideas about Moses well-suited to the notion of "baptism into" him. Paul's expression can be counted among the texts attesting such ideas. This chapter went on to suggest, contrary to usual opinion, that Paul's doctrine of baptism into Christ might owe something to the idea of baptism into Moses, and not the other way round.

Already, in connection with other aspects of the figure of Moses, earlier chapters of this study had noted attributions to Moses of features of a more extraordinary character. Chapter Seven took particular notice of these in arguing for Jewish veneration of Moses as a personal focus of loyalty. References in Jewish literature to Moses as a divine or angelic figure, the wide ascription to Moses of disciples (comprising either all Jews or especially devout groups of them) and the equally widespread description of Moses as somehow an effective overseer and personal authority over the Jews, help to establish Moses as an appropriate object for Jewish faith and hope and a personal focus for Jewish allegiance. The New Testament offers texts that describe precisely these attitudes toward Moses. Acts especially goes beyond merely ascribing dignity and general importance to Moses, to making loyalty to him the litmus test of right standing as a Jew, or, one might say, of true Jewishness. This aspect of Moses has not been generally recognized.

In the first century, a view of Moses at the head of the Jewish people would both have scriptural support and also be implied by the extrabiblical literature of the day. The New Testament puts a higher premium on allegiance to Moses than does most other Jewish literature but in the New Testament, as well as outside it, Moses is for Jews in some respects what Christ is for the Church.

Partly in response to this observation, Chapter Eight gathered together points of contact between NT Christology and the NT Moses that earlier chapters had left to one side. These parallels seem, based on the survey of scholarship in Chapter Eight, not to have received the kind of thorough consideration that this study suggests they might deserve. Although Moses Christology has not been totally ignored up until now, this study points out, in two surveys of relevant scholarship, that scholarly predispositions have tended not to bring the fuller picture of Moses into focus. This in turn appears to have tended toward the undue minimization of the probable role of the figure of Moses in early Christology. It now seems likely that Jesus was seen as a Mosaic Messiah in senses heretofore not properly appreciated.

9.2 Contributions to Research

The contributions of this study fall under four headings.

9.2.1 Ancient Jewish Thought and Belief

The first, and overarching, aim of this study was to contribute to knowledge of ancient Judaism, by broadening understanding of the ancient Jewish conception of Moses, especially of Moses in relation to Israel. As

should now be apparent, the NT portrayal of Moses' relationship to Israel
is particularly robust. In some respects the New Testament simply is
clearer or more detailed in its statements than other Jewish literature. In a
few cases it adds entirely new stones to the first-century Mosaic mosaic,
but the overall NT impression integrates well enough with other Jewish
portrayals to demonstrate that the NT figure of Moses is not merely a
Christian reflection of Christ onto Moses. Rather the New Testament reveals its authors' familiarity with explicit and powerful ideas about Moses
already present in contemporary Jewish thought, ideas which apparently
were also current within the early Church.

The views of Moses that appear in the New Testament corroborate and
broaden the (at times tenuous) continuity between Hellenistic writers like
Artapanus and the obviously much later rabbinic midrash. This demonstra-
tion of diachronic continuity is complemented by the New Testament's
reflection of Jewish diversity: a very broad range of Second Temple Jewish
tradition about Moses is reflected in a similarly broad range of NT positions. Certain more unusual ideas about Moses, which have a tendency to
be traced back to an allegedly esoteric Alexandria, are shown by the New
Testament (and related sources) to be at home in the Palestinian environment as well. The NT Moses therefore witnesses to an underlying continuity between what have at times been misconceived as Palestinian and
Alexandrian/Egyptian "compartments" in ancient Judaism, as well as to the
continuity of Moses traditions across several epochs of Jewish history.

9.2.2 New Testament Studies and Early Christian Hermeneutics

Second, study centered on the New Testament naturally has implications
for NT studies. The New Testament is shown (in this as in other areas) to
be comprehensible as one of many ancient Jewish interpretations of the
Hebrew Scriptures. Its different portrayals of Moses display points of
contact with other witnesses to Jewish hermeneutical traditions, and the
NT, "Christian" view of Moses turns out to be at home among contemporary, less ambiguously Jewish views. In both its unity and its diversity
the NT Moses blends well with the representation(s) of Moses found in
other Jewish sources, and demonstrates the importance of Jewish traditions
for Christian thought.

9.2.3 Christology

Third, although this study has at points criticized the way NT scholars frequently approach the subject of Moses with strictly christological interest,
those scholars have not been mistaken in supposing Moses to be important
for early Christology. This study specifically set out to place the study of
Moses Christology on more solid footing by making a fresh assessment of
Moses as he seems to have been understood by the NT writers, and so by

the early Church. Resemblances between the NT figures of Moses and Christ were pointed out occasionally throughout this study, while the final chapter attempted to bring these together to demonstrate the extent of the overlap between the NT presentations of the two figures.

All aspects of Moses that surface in the New Testament turn out to compare well with the NT view of Christ, even as they are seen to cohere just as well with contemporary Jewish concepts. Most of these parallels, though not all, have been observed before in the study of NT Christology. What has been relatively neglected is the impact of the total picture, which suggests much more than passing references to Moses in the framing of early Christology. Rather, Christology must from the first have been undertaken with the strongest possible consciousness of Moses, and with explicit borrowing from Moses to describe Christ.

9.2.4 Ecclesiology

Fourth, this study has implications, too extensive to be fully explored here, for the origin and description of early ecclesiology. The concentration of this study on Moses' relationship toward Israel means that it has implications for Jewish self-definition. Just as the Jewish conception of Moses played a part in the origins of Christology so Jewish traditions of Israelite self-awareness had an important role in the formation of Christian ecclesiology. The role of Jewish traditions about the constitution of Israel in Jewish self-definition, however, let alone in early Christian ecclesiology, tends to be sparsely treated, while the influence of the figure of Moses in these respects has been fairly thoroughly neglected. Yet the constitution of Israel as a unified nation under Moses seems, in light of findings in this study, to have been more important to Jews than has always been allowed, and such Jewish perspectives, as well as allied concepts such as those related to baptism, are likely to have had a strong impact on conceptions of the Church as a unified body or kingdom under Christ.

9.3 Summation

What portrait of Moses and Israel emerges from the New Testament? Moses appears there as the greatest of Israel's prophets, as Israel's king and redeemer, and as her lawgiver — though neither the height of his exaltation in these individual capacities, nor the cumulative effect of them all together, has always been appreciated. Nor, going beyond these, has it always been appreciated that the New Testament in one place suggests that Moses was capable of being regarded as a spiritual being with whom Israel was united through baptism. Perfect prophet, redeeming king, authoritative lawgiver, spiritual unifier: perhaps it was this lofty appraisal of Moses which suited him for his role as the focus of Jewish loyalty and the source of Jewish identity. This central position of Moses in relation to Israel seems to be particularly prominent in the New Testament, although it can be detected in other Jewish sources.

While the portrait of Moses that emerges from the New Testament is generally consistent with that arising from other ancient Jewish writings, at the same time the New Testament contributes important insights into how Jews believed Moses functioned toward them, and into how they characterized their relationship with him. The portrait of Moses in the New Testament also forms an under-appreciated key to NT Christology and ecclesiology, and especially to the Christian conception of the relationship between Christ and the Church.

Bibliography

1. Reference Works Employed

Alexander, Patrick H., et al., eds. The SBL Handbook of Style for Ancient Near Eastern, Biblical, and Early Christian Studies. Peabody, Massachusetts: Hendrickson, 1999.

Bauer, Walter. *A Greek-English Lexicon of the New Testament*, 4th ed. Translated and adapted by William F. Arndt and F. Wilbur Gingrich. 2d ed., revised by F. Wilbur Gingrich and Frederick W. Danker. Chicago: The University of Chicago Press, 1979.

Dutripon, F. P. *Bibliorum Sacrorum Concordantiae*, 8th ed. Hildesheim and New York: Georg Olms Verlag, 1986; first published, Paris: Bloud et Barral, Bibliopolas, 1880.

Hatch, Edwin and Henry A. Redpath, eds. *A Concordance to the Septuagint and the Other Greek Versions of the Old Testament (Including the Apocryphal Books)*, 2d ed. With introduction by Robert A. Kraft and Emanuel Tov. Hebrew/Aramaic index by Takamitsu Muraoka. Grand Rapids: Baker Book House, 1998.

Jastrow, Marcus. *A Dictionary of the Targumim, the Talmud Babli and Yerushalmi, and the Midrashic Literature, with an Index of Scriptural Quotations.* 2 vols. 1886-1903; reprint, New York: The Judaica Press, 1971; reprint in one volume, 1996.

Kautzsch, E. editor. *Gesenius' Hebrew Grammar*, 2d English ed. Revised by A. E. Cowley. With a facsimile of the Siloam inscription by J. Euting, and a table of alphabets by M. Lidzbarski. Oxford: Clarendon Press, 1910.

Lewis, Charlton T. and Charles Short. *A Latin Dictionary.* Oxford: Clarendon Press, 1879; reprint, 1998.

Liddell, Henry George and Robert Scott. *A Greek-English Lexicon*, 9th ed. Revised by Henry Stuart Jones, with Roderick McKenzie. Revised supplement edited by P. G. W. Glare with A. A. Thompson. Oxford: Clarendon Press, 1996.

Lisowsky, Gerhard, with Leonhard Rost. *Konkordanz zum hebräischen Alten Testament*, 2d ed. Stuttgart: Würtembergische Bibelanstalt, 1958.

Mayer, Günter. *Index Philoneus.* Berlin: Walter de Gruyter, 1974.

Rengstorf, Karl Heinrich, ed. *A Complete Concordance to Flavius Josephus*, 4 vols. Leiden: E. J. Brill, 1973-1983.

Schalit, Abraham. *Namenwörterbuch zu Flavius Josephus.* Supplement 1 to *A Complete Concordance to Flavius Josephus*, ed. Karl Heinrich Rengstorf. Leiden: E. J. Brill, 1968.

Schmoller, Alfred. *Pocket Concordance to the Greek New Testament*, 8th ed. Stuttgart: German Bible Society, 1989.

Sokoloff, Michael. *A Dictionary of Jewish Palestinian Aramaic of the Byzantine Period.* Dictionaries of Talmud, Midrash and Targum, vol. 2. Ramat-Gan, Israel: Bar Ilan University Press, 1990.

Turabian, Kate. L. *A Manual for Writers of Term Papers, Theses, and Dissertations*, 6th ed. Revised by John Grossman and Alice Bennett. Chicago and London: The University of Chicago Press, 1996.

2. Bibles and Versions (excluding Targumim)

2.1 Old Testament and Apocrypha

Barnes, William Emery, ed. *The Peshitta Psalter according to the West Syrian Text.* Cambridge: The University Press, 1904.

Beentjes, Pancratius C., ed. *The Book of Ben Sira in Hebrew: A Text Edition of All Extant Hebrew Manuscripts and a Synopsis of All Parallel Hebrew Ben Sira Texts.* Supplements to *Vetus Testamentum*, ed. John A. Emerton, et al., vol. 68. Leiden: E. J. Brill, 1997.

Brooke, Alan England, Norman McLean, and Henry St John Thackeray, eds. *The Old Testament in Greek.* Vol. 2, *The Later Historical Books.* Pt. 2, *I and II Kings.* Cambridge: The University Press, 1930.

Charles, R. H. *The Apocrypha and Pseudepigrapha of the Old Testament in English.* 2 vols. Oxford: Clarendon Press, 1913.

Elliger, K. and W. Rudolph, eds. *Biblia Hebraica Stuttgartensia*, 3d ed. revised by W. Rudolph and H. P. Rüger. Stuttgart: Deutsche Bibelgesellschaft, 1967/1977.

Field, Frederick, ed. *Origenis Hexaplorum Quae Supersunt: Sive Veterum Interpretum Graecorum in Totum Vetus Testamentum Fragmenta.* 2 vols.; vol. 1: *Prolegomena, Genesis-Esther*, vol. 2: *Job-Malachi.* Oxford: Clarendon, 1875.

Metzger, Bruce M. and Roland E. Murphy, eds. *The New Oxford Annotated Apocrypha: The Apocryphal/Deuterocanonical Books of the Old Testament.* New Revised Standard Version. New York: Oxford University Press, 1991.

Ralhfs, Alfred, ed.. *Psalmi cum Odis. Septuaginta: Auctoritate Societatis Litterarum Gottingensis Editum*, vol. 10. Göttingen: Vandenhoeck & Ruprecht, 1931.

Smend, Rudolf. *Die Weisheit des Jesus Sirach: Hebräisch und deutsch mit einem hebräischen Glossar*, 2 vols., *Text* and *Notes.* Berlin: Georg Reimer, 1906.

Weber, Robert, ed. *Biblia Sacra iuxta Vulgatem Versionem.* 2 vols., *Genesis-Psalmi* and *Proverbia-Apocalypsis, Appendix.* Stuttgart: Württembergische Bibelanstalt 1969.

Wevers, John William, with U. Quast, eds. *Deuteronomium. Septuaginta: Vetus Testamentum Graecum Auctoritate Societatis Litterarum Gottingensis Editum*, vol. 3.2. Göttingen: Vandenhoeck & Ruprecht, 1977.

____. *Exodus. Septuaginta: Vetus Testamentum Graecum Auctoritate Societatis Litterarum Gottingensis Editum*, vol. 2.1. Göttingen: Vandenhoeck & Ruprecht, 1991.

Ziegler, Joseph, ed. *Ieremias, Baruch, Threni, Epistula Ieremiae. Septuaginta: Vetus Testamentum Graecum, Auctoritate Societatis Litterarum Gottingensis Editum*, vol. 15. Göttingen: Vandenhoeck & Ruprecht, 1957.

___. *Sapientia Iesu Filii Sirach.* Septuaginta: Vetus Testamentum Graecum, Auctoritate Societatis Litterarum Gottingensis Editum, vol. 12.2. Göttingen: Vandenhoeck & Ruprecht, 1965.

___. *Sapientia Solomonis.* Septuaginta: Vetus Testamentum Graecum, Auctoritate Societatis Litterarum Gottingensis Editum, vol. 12.1. Göttingen: Vandenhoeck & Ruprecht, 1962.

___. *Susanna, Daniel, Bel et Draco.* Septuaginta: Vetus Testamentum Graecum, Auctoritate Societatis Litterarum Gottingensis Editum, vol. 16.2. Göttingen: Vandenhoeck & Ruprecht, 1954.

2.2 New Testament

Bell, H. Idris and T. C. Skeat, eds. *Fragments of an Unknown Gospel and Other Early Christian Papyri.* London: The British Museum, 1935.

Nestle, E. and K. Aland, eds. *Novum Testamentum Graece,* 27th ed. Stuttgart: Deutsche Bibelgesellschaft, 1993.

Weber, Robert, ed. *Biblia Sacra iuxta Vulgatem Versionem.* 2 vols., *Genesis-Psalmi* and *Proverbia-Apocalypsis, Appendix.* Stuttgart: Württembergische Bibelanstalt 1969.

3. Targumim

3.1 Onqelos

Drazin, Israel, trans. *Targum Onkelos to Deuteronomy: An English Translation of the Text with Analysis and Commentary (Based on A. Sperber's Edition).* N.p. (USA): Ktav Publishing House, 1982.

___. *Targum Onkelos to Exodus: An English Translation of the Text with Analysis and Commentary (Based on the A. Sperber and A. Berliner Edition).* N.p. (USA): Ktav Publishing House, 1990.

___. *Targum Onkelos to Numbers: An English Translation of the Text with Analysis and Commentary (Based on the A. Sperber and A. Berliner Edition).* N.p. (USA): Ktav Publishing House, the Center for Judaic Studies of the University of Denver, and the Society for Targumic Studies, 1982.

Etheridge, J. W., trans. *The Targums of Onkelos and Jonathan Ben Uzziel on the Pentateuch with the Fragments of the Jerusalem Targum: From the Chaldee.* Two vols. in one. New York: Ktav Publishing House, 1968; first published 1862, 1865.

Grossfeld, Bernard, trans. *Targum Onqelos to Deuteronomy, Translated with Apparatus and Notes.* The Aramaic Bible: The Targums, ed. Martin McNamara, et al., vol. 9. Edinburgh: T. & T. Clark, 1988.

___. *The Targum Onqelos to Exodus: Translated, with Apparatus and Notes.* The Aramaic Bible: The Targums, ed. Kevin Cathcart, Michael Maher, and Martin McNamara, vol. 7. Edinburgh: T. & T. Clark, 1988.

Sperber, Alexander, ed. *The Pentateuch According to Targum Onqelos. The Bible in Aramaic Based on Old Manuscripts and Printed Texts,* 5 vols., vol. 1. Leiden: E. J. Brill, 1959.

3.2 Pseudo-Jonathan

Clarke, Ernest G., with Shirley Magder, trans. *Targum Pseudo-Jonathan: Numbers.* Bound with *Targum Neofiti 1: Numbers,* trans. Martin McNamara, in The Aramaic Bible: The Targums, ed. Kevin Cathcart, Michael Maher, and Martin McNamara, vol. 4. Edinburgh: T. & T. Clark, 1995.

Clarke, Ernest G., with Sue Magder, trans. *Targum Pseudo-Jonathan: Deuteronomy.* The Aramaic Bible: The Targums, ed. Martin McNamara, et al., vol. 5B. Edinburgh: T. & T. Clark, 1998.

Etheridge, J. W., trans. *The Targums of Onkelos and Jonathan Ben Uzziel on the Pentateuch with the Fragments of the Jerusalem Targum: From the Chaldee.* Two vols. in one. New York: Ktav Publishing House, 1968; first published 1862, 1865.

Ginsburger, M., ed. *Pseudo-Jonathan (Thargum Jonathan ben Usiël zum Pentateuch) nach der Londoner Handschrift (Brit. Mus. add. 27031).* Berlin: S. Calvary & Co., 1903.

Maher, Michael, trans. *Targum Pseudo-Jonathan: Exodus.* Bound with *Targum Neofiti 1: Exodus,* trans. Martin McNamara, with notes by Robert Hayward, in The Aramaic Bible: The Targums, ed. Martin McNamara, vol. 2. Edinburgh: T. & T. Clark, 1994.

_____. *Targum Pseudo-Jonathan: Leviticus.* Bound with *Targum Neofiti 1: Leviticus,* trans. Martin McNamara, with in introduction and notes by Robert Hayward, in The Aramaic Bible: The Targums, ed. Kevin Cathcart, Michael Maher, and Martin McNamara, vol. 3. Edinburgh: T. & T. Clark, 1994.

3.3 Neophyti I

Díez Macho, Alejandro, ed. *Deuteronomio: Edición Príncipe, Introducción y Versión Castellana.* English translation by Martin McNamara and Michael Maher. Parallels to Deuteronomy from Pseudo-Jonathan and Neophyti I by Etan B. Levine. Vol. 5 of *Neophyti 1: Targum Palestinense MS de la Biblioteca Vaticana.* Textos y Estudios, ed. Federico Pérez Castro, no. 10. Madrid: Consejo Superior de Investigaciones Científicas, 1978.

_____. *Neophyti 1. Targum Palestinense MS de la Biblioteca Vaticana.* 6 vols. Textos y Estudios, ed. Federico Pérez Castro, nos. 7-11, 20 (*Apéndices*). Madrid: Consejo Superior de Investigaciones Científicas, 1968, 1970, 1971, 1974, 1978, 1979.

McNamara, Martin, trans. *Targum Neofiti 1: Deuteronomy.* The Aramaic Bible: The Targums, ed. Kevin Cathcart, Michael Maher, and Martin McNamara, vol. 5A. Edinburgh: T. & T. Clark, 1997.

_____. *Targum Neofiti 1: Exodus.* With notes by Robert Hayward. Bound with *Targum Pseudo-Jonathan: Exodus,* trans., Michael Maher, in The Aramaic Bible: The Targums, ed. Martin McNamara, vol. 2. Edinburgh: T. & T. Clark, 1994.

_____. *Targum Neofiti 1: Leviticus.* With introduction and notes by Robert Hayward. Bound with *Targum Pseudo-Jonathan: Leviticus,* trans., Michael Maher, in The Aramaic Bible: The Targums, ed. Kevin Cathcart, Michael Maher, and Martin McNamara, vol. 2. Edinburgh: T. & T. Clark, 1994.

3.4 Fragment-Targum

Etheridge, J. W., trans. *The Targums of Onkelos and Jonathan Ben Uzziel on the Pentateuch with the Fragments of the Jerusalem Targum: From the Chaldee.* Two Volumes in One. New York: Ktav Publishing House, 1968; first published 1862, 1865.

Klein, Michael L. *The Fragment-Targums of the Pentateuch According to Their Extant Sources*. 2 vols. Vol. 1: *Texts, Indices and Introductory Essays*, vol. 2: *Translation*. Analecta Biblica: Investigationes Scientificae in Res Biblicas, no. 76. Rome: Biblical Institute Press, 1980.

3.5 Cairo Genizah

Klein, Michael L. *Genizah Manuscripts of Palestinian Targum to the Pentateuch*. 2 vols. Cincinnati: Hebrew Union College Press, 1986.

3.6 Jonathan on the Prophets

Sperber, Alexander, ed. *The Former Prophets According to Targum Jonathan*, and *The Latter Prophets According to Targum Jonathan*. Vols. 2 and 3 of *The Bible in Aramaic Based on Old Manuscripts and Printed Texts* (5 vols). Leiden: E. J. Brill, 1959, 1962.

3.7 Psalms

Diez Merino, Luis, ed. *Targum de Salmos: Edición Principe del Ms. Villa-Amil n. 5 de Alfonso de Zamora*. Biblia Poliglota Complutense, Tradición sefardí de la Biblia Aramea 4.1. Bibliotheca Hispana Biblica, ed. Domingo Muñoz León, vol. 6. Madrid: Consejo Superior de Investigaciones Científicas, Instituto "Franciso Suarez," 1982.

3.8 Isaiah

Stenning, J. F., ed. and trans. *The Targum of Isaiah*. Oxford: Clarendon Press, 1949.

4. Pseudepigrapha

4.1 Assumption of Moses

Charles, R. H., ed. and trans. *The Assumption of Moses, Translated from the Latin Sixth Century MS*. London: Adam and Charles Black, 1897.

Priest, J., trans. In *The Old Testament Pseudepigrapha*, ed. James H. Charlesworth, vol. 2, *Expansions of the "Old Testament" and Legends, Wisdom and Philosophical Literature, Prayers, Psalms and Odes, Fragments of Lost Judeo-Hellenistic Works*, 919-934. The Anchor Bible Reference Library. New York:Doubleday, 1985.

Tromp, Johannes, ed. and trans. *The Assumption of Moses: A Critical Edition with Commentary*. Studia in Veteris Testamenti Pseudepigrapha, ed. A.-M. Denis and M. de Jonge, vol. 10. Leiden: E. J. Brill, 1993.

4.2 (Syriac Apocalypse of) Baruch

Klijn, A. F. J., trans. In *The Old Testament Pseudepigrapha*, ed. James H. Charlesworth, vol. 1, *Apocalyptic Literature and Testaments*, 615-652. The Anchor Bible Reference Library. New York: Doubleday, 1983.

4.3 First (Ethiopic Apocalypse of) Enoch

Charles, R. H. *The Book of Enoch*. Translations of Early Documents, Series 1, Palestinian Jewish Texts (Pre-Rabbinic). London: SPCK, 1921.

Fleming, Joh. and L. Radermacher, trans. *Das Buch Henoch.* Die Griechischen Christlichen Schriftsteller der Ersten Drei Jahrhunderte. Leipzig: J. C. Hinrichs'sche Buchhandlung, 1901.

Isaac, E., trans. In *The Old Testament Pseudepigrapha*, ed. James H. Charlesworth, vol. 1, *Apocalyptic Literature and Testaments*, 5-89. The Anchor Bible Reference Library. New York: Doubleday, 1983.

Knibb, Michael A., with Edward Ullendorff. *The Ethiopic Book of Enoch: A New Translation in the Light of the Dead Sea Fragments.* 2 vols., *Text and Apparatus*, and *Introduction, Translation and Commentary*. Oxford: Clarendon Press, 1978.

Martin, François, et al., trans. *Le livre d'Hénoch traduit sur le texte Éthiopien.* Documents pour l'Étude de la Bible, ed. François Martin, Les Apocryphes de l'Ancien Testament. Paris: Letouzey et Ané, 1906; reprint, Paris: Archè, 1996.

4.4 Third (Hebrew Apocalypse of) Enoch

Alexander, P., trans. In *The Old Testament Pseudepigrapha*, ed. James H. Charlesworth, vol. 1, *Apocalyptic Literature and Testaments*, 223-315. The Anchor Bible Reference Library. New York: Doubleday, 1983.

4.5 Fourth Ezra

Metzger, B. M., trans. In *The Old Testament Pseudepigrapha*, ed. James H. Charlesworth, vol. 1, *Apocalyptic Literature and Testaments*, 516-559. The Anchor Bible Reference Library. New York: Doubleday, 1983.

4.6 Jubilees

Wintermute, O. S., trans. In *The Old Testament Pseudepigrapha*, ed. James H. Charlesworth, vol. 2, *Expansions of the "Old Testament" and Legends, Wisdom and Philosophical Literature, Prayers, Psalms and Odes, Fragments of Lost Judeo-Hellenistic Works*, 35-142. The Anchor Bible Reference Library. New York: Doubleday, 1985.

4.7 Martyrdom and Ascension of Isaiah

Knibb, M. A., trans. In *The Old Testament Pseudepigrapha*, ed. James H. Charlesworth, vol. 2, *Expansions of the "Old Testament" and Legends, Wisdom and Philosophical Literature, Prayers, Psalms and Odes, Fragments of Lost Judeo-Hellenistic Works*, 143-176. The Anchor Bible Reference Library. New York: Doubleday, 1985.

4.8 Paraleipomena Jeremiou

Kraft, Robert A. and Ann-Elizabeth Purintim, ed. and trans. Texts and Translations, ed. Robert W. Funk, et al., no. 1. Pseudepigrapha Series, ed. Robert A. Kraft, et al., no. 1. Missoula, Montana: Society of Biblical Literature, 1972.

4.9 The Sibylline Oracles

Collins, J. J., trans. In *The Old Testament Pseudepigrapha*, ed. James H. Charlesworth, vol. 1, *Apocalyptic Literature and Testaments*, 317-472. The Anchor Bible Reference Library. New York: Doubleday, 1983.

Geffcken, Joh., ed. *Die Oracula Sibyllina.* Die griechischen christlichen Schriftsteller der ersten drei Jahrhunderte. Leipzig: J. C. Hinrichs'sche Buchhandlung, 1902.

4.10 Testaments of the Twelve Patriarchs

Kee, H. C., trans. In *The Old Testament Pseudepigrapha*, ed. James H. Charlesworth, vol. 1, *Apocalyptic Literature and Testaments*, 775-828. The Anchor Bible Reference Library. New York: Doubleday, 1983.

5. Ancient Near Eastern Literature

Pritchard, James B. ed. *Ancient Near Eastern Texts Relating to the Old Testament*. W. F. Albright, et al., translators. Princeton, New Jersey: Princeton University Press, 1950.

6. Qumran and Judaean Desert Texts

García Martínez, Florentino and Eibert J. C. Tigchelaar, eds., *The Dead Sea Scrolls Study Edition*. 2 vols. Vol. 1: *1Q1-4Q273*, vol. 2: *4Q274-11Q31*. Leiden: Brill, 1997, 1998.

Puech, Émile, ed. *Qumrân Grotte 4 XXII: Textes Araméens, première partie, 4Q529-549*. Discoveries in the Judaean Desert, ed. Emanuel Tov, vol. 31, edited with James Vanderkam and Monica Brady. Oxford: Clarendon Press, 2001.

Vanderkam, James and M. Brady. "[4Q]377: 4QApocryphal Pentateuch B." In *Wadi Daliyeh II and Qumran Cave 4 XXVIII*, ed. Douglas M. Gropp (Wadi Daliyeh) and Moshe Bernstein, et al. (Qumran Cave 4), 205-217. Discoveries in the Judaean Desert, ed. Emanuel Tov, vol. 28. Oxford: Clarendon Press, 2001.

Yadin, Y. "Expedition D." *Israel Exploration Journal* 11, nos. 1-2 (The Expedition to the Judean Desert, 1960) (1961): 36-52.

Yadin, Yigael, et al., eds. *The Documents from the Bar Kokhba Period in the Cave of Letters: Hebrew, Aramaic, and Nabatean-Aramaic Papyri*. Judean Desert Studies. Jerusalem: Israel Exploration Society, Hebrew University Institute of Archaeology, Israel Museum Shrine of the Book, 2002.

7. Greek Jewish Literature

7.1 Aristeas, Letter of

Meecham, Henry G. *The Letter of Aristeas: A Linguistic Study with Special Reference to the Greek Bible*. Publications of the University of Manchester, no. 241. Manchester: Manchester University Press, 1935. [Includes the Greek text edited by H. St. J. Thackeray, contained in an appendix to Henry Barclay Swete, *An Introduction to the Old Testament in Greek* (Cambridge: Cambridge University Press, 1914).]

Pelletier, André, ed. *Lettre d'Aristée a Philocrate: Introduction, texte critique, traduction et notes, index complet des mots grecs*. Sources Chrétiennes, ed. C. Mondésert, no. 89. Série Annexe de textes non-chrétiens. Paris: Les Éditions du Cerf, 1962.

Shutt, R. J. H., trans. In *The Old Testament Pseudepigrapha*, ed. James H. Charlesworth, vol. 2, *Expansions of the "Old Testament" and Legends, Wisdom and Philosophical Literature, Prayers, Psalms and Odes, Fragments of Lost Judeo-Hellenistic Works*, 831-842. The Anchor Bible Reference Library. New York: Doubleday, 1985.

7.2 Aristobulus

Collins, A. Yarbro, trans. In *The Old Testament Pseudepigrapha*, ed. James H. Charlesworth, vol. 2, *Expansions of the "Old Testament" and Legends, Wisdom and Philosophical Literature, Prayers, Psalms and Odes, Fragments of Lost Judeo-Hellenistic Works*, 831-842. The Anchor Bible Reference Library. New York: Doubleday, 1985.

Holladay, Carl R, ed. *Aristobulus. Fragments from Hellenistic Jewish Authors*, vol. 1. Society of Biblical Literature Texts and Translations Pseudepigrapha Series, ed. Martha Himmelfarb, Texts and Translations no. 39, Pseudepigrapha no. 13. Atlanta: Scholars Press, 1995.

7.3 Artapanus

Collins, J. J., trans. In *The Old Testament Pseudepigrapha*, ed. James H. Charlesworth, vol. 2, *Expansions of the "Old Testament" and Legends, Wisdom and Philosophical Literature, Prayers, Psalms and Odes, Fragments of Lost Judeo-Hellenistic Works*, 889-903. The Anchor Bible Reference Library. New York: Doubleday, 1985.

7.4 Eupolemus

Fallon, F. trans. In *The Old Testament Pseudepigrapha*, ed. James H. Charlesworth, vol. 2, *Expansions of the "Old Testament" and Legends,Wisdom and Philosophical Literature, Prayers, Psalms and Odes, Fragments of Lost Judeo-Hellenistic Works*, 861-872. The Anchor Bible Reference Library. New York:Doubleday, 1985.

7.5 Ezekiel the Tragedian

Jacobson, Howard, ed. and trans. *The* Exagoge *of Ezekiel*. Cambridge: Cambridge University Press, 1983.

Robertson. R. G., trans. In *The Old Testament Pseudepigrapha*, ed. James H. Charlesworth, vol. 2, *Expansions of the "Old Testament" and Legends, Wisdom and Philosophical Literature, Prayers, Psalms and Odes, Fragments of Lost Judeo-Hellenistic Works*, 803-819. The Anchor Bible Reference Library. New York: Doubleday, 1985.

7.6 Pseudo-Philo

Harrington, D. J., trans. In *The Old Testament Pseudepigrapha*, ed. James H. Charlesworth, vol. 2, *Expansions of the "Old Testament" and Legends, Wisdom and Philosophical Literature, Prayers, Psalms and Odes, Fragments of Lost Judeo-Hellenistic Works*, 297-377. The Anchor Bible Reference Library. New York: Doubleday, 1985.

Jacobson, Howard, ed. *A Commentary on Pseudo-Philo's* Liber Antiquitatum Biblicarum *with Latin Text and English Translation*, 2 vols. Arbeiten zur Geschichte des antiken Judentums und des Urchristentums, ed. Martin Hengel, et al., no. 31. Leiden: E. J. Brill, 1996.

7.7 Orphica

Holladay, Carl R., trans. *Orphica. Fragments from Hellenistic Jewish Authors*, vol. 4. Society of Biblical Literature Texts and Translations Pseudepigrapha Series, ed. Martha Himmelfarb, Texts and Translations no. 40, Pseudepigrapha no. 14. Atlanta: Scholars Press, 1996.

Lafargue, M., trans. "Orphica." In *The Old Testament Pseudepigrapha*, ed. James H. Charlesworth, vol. 2, *Expansions of the "Old Testament" and Legends, Wisdom and Philosophical Literature, Prayers, Psalms and Odes, Fragments of Lost Judeo-Hellenistic Works*, 795-801. The Anchor Bible Reference Library. New York: Doubleday, 1985.

7.8 Philo

Philo. 10 vols. and 2 supplements. Translated by F. H. Colson and G. H. Whitaker (vols 1-10), and Ralph Marcus (supplements), with index by J. W. Earp (in vol. 10). Loeb Classical Library, ed. T. E. Page, et al. London: William Heinemann; New York: G. P. Putnam's Sons, 1929, 1929, 1930, 1932, 1934; Cambridge, Massachusetts: Harvard University Press; London: William Heinemann, 1935, 1937, 1939, 1941, 1942, 1953, 1953.

7.9 Josephus

Josephus. 13 vols. Translated by H. St. J. Thackeray, Ralph Marcus, Allen Wikgren, and L. H. Feldman. Loeb Classical Library. Cambridge, Massachusetts and London: Harvard University Press, in 10 vols., 1926, 1927, 1928, 1930, 1934, 1937, 1933, 1963, 1965, 1965, reprinted 1997, 1998, at which dates *War* rebound from two vols to three, and *Antiquities* from six vols. to nine.

7.10 Collections

Holladay, Carl R, ed. *Historians. Fragments from Hellenistic Jewish Authors*, vol. 1. Society of Biblical Literature Texts and Translations Pseudepigrapha Series, ed. Harold W. Attridge, Texts and Translations no. 20, Pseudepigrapha no. 10. Chico, California: Scholars Press, 1983.

___. *Poets. Fragments from Hellenistic Jewish Authors*, vol. 2. Society of Biblical Literature Texts and Translations Pseudepigrapha Series, ed. James C. Vanderkam, Texts and Translations no. 30, Pseudepigrapha no. 12. Atlanta: Scholars Press, 1989.

8. Samaritan Texts

Bowman, John, trans. and ed. *Samaritan Documents Relating to Their History, Religion and Life*. Pittsburgh Original Texts and Translations Series, ed. Dikran Y. Hadidian, no. 2. Pittsburgh: The Pickwick Press, 1977.

Memar Marqah: The Teaching of Marqah. 2 vols. Vol. 1: *The Text*, vol. 2: *The Translation*. Edited and translated by John MacDonald. Beihefte zur Zeitschrift für die alttestamentliche Wissenschaft, ed. Georg Fohrer, no. 84. Berlin: Alfred Töpelmann, 1963.

Plummer, Reinhard. *Samaritan Marriage Contracts and Deeds of Divorce.* 2 vols. Vol. 1, Wiesbaden: Otto Harrassowitz, 1993. Vol. 2, with the collaboration of Abraham Tal. Wiesbaden: Harrassowitz Verlag, 1997.

9. Classical Authors

Cicero. *The Speeches: Pro Sestio and In Vatinium.* Translated by R. Gardner. Loeb Classical Library. London: Heinemann, 1958.
Juvenal. *Juvenal and Persius.* Translated by G. G. Ramsay. Loeb Classical Library. Cambridge, Massachusetts: Harvard University Press and London: William Heinemann, 1979.
Stern, Menachem, ed. and trans. *Greek and Latin Authors on Jews and Judaism Edited with Introductions, Translations, and Commentary,* 3 vols. Vol. 1, *From Herodotus to Plutarch,* vol. 2, *From Tacitus to Simplicitus,* vol. 3, *Appendixes and Indexes.* Fontes and Res Judaicas Spectantes. Jerusalem: The Israel Academy of Sciences and Humanities, 1974, 1980, 1984.
Strabo. *The Geography,* 8 vols. Translated by Horace Leonard Jones. Loeb Classical Library. Cambridge, Massachusetts: Harvard University Press and London: William Heinemann, 1917-1949.
Virgil. *Eclogues, Georgics, Aeneid 1-6.* Translated by H. Rushton Fairclough. Revised by G. P. Goold. Loeb Classical Library. Cambridge, Massachusetts: Harvard University Press, 1999.

10. Ecclesiastical Writers

Augustine of Hippo. *Sancti Aurelii Augustini Hipponensis Episcopi Opera Omnia,* 16 vols. ed. J.-P. Migne. Patrologiae Cursus Completus, Series Latina. Paris: *n.p.,* 1865.
Basil the Great. *The Book of Saint Basil the Great Bishop of Caesarea in Cappadocia On the Holy Spirit Written to Amphilochius, Bishop of Iconium, against the Pneumatomachi,* ed. C. F. H. Johnston. Oxford: Clarendon Press, 1892.
Clement of Alexandria. *Clemens Alexandrinus.* Vol. 1, *Protrepticus und Paedagogus;* vol. 2, *Stromata Buch I-VI;* vol. 3, *Stromata Buch VII und VIII, Excerpta ex Theodoto, Eclogae Propheticae, Quis Dives Salvetur, Fragmente.* Edited by Otto Stählin. Die griechischen christlichen Schriftsteller der ersten drei Jahrhunderte. Leipzig: J. C. Hinrichs'she Buchhandlung, 1905, 1906, 1909.
Les Constitutions Apostolique. 3 vols. Sources Chrétiennes, nos. 320, 329, 336. Paris: Les Éditions du Cerf, 1985, 1986, 1987.
Constitutiones Apostolorum. Edited by P. A. de Lagarde. Leipzig: B. G. Teubner and London: Williams & Norgate, 1862.
Didascalia Apostolorum: The Syriac Version Translated and Accompanied by the Verona Latin Fragments. Translated with Introduction and Notes by R. Hugh Connolly. Oxford: Clarendon Press, 1929.
Eusebius of Caesarea. *Ecclesiastical History,* 2 vols. Vol. 1, *Books I-V,* translated by Kirsopp Lake; vol. 2, *Books VI-X,* translated by J. E. L. Oulton with H. J. Lawlor. Loeb Classical Library, ed. G. P. Goold. Cambridge, Massachusetts: Harvard University Press, 1926, 1932; reprint 1998, 2000. [The text is that of E. Schwartz in

Die griechischen christlichen Schriftsteller der ersten drei Jahrhunderte, vols. 1 and 2 of Part II.]

Eusebius of Caesarea. *Eusebii Caesariensis Opera*, ed. William Dindorf. Vol. 1, *Praeparationis Evangelicae Libri I-X*; vol. 2, *Praeparationis Evangelicae Libri XI-XV*. Lipsiae: B. G. Teubner, 1867.

Justin Martyr. *Iustini Martyris Dialogus cum Tryphone*. Edited by Miroslav Marcovich. Patristische Texte und Studien, ed. H. C. Brennecke and E. Mühlenberg, vol. 47. Berlin: Walter de Gruyter, 1997.

Justin Martyr. *Iustini Philosophi et Martyris Opera Quae Feruntur Omnia*, 3d ed., 2 vols. Edited by Johann Karl von Otto. Vol. 1, *Opera Iustini Indubitata*, vol. 2, *Opera Iustini, Addubitata*. Corpus Apologetarum Christianorum, 2d series, vol. 1, Iustinus Philosophus et Martyr. Jena: Hermann Dufft, 1876; Gustav Fischer, 1879.

Pseudo-Phocylides. *The Sentences of Pseudo-Phocylides with Introduction and Commentary*. Edited by P. W. van der Horst. Studia in Veteris Testamenti Pseudepigrapha, ed. A. M. Denis and M. de Jonge, no. 4. Leiden: E. J. Brill, 1978.

11. Talmud and Midrash

11.1 Mishnah

Blackman, Philip, ed. and trans. *Mishnayoth*, 2d ed. 7 vols., including supplement and index vol. New York: The Judaica Press, 1963-1964.

Danby, Herbert. *The Mishnah*. London: Oxford University Press, 1933; reprint, 1950.

11.2 Tosefta

Neusner, Jacob. *The Tosefta Translated from the Hebrew*. 6 vols. New York: Ktav, 1977-1986.

Zuckermandel, M. S., ed. *Tosephta: Based on the Erfurt and Vienna Codices*, 2d ed. With "Supplement to the Tosephta," by Saul Liebermann. Jerusalem: Bamberger & Wahrmann, 1937.

11.3 Talmud

Talmud Yerushalmi. קראטאשין (Krotoschin), 1866; reprint: Jerusalem, 1969.

Epstein, I., ed. *Hebrew-English Edition of the Babylonian Talmud*, rev. ed. 30 vols. London: Soncino, 1967-1989.

Neusner, Jacob, et al. *The Talmud of the Land of Israel: A Preliminary Translation and Explanation*. 35 vols. Chicago Studies in the History of Judaism. Chicago: University of Chicago Press, 1982-1994. [This translation was consulted, but not depended on.]

11.4 Midrash

Agadath Bereschith: Midraschische Auslegungen zum ersten Buche Mosis. Edited by Salomon Buber. Krakow: Josef Fischer, 1902.

Mekilta de-Rabbi Ishmael: A Critical Edition on the Basis of Manuscripts and Early Editions. 3 vols. Translated by Jacob Z. Lauterbach. The JPS Library of Jewish Classics. Philadelphia: Jewish Publication Society of America, 1933.

The Midrash on Psalms. 2 vols. Translated by William G. Braude. Yale Judaica Series, ed. Leon Nemoy, Saul Lieberman, and Harry A. Wolfson, vol. 13. New Haven: Yale University Press, 1959.

Midrash Rabbah. 10 vols. Edited by H. Freedman and Maurice Simon. With a foreword by I. Epstein. Vols. 1 and 2: *Genesis 1* and *Genesis 2*, trans. H. Freedman; vol. 3: *Exodus*, trans. S. M. Lehrman; vol. 4: *Leviticus*, trans. J. Israelstam (chaps. 1-19) and Judah J. Slotki (chaps. 20-37); vols. 5 and 6: *Numbers 1* and *Numbers 2*, trans. Judah J. Slotki; vol. 7: *Deuteronomy*, trans. J. Rabbinowitz and *Lamentations*, trans. A. Cohen; vol. 8: *Ruth*, trans. L. Rabinowitz and *Ecclesiastes*, trans. A. Cohen; vol. 9: *Esther* and *Song of Songs*, trans. Maurice Simon; vol. 10: *Indices*. London: The Soncino Press, 1939.

Midrás Sifre Números: Versión Crítica, Introducción y Notas. Edited by Miguel Pérez Fernández. Biblioteca Midrásica, ed. Miguel Pérez Fernández, no. 9. Valencia: Institución San Jerónimo, 1989.

Midrash Sifre on Numbers: Selections from Early Rabbinic Scriptural Interpretations. Translated and annotated by Paul P. Levertoff. Introduction by G. H. Box. Translations of Early Documents, Series 3: Rabbinic Texts. London: Society for Promoting Christian Knowledge, 1926.

Midrash Tanḥuma: Translated into English (S. Buber Recension). Translated by John T. Townsend. Vol. 1: *Genesis*, vol. 2: *Exodus and Leviticus* (Hoboken, New Jersey: Ktav Publishing House, 1989, 1997.

Midrasch Tannaïm zum Deuteronomium aus der in der Königlichen Bibliothek zu Berlin befindlichen Handschrift des „Midrasch haggadol" gesammelt und mit Anmerkungen versehen. Edited by D. Hoffmann. 2 vols., *Deut. 1,1-20,9* and *Deut. 20, 10-Ende*. Berlin: M. Poppelauer, 1908, 1909.

Midrash Rabbah. 2 vols. Wilna: Romm, 1878; reprint, Jerusalem, 1961.

Pesikta Rabbati: Discourses for Feasts, Fasts, and Special Sabbaths, 2 vols. Translated by William G. Braude. Yale Judaica Series, ed. Leon Nemoy, Saul Lieberman, and Harry A. Wolfson, vol. 18. New Haven and London: Yale University Press, 1968.

Pirḳê de Rabbi Eliezer (The Chapters of Rabbi Eliezer the Great) According to the Text of the Manuscript Belonging to Abraham Epstein of Vienna. Edited and translated by Gerald Friedlander. London: Kegan Paul, Trench, Trubner & Co. and New York: The Bloch Publishing Company, 1916.

Pesikta de Rav Kahana according to an Oxford Manuscript with Variants from All Known Manuscripts, 2d ed. 2 vols. Edited by Bernard Mandelbaum. New York: The Jewish Theological Seminary of America, 1987.

Sifra. Edited by I. H. Weiss. Vienna: Jacob Schlossberg, 1862.

Sifra: An Analytical Translation. 3 vols. Translated by Jacob Neusner. Brown Judaic Studies, ed. Jacob Neusner, et al., nos. 138-140. Atlanta: Scholars Press, 1988.

Sifre: A Tannaitic Commentary on the Book of Deuteronomy. Translated with introduction and notes by Reuven Hammer. Yale Judaica Series, ed. Leon Nemoy, Judah Goldin, and Isadore Twersky, vol. 24. New Haven: Yale University Press, 1986.

Sifre on Deuteronomy. Edited by Louis Finkelstein. Corpus Tannaiticum, Section 3, Part 3, Siphre d'be Rab, fascicle 2. Berlin: Gesellschaft zur Förderung der Wissenschaft des Judentums, 1939; republished New York: Jewish Theological Seminary of America, 1969.

12. Piyyut

Klein, Michael L. *Genizah Manuscripts of Palestinian Targum to the Pentateuch.* 2 vols. Cincinnati: Hebrew Union College Press, 1986.
Sokoloff, Michael and Joseph Yahalom. *Jewish Palestinian Aramaic Poetry from Late Antiquity.* Jerusalem: Israel Academy of Sciences, 1999.
Yahalom, Joseph. "Ezel Moshe — According to the Berlin Papyrus." *Tarbiz* 47, nos. 3-4 (April-September 1978): 173-184. [Berlin Stadtmuseum P8498.]

13. Secondary Sources

Aalen, S. "A Rabbinic Formula in I Cor. 14,34." In *Studia Evangelica*, vol. 2, *Papers Presented to the Second International Congress on New Testament Studies Held at Christ Church, Oxford, 1961*, part I, *The New Testament Scriptures*, ed. F. L. Cross, 513-525. Texte und Untersuchungen zur Geschichte der altchristlichen Literatur, vol. 87. Berlin: Akademie-Verlag, 1964.
___. "'Reign' and 'House' in the Kingdom of God in the Gospels," including supplement, "'Kingdom' and 'House' in Pre-Christian Judaism." *New Testament Studies* 8 (1961-1962), no. 3 (1962): 215-240 (supplement, 233-240).
Aitken, James K. "Hebrew Study in Ben Sira's *Beth Midrash*." In *Hebrew Study from Ezra to Ben-Yehuda*, ed. William Horbury, 27-37. Edinburgh: T. & T. Clark, 1999.
Allen, E. L. "Jesus and Moses in the New Testament." *The Expository Times* 67 (1955-1956): 104-106.
Allison, Dale C., Jr. *The New Moses: A Matthean Typology.* Edinburgh: T. & T. Clark, 1993.
___. "Psalm 23(22) in Early Christianity: A Suggestion." *Irish Biblical Studies* 5 (July 1983): 132-137.
Amir, Yehoshua. *Die hellenistische Gestalt des Judentums bei Philon von Alexandrien.* Forschungen zum jüdisch-christlichen Dialog, ed. Yehuda Aschkenasy and Heinz Kremers, vol. 5. Neukirchen-Vluyn: Neukirchener Verlag, 1983.
Anderson, H. "The Jewish Antecedents of the Christology in Hebrews." In *The Messiah:Developments in Earliest Judaism and Christianity*, ed. James H. Charlesworth with J. Brownson, M. T. Davis, S. J. Kraftchick, and A. F. Segal, 512-535. Minneapolis: Fortress Press, 1992.
Anderson, Paul N. *The Christology of the Fourth Gospel: Its Unity and Disunity in the Light of John 6.* Wissenschaftliche Untersuchungen zum Neuen Testament, 2d series, ed. Martin Hengel and Otfried Hofius, no. 78. Tübingen: J. C. B. Mohr (Paul Siebeck), 1996.
Aune, D. E. "The Problem of the Genre of the Gospels: A Critique of C. H. Talbert's *What Is a Gospel?*." In *Gospel Perspectives: Studies of History and Tradition in the Four Gospels*, vol. 2, ed. R. T. France and David Wenham, 9-60. Sheffield: JSOT Press, 1981.
Avi-Yonah, Michael. "Goodenough's Evaluation of the Dura Paintings: A Critique." In *The Dura-Europos Synagogue: A Re-evaluation (1932-1992)*, ed. Joseph Gutmann, 117-136. South Florida Studies in the History of Judaism, ed. Jacob Neusner, et al., no. 25. Atlanta: Scholars Press, 1992.
Badke, William B. "Baptised into Moses — Baptised into Christ: A Study in Doctrinal Development." *The Evangelical Quarterly* 88, no. 1 (1988): 23-29.

Bammel, E. "The Feeding of the Multitude." In *Jesus and the Politics of His Day*, ed. Ernst Bammel and C. F. D. Moule, 211-240. Cambridge: Cambridge University Press, 1984.

___. "'John did no miracle': John 10.41." In *Miracles: Cambridge Studies in Their Philosophy and History*, ed. C. F. D. Moule, 179-202. London: A. R. Mowbray & Co., 1965.

Bandstra, Andrew. "Interpretation in 1 Corinthians 10:1-11." *Calvin Theological Journal* 6, no. 1 (April 1971): 5-21.

Banks, Robert. "The Eschatological Role of Law in Pre- and Post-Christian Jewish Thought." In *Reconciliation and Hope: New Testament Essays on Atonement and Eschatology presented to L. L. Morris on his 60th Birthday*, ed. Robert Banks, 173-185. Exeter: Paternoster Press, 1974.

Barclay, John M. G. *Jews in the Mediterranean Diaspora from Alexander to Trajan (323 BCE-117 CE)*. Edinburgh: T. & T. Clark, 1996.

Bar-Kochva, Bezalel. *Pseudo-Hecataeus' On the Jews: Legitimizing the Jewish Diaspora*. Hellenistic Culture and Society, ed. Anthony W. Bulloch, et al., no. 21. Berkeley: University of California Press, 1996.

Barrett, C. K. *A Critical and Exegetical Commentary on the Acts of the Apostles*, vol. 1, *Preliminary Introduction and Commentary on Acts I-XIV* and vol. 2, *Introduction and Commentary on Acts XV-XXVIII*. The International Critical Commentary on the Holy Scriptures of the Old and New Testaments, ed. J. A. Emerton, C. E. B. Cranfield, and G. N. Stanton. Edinburgh: T. & T. Clark, 1994, 1998.

___. *From First Adam to Last: A Study in Pauline Theology*. London: Adam & Charles Black, 1962.

___. *The Gospel According to St John: An Introduction with Commentary and Notes on the Greek Text*, 2d ed. London: SPCK, 1978.

Barton, John. *Oracles of God: Perceptions of Ancient Prophecy in Israel after the Exile*. London: Darton, Longman and Todd, 1986.

Bauckham, Richard. *God Crucified: Monotheism and Christology in the New Testament*. Didsbury Lectures, 1996. Carlisle, Cumbria: Paternoster Press, 1998.

___. "The Throne of God and the Worship of Jesus." In *The Jewish Roots of Christological Monotheism: Papers from the St. Andrews Conference on the Historical Origin of the Worship of Jesus*, ed. Carey C. Newman, James R. Davila, and Gladys S. Lewis, 43-69. Supplements to the *Journal for the Study of Judaism*, ed. John J. Collins with Florentino García Martínez, vol. 63. Leiden: Brill, 1999.

Beasley-Murray, G. R. "Baptism." In *Dictionary of Paul and His Letters*, ed. Gerald F. Hawthorne, Ralph P. Martin, and Daniel G. Reid, 60-66. Downers Grove, Illinois: InterVarsity Press, 1993.

___. *Baptism in the New Testament*. London: Macmillian & Co.; New York: St. Martin's Press, 1962.

Beckwith, Roger. *The Old Testament Canon of the New Testament Church and Its Background in Early Judaism*. Grand Rapids: William B. Eerdmans, 1985.

Bell, H. Idris and T. C. Skeat, eds. *Fragments of an Unknown Gospel and Other Early Christian Papyri*. London: The British Museum, 1935.

Bentzen, Aage. *King and Messiah*. Translated by the author. Lutterworth Studies in Church and Bible. London: Lutterworth Press, 1955. (Originally published as *Messias-Moses Redivivus-Menschensohn*. Zürich: Zwingli-Verlag, *n.d.*).

Berger, Klaus. "Die königlichen Messiastraditionen des Neuen Testaments." *New Testament Studies* 20 (1974): 1-44.

___. "Der traditionsgeschichtliche Ursprung der 'Traditio Legis'." *Vigiliae Christianae* 27 (1973): 104-122.

Bernard, J. H. *A Critical and Exegetical Commentary on the Gospel According to St. John*, ed. A. H. McNeile, 2 vols. The International Critical Commentary. Edinburgh: T. & T. Clark, 1928; reprint, 1942.

Bertholet, Alfred. *Deuteronomium*. Kurzer Hand-Commentar zum Alten Testament, ed. Karl Marti, vol. 5. Freiburg i. B., Leipzig, and Tübingen: J. C. B. Mohr (Paul Siebeck), 1899.

Best, Ernest. *One Body in Christ: A Study in the Relationship of the Church to Christ in the Epistles of the Apostle Paul*. London: SPCK, 1955.

Betz, Hans Dieter. *Galatians: A Commentary on Paul's Letter to the Churches in Galatia*. Hermeneia: A Critical and Historical Commentary on the Bible, New Testament Editorial Board, Helmut Koester, et al. Philadelphia: Fortress Press, 1979.

Blau, Ludwig. *Die jüdische Ehescheidung und der jüdische Scheidebrief: Eine historische Untersuchung*. Part One: "Die jüdische Ehescheidung." Part Two: [no separate title]. Budapest: In conjunction with *Jahresbericht der Landes-Rabbinerschule in Budapest für das Schuljahr 1910-1911*; part one, 1911; part two, 1912; reprinted in one volume, Westmead, Farnborough, Hants., England: Gregg International Publishers, 1970.

Bloch, Renée. "Quelques aspects de la figure de Moïse dans la tradition rabbinique." *Cahiers Sioniens* 8, nos. 2, 3, and 4 (*Moïse: L'homme de l'alliance*, 1954): 93-167 in this fascicle (211-285 in the volume).

Bock, Darrell L. *Proclamation from Prophecy and Pattern: Lucan Old Testament Christology*. Journal for the Study of the New Testament Supplement Series, ed. David Hill, publishing ed. David E. Orton, vol. 12. Sheffield: JSOT Press, 1987.

___. *Luke*. 2 vols., *1:1-9:50* and *9:51-24.53*. Baker Exegetical Commentary on the New Testament, ed. Moisés Silva, vols. 3A, 3B. Grand Rapids: Baker Books, 1996.

Boismard, M.-É. *Moses or Jesus: An Essay in Johannine Christology*. Translated by B. T. Viviano. Bibliotheca Ephemeridum Theologicarum Lovaniensum LXXXIV-A. Louvain: Leuven University Press, 1993.

Borgen, P. "'There Shall Come Forth a Man': Reflections on Messianic Ideas in Philo." In *The Messiah: Developments in Earliest Judaism and Christianity*, ed. James H. Charlesworth with J. Brownson, M. T. Davis, S. J. Kraftchick, and A. F. Segal, 341-361. Minneapolis: Fortress Press, 1992.

Bovon, Francois. "La figure de Moïse dans l'oeuvre de Luc." In *La figure de Moïse: Ecriture et relectures*, by Robert Martin-Achard, et al., 47-65. Publications de la Faculté de Théologie de l'Université de Genève, no. 1. Geneva: Labor et Fides, 1978.

Bowman, John, translator and editor. *Samaritan Documents Relating to Their History, Religion and Life*. Pittsburgh Original Texts and Translations Series, ed. Dikran Y. Hadidian, no. 2. Pittsburgh: The Pickwick Press, 1977.

___. "Samaritan Studies." *Bulletin of the John Rylands Library* 40 (1957-1958): 298-327.

Braumann, Georg. *Vorpaulinische christliche Taufverkündigung bei Paulus*. Beiträge zur Wissenschaft vom Alten und Neuen Testament, 5th series, ed. Karl Heinrich Rengstorf and Leonhard Rost, vol. 2 (vol. 82 of the entire collection). Stuttgart: W. Kohlhammer, 1962.

Braun, Martin. *History and Romance in Graeco-Oriental Literature*. With a preface by Arnold Toynbee. Oxford: Basil Blackwell, 1938.

Brown, Raymond E. *The Gospel According to John (i-xii)* and *The Gospel According to John (xiii-xxi)*. The Anchor Bible, ed. William Foxwell Albright and David Noel Freedman, unnumbered and vol. 29A respectively. Garden City, New York: Doubleday and Co., 1966, 1970.

Büchsel, F., with O. Proksch. "λύω κτλ." *Theological Dictionary of the New Testament*, ed. Gerhard Kittel, trans. and ed. Geoffrey W. Bromiley, vol. 4, *Λ-Ν*, 328-356. Grand Rapids: Wm. B. Eerdmans, 1967.

Bühner, Jan-Adolf. *Der Gesandte und sein Weg im 4. Evangelium: Die kultur- und religionsgeschichtlichen Grundlagen der johanneischen Sendungschristologie sowie ihre traditionsgeschichtliche Entwicklung*. Wissenschaftliche Untersuchungen zum Neuen Testament, 2d series, ed. Martin Hengel, Joachim Jeremias, and Otto Michel, no. 2. Tübingen: J. C. B. Mohr (Paul Siebeck), 1977.

Bultmann, Rudolf. *Das Evangelium des Johannes*, 11th ed. (2d ed. by Bultmann). Kritisch-exegetischer Kommentar über das Neue Testament, part 2, 11th ed. Göttingen: Vandenhoeck & Ruprecht, 1950.

___. *Der zweite Brief an die Korinther*, ed. Erich Dinkler. Kritisch-exegetischer Kommentar über das Neue Testament, ed. Ferdinand Hahn. Göttingen: Vandenhoeck & Ruprecht, 1976.

Burkitt, F. Crawford. *Jewish and Christian Apocalypses*. The Schweich Lectures, 1913. London: Oxford University Press, 1914.

Camponovo, Odo. *Königtum, Königsherrschaft und Reich Gottes in den frühjüdischen Schriften*. Orbis Biblicus et Orientalis, ed. Othmar Keel, with Erich Zenger and Albert de Pury, no. 58. Freiburg, Switzerland: Universitätsverlag Freiburg; Göttingen: Vandenhoeck & Ruprecht, 1995.

Carson, D. A. *The Gospel According to John*. Leicester: Inter-Varsity Press; Grand Rapids: Wm. B. Eerdmans, 1991.

Casey, P. M. *From Jewish Prophet to Gentile God: The Origins and Development of New Testament Christology*. Cambridge, England: James Clarke & Co.; Louisville, Kentucky: Westminster/John Knox Press, 1991.

Cazelles, Henri, with H.-J. Fabry. "מֹשֶׁה mōšeh." *Theological Dictionary of the Old Testament*, ed. G. Johannes Botterweck, Helmer Ringgren, and Heinz-Josef Fabry. Translated by David E. Green, vol. 9, נָשָׂה־מָרַד *mārad-nāqâ* [sic], 28-43. Grand Rapids: William B. Eerdmans, 1998.

Chadwick, Henry. *The Church in Ancient Society from Galilee to Gregory the Great*. Oxford: Oxford University Press, 2001.

Charlesworth, James Hamilton. *The Old Testament Pseudepigrapha and the New Testament: Prolegomena for the Study of Christian Origins*. Society for New Testament Studies Monograph Series, ed. G. N. Stanton, vol. 54. Cambridge: Cambridge University Press, 1985.

Cohen, Shaye J. D. *The Beginnings of Jewishness: Boundaries, Varieties, Uncertainties*. Hellenistic Culture and Society, ed. Anthony W. Bulloch, et al., no. 31. Berkeley and Los Angeles: University of California Press, 1999.

___. "Is 'Proselyte Baptism' Mentioned in the Mishnah?: The Interpretation of *m. Pesahim* 8.8 (= *m. Eduyot* 5.2)." In *Pursuing the Text: Studies in Honor of Ben Zion Wacholder on the Occasion of his Seventieth Birthday*, ed. John C. Reeves and John Kampen, 278-292. Journal for the Study of the Old Testament Supplement Series, ed. David J. A. Klines and Philip R. Davies, no. 184. Sheffield: Sheffield Academic Press, 1994.

___. "The Rabbinic Conversion Ceremony." *Journal of Jewish Studies* 41 (1990): 177-203.

Collange, J.-F. *Énigmes de la deuxième épître de Paul aux Corinthiens: Étude exégetique de 2 Cor. 12:14-7:4.* Society for New Testament Studies Monograph Series, ed. Matthew Black, no. 18. Cambridge: The University Press, 1972.

Collins, Adela Yarbro. "The Worship of Jesus and the Imperial Cult." In *The Jewish Roots of Christological Monotheism: Papers from the St. Andrews Conference on the Historical Origin of the Worship of Jesus,* ed. Carey C. Newman, James R. Davila, and Gladys S. Lewis, 234-257. Supplements to the *Journal for the Study of Judaism,* ed. John J. Collins with Florentino García Martínez, vol. 63. Leiden: Brill, 1999.

Collins, John J. "The Date and Provenance of the Testament of Moses." In *Studies on the Testament of Moses,* ed. George W. E. Nickelsburg, Jr., 15-32. Septuagint and Cognate Studies, no. 4. Cambridge, Massachusetts: Society of Biblical Literature, 1973.

___. *The Sibylline Oracles of Egyptian Judaism.* SBL Dissertation Series, no. 13. Missoula, Montana: Society of Biblical Literature, 1974.

___. "Jewish Monotheism and Christian Theology." In *Aspects of Monotheism: How God Is One,* ed. Hershel Shanks and Jack Meinhardt, 81-105. Symposium at the Smithsonian Institution October 19, 1996. Washington, D.C.: Biblical Archaeology Society, 1997.

Craigie, Peter C. *The Book of Deuteronomy.* The New International Commentary on the Old Testament, ed. R. K. Harrison. Grand Rapids: William B. Eerdmans, 1976.

Cranfield, C. E. B. *The Gospel According to Saint Mark,* rev. ed. Cambridge Greek Testament Commentary, ed. C. F. D. Moule. Cambridge: Cambridge University Press, 1972.

Cullmann, Oscar. *Die Christologie des Neuen Testaments.* Tübingen: J. C. B. Mohr (Paul Siebeck), 1957

___. *The Christology of the New Testament,* 2d ed. E.T. London: SCM Press, 1963.

Dahl, Nils Alstrup. *Jesus the Christ: The Historical Origins of Christological Doctrine.* Edited by Donald H. Juel. Minneapolis: Fortress Press, 1991.

___., revised by D. H. Juel. "Messianic Ideas and the Crucifixion of Jesus." In *The Messiah: Developments in Earliest Judaism and Christianity,* ed. James H. Charlesworth, with J. Brownson, M. T. Davis, S. J. Kraftchich, and A. F. Segal, 382-403. Minneapolis: Fortress Press, 1992.

___. *Das Volk Gottes: Eine Untersuchung zum kirchenbewusstsein des Urchristentums.* Skrifter Utgitt Av Det Norske Videnskaps-Akademi I Oslo (Writings published by the Norwegian Science Academy of Oslo), II. Hist.-Filos. Klasse, 1941, no. 2. Oslo: Jacob Dybwad, 1941.

D'Angelo, Mary Rose. *Moses in the Letter to the Hebrews.* Society of Biblical Literature Dissertation Series, ed. Howard Clark Kee, no. 42. Missoula, Montana: Scholars Press, 1979.

Davies, W. D. "Jewish Sources of Matthew's Messianism." In *The Messiah: Developments in Earliest Judaism and Christianity,* ed. James H. Charlesworth, with J. Brownson, M. T. Davis, S. J. Kraftchick, and A. F. Segal, 494-511. Minneapolis: Fortress Press, 1992.

___. *Paul and Rabbinic Judaism: Some Rabbinic Elements in Pauline Theology,* 4th ed., with new preface. Philadelphia: Fortress Press, 1980.

___. *The Setting of the Sermon on the Mount.* Cambridge: The University Press, 1964.

___. *Torah in the Messianic Age and/or the Age to Come.* Journal of Biblical Literature Monograph Series, ed. Ralph Marcus, vol. 7. Philadelphia: Society of Biblical Literature, 1952.

Davies, W. D. and Dale Allison. *A Critical and Exegetical Commentary on the Gospel According to Saint Matthew.* 3 vols. Volume 1, *Introduction and Commentary on Matthew 1-7*; vol. 2, *Commentary on Matthew 8-18*; vol. 3, *Commentary on Matthew 19-28.* The International Critical Commentary on the Holy Scriptures of the Old and New Testaments, ed. J. A. Emerton, C. E. B. Cranfield, and G. N. Stanton. Edinburgh: T. & T. Clark, 1988, 1991, 1997.

Davila, James R. "Of Methodology, Monotheism and Metatron: Introductory Reflections on Divine Mediators and the Origins of the Worship of Jesus." In *The Jewish Roots of Christological Monotheism: Papers from the St. Andrews Conference on the Historical Origin of the Worship of Jesus*, ed. Carey C. Newman, James R. Davila, and Gladys S. Lewis, 3-18. Supplements to the *Journal for the Study of Judaism*, ed. John J. Collins with Florentino García Martínez, vol. 63. Leiden: Brill, 1999.

Day, John. "Prophecy." In *It Is Written: Scripture Citing Scripture: Essays in Honour of Barnabas Lindars, SSF*, ed. D. A. Carson and H. G. M. Williamson, 39-55. Cambridge: Cambridge University Press, 1988.

de Jonge, Marinus. *Christology in Context: The Earliest Christian Responses to Jesus.* Philadelphia: The Westminster Press, 1998.

___. *God's Final Envoy: Early Christology and Jesus' Own View of His Mission.* Grand Rapids, Michigan and Cambridge, England: William B. Eerdmans, 1998.

___. "Jesus as Prophet and King in the Fourth Gospel." *Ephemerides Theologicae Lovaniensis* 49, no. 1 (May 1973): 160-177.

___. *Jesus: Stranger from Heaven and Son of God: Jesus Christ and the Christians in Johannine Perspective.* Edited and translated by John E. Steely. Society of Biblical Literature Sources for Biblical Study, ed. Wayne A. Meeks, no. 11. Missoula, Montana: Scholars Press, 1977.

Delling, Gerhard. "ἄρχω κτλ." In *Theological Dictionary of the New Testament*, ed. Gerhard Kittel, trans. and ed. Geoffrey W. Bromiley, vol. 4, *Α-Γ*, 478-489. Grand Rapids: Wm. B. Eerdmans, 1964.

Démann, Paul. "Moïse et la Loi dans la pensée de Saint Paul." *Cahiers Sioniens* 8, nos. 2, 3, and 4 (*Moïse: L'homme de l'alliance*, 1954): 189-242 in this fascicle (307-360 in the volume).

Descamps, Albert. "Moïse dans les évangiles et dans la tradition apostolique." *Cahiers Sioniens* 8, nos. 2, 3, and 4 (*Moïse: L'homme de l'alliance*, 1954): 171-187 in this fascicle (290-305 in the volume).

Dexinger, Ferdinand. "Die Moses-terminologie in Tibåt Mårqe — Einige Beobachtungen." *Frankfurter Judaistische Beiträge* 25 (1998): 51-62.

___. "Samaritan Eschatology." In *The Samaritans*, ed. Alan D. Crown, 266-292. Tübingen: J. C. B. Mohr (Paul Siebeck), 1989.

Dogniez, Cécile and Marguerite Harl. *Le Deutéronome: Traduction du texte grec de la Septante, Introduction et Notes.* La Bible d'Alexandrie, ed. Marguerite Harl, vol. 5. Paris: Les Éditions du Cerf, 1992.

du Mesnil du Buisson, Comte. *Les peintures de la synagogue de Doura-Europos, 245-256 après J.-C.* Introduction by Gabriel Millet. Scripta Pontificii Instituti Biblici, no. 86. Rome: Pontifical Biblical Institute, 1939.

Dunn, James D. G. *The Acts of the Apostles.* Epworth Commentaries, ed. Ivor H. Jones. Peterborough, England: Epworth Press, 1996.

___. *Baptism in the Holy Spirit: A Re-examination of the New Testament Teaching on the Gift of the Spirit in relation to Pentecostalism Today.* Studies in Biblical Theology, 2d series, ed. C. F. D. Moule, et al., no. 15. London: SCM Press, 1970.

___. *Christology in the Making: A New Testament Inquiry into the Origins of the Doctrine of the Incarnation*, 2d ed. London: SCM Press, 1989.

___. *The Theology of Paul the Apostle*. Edinburgh: T. & T. Clark, 1998.

Ellis, E. Earle. *Paul's Use of the Old Testament*. Edinburgh: Oliver and Boyd, 1957.

___. "Traditions in 1 Corinthians." *New Testament Studies* 32 (1986): 481-502.

Ellis, Peter F. *The Genius of John: A Composition-Critical Commentary on the Fourth Gospel*. Collegeville, Minnesota: The Liturgical Press, 1984.

Ellison, H. L. *The Centrality of the Messianic Idea for the Old Testament*. Tyndale Monographs. London: Tyndale Press, 1953.

Emerton, J. A. "Some New Testament Notes." *Journal of Theological Studies*, NS, 11 (1960): 329-336.

Enns, Peter. *Exodus Retold: Ancient Exegesis of the Departure from Egypt in Wis 15-21 and 19:1-9*. Harvard Semitic Museum Publications, ed. Lawrence E. Stager, Harvard Semitic Monographs, ed. Peter Machinist, no. 57. Atlanta: Scholars Press, 1997.

Evans, C. F. "The Central Section of St. Luke's Gospel." *Studies in the Gospels: Essays in Memory of R. H. Lightfoot*, ed. D. E. Nineham, 37-53. Oxford: Basil Blackwell, 1955.

Fee, Gordon D. *The First Epistle to the Corinthians*. The New International Commentary on the New Testament, ed. F. F. Bruce. Grand Rapids: William B. Eerdmans, 1987.

Fitzmyer, Joseph A. *The Acts of the Apostles: A New Translation with Introduction and Commentary*. The Anchor Bible, ed, William Foxwell Albright and David Noel Freedman, vol. 31. New York: Doubleday, 1998.

___. *Paul and His Theology: A Brief Sketch*, 2d ed. Englewood Cliffs, New Jersey: Prentice Hall, 1989.

Fletcher-Louis, Crispin H. T. "4Q374: A Discourse on the Sinai Tradition: The Deification of Moses and Early Christology." *Dead Sea Discoveries* 3 (1996): 236-252.

___. *All the Glory of Adam: Liturgical Anthropology in the Dead Sea Scrolls*. Studies on the Texts of the Desert of Judah, edited by F. García Martínez with P. W. Flint, vol. 42. Leiden: E. J. Brill, 2002.

___. *Luke-Acts: Angels, Christology and Soteriology*. Wissenschaftliche Untersuchungen zum Neuen Testament, 2d series, ed. Martin Hengel and Otfried Hofius, vol. 94. Tübingen: J. C. B. Mohr (Paul Siebeck), 1997.

___. "The Revelation of the Son of Man: The Genre, History of Religions Context and the Meaning of the Transfiguration." In *Auferstehung-Resurrection*, ed. Friedrich Avemarie and Hermann Lichtenberger. Wissenschaftliche Untersuchungen zum Neuen Testament, ed. Martin Hengel and Otfried Hofius, vol. 135. Tübingen: J. C. B. Mohr (Paul Siebeck), 2001.

Fossum, Jarl E. *The Image of the Invisible God: Essays on the Influence of Jewish Mysticism on Early Christianity*. Novum Testamentum et Orbis Antiquus, ed. Max Küchler, with Gerd Theissen, no. 30. Freiburg, Switzerland: Universitätsverlag Freiburg; Göttingen: Vandenhoeck & Ruprecht, 1995.

___. *The Name of God and the Angel of the Lord: Samaritan and Jewish Concepts of Intermediation and the Origin of Gnosticism*. Wissenschaftliche Untersuchungen zum Neuen Testament, ed. Martin Hengel and Otfried Hofius, no. 36. Tübingen: J. C. B. Mohr (Paul Siebeck), 1985.

___. "Sects and Movements." In *The Samaritans*, ed. Alan D. Crown, 293-389. Tübingen: J. C. B. Mohr (Paul Siebeck), 1989.

Franke, Peter. "Traditio Legis und Petrusprimat." *Vigiliae Christianae* 26 (1972): 263-271.

Fraser, P. M. *Ptolemaic Alexandria*, 3 vols. divided into 4 parts; vol. 1, *Text*, vol. 2a, *Notes to Chapters 1-7*; vol. 2b, *Notes to Chapters 8-11 and Epilogue*; vol. 3, *Indexes*. Oxford: Clarendon Press, 1972; reprint, 1984, still in three tomes, but with volume 2 broken into 2a and 2b, with vol. 2a bound separately and vol. 2b bound together with vol. 3 in the third tome.

Fredriksen, Paula. *From Jesus to Christ: The Origins of the New Testament Images of Jesus*. New Haven, Connecticut and London: Yale University Press, 1988.

Freudenthal, J. *Alexander Polyhistor und die von ihm erhaltenen Reste judäischer und samaritanischer Geschichtswerke*. Vol. 2 in *Hellenistische Studien von Dr. J. Freudenthal*, vols. 1 and 2. Breslau: H. Skutsch, 1875.

Freund, Richard A. "From Kings to Archons: Jewish Political Ethics and Kingship Passages in the LXX." *Scandinavian Journal of the Old Testament* (1990, part 2): 58-72.

Friedrich, Gerhard. "εὐαγγελίζομαι κτλ." In *Theological Dictionary of the New Testament*, ed. Gerhard Friedrich, trans. and ed. Geoffrey W. Bromiley, vol. 2, *Δ-Η*, 707-737. Grand Rapids: Wm. B. Eerdmans, 1964.

Fuller, Reginald H. *The Foundations of New Testament Christology*. Lutterworth Library, ed. James Barr, et al. London: Lutterworth Press, 1965.

Furnish, Victor Paul. *II Corinthians: Translated with Introduction, Notes, and Commentary*. The Anchor Bible, ed. William Foxwell Albright and David Noel Freedman, vol. 32A. Garden City, New York: Doubleday & Co., 1984.

Gager, John G. *Moses in Greco-Roman Paganism*. Society of Biblical Literature Monograph Series, ed. Robert A. Kraft, no. 16. Nashville and New York: Abingdon Press, 1972.

Gardner-Smith, P. *Saint John and the Synoptic Gospels*. Cambridge: The University Press, 1938.

Gavin, F. *The Jewish Antecedents of the Christian Sacraments*. London: Society for Promoting Christian Knowledge, 1928.

Gelin, Albert. "Moïse dans l'Ancient Testament." *Cahiers Sioniens* 8, nos. 2, 3, and 4 (*Moïse: L'homme de l'alliance*, 1954): 29-52 in this fascicle (147-170 in the volume).

Gieschen, Charles A. *Angelomorphic Christology: Antecedents and Early Evidence*. Arbeiten zur Geschichte des Antiken Judentums und des Urchristentums, ed. Martin Hengel, et al., no. 42. Leiden: Brill, 1998.

Ginzberg, Louis. *The Legends of the Jews*. 7 vols. Vols. 1 and 2 translated by Henrietta Szold. Vol. 3 translated by Paul Radin. Vol. 7, *Index*, by Boaz Cohen. Philadelphia: The Jewish Publication Society of America, 1913, 1920[*sic*], 1911[*sic*], 1913, 1925, 1928, 1938.

Glasson, T. F. *Moses in the Fourth Gospel*. Studies in Biblical Theology, ed. C. F. D. Moule, et al., no. 40. London: SCM Press, 1963.

Goldin, Judah. "Not by Means of an Angel and Not by Means of a Messenger." *Religions in Antiquity: Essays in Memory of Erwin Ramsdell Goodenough*, ed. Jacob Neusner, 412-424. Studies in the History of Religion (Supplements to *Numen*), no. 14. Leiden: E. J. Brill, 1968.

Goodenough, Erwin R. *By Light, Light: The Mystic Gospel of Hellenistic Judaism*. New Haven, Connecticut: Yale University Press, 1935; reprint, Amsterdam: Philo Press, 1969.

___. *Jewish Symbols in the Greco-Roman Period.* 12 vols. + vol. 13, *Indexes and Maps*, prepared by Delight Ansley and Liam Dunne, with Irene J. Winter. Bollingen Series, no 37. New York: Pantheon Books, 1953 (vols. 1-3), 1954 (vol. 4), 1956 (vols. 5-6), 1958 (vols. 7-8), 1964 (vols. 9-11), 1965 (vol. 12); Princeton, New Jersey: Princeton University Press, 1968 (vol. 13).

___. "The Political Philosophy of Hellenistic Kingship." In *Yale Classical Studies*, ed. Austin M. Harmon, vol. 1. New Haven: Yale University Press, 1928.

___. *The Politics of Philo Judaeus: Practice and Theory.* With bibliography of Philo by Howard L. Goodhart and Erwin R. Goodenough. New Haven: Yale University Press, 1938.

Goodman, Martin. *Mission and Conversion: Proselytizing in the Religious History of the Roman Empire.* Oxford: Clarendon Press, 1994.

Grabbe, Lester L. *Judaic Religion in the Second Temple Period: Belief and Practice from the Exile to Yavneh.* London and New York: Routledge, 2000.

Gray, Rebecca. *Prophetic Figures in Late Second Temple Jewish Palestine: The Evidence from Josephus.* New York and Oxford: Oxford University Press, 1993.

Green, E. M. B. *2 Peter Reconsidered.* Tyndale Monographs. London: Tyndale Press, 1960.

Gruen, Erich S. *Heritage and Hellenism: The Reinvention of Jewish Tradition.* Hellenistic Culture and Society, ed. Anthony W. Bulloch, et al., no. 30. Berkeley: University of California Press, 1998.

Grundmann, Walter. "The Decision of the Supreme Court to Put Jesus to Death (John 11:47-57) in Its Context: Tradition and Redaction in the Gospel of John." In *Jesus and the Politics of His Day*, ed. Ernst Bammel and C. F. D. Moule, 295-318. Cambridge: Cambridge University Press, 1984.

Gundry, Robert H. *Mark: A Commentary on His Apology for the Cross.* Grand Rapids: William B. Eerdmans, 1993.

Gutbrod, W. with H. Kleinknecht. "νόμος." In *Theological Dictionary of the New Testament*, ed. Gerhard Kittel, trans. and ed. Geoffrey W. Bromiley, vol. 4, *Λ-Ν*, 1022-1091. Grand Rapids: Wm. B. Eerdmans, 1967.

Gutmann, Joseph, ed. *The Dura-Europos Synagogue: A Re-evaluation (1932-1992).* South Florida Studies in the History of Judaism, ed. Jacob Neusner, et al., no. 25. Atlanta: Scholars Press, 1992.

von Haacker, Klaus and Peter Schäfer. "Nachbiblische Traditionen vom Tod des Mose." In *Josephus-Studien: Untersuchungen zu Josephus dem antiken Judentum und dem Neuen Testament: Otto Michel zum 70. Geburtstag gewidmet*, ed. Otto Betz, Klaus Haacker, and Martin Hengel, 147-174. Göttingen: Vandenhoeck & Ruprecht, 1974.

Habel N. "The Form and Significance of the Call Narratives ." *Zeitschrift fur die alttestamentliche Wissenschaft* 77, no. 3 (1965): 305-23.

Hadas, Moses, editor and translator. *Aristeas to Philocrates (Letter of Aristeas).* Dropsie College Edition. Jewish Apocryphal Literature, ed. Solomon Zeitlin, et al. New York: Harper & Brothers, 1951.

Haenchen, Ernst. *The Acts of the Apostles: A Commentary.* Translated from 14th German ed. (Göttingen: Vandenhoeck and Ruprecht, 1965) by Bernard Noble and Gerald Shinn, under the supervision of Hugh Anderson. Translation revised and updated by R. McL. Wilson. Oxford: Basil Blackwell, 1971.

___. *John 1: A Commentary on the Gospel of John Chapters 1-6.* Translated by Robert W. Funk. Edited by Robert W. Funk with Ulrich Busse. Hermeneia — A

Critical and Historical Commentary on the Bible, ed. Frank Moore Cross, Helmut Koester, et al. Philadelphia: Fortress Press, 1984.

Hafemann, Scott J. "Moses in the Apocrypha and Pseudepigrapha: A Survey." *Journal for the Study of the Pseudepigrapha* 7 (1990): 79-104.

____. *Paul, Moses, and the History of Israel: The Letter/Spirit Contrast and the Argument from Scripture in 2 Corinthians 3.* Wissenschaftliche Untersuchungen zum Neuen Testament, ed. Martin Hengel and Otfried Hofius, no. 81. Tübingen: J. C. B. Mohr (Paul Siebeck), 1995.

Hahn, Ferdinand. *Christologische Hoheitstitel: Ihre Geschichte im frühen Christentum.* Forschungen zur Religion und Literatur des Alten und Neuen Testamentes, ed. Ernst Käsemann and Ernst Würthwein, no. 83. Göttingen: Vandenhoeck & Ruprecht, 1963.

____. *The Titles of Jesus in Christology: Their History in Early Christianity.* Translated by Harold Knight and George Ogg. Lutterworth Library, ed. James Barr, et al. London: Lutterworth Press, 1969.

Hamerton-Kelly, R. G. *Pre-existence, Wisdom, and the Son of Man: A Study of the Idea of Pre-existence in the New Testament.* Society for New Testatment Studies Monograph Series, ed. Matthew Black and R. McL. Wilson, no. 21. Cambridge: The University Press, 1973.

Harris, Murray J. "Prepositions and Theology in the Greek New Testament." In *The New International Dictonary of New Testament Theology*, ed. Colin Brown, trans. G. H. Boobyer, et al., vol. 3, *Pri-Z.* Exeter: Paternoster Press, 1978.

Harstine, Stan. *Moses as a Character in the Fourth Gospel: A Study of Ancient Reading Techniques.* Journal for the Study of the New Testament Supplement Series, ed. Stanley E. Porter, et al., no. 229. London and New York: Sheffield Academic Press, 2002.

Hayes, Christine E. *Gentile Impurities and Jewish Identities: Intermarriage and Conversion from the Bible to the Talmud.* Oxford: Oxford University Press, 2002.

Haykin, Michael A. G. "'In the Cloud and in the Sea': Basil of Caesarea and the Exegesis of 1 Cor 10:2." *Vigiliae Christianae* 40 (1986): 135-144.

Hays, Richard B. *First Corinthians.* Interpretation: A Bible Commentary for Teaching and Preaching, ed. James Luther Mays, Patrick D. Miller, and Paul J. Achtemeier. Louisville, Kentucky: John Knox Press, 1997.

Hengel, Martin. "Das Johannesevangelium als Quelle für die Geschichte des antiken Judentums." In *Judaica, Hellenistica, et Christiana: Kleine Schriften II*, ed. Martin Hengel with Jörg Frey and Dorothea Betz, 293-334. Wissenschaftliche Untersuchungen zum Neuen Testament, ed. Martin Hengel and Otfried Hofius, no. 109. Tübingen: J. C. B. Mohr (Paul Siebeck), 1999.

____. *The Four Gospels and the One Gospel of Jesus Christ: An Investigation of the Collection and Origin of the Canonical Gospels.* London: SCM Press, 2000.

____. "Präexistenz bei Paulus?" In *Jesus Christus als die Mitte der Schrift: Studien zur Hermeneutik des Evangeliums*, ed. Christof Landmesser, Hans-Joachim Eckstein, and Hermann Lichtenberger. Beihefte zur Zeitschrift für die neutestamentliche Wissenschaft und die Kunde der älteren Kirche, ed. Erich Gräßer, no. 86, 479-518. Berlin and New York: Walter de Gruyter, 1997.

____. *Studies in Early Christology.* Edinburgh: T. & T. Clark, 1995.

____. *The Zealots: Investigations into the Jewish Freedom Movement in the Period from Herod I until 70 A.D.* Translated by David Smith. Edinburgh: T. & T. Clark, 1989.

Héring, J. *La première épître de saint Paul aux Corinthiens.* Commentaire du Nouveau Testament, ed. P. Bonnard, et al., no. 7. Paris: Delachaux & Niestlé, 1949.

Hickling, C. J. A. "Paul's Use of Exodus in the Corinthian Correspondence." In *The Corinthian Correspondence*, ed. R. Bieringer, 367-376. Bibliotheca Ephemeridum Theologicarum Lovaniensum, no. 125. Leuven-Louvain: Leuven University Press, 1996.

Hooker, Morna D. "Paul and 'Covenantal Nomism'." In *Paul and Paulinism: Essays in Honour of C. K. Barrett*, ed. M. D. Hooker and S. G. Wilson, 47-56. London: SPCK, 1982.

___. *The Signs of a Prophet: The Prophetic Actions of Jesus.* London: SCM Press, 1997.

Hopkins, Clark. *The Discovery of Dura-Europos*, ed. Bernard Goldman. New Haven and London: Yale University Press, 1979.

Horbury, William. "The Aaronic Priesthood in the Epistle to the Hebrews." *Journal for the Study of the New Testament* 19 (October 1983): 43-71.

___. "Jewish-Christian Relations in Barnabas and Justin Martyr." In *Jews and Christians: The Parting of the Ways A.D. 70 to 135*, ed. James D. G. Dunn, 315-345. Wissenschaftliche Untersuchungen zum Neuen Testament, ed. Martin Hengel and Otfried Hofius, no. 66. Tübingen: J. C. B. Mohr (Paul Siebeck), 1992.

___. *Jewish Messianism and the Cult of Christ.* London: SCM Press, 1998.

___. *Jews and Christians in Contact and Controversy.* Edinburgh: T. &. T. Clark, 1998.

___. "The Messianic Associations of 'The Son of Man'." *Journal of Theological Studies*, NS 36, no. 1 (April 1985): 34-55.

___. *Messianism Among Jews and Christians: Twelve Biblical and Historical Studies.* London and New York. T. & T. Clark, 2003.

___. "Moses and the Covenant in *The Assumption of Moses* and the Pentateuch." In *Covenant as Context*, ed. A. D. H. Mayes and R. B. Salters. Oxford: Clarendon Press, 2003.

___. "Old Testament Interpretation in the Writings of the Church Fathers." In *Mikra: Text, Translation, Reading and Interpretation of the Hebrew Bible in Ancient Judaism and Early Christianity*, ed. Martin Jan Mulder, 727-789. Compendia Rerum Iudaicarum ad Novum Testamentum, ed. W. J. Burgers, H. Sysling, and P. J. Tomson, Section Two, The Literature of the Jewish People in the Period of the Second Temple and the Talmud, Volume 1. Assen and Maastricht: Van Gorcum; Philadelphia: Fortress Press, 1988.

___. "Septuagintal and New Testament Conceptions of the Church." In *A Vision for the Church: Studies in Early Christian Ecclesiology in Honour of J. P. M. Sweet*, ed. Markus Bockmuehl and Michael B. Thompson, 1-17. Edinburgh: T. & T. Clark, 1997.

___. "The Twelve and the Phylarchs." *New Testament Studies* 32 (1986): 503-527.

___. "Women in the Synagogue." In *The Cambridge History of Judaism*, vol. 3, *The Early Roman Period*, ed. William Horbury, W. D. Davies, and John Sturdy, 358-401. Cambridge: Cambridge University Press, 1999.

___. Review of *The Office of Apostle in the Early Church*, by Walter Schmithals, translated by J. E. Steely. *Journal of Theological Studies*, NS 23 (1972): 216-219.

Horsley, Richard A. "'How can some of you say that there is no resurrection of the dead?': Spiritual Elitism in Corinth." *Novum Testamentum* 20 (1978): 203-231.

____. "Popular Prophetic Movements at the Time of Jesus: Their Principal Features and Social Origins." *Journal for the Study of the New Testament* 26 (February 1986): 3-27.

Horsley, Richard A. and John S. Hanson. *Bandits, Prophets, and Messiahs: Popular Movements in the Time of Jesus*. New Voices in Biblical Studies, ed. Adela Yarbro Collins and John J. Collins. Minneapolis: Winston Press, 1985.

Hurtado, Larry W. *Mark*. New International Biblical Commentary, New Testament ed., W. Ward Gasque. Peabody, Massachusetts: Hendrickson, 1989.

____. *One God, One Lord: Early Christian Devotion and Ancient Jewish Monotheism*. London: SCM Press, 1988.

Instone-Brewer, David. "1 Corinthians 7 in the Light of the Jewish Greek and Aramaic Marriage and Divorce Papyri." *Tyndale Bulletin* 52, no. 1 (2001): 101-116.

Jacobs, Louis. "Moses (Rabbinic View)." *Encyclopaedia Judaica*, ed. Cecil Roth, et al., 12.393-395. Jerusalem: Keter Publishing House, 1972.

Jepsen, Alfred. *Nabi: Soziologische Studien zur alttestamentlichen Literatur und Religionsgeschichte*. München: C. B. Beck'sche Verlagsbuchhandlung, 1934.

Jeremias, Gert. *Der Lehrer der Gerechtigkeit*. Studien zur Umwelt des Neuen Testaments, ed. Karl Georg Kuhn, vol. 2. Göttingen: Vandenhoeck & Ruprecht, 1963.

Jeremias, Joachim. "Μωυσῆς." In *Theological Dictionary of the New Testament*, ed. Gerhard Kittel, trans. and ed. Geoffrey W. Bromiley, vol. 4, *Λ-Ν*, 848-873. Grand Rapids: Wm. B. Eerdmans, 1967.

____. "Μωυσῆς." In *Theologisches Wörterbuch zum Neuen Testament*, ed. Gerhard Kittel, vol. 4, *Λ-Ν*, 852-878. Stuttgart: W. Kohlhammer, 1942.

____. "Paulus als Hillelit." In *Neotestamentica et Semitica: Studies in Honour of Matthew Black*, ed. E. Earle Ellis and Max Wilcox, 88-94. Edinburgh: T. & T. Clark, 1969.

____. "ποιμήν κτλ." In *Theological Dictionary of the New Testament*, ed. Gerhard Friedrich, trans. and ed. Geoffrey W. Bromiley, vol. 6, *Πε-Ρ*, 485-502. Grand Rapids: Wm. B. Eerdmans, 1968.

____. "Proselytentaufe und Neues Testament." *Theologische Zeitschrift* 5 (1949): 418-428.

____. "Der Ursprung der Johannestaufe." *Zeitschrift für die Neutestamentliche Wissenschaft* 28 (1929): 312-320.

Jeske, Richard L. "The Rock was Christ: The Ecclesiology of 1 Corinthians 10." In *Kirche: Festschrift für Günther Bornkamm zum 75. Geburtstag*, ed. Dieter Lührmann and Georg Strecker, 245-255. Tübingen: J. C. B. Mohr (Paul Siebeck), 1980.

Johnson, Luke Timothy. *The Acts of the Apostles*. Sacra Pagina Series, ed. Daniel J. Harrington, vol. 5. Collegeville, Minnesota: The Liturgical Press, 1992.

Johnston, Edwin D. "The Johannine Version of the Feeding of the Five Thousand — An Independent Tradition?." *New Testament Studies* 8 (1961-1962): 151-154.

Jones, Peter Rhea. "The Figure of Moses as a Heuristic Device for Understanding the Pastoral Intent of Hebrews." *Review and Expositor* 76 (1979): 95-107.

Kastner, Josef M. "Moses im Neuen Testament." Th.D. Dissertation, Ludwig-Maximilians-Universität Munich, 1967.

Kistemaker, Simon J. *Exposition of the First Epistle to the Corinthians*. New Testament Commentary. Grand Rapids: Baker Books, 1993.

Knox, Wilfred L. *St Paul and the Church of the Gentiles*. Cambridge: Cambridge University Press, 1939.

____. *Some Hellenistic Elements in Primitive Christianity*. The Schweich Lectures of the British Academy, 1942. London: Oxford University Press, 1944.

Koester, Craig R. *Hebrews: A New Translation with Introduction and Commentary.* The Anchor Bible, ed. William Foxwell Albright and David Noel Freedman, vol. 36. New York: Doubleday, 2001.

Küchler, Max. *Schweigen, Schmuck und Schleier: Drei neutestamentliche Vorschriften zur Verdrängung der Frauen auf dem Hintergrund einer frauenfeindlichen Exegese des Alten Testaments im antiken Judentum.* Novum Testamentum et Orbis Antiquus, ed. Max Küchler with Gerd Theissen, no. 1. Freiburg, Switzerland: Universitätsverlag; Göttingen: Vandenhoeck & Ruprecht, 1986.

Kümmel, Werner Georg. *Introduction to the New Testament,* rev. ed. Translated by Howard Clark Kee from the 17th revised edition (Heidelberg: Quelle Meyer, 1973). London: SCM Press, 1975.

LaGrange, M.-J. *Évangile selon Saint Jean,* 2d ed. Études Bibliques. Paris: Librairie Victor LeCoffre, 1925.

Lane, William L. *Hebrews 1-8.* Word Biblical Commentary, ed. David A. Hubbard and Glenn W. Barker, New Testament Editor, Ralph P. Martin, vol. 47A. Dallas: Word Books, 1991.

Lebram, Jürgen C. H. "Der Idealstaat der Juden." In *Josephus-Studien: Untersuchungen zu Josephus, dem antiken Judentum, und dem Neuen Testament, Otto Michel zum 70. Geburtstag gewidmet,* ed. Otto Betz, Klaus Haacker, and Martin Hengel, 233-253. Göttingen: Vandenhoeck & Ruprecht, 1974.

Levine, Etan. *The Aramaic Version of the Bible: Contents and Context.* Beiheft zur Zeitschrift für die alttestamentliche Wissenschaft, ed. Otto Kaiser, no. 174. Berlin: Walter de Gruyter, 1988.

Lietzmann, Hans. *An die Korinther I/II,* expanded ed. Handbuch zum Neuen Testament, ed. Günther Bornkamm, vol. 9. Tübingen: J. C. B. Mohr (Paul Siebeck), 1949.

Lindars, Barnabas. *The Gospel of John.* New Century Bible, ed. Ronald E. Clements and Matthew Black. London: Oliphants, 1972.

Loewenstamm, Samuel E. "The Death of Moses." In *Studies on the Testament of Abraham,* ed. George W. E. Nickelsburg, Jr., 185-217. Septuagint and Cognate Studies, ed. Harry M. Orlinsky, no 6. Missoula, Montana: Scholars Press, 1972. [Revised version of article in *Tarbiz* 27 (1958): 142-157.]

Longenecker, Richard N. *Biblical Exegesis in the Apostolic Period.* Grand Rapids: William B. Eerdmans, 1975.

___. *The Christology of Early Jewish Christianity.* Studies in Biblical Theology, 2d series, ed. C. F. D. Moule, et al., no. 17. London: SCM Press, 1970.

MacDonald, John. *The Theology of the Samaritans.* The New Testament Library, ed. Alan Richardson, C. F. D. Moule, and Floyd V. Filson. London: SCM Press, 1964.

Maher, Michael. "Targum Pseudo-Jonathan of Exodus 2.21." *Targumic and Cognate Studies: Essays in Honour of Martin MacNamara,* ed. Kevin J. Cathcart and Michael Maher, 81-99. Journal for the Study of the Old Testament Supplement Series, ed. David J. A. Clines and Philip R. Davies, no. 230. Sheffield: Sheffield Academic Press, 1996.

Mánek, Jindřich. "The New Exodus in the Books of Luke." *Novum Testamentum* 2, no. 1 (January 1957): 8-23.

Manson, William. *The Epistle to the Hebrews: An Historical and Theological Reconsideration.* The Baird Lecture, 1949. London: Hodder and Staughton, 1951.

Marcus, Joel. *Mark 1-8: A New Translation with Introduction and Commentary.* The Anchor Bible, ed. William Foxwell Albright and David Noel Freedman, vol. 27. New York: Doubleday, 2000.

Martin, Ralph P. *2 Corinthians*. Word Biblical Commentary, ed. David A. Hubbard and Glenn W. Barker, New Testament Editor, Ralph P. Martin, vol. 40. Waco, Texas: Word Books, 1986.

Matera, Frank J. *New Testament Christology*. Louisville, Kentucky: Westminster John Knox Press, 1999.

Meeks, Wayne A. "'And Rose Up to Play': Midrash and Paraenesis in 1 Corinthians 10:1-22." *Journal for the Study of the New Testament* 16 (1982): 64-78.

___. "Moses as God and King." In *Religions in Antiquity: Essays in Memory of Erwin Ramsdell Goodenough*, ed. Jacob Neusner, 354-371. Studies in the History of Religions (Supplements to *Numen*), no. 14. Leiden: E. J. Brill, 1968.

___. *The Prophet-King: Moses Traditions and the Johannine Christology*. Supplements to *Novum Testamentum*, ed. W. C. van Unnik, et al., vol. 14. Leiden: E. J. Brill, 1967.

Menzies, Allan. *The Second Epistle of the Apostle Paul to the Corinthians: Introduction, Text, English Translation and Notes*. London: Macmillan and Co., 1912.

Merkel, Helmut. "The Opposition between Jesus and Judaism." In *Jesus and the Politics of His Day*, ed. Ernst Bammel and C. F. D. Moule, 129-144. Cambridge: Cambridge University Press, 1984.

Meshorer, Ya'akov. *Jewish Coins of the Second Temple Period*. Translated from the Hebrew by I. H. Levine. Tel-Aviv: Am Hassefer, 1967.

Metzger, Bruce, on behalf of and in cooperation with the Editorial Committee of the United Bible Societies' Greek New Testament. *A Textual Commentary on the Greek New Testament: A Companion Volume to the* United Bible Societies' Greek New Testament, 4th rev. ed., 2d ed. Stuttgart: German Bible Society and United Bible Societies, 1994.

Meyer, Rudolf, with Helmut Krämer, Rolf Rendtorff, and Gerhard Friedrich. "προφήτης κτλ." In *Theological Dictionary of the New Testament*, ed. Gerhard Friedrich, trans. and ed. Geoffrey W. Bromiley, vol. 6, *Πε-Ρ*, 781-861 (Meyer, 812-828). Grand Rapids: William B. Eerdmans, 1968, reprint, 1988.

Milgrom, Jacob. *Leviticus 1-16: A New Translation with Introduction and Commentary*. The Anchor Bible, ed. William Foxwell Albright and David Noel Freedman, vol. 3. New York: Doubleday, 1991.

Montefiore, Hugh. "Revolt in the Desert? (Mark VI.30ff)." *New Testament Studies* 8 (1961-1962): 135-141.

Montgomery, James Alan. *The Samaritans, the Earliest Jewish Sect: Their History, Theology and Literature*. Introduction by Abraham S. Halkin. New York: Ktav Publishing House, 1968; reprinted from first edition, 1907.

Moore, George Foote. *Judaism in the First Centuries of the Christian Era: The Age of the Tannaim*, 3 vols. Cambridge, Massachusetts: Harvard University Press, 1927, 1927, 1930.

Morray-Jones, C. R. A. "Transformational Mysticism in the Apocalyptic-Merkabah Tradition." *Journal of Jewish Studies* 43, no. 1 (1992): 1-31.

Morris, Leon. *The Gospel according to John*, rev. ed. The New International Commentary on the New Testament, ed. Gordon D. Fee. Grand Rapids: William B. Eerdmans, 1995.

Mowinckel, Sigmund. "General Oriental and Specific Israelite Elements in the Israelite Conception of the Sacral Kingdom." In *The Sacral Kingship: Contributions to the Central Theme of the VIIIth International Congress for the History of Religions*, 283-293. Studies in the History of Religions (Supplements to *NVMEN*), no. 4. Leiden: E. J. Brill, 1959.

Murphy, Frederick J. *Pseudo-Philo: Rewriting the Bible.* New York and Oxford: Oxford University Press, 1993.

Neusner, Jacob. "Judaism at Dura-Europos." In *The Dura-Europos Synagogue: A Reevaluation (1932-1992),* ed. Joseph Gutmann, 155-192. South Florida Studies in the History of Judaism, ed. Jacob Neusner, et al., no. 25. Atlanta: Scholars Press, 1992.

Newport, Kenneth G. C. "A Note on 'the Seat of Moses'." *Andrews University Seminary Studies* 28, no. 1 (1990): 53-58.

Nickelsburg, George W. E., Jr. "An Antiochan Date for the Testament of Moses." In *Studies on the Testament of Moses,* ed. George W. E. Nickelsburg, Jr., 33-37. Septuagint and Cognate Studies, no. 4. Cambridge, Massachusetts: Society of Biblical Literature, 1973.

___. "Introduction." In *Studies on the Testament of Moses,* ed. George W. E. Nickelsburg, Jr., 5-14. Septuagint and Cognate Studies, no. 4. Cambridge, Massachusetts: Society of Biblical Literature, 1973.

Niehr, H. "נָשִׂיא nāśî'." *Theologisches Wörterbuch zum Neuen Testament,* ed. G. Johannes Botterweck, Helmer Ringgren, and Heinz-Josef Fabry, vol. 4, מָרַד-עֹזֵב, 647-657. Stuttgart: W. Kohlhammer, 1986.

Nixon, R. E. *The Exodus in the New Testament.* Tyndale Monographs. London: The Tyndale Press, 1962.

Oepke, Albrecht. "βάπτω κτλ." In *Theological Dictionary of the New Testament,* ed. Gerhard Kittel, trans. and ed. Geoffrey W. Bromiley, vol. 1, *Α-Γ,* 529-546. Grand Rapids: William B. Eerdmans, 1964.

___. "μεσίτης κτλ." In *Theological Dictionary of the New Testament,* ed. Gerhard Kittel, trans. and ed. Geoffrey W. Bromiley, vol. 4, *Λ-Ν,* 598-624. Grand Rapids: William B. Eerdmans, 1967.

Oesterley, W. O. E. *The Wisdom of Jesus the Son of Sirach or Ecclesiasticus in the Revised Version with Introduction and Notes.* The Cambridge Bible for Schools and Colleges, ed. (Old Testament) A. F. Kirkpatrick. Cambridge: Cambridge University Press, 1912.

Ostmeyer, Karl-Heinrich. *Taufe und Typos: Elemente und Theologie der Tauftypologien in 1. Korinther 10 und 1. Petrus 3.* Wissenschaftliche Untersuchungen zum Neuen Testament, 2d series, ed. Martin Hengel and Otfried Hofius, no. 118. Tübingen: J. C. B. Mohr (Paul Siebeck), 2000.

Pamment, Margaret. "Moses and Elijah in the Story of the Transfiguration. *The Expository Times* 92 (1980-1981): 338-339.

Pérez Fernández, Miguel. *Tradiciones Mesiánicas en el Targum Palestinense: Estudios Exegéticos.* Institución San Jerónimo, no. 12. Valencia and Jerusalem: Institución San Jerónimo para la Investigación Bíblica, in collaboration with the Instituto Español Bíblico y Arqueológico (Casa de Santiago) de Jerusalén, 1981.

Polzin, Robert. "Deuteronomy." In *The Literary Guide to the Bible,* ed. Robert Alter and Frank Kermode, 92-101. London: William Collins & Sons, 1987.

Porter, J. R. *Moses and Monarchy: A Study in the Biblical Tradition of Moses.* Oxford: Basil Blackwell, 1963.

Powys, David. *"Hell": A Hard Look at a Hard Question: The Fate of the Unrighteous in New Testament Thought.* Foreword by Graham Stanton. Paternoster Biblical and Theological Monographs. Carlisle, Cumbria, U.K.: Paternoster Press, 1998.

Priest, J., trans. "The Testament of Moses." In *The Old Testament Pseudepigrapha,* ed. James H. Charlesworth, vol. 2, *Expansions of the "Old Testament" and Legends, Wisdom and Philosophical Literature, Prayers, Psalms and Odes, Fragments of Lost Judeo-Hellenistic Works*, 919-934. The Anchor Bible Reference Library. New York: Doubleday, 1985.

Quesnel, Michel. "La figure de Moïse en Romains 9-11." *New Testament Studies* 49 no. 3 (July 2003): 321-335.

Rendtorff, Rolf, with Rudolf Meyer, Helmut Krämer, and Gerhard Friedrich. "προφήτης κτλ." In *Theological Dictionary of the New Testament*, ed. Gerhard Friedrich, trans. and ed. Geoffrey W. Bromiley, vol. 6, *Πε-Ρ*, 781-861 (Rendtorff, 796-812). Grand Rapids: William B. Eerdmans, 1968, reprinted 1988.

Rengstorf, Karl Heinrich. "ἀποστέλλω κτλ." In *Theological Dictionary of the New Testament*, ed. Gerhard Kittel, trans. and ed. Geoffrey W. Bromiley, vol. 1, *Α-Γ*, 398-447. Grand Rapids: William B. Eerdmans, 1964.

___. "σημεῖον κτλ." In *Theological Dictionary of the New Testament*, ed. Gerhard Friedrich, trans. and ed. Geoffrey W. Bromiley, vol. 7, *Σ*, 200-269. Grand Rapids: William B. Eerdmans, 1964.

Renov, I. "The Seat of Moses." *Israel Exploration Journal* 5, no. 4 (1955): 262-267.

Ribera, Josep. "Prophecy according to Targum Jonathan to the Prophets and the Palestinian Targum to the Pentateuch." Translated by Fiona Ritchie. In *Targum Studies*, vol. 1, *Textual and Contextual Studies in the Pentateuchal Targums*, ed. Paul V. M. Flesher, 61-74. South Florida Studies in the History of Judaism, ed. Jacob Neusner, et al., no. 55. Atlanta, Georgia: Scholars Press, 1992.

Richter, Wolfgang. *Die sogenannten vorprophetischen Berufungberichte: Eine literaturwissenschaftliche Studie zu 1 Sam 9,1-10, Ex 3f. und Ri 6,11b-17*. Forschungen zur Religion und Literatur des Alten und Neuen Testaments, ed. Ernst Käsemann and Ernst Wurthwein, no. 101. Göttingen: Vandenhoeck & Ruprecht, 1970.

Ringgren, Helmer. *The Faith of Qumran: Theology of the Dead Sea Scrolls*. Translated by Emilie T. Sander. Edited with new introduction by James H. Charlesworth. Christian Origins Library. New York: Crossroads, 1995. [Text is translation of *Tro och liv enligt Döda-havsrullarna* (Stockholm, 1961).]

Robertson, Archibald and Alfred Plummer. *A Critical and Exegetical Commentary on the First Epistle of St Paul to the Corinthians*, 2d ed. The International Critical Commentary on the Holy Scriptures of the Old and New Testaments, ed. Samuel Rolles Driver, Alfred Plummer, and Charles Augustus Briggs. Edinburgh: T. & T. Clark, 1914, reprint, 1929.

Robinson, J. A. T. "'His Witness is True': A Test of the Johannine Claim." In *Jesus and the Politics of His Day*, ed. Ernst Bammel and C. F. D. Moule, 453-476. Cambridge: Cambridge University Press, 1984.

Rofé, Alexander. "Qumranic Paraphrases, the Greek Deuteronomy and the Late History of the Biblical נשיא." *Textus* 14 (1988): 163-174.

Rost, Leonhard. *Die Vorstufen von Kirche und Synagoge im Alten Testament: Eine wortgeschichtliche Untersuchung*. Beiträge zur Wissenschaft vom Alten und Neuen Testament, 4th series, ed. Albrecht Alt and Gerhard Kittel, vol. 24 (76 of whole collection). Stuttgart: W. Kohlhammer, 1938.

Roth, Cecil. "The 'Chair of Moses' and Its Survivals." *Palestine Exploration Quarterly* (July-October 1949): 100-111.

Rowland, Christopher. *The Open Heaven: A Study of Apocalyptic in Judaism and Early Christianity*. London: SPCK, 1982.

Rowley, H. H. "Jewish Proselyte Baptism and the Baptism of John." *Hebrew Union College Annual* 15 (1940): 313-334.

Rudolph, Kurt. "The Baptist Sects." In *The Cambridge History of Judaism*, vol. 3, *The Early Roman Period*, ed. William Horbury, W. D. Davies, and John Sturdy, 471-500. Cambridge: Cambridge University Press, 1999.

Runia, D. T. "God and Man in Philo of Alexandria." *Journal of Theological Studies*, NS 39, part 1 (April 1988): 48-75.

Sahlin, Harald. "The New Exodus of Salvation according to St Paul." In *The Root of the Vine: Essays in Biblical Theology*, Anton Fridrichsen, et al., 81-95. London: Dacre Press, 1953.

Sanders, J. N. *A Commentary on the Gospel according to St. John.* Edited and completed by B. A. Mastin. Black's New Testament Commentaries, ed. Henry Chadwick. London: Adam & Charles Black, 1968.

Savage, Timothy B. *Power through Weakness: Paul's Understanding of the Christian Ministry in 2 Corinthians.* Society for New Testament Studies Monograph Series, ed. Margaret E. Thrall, no. 86. Cambridge: Cambridge University Press, 1996.

Schiffman, Lawrence H. "At the Crossroads: Tannaitic Perspectives on the Jewish-Christian Schism." In *Jewish and Christian Self-Definition*, vol. 2, *Aspects of Judaism in the Graeco-Roman Period*, ed. E. P. Sanders with A. I. Baumgarten and Alan Mendelson, 115-156. Philadelphia: Fortress Press, 1981.

___. *Who Was a Jew?: Rabbinic and Halakhic Perspectives on the Jewish Christian Schism.* Hoboken, New Jersey: Ktav Publishing House, 1985.

Schille, Gottfried. *Die Apostelgeschichte des Lukas.* Theologischer Handkommentar zum Neuen Testament, ed. Erich Fascher, Joachim Rohde and Christian Wolff, no. 5. Berlin: Evangelische Verlagsanstalt, 1983.

Schmithals, Walter. *The Office of Apostle in the Early Church.* Translated by John E. Steely. London: SPCK, 1971. Originally, *Das Kirchliche Apostelamt: Eine historische Untersuchung.* Gottingen: Vandenhoeck & Ruprecht, 1961.

Schnackenburg, Rudolf. *Baptism in the Thought of St. Paul: A Study in Pauline Theology.* Translated by G. R. Beasley-Murray. Oxford: Basil Blackwell, 1964.

___. *The Gospel According to St John.* 3 vols. Vol. 1: *Introduction and Commentary on 1-4*, translated by Kevin Smyth; vol. 2: *Commentary on Chapters 5-12*, translated by Cecily Hastings, et al.; vol. 3: *Commentary on Chapters 13-21*, translated by David Smith and G. A. Kon. Herder's Theological Commentary on the New Testament, ed. Serafin de Ausejo, et al. London: Burns and Oates, 1968, 1980, 1982.

___. *Jesus in the Gospels: A Biblical Christology.* Translated by O. C. Dean, Jr. Louisville, Kentucky: Westminster John Knox Press, 1995.

Schrage, Wolfgang. *Der erste Brief an die Korinther.* 3 vols. Evangelisch-Katholischer Kommentar zum Neuen Testament, ed. Norbert Brox, et al., vols. 7/1, 7/2, 7/3. Düsseldorf: Benziger and Neukirchen-Vluyn: Neukirchener, 1991, 1995, 1999.

Schreiber, Stefan. *Gesalbter und König: Titel und Konzeptionen der königlichen Gesalbtenerwartung in frühjüdischen und urchristlichen Schriften.* Beihefte zur Zeitschrift für die neutestamentliche Wissenschaft und die Kunde der älteren Kirche, ed. Michael Wolter, vol. 105. Berlin: Walter de Gruyter, 2000.

Schur, Nathan. *History of the Samaritans.* Beiträge zur Erforschung des Alten Testamentes und des antiken Judentums, ed. Matthias Augustin and Michael Mach, no. 18. Frankfurt am Main: Verlag Peter Lang, 1989.

Schürer, Emil. *The History of the Jewish People in the Age of Jesus Christ (175 BC-AD 135).* Vols. 1, 2, 3.1, and 3.2. Revised and edited by Geza Vermes, Fergus Millar, and Martin Goodman. Literary Editor, Pamela Vermes. Organizing Editor, Matthew Black. Edinburgh: T. & T. Clark, 1973, 1979, 1986, 1987.

Segal, A. F. "Conversion and Messianism: Outline for a New Approach." In *The Messiah: Developments in Earliest Judaism and Christianity*, ed. James H. Charlesworth, with J. Brownson, M. T. Davis, S. J. Kraftchick, and A. F. Segal, 296-340. Minneapolis: Fortress Press, 1992.

Sheehan, John F. X. "Feed My Lambs." *Scripture* 16 (1964): 21-27.

Siegert, Folker. *Philon von Alexandrien: Über die Gottesbezeichnung "wohltätig verzehrendes Feuer" (de Deo): Rückübersetzung des Fragments aus dem Armenischen, deutsche Übersetzung und Kommentar.* Wissenschaftliche Untersuchungen zum Neuen Testament, ed. Joachim Jeremias and Otto Michel, no. 46. Tübingen: J. C. B. Mohr (Paul Siebeck), 1988.

Simian-Yofre, H. "מַטֶּה maṭṭeh." In *Theological Dictionary of the Old Testament*, ed. G. Johannes Botterweck, Helmer Ringgren, and Heinz-Josef Fabry. Translated by Douglas W. Stott, vol. 8, מֹר־לָכַד *lakad-mor*, 241-249. Grand Rapids: William B. Eerdmans, 1997.

Simon, Marcel. *St Stephen and the Hellenists in the Primitive Church*. London: Longmans, Green and Co., 1958.

Smedes, Lewis B. *All Things Made New: A Theology of Man's Union with Christ*. Grand Rapids: William B. Eerdmans, 1970.

Smend, Rudolf. *Das Mosebild von Heinrich Ewald bis Martin Noth*. Beiträge zur Geschichte der biblischen Exegese, ed. Oscar Cullmann, et al., no. 3. Tübingen: J. C. B. Mohr (Paul Siebeck), 1959.

Smith, D. Moody. "The Pauline Literature." In *It Is Written: Scripture Citing Scripture: Essays in Honour of Barnabas Lindars, SSF*, ed. D. A. Carson and H. G. M. Williamson, 265-291. Cambridge: Cambridge University Press, 1988.

Smolar, Leivy and Moses Aberbach. *Studies in Targum Jonathan to the Prophets*. The Library of Biblical Studies, ed. Harry M. Orlinsky. New York and Baltimore: Ktav Publishing House and the Baltimore Hebrew College, 1983. Bound together with Pinkhos Churgin, *Targum Jonathan to the Prophets*, first published by Yale University Press, 1927.

Sokoloff, Michael and Joseph Yahalom. *Jewish Palestinian Aramaic Poetry from Late Antiquity*. Jerusalem: Israel Academy of Sciences, 1999.

Spilsbury, Paul. *The Image of the Jew in Flavius Josephus' Paraphrase of the Bible*. Texte und Studien zum Antiken Judentum, ed. Martin Hengel and Peter Schäfer, no. 69. Tübingen: J. C. B. Mohr (Paul Siebeck), 1998.

St John Parry, R. *The First Epistle of Paul the Apostle to the Corinthians*, 2d ed. Cambridge Greek Testament for Schools and Colleges. Cambridge: The University Press, 1926, reprint 1937.

Stadelmann, Helge. *Ben Sira als Schriftgelehrter: Eine Untersuchung zum Berufsbild des vor-makkabäischen Sofer unter Berücksichtigung seines Verhältnisses zu Priester-, Propheten- und Weisheitslehrertum.* Wissenschaftliche Untersuchungen zum Neuen Testament, 2d series, ed. Martin Hengel, Otfried Hofius, and Otto Michel, no. 6. Tübingen: J. C. B. Mohr (Paul Siebeck), 1980.

Stählin, Gustav. *Die Apostelgeschichte*. Das Neue Testament Deutsch, ed. Paul Althaus and Gerhard Friedrich, no. 5. Göttingen: Vandenhoeck & Ruprecht, 1966.

Stern, Sacha. *Jewish Identity in Early Rabbinic Writings*. Arbeiten zur Geschichte des antiken Judentums und des Urchristentums, ed. Martin Hengel, et al., no. 23. Leiden: E. J. Brill, 1994.

Stewart, Roy A. *Rabbinic Theology: An Introductory Study*. With a foreword by Raphael Loewe. Edinburgh and London: Oliver and Boyd, 1961.

Stone, Michael Edward. *Fourth Ezra: A Commentary on the Book of Fourth Ezra.* Edited by Frank Moore Cross. Hermeneia — A Critical and Historical Commentary on the Bible. Old Testament Editorial Board, Frank Moore Cross, et al. Minneapolis: Fortress Press, 1990.

Strachan, R. H. *The Second Epistle of Paul to the Corinthians.* The Moffatt New Testament Commentary, ed. James Moffatt. London: Hodder and Stoughton, 1935.

Strack, Herman L. and Paul Billerbeck. *Kommentar zum Neuen Testament aus Talmud und Midrasch,* 4 vols. Vol. 1, *Das Evangelium nach Matthäus,* vol. 2, *Das Evangelium nach Markus, Lukas, und Johannes und die Apostelgeschichte,* vol. 3, *Die Briefe des Neuen Testaments und die Offenbarung Johannis,* vol. 4 *Exkurse zu einzelnen Stellen des Neuen Testaments abhandlungen zur neutestamentliche Theologie und Archäologie,* parts 1 and 2. Vol. 5, *Rabbinischer Index,* and vol. 6, *Verzeichnis der Schriftgelehrten; Geographisches Register,* ed. Joachim Jeremias with Kurt Adolph. Munich: C. H. Beck'sche Verlagsbuchhandlung (Oskar Beck), 1922, 1924, 1926, 1928, 1956, 1956.

Sukenik, E. L. *Ancient Synagogues in Palestine and Greece.* The Schweich Lectures of the British Academy, 1930. London: Published for the British Academy by Oxford University Press, 1934.

Taylor, Vincent. *The Names of Jesus.* London: Macmillan and Co., 1953.

Tcherikover, Victor. "Jewish Apologetic Literature Reconsidered." *Eos* 48, no. 3 (1956): 169-193.

Teeple, Howard M. *The Mosaic Eschatological Prophet.* Journal of Biblical Literature Monograph Series, vol. 10. Philadelphia: Society of Biblical Literature, 1957.

Thoma, Clemens. "The High Priesthood in the Judgment of Josephus." In *Josephus, the Bible, and History,* ed. Louis H. Feldman and Gohei Hata, 196-215. Leiden: E. J. Brill, 1989.

Thrall, Margaret, E. *A Critical and Exegetical Commentary on the Second Epistle to the Corinthians,* 2 vols., vol. 1, *Introduction and Commentary on II Corinthians I-VII,* vol. 2, *Commentary on II Corinthians VIII-XIII.* The International Critical Commentary on the Holy Scriptures of the Old and New Testaments, ed. J. A. Emerton, C. E. B. Cranfield, and G. N. Stanton. Edinburgh: T. & T. Clark, 1994, 2000.

Tiede, David Lenz. *The Charismatic Figure as Miracle Worker.* Society of Biblical Literature Dissertation Series, no. 1. Missoula, Montana: Society of Biblical Literature, 1972. [Includes a Greek text of Artapanus.]

___. "The Figure of Moses in *The Testament of Moses.*" In *Studies on the Testament of Moses: Seminar Papers,* ed. George W. E. Nickelsburg, Jr., 86-92. Society of Biblical Literature Pseudepigrapha Group, Septuagint and Cognate Studies, no. 4. Cambridge, Massachusetts: Society of Biblical Literature, 1973.

Tigay, Jeffrey H. *Deuteronomy: The Traditional Hebrew Text with the New JPS Translation.* The JPS Torah Commentary, ed. Nahum M. Sarna, Chaim Potok, and (this volume) Jeffrey H. Tigay. Philadelphia and Jerusalem: The Jewish Publication Society, 1996.

Urbach, Ephraim E. *The Sages: Their Concepts and Beliefs,* 2 vols. Translated by Israel Abrahams. Publications of the Perry Foundation in the Hebrew University of Jerusalem. Jerusalem: Magnes Press, The Hebrew University, 1979.

van der Horst, Pieter W. "Moses' Throne Vision in Ezekiel the Dramatist." *Journal of Jewish Studies* 34 (1983): 21-29.

___. "Some Notes on the *Exagoge* of Ezekiel." *Mnemosyne* 37, nos. 3-4 (1984): 354-375.

Van De Water, Rick. "Moses' Exaltation: Pre-Christian?." *Journal for the Study of the Pseudepigrapha* 21 (2000): 59-69.

Vanhoozer, Kevin J. *Is There a Meaning in This Text?: The Bible, the Reader and the Morality of Biblical Knowledge.* Grand Rapids, Michigan: Zondervan, 1998.

Vermes, Geza. "La figure de Moïse au tournant des deux Testaments." *Cahiers Sioniens* 8, nos. 2, 3, and 4 (*Moïse: L'homme de l'alliance*, 1954): 63-92 in this fascicle (180-210 in the volume).

___. *Jesus the Jew: A Historian's Reading of the Gospels.* London: William Collins Sons & Co., 1973.

___. *Scripture and Tradition in Judaism: Haggadic Studies.* Studia Post-Biblica, ed. P. A. H. de Boer, vol. 4. Leiden: E. J. Brill, 1961.

Volz, Paul. *Die Eschatologie der jüdischen Gemeinde im neutestamentlichen Zeitalter: Nach den Quellen der rabbinischen, apokalyptischen und apokryphen Literatur.* Hildesheim: Georg Olms Verlagsbuchhandlung, 1966.

Weiss, Bernhard. *Das Johannes-Evangelium*, 6th ed. Kritisch-exegetischer Kommentar über das Neue Testament, 9th ed. Göttingen: Vandenhoeck & Ruprecht, 1902.

Wevers, John William. *Notes on the Greek Text of Deuteronomy.* Society of Biblical Literature Septuagint and Cognate Studies Series, ed. Bernard A. Taylor, no. 39. Atlanta: Scholars Press, 1995.

___. *Notes on the Greek Text of Exodus.* Society of Biblical Literature Septuagint and Cognate Studies Series, ed. Claude E. Cox, no. 30. Atlanta: Scholars Press, 1990.

___. *Notes on the Greek Text of Numbers.* Society of Biblical Literature Septuagint and Cognate Studies Series, ed. Bernard A. Taylor, no. 46. Atlanta: Scholars Press, 1998.

Widengren, Geo. *The Ascension of the Apostle and the Heavenly Book (King and Saviour III).* Uppsala Universiteits Årsskrift, no. 7. Uppsala: A. B. Lundequistska Bokhandeln, 1950.

Wieder, Naphtali. *The Judean Scrolls and Karaism.* East and West Library. London: Horovitz Publishing Company, 1962.

___. "The 'Law-Interpreter' of the Sect of the Dead Sea Scrolls: The Second Moses." *Journal of Jewish Studies* 4, no. 4 (1953): 158-175.

Williamson, H. G. M. "History." In *It Is Written: Scripture Citing Scripture: Essays in Honour of Barnabas Lindars, SSF*, ed. D. A. Carson and H. G. M. Williamson, 25-38. Cambridge: Cambridge University Press, 1988.

Wolfson, Harry Austryn. *Philo: Foundations of Religious Philosophy in Judaism, Christianity, and Islam*, 2 vols. Structure and Growth of Philosophic Systems from Plato to Spinoza, II. Cambridge, Massachusetts: Harvard University Press, 1947.

Yadin, Y. "Expedition D." *Israel Exploration Journal* 11, nos. 1-2 (The Expedition to the Judean Desert, 1960) (1961): 36-52.

Yahalom, Joseph. "Ezel Moshe — According to the Berlin Papyrus." *Tarbiz* 47, nos. 3-4 (April-September 1978): 173-184. [Berlin Stadtmuseum P8498.]

Zuntz, G. *The Text of the Epistles: A Disquisition upon the* Corpus Paulinum. Schweich Lectures of the British Academy, 1946. London: Oxford University Press for the British Academy, 1953.

Citation Index

Contents: 1. Old Testament; 2. Apocrypha; 3. New Testament; 4. Pseudepigrapha; 5. Philo; 6. Josephus; 7. Secular Authors; 8. Ecclesiastical Authors; 9. Qumran; 10. Targums; 11. Mishnah; 12. Tosefta; 13. Babylonian Talmud; 14. Jerusalem Talmud; 15. Midrash; 16. Samaritan Literature; 17. Piyyut; 18. Papyri and Manuscripts

3. New Testament

De Mutatione Nominum

7. Secular Authors

16. Samaritan Literature

17. Piyyut

18. Jewish Liturgy

19. Papyri and Manuscripts

Author Index

Subject Index

Aaron 66-67, 68, 76, 103, 107, 148, 230, 231, 241, 272, 273
-as angel 239, 242
-exalted as divine being 242-43
Abraham 218 n 49, 222, 233
Adam as angel 243
Agrippa II 106
Ahab 108
Amram 69, 137, 239, 240, 241
Angels
-Aaron as 242-43
-Adam as 243
-as gods 237-38
-as mediators of the Law 168, 171
-men as 238-44
-Moses as 240, 244-46
-worshipping with men 238
apostolus 71
Apostasy from Moses 157, 253-56
Apostleship
-of Paul
  -compared with ministry of Moses 168-72
  -defended 168-72
-signs of 61-62
Aqiba 116, 214 n 26
Aquila 114, 147
Aristobulus 23, 24, 36, 129, 233
Artapanus 15, 22, 23, 25, 26, 29, 55, 210, 211, 214, 233 n 111, 292
Assumption of Moses 259
Authority
-personal 125-26, 128, 142, 149-58
-derived 159, 161

Baptism
-into Christ
  -meaning of 185-86
  -priority of 180-81, 277
-into Moses 175-208, 277
  -meaning of 186-87
-Jewish 180-82
  -biblical basis for 182-84
  -mode of 183-84

-priority of 179-80
-meaning of 185-87
-proselyte, Jewish 178-85, 207, 277
  purpose of 180-82, 185
-resulting in inspiration 184
Bar Kokhba 116-17, 214 n 26
Basil the Great 252
Beth Midrash 155
Bezalel 191
Bills of Marriage and Divorce
-Jewish 144, 150
-Samaritan 69, 89, 245, 247-48
-utility for NT study 69, 144
Blasphemy of Moses 157-58, 226-29, 247, 253-54

Cairo Genizah 72, 82
Chorazin 153
Christ
-activity after death 284-85
-as lawgiver 275-76, 282
-as living being 186
-as prophet 259, 264
-as second Moses 260, 275-76, 281-82
-as spirit 186, 277
-baptism into 185-87, 277, 286
-pre-existence of 283-84
-session of 285-86
Christology 10, 13, 21, 258-88
-angel 260
-by titles 259
-Davidic 267-69
  -accomodating Mosaic Christology 267-69
-Johannine 265
-Lukan 260, 261-62, 265, 267-69, 271-72
-Matthean 65, 267
-Moses 31, 73-76, 110, 121, 196, 208, 225, 258-70, 274, 279-88, 292-93
  -as earliest Christology 260-61, 264
  -as prophet Christology 219, 261-70
-study of Moses as adjunct to 9, 31, 270-71
-influencing portrayal of Moses 13-14, 15, 16, 76, 218

Wissenschaftliche Untersuchungen zum Neuen Testament

Alphabetical Index of the First and Second Series

Bosman, Philip: Conscience in Philo and Paul. 2003. *Volume II/166.*

Bovon, François: Studies in Early Christianity. 2003. *Volume 161.*

Brocke, Christoph vom: Thessaloniki – Stadt des Kassander und Gemeinde des Paulus. 2001. *Volume II/125.*

Brunson, Andrew: Psalm 118 in the Gospel of John. 2003. *Volume II/158.*

Büchli, Jörg: Der Poimandres – ein paganisiertes Evangelium. 1987. *Volume II/27.*

Bühner, Jan A.: Der Gesandte und sein Weg im 4. Evangelium. 1977. *Volume II/2.*

Burchard, Christoph: Untersuchungen zu Joseph und Aseneth. 1965. *Volume 8.*

– Studien zur Theologie, Sprache und Umwelt des Neuen Testaments. Ed. von D. Sänger. 1998. *Volume 107.*

Burnett, Richard: Karl Barth's Theological Exegesis. 2001. *Volume II/145.*

Byron, John: Slavery Metaphors in Early Judaism and Pauline Christianity. 2003. *Volume II/162.*

Byrskog, Samuel: Story as History – History as Story. 2000. *Volume 123.*

Cancik, Hubert (Ed.): Markus-Philologie. 1984. *Volume 33.*

Capes, David B.: Old Testament Yaweh Texts in Paul's Christology. 1992. *Volume II/47.*

Caragounis, Chrys C.: The Son of Man. 1986. *Volume 38.*

– see *Fridrichsen, Anton.*

Carleton Paget, James: The Epistle of Barnabas. 1994. *Volume II/64.*

Carson, D.A., O'Brien, Peter T. and *Mark Seifrid* (Ed.): Justification and Variegated Nomism: A Fresh Appraisal of Paul and Second Temple Judaism. Volume 1: The Complexities of Second Temple Judaism. *Volume II/140.*

Ciampa, Roy E.: The Presence and Function of Scripture in Galatians 1 and 2. 1998. *Volume II/102.*

Classen, Carl Joachim: Rhetorical Criticsm of the New Testament. 2000. *Volume 128.*

Colpe, Carsten: Iranier – Aramäer – Hebräer – Hellenen. 2003. *Volume 154.*

Crump, David: Jesus the Intercessor. 1992. *Volume II/49.*

Dahl, Nils Alstrup: Studies in Ephesians. 2000. *Volume 131.*

Deines, Roland: Jüdische Steingefäße und pharisäische Frömmigkeit. 1993. *Volume II/52.*

– Die Pharisäer. 1997. *Volume 101.*

Dettwiler, Andreas and *Jean Zumstein (Ed.):* Kreuzestheologie im Neuen Testament. 2002. *Volume 151.*

Dickson, John P.: Mission-Commitment in Ancient Judaism and in the Pauline Communities. 2003. *Volume II/159.*

Dietzfelbinger, Christian: Der Abschied des Kommenden. 1997. *Volume 95.*

Dobbeler, Axel von: Glaube als Teilhabe. 1987. *Volume II/22.*

Du Toit, David S.: Theios Anthropos. 1997. *Volume II/91*

Dunn, James D.G. (Ed.): Jews and Christians. 1992. *Volume 66.*

– Paul and the Mosaic Law. 1996. *Volume 89.*

Dunn, James D.G., Hans Klein, Ulrich Luz and *Vasile Mihoc* (Ed.): Auslegung der Bibel in orthodoxer und westlicher Perspektive. 2000. *Volume 130.*

Ebertz, Michael N.: Das Charisma des Gekreuzigten. 1987. *Volume 45.*

Eckstein, Hans-Joachim: Der Begriff Syneidesis bei Paulus. 1983. *Volume II/10.*

– Verheißung und Gesetz. 1996. *Volume 86.*

Ego, Beate: Im Himmel wie auf Erden. 1989. *Volume II/34*

Ego, Beate and *Lange, Armin* with *Pilhofer, Peter (Ed.):* Gemeinde ohne Tempel – Community without Temple. 1999. *Volume 118.*

Eisen, Ute E.: see *Paulsen, Henning.*

Ellis, E. Earle: Prophecy and Hermeneutic in Early Christianity. 1978. *Volume 18.*

– The Old Testament in Early Christianity. 1991. *Volume 54.*

Endo, Masanobu: Creation and Christology. 2002. *Volume 149.*

Ennulat, Andreas: Die 'Minor Agreements'. 1994. *Volume II/62.*

Ensor, Peter W.: Jesus and His 'Works'. 1996. *Volume II/85.*

Eskola, Timo: Messiah and the Throne. 2001. *Volume II/142.*

– Theodicy and Predestination in Pauline Soteriology. 1998. *Volume II/100.*

Fatehi, Mehrdad: The Spirit's Relation to the Risen Lord in Paul. 2000. *Volume II/128.*

Feldmeier, Reinhard: Die Krisis des Gottessohnes. 1987. *Volume II/21.*

– Die Christen als Fremde. 1992. *Volume 64.*

Feldmeier, Reinhard and *Ulrich Heckel* (Ed.): Die Heiden. 1994. *Volume 70.*

Fletcher-Louis, Crispin H.T.: Luke-Acts: Angels, Christology and Soteriology. 1997. *Volume II/94.*

Förster, Niclas: Marcus Magus. 1999. *Volume 114.*

Forbes, Christopher Brian: Prophecy and Inspired Speech in Early Christianity and its Hellenistic Environment. 1995. *Volume II/75.*

Fornberg, Tord: see *Fridrichsen, Anton.*

Fossum, Jarl E.: The Name of God and the Angel of the Lord. 1985. *Volume 36.*

Fotopoulos, John: Food Offered to Idols in Roman Corinth. 2003. *Volume II/151.*

Frenschkowski, Marco: Offenbarung und Epiphanie. Volume 1 1995. *Volume II/79 –* Volume 2 1997. *Volume II/80.*

Frey, Jörg: Eugen Drewermann und die biblische Exegese. 1995. *Volume II/71.*

– Die johanneische Eschatologie. Volume I. 1997. *Volume 96.* – Volume II. 1998. *Volume 110.*

– Volume III. 2000. *Volume 117.*

Freyne, Sean: Galilee and Gospel. 2000. *Volume 125.*

Fridrichsen, Anton: Exegetical Writings. Edited by C.C. Caragounis and T. Fornberg. 1994. *Volume 76.*

Garlington, Don B.: 'The Obedience of Faith'. 1991. *Volume II/38.*

– Faith, Obedience, and Perseverance. 1994. *Volume 79.*

Garnet, Paul: Salvation and Atonement in the Qumran Scrolls. 1977. *Volume II/3.*

Gese, Michael: Das Vermächtnis des Apostels. 1997. *Volume II/99.*

Gheorghita, Radu: The Role of the Septuagint in Hebrews. 2003. *Volume II/160.*

Gräbe, Petrus J.: The Power of God in Paul's Letters. 2000. *Volume II/123.*

Gräßer, Erich: Der Alte Bund im Neuen. 1985. *Volume 35.*

– Forschungen zur Apostelgeschichte. 2001. *Volume 137.*

Green, Joel B.: The Death of Jesus. 1988. *Volume II/33.*

Gregory, Anthony: The Reception of Luke and Acts in the Period before Irenaeus. 2003. *Volume II/169.*

Gundry Volf, Judith M.: Paul and Perseverance. 1990. *Volume II/37.*

Hafemann, Scott J.: Suffering and the Spirit. 1986. *Volume II/19.*

– Paul, Moses, and the History of Israel. 1995. *Volume 81.*

Hahn, Johannes (Ed.): Zerstörungen des Jerusalemer Tempels. 2002. *Volume 147.*

Hannah, Darrel D.: Michael and Christ. 1999. *Volume II/109.*

Hamid-Khani, Saeed: Relevation and Concealment of Christ. 2000. *Volume II/120.*

Harrison; James R.: Paul's Language of Grace in Its Graeco-Roman Context. 2003. *Volume II/172.*

Hartman, Lars: Text-Centered New Testament Studies. Ed. von D. Hellholm. 1997. *Volume 102.*

Hartog, Paul: Polycarp and the New Testament. 2001. *Volume II/134.*

Heckel, Theo K.: Der Innere Mensch. 1993. *Volume II/53.*

– Vom Evangelium des Markus zum viergestaltigen Evangelium. 1999. *Volume 120.*

Heckel, Ulrich: Kraft in Schwachheit. 1993. *Volume II/56.*

– Der Segen im Neuen Testament. 2002. *Volume 150.*

– see *Feldmeier, Reinhard.*

– see *Hengel, Martin.*

Heiligenthal, Roman: Werke als Zeichen. 1983. *Volume II/9.*

Hellholm, D.: see *Hartman, Lars.*

Hemer, Colin J.: The Book of Acts in the Setting of Hellenistic History. 1989. *Volume 49.*

Hengel, Martin: Judentum und Hellenismus. 1969, ³1988. *Volume 10.*

– Die johanneische Frage. 1993. *Volume 67.*

– Judaica et Hellenistica. Kleine Schriften I. 1996. *Volume 90.*

– Judaica, Hellenistica et Christiana. Kleine Schriften II. 1999. *Volume 109.*

– Paulus und Jakobus. Kleine Schriften III. 2002. *Volume 141.*

Hengel, Martin and Ulrich Heckel (Ed.): Paulus und das antike Judentum. 1991. *Volume 58.*

Hengel, Martin and Hermut Löhr (Ed.): Schriftauslegung im antiken Judentum und im Urchristentum. 1994. *Volume 73.*

Hengel, Martin and Anna Maria Schwemer: Paulus zwischen Damaskus und Antiochien. 1998. *Volume 108.*

– Der messianische Anspruch Jesu und die Anfänge der Christologie. 2001. *Volume 138.*

Hengel, Martin and Anna Maria Schwemer (Ed.): Königsherrschaft Gottes und himmlischer Kult. 1991. *Volume 55.*

– Die Septuaginta. 1994. *Volume 72.*

Hengel, Martin; Siegfried Mittmann and Anna Maria Schwemer (Ed.): La Cité de Dieu / Die Stadt Gottes. 2000. *Volume 129.*

Herrenbrück, Fritz: Jesus und die Zöllner. 1990. *Volume II/41.*

Herzer, Jens: Paulus oder Petrus? 1998. *Volume 103.*

Hoegen-Rohls, Christina: Der nachösterliche Johannes. 1996. *Volume II/84.*

Hofius, Otfried: Katapausis. 1970. *Volume 11.*

– Der Vorhang vor dem Thron Gottes. 1972. *Volume 14.*

– Der Christushymnus Philipper 2,6-11. 1976, ²1991. *Volume 17.*
– Paulusstudien. 1989, ²1994. *Volume 51.*
– Neutestamentliche Studien. 2000. *Volume 132.*
– Paulusstudien II. 2002. *Volume 143.*

Hofius, Otfried and *Hans-Christian Kammler:* Johannesstudien. 1996. *Volume 88.*

Holtz, Traugott: Geschichte und Theologie des Urchristentums. 1991. *Volume 57.*

Hommel, Hildebrecht: Sebasmata. Volume 1 1983. *Volume 31* – Volume 2 1984. *Volume 32.*

Hvalvik, Reidar: The Struggle for Scripture and Covenant. 1996. *Volume II/82.*

Johns, Loren L.: The Lamb Christology of the Apocalypse of John. 2003. *Volume II/167.*

Joubert, Stephan: Paul as Benefactor. 2000. *Volume II/124.*

Jungbauer, Harry: „Ehre Vater und Mutter". 2002. *Volume II/146.*

Kähler, Christoph: Jesu Gleichnisse als Poesie und Therapie. 1995. *Volume 78.*

Kamlah, Ehrhard: Die Form der katalogischen Paränese im Neuen Testament. 1964. *Volume 7.*

Kammler, Hans-Christian: Christologie und Eschatologie. 2000. *Volume 126.*
– Kreuz und Weisheit. 2003. *Volume 159.*
– see *Hofius, Otfried.*

Kelhoffer, James A.: Miracle and Mission. 1999. *Volume II/112.*

Kieffer, René and *Jan Bergman (Ed.):* La Main de Dieu / Die Hand Gottes. 1997. *Volume 94.*

Kim, Seyoon: The Origin of Paul's Gospel. 1981, ²1984. *Volume II/4.*
– "The 'Son of Man'" as the Son of God. 1983. *Volume 30.*

Klauck, Hans-Josef: Religion und Gesellschaft im frühen Christentum. 2003. *Volume 152.*

Klein, Hans: see *Dunn, James D.G..*

Kleinknecht, Karl Th.: Der leidende Gerechtfertigte. 1984, ²1988. *Volume II/13.*

Klinghardt, Matthias: Gesetz und Volk Gottes. 1988. *Volume II/32.*

Koch, Stefan: Rechtliche Regelung von Konflikten im frühen Christentum. 2004. *Volume II/174.*

Köhler, Wolf-Dietrich: Rezeption des Matthäusevangeliums in der Zeit vor Irenäus. 1987. *Volume II/24.*

Kooten, George H. van: Cosmic Christology in Paul and the Pauline School. 2003. *Volume II/171.*

Korn, Manfred: Die Geschichte Jesu in veränderter Zeit. 1993. *Volume II/51.*

Koskenniemi, Erkki: Apollonios von Tyana in der neutestamentlichen Exegese. 1994. *Volume II/61.*

Kraus, Thomas J.: Sprache, Stil und historischer Ort des zweiten Petrusbriefes. 2001. *Volume II/136.*

Kraus, Wolfgang: Das Volk Gottes. 1996. *Volume 85.*
– and *Karl-Wilhelm Niebuhr* (Ed.): Frühjudentum und Neues Testament im Horizont Biblischer Theologie. 2003. *Volume 162.*
– see *Walter, Nikolaus.*

Kreplin, Matthias: Das Selbstverständnis Jesu. 2001. *Volume II/141.*

Kuhn, Karl G.: Achtzehngebet und Vaterunser und der Reim. 1950. *Volume 1.*

Kvalbein, Hans: see *Ådna, Jostein.*

Laansma, Jon: I Will Give You Rest. 1997. *Volume II/98.*

Labahn, Michael: Offenbarung in Zeichen und Wort. 2000. *Volume II/117.*

Lambers-Petry, Doris: see *Tomson, Peter J.*

Lange, Armin: see *Ego, Beate.*

Lampe, Peter: Die stadtrömischen Christen in den ersten beiden Jahrhunderten. 1987, ²1989. *Volume II/18.*

Landmesser, Christof: Wahrheit als Grundbegriff neutestamentlicher Wissenschaft. 1999. *Volume 113.*
– Jüngerberufung und Zuwendung zu Gott. 2000. *Volume 133.*

Lau, Andrew: Manifest in Flesh. 1996. *Volume II/86.*

Lawrence, Louise: An Ethnography of the Gospel of Matthew. 2003. *Volume II/165.*

Lee, Pilchan: The New Jerusalem in the Book of Relevation. 2000. *Volume II/129.*

Lichtenberger, Hermann: see *Avemarie, Friedrich.*

Lierman, John: The New Testament Moses. 2004. *Volume II/173.*

Lieu, Samuel N.C.: Manichaeism in the Later Roman Empire and Medieval China. ²1992. *Volume 63.*

Loader, William R.G.: Jesus' Attitude Towards the Law. 1997. *Volume II/97.*

Löhr, Gebhard: Verherrlichung Gottes durch Philosophie. 1997. *Volume 97.*

Löhr, Hermut: Studien zum frühchristlichen und frühjüdischen Gebet. 2003. *Volume 160.*
– : see *Hengel, Martin.*

Löhr, Winrich Alfried: Basilides und seine Schule. 1995. *Volume 83.*

Luomanen, Petri: Entering the Kingdom of Heaven. 1998. *Volume II/101.*

Luz, Ulrich: see *Dunn, James D.G.*

Maier, Gerhard: Mensch und freier Wille. 1971. *Volume 12.*

– Die Johannesoffenbarung und die Kirche. 1981. *Volume 25.*

Markschies, Christoph: Valentinus Gnosticus? 1992. *Volume 65.*

Marshall, Peter: Enmity in Corinth: Social Conventions in Paul's Relations with the Corinthians. 1987. *Volume II/23.*

Mayer, Annemarie: Sprache der Einheit im Epheserbrief und in der Ökumene. 2002. *Volume II/150.*

McDonough, Sean M.: YHWH at Patmos: Rev. 1:4 in its Hellenistic and Early Jewish Setting. 1999. *Volume II/107.*

McGlynn, Moyna: Divine Judgement and Divine Benevolence in the Book of Wisdom. 2001. *Volume II/139.*

Meade, David G.: Pseudonymity and Canon. 1986. *Volume 39.*

Meadors, Edward P.: Jesus the Messianic Herald of Salvation. 1995. *Volume II/72.*

Meißner, Stefan: Die Heimholung des Ketzers. 1996. *Volume II/87.*

Mell, Ulrich: Die „anderen" Winzer. 1994. *Volume 77.*

Mengel, Berthold: Studien zum Philipperbrief. 1982. *Volume II/8.*

Merkel, Helmut: Die Widersprüche zwischen den Evangelien. 1971. *Volume 13.*

Merklein, Helmut: Studien zu Jesus und Paulus. Volume 1 1987. *Volume 43.* – Volume 2 1998. *Volume 105.*

Metzdorf, Christina: Die Tempelaktion Jesu. 2003. *Volume II/168.*

Metzler, Karin: Der griechische Begriff des Verzeihens. 1991. *Volume II/44.*

Metzner, Rainer: Die Rezeption des Matthäusevangeliums im 1. Petrusbrief. 1995. *Volume II/74.*

– Das Verständnis der Sünde im Johannesevangelium. 2000. *Volume 122.*

Mihoc, Vasile: see *Dunn, James D.G.*.

Mineshige, Kiyoshi: Besitzverzicht und Almosen bei Lukas. 2003. *Volume II/163.*

Mittmann, Siegfried: see *Hengel, Martin.*

Mittmann-Richert, Ulrike: Magnifikat und Benediktus. *1996. Volume II/90.*

Mußner, Franz: Jesus von Nazareth im Umfeld Israels und der Urkirche. Ed. von M. Theobald. 1998. *Volume 111.*

Niebuhr, Karl-Wilhelm: Gesetz und Paränese. 1987. *Volume II/28.*

– Heidenapostel aus Israel. 1992. *Volume 62.*

– see *Kraus, Wolfgang*

Nielsen, Anders E.: "Until it is Fullfilled". 2000. *Volume II/126.*

Nissen, Andreas: Gott und der Nächste im antiken Judentum. 1974. *Volume 15.*

Noack, Christian: Gottesbewußtsein. 2000. *Volume II/116.*

Noormann, Rolf: Irenäus als Paulusinterpret. 1994. *Volume II/66.*

Novakovic, Lidija: Messiah, the Healer of the Sick. 2003. *Volume II/170.*

Obermann, Andreas: Die christologische Erfüllung der Schrift im Johannesevangelium. 1996. *Volume II/83.*

Öhler, Markus: Barnabas. 2003. *Volume 156.*

Okure, Teresa: The Johannine Approach to Mission. 1988. *Volume II/31.*

Oropeza, B. J.: Paul and Apostasy. 2000. *Volume II/115.*

Ostmeyer, Karl-Heinrich: Taufe und Typos. 2000. *Volume II/118.*

Paulsen, Henning: Studien zur Literatur und Geschichte des frühen Christentums. Ed. von Ute E. Eisen. 1997. *Volume 99.*

Pao, David W.: Acts and the Isaianic New Exodus. 2000. *Volume II/130.*

Park, Eung Chun: The Mission Discourse in Matthew's Interpretation. 1995. *Volume II/81.*

Park, Joseph S.: Conceptions of Afterlife in Jewish Insriptions. 2000. *Volume II/121.*

Pate, C. Marvin: The Reverse of the Curse. 2000. *Volume II/114.*

Peres, Imre: Griechische Grabinschriften und neutestamentliche Eschatologie. 2003. *Volume 157.*

Philonenko, Marc (Ed.): Le Trône de Dieu. 1993. *Volume 69.*

Pilhofer, Peter: Presbyteron Kreitton. 1990. *Volume II/39.*

– Philippi. Volume 1 1995. *Volume 87.* – Volume 2 2000. *Volume 119.*

– Die frühen Christen und ihre Welt. 2002. *Volume 145.*

– see *Ego, Beate.*

Pöhlmann, Wolfgang: Der Verlorene Sohn und das Haus. 1993. *Volume 68.*

Pokorný, Petr and *Josef B. Souček:* Bibelauslegung als Theologie. 1997. *Volume 100.*

Pokorný, Petr and *Jan Roskovec* (Ed.): Philosophical Hermeneutics and Biblical Exegesis. 2002. *Volume 153.*

Porter, Stanley E.: The Paul of Acts. 1999. *Volume 115.*

Prieur, Alexander: Die Verkündigung der Gottesherrschaft. 1996. *Volume II/89.*

Probst, Hermann: Paulus und der Brief. 1991. *Volume II/45.*

Räisänen, Heikki: Paul and the Law. 1983,
²1987. *Volume 29.*

Rehkopf, Friedrich: Die lukanische Sonderquel-
le. 1959. *Volume 5.*

Rein, Matthias: Die Heilung des Blindgeborenen
(Joh 9). 1995. *Volume II/73.*

Reinmuth, Eckart: Pseudo-Philo und Lukas.
1994. *Volume 74.*

Reiser, Marius: Syntax und Stil des Markusevangeliums. 1984. *Volume II/11.*

Richards, E. Randolph: The Secretary in the
Letters of Paul. 1991. *Volume II/42.*

Riesner, Rainer: Jesus als Lehrer. 1981, ³1988.
Volume II/7.

– Die Frühzeit des Apostels Paulus. 1994.
Volume 71.

Rissi, Mathias: Die Theologie des Hebräerbriefs.
1987. *Volume 41.*

Roskovec, Jan: see *Pokorný, Petr.*

Röhser, Günter: Metaphorik und Personifikation
der Sünde. 1987. *Volume II/25.*

Rose, Christian: Die Wolke der Zeugen. 1994.
Volume II/60.

Rothschild, Clare K.: Luke Acts and the
Rhetoric of History. 2004. *Volume II/175.*

Rüegger, Hans-Ulrich: Verstehen, was Markus
erzählt. 2002. *Volume II/155.*

Rüger, Hans Peter: Die Weisheitsschrift aus der
Kairoer Geniza. 1991. *Volume 53.*

Sänger, Dieter: Antikes Judentum und die
Mysterien. 1980. *Volume II/5.*

– Die Verkündigung des Gekreuzigten und
Israel. 1994. *Volume 75.*

– see *Burchard, Christoph*

Salzmann, Jorg Christian: Lehren und
Ermahnen. 1994. *Volume II/59.*

Sandnes, Karl Olav: Paul – One of the
Prophets? 1991. *Volume II/43.*

Sato, Migaku: Q und Prophetie. 1988.
Volume II/29.

Schaper, Joachim: Eschatology in the Greek
Psalter. 1995. *Volume II/76.*

Schimanowski, Gottfried: Die himmlische
Liturgie in der Apokalypse des Johannes.
2002. *Volume II/154.*

– Weisheit und Messias. 1985. *Volume II/17.*

Schlichting, Günter: Ein jüdisches Leben Jesu.
1982. *Volume 24.*

Schnabel, Eckhard J.: Law and Wisdom from
Ben Sira to Paul. 1985. *Volume II/16.*

Schutter, William L.: Hermeneutic and
Composition in I Peter. 1989. *Volume II/30.*

Schwartz, Daniel R.: Studies in the Jewish
Background of Christianity. 1992.
Volume 60.

Schwemer, Anna Maria: see *Hengel, Martin*

Scott, James M.: Adoption as Sons of God.
1992. *Volume II/48.*

– Paul and the Nations. 1995. *Volume 84.*

Shum, Shiu-Lun: Paul's Use of Isaiah in
Romans. 2002. *Volume II/156.*

Siegert, Folker: Drei hellenistisch-jüdische
Predigten. Teil I 1980. *Volume 20* – Teil II
1992. *Volume 61.*

– Nag-Hammadi-Register. 1982. *Volume 26.*

– Argumentation bei Paulus. 1985. *Volume 34.*

– Philon von Alexandrien. 1988. *Volume 46.*

Simon, Marcel: Le christianisme antique et son
contexte religieux I/II. 1981. *Volume 23.*

Snodgrass, Klyne: The Parable of the Wicked
Tenants. 1983. *Volume 27.*

Söding, Thomas: Das Wort vom Kreuz. 1997.
Volume 93.

– see *Thüsing, Wilhelm.*

Sommer, Urs: Die Passionsgeschichte des
Markusevangeliums. 1993. *Volume II/58.*

Souček, Josef B.: see *Pokorný, Petr.*

Spangenberg, Volker: Herrlichkeit des Neuen
Bundes. 1993. *Volume II/55.*

Spanje, T.E. van: Inconsistency in Paul? 1999.
Volume II/110.

Speyer, Wolfgang: Frühes Christentum im
antiken Strahlungsfeld. Volume I: 1989.
Volume 50.

– Volume II: 1999. *Volume 116.*

Stadelmann, Helge: Ben Sira als Schriftgelehrter. 1980. *Volume II/6.*

Stenschke, Christoph W.: Luke's Portrait of
Gentiles Prior to Their Coming to Faith.
Volume II/108.

Stettler, Christian: Der Kolosserhymnus. 2000.
Volume II/131.

Stettler, Hanna: Die Christologie der Pastoral-
briefe. 1998. *Volume II/105.*

Stökl Ben Ezra, Daniel: The Impact of
Yom Kippur on Early Christianity. 2003.
Volume 163.

Strobel, August: Die Stunde der Wahrheit. 1980.
Volume 21.

Stroumsa, Guy G.: Barbarian Philosophy. 1999.
Volume 112.

Stuckenbruck, Loren T.: Angel Veneration and
Christology. 1995. *Volume II/70.*

Stuhlmacher, Peter (Ed.): Das Evangelium und
die Evangelien. 1983. *Volume 28.*

– Biblische Theologie und Evangelium. 2002.
Volume 146.

Sung, Chong-Hyon: Vergebung der Sünden.
1993. *Volume II/57.*

Tajra, Harry W.: The Trial of St. Paul. 1989.
Volume II/35.

- The Martyrdom of St.Paul. 1994. *Volume II/67.*

Theißen, Gerd: Studien zur Soziologie des Urchristentums. 1979, ³1989. *Volume 19.*

Theobald, Michael: Studien zum Römerbrief. 2001. *Volume 136.*

Theobald, Michael: see *Mußner, Franz.*

Thornton, Claus-Jürgen: Der Zeuge des Zeugen. 1991. *Volume 56.*

Thüsing, Wilhelm: Studien zur neutestamentlichen Theologie. Ed. von Thomas Söding. 1995. *Volume 82.*

Thurén, Lauri: Derhethorizing Paul. 2000. *Volume 124.*

Tomson, Peter J. and *Doris Lambers-Petry* (Ed.): The Image of the Judaeo-Christians in Ancient Jewish and Christian Literature. 2003. *Volume 158.*

Treloar, Geoffrey R.: Lightfoot the Historian. 1998. *Volume II/103.*

Tsuji, Manabu: Glaube zwischen Vollkommenheit und Verweltlichung. 1997. *Volume II/93*

Twelftree, Graham H.: Jesus the Exorcist. 1993. *Volume II/54.*

Urban, Christina: Das Menschenbild nach dem Johannesevangelium. 2001. *Volume II/137.*

Visotzky, Burton L.: Fathers of the World. 1995. *Volume 80.*

Vollenweider, Samuel: Horizonte neutestamentlicher Christologie. 2002. *Volume 144.*

Vos, Johan S.: Die Kunst der Argumentation bei Paulus. 2002. *Volume 149.*

Wagener, Ulrike: Die Ordnung des „Hauses Gottes". 1994. *Volume II/65.*

Walker, Donald D.: Paul's Offer of Leniency (2 Cor 10:1). 2002. *Volume II/152.*

Walter, Nikolaus: Praeparatio Evangelica. Ed. von Wolfgang Kraus und Florian Wilk. 1997. *Volume 98.*

Wander, Bernd: Gottesfürchtige und Sympathisanten. 1998. *Volume 104.*

Watts, Rikki: Isaiah's New Exodus and Mark. 1997. *Volume II/88.*

Wedderburn, A.J.M.: Baptism and Resurrection. 1987. *Volume 44.*

Wegner, Uwe: Der Hauptmann von Kafarnaum. 1985. *Volume II/14.*

Weissenrieder, Annette: Images of Illness in the Gospel of Luke. 2003. Volume II/164.

Welck, Christian: Erzählte ,Zeichen'. 1994. *Volume II/69.*

Wiarda, Timothy: Peter in the Gospels . 2000. *Volume II/127.*

Wilk, Florian: see *Walter, Nikolaus.*

Williams, Catrin H.: I am He. 2000. *Volume II/113.*

Wilson, Walter T.: Love without Pretense. 1991. *Volume II/46.*

Wisdom, Jeffrey: Blessing for the Nations and the Curse of the Law. 2001. *Volume II/133.*

Wucherpfennig, Ansgar: Heracleon Philologus. 2002. *Volume 142.*

Yeung, Maureen: Faith in Jesus and Paul. 2002. *Volume II/147.*

Zimmermann, Alfred E.: Die urchristlichen Lehrer. 1984, ²1988. *Volume II/12.*

Zimmermann, Johannes: Messianische Texte aus Qumran. 1998. *Volume II/104.*

Zimmermann, Ruben: Geschlechtermetaphorik und Gottesverhältnis. 2001. *Volume II/122.*

Zumstein, Jean: see *Dettwiler, Andreas*

For a complete catalogue please write to the publisher
Mohr Siebeck • P.O. Box 2030 • D–72010 Tübingen/Germany
Up-to-date information on the internet at www.mohr.de